Public Relations
The Profession and the Practice

THIRD EDITION

DAN LATTIMORE

OTIS BASKIN

SUZETTE T. HEIMAN

ELIZABETH L. TOTH

 Higher Education

Boston Burr Ridge, IL Dubuque, IA New York San Francisco St. Louis
Bangkok Bogotá Caracas Kuala Lumpur Lisbon London Madrid Mexico City
Milan Montreal New Delhi Santiago Seoul Singapore Sydney Taipei Toronto

Higher Education

Published by McGraw-Hill, an imprint of The McGraw-Hill Companies, Inc., 1221 Avenue of the Americas, New York, NY 10020. Copyright © 2009, 2007, 2004. All rights reserved. No part of this publication may be reproduced or distributed in any form or by any means, or stored in a database or retrieval system, without the prior written consent of The McGraw-Hill Companies, Inc., including, but not limited to, in any network or other electronic storage or transmission, or broadcast for distance learning.

2 3 4 5 6 7 8 9 0 VNH/VNH 0 9

ISBN: 978-0-07-337887-9
MHID: 0-07-337887-9

Editor in Chief: *Michael Ryan*
Publisher: *Frank Mortimer*
Executive Sponsoring Editor: *Katie Stevens*
Developmental Editor: *Phil Butcher*
Editorial Coordinator: *Erika Lake*
Executive Marketing Manager: *Leslie Oberhuber*
Senior Production Editor: *Carey Eisner*
Manuscript Editor: *Darlene Bledsoe*
Cover: (Clockwise from left) U.S. Air Force photo by Tech. Sgt. Tracy L. DeMarco; © Ryan McVay/Getty Images; © Photodisc/Getty Images; © Ryan McVay/Getty Images; Royalty-Free/CORBIS.

Design Manager: *Ashley Bedell*
Cover Designer: *Mary-Presley Adams*
Interior Design: *Glenda King*
Senior Photo Research Coordinator: *Natalia Peschiera*
Senior Production Supervisor: *Tandra Jorgensen*
Composition: *10/12 Minion by Macmillan Publishing Solutions*
Printing: *45# New Era Matte Plus, Courier, Inc.*

Library of Congress Cataloging-in-Publication Data

Public relations : the profession and the practice / Dan Lattimore . . . [et al.]. – 3rd ed.
    p. cm.
  Includes bibliographical references and index.
  ISBN-13: 978-0-07-337887-9 (alk. paper)
  ISBN-10: 0-07-337887-9 (alk. paper)
  1. Public relations. 2. Public relations–United States. I. Lattimore, Dan.
  HM1221.P82 2008
  659.2–dc22

                                                        2008045186

Brief Contents

iii

Contents

PART FOUR The Practice 295

Preface

Social media, crisis communication, global practice, and a changing organizational structure are powerful influences on the practice of public relations in the 21st century. The *profession* of public relations continues to emerge as a major force in global society. The *practice* of public relations is seeing revolutionary change as new, interactive media and instantaneous communication possibilities increase rapidly each year. While traditional media are still the foundation of public communication, new social media provide for a much more personal and interactive form of public relations.

The *process* of public relations continues to be grounded in the research, planning, action, and evaluation of the past, but many techniques of actually carrying out that process are being changed by technology. Surveys once done by interviewers door-to-door, or even by telephone, are more often done through the Internet today. The *publics* of public relations are still the major stakeholders for an organization whether they are employees, media, community members, consumers, or investors.

These critical changes in society and technology lend importance to the increasing emphasis in the *management function* of public relations. The practitioner may be a counselor in a public relations firm advising business and organizations on the important public relations positions and operations, or a vice president of a corporation sitting at the executive roundtable advising his or her peers of the consequences of some action. Practitioners are no longer mere technicians who shape and transmit messages from their organizations. They are professionals who manage the public relations function and *build the relationships* an organization has with its various constituencies. Public relations practitioners must possess the communication expertise and social sensitivity necessary to enable organizations to adapt to the changing environment.

Public relations professionals today must bring to their broadened role not only the traditional communication skills, but also the abilities to research and understand problems, to strategically plan public relations programs, to create effective messages using both the new social media as well as the traditional media, and to evaluate the effectiveness of these programs. The goal of this book is to provide you with an understanding of the principles underlying the practice of public relations while giving you a look at both the new communication opportunities and the trusted older tools for public relations practice. This we have tried to do within the historical context, the theoretical framework, and the legal and ethical foundation for the profession of public relations.

APPROACH OF THE TEXT

A multidisciplinary approach has characterized the text from its inception and is continued in this edition. We believe that by drawing on the experience of journalism, business, psychology, and communication professionals, we can present a comprehensive and inclusive overview of public relations. The education, research, and teaching experience of the authors in each of these disciplines addresses the needs of students who will be practicing in diverse environments.

We have tried to maintain an easy-to-read, personal style throughout the text. To that end, we have kept the jargon to a minimum and have provided definitions for all terms that are particular to the profession. In addition, we have attempted to give public relations students and practitioners the tools and knowledge they need in ways that reflect the reality of public relations. For example, **Mini-cases** provide insight into real-time activities conducted by organizations. Public relations **Spotlights** provide helpful information on topics such as lessons learned from the Enron scandal and the PRSA Code of Ethics.

ORGANIZATION OF THE TEXT

This edition retains the four-part organization of earlier editions: the profession, the process, the publics, and the practice. Part 1 describes the current public relations situation, its historical roots, theories, and ethical and legal concerns. Part 2 examines the core issues of the process that underlie public relations, whereas part 3 focuses on the publics that are the object of these efforts. Finally, part 4 summarizes the practice of public relations and looks at the emerging trends of the profession. We believe that this structure truly reflects the growth and development of public relations as an emerging profession.

PEDAGOGY

- Chapters have been updated, while the classic material has been retained. The content truly reflects the direction of public relations in the 21st century.
- Each chapter opens with a *preview* that engages the student in a real-life public relations situation.
- Two appendixes provide practical guidelines for writing and speaking.
- *Mini-cases* in each chapter allow students to "see" public relations in action.
- *Spotlights* in each chapter add material to enhance students' understanding of the chapter's concepts.
- Numerous figures and tables explain and clarify concepts under discussion.
- An *integrating case study* runs through each of the four chapters of part two to help pull together the process.
- A *case study* at the end of each chapter provides opportunities for student discussion and interaction with the concepts in the chapter.
- Each chapter includes end-of-chapter references.
- Highlighted glossary terms in the text, and a complete end-of-book glossary, focus on terms that are particular to the profession.

WHAT'S FEATURED IN EACH CHAPTER

Chapter One: The Nature of Public Relations

This chapter introduces the reader to the changing nature of public relations, including the new social media. A new spotlight features the Public Relations Student Society of America. A new mini-case on MTV's campaign to make global climate change a priority is featured along with an end-of-chapter case study on work as a student intern.

Chapter Two: The History of Public Relations

This chapter looks at the historical development of public relations through four overlapping traditions. It highlights key public relations professionals throughout history, and a spotlight provides short biographical sketches of these professionals. Included are two new professionals—Moss Kendrix, a pioneering African American practitioner, and Chester Burger, a counselor to counselors and CEOs.

Chapter Three: A Theoretical Basis for Public Relations

Persuasion and social influence theories are illustrated through a mini-case on DaimlerChrysler's StreetWise computer game. The chapter also links the new mixed motive model of public relations with strategies of conflict resolution. A spotlight summarizes nine key research theories in four categories.

Chapter Four: Law and Ethics

The developing legal consideration of the Internet is considered in depth, and the chapter has a new focus on financial law looking at the Sarbanes-Oxley Act. The USA Patriot Act is also introduced, and a new end-of-chapter case study features baseball and steroid use.

Chapter Five: Research: Understanding Public Opinion

The research chapter begins the process section with the initial part of the case study that runs throughout the four chapters in this section. The research terms are explained in lay language with a spotlight. Usability research for Web-based material is included, along with an examination of Internet, library, and database resources.

Chapter Six: Strategic Planning for Public Relations Effectiveness

This chapter features a sample plan and budget, along with the second part of the case study that runs throughout this section. A new case study highlights Kodak Galleries.

Chapter Seven: Action and Communication

The chapter highlights the importance of Internet writing and includes a spotlight on guidelines for effective Web sites.

Chapter Eight: Evaluating Public Relations Effectiveness

Evaluation software, an examination of Ketchum's extranet efforts, and additional measurement strategies are included in this chapter. A new emphasis on measurements that matter is included.

Chapter Nine: Media Relations

The new social media are highlighted in this chapter with a section explaining the personal, interactive media and how it is changing media relations. Spotlights are on social media terms and the Blogosphere.

Chapter Ten: Employee Communication

This chapter considers the new labor force of the 21st century and its influence on employee communication. It presents the use of blogs as an employee communication tool. The chapter has a case study on maintaining employee relationships during a tragedy.

Chapter Eleven: Community Relations

This chapter provides emphasis on corporate social philanthropy as well as community activism. A new spotlight features Kodak's commitment to community relations.

Chapter Twelve: Consumer Relations and Marketing

New to this chapter is an expanded discussion of corporate social responsibility. Also, there is a new section on viral marketing.

Chapter Thirteen: Investor Relations

The WorldCom case, along with a discussion of such influences on investor relations as the Sarbanes-Oxley Act, highlight this chapter.

Chapter Fourteen: Public Affairs: Relations with Government

A new end case study on the U.S. Treasury teaming with Weber Shandwick Public Relations for a several-year campaign to entice more federal government retirees to use direct deposit.

Chapter Fifteen: Public Relations in Nonprofit Organizations

This chapter provides a global perspective on nonprofit work, going far beyond small, well-intentioned community-based programs, and includes a discussion of the challenges faced by nonprofits. A new case study on creating a national identity is presented.

Chapter Sixteen: Corporate Public Relations

The role of the chief executive officer in corporate public relations has been expanded, citing recent scandals. This chapter discusses the crucial role that public relations plays in creating and developing a corporation's image and reputation with its key publics, particularly life after corporate scandals. A section on "12 steps on restoring a company's reputation" has been added. A new end-of-chapter case study on MasterCard's *Project Math* is included.

Chapter Seventeen: Issues in Public Relations: Crisis Communication, Social Media, and Global Advances

Handling crisis communication is increasingly becoming a major need in public relations. A new section on crisis communication has been added to the list of pressing issues in public relations. The chapter also examines social media's use for public relations and its possibilities for the future. A new mini-case on lead in Chinese-imported toys highlights both the global and crisis issues. Global and organizational issues are also examined.

Appendix 1 and Appendix 2

Two appendixes provide additional help for students with two basic public relations skills: writing and speaking.

The Online Learning Center, available for students and instructors alike, can be found at **www.mhhe.com/lattimore3e**. This useful resource contains a number of assets that students and instructors will want to use throughout the duration of the course.

For the student, these assets include:

- *Self-Quizzes:* Students can assess their comprehension of the chapter concepts by taking practice tests that provide feedback for each answer.
- A glossary provides definitions of terms.
- Chapter Overviews aid students in their review of chapters.
- *Video:* with Public Relations Professionals: The 15 original video interviews conducted by the book's authors are also available on the Online Learning Center. Instructors can also use the clips as discussion starters.

For the instructor, these assets include:

- An Instructor's Manual containing Chapter Summaries, Objectives, In-Class Exercises and Individual Learning Activities, and Essay Questions.
- A comprehensive test item bank with numerous multiple-choice questions for use with each chapter of the textbook.

The following academics reviewed our manuscript and helped us to make it as useful as possible for students and professors:

ACKNOWLEDGMENTS

Coy Callison
Texas Tech University

Todd Chambers
Texas Tech University

Scott Dickmeyer
University of Wisconsin

Shearlean Duke
Western Washington University

Dina Gavrilos
Walter Cronkite School, Arizona State University

Judith A. Linville
University of Missouri–St. Louis

Kenneth Plowman
Brigham Young University

Christine Russell
East Carolina University

Andi Stein
Cal State Fullerton

We deeply appreciate those who distilled from their professional or teaching experiences the cases and spotlights that appear in each chapter. Our appreciation also goes to our universities for their support, services, and resources. Finally, we give our sincere thanks to the professionals at McGraw-Hill Publishing who worked so hard and long assisting us in putting the project together.

Dan Lattimore, *University of Memphis*
Otis Baskin, *Pepperdine University*
Suzette T. Heiman, *University of Missouri–Columbia*
Elizabeth L. Toth, *University of Maryland*

About the Authors

Dan Lattimore is vice provost for extended programs, dean of University College, professor of journalism at the University of Memphis, and an accredited public relations practitioner. He is the author of five books and represents PRSA on the Commission for Public Relations Education.

Otis Baskin is professor of management at the George L. Graziadio School of Business and Management at Pepperdine University where he served as dean from 1995 to 2001. Dr. Baskin has served as an adviser to management for public and private organizations around the world. He is a frequent speaker to industry and executive groups including the Conference Board, the Family Business Network (Europe), and the International Security Management Network. Dr. Baskin's scholarly achievements include six books, in addition to numerous articles and published papers.

Suzette T. Heiman is director of planning and communication and an associate professor at the Missouri School of Journalism at the University of Missouri–Columbia. Her professional background includes experience in public relations and advertising for nonprofits, and she serves as a consultant to industry. She is an accredited member of PRSA.

Elizabeth L. Toth, PhD, is a full professor and the chair of the Department of Communication of the University of Maryland–College Park. Toth has co-authored *Women and Public Relations: How Gender Influences Practice; The Velvet Ghetto: The Increasing Numbers of Women in Public Relations; Beyond the Velvet Ghetto;* and the PRSA Glass Ceiling Studies. She co-edited *The Gender Challenge to Media: Diverse Voices from the Field.* Toth edited the *Journal of Public Relations Research* for six years. Currently, she co-edits *Journalism Studies,* an international journal. Her co-edited book, *Rhetorical and Critical Approaches to Public Relations,* won the NCA PRIDE Award. She has published over 75 articles, book chapters, and papers. Toth is the recipient of the PRSA Outstanding Educator Award; the Institute for Public Relations Pathfinder Award; and the Jackson, Jackson & Wagner Behavior Science Prize for research. Her professional public relations experience was in government relations.

Visual Preview

The Profession and the Practice: A Structure That Reflects the Growth and Development of Public Relations

Unique four-part organization ensures that students will leave the course with a thorough understanding of public relations and a basis for successful practice today and in the future.

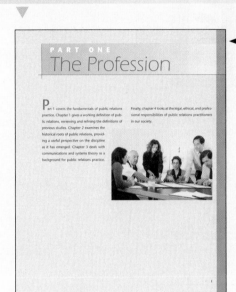

Part 1 describes the current public relations climate, its history, theories, ethics, and legal concerns.

Part 2 examines the core issues of the process that underlies public relations.

Part 3 focuses on the publics that are the object of the public relations efforts.

Part 4 summarizes the practice of public relations and looks at the emerging trends of the profession.

The Profession and the Practice: Tools and Knowledge That Reflect the Reality of Public Relations

Mini-cases—Provide insight into real-time activities conducted by organizations.

Mini-Case 9.1 — Fatal Tiger Attack at San Francisco Zoo

Laurie Volkmann, Ph.D.
Dominican University

Shortly after 5 p.m. on Christmas Day 2007, a 300-pound Siberian tiger escaped from his outdoor grotto at the San Francisco Zoo, chasing down three young men, mauling two and killing one. In the investigation that followed over the next several days, it was found that the teenage boys had taunted the tiger but also that the 12½-foot fence of the grotto was 4 feet below the standard and 7½ feet below what officials had reported the fence to be, making it possible for an agitated animal to jump over and escape. The San Francisco Zoo closed down for several days following the incident and kept the tiger exhibit closed for several months. The two injured young men filed suit against the city three months after the attack.

As the current director of public relations for the SF Zoo, consider your short-term and long-term actions in response to the crisis.

Questions

1. How do you address the media and the public about the fatality

and injuries to the three young men? Draft a 200-word statement you would present at a press conference.
2. Write 10 questions you would expect the reporters to ask at your initial press conference.
3. How do you handle your communication with the families of the boys?
4. What do you do—and what is your timeline—for addressing the fencing issue?
5. Provide descriptions of three strategies for restoring the public's confidence in zoo safety and avoiding a major blow to attendance.
6. Research what was done by the zoo to deal with the media over the year following the incident, and report what you think worked and what may not have worked as well.

Sources: Steve Rubenstein, "Beloved but beleaguered zoo," San Francisco Chronicle, Dec. 30, 2007, A-1; Kevin Fagan, Cecilia M. Vega, Steve Rubenstein, "Wall below standard, shorter than zoo said," San Francisco Chronicle, Dec. 28, 2007, A-1.

responding to the public's need to know. Practitioners know that they must facilitate the work of journalists if they expect their organizations to get covered.

Because of this dependency, practitioners' selection and presentation of information often conforms more to journalistic standards than to the desires of their superiors in their own organizations. In a sense, both the journalist and the practitioner, in dealing with each other, are caught between the demands of the organizations they represent and the demands of the opposite party. In short, the relationship between public relations practitioners and journalists is one of mutual dependency. Public relations practitioners, as boundary spanners, are often caught in the middle between journalistic and other institutions, trying to explain each to the other.

Mutual Dependence

Although journalists like to picture themselves as reluctant to use public relations information, economic considerations force them to do otherwise. A news staff capable of ferreting information from every significant organization in a city without the assistance of representatives for those organizations would be prohibitively expensive. Through the efforts of public relations practitioners, the media receive a constant flow of free information. Facts that journalists might not have acquired otherwise become available

174

Spotlights—Provide helpful information on topics such as the PRSA Code of Ethics and the lessons learned from the Enron scandal.

Spotlight 9.1 — Social Media Terms

API (Application Programming Interface) Ease of creating content and moving it into a variety of Web sites is often the result of using an open API provided by these sites.

Blog Technically a Web log. The author writes blogs like a journalist writes a column except that people can interact and post responses to the information on the blog.

Blogosphere The collective universe of bloggers.

Open Source Most commonly applied to the source code of software that is made available to the general public with relaxed or nonexistent intellectual property restrictions. This allows users to create user-generated software content through incremental individual effort or through collaboration. Open source is part of the whole Web 2.0 movement and now means more than just software. It's evolved to mean partly a group of people coming together, regardless of traditional organizational structures, to create something all benefit from but none can do alone.

Podcast Digital media files that can be audio and/or video that are distributed over the Internet for playback on portable media players or computers. The term originated with delivery to the Apple iPod combined with the term broadcast; it has much wider application now. Podcasts may be downloaded, streamed, or fed through feed

formats such as RSS. The **Podcaster** is the producer or author of the podcast.

Portal A gateway. **Web portal** is a site that functions as a point of access for more information on other pages at that Web site. **Enterprise portal** is a gateway on enterprise Web software to provide a single point of access to a variety of information or tools that the organization wants you to have in one place.

Remix/Mashups An open approach to content. The "remix" society takes content, personalizes it by changing it or "mashing" it with other content to make something entirely new.

RSS (Real Simple Syndication) Feed of information to Web sites and services updated whenever something changes. Data is pushed to the user when it is new and doesn't require someone to go get it. Putting multiple RSS feed into one feed makes viewing, organizing, and understanding vast amounts of information that is being generated much easier to understand.

Social Bookmarking Method for Web users to store, organize, search, and manage bookmarks of Web pages with the help of metadata. Users save links to Web pages privately and share with specified people or groups inside a special network or some domain. Much of the bookmarking is done informally, but

others use bookmarking services. Many of the services provide ratings or comments and other social networking features.

Tagging User-generated way of describing content by adding "tags" to writing, images, videos, posts, or other social media content.

Web 2.0 Internet use that facilitates creativity and collaboration among users. It usually involves the new social media such as wikis, blogs, and social-networking sites. Rather than referring to any technical changes, it refers to changes in the ways software developers and other people make use of Web technology.

Wiki Short for a wikipedia. A wiki is a technology for creating collaborative Web sites. **Wikipedia** is now used as a term that combines "wiki" with "encyclopedia" to prove an Internet reference site begun in 2001 by Jimmy Wales and Larry Sanger.

Sources: Audrey Williams, "Best Practices and Innovation in Distance Learning: Using Web 2.0," presentation at Tennessee Alliance for Continuing Higher Education, Nashville, TN, Fall 2007; www.digitalcenter.org/, retrieved March 9, 2008; Vocus, "Five Golden Rules for Blogger Relations," Vocus White Paper, 2008; en.wikipedia.org/

You are the community relations director of the local police force. A reporter calls to request a meeting with your chief about low police morale resulting from the city's inability to meet rank-and-file demands for pay raises. When you attempt to arrange an interview for the following afternoon, the chief berates you, saying, "It's your job to keep the press off my back. Why can't you handle the guy's questions?" You convince the chief that the reporter would not talk to you because he said he was tired of the chief hiding behind his "flack." You tell him departmental integrity and morale depend on his willingness to deal with the press. You promise to help him prepare. He reluctantly agrees to the interview.

180

MasterCard Project Math

Case Study

Summary

The current state of U.S. math achievement has serious implications for tomorrow's workforce, especially for technology-based companies such as MasterCard Worldwide. In St. Louis, home to the MasterCard global technology and operations headquarters, the company's communications team with its agency colleagues at Weber Shandwick examined local math achievement and decided to focus its local support of education on one cause—improving the teaching of math—that not only helps the community but is also good for business. The result was Project Math, a community program to maximize the visibility and impact of the company's local grants while helping advance regional math achievement and build workforce employability.

Research

Research was critical to the success of the program, as MasterCard did not consider itself in a position to dictate a solution for advancing the teaching of math, but rather, to serve as the means to activate a solution defined by math education experts. The team conducted both primary and secondary research in order to ensure that the program was relevant, meaningful, and successful.

Secondary Research

The team researched the state of math achievement in Missouri and St. Louis and reached out to Missouri Governor Matt Blunt's Math, Engineering, Technology and Science (METS) initiative for data to illustrate the need for improvement.

STRATEGIC PLANNING

Public relations strategic planning provides organization to the public relations process. "Strategic planning is a process of assessing what you have and where you want to go."[1] The caliber and thoroughness of thinking preceding the execution of public relations activities will determine the value of the public relations operation. Understanding how to develop a public relations plan, then, is one of the main criteria that separates entry-level positions from top management in public relations.

Planning moves public relations from a reactive activity to a **proactive** process. Public relations practitioners, like most other managers, tend to be action oriented. The constant changes that take place both inside and outside any organization produce an endless procession of public relations problems. Too often, because of the number of pressing problems, managers find themselves responding only to exceptional situations. Such situations are usually negative in that they require the practitioner to intervene after a problem has already gotten out of control.

Although putting out fires is certainly part of the public relations function, it cannot be allowed to dominate all actions. If it does, the practitioner becomes a victim of circumstances, able to react only to the situation at hand. Perhaps the most frequent complaint of public relations practitioners is that other managers ask for their services only after the problem has become unmanageable. When damage to the organization's image has already been done, the public relations manager is often directed to "fix it." This may prove to be a no-win situation both for the organization and for the practitioner who must engage in usually fruitless remedial public relations.

For a long time, public relations practitioners have been advocating preventive public relations to avoid such problems. Part of this approach involves the type of fact-finding research we discussed in chapter 5. If practitioners detect potential problems before they erupt into damaging situations, they can give management early warning and advice. Sometimes even early detection cannot forestall some negative impact. When advanced warning is coupled with adequate planning, however, negative effects can be minimized, and public relations management can provide well-designed, positive actions rather than hastily conceived reactions. As we continue the integrating case begun in chapter 5, notice how the pitfalls of hasty reaction were avoided.

Integrating Case Study

Cedar Springs Community Hospital
Segment 2

You may remember that the physicians at Cedar Springs Hospital (chapter 5) were calling for immediate action to correct what they saw as a potentially life-threatening situation in patient care. Reaction to the problem as it appeared at the time would have generated a campaign to make employees more aware of the need for quality patient care and emphasize their responsibility for providing the best care possible. However, before taking action, the public relations director conducted some research to help him better understand the problem. The results were surprising and showed that the first action contemplated would have only made things worse. Employees already believed that the quality of patient care in the hospital was subpar and were frustrated because they felt they personally were doing a good job. In addition, research revealed that recently released patients rated the quality of care significantly better than the employees did.

The Profession and the Practice: Pedagogy That Reflects a Solid Public Relations Text

For self-testing and additional chapter resources, go to the Online Learning Center at
www.mhhe.com/lattimore3e.

PART ONE
The Profession

art 1 covers the fundamentals of public relations practice. Chapter 1 gives a working definition of public relations, reviewing and refining the definitions of previous studies. Chapter 2 examines the historical roots of public relations, providing a useful perspective on the discipline as it has emerged. Chapter 3 deals with communications and systems theory as a background for public relations practice.

Finally, chapter 4 looks at the legal, ethical, and professional responsibilities of public relations practitioners in our society.

The Nature of Public Relations

OUTLINE

PREVIEW

Marissa has just been promoted to account executive at the up-and-coming public relations and strategic communications agency where she works. Her client is the software giant Microsoft. Settling into her office, Marissa checks her e-mails and daily media tracking report to see what the media have reported about her Microsoft product over the past 24 hours. She also checks to see what, if anything, has been said or written about her client's competitors. Then she summarizes the highlights and e-mails them to her clients and to the other members of her Microsoft product team.

Next is her project with *Wired,* a computer publication. Marissa has been working with a *Wired* reporter to ensure that Microsoft's new-product launch announcement will be the featured article in an upcoming issue, with front-cover placement. Today she begins organizing artwork to accompany the announcement, then takes the art to an account team meeting where team members will synchronize the *Wired* feature with follow-up stories in other trade publications, consumer electronics magazines, and the financial press.

Over lunch with a group of volunteers organizing a summer reading program for kids, Marissa suggests some local business partnerships as ways to sponsor the program and provide transportation to and from the library for the children. The afternoon's agenda includes locating a Microsoft executive to field questions from a reporter writing about Internet regulation and starting a new line of research for a Microsoft brand manager looking for help with a marketing program. In just a few hours Marissa has demonstrated the communication, leadership, and management skills on which successful public relations practitioners rely.

WHAT IS PUBLIC RELATIONS?

We examine other aspects of a job like Marissa's throughout this chapter and the entire book, but first let's define public relations and its key dimensions. Attempts to define public relations as a professional field and academic discipline are many and varied. The very nature of the profession and its constant adaptation to the needs of society make it at best a moving target for definition. Public relations is practiced in organizations that range from giant, multinational telecommunications companies to small human service agencies and fledgling social movement organizations. A public relations manager for a private university may devote most of her or his efforts to fund-raising and student recruitment. In contrast, the public relations staff of a large corporation may be responsible for the firm's relationships with customers, suppliers, investors, employees, and even foreign governments.

A Working Definition

Public relations practitioners help others establish and maintain effective relationships with third parties. They usually work in businesses like public relations firms or agencies such as Marissa's, or as independent consultants, or on the communication staffs of corporations, not-for-profit organizations, or government agencies. For the purposes of this book—and to establish a broad, realistic, and accurate description of the public relations function—we offer the following working definition:

> **Public relations** is a leadership and management function that helps achieve organizational objectives, define philosophy, and facilitate organizational change. Public relations practitioners communicate with all relevant internal and external publics to develop positive relationships and to create consistency between organizational goals and societal expectations. Public relations practitioners develop, execute, and evaluate organizational programs that promote the exchange of influence and understanding among an organization's constituent parts and publics.

We review the key dimensions of the definition on the following pages. Also be sure to look at spotlight 1.1, the official statement on public relations outlined by the Public Relations Society of America (PRSA). PRSA is the oldest and largest professional association serving public relations practitioners.

Public Relations Practitioners' Work

Public relations continues to be one of the most dynamic disciplines in organizational life throughout the world. One reason is that public relations practitioners bring such a diversity of skills and programmatic capabilities to their jobs. You can appreciate the broad nature of the discipline when you realize it can include any of the following:

Research	Media relations
Counseling/advising	Public affairs
Government affairs	Community relations
Investor relations	Employee relations
Development or fund-raising	Publicity
Multicultural affairs	Marketing communication
Issues management	Promotion

We look at these and other aspects of public relations throughout the remainder of the book.

Public relations helps our complex, pluralistic society to reach decisions and function more effectively by contributing to mutual understanding among groups and institutions. It serves to bring the public and public policies into harmony.

Public relations serves a wide variety of institutions in society, such as businesses, trade unions, government agencies, voluntary associations, foundations, hospitals, and educational and religious institutions. To achieve their goals, these institutions must develop effective relationships with many different audiences or publics, such as employees, members, customers, local communities, shareholders, and other institutions, and with society at large.

The leadership of institutions needs to understand the attitudes and values of their publics in order to achieve institutional goals. The goals themselves are shaped by the external environment. The public relations practitioner acts as a counselor to management and as a mediator, helping to translate private aims into reasonable, publicly acceptable policy and action. As a management function, public relations encompasses the following:

1. Anticipating, analyzing, and interpreting public opinion, attitudes, and issues that might impact, for good or ill, the operations and plans of the organization.
2. Counseling management at all levels in the organization with regard to policy decisions, courses of action, and communication, taking into account their public ramifications and the organization's social or citizenship responsibilities.
3. Researching, conducting, and evaluating, on a continuing basis, programs of action and communication to achieve informed public understanding necessary to the success of an organization's aims. These may include marketing, financial, fund-raising, employee, community or government relations, and other programs.
4. Planning and implementing the organization's efforts to influence or change public policy.
5. Setting objectives, planning, budgeting, recruiting and training staff, developing facilities—in short, managing the resources needed to perform all of the above.
6. Examples of the knowledge that may be required in the professional practice of public relations include communication arts, psychology, social psychology, sociology, political science, economics, and the principles of management and ethics. Technical knowledge and skills are required for opinion research, public issue analysis, media relations, direct mail, institutional advertising, publications, film/video productions, special events, speeches, and presentations.

In helping to define and implement policy, the public relations practitioner utilizes a variety of professional communications skills and plays an integrative role both within the organization and between the organization and the external environment.

Source: "Public Relations: An Overview" (New York: PRSA Foundation, 1991), pp. 4–5. Statement formally adopted by PRSA Assembly, November 6, 1982.

Public relations work is all about developing effective relationships between organizations and groups that are important to them, including the media, customers, employees, investors, community leaders and members, activist groups, and government agencies. These relationships should benefit both parties. Creating that kind of lasting, win-win situation requires a great deal of give-and-take based on a mutual understanding of each other's interests. Effective two-way communication also implies doing well by doing good, as the MTV mini-case study shows. The climate change campaign in mini-case 1.1 is both a public relations and a social marketing program. **Social marketing** is a special form of public relations that tries to change public attitudes and behaviors on behalf of a social cause whose work benefits society as a whole, rather than on behalf of the sponsoring organization.

DEVELOPING RELATIONSHIPS BASED ON TWO-WAY COMMUNICATION

Much of the communicating that public relations practitioners do is both persuasive and purposive. That's why our definition talks about promoting the exchange of influence among an organization's constituent parts and publics. From the earliest times public relations has been seen as the planned effort to influence public opinion, generally through persuasive communication. Marketing communication campaigns,

INFLUENCING GROUPS, POLICIES, AND ISSUES

for example, utilize product publicity to introduce products. Social marketing programs are persuasion efforts designed to inform people and to change their behaviors regarding some public good. An example is the HIV Alliance campaign promoting safer sex through neighborhood needle exchange programs. The public relations practitioner writes the message and selects the communication channel, while the marketing specialists make sure that the messages and condoms are distributed.

THE PUBLICS IN PUBLIC RELATIONS

All definitions and discussions of public relations refer to *publics* and *public opinion.* How do people who study and practice public relations make use of these terms? To begin, groups that are almost always important to organizations are called **publics,** and we generally define them in terms of their organizational relationships to us, including the media, employees, governmental officials, community leaders, and financial analysts, for example.

In other instances, we define publics as categories of people who become important to our organization because it has purposely or even inadvertently galvanized them. Perhaps they are community members who resent our organization building a new office addition immediately adjacent to a wetlands area. They become a public once they recognize an issue, understand its relevance to them, and then talk about it or even organize to do something about it.

Alert public relations practitioners communicate with these groups very early in the process, perhaps even before they become organized activists or a social movement organization. Chances are, though, that these activists understand the processes by which people begin to make up their minds on an issue once it gets publicized in local newspapers, on radio, and on television newscasts.

As the general citizenry learns about an issue, individuals begin to express opinions, talk with others about the issue, and reconcile their opinions with long-standing attitudes, values, and group affiliations. It's not surprising, therefore, that public relations practitioners monitor public opinion formation and change around many issues; it's in their best interests. Moreover, the study of public relations has always included the investigation of public opinion, attitude change processes, and social psychology. If public relations practitioners are to build and maintain an organization's reputation, they'll need to understand that public opinion formation is a dynamic process in which each of the major interests competes to frame the issue a particular way in the media. In addition, public relations practitioners influence public opinion by helping organizations attract and mobilize supporters.

This billboard encourages community relations involvement by employees mentoring young people and inspiring them to reach their dreams.

MTV Global Climate Change

When the largest TV network in the world, with a potential audience of more than 1.5 billion people in more than 150 countries, decides to make global climate change a top priority, people take notice.

MTV launched its climate change campaign in June 2007 on MTV Switch at www.mtvswitch.org. The campaign's mission is "Who on earth are we? We're MTV's International climate change campaign, and we're on a mission to make y'all green."

The portal was launched to provide information on the environment and as a gathering place for MTV viewers or visitors interested in learning about ways to live an environmentally friendly lifestyle. MTV feels "a responsibility to address an issue that research shows is the number-one concern among its viewers, apart from family and personal issues."

MTV plans a splash of media activity every three or four months to sustain interest in its global change effort. In December 2007 the network premiered a documentary and about 10 public service announcements. Some play on its MTVswitch Web site, and some are in places like YouTube that are designed to drive traffic to its campaign Web site. Nokia sponsored the documentary. The PSAs were prepared pro bono by ad agencies Lowe Worldwide and Ogilvy. The Web site serves as the focal point for the environmental campaign.

John Jackson, director of MTV International's public affairs group, said the goal of the messages on the Web site is to focus on "positive, achievable changes we can make."

1. Go to the Web site and write a 250-word description of your evaluation of it and its effort to raise awareness and change behavior on environmental issues.
2. Write a comment on the blog at www.mtvswitch.blogspot.com.
3. What different channels of communication can you find that MTV is using to push its climate change campaign?

In many respects the heart of public relations work—at least for entry-level positions—is the ability to write, design, and produce materials for all media; public relations practitioners must also possess public speaking, group leadership, and event planning skills. Thus, a big share of day-to-day public relations work is

USING COMMUNICATION SKILLS EFFECTIVELY

identifying key messages and choosing the best combination of communication channels for directing those messages to target audiences. The integrated public relations media model developed by Professor Kirk Hallahan and shown in table 1.1 illustrates the range of communication channels for which public relations students learn to write, design, and produce.

Because the words *public relations* are very general, it's not surprising that different organizations label the function very differently; for example, the words *communication* and *corporate communication* are now more commonly

DISTINGUISHING PUBLIC RELATIONS FROM RELATED FIELDS

used to label the public relations function in many corporate and nonprofit settings. Government agencies often use the terms *public information* or *public affairs* to delineate the public relations and communication functions, even though **public affairs** generally refers to relationships between organizations and governments. Other terms are *corporate relations* and *marketing communication*. The labeling issue is further complicated by the fact that public relations practitioners are sometimes assigned to various departments throughout an organization rather than being housed together in a common public relations or communications department.

The terms *public relations* and *advertising* are often confused as well. Advertising refers to paid space and time in the media, whereas public relations describes publicity or stories that run without charge in the news columns of the media. Paid ads and commercials run almost exclusively in major mass media, including television, newspapers, radio, magazines, and the Internet.

TABLE 1.1   An Integrated Public Relations Media Model

Characteristic	Public Media	Interactive Media	Controlled Media	Events/Groups	One-on-One
Key use	Build awareness	Respond to queries; exchange information	Promotion; provide detailed information	Motivate attendees; reinforce attitudes	Obtain commitments; resolve problems
Examples	Newspapers, magazines, television, radio	Phone-based: automated response; audio text Computer-based: Internet, database, e-mail, listservs, newsgroups, chatrooms, bulletin boards, CD-ROMs	Brochures, newsletters, sponsored magazines, annual reports, books, direct mail, point of purchase displays, video, Web pages, e-mail	Speeches, trade shows, exhibits, meetings/ conferences, demonstrations, rallies, sponsorships, anniversaries, sweepstakes/ contests, recognitions/ awards	Personal visits, lobbying, personal letters, telephone calls, telemarketing/ solicitation
Nature of communications	Nonpersonal	Nonpersonal	Nonpersonal	Quasi-personal	Personal
Direction of communications	One-way	Quasi-two-way	One-way	Quasi-two-way	Two-way
Technological sophistication	High	High	Moderate	Moderate	Low
Channel ownership	Media organizations	Common carrier or institution	Sponsor	Sponsor or other organization	None
Message chosen by	Third parties and producers	Receiver	Sponsor	Sponsor or joint organization	Producer and audience
Audience involvement	Low	High	Moderate	Moderate	High
Reach	High	Moderate-low	Moderate-low	Low	Low
Cost per impression	Extremely low	Low	Moderate	Moderate	High
Key challenges to effectiveness	Competition; media cutter	Availability, accessibility	Design, distribution	Attendance, atmosphere	Empowerment, personal dynamics

Source: Kirk Hallahan, *Strategic Media Planning: Toward a Public Relations Model* (Thousand Oaks, CA: Sage, 2001), pp. 461–70.

Marketing is a sales and distribution function whose principal publics are customers, retailers, and distributors. In contrast, public relations deals with many publics, whose interests sometimes collide with customer interests. In addition to customers, important public relations publics include the media, employees, community leaders, government regulators, investment analysts, activist groups, and more.

Finally, *journalism* is distinct from *public relations* in two ways. Journalists do not represent the organizations about which they write, but public relations practitioners do, and this may influence their objectivity and the way they frame ideas and present facts. Journalists are trained to write for news media. Public relations practitioners must master the basic writing, graphic design, and journalistic conventions of all mass media along with more specialized media whose content they control, such as direct mail, pamphlets, posters, newsletters, trade publications, and their organization's Web site.

Public relations departments range in size from more than 400 members in large corporations to one or two individuals in small organizations. The public relations function in large corporations is frequently led by a vice president who helps develop overall policy as a member of top management. Large

organizations also typically include various other public relations managers at both corporate and division levels, and they may employ a number of public relations specialists such as writers, researchers, and representatives to the media. In a small organization, however, one individual may handle all these responsibilities. Public relations counseling firms may contain specialists in a particular practice area, such as health care or financial services, as well as functional specialists for managing corporate culture change or coordinating content on the internal intranet.

This great diversity in the duties of public relations practitioners is clear in the list of public relations functions published in PRSA's booklet *Careers in Public Relations:*

1. *Programming.* Programming means analyzing problems and opportunities; defining goals and the publics (or groups of people whose support or understanding is needed); and recommending and planning activities. It may include budgeting and assignment of responsibilities to the appropriate people, including non–public relations personnel. For example, an organization's president or executive director is often a key figure in public relations activities.

2. *Relationships.* Successful public relations people develop skill in gathering information from management, from colleagues in their organizations, and from external sources. They do this to strengthen their organization's ties to external groups, including the media, community leaders, government policymakers and regulators, investors, financial analysts, educational institutions, activist groups, and so on. They also build relationships with internal employee audiences and departments with which they maintain daily contact, such as marketing, human resources, and the legal department.

3. *Writing and Editing.* Because the public relations worker is often trying to reach large groups of people, the printed word is an important tool for creating reports, news releases, booklets, speeches, film scripts, trade magazine articles, product information and technical material, employee publications, newsletters, shareholder reports, and other management communications directed to both organizational personnel and external groups. A sound, clear style of writing that communicates effectively is a must for public relations work.

4. *Information.* An important public relations task is sharing information with appropriate newspaper, broadcast, and general and trade publication editors to enlist their interest in publishing an organization's news and features. This requires knowing how newspapers and other media operate, their areas of specialization, and the interests of individual editors. (Competition is keen for the attention of editors and broadcasters, who have a limited amount of space and time at their disposal.)

As one public relations practitioner puts it, "You have to get to the right editor of the right publication with the right story at the right time." Although ideas are accepted on the basis of newsworthiness and other readership values, successful practitioners develop relationships of mutual respect and cooperation with the news media that are useful to both the practitioners and the news people.

5. *Production.* Various publications, special reports, films, and multimedia programs are important ways of communicating. The public relations practitioner need not be an expert in art, layout, typography, and photography, but he or she should have background knowledge of the techniques in order to intelligently plan and supervise their use.

6. *Special Events.* News conferences, convention exhibits and special showings, new facility and anniversary celebrations, contests and award programs, and tours and special meetings are only a few of the special events used to gain attention and acceptance. They require careful planning and coordination, attention to detail, and the preparation of special booklets, publicity, and reports.

7. *Speaking.* Public relations work often requires face-to-face communication—finding appropriate platforms, delivering speeches, and preparing speeches for others. Those with public speaking skills will enjoy an advantage.

8. *Research and Evaluation.* All public relations work is underpinned by research—research on issues, organizations, publics, competition, opportunities, threats, and so on. Public relations practitioners spend considerable time incorporating their research findings into position statements, public relations plans, communication campaigns, media briefing materials, and so on. They gather research through interviews, informal conversation, and review of library materials, databases, and Web sites. They may also conduct surveys or hire firms specializing in designing and conducting opinion research.

Research findings influence a public relations program's objectives and strategies, which in turn form the basis for evaluating its planning, implementation, and effectiveness. More and more managers expect research and evaluation from their public relations advisers or staffs.

An employment psychological testing firm, RembrandtAdvantage, found in its research comparing mid- and senior-level public relations professionals at top public relations firms that high-performing public relations practitioners typically share three common traits: urgency, analytical problem solving, and flexibility. In its Web booklet *Careers in Public Relations* the Council of Public Relations Firms put together a comparison for the three traits to give aspiring public relations practitioners a test to indicate the likelihood that they would have the ability to become top public relations executives.[1] See table 1.2 for the comparison.

THE MANAGEMENT AND LEADERSHIP FUNCTIONS OF PUBLIC RELATIONS

Public relations calls upon both leadership and management functions, and we distinguish between the two in this section. We also address the roles that public relations practitioners and leaders play in advancing socially responsible behavior. And finally, we consider how public relations practitioners help make decisions in their organizations.

Business scholars often distinguish leadership from management by saying that leadership means doing the right things and making the right choices, whereas management means doing things right. As managers, public relations practitioners design and

TABLE 1.2   Comparison with PR Professionals

Compare yourself with successful public relations professionals.

Are you "urgent"?

_____   Do you move through work faster than most people?

_____   Do you become restless when there is a lull in activity?

_____   Do you consider yourself more intense than most people?

Are you an "analytical problem solver"?

_____   Do complex games and puzzles hold your interest?

_____   Do you find that solutions to various problems come to you more easily than they do to other people?

_____   Do you instinctively want to address the root cause behind various issues/problems?

Are you "flexible" in your approach to work and interactions?

_____   When people's views differ from yours, do you thoughtfully consider their perspective?

_____   Do you find that you can have many interruptions and still complete the goals that you set for the day?

_____   Do shifts to your plans add to the excitement of your day?

If you answered yes to most or all the statements above, you may have what it takes to become a PR professional.

Source: *Careers in Public Relations: A Guide to Opportunities in a Dynamic Industry,* Council of Public Relations Firms, retrieved from www.prfirms.org on Feb. 20, 2008.

organize communication programs and campaigns. They're the communication experts for their organizations. Like leaders, communication managers are steeped in planning, but this is generally intermediate-range planning, such as developing the communication for a multiyear marketing plan, determining the key messages for an organization's "cultural change" training program, or developing the content guidelines for the company's Web pages and its various intranet and extranet uses.

Traditionally, public relations professionals have been viewed more as communication managers than as organizational leaders. Leaders are the individuals charged with building and maintaining an organization's long-term reputation, helping to meet profit goals, and advising organizations on how to act responsibly in the public interest. They reconcile strategic plans at the highest organizational levels with the interests and concerns of groups whose support is needed, whether those groups are inside the organization, in the community, or even elsewhere in the world. Let's examine several dimensions of public relations leadership.

Advancing Socially Responsible Behavior

Public relations leaders help keep organizations profitable and long-lasting through socially responsible behavior that serves the public interest as well as their own. Events like the Enron debacle, the September 11, 2001, terrorist attacks, and regional conflicts throughout the world underscore how critical it is for businesses, governments, and nonprofit organizations to be viewed as credible and responsible in all places at all times. And yet the technology boom of the past two decades, together with overpaid executives at home and underpaid factory workers abroad, show that the public reputations of many organizations are in serious jeopardy. Against this backdrop,

Public relations practitioners discuss campaign tactics.

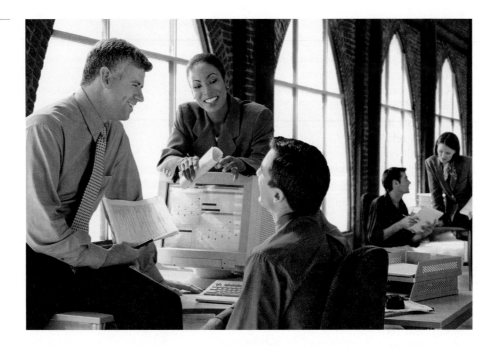

thoughtful observers today argue that institutions should assume more responsibility for the consequences of their actions. Insightful public relations practitioners recognize that socially responsive and responsible behavior helps prevent labor unrest and strikes, customer boycotts, environmental lawsuits, and random attacks by disaffected individuals and activist groups.

Veteran public relations practitioner and academic Rex Harlow believed that the public relations practitioner defines and emphasizes the responsibility of management to serve in the public interest. Former Hill & Knowlton CEO Robert Dilenschneider takes an even stronger stand, arguing that socially responsive behavior from 2000 to 2020 will determine the extent to which globalization and the world economy will survive.

Public Relations Leaders and Decision Making

What gives public relations leaders and practitioners the responsibility or the right to determine and influence socially responsive organizational behavior in the public interest? In truth, public relations leaders do not make all the decisions that lead to change within organizations, but because they constantly monitor and interact with all the publics in the organization's environment, they often possess information that suggests a need for change or indicates the direction change should take. Public relations practitioners can discover a problem when it is still manageable, thus avoiding unnecessary crises. Indeed, the late Scott Cutlip, renowned public relations educator, believed that the public relations practitioner's most important responsibility is to interpret the public opinion climate to management.

Because they understand the interests of different publics, public relations leaders can help organizations set policy and make strategic plans, establish philosophies, achieve objectives, adapt to changing environments, and successfully compete in today's markets. Public relations can make important contributions to forming an organization's ideas about itself—what it should do and what society wants and expects from it. Charles Steinberg described this aspect of public relations as the "structuring of company philosophy and carrying out that philosophy in practice so that what the institution says is not at variance with what it does."[2] In essence, then, public relations leaders spend considerable time gauging the implications that social, political, and economic issues at home and abroad have on maintaining the organization's long-term reputation.

One reason we distinguish public relations leadership from the management of an organization's communication functions is that the public's perceptions of business and organizational life are too far-reaching for public relations to address them alone. Indeed, public relations is increasingly the responsibility of executives as well as the province of public relations staffers. We see the need to reinvent the "good" in business and organizational life, as government agencies at all levels retrench in the face of new fiscal limitations. Hospitals struggle with regulations, rising costs, new technologies, and changing customer demands. Arts organizations seek new sources of funds as Congress plans to reduce or withdraw government support. Businesses deal with global competition, uncertain economic conditions, and a skeptical public. Thus successful leaders in all organizations incorporate public relations savvy and perspectives into their work.

Chief executive officers of major corporations are well aware that public relations contributes to decision making. Sir Gordon White, who as chairman of Hanson Industries made a career of buying companies and eliminating their corporate staffs, had a staff of only 12, but it included a public relations officer. Perhaps the most important task of public relations practitioners is to ensure that public relations considerations are in the mainstream of managerial decision making.

THE SCOPE OF THE PUBLIC RELATIONS INDUSTRY

Because the global reach of public relations practice is changing so quickly, it's hard to know exactly how many public relations practitioners there are around the world, but the Bureau of Labor Statistics estimated that there were 243,000 public relations specialists in the United States in 2006 and forecast that to rise to 286,000 by 2016.[3] In fact, U.S. organizations spend more than $10 billion annually on public relations. Worldwide, the public relations industry in Europe, including the Commonwealth of Independent States and former Soviet-bloc countries, is roughly one-third the size of the U.S. industry. Next come Asian countries, especially Japan, China, Hong Kong, Korea, Singapore, and Malaysia. The field is growing rapidly in Latin America and somewhat in Africa's fastest growing economies.

As shown in figure 1.1, within the United States, it's estimated that roughly one-third of all public relations practitioners work for agencies. Some of those agencies focus on public relations, but others combine public relations with marketing communication or advertising. Another third of practitioners work for corporations, including consumer goods such as consumer electronics, manufacturing, financial, and investment businesses; insurance firms; industrial firms; and the entertainment and media industries. Trade associations, educational institutions, and foundations employ about one-seventh of the practitioners, and health care about one-tenth. Municipal, county, state, and federal government agencies account for about 5 percent, as do social welfare, charitable, and religious associations.

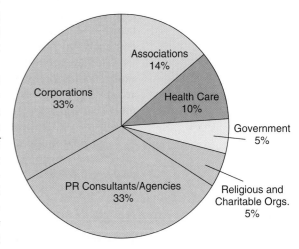

FIGURE 1.1   Where U.S. Public Relations Practitioners Work

A PROFILE OF PUBLIC RELATIONS PRACTITIONERS

More than at any time in the past, today's public relations practitioner is better educated, better paid, and more prepared to take on a range of strategic planning and communication functions for organizations of all kinds. The following subsections describe the principal findings from a large-scale U.S. and Canadian study of the profession.[4] The study was conducted by the two largest professional associations in public relations—the Public Relations Society of America (PRSA) and the International Association of Business Communicators (IABC).

Education

Two-thirds (65%) of public relations practitioners are college and university graduates with bachelor's degrees, and almost half say their degree programs focused on public relations. Almost 300 universities have student public relations chapters. In 2007–08 nearly 10,000 students were members of PRSSA, the Public Relations Student Society of America (see spotlight 1.2).

Increasingly more practitioners have not only a bachelor's degree but advanced degrees as well. More than 30 percent, or almost a third, had master's degrees, up from 27 percent five years earlier. Of those, close to half the master's degrees were in communications, public relations, or journalism or related media fields. Another 40 percent were master of business administration (MBA) degrees. The remaining 10 to 15 percent came from a range of related graduate majors. And surprisingly, an additional 2 percent of those surveyed held doctorate or PhD degrees.

Just under one-fourth (24%) of communicators surveyed have also passed national accreditation exams administered by either the IABC or the PRSA.[5]

Salaries

Salary figures can change dramatically from year to year. A good place to check a variety of salary figures for public relations is www.salary.com (search by using "public relations" as keywords and put in your desired location). According to salary.com, in 2008 the median salary for a beginning public relations specialist in Chicago was $46,035 plus benefits and bonuses. A public relations director in Chicago had a median salary of $136,712 plus benefits and bonuses. The top public relations executives at a few major corporations, however, make more than $500,000 annually.[6]

The Council of Public Relations Firms says that account executives with 2–5 years experience typically make between $35,000 and $50,000 plus benefits and bonuses. An account supervisor with 5–10 years experience makes between $55,000 and $85,000 plus benefits and bonuses. The senior vice president with 10 or more years of experience is likely to make between $120,000 and $175,000 plus benefits and bonuses.[7]

The latest salary survey done by PRSA found the average public relations practitioner's salary was $69,000 plus $10,000 bonus. The average public relations consultant made $110,000 with $20,000 in bonuses.[8]

Age and Gender

The average age for those PRSA and IABC members surveyed was 39. It's important to note that the average age of practitioners has been dropping annually for at least the past decade.

Public Relations Student Society of America

Today students in public relations can be involved in one of 284 chapters of the Public Relations Student Society of America, an educational division of the parent Public Relations Society of America. In 2007, there were more than 9,600 student members of PRSSA across the United States. This was not always the case.

PRSSA was founded at the annual meeting of PRSA on November 11, 1967, in Philadelphia, with the support of J. Carroll Bateman, president of the society that year. Today, the PRSSA case study competition is named for Bateman. Public relations professionals had been looking at involving students in the professional society since 1950. The first nine chapters were charted in early 1968, with five more added before the year ended.

Dr. Frederick Teahan, APR, vice president for education for PRSA and founding father of PRSSA, wrote the following about PRSSA's first two decades: "What an unlikely time it was for the PRSA leadership to create a junior branch of the society. . . . Riots devastated cities. Violent protests about involvement in Vietnam were commonplace. The assassination of public figures both sickened and frightened. Widespread radicalism assaulted all American institutions—religion, government, the military, democracy. Universities themselves were denounced as 'irrelevant.' And all of this was inevitably connected in the popular mind with students. The champions of a public relations society of young collegiates, however, were undaunted. Radicalism appeared to be absent from the ranks of these pre-professionals."

It may have been an unlikely time to start, but PRSSA grew rapidly. It created its own national conference in 1976. One major requirement for a chapter was the number of public relations courses offered by the unit in which public relations was taught. That number increased to five public relations courses offered by the unit in 1988. That remains the standard. In its 40th anniversary year, 2007, the friends of PRSSA, called Champions, published *PRSSA, A Brief History* as a gift to the 81,000 PRSSA alumni and the generations of future students to come.

Source: F. H. "Chris" Teahan, *A Brief History: The First Two Decades,* and Susan Gonders and Barbara DeSanto, *A Brief History: The Second Two Decades* (New York: Public Relations Society of America, 2007).

More than 7 in 10 of the practitioners (71%) were female. In fact, the female:male ratio has nearly reversed itself in the last 25 or 30 years. Even so, men continue to hold proportionately more of the top managerial public relations posts, primarily because they have spent a greater number of years in the field. Salary differences between males and females is but one of the gender issues we consider later.[9]

The Intern Assignment

Case Study

You have been fortunate to get a paid internship for the summer working with Marissa and the public relations agency handling the Microsoft account. Marissa wants to do something this summer as a social marketing project. Your first assignment is to think about various social marketing projects that Microsoft might be involved with and to look at what publics and communication tools might be used. Answer the following questions:

1. What social projects would fit best with Microsoft in its northwestern United States location? Provide three ideas.
2. Who might be Microsoft's key external publics for one of these projects?
3. Who are Microsoft's key internal publics, and how would you want to involve them?
4. What media would you want to use in this project?
5. What other communication tools might work well?

Summary

For self-testing and additional chapter resources, go to the Online Learning Center at **www.mhhe.com/lattimore3e.**

Public relations is a management and relationship-building function based on effective two-way communication between an organization and its stakeholders. This function is carried out by public relations practitioners whose duties include a wide range of skills from effective writing to strategic planning. The public relations practitioner today is better educated, better paid, and better prepared to work in all types of organizations. At advanced levels public relations leaders design and execute communication campaigns, contribute to organizational strategic planning and decision-making, and assume responsibility for building and maintaining the organization's image and reputation.

While no exact figure of public relations practitioners in the United States is available, the Labor Bureau estimates there are about a quarter of a million public relations professionals here. However, public relations is a global function that is particularly fast-growing in Eastern Europe. Europe itself has about one-third the number of public relations practitioners in the United States. Asia is also a fast-growing region of the world for public relations followed by Latin America and then Africa.

Key Terms

public affairs
public relations

publics
social marketing

Notes

1. *Careers in Public Relations: A Guide to Opportunities in a Dynamic Industry,* Council of Public Relations Firms, retrieved from www.prfirms.org on Feb. 20, 2008, p. 8.

2. Charles S. Steinberg, *The Creation of Consent: Public Relations in Practice* (New York: Hastings House, 1975), p. 9.

3. Bureau of Labor Statistics. http://stats.bls .gov/oco/ocos086.htm, on Feb. 14, 2008.

4. *Profile 2000—A Survey of the Profession* (International Association of Business Communicators and Public Relations Society of America, 2001), p. A22.

5. Ibid., p. A5.

6. Retrieved from www.salary.com on Feb. 20, 2008.

7. Council of Public Relations Firms, *Careers in Public Relations: A Guide to Opportunities in a Dynamic Industry,* retrieved from www.prfirms.org on Feb. 18, 2008, p. 8.

8. *Profile 2000—A Survey of the Profession,* p. A5.

9. Ibid.

CHAPTER 2

The History of Public Relations

Newspapers have carried advertising since the days of the American Revolution. Benjamin Franklin, who was also a writer and an editor, published the most widely read newspaper in the American colonies. His *Pennsylvania Gazette* carried advertising for such everyday items as soap, books, and stationery. Franklin even wrote some of his own ads, one of which praises the superior features of the pot-bellied stove he invented.

People with a message to communicate have long recognized the power of public opinion to move others to action. That's why public opinion is one of the three factors responsible for the growth of public relations as a communications medium. The other two are competition among the many institutions that rely on public support and the development of media through which these organizations can reach the public. These three factors have motivated the evolution of public relations through four different traditions:

- The rhetorician and press agent tradition
- The journalistic and publicity tradition
- The persuasive communication campaign tradition
- The relationship-building and two-way communication tradition

As we look at each of these traditions throughout the chapter, you'll see that like many historical trends, they overlap somewhat. Each has been a product of the larger economic, political, social, and cultural forces of the time, as well as of the growth of mass media and specialized communications channels. We can think of them as a historical continuum of the strategic uses of communication by business organizations, social movements, not-for-profit groups, government agencies, and community groups.

But it is the lessons we learn from history that make its study important for us. In public relations we have the benefit of important principles developed and employed by many 20th-century practitioners. Ivy Lee teaches us that we must take positive action in order to have something worth communicating. Harold Burson, who built the largest public relations agency in the world, stresses a business culture of "caring and sharing," or "prize the individual and celebrate the team." Edward Bernays teaches us the importance of applying social science techniques to influence behavior.

This chapter presents the many individuals and social movements that have shaped our practice of public relations today. Learn the principles they developed, and be creative in applying them to the public relations discipline of the future.

RHETORICIAN AND PRESS AGENT TRADITION

The forerunner to modern-day public relations practice can be found in the work of **rhetoricians, press agents,** and other promoters. Since early times speechmakers, called rhetoricians, provided such communication services as speech-writing, speaking on clients' behalf, training for difficult questions, and persuasion skills.

For example, by Plato's day, ca. 427 to 347 BC, rhetoric as a distinct discipline was well established in Greece. The foremost rhetorician was Gorgias of Leontinium in Sicily (ca. 483–375 BC) who believed that the rhetorician's job was to foster persuasive skills more than it was to determine if arguments and claims were true or false, according to Helio Fred Garcia.[1] Garcia also noted that even in classical Athens, public opinion determined matters both large and small, from important public works projects such as building city walls to the appointment of generals and other high officeholders to settling matters of criminal justice.[2]

Persuasive skills have been used to influence the public and public opinion for hundreds of years. Artifacts of what can be construed as public relations materials survive from ancient India, Mesopotamia, Greece, and Rome. The Crusades, the exploits of Lady Godiva, the actions of Martin Luther, and the adventures of the conquistadores seeking El Dorado have all been explained as examples of ancient public relations activities. The creation in the 17th century of the Congregatio de Propaganda (the congregation for propagating the faith) by the Roman Catholic Church is often pointed to as a keystone in the development of public relations. The action brought us the term *propaganda* but was not a significant development in a church that exists to propagate the faith.

American Antecedents to Public Relations

Numerous examples of public relations–like activities were identifiable in the early days of American settlement as each of the colonies used publicity techniques to attract settlers. In 1641, Harvard College initiated the first systematic U.S. fund-raising campaign, which was supported by the first fund-raising brochure, *New England's First Fruits.*

Boston Tea Party staged by Samuel Adams.

In 1758, King's College (now Columbia University) issued the first press release—to announce graduation exercises.

Publicity techniques were even more prevalent at the time of the American Revolution and all subsequent conflicts or situations when power has been threatened or when public support is needed. Indeed, public relations has prospered most in times of extreme pressure or crisis. Such were the circumstances preceding the American Revolutionary War, when Samuel Adams initiated what can be called a public relations campaign. Adams was to the communication dimension of the Revolutionary War what George Washington was to the military dimension. Adams recognized the value of using symbols like the Liberty Tree that were easily identifiable and aroused emotions.

Adams also used slogans that are still remembered, like "taxation without representation is tyranny." Because he got his side of the story to a receptive public first, shots fired into a group of rowdies became known as "the Boston Massacre." Adams directed a sustained-saturation public relations campaign using all available media. He staged the Boston Tea Party to influence public opinion. In the Sons of Liberty and Committees of Correspondence, he provided the organizational structure to implement the actions made possible by his public relations campaign.[3]

Public Relations in a Young Nation

In the infancy of the United States, public relations was practiced primarily in the political sphere. The publication and dissemination of the Federalist Papers, which led to the ratification of the U.S. Constitution, has been called "history's finest public relations job."[4]

Early in his presidency, Andrew Jackson appointed Amos Kendall, a member of the famous Kitchen Cabinet, to serve as the candidate's pollster, counselor, ghostwriter, and publicist. Although he did not hold the title, Kendall effectively served as the first presidential press secretary and congressional liaison. Jackson, who could not express himself very well, used Kendall as a specialist to convey his ideas to Congress and the

American people through the newspapers of the day. Newspapers, for the first time, were beginning to reach a rising middle class as a result of urbanization and advances in public education and literacy rates. Still, communication was primarily face-to-face because the majority of Americans lived on farms or in small communities.

Publicity drove the settlement of the American western frontier, the biggest issue of the time. From Daniel Boone to Davy Crockett to Buffalo Bill, skillful and sometimes exaggerated promotion was the way to move easterners to the west. Even Jesse James got into the act when he issued a news release about one of his particularly daring train robberies. Business leaders, too, became aware of publicity's virtues. When Burlington Railroad initiated its 1858 publicity campaign, Charles Russell Lowell stated, "We must blow as loud a trumpet as the merits of our position warrants."[5]

P. T. Barnum and Press Agentry

Phineas T. Barnum has always been considered the master of press agentry, a promoter with endless imagination. Barnum promoted the midget General Tom Thumb; Jenny Lind, the "Swedish Nightingale"; Jumbo, the elephant; and Joice Heath, a 161-year-old woman (it was claimed, although an autopsy report after her death put her age at 70–80). Barnum used publicity to make money, pure and simple.

When P. T. Barnum died, the *London Times* fondly called him a "harmless deceiver." As long as press agentry is used to promote circuses, entertainment, and professional sports, its negative potential is limited. Its use in business and politics, however, is more threatening.

The Downside of Press Agentry

In the quest to gain media and public attention, press agentry can become increasingly outrageous, exploitive, and manipulative. Moreover, the manipulative attempt to gain the attention of the public through the media has an even darker side.

In 1878, French sociologist Paul Brousse described what he called the **"propaganda of the deed."** The term refers to a provocative act committed to draw attention toward an idea or grievance in order to get publicity. For European anarchists in the late 19th and early 20th centuries, propaganda of the deed meant bombing, murder, and assassination. European sociologists feared that press agents and rhetoricians could incite mob rule, thereby making governments and societies less stable. This is the same tactic used by terrorist organizations through attacks such as the 9/11 suicide flights into the World Trade Center and the Pentagon. Terrorists try to use their attacks to draw attention to their propaganda.

JOURNALISTIC AND PUBLICITY TRADITION

Societal conditions surrounding the 19th-century American Industrial Revolution paved the way for a new dominant model of public relations practice. The Industrial Revolution hit America with full force during the last quarter of the 19th century. The nation's population doubled as immigrants rushed to the land of opportunity. New products and new patterns of life rapidly emerged. The enforced rhythm of the factory, the stress of urban life, and the vast distinction between the bosses and the workers were new and not always pleasant realities of American life. In fact, social harmony was generally breaking down as evidenced by rising conflict and confrontation.

Businesses were racking up enormous profits but were losing public support in the process. Workers began to organize themselves into unions, and they perceived their interests in many cases as directly opposed to those of business owners. Business was at once highly successful and increasingly besieged. Historian Merle Curti wrote that corporations gradually began to realize the importance of combating hostility and to court public favor. The expert in the field of public relations was an inevitable phenomenon in view of the need for the services he or she could provide.[6]

In short, industrialization altered the structure of society and gave rise to conditions requiring public relations expertise. By the early 1900s, business was forced to submit to more and more governmental regulations and encountered increasingly hostile criticism from the press. Corporations recognized that deception, manipulation, and self-serving half-truths were inappropriate responses to challenges raised by media and government. As a result, public relations became a specialized function broadly accepted in major corporations in order to counter hostility by courting public support.

Not surprisingly, the term *public relations* came into use at this time; its earliest appearance was probably in Dorman B. Eaton's 1882 address to the graduating class of the Yale Law School. The concept, as noted, was not new, but the coining of the term suggested a new level of importance and consciousness. As historian Marc Bloch has commented, "The advent of a name is a great event even when the object named is not new, for the act of naming signifies conscious awareness."[7]

Early Public Relations Consultants

Former journalists began to find it possible to make a living in the public relations business. In 1900, George V. S. Michaelis established the Publicity Bureau in Boston. His job, as he saw it, was to gather factual information about his clients for distribution to newspapers. By 1906, his major clients were the nation's railroads. The railroads engaged the Publicity Bureau to head off adverse regulations being promoted by Theodore Roosevelt. The agency used fact-finding publicity and personal contact to push its clients' position, but it kept secret its connection with the railroad. The Publicity Bureau staff increased dramatically, with offices set up in New York, Chicago, Washington, D.C., St. Louis, and Topeka and with agents in California, South Dakota, and elsewhere.

President Theodore Roosevelt, who saw the presidency as "a bully pulpit," proved to be more than a match for the Publicity Bureau. The first president to make extensive use of press conferences and interviews, Roosevelt was said to rule the country from the newspapers' front pages. The passage of the Hepburn Act extended government control over the railroad industry and represented a clear victory for the Roosevelt administration.

The father of public relations and the man most credited with nurturing the fledgling public relations profession was Ivy Ledbetter Lee, son of a Georgia preacher. Lee was a reporter who, early on, saw better prospects in the publicity arena. After working in New York's 1903 mayoral campaign and for the Democratic National Committee, Lee joined George Parker, another newspaper veteran, to form the nation's third publicity agency in 1904.

Two years later, coal operators George F. Baer and Associates hired the partnership to represent their interests during a strike in the anthracite mines. John Mitchell, leader of the labor forces, was quite open and conversant with the press, which treated him and his cause with considerable sympathy. The tight-lipped Baer would not even talk to the president of the United States.

Lee took the assignment and persuaded Baer to open up. Then he promptly issued a Declaration of Principles to all newspaper city editors. The sentiments expressed in this document clearly indicated that public relations had entered its second stage.

As Eric Goldman observed, "The public was no longer to be ignored, in the traditional manner of business, nor fooled, in the continuing manner of the press agent."[8] Lee declared that the public was to be informed:

> This is not a secret press bureau. All our work is done in the open. We aim to supply news. This is not an advertising agency; if you think any of our matter ought properly to go to your business office, do not use it. Our matter is accurate. Further details on any subject treated will be supplied promptly, and any editor will be assisted most cheerfully in verifying directly any statement of fact. . . . In brief, our plan is, frankly and openly, on behalf of business concerns and public institutions, to supply to the press and public of the United States prompt and accurate information concerning subjects which it is of value and interest to the public to know about.[9]

In short, then, Lee's idea was to tell the truth about his client organizations' actions. He believed that if telling the truth damaged the organization, the organization should correct the problem so that the truth could be told without fear. That said, Lee's railroad clients did not react well to this treatise. Public relations historian Ray Hiebert wrote, "Many an old-timer with the railroad was dismayed when, almost immediately, Lee began revolutionizing things, putting into effect his theories about absolute frankness with the press."[10]

Lee's publicity arsenal was not limited to news releases. In helping stave off railroad freight regulations, Lee published leaflets, folders, and bulletins for customers; company news for employees; and other material for important decision makers, including congressmen, state legislators, mayors and city councilmen, economists, bankers, college presidents, writers, and clergymen.[11]

Lee realized that a corporation could not hope to influence the public unless its publicity was supported by good works. Performance determines publicity. To achieve necessary and positive consistency between words and actions, Lee urged his clients in business and industry to align their senses and their policies with the public interest. The public, Lee thought, was made up of rational human beings who, if they are given complete and accurate information, would make the right decisions. As a result, he said that his job was interpreting the Pennsylvania Railroad to the public and interpreting the public to the Pennsylvania Railroad. In short, Lee saw himself as a mediator bridging the concerns of business and the public's interests.

Then, in 1914, Lee was hired to remake the image of John D. Rockefeller, the owner of Standard Oil of New Jersey. Nine thousand coal miners went on strike in southern Colorado in September 1913. The Rockefellers were the principal stockholders in the largest company involved, the Colorado Fuel and Iron Company. In April 1914, an accidental shot resulted in a battle in which several miners, two women, and 11 children were killed. The Rockefellers were blamed, and their name was damaged. Lee advised the younger Rockefeller to practice a policy of openness. After the strike, Lee advised Rockefeller to visit the mining camps to observe conditions firsthand.

Lee died in disgrace, the victim of his own public relations policies. In the early 1930s, Lee advised the Interessen Gemeinschaft Farben Industrie, more commonly known as I. G. Farben, or the German Dye Trust. Eventually the Nazis took over, and the company asked Lee for advice on how to improve German–American relations. He told the company to be open and honest. Shortly before his death, Lee's connections with the Germans were investigated by the House Special Committee on Un-American

Activities. Headlines screamed "Lee Exposed as Hitler Press Agent," and his name was blackened throughout the United States.

Other early publicity offices were established by William Wolf Smith in Washington, D.C., in 1902; Hamilton Wright, San Francisco, 1908; Pendleton Dudley, New York's Wall Street district, 1909; Rex Harlow, Oklahoma City, 1912; and Fred Lewis and William Seabrook, Atlanta, 1912.

Not-for-Profit Organizations and Social Movements

Not-for-profit organizations, including colleges, churches, charitable causes, and health and welfare agencies, began to use publicity extensively in the early 20th century. In 1899, Anson Phelps Stokes converted Yale University's Office of the Secretary into an effective alumni and public relations office. Harvard president Charles W. Eliot, who spoke as early as 1869 on the need to influence public opinion toward advancement of learning, was among the Publicity Bureau's first clients in 1900. The University of Pennsylvania and the University of Wisconsin set up publicity bureaus in 1904. By 1917, the Association of American College News Bureaus was formed.

In 1905, the Washington, D.C., YMCA sought $350,000 for a new building. For the first time, a full-time publicist was engaged in a fund-raising drive. By 1908, the Red Cross and the National Tuberculosis Association were making extensive use of publicity agents. The New York Orphan Asylum was paying a publicity man $75 per month.

Churches and church groups were quick to recognize the value of an organized publicity effort. New York City's Trinity Episcopal Church was one of Pendleton Dudley's first clients in 1909. The Seventh-Day Adventist Church established its publicity office in 1912. George Parker, Ivy Lee's old partner, was appointed to handle publicity for the Protestant Episcopal Church in 1913.

Though largely neglected in histories of public relations, the social movements of the day adopted the same public relations techniques that were used by other not-for-profit organizations, according to public relations scholar Karen Miller. Moreover, she notes that public relations texts give virtually no attention to the women who headed such movements, including Clara Barton, Margaret Sanger, Susan B. Anthony, Ida B. Wells, and Elizabeth Cady Stanton. Each of these women used public relations techniques of the day most effectively to inform the public about controversial issues despite the fact that their work is generally considered to be outside the business frame of the field.[12]

Early Corporate Communications Departments

As early as 1883, AT&T leader Theodore Vail expressed concern about the company's relationship with the public and the public's conflicts with the company. He built support from the middle class for AT&T programs by implementing cut-rate phone bills, friendly greetings from the telephone operator, employee morale programs, and paid advertising. In 1907, he hired James Drummond Ellsworth for AT&T's public relations. Ellsworth promoted efficient operation and consideration of customers' needs, a systematic method for answering complaints, and acceptance of governmental regulation as the price for operating a privately owned natural monopoly.

By 1888, the Mutual Life Insurance Company employed Charles J. Smith to manage a "species of literary bureau." A year later, George Westinghouse, head of Westinghouse Electric, established the first corporate communications department. Samuel Insull, an associate of George Westinghouse, rose to head the Chicago Edison Company, an electric utility. In 1903, he began to publish *The Electric City*, a magazine aimed at gaining the understanding and goodwill of the community. He pioneered films for public relations purposes in 1909, and in 1912 he introduced bill stuffers, messages to customers in their monthly statements.

Among the greatest of industrial publicity users was Henry Ford. The Ford Company pioneered use of several public relations tools. The employee periodical *Ford Times* was begun in 1908 and continues today. In 1914, a corporate film department was established. Ford also surveyed 1,000 customers to gain insights into their attitudes and concerns.

Astute corporate communicators began recognizing that well-informed employees could serve as ambassadors of corporate goodwill. In fact, George Michaelis, who had founded the Publicity Bureau in Boston, advised George Westinghouse in 1914 to pay more attention to internal "human relations." Thus, employees became recognized as a significant public and an appropriately important audience for public relations efforts. By 1925, more than half of all manufacturing companies were publishing employee magazines.

Early Government Public Relations

The greatest public relations effort in history, up to its time, was the one mounted in support of the U.S. effort in World War I. The military had utilized publicity for several years; the Marine Corps established a publicity bureau in Chicago in 1907. Never before had such a massive, multifaceted, coordinated program been mounted. Moreover, though often used by big business in a defensive fashion, public relations took the offensive when it came to war.

THE PERSUASIVE COMMUNICATION CAMPAIGN TRADITION

In many respects, the beginnings of the persuasive campaign tradition are imbedded in the U.S. World War I publicity and propaganda program.

The Creel Committee

Woodrow Wilson set up a Committee on Public Information in 1917, and newspaperman George Creel was asked to run it. With a staff of journalists, scholars, artists, and others skilled at manipulating words and symbols, Creel mobilized the home front with a comprehensive propaganda bureau that utilized all media, including film and photography.

Creel did not just work out of a central office; he decentralized the organization and the effort. Every industry had a special group of publicity workers tending to their particular contributions to the war effort. Political scientist Harold D. Lasswell was involved in the Creel organization. Looking back to assess the situation, Lasswell concluded, "Propaganda is one of the most powerful instrumentalities in the modern world."[13]

Although the methods used by Creel's committee were fairly standard tools of the public information model, the Creel committee achieved great success because it made use, without knowing it, of psychological principles of mass persuasion. Committee members constructed messages that appealed to what people believed and wanted to hear. Clearly, the Creel committee demonstrated the power of mass persuasion and social influence at a national level.

The success prompted thoughtful Americans to give more concerted attention to the nature of public opinion and the role of the public in society. Educational philosopher John Dewey and his supporters believed that wartime propaganda and postwar societal focus on business development signaled that the citizenry was losing interest in civic life. In contrast, well-spoken political commentator Walter Lippmann professed that American society had grown too complex for the average citizen to understand. The government, he thought, should be influenced and run by experts who could interpret the public will in light of national needs and concerns. The Lippmann interpretation prompted professional persuaders like Edward Bernays to emphasize that the function of public relations was to change images and influence public perception of issues.

Given the pro-business attitudes of the 1920s and 1930s, it's little wonder that Lippmann's ideas swamped Dewey's. Critical scholar Margaret Duffy notes that Lippmann's ideas were "grafted" by Edward Bernays, the focal practitioner of the persuasive communication campaign tradition.[14]

Edward Bernays

The leading proponent of persuasion was clearly Edward Bernays, the nephew of psychoanalyst Sigmund Freud. Bernays grew up with dinner-table social science discussions prior to joining Creel's public information committee. After World War I he became a science writer and then a theater promoter, where he combined his journalistic and persuasion interests.

Bernays understood that publics could be persuaded if the message supported their values and interests. In many ways, the thrust of his philosophy is made clear in his first book, *Crystallizing Public Opinion*. At the time, he saw public relations as being more or less synonymous with propaganda, which he defined as "the conscious and intelligent manipulation of the organized habits and opinions of the masses."[15]

Throughout his career Bernays described public relations as the science of creating circumstances, mounting events that are calculated to stand out as newsworthy, yet at the same time do not appear to be staged. Staged "media events" were clearly a defining characteristic of the agency that Bernays started in 1919 with Doris Fleischman, his future wife and partner. Bernays's most well-known event was "Lights Golden Jubilee." Underwritten in 1929 by General Electric and the National Electric Light Association, the jubilee media event recognized the 50-year anniversary of Thomas Edison's invention of the electric lightbulb. Bernays cast the celebration as a premier testimony to the genius of American business and entrepreneurial spirit. It was staged as a massive display of lighting in Dearborn, Michigan, and at other locations around the world. Prior to the event Bernays orchestrated tremendous press coverage and magazine features, salutatory proclamations and endorsements from mayors, governors, and other statesmen throughout the United States and western Europe. The real newsworthiness, however, came on the day of the event when the assembled dignitaries on the Dearborn platform included President Herbert Hoover, J. P. Morgan, John D. Rockefeller Jr., Orville Wright, Madame Curie, and *The New York Times* publisher Adolph Ochs.

RELATIONSHIP-BUILDING AND TWO-WAY COMMUNICATION TRADITION

While Bernays was championing the persuasive campaign approach to public relations, a very different perspective was being set forth by Arthur Page, a successful businessman, public servant, writer, and editor.

Arthur Page

Arthur Page was approached with an offer to become vice president of AT&T, succeeding the pioneer public relations specialist James D. Ellsworth. Page agreed to accept the position only on the condition that he would not be restricted to publicity in the traditional sense. He demanded and received a voice in company policy and insisted that the company's performance be the determinant of its public reputation. Page maintained that all business in a democratic country begins with public permission and exists by public approval. If that be true, it follows that business should be cheerfully willing to tell the public what its policies are, what it is doing, and what it hopes to do. This seems practically a duty.[16]

Page viewed public relations as a broad-based management function that transcended both the journalistic publicity and persuasive communication campaign traditions. Under Page's leadership, however, the company recognized that winning public confidence required not merely ad hoc attempts to answer criticism. Rather, a continuous and planned program of positive public relations using institutional advertising, the usual stream of information flowing through press releases, and other methods were needed. Bypassing the conventional print media, the company went directly to the public, establishing, for instance, a film program to be shown to schools and civic groups.

AT&T sought to maintain direct contact with as many of its clients as possible. The company made a total commitment to customer service. Moreover, money was deposited into a number of different banks, legal business was given to attorneys throughout the country, and contracts for supplies and insurance were made with many local agencies. AT&T paid fees for employees to join outside organizations, knowing that through their presence the company would be constantly represented in many forums. Finally, the company sought to have as many people as possible own its stock. Today, AT&T and the successor companies that were created by divestiture in 1984 are the most widely held of all securities.

What truly set Page apart and established him as a pioneer was his insistence that the publicity department act as an interpreter of the public to the company, drawing on a systematic and accurate diagnosis of public opinion. Page wanted data, not hunches. Under his direction, the AT&T publicity department (as it was still called) kept close check on company policies, assessing their impact on the public. Thus, Page caused the company "to act all the time from the public point of view, even when that seems in conflict with the operating point of view."[17]

Page insisted that his staff practice six principles of public relations:

1. *Tell the Truth.* Let the public know what's happening and provide an accurate picture of the company's character, ideals, and practices.

2. *Prove It with Action.* Public perception of an organization is determined 90 percent by doing and 10 percent by talking.

3. *Listen to the Customer.* To serve the company well, understand what the public wants and needs. Keep top decision makers and other employees informed about company products, policies, and practices.

4. *Manage for Tomorrow.* Anticipate public relations and eliminate practices that create difficulties. Generate goodwill.

5. *Conduct Public Relations as if the Whole Company Depends on It.* Corporate relations is a management function. No corporate strategy should be implemented without considering its impact on the public. The public relations professional is a policymaker capable of handling a wide range of corporate communications activities.

6. *Remain Calm, Patient, and Good-Humored.* Lay the groundwork for public relations miracles with consistent, calm, and reasoned attention to information and contacts. When a crisis arises, remember that cool heads communicate best.

Public relations historian Karen Miller Russell believes that Page may come closest among early practitioners of representing the sense of the relationship-building and two-way communication tradition. This shows up, says Russell, in Page's continual quest for government-industry accommodation. He led the effort with Columbia University social scientist Paul Lazarsfeld to conduct regularly scheduled research with customers, employees, and other key publics to assess AT&T's standing among those groups. In turn, he used that feedback both to encourage organizational change and to fine-tune messages regarding the company's identity. (See spotlight 2.1 for a brief biographical sketch of leading public relations pioneers.)

The Depression and World War II

Although corporate and agency public relations practice grew handily as part of the 1920s business boom, it was the Great Depression of the 1930s and the personal leadership of President Franklin Roosevelt that further transformed the practice. With help from public relations practitioners like Carl Byoir, Roosevelt built public support and changed public opinion toward his New Deal recovery programs with weekly radio broadcasts and numerous other techniques, including those described in mini-case 2.1 featuring counselor Carl Byoir.

Roosevelt's presidency was highlighted by both the Great Depression and World War II. In June 1942, with America fully engaged in worldwide war, the Office of War Information (OWI) was established. Similar to Creel's effort in World War I, a massive public relations effort was mounted to rally the home front. Elmer Davis directed the program. The goals of the OWI included selling war bonds; rationing food, clothing, and gasoline; planting victory gardens; and recruiting military personnel. Other issues promoted were factory productivity and efficiency.

Post–World War II

The period following World War II represented a high point in professional growth and development of public relations practice. Many leading practitioners from the 1950s to the 1980s were among the nearly 75,000 Americans who had the "ultimate public relations internship," learning public relations practice during wartime while working for the OWI.

Several important communication agencies still active today trace their beginnings to the OWI. These include the Voice of America, the American Advertising Council, and the United States Information Agency, which sponsors scholarly and cultural exchanges. Many OWI veterans applied their wartime skills to initiate public information and public relations programs for government agencies, nonprofit organizations, schools, colleges, and hospitals. Moss Kendrix, a pioneer African American public relations practitioner, was one of those whose career paths were launched while working with the Treasury Department promoting war bonds.[23]

And yet the hallmark of postwar public relations growth took place in the private sector, in corporations and agencies. A consumer economy made use of both public relations and advertising to market products. Agencies came into full being, providing media relations and media contact capabilities not always available on the corporate side. The need for these skills was driven in part by the explosive growth of media outlets not available before the war—including FM radio, general magazines, suburban community newspapers, and trade and professional association publications. Their services expanded from a base of counseling and media relations to include public affairs or government relations, financial and investor relations, crisis communication, and media relations training for executives.

P. T. Barnum. A consummate showman during the middle and late 1800s, Barnum originated many methods for attracting public attention. He didn't let truth interfere with his publicity and press agentry techniques. Although he contributed positively to our understanding of the power of publicity, his lack of honesty led to a legacy of mistrust of publicity efforts that exists sometimes even today.

George Michaelis. Organizer of the nation's first publicity firm, the Publicity Bureau in Boston in 1900, Michaelis used fact-finding publicity and personal contact to saturate the nation's press.

Ivy Lee. Often called the father of modern public relations, Lee believed the public should be informed. He recognized that good words had to be supported by positive actions on the part of individuals and organizations. His emphasis on public relations as a management function put public relations on the right track with corporate America.

George Creel. As head of the Committee on Public Information during World War I, Creel used public relations techniques to sell liberty bonds, build the Red Cross, and promote food conservation and other war-related activities. In so doing, he proved the power of public relations and trained a host of the 20th century's most influential practitioners.

Edward Bernays. An intellectual leader in the field, Bernays coined the phrase *public relations counsel,* wrote *Crystallizing Public Opinion* (the first book on public relations), and taught the first college-level public relations course at New York University in 1923. Bernays emphasized the social science contribution to public relations and was a leading advocate for public relations professionalism through practitioner licensing or credentialing. He remained an active counselor, writer, and speaker until his death in 1995 at age 103.

Arthur Page. When offered a vice presidency at AT&T, Page insisted he have a voice in shaping corporate policy. He maintained that business in a democratic country depends on public permission and approval.

John Hill. Along with Don Knowlton, John Hill opened a public relations agency in Cleveland, Ohio, in 1927. When John Hill moved to New York a few years later to open Hill & Knowlton, Knowlton was not part of the agency. The New York–based agency, though, continued to bear both their names. It became the largest public relations agency in the world and continues to rank in the top grouping. John Hill had major steel and tobacco accounts in his counseling career. His agency was sold to J. Walter Thompson in 1980 for $28 million. In 1987, it was sold to the English-based WPP Group for $85 million.

Doris Fleischman Bernays. Doris Fleischman Bernays was Edward Bernays's counselor partner from their marriage in 1922 until retirement in 1952. She counseled corporations, government agencies, and presidents along with her husband. She struggled for equality, not with her husband, but with the attitudes of American business that often paid less attention to the advice given by a female public relations practitioner.

Leone Baxter. She and her husband, Clem Whitaker, developed the public relations specialty of political media consultant. They met at a meeting in support of the Central Valley Project in California in 1933. Out of that meeting came an offer for the two to organize a campaign to defeat a Pacific Gas & Electric–sponsored referendum. They were successful, winning by 33,000 votes. PG&E then hired the pair on a $10,000-a-year retainer, an account they kept for more than 25 years. This account led to a partnership as Whitaker and Baxter International.[18] It also led to their marriage. In their professional partnership they rotated every year as president of the company and divided their profits evenly. *Time* magazine called them the "acknowledged originals in the field of political public relations."

Carl Byoir. Carl Byoir, like Edward Bernays, was another member of George Creel's Committee on Public Information in World War I. After the war he founded Carl Byoir and Associates in 1930 to promote tourism to Cuba. He was known

On the organizational or client side, new services areas were added to complement the existing areas of publicity/media relations, employee publications, community relations, and audiovisual services. Chief among these was a new public affairs component to develop relationships with governmental offices in the legislative and executive branches of government. Initially, governmental affairs, or public affairs, built on community relations practices, but it soon came into its own, oftentimes as a result of new federal Great Society programs begun in the 1960s and 1970s. Civil rights, environmental, urban development, and similar programs all mandated citizen involvement or public participation assessments to determine how various **stakeholders** and established publics were affected by changes in land use, zoning, and community development activities.

for his use of third-party endorsements, use of newspaper advertising as a public relations tool, and development of lobbying in legislative battles for clients such as A&P, Libby-Owens-Ford, and Eastern Railroads.

Rex Harlow. Harlow was a leading public relations educator. He began teaching a public relations course at Stanford in 1939 and may have been the first full-time professor of public relations. He also founded the American Council on Public Relations in 1939. The council eventually merged with the National Association of Public Relations Councils to form the Public Relations Society of America in 1947. Harlow founded the *Public Relations Journal* in 1944 and the *Social Science Reporter* in 1952.

Moss Kendrix. Kendrix, an African American public relations pioneer, developed numerous public relations and advertising campaigns and messages for such clients as Coca-Cola, Carnation, Ford Motor Company, and the National Education Association. Born in 1917 in Atlanta and educated at Morehouse College, Kendrix was editor of his college newspaper and co-founder of Phi Delta Delta Journalism Society, the only African American journalism society for decades.[19]

Kendrix was drafted in World War II and served in the U.S. Army working for the War Finance Office. There he received his on-the-job public relations experience traveling throughout the country with African American celebrities promoting war bonds.

In 1944, Moss Kendrix established his own public relations firm in Washington, D.C. His highly successful public relations work for the Republic of Liberia's Centennial Celebration launched his future career in public relations working with major corporations and national nonprofit agencies such as the National Dental Association and NEA.[20]

In addition to his public relations consulting, Kendrix also hosted the weekly radio program *Profiles of Our Times.* He died in 1989.

Denny Griswold. Griswold founded and served for almost 40 years as editor of *Public Relations News,* the first weekly newsletter devoted to public relations. Her professional experience included work for broadcasting networks, *Forbes, BusinessWeek,* and Bernays's public relations firm. Her newsletter published thousands of case studies. She not only covered the profession, but she helped give it identity by honoring many of its leaders in her newsletter.[21]

Chester Burger. A "counselor to counselors" in public relations, was honored as the first life member of the Counselor's Academy. He is renowned for his many public relations campaigns in civil rights and public diplomacy. His public relations career began, though, like many early public relations practitioners with work in the media. He joined CBS in 1941 as a page and left there in 1955 after he had risen to National Manager of CBS News. World War II interrupted his career with CBS. He served in the U.S. Army Air Force and produced the army's

first broadcasts. In 1946, he returned to CBS from the army and was the nation's first television news reporter.[22]

Chester Burger & Co., his communications management consulting firm, included clients such as AT&T, Sears, American Bankers Association, American Cancer Society, Texas Instruments, and Occidental Petroleum Corporation. He is the author of six books on management.

Patrick Jackson. Highly regarded public relations counselor Patrick Jackson served the profession with distinction for more than 30 years until his death in 2001. He published the trade newsletter *pr reporter,* where he reported on current research affecting public relations practice with an emphasis on applying communication and behavioral science research findings. He also served as president of the Public Relations Society of America.

Harold Burson. A native of Memphis, Burson founded Burson-Marsteller Public Relations with Bill Marsteller, an advertising agency owner, in 1953. While the Marsteller ad agency owned 51 percent of the public relations agency, the public relations firm was a freestanding, separate company. The agency grew to become the world's largest public relations agency by expanding both in the United States and to 35 countries around the world and remains at or near the top today. Burson believes behavioral change should be the goal of most public relations objectives. He remains on Burson-Marsteller's executive board as founding chairman.

The new mandated citizen involvement and public participation programs exemplified the growing relationship-building and two-way communication tradition. The two-way tradition involved building long-term relationships with publics and important stakeholders for organizations to recognize. Programs were geared not toward persuasion but rather toward mutual understanding, compromise, and creating win-win situations for organizations and their affected publics and stakeholders. In many respects this approach had already been adopted across regulated industries such as public utilities, cable television businesses, and others for which license renewals and rate increases were contingent on government approval. In turn, that approval was contingent on the licensee demonstrating community support by showing that the needs of various publics had been addressed in the renewal application.

Franklin Delano Roosevelt became ill with polio in 1921 while vacationing a few months after his defeat as vice president on the James Cox Democratic ticket of 1920. Roosevelt narrowly escaped death from the polio and fought the crippling effects of the disease for the rest of his life.

In 1926, Roosevelt bought a rundown spa in Warm Springs, Georgia, from friend and philanthropist George Peabody. The spa—with 1,200 acres, a hotel, and cottages—was in poor shape, but the curative powers of the hot mineral springs held promise for many polio victims.

When Roosevelt was elected governor of New York in 1928, he realized he wouldn't have time to oversee the rehabilitation effort at Warm Springs, so he asked his law partner, Basil O'Conner, to lead the effort. O'Conner formed the Warm Springs Foundation to raise money for the refurbishing of the health resort, but the stock market crash in 1929 made fund-raising difficult.

When Roosevelt became president in 1932, the foundation was nearly bankrupt. However, one of the foundation fund-raisers, Keith Morgan, hired a public relations counselor, Carl Byoir, to do the job. Byoir had founded his own public relations agency in 1930 to promote tourism to Cuba. Byoir's fund-raising idea for the Warm Springs Foundation was to create a special event to raise the money. That event turned out to be birthday balls around the country to celebrate President Roosevelt's birthday on January 30, 1934.

Byoir sent letters to newspaper editors around the country asking them to nominate a birthday ball director for their area. If an editor didn't respond, he went to either the Democratic Party chairman in the area or to the Roosevelt-appointed postmaster to ask them to do the ball. Media were besieged with information about the balls. National syndicated columnist and broadcaster Walter Winchell presented an appeal that was so good it would be used for years for both birthday balls and the March of Dimes. Radio personalities tried to outdo one another in promoting the balls. In the end 6,000 balls were held in 3,600 communities, and more than $1 million was raised for the foundation.

The next two years the event was changed to split the proceeds, with 70 percent going to local communities and 30 percent to a newly created national polio research commission.

Carl Byoir led the first three birthday balls. He then left because he had become disillusioned with President Roosevelt when FDR "packed" the Supreme Court in 1937.

But out of Byoir's effort came not only the birthday balls but also the March of Dimes, the National Foundation for Infantile Paralysis, and finally victory over polio. Carl Byoir had elevated fund-raising to a new level through his public relations efforts and had given new insight into techniques that public relations practitioners continue to use today.

Questions

1. What have other not-for-profits done that build on this concept of a national special event?
2. Check out the St. Jude Children's Research Hospital Web site (www.stjude.org) to find out about its Thanks & Giving Program. How does it capitalize on a national audience to give to St. Jude?

Source: Scott M. Cutlip, *The Unseen Power* (Hillsdale, NJ: Erlbaum, 1994), pp. 553–63.

Harold Burson

Harold Burson personifies this post–World War II growth of public relations. The cofounder of Burson-Marstellar Public Relations, one of the world's largest and most respected agencies, Burson came from humble beginnings. He grew up in Memphis, Tennessee. His parents were immigrants. They couldn't afford to put him through college, so he paid his way through Ole Miss by serving as a campus reporter for the *Memphis Commercial Appeal*. He served as an enlisted man in the combat engineers in World War II and later covered the Nuremberg trials for army radio network.[24]

In 1946 Burson began his own public relations agency. He soon became a leader in the postwar boom of public relations that saw a small discipline of less than 20,000 practitioners grow to a major career opportunity today, with more than 400,000 practitioners estimated by the U.S. Department of Labor.

Burson joined with Bill Marsteller in 1953 to form Burson-Marsteller, which became the world's largest public relations agency. It continues to be among the top three agencies in the world today. Burson was CEO for 35 years and managed the expansion of the agency into more than 35 countries. Crediting much of the success of the agency to hiring valuable people who often spent their entire careers with the agency, Burson says that if he were to start again, he would pay even more attention to "recruiting, training, developing, motivating, and rewarding key employees." He suggests that the success of his agency is primarily related to four key actions:

1. Hiring a cadre of *dedicated employees* who worked for the firm for many years.
2. Developing a *family atmosphere* with a team approach for the business.
3. Creating a *corporate culture* proactively by seeding new offices with experienced Burson-Marsteller employees who hired and trained local people.
4. Positioning the firm as a *leader* by being the first to use multimedia (including its own broadcast studio with satellite uplink and downlink), crisis simulation, health care practice, and personal computers.[25]

See video clip #5 on the Online Learning Center for the interview with Harold Burson.[26]

Moss Kendrix

Moss Kendrix, an African American public relations pioneer, developed numerous public relations and advertising campaigns and messages for such clients as Coca-Cola, Carnation, Ford Motor Company, and the National Education Association. Kendrix was born in 1917 in Atlanta and educated at Morehouse College.[27]

Kendrix was drafted in World War II and served in the U.S. Army working for the War Finance Office, where he received his on-the-job public relations experience traveling throughout the country with African American celebrities promoting war bonds.

In 1944, Moss Kendrix established his own public relations firm in Washington, D.C. He successfully did the public relations work for the Republic of Liberia's Centennial Celebration, which launched his future career in public relations.

In addition to his public relations consulting, Kendrix also hosted a weekly radio program called *Profiles of Our Times.* He died in 1989.

Fund-raising events, such as this WalkAmerica for March of Dimes, use public relations tools to make them successful events.

Professionalization of the Field

More important, perhaps, were the concerted measures taken to establish public relations as a defined, respectable, and accepted field of professional practice. In fact, the 40 years from 1960 to 2000 are perhaps best characterized as the professional-development-building era in public relations. In 1947, Boston University established the first school of public relations. Two years later, 100 colleges and universities offered classes in the subject.

Perhaps more than anything else, the 50-year period between the end of World War II and the Internet explosion was characterized by professionalizing the practice. Two major national professional associations were formed from mergers of smaller groups. The largest, the PRSA, began in 1948 and now maintains a membership of 20,000, including more than 110 local chapters as well as university student organizations under the name of the Public Relations Student Society of America. In 1954 the PRSA developed the first code of ethics for the profession. The society set up a grievance board for code enforcement in 1962, a program of voluntary accreditation in 1964, and a rewritten ethics code in 2000.

In 1970 the International Association of Business Communicators (IABC) was formed by the merger of the International Council of Industrial Editors and the Association of Industrial Editors. The IABC has been at the forefront in underwriting research studies, examining the current state and future of the public relations profession. Both PRSA and IABC now administer professional continuing education programs for their members and an accreditation program. Practitioners who pass both oral and written accreditation exams are deemed accredited and allowed to place the initials APR or ABC after their names on their business cards. PRSA uses APR (Accredited Public Relations); IABC uses ABC (Accredited Business Communicator).

In addition to PRSA and IABC, today more than a dozen national public relations organizations are based in the United States, not to mention those whose membership is largely outside the United States. They're listed here to indicate the range of professionally organized specialties within public relations:

Religious Public Relations Council, founded in 1929.

National School Public Relations Association, founded in 1935.

Public Relations Society of America, founded in 1948. Includes 21,000 members, not counting members of the affiliated Public Relations Student Society of America.

Agricultural Relations Council, founded in 1953.

International Public Relations Association, founded in 1955.

National Society of Fund-Raising Executives, founded in 1960.

National Investor Relations Institute, founded in 1969.

International Association of Business Communicators, founded in 1970 and now with 13,000 members.

Council for the Advancement and Support of Education (CASE), founded in 1975.

National Association of Government Communicators, founded in 1976.

Issue Management Council, founded in 1982.

The Arthur Page Society, founded in 1983.

Society of Healthcare Strategy and Marketing Development, founded in 1996 and subsuming previous hospital and health care public relations associations.

Association of Counseling Firms, founded in 1999.

1920s: Systematic understanding of the importance and nature of public opinion emerged not only in terms of polling and scientific measurement but also as a social organizing process around issues.

1950s: Persuasion and social influence principles, and especially those set forth with the Yale Communication Program, provided the strategies for establishing, maintaining, and changing opinions and attitudes.

1960s: The diffusion of innovations research tradition served as a conceptual framework for public relations practitioners, health communicators, and Peace Corps officials on how to combine interpersonal and media communication to change behaviors. Most recently, the diffusion framework has been used to illustrate the use of marketing communication elements, including publicity, advertising, sales promotion, and direct selling.

1970s: Situational theory of publics was put forth. While public relations practitioners use a range of audience segmentation techniques, J. Grunig's situational theory explains which publics will become most active regarding specific issues. Relational communication, with its roots in interpersonal communication, set forth by Rogers and Millar, accounts for conditions prompting and inhibiting relational development.

1960s–1990s: Social psychological foundations underpinning public relations practice flourished alongside specific public relations theories. Many of these theories are used to study cognitive or knowledge change and information processing in public relations and health communication. These include attitude/action consistency, expectancy value theory, co-orientation, theory of reasoned action, framing theory, social cognitive theory, and game theory.

1970s–2000: Normative influences on the practice of public relations have underpinned important research on practitioner roles, feminization of the field, and other gender-related effects.

1980s–2000: J. Grunig's four models of public relations based on one-way/two-way and balanced/unbalanced communication have prompted the greatest amount of recent research and theory development in public relations.

Social and organizational structural influences on the growth and nature of public relations work, including research on public relations in different industry categories, structurally determined cross-cultural impacts on the practice, and encroachment on the public relations functions by related areas, became evident.

1990s–2010: Critical theory approaches emerged. Scholars in this tradition believe that the practice and study of public relations from a business and organizational standpoint mask power differences in society and ignore nonmainstream groups, including social movements and third-party candidates.

Professional and specialized public relations organizations also started professional magazines and newsletters, such as the *Public Relations Journal* and *Communication World*, which were followed by other private newsletters and trade magazines, such as the *Ragan Report, PR News, PR Tactics, PR Week, pr reporter*, and *Public Relations Quarterly*. Taken together, these professional publications form a distinctive literature aimed at those practitioners.

Public relations texts were published once college-level courses were offered, first as a concentration within the journalism or mass communication major and later within speech communication or integrated communication. Then came the academic journals, where university professors published research findings or developed new theoretical traditions to explain the practice of public relations. The principal journals were *Public Relations Review, Public Relations Research and Education, Public Relations Research Annual*, and the *Journal of Public Relations Research*. A public relations literature or body of knowledge was developing separately from related fields such as advertising, journalism, public opinion, and interpersonal communication. Those conceptual underpinnings were grounded in theory and are outlined chronologically in spotlight 2.2.

Taken together, these new professional magazines, texts, and research publications all reinforced the growing consensus that public relations work could be organized in terms of a four-step process—research, planning, communication and action (implementation), and evaluation. As time went on, the field gained even more respect as program plans expanded to include measurable objectives and follow-up evaluation measures to assess the impact, the cost, and ways to improve future campaigns and programs.

New Stakeholder Groups

In the late 1960s and the 1970s, democratically inspired social movements used effective public relations techniques to oppose business interests. With little money or staff, environmental group members, for example, became proficient at staging tree huggings, roadblocks, and other events whose conflict themes were almost guaranteed to generate television footage. They effectively used not only alternative and specialized media but also journalistic conventions, sometimes at the expense of losing their hard edge, according to sociologists Todd Gitlin and Charlotte Ryan.[28]

Societal concerns during the late 1960s and 1970s prompted businesses and their public relations agencies to place new emphasis on governmental and community relations, issue tracking, issue management, and strategic planning. This was especially the case with regulated businesses, such as utilities and telecommunication firms whose rate structures, franchises, and licensing requirements placed a premium on effective relationship building among key constituencies.

THE GLOBAL INFORMATION SOCIETY

Another distinct phase in public relations history emerged around 1990 and was characterized by (1) the use of the Internet and other new communication technologies and (2) the growth of public relations agencies, which occurred oftentimes either by merging with larger public relations agencies or advertising agencies or by forming alliances with other firms in regional cities.

The 1990s were also characterized by the growth of specialty practices in public relations. Investor relations, though begun 20 years earlier, came into its own as technology companies sought venture capital, became stock-held corporations through initial public offerings, and later merged with other public corporations. Thus, keeping stockholders informed and attracting new investors became a central, rather than peripheral, public relations function.

By 1990 leading firms had aligned their corporate giving with ongoing community relations programs. As well, their global reach throughout the 1990s led to more focus on corporate social responsibility in general rather than corporate giving in a narrow sense. Issues management and environmental scanning functions became more systematic, owing to computer databases and tracking systems in which organizations could join chat groups, listservs, and blogs.

The opening of new markets on a global scale led to systems of global strategic design with local implementation and a noticeably heavier emphasis given to intercultural issues or differences in the ways companies could offer themselves and their products in different cultures and regions of the world.

At home, a much greater degree of specialization began occurring at agencies as they sought to develop more subject matter competence in key industrial niches, including technology, health care, financial and investor institutions, and international practice.

Another milestone was reached when it became known that more and more public relations practitioners were seeking master's degrees either to become more specialized within the field of public relations or as a way of taking on more general management responsibilities.

The 1990s was a time of explosive growth for public relations and corporate communication stemming in large part from (1) growth and use of the Internet, (2) global communication demands, and (3) proliferating communication channels.

The Internet

It's little wonder that the Internet changed the nature of public relations work. In its early days, seven people every second logged on for the first time. Public relations Internet expert Don Middleberg forecasted 1 billion Internet users by 2010, with most of the new users coming from outside the United States.[29] To put the impact of the Internet in perspective, those who study media adoption note that it took radio 30 years to reach an audience of 50 million, and TV took 13 years; by contrast, the Internet took just 4 years. By 2000, e-mail had become the preferred medium for reaching reporters with whom an organization had already developed relationships.

Before the Internet, the thrust of media relations work was "pushing" information from the organization to the desks of media reports, producers, and editors via news releases, news tips, and press kits. That all changed because the Web gives the reporter the opportunity to pull and parse needed company information from the Web site and all of its links without ever going through the public relations or media relations office. Dot-com journalists believe they have deadlines every second. As media relations expert Carole Howard notes, "The media day has turned into the media hour and now the media minute or second."[30] The key point here is that the Internet is a very different and more powerful media relations tool than almost any over the preceding 50 years.

It is now commonplace for reporters to check Web sites while writing their stories, especially broad-based pieces. This requires organizations to update their Web sites regularly and to make all the media "pages" and links readily accessible so that reporters who cover an organization come to consider its Web site a current, useful, and trusted source.

Search engines like Google have also revolutionized the way journalists and public relations practitioners gather information. Likewise, blogs of a given subject give readers a pulse on current issues. Finally, Webcasting by particular organizations or promoting specific issues is readily available for the Internet savvy.

Journalists and public relations practitioners are not the only ones reaping the benefits of the Internet. Fund-raising groups, nonprofit organizations, and political/social movements all use these new and relatively "free" technologies to meet their needs, allowing them to operate more competitively within their limited budgets. See chapter 9 for more about the technical changes in media relations.

Global Communication Demands

Just as Internet Web sites and e-mail functions have reshaped public relations practice, so too has the creation of new consumer and financial markets around the world. Competition for worldwide markets speeds product introduction times. As a result, trade magazine editors and financial reports clamor for updated information almost by the hour. Gone, then, are the days when publicity releases could be planned and scheduled weeks and months in advance.

The new worldwide public relations environment means working simultaneously with the media across various cultures, nations, and regions. Under these conditions, public relations practitioners are forced to be better versed in intercultural communication practices and to understand differences in the ways media reporters and editors are approached or contacted in different cultures.

In Japan, for example, contact with the media is made through "press clubs" maintained separately by each industry or at government press rooms maintained by each government minister. Press club secretaries decide whether to issue press releases, call press conferences, or do nothing. The press club seal of endorsement—especially regarding press conferences—markedly increases newspaper coverage.

Proliferating Communication Channels

The proliferation of media channels—especially cable channels and new magazine titles—continues in response to individual and media desires for more specialized information tailored to the various reading and viewing interests of investors, customers, employees, donors, and so on. For public relations practitioners this means matching the qualities of traditional and **online** media to the information needs of their target audiences. Ray Kotcher, senior partner and CEO of Ketchum, explains how channel proliferation affects media relations work: "At the moment we are being asked to deal on a more strategic level (make this a new development) because of this incredible momentum in the media, messaging, and information that's out there. Think about it. We only had one NBC network 15 years ago. Now we have CNBC, MSNBC, and I don't know how many NBC's online."[31]

Wreck on the Pennsylvania Railroad, 1906

By Craig E. Aronoff
Kennesaw State College

Severe railroad regulations passed in 1903 and 1906 caused Alexander J. Cassatt, president of the Pennsylvania Railroad, to seek the counsel of Ivy Ledbetter Lee concerning how to deal better with the press and the public. Lee went right to work. He believed in absolute frankness with the press. Veteran railroad men were distressed at Lee's behavior. They were convinced that revealing facts about accidents would frighten customers.

A golden opportunity for Lee to put his ideas into practice soon arose. A train wrecked on the Pennsylvania Railroad main line near the town of Gap, Pennsylvania. As was its time-honored practice, the company sought to suppress all news of the accident.

When Ivy Lee learned of the situation, he took control. He contacted reporters, inviting them to come to the accident scene at company expense. He provided facilities to help them in their work. He gave out information for which the journalists had not asked.

The railroad's executives were appalled at Lee's actions. His policies were seen as unnecessary and destructive. How could the propagation of such bad news do anything but harm the railroad's freight and passenger business?

At about the time of the wreck on the Pennsylvania, another train accident struck the rival New York Central. Sticking with its traditional policy, the Central sought to avoid the press and restrict information flow concerning the situation. Confronted with the Central's behavior, and having tasted Lee's approach to public relations, the press was furious with the New York line. Columns and editorials poured forth chastising the Central and praising the Pennsylvania.

Lee's efforts resulted in positive publicity, increased credibility, comparative advantages over the Central, and good, constructive press coverage and relations. Lee's critics were silenced.

Earl Newsom, himself a public relations giant, looked back at this accident nearly 60 years later and said:

> This whole activity of which you and I are a part can probably be said to have its beginning when Ivy Lee persuaded the directors of the Pennsylvania Railroad that the press should be given all the facts on all railway accidents—even though the facts might place the blame on the railroad itself.*

When Ivy Lee died in 1934, among the many dignitaries at his funeral were the presidents of both the Pennsylvania and the New York Central railroads.

Source: Material for this case was gathered from Ray Hiebert's *Courtier to the Crowd* (Ames, IA: Iowa State University Press, 1966), pp. 55–61, and Eric Goldman's *Two-Way Street* (Boston: Bellman Publishing, 1948), p. 8.
*Earl Newsom, "Business Does Not Function by Divine Right," *Public Relations Journal* (January 1963), p. 4.

Questions

1. Were Lee's actions in response to the railroad accident consistent with practice today? Explain.
2. Had the New York Central accident not occurred, what do you think would have happened to Ivy Lee and his relationship with the Pennsylvania Railroad? Do you think the course of public relations development would have been affected?
3. In certain totalitarian states, news of accidents and disasters is often largely suppressed. What do you consider their reasons to be for retaining a posture given up by American public relations practice more than 80 years ago?

Summary

The scope of public relations work today is clearly nothing like it was in early times or even during the jump-start period following World War I. Even so, the pattern of development can be seen in the four orienting traditions: the rhetorician and press agent tradition, the journalistic publicity tradition, the persuasive communication campaign tradition, and, finally, a relationship-building and two-way communication tradition. We close with a quote from veteran public relations educator and historian Scott M. Cutlip who wrote in *The Unseen Power*, "The essentiality of public relations as a management function that Ivy Lee envisaged in the early 1900s becomes clearer each passing day as our global society becomes even more dependent on effective communication and on an interdependent, competitive world."[32]

For self-testing and additional chapter resources, go to the Online Learning Center at **www.mhhe.com/lattimore3e.**

Key Terms

online
press agents
propaganda of the deed

rhetoricians
stakeholders

Notes

1. Helio Fred Garcia, "Really-Old-School Public Relations," *Public Relations Strategist* (Summer 1998), p. 18.

2. Ibid., pp. 16–18.

3. Philip Davidson, *Propaganda and the American Revolution, 1763–1783* (Chapel Hill: University of North Carolina Press, 1941), p. 3.

4. Allan Nevins, *The Constitution Makers and the Public, 1785–1790* (New York: Foundation for Public Relations Research and Education, 1962), p. 10.

5. Richard Overton, *Burlington West* (Cambridge, MA: Harvard University Press, 1941), pp. 158–59.

6. Merle Curti, *The Growth of American Thought,* 3rd ed. (New York: Harper & Row, 1964), p. 634.

7. Marc Bloch, *The Historian's Craft* (New York: Knopf, 1953), p. 168.

8. Eric F. Goldman, *Two-Way Street* (Boston: Bellman Publishing, 1948), p. 21.

9. Quoted in Sherman Morse, "An Awakening on Wall Street," *American Magazine* 62 (September 1906), p. 460.

10. Ray E. Hiebert, *Courtier to the Crowd: The Story of Ivy Lee and the Development of Public Relations* (Ames: Iowa State University Press, 1966), p. 57.

11. Ibid., p. 65.

12. Karen S. Miller, "U.S. Public Relations History: Knowledge and Limitations," *Communication Yearbook* 23 (2000), pp. 381–420.

13. Harold D. Lasswell, *Propaganda Techniques in the World War* (New York: Knopf, 1927), p. 220.

14. Margaret E. Duffy, "There's No Two-Way Symmetric About It: A Postmodern Examination of Public Relations Textbooks," *Critical Studies in Media Communication* 17, no. 3 (September 2000), pp. 294–313.

15. Stuart Ewan, *A Social History of Spin* (New York: Basic Books, 1996), p. 34.

16. George Griswold Jr., "How AT&T Public Relations Policies Developed," *Public Relations Quarterly* 12 (Fall 1967), p. 13.

17. Allan R. Raucher, *Public Relations and Business, 1900–1929* (Baltimore: Johns Hopkins University Press, 1968), pp. 80–81.

18. Scott Cutlip, *The Unseen Power: Public Relations—A History* (Hillsdale, NJ: Erlbaum, 1994), pp. 595–96.

19. "Moss Kendrix, A Retrospective," The Museum of Public Relations, retrieved from www.prmuseum.com/kendrix/life/html on March 3, 2008.

20. Ibid.

21. "In Memoriam: Denny Griswold," PRSA, retrieved from www.prsa.org on Sept. 23, 2005, and "Arthur W. Page Society Will Honor Two Public Relations Legends," retrieved from www.awpagesociety.com on Sept. 25, 2005.

22. "Chester Burger," The Museum of Public Relations, March 2000, retrieved from www.prmuseum.com/burger/chet1.html on March 3, 2008.

23. Moss Kendrix: A Retrospective," Public Relations Museum, retrieved from www.prmuseum.com/kendrix/life.html on March 3, 2008.

24. Harold Burson, *E Pluribus Unum: The Making of Burson-Marsteller* (New York: Burson-Marsteller, 2002).

25. Ibid. p. 161.

26. Dan Lattimore, video interview with Harold Burson, Memphis, TN, 2002.

27. "Moss Kendrix: A Retrospective," Public Relations Museum, retrieved from www.prmuseum.com/kendrix/life.html on March 3, 2008.

28. Todd Gitlin, *The Whole World Is Watching: Mass Media in the Making and Unmaking of the New Left* (Berkeley: University of California Press, 1980), and Charlotte, Ryan, *Media Strategies for Grassroots Organizing* (Boston, MA: South End Press, 1991).

29. Don Middleberg and Steven Ross, "The Middleberg/Ross Media Survey: Change and Its Impact on Communication," Eighth Annual National Survey, 2002.

30. Carole Howard, "Technologies and Tabloids: How the New Media World Is Changing Our Jobs," *Public Relations Quarterly* 45 (Spring 2000), p. 9.

31. Ray Kotcher, "Roundtable: Future Perfect? Agency Leaders Reflect on the 1990s and Beyond," *Public Relations Strategist* 8 (Summer 2001), p. 11.

32. Cutlip, *The Unseen Power,* p. 761.

A Theoretical Basis for Public Relations

Why have a chapter on theory in a beginning public relations principles textbook? Whereas most textbooks describe public relations—its history, its practices, and its processes—we believe that it is also important to provide some perspective about why and how public relations is practiced as it is. More important, theory explains how to make public relations most effective for organizations and society.

Theories predict the way things work or happen. They provide an understanding of the relationship between actions and events. As a public relations practitioner, you will need to be able to explain why and how your plans and proposals will work. Your supervisor and your co-workers will be more convinced to support your opinions if you have theories and evidence to back them up.

There is no one theory that will explain all public relations practices. Public relations practitioners consider several theories when they make decisions about how they can build successful relationships with their publics. This chapter introduces six types of theories that public relations practitioners use every day: relationship theory, persuasion and social influence, mass communication, roles, models, and approaches to conflict resolution.

THEORY DEFINED

What would happen if we used a Web site to reach our volunteers? Why did our audience agree to donate money? How will investors learn about our stocks? Questions like these should sound familiar to anyone working in public relations. Public relations practitioners evaluate why a plan worked or didn't work so that they can adjust their strategies for future efforts.

Some of the questions we ask as practitioners are routine, and some are not so routine. When someone knows answers to routine questions, we say that person has common sense. When someone can correctly answer the nonroutine, we say that person is astute or experienced. But to answer either type of question, a person needs to understand the relationships between actions and events.

A **theory** is a prediction of how events and actions are related. For example, *pr reporter* described as a failure a federally funded message campaign to frighten kids off drugs.[1] Research showed that kids who reported seeing the ads were using marijuana even more than those who had not seen the ads. What caused this waste of $180 million a year? One expert said, "Scaring kids doesn't work. When people try pot for the first time, they wonder what the big deal is. Then, they don't believe the other stuff. The ads are not realistic."[2] This opinion reflects a great deal of theory on the use of fear appeals. Fear appeals theory predicts that there will be little change with an overreliance on fear appeals that threaten physical harm. More persuasive are balanced arguments with incentives for changing behavior.[3] We call this prediction a theory.

We have theories about many actions and events in public relations. Some theories serve us well because we test them regularly and observe the same relationships over time. For example, thank-you notes to express appreciation will almost always lead to an improved relationship between an organization and its customers, clients, employees, and other stakeholders. Other theories are dynamic and evolving and need more testing and refinement so that they will have better predictive value.

As a public relations manager, you should have knowledge of different theoretical models so that you can make the right decisions for your public relations plans and programs. Your value to your employer or client will be directly related to how well you use theory in your work. Read some of former PRSA president Pat Jackson's lasting theories for public relations in spotlight 3.1.

No single theory covers all you need to know in public relations or any other discipline; therefore, it is valuable to look at theories by grouping them according to how they are used. We start with theories of relationships. Then, we discuss theories of persuasion and social influence; that is, theories about how people take in information and what moves them to act. Next, we consider theories of mass communication. Finally, we look at ways to describe what public relations people do and how organizations approach public relations.

THEORIES OF RELATIONSHIPS

Both systems theory and situational theory are considered *theories of relationships*. We look at each theory here.

Systems Theory

Systems theory is useful in public relations because it gives us a way to think about relationships. Generally, systems theory looks at organizations as made up of interrelated parts, adapting and adjusting to changes in the political, economic, and social environments in which they operate. Organizations have recognizable boundaries, within which

- Any profession exists by public consent only. Public relations provides an overriding social benefit when people have a voice.
- Harmony is an outcome of public relations practiced over a long time.
- Harmonious relationships, not just relations, fortified with trust require co-authorship.
- Remind managers that their communication role is to transmit not only information but also emotions and intuition.

- The most important effect is to change behavior.
- The public relations practitioner's chief role is to serve as a catalyst.

_____

Source: From *pr reporter*, April 2, 2001, pp. 1–2.

Pat Jackson

there must be a communication structure that guides the parts of the organization to achieve organizational goals. The leaders of the organization create and maintain these internal structures.

Grunig, Grunig, and Dozier state that the systems perspective emphasizes the interdependence of organizations with their environments, both internal and external to the organization.[4] According to the systems perspective, organizations depend on resources from their environments, such as "raw materials, a source of employees, and clients or customers for the services or products they produce. The environment needs the organization for its products and services."[5] Organizations with **open systems** use public relations people to bring back information on how productive their relationships are with clients, customers, and other stakeholders. Organizations with **closed systems** do not seek new information. The decision makers operate on what happened in the past or their personal preferences.

Organizations are part of a greater environment made up of many systems. We use as an example a hypothetical organization—United PRworks. It is depicted as an oval in the center of figure 3.1. Moving out from the organization, you can see that it has an environment—the area between the large circle and our organization. In that environment we see most of the groups we considered in chapter 1—customers, media, community, financial institutions, and government. These groups are called **stakeholders** because "they and the organization have consequences on each other"[6]—they create problems and opportunities for one another.

We can use systems theory not only to examine relationships with our external stakeholders but also to look at the internal functions and stakeholders of our organizations. Organizations structure their employees by specific jobs and functions. Many different departments, such as accounting, legal, and public relations, make up the managerial function. The production function of an organization might include skilled and

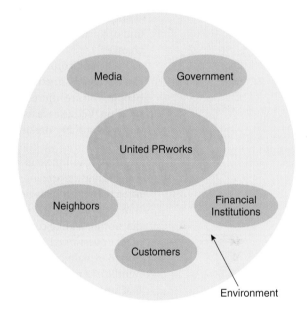

FIGURE 3.1 Systems Model of an Organization and Its Environment

unskilled employees who actually make the product or provide the service to customers. The marketing function is made up of sales staff. All of these different employees are interdependent.

Consider this real-world example of systems thinking by a corporate social responsibility director at Merck & Co., Inc., a worldwide pharmaceutical company. Merck helps fight AIDS by creating stakeholder partnerships: Merck corporate directors, the government of Botswana, and the Bill and Melinda Gates Foundation. This requires constant communication and problem solving. To prepare for a presentation at an international AIDS conference in Bangkok, Maggie Kohn described her efforts to bridge effectively many different internal and external systems: "I had weekly meetings with the two Merck representatives, daily communication with the Botswana communication director, and bimonthly calls with Gates Foundation communicators."[7]

The monitoring of relationships is a major one for public relations people. Through systems theory, we think of public relations people as **boundary spanners,** straddling the edge of an organization—looking inside and outside of an organization. Public relations practitioners are the go-betweens, explaining the organization to its stakeholders and interpreting the environment to the organization. Public relations people advise the **dominant coalition,**[8] the primary decision makers of the organization, about problems and opportunities in the environment and help these decision makers respond to these changes.

The **environment** imposes constraints on organizations. For example, customers can boycott an organization's products. The courts can make a business pay damages to people who are injured by its products. Banks can choose not to lend money to an organization. Because we use systems theory, we can identify an organization's stakeholders, and by spanning organizational boundaries, we can anticipate each side's relationship needs.

If decision makers keep their systems open, they allow for the two-way flow of resources and information between the organization and its environment. They use that information for adapting to the environment, or they may use the incoming information to try to control the environment. For example, to control potentially negative media stories, a Nike corporate communicator created the "Issues Brief" to be used when media questioned Nike products. The Issues Brief gave Nike spokespersons information to explain company policies or positions. "For example, if a top athlete were in the middle of a marathon and a Nike running shoe fell apart, we have a one-page document that provides in a very concise fashion the history of that product or issue, approved legal statements and language that can be used when discussing the issues, and a list of the most-likely questions that the media or other external stakeholders will ask."[9]

Using the concepts of organizations and environments we can begin to create theoretical statements about relationships with stakeholders. For example, we might say: The more turbulent the environment, the more flexible the public relations department needs to be because the stakeholders that could have positive or negative consequences for the organization are constantly changing. Organizations that remain closed to new information from the environment are less likely to build effective relationships with key publics. If organizations have closed systems, it may take a crisis for an organization to accept environmental changes.

Situational Theory

Grunig and Repper agreed that it was a good start to use the concept of stakeholders as a way of describing relationships.[10] However, they concluded that not all people in stakeholder groups would be equally likely to communicate with the organization. They felt that public relations people could more effectively manage communications by identifying specific publics within stakeholder groups. These **publics** were subgroups that were more or less active in their communication behavior. An example of a stakeholder public would be active voters within the broader group of all registered voters. Candidates for political office focus their communication efforts on those voters who can be counted on to go to polls on election day. Grunig and Hunt proposed what they call a situational theory of publics to give us more specific information about their communication needs.[11]

Grunig and Hunt theorized that publics range from those who actively seek and process information about an organization or an issue of interest, to those publics who passively receive information. According to these researchers, three variables predict when publics will seek and process information about an issue: problem recognition, constraint recognition, and level of involvement. The key is that publics are situational. That is, as the situation, problem, opportunity, or issue changes, the publics, with which the organization must communicate, change.

Problem Recognition   Publics facing an issue must first be aware of it and recognize its potential to affect them. For example, parents of school-age children will be more aware of subpar school facilities than will taxpayers without children.

Constraint Recognition   This variable describes how publics perceive obstacles that may stand in the way of a solution. If they believe they have a real shot at influencing an issue, they will tend to seek and process information on that issue. Think again about parents with school-age children. They have more access to school decision makers because they have more contact with school principals, teachers, and administrators than do taxpayers without children.

Level of Involvement   This variable refers to how much an individual cares about an issue. Those who care a lot would likely be active communicators on an issue. Those who care little would likely be more passive in seeking and processing information. We anticipate that the level of involvement would be much higher for those who saw firsthand substandard school facilities than those who had not.

Using these three variables, Grunig and Hunt described four responses that follow from being high or low in these dimensions. For example, those publics who have high problem recognition, low constraint recognition, and high involvement in an issue are much more likely to actively engage in communication about it.

Situational theory also helps explain why some groups are active on a single issue, others are active on many issues, and others are uniformly apathetic. The specific relationship is determined by the type of group (active, passive) and how an organization is linked with the issue. Public relations people can plan their communication strategies much more accurately if they know how actively their stakeholder publics will seek information.

THEORIES OF PERSUASION AND SOCIAL INFLUENCE

Public relations people try to persuade audiences to learn new information, to change emotions, and to act in certain ways. As Miller and Levine stated, "At a minimum a successful persuasive attempt generates some type of cognitive, affective, or behavioral modification in the target."[12] We use the following terms to talk about **persuasion:**

Mini·Case 3.1 | DaimlerChrysler: Road Ready Teens

Teenagers aged 16 to 19 are far more likely to be killed in a car crash than any other group. This is primarily due to driver inexperience, or lack of maturity behind the wheel. Research shows that when teens are eased into driving and when parents take an active role in their teens' driver education by setting driving guidelines, their teens' chances of being in a car crash can be reduced by up to one-third. DaimlerChrysler sought to reinforce its position as a safety leader with consumers by raising awareness among teens and their parents about the risks teens face as new drivers and by providing them with tools and tactics to survive the high-risk years. To this end, DaimlerChrysler made available free and on the Internet (www.roadreadyteens.org in English and Spanish) a video game called StreetWise. Results showed that more than 1.8 million games of StreetWise were played, with game play averaging 19 minutes per player.

Questions

1. DaimlerChrysler wanted what kinds of persuasive effects for this campaign: awareness, attitude, belief, or behavior change?
2. How did this campaign consider the source, the message, and the receiver to create its effects?
3. Can you apply the theories of persuasion and social influence to this case: Social exchange? Social learning? Diffusion? Elaborated likelihood model?

Source: DaimlerChrysler, Road Ready Teens, accessed March 27, 2008, http://69.20.125.164/dbtw-wpd/exec/dbtwpub.dll.

Awareness: accepting information for the first time

Attitudes: predispositions to like or dislike things

Beliefs: assessments that things are true or false

Behavior: observable actions[13]

Sometimes we are not even aware that we are being persuaded. Consider a common activity, like going to the bank. When you enter the bank, there are tent cards and brochures explaining how to open an account and new services that the bank says will save you money. Free coffee and popcorn are available. With each of these subtle "touches" the bank's public relations people are seeking to change your awareness, attitudes, beliefs, and behavior. (See mini-case 3.1 for another example of these terms in use.)

Several factors will influence how persuasive public relations messages or actions will be. Among them are the **source** of the message, the **message** itself, and the **receiver.** Not surprisingly, researchers have found that the more credible or believable the source is, the more likely we will accept the message. Studies of effective messages consider such characteristics as language intensity, message-sidedness, and the quality and quantity of the evidence.[14] Gender, personality traits, and the argumentativeness of the receiver will also influence the impact of persuasive messages.[15]

We will discuss four theories of persuasive and social influences: social exchange, diffusion, social learning, and elaborated likelihood model.

Social Exchange Theory

Social exchange theory uses the economic metaphor of costs and benefits to predict behavior. It assumes that individuals and groups choose strategies based on perceived rewards and costs. This theory, developed by John Thibaut and Harold Kelley, applies to many fields of study, including interpersonal communication, public relations, and theories of organizations.[16]

Social exchange theory asserts that people factor in the consequences of their behavior before acting. In general, people want to keep their costs low and their rewards high. Get-rich-quick schemes have been using this principle for a long time.

But what does this have to do with public relations? Let's say we want people to respond to a survey. Remember, we want to keep costs to potential respondents low and perceived rewards high. What can we do to keep costs low?

- Keep the instructions simple.
- Keep the survey short.
- If mailing is required, provide a prepaid return envelope.
- If returning by fax, use an 800 number.
- Avoid open-ended, complex, and personal questions.

Now, how can we increase the rewards for the respondent?

- Make the survey interesting.
- Emphasize that the person is being "consulted" for his or her thoughts and that her or his ideas are important.
- Tell respondents how the results will be used—presumably to contribute to something worthwhile.
- Offer an opportunity for a tangible reward, for example, a copy of the results or a chance to win something of value.

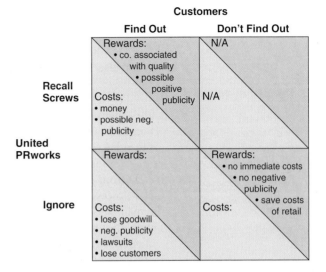

FIGURE 3.2 Payoff Matrix Showing Costs and Rewards Involved in a Recall Decision

This same logic can be applied to more complex behavior by using a payoff matrix. Let's say our company, United PRworks, becomes aware of defects in a product that has already been shipped to customers. The defect may mean that the product will need repairs much sooner than a promised three-year guarantee. We can look at this situation as a set of possible decisions, with each decision having costs and rewards. In figure 3.2, the upper part of each cell contains perceived rewards, and the lower part, possible costs. Some of the consequences, like recall costs, are certain. Others, like the possibility of lawsuits and negative publicity, have some probability associated with them.

If the head of United PRworks could see the decision this way, the company would recall the products and accept the short-term loss. The trouble is that human nature can blind us to the information in the cells associated with customers finding out about the defect. It would be human nature to ignore the problem, hoping it would go away. The public relations practitioner's job is to let the decision maker see a whole range of options along with the associated costs and rewards.

Diffusion Theory

Diffusion theory is another way to look at how people process and accept information. Diffusion theory says that people adopt an idea only after going through the following five discrete steps (or stages):

1. *Awareness.* The individual has been exposed to the idea.
2. *Interest.* The idea has to arouse the individual.
3. *Evaluation.* The individual must consider the idea as potentially useful.
4. *Trial.* The individual tries out the idea on others.

5. *Adoption.* This represents final acceptance of the idea after having successfully passed through the four earlier stages.[17]

This theory is useful for explaining how we reach important decisions—not acts of impulse. We know from testing this model that mass media are important in the first two stages; personal contacts are important for the next two.

Let's take an example. United PRworks's annual family picnic is two weeks away. You are selling tickets at $1 per family as a way to plan how much food to order. You tell the boss at the morning staff meeting that ticket sales have been slow. If your boss is typical, she or he will say, "Make sure every employee gets a flyer."

Sending out more flyers virtually guarantees awareness, but you are still four steps away from getting people to decide to go (adoption). By knowing how people accept and process information, you plan systematically to move the employees through the remaining stages. The next step is to arouse interest in attending the picnic by sending individual invitations that tell employees how their families will enjoy the event. How about entertainment for the old and young? A special "snack" table for the kids, games and door prizes for adults and kids. Then, have your picnic organizers asked employees for their evaluations for how to make the event mesh with their interests. Free parking? Baby-sitting service? Get some "buzz" going by having the CEO talk about the picnic with employees. Finally, you will need lots of people at the shop level to talk about the picnic to their fellow workers. Then, they need to go sell the tickets.

Social Learning Theory

So far, we have discussed theories that consider the receiver to be actively involved in information processing. **Social learning theory** attempts to explain and predict behavior by looking at another way individuals process information. This theory helps us understand that personal example and mass media can be important to acquiring new behaviors.

Social psychologist Albert Bandura says that we can learn new behaviors merely by observing others.[18] When we see behavior that interests us, we note whether that behavior seems to be rewarding the actor. These rewards can be external, as in praise, or internal, as in "it looks cool." Bandura says that we vicariously try out the behavior in our minds. If we agree that the behavior is potentially useful to us, it can lie dormant for long periods until we need it. The likelihood that a specific behavior will occur is determined by the expected consequences from performing that behavior. The more positive and rewarding the consequences, the more likely the behavior will occur.

Knowing this, public relations people can anticipate that new or inexperienced employees will model the behavior of more experienced employees, particularly if that behavior is rewarded. If a company recognizes with achievement awards the employees who are willing to give their best efforts to satisfy customers, then you can predict that those wanting to get ahead will model those behaviors.

Remember: You get the behavior you reward. Social learning theory explains one of the routes to this behavior.

Elaborated Likelihood Model

The notion of "routes" is central to a theory that describes two ways that people are influenced. Richard Petty and John Cacioppo describe the first route as the "central route"—the situation in which people actively think about an idea.[19] Relying on this route presumes people are interested in your message, have the time to attend to your arguments, and can evaluate your evidence with an open mind. This is how public relations people usually attempt to influence attitudes and behavior.

But what if the target group is not interested, is too busy, or just can't understand the issues? How do you proceed?

The **elaborated likelihood model** proposes a "peripheral route" in which people are influenced by such things as repetition, a highly credible spokesperson, or even tangible rewards. Public relations practitioners frequently use this route when designing their messages. For example, candidates for local office can't engage all the voters in a discussion of the issues, so they take the peripheral route and blanket the town with yard signs. Message repetition provides familiarity with the candidate's name, and sign location suggests that many voters actively support that candidate. People who are not politically active don't have to think about the issues; they just vote for the obvious popular choice.

When long-distance phone companies claim they can save you money on plans that are not easily compared, it becomes difficult to make an informed decision. That's when the credibility of the spokesperson may be the deciding factor on which plan you select.

Other successful peripheral routes to changing behavior are found in the public relations efforts of weight-loss companies. They offer coupons and discounts to join their programs. They provide free counseling by phone if the weight management plan is too complicated. You are likely to receive free exercise videos and diaries and recognition for weight loss. Celebrities are paid to lose weight and publicize their weight losses right along with you. Even though weight control prevents many health problems, this is not the central message that will help people with weight problems. It is direct but not usually persuasive.

Two popular theories that apply especially to the mass media are uses and gratifications theory and agenda setting.

THEORIES OF MASS COMMUNICATION

Uses and Gratifications Theory

It's important to remember that not everyone regularly reads the daily paper, watches the 6 o'clock news, or listens to talk radio. Papers, TV, and radio are called mass media, but each person chooses how and when to use mass media. Similarly, you shouldn't presume that employees uniformly read internal publications or view company videos. Even a note in every pay envelope could go straight into the wastebasket.

How do we explain this behavior? **Uses and gratifications theory** asserts that people are active users of media and select how they will use it.[20] Researchers have found that people use media in the following ways:

As entertainment

To scan the environment for items important to them personally

As a diversion

As a substitute for personal relationships

As a check on personal identity and values

For public relations practitioners this means that not everyone will see or hear the bad news about a company or product. It also means you can't count on people seeing or hearing the good news. Just because a message is available in some medium does not mean that people attend to it and remember it.

Public relations practitioners should expect that messages in the mass media will be shaped, selected, and interpreted in multiple ways if these messages are seen or heard at all! For example, the American public never did understand why President Clinton's personal life should interfere with his presidency, even with hours of televised hearings and printed transcripts. Plenty of opinions were aired, even by Jay Leno and *Saturday Night Live*. But American opinion never changed from a position of distaste for Clinton's morals and support for his presidency, despite the media.

Agenda Setting Theory

Bernard Cohen noted that although the media can't tell people what to think, they are stunningly successful in telling them what to think about.[21] This was an interesting idea but not widely accepted in 1963. About a decade later journalism scholars Maxwell McCombs and Donald Shaw demonstrated that Cohen was onto something.[22] During the 1968 presidential campaign, they followed public opinion and media reports of the key issues in Chapel Hill, North Carolina. They found that a strong positive relationship existed between what voters said was important and what media were reporting as important. Because the issues were evident in the media several weeks before they appeared in public opinion, McCombs and Shaw were reasonably sure that the media set the agenda and not the reverse. Even more amazing was that voters were more likely to agree with the composite media agenda than with the position of the candidate they claimed they favored.

McCombs and Shaw do not say that simple agreement with the media changed voting behavior. They simply demonstrated that the media can set the agenda for what we talk and think about.

This talking and thinking can lead to information seeking and processing, following the situational theory of publics, but only if other conditions are met. That's an important point for public relations practitioners to remember when their organization is taking a beating in the press. People may be talking about you, but it doesn't necessarily mean that strong opinions about your organization will be changed. You will need to do some research before you can draw such a conclusion.

Public relations practitioners attempt to influence the **media agenda** by providing news items for public consumption. To accomplish this, they identify subjects that editors and news directors consider news, localize their messages, and help media representatives cover the story. (See spotlight 3.2 for a summary of the public relations theories.)

PUBLIC RELATIONS ROLES

Some of the most important theory building that has been developed in public relations is about the roles of practitioners in organizational life. Some of these roles are managerial; some are tied to marketing. There are communication demands from the human resources function. Even the legal department influences public relations activities when there is an organizational crisis. At issue is whether public relations practitioners play the right roles to achieve organizational effectiveness.

Roles are the collection of daily activities that people perform. Glen Broom and David Dozier have studied public relations roles for more than 20 years. Their role types have helped us learn about the power of the public relations function in the organization and how the activities of public relations people produce the right programs, influence strategic planning, and affect the short-range (bottom-line) and long-range (survival) goals of organizations.[23]

In research on public relations activities, two broad roles consistently emerge in public relations: the technician and the manager. The **technician role** represents the craft side of public relations: writing, editing, taking photos, handling communication production, running special events, and making telephone calls to the media. These

The nine theories highlighted in the chapter are summarized as follows:

I. Theories of Relationships

1. Systems theory: evaluates relationships and structure as they relate to the whole.
2. Situational theory: maintains that situations define relationships.

II. Theories of Cognition and Behavior

3. Social exchange theory: predicts behavior of groups and individuals and is based on perceived rewards and costs.
4. Diffusion theory: suggests that people adopt an important idea or innovation after going through five discrete steps: awareness, interest, evaluation, trial, and adoption.
5. Social learning theory: states that people use information processing to explain and predict behavior.
6. Elaborated likelihood model: suggests decision making is influenced through repetition, rewards, and credible spokespersons.

III. Theories of Mass Communication

7. Uses and gratifications theory: states that people are active users of media and select media based on its gratification for them.
8. Agenda setting theory: suggests that media content that people read, see, and listen to set the agendas for society's discussion and interaction.

IV. Approaches to Conflict Resolution

9. Nine strategies: contention; cooperation; accommodation; avoidance; unconditional constructive; compromise; principled; win-win or no deal; mediated.

activities focus on the implementation of the management's overall communication strategies. The **manager role** focuses on activities that help identify and solve public relations problems. Public relations managers advise senior managers about communication needs and are responsible for broad organizational results. Public relations managers carry out three roles:

Expert prescriber: the person who operates as a consultant to define the problem, suggests options, and oversees implementation.

Communication facilitator: the person on the boundary between the organization and its environment who keeps two-way communication flowing.

Problem-solving facilitator: the person who partners with senior management to identify and solve problems.[24]

To perform all three roles, much depends on the knowledge of the individual manager. If managers can deliver both manager and technical functions, they achieve higher status in organizational decision making. Public relations professionals cannot expect to achieve a "seat at the table" where they can influence how to achieve beneficial relationships with stakeholders unless they perform both roles. They especially must execute the manager role in such a way that top management will understand its value and demand it of the public relations function.[25]

MODELS OF PUBLIC RELATIONS

One of the most useful ways of thinking about public relations has been through the description of public relations **models** that identify the central ideas of public relations and how they are related to each other. In 1984 James E. Grunig and Todd Hunt proposed four models of public relations that are based on communication, research, and ethics. Since that time Grunig and a team of scholars have proposed new models that have enriched our understanding of how public relations is practiced.

The original four models were press agentry, public information, the two-way asymmetrical model, and the two-way symmetrical model.[26] The first three models reflect a practice of public relations that attempts through persuasion to achieve the organization's goals. The fourth focuses on balancing self-interests and the interests of the other group or public.

Press agentry is the model where information moves one way—from the organization to its publics. It is perhaps the oldest form of public relations and is synonymous with promotions and publicity. Public relations practitioners operating under this model are always looking for opportunities to get their organization's name favorably mentioned in the media. They do not conduct much research about their publics, beyond "counting the house." This model includes propaganda tactics such as use of celebrity names and attention-gaining devices such as giveaways, parades, and grand openings. Although press agents are not unethical, they don't desire to be ethical either. The louder the noise, the more attention-getting the story, whether true or face, the better they are doing their jobs.

Public information differs from press agentry because the intent is to inform rather than to press for promotion and publicity, but the communication is still essentially one-way. Today this model represents public relations practices in government, educational institutions, nonprofit organizations, and even in some corporations. Practitioners operating under this model do very little research about their audiences beyond testing the clarity of their messages. They are "journalists-in-residence," who value accuracy but decide what information is best to communicate to their publics.

The *two-way asymmetrical model* considers public relations to be scientific persuasion. This model employs social science research methods to increase the persuasiveness of messages. Public relations practitioners use surveys, interviews, and focus groups to measure public relationships so the organization can design public relations programs that will gain the support of key publics. Although feedback is built into the process, the organization is much more interested in having the publics adjust to the organization than the reverse.

The *two-way symmetrical model* depicts a public relations orientation in which organizations and their publics adjust to each other. It focuses on the use of social science research methods to achieve mutual understanding and two-way communication rather than one-way persuasion. In 2001 James E. Grunig created other names for the symmetrical model: mixed motives, collaborative advocacy, and cooperative antagonism. His intent was to present a model that "balanced self-interests with the interest of others in a give-and-take process that can waver between advocacy and collaboration."[27] Grunig argued that this model was the most ethical because all groups were part of the resolution of problems.

In 1995 David M. Dozier, Larissa A. Grunig, and James E. Grunig presented a new model of public relations that came from their research on excellence in public relations and communication management. They found in a study of 321 organizations in three countries that public relations practitioners who exhibited the most effective or excellent public relations practices used the "new model of symmetry as two-way practice."[28] This depiction of public relations placed the organization and its publics on a continuum (see figure 3.3). Because in the best practice of public relations, public relations practitioners and their supervisors reported using both two-way symmetrical and two-way asymmetrical models, Dozier, Grunig, and Grunig reasoned that given each specific public relations situation, organizations *and* their publics would seek to persuade each other as much as possible. They are pictured at opposite ends of the continuum, either as a pure asymmetry model in which the dominant coalition tries to force a public into accepting the organization's position or as a pure cooperation model in which the public uses communication to convince the dominant coalition to accept the public's position. The middle of the continuum is the "win-win" zone in which the organization and

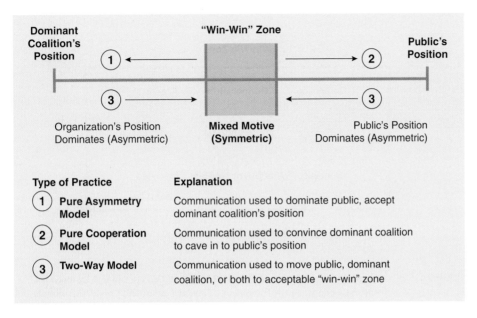

FIGURE 3.3   New Model of Symmetry as Two-Way Practice

the public use communication to achieve a decision acceptable to both sides. This new model advances our thinking about the practice of public relations because it considers both parties in the public relations situation. Because the organization and its publics will be employing communication strategies as well, we have to be as savvy about our publics' communication strategies as we are our own.

The work on developing models of public relations that more effectively describe how public relations is carried out continued in 1996, with the report of two different models: the **cultural interpreter model** and the **personal influence model.** Although both models fall into the asymmetrical category, they give us more to think about in our understanding of the practice of public relations. Both models were found in research by University of Maryland graduate students who returned to their home countries of India, Greece, and Taiwan to test whether practitioners in these countries were using the four original models of public relations. Although these two new models may represent public relations practiced in other cultures, we see applications of them to practices in the United States. A brief summary of the two models follows:

> The *cultural interpreter model* depicts the practice of public relations in organizations that do business in other countries, "where it needs someone who understands the language, culture, customs, and political system of the host country."

> The *personal influence model* depicts a practice of public relations in which practitioners try to establish personal relationships with key individuals, "as contacts through favors can be sought."[29]

If we begin with the notion that **conflict resolution** is just one of many states a relationship can take, we have a better theory about conflict and how to deal with it. All of us have a common understanding of conflict. It involves an individual or group actively

APPROACHES TO CONFLICT RESOLUTION

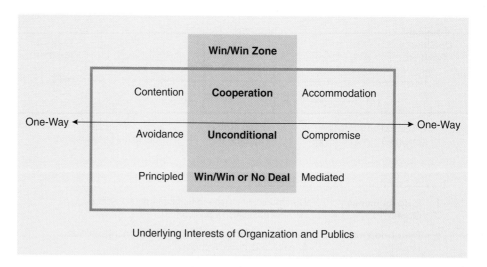

FIGURE 3.4   **Mixed-Motive Model of Public Relations**   Source: Kenneth D. Plowman, William G. Briggs, and Yi-Hui Huang, "Public Relations and Conflict Resolutions," in *Handbook of Public Relations,* ed. R.L. Heath (Thousand Oaks, CA: Sage, 2001), p. 304.

opposing another's values or goals. As with individuals, corporate conflict occurs when a stakeholder moves in a direction different from the organization, producing friction among the parties.[30] When this occurs, public relations professionals must often move the organization and its public toward a resolution.

Plowman, Briggs, and Huang identified nine types of conflict resolution strategies and linked them to the motives of organizations and publics (see figure 3.4):

1. *Contention.* Involves one party forcing its position on another.
2. *Cooperation.* Both parties work together to reach a mutually beneficial solution.
3. *Accommodation.* One party partially yields on its position and lowers its aspirations.
4. *Avoidance.* One or both parties leave the conflict either physically or psychologically.
5. *Unconditional Constructive.* The organization reconciles the strategic interests of both the organization and its publics, whether the public follows guidelines or not, even if the other party to the conflict does not reciprocate.
6. *Compromise.* An alternative agreement that stands part way between the parties' preferred positions.
7. *Principled.* Both parties hold to higher ethics that cannot be compromised.
8. *Win-Win or No Deal.* Both parties hold off on any agreement until they are ready for the deal to be struck.
9. *Mediated.* Involves use of an outside disinterested party.[31]

Plowman has substituted *perseverance* for mediation because he reasoned that mediation was useful across all nine strategies.[32] He offered a new word—"humwillity"—combining humility and strength of will or perseverance.[33] Clearly, not all of these strategies will result in mutually satisfied parties. The conflict may be "resolved," but the public relations practitioner's job is far from over.

Citizens to Stop the Coal Trains: Extension of Public Comment Period

Overview

Citizens to Stop the Coal Train (CSCT), a coalition of leaders who represent all facets of the Rochester, Minnesota, community, launched an aggressive grassroots campaign against a $1.4 billion coal train proposal proffered by the Dakota, Minnesota & Eastern Railroad (DM&E). If approved, the coal train proposal would be devastating to Rochester, resulting in a mile-long, open-car coal train rumbling through the heart of this bucolic downtown every 40 minutes, 365 days per year. Traffic delays at Rochester's railroad crossings would total nearly three hours per day.

More than 1.5 million national and international visitors come each year to Rochester, which has a population of approximately 80,000. The vast majority of these visitors come because of the world-renowned Mayo Clinic, which is the third largest private employer in Minnesota. Rochester's economy is of course heavily dependent on caring for these visitors, as well as for their families, while they're in town.

Thirty-seven coal trains barreling through Rochester every day would endanger public safety, threaten economic vitality, and erode quality of life in this community, which is often near the top of national "Best Places to Live" rankings.

CSCT formed in July 2000 in anticipation of the Surface Transportation Board's (STB) release of its Draft Environmental Impact Statement (DEIS). One of CSCT's primary objectives was to persuade the federally appointed independent STB to expand the public comment period of the DEIS from the given 90 days to 180 days. An extension of this comment period would

- Give experts in the legal and environmental fields adequate time to address problematic findings within the DEIS report and submit meaningful analysis to the STB.
- Allow more time for CSCT to garner support from Rochester citizens and send personal letters to the STB.
- Slow the railroad's momentum for this project.
- Send a strong message to DM&E that Rochester is capable of thwarting its coal train project.

Research

We learned that the STB is an independent adjudicatory body, which enables this group of three appointed people to make decisions independent of any other federal office. However, the STB must consider all statements submitted during the public comment period for this coal train project, so we hoped we could sway the STB to grant an extension based on volume and quality of requests for an extension from citizens and their elected officials.

To help make CSCT's case to the Rochester public, we researched statistics about the railroad as well as Rochester's safety, economy, and quality of life.

We discovered that the DM&E has the worst safety record of any in its class in the nation. We demonstrated how dependent Rochester's emergency response units were on clear access to roads in order to determine how congestion at railroad crossings would increase response times and threaten lives.

To better understand which statistics concerned Rochester citizens most, we interviewed citizens representing the groups we were attempting to mobilize—businesses, health care, schools, and senior citizens. We then incorporated these statistics into every news release, interview, and speaking opportunity, tailoring the statistics to the specific audience we were trying to reach.

Planning

We developed a comprehensive plan to increase our odds of securing an extension to the 90-day public comment period. Tactical elements of this plan included the following:

- Position the CSCT as a leader in advocacy for the city of Rochester and its citizens.
- Educate all Rochester citizens—not just those who live near the railroad tracks—about the dangers of the coal train proposal and how the coal trains would affect their lives every day.
- Gain media attention and coverage about the coal train issue and emphasize Rochester's concerns in clear, concise language. Add credibility by involving well-respected members of the community who represent affected sectors—business, health care, schools, and seniors.
- Bring Rochester's concerns about the coal train project to the attention of candidates and elected representatives at the local, state, and federal levels and persuade these representatives to submit their own statements and letters to the STB.
- Provide citizens modes of easy access in contacting the STB to voice their concerns. Drive traffic to the CSCT Web site and encourage mailing of response cards to the STB.

With objectives in place and a budget set at $150,000 for project management, media relations, video and advertising production, event management, and Web site creation, we set out to implement this aggressive plan within a short time frame—five months.

Execution

We gained momentum as each tactic within our program was executed. Some of our milestone efforts included the following:

- Holding a CSCT press conference the same day that the DEIS was released. The press conference drew more than 100 people and garnered numerous print and broadcast stories.
- Sending a CSCT delegation to Washington, D.C., to meet with key members of Congress. This trip prompted letters of support from Governor Ventura and Rep. Gutknecht for an extension to the public comment period.

- Producing a 10-minute video to capture the attention of local residents by showing how devastating the effects of coal trains would be for Rochester.
- Arranging dozens of speaking engagements across the Rochester community.
- Launching a local print and broadcast advertising campaign. This ad campaign was phased to target our key audiences—businesses, schools, heath care, and seniors. The print ads provided response cards that readers could fill out and send to the STB, while broadcast ads drove traffic to the CSCT Web site.
- Developing a Web site to inform concerned citizens and provide them with the means to voice their own concerns to the STB.
- Promoting a public rally and town hall meeting. These events were a huge show of force, attracting hundreds of button-wearing, sign-carrying residents who supported our efforts.

Evaluation

On December 14, the STB announced that it was extending the public comment period by 60 days, and there's no doubt CSCT influenced that decision. Our four-month campaign resulted in front-page newspaper coverage of more than 300 citizens who turned out for the CSCT rally; 75,000 visitor sessions and more than 8,000 letters to the STB generated by www.stopthecoaltrain .com; many hundreds of response cards mailed from our advertising campaign; and letters of support from congressional delegates following our Washington, D.C., tour.

Our campaign was featured in Ragan's *Interactive Public Relations* February 2001 issue. Here is an excerpt: "The extension is a significant win for us—one that'll give more time to fully review the 5,000 page document" that outlines the environmental impact of the train proposal, says John Wade, co-chair of Citizens to Stop the Coal Train.

Further, the time delay adds cost and aggravation for the DM&E, which proposed the rail line.

"As the process gets longer and more complex, the market changes, the economy changes, and prices change. There could come a point when we're no longer able to afford the project," says Rick Daugherty, public affairs officer for the DM&E. "The billion dollar question remains: How long will that be?"

Source: PRSA Silver Anvil Awards, 2001, Public Affairs section. Citizens to Stop the Coal Trains with Weber Shandwick Worldwide.

Questions

1. How could you use figure 3.2 to look at the costs and consequences to the DM&E's proposal?
2. How did the citizens use diffusion theory to get citizens to act?
3. How is the elaborated likelihood model illustrated in this case?
4. How did the citizens take advantage of agenda setting theory?

Summary

For self-testing and additional chapter resources, go to the Online Learning Center at **www.mhhe.com/lattimore3e.**

Theories of how public relations is practiced continue to develop. The original four models of public relations were a good starting point for describing the key activities that public relations practitioners perform: communication, research, and ethics. They gave us a way of organizing our concepts by types of public relations practice. James E. Grunig proposed to move on from the models of public relations to more specific sets of measurable variables: symmetry and asymmetry (research method choices); the extent of one-way versus two-way communication; the use of mediated and interpersonal forms of communication; and the extent to which public relations is practiced ethically.[34] These four dimensions give us even deeper and more sophisticated ways of thinking about public relations than did the original models. They help us predict more effectively what will and will not work in our practice of public relations.

Key Terms

boundary spanners	**persuasion**
closed system	**publics**
conflict resolution	**receiver**
cultural interpreter model	**roles**
diffusion theory	**situational theory**
dominant coalition	**social exchange theory**
elaborated likelihood model	**social learning theory**
environment	**source**
manager role	**stakeholders**
media agenda	**systems theory**
message	**technician role**
models	**theory**
open system	**uses and gratifications theory**
personal influence model	

Notes

1. Doug McVay, "In Fighting the Drug War, Keep Kids' Behavior Focused on Positive Actions; Lessons Applicable for All," *pr reporter*, June 3, 2002, pp. 1–2.

2. Ibid., p. 1.

3. Charles Atkin and Alicia Marshall, "Health Communication," in *An Integrated Approach to Communication Theory and Research,* ed. Michael B. Salwen and Don W. Stacks (Mahwah, NJ: Erlbaum, 1996), pp. 479–96.

4. Larissa A. Grunig, James E. Grunig, and David M. Dozier, *Excellence in Public Relations and Effective Organizations:* *A Study of Communication Management in Three Countries* (Mahwah, NJ: Erlbaum, 2002).

5. Ibid., p. 5.

6. J. E. Grunig and Fred C. Repper, "Strategic Management, Publics, and Issues," in *Excellence in Public Relations and Communication Management,* ed. J. E. Grunig (Hillsdale, NJ: Erlbaum, 1992), pp. 117–58.

7. Maggie M. Kohn, "Integrating Responsibility Communications at Merck," *Strategic Communication Management* 8 (2004), p. 32.

8. David M. Dozier, Larissa A. Grunig, and J. E. Grunig, *The Manager's Guide*

to Public Relations and Communication Management (Mahwah, NJ: Erlbaum, 1995), p. 15.

9. Vada Manager, "Integrated Issues Management," *Strategic Communication Management* 8, no. 6 (2004), p. 4.

10. Grunig and Repper, "Strategic Management," pp. 117–58.

11. James E. Grunig and Todd Hunt, *Managing Public Relations* (New York: Holt, Rinehart & Winston, 1984).

12. Michael D. Miller and Timothy R. Levine, "Persuasion," in *An Integrated Approach to Communication Theory and Research,* ed. Michael B. Salwen and Don W. Stacks (Mahwah, NJ: Erlbaum, 1996), p. 261.

13. Ibid., p. 262.

14. Ibid., pp. 262–63.

15. Ibid., p. 262.

16. John W. Thibaut and Harold H. Kelley, *The Social Psychology of Groups* (New York: Wiley, 1959).

17. Herbert F. Lionberger, *Adoption of New Ideas and Practices* (Ames: Iowa State University Press, 1960), p. 32.

18. Albert Bandura, *Social Learning Theory* (Englewood Cliffs, NJ: Prentice-Hall, 1977).

19. Richard E. Petty and John T. Cacioppo, *Communication and Persuasion: Central and Peripheral Routes to Attitude Change* (New York: Springer-Verlag, 1986).

20. Elihu Katz, Jay G. Blumler, and Michael Gurevitch, "Utilization of Mass Communication by the Individual," in *The Uses of Mass Communications: Current Perspectives on Gratifications Research,* ed. J. G. Blumler and E. Katz (Beverly Hills, CA: Sage, 1974), pp. 19–32.

21. Bernard C. Cohen, *The Press and Foreign Policy* (Princeton, NJ: Princeton University Press, 1963).

22. Donald E. Shaw and Maxwell E. McCombs, *The Emergence of American Political Issues: The Agenda Setting Function of the Press* (St. Paul, MN: West, 1977).

23. Dozier, Grunig, and Grunig, *The Manager's Guide.*

24. Scott M. Cutlip, Allen H. Center, and Glen M. Broom, *Effective Public Relations* (Upper Saddle River, NJ: Prentice-Hall, 2000), pp. 41–44.

25. Dozier, Grunig, and Grunig, *The Manager's Guide.*

26. Grunig and Hunt, *Managing Public Relations.*

27. James E. Grunig, "Two-Way Symmetrical Public Relations: Past, Present, Future," in *The Handbook of Public Relations,* ed. Robert L. Heath (Thousand Oaks, CA: Sage, 2000), p. 28.

28. Dozier, Grunig, and Grunig, *The Manager's Guide,* p. 48.

29. James E. Grunig, Larissa A. Grunig, K. Sriramesh, Yi-Hui Huang, and Anastasia Lyra, "Models of Public Relations in an International Setting," *Journal of Public Relations Research* 7, no. 3 (1995), p. 183.

30. Larissa A. Grunig, "Power in the Public Relations Department," in *Public Relations Research Annual,* ed. Larissa A. Grunig and James E. Grunig (1990), pp. 115–56.

31. Kenneth D. Plowman, William G. Briggs, and Yi-Hui Huang, "Public Relations and Conflict Resolution," in *Handbook of Public Relations,* ed. Robert L. Heath (Thousand Oaks, CA: Sage, 2001), p. 304. See also Kenneth D. Plowman et al., "Walgreens: A Case Study in Health Care Issues and Conflict Resolution," *Journal of Public Relations Research* 7, no. 4 (1995), pp. 231–58; and Kenneth D. Plowman, "Power in Conflict for Public Relations," *Journal of Public Relations Research* 10 (1998), pp. 237–62.

32. Kenneth D. Plowman. "Public Relations, Conflict Resolution, and Mediation," in *The Future of Excellence in Public Relations and Communication Management: Challenges for the Next Generation,* ed. Elizabeth L. Toth (Mahwah, NJ: Erlbaum, 2007), p. 96.

33. Ibid.

34. Grunig, "Power in the Public," p. 28.

CHAPTER 4

Law and Ethics

OUTLINE

PREVIEW

It's been a long day. You're tired, but your brain is awhirl, and you can't sleep. What you really need is to spend a little time relaxing with a good book, so you get up, go to your computer, download the latest John Grisham thriller from Google for free, and settle down to read.

Impossible? For now, yes. But many publishers and authors are afraid that Google's *Print for Libraries* program, intended to offer users searchable, digitized versions of public-domain books from great American and British research libraries, could morph into a free, unauthorized giveaway of copyrighted texts. Five publishers have already filed a lawsuit claiming the program violates federal copyright laws.

Some publishing executives think the proposed program could benefit both publishers and authors, while others fear not only copyright infringement but also the possibility of piracy as well. Google is assuring publishers and the public alike that only "snippets" of copyrighted texts will be made available, and they will be accompanied by links to Web sites where the books can be purchased. A Google executive noted that Google has nurtured a "respectful relationship" with the owners of content it distributes.[1]

Will Google and the publishers come to an agreement about what constitutes "fair use," or will they fight it out in court? How will each party shape the reading public's perception of its side of the argument? In either case, the public relations practitioners for Google and the publishers association will be busy.

THE LEGAL ENVIRONMENT

According to a survey of public relations practitioners, "Many public relations professionals may be placing themselves and their client organizations at risk of legal liability because they have little or no familiarity with important legal issues that affect public relations activities."[2] Thus, because public relations practitioners are increasingly vulnerable to legal liability, it is more important than ever that they be acquainted with key legal issues such as **First Amendment** rights and limits, libel, privacy, copyright contracts, commercial speech, and numerous federal, state, and local government **regulations.** Also, public relations practitioners work with organizational lawyers in the area of litigation. When an employer or client gets sued, public relations is involved in a court of law and, at the courthouse steps, maintaining relationships that come under scrutiny.

First Amendment Rights and Limits

One of the most strongly supported rights of U.S. citizens is the right to freedom of speech, which is guaranteed under the First Amendment to the Constitution:

> Congress shall make no law respecting an establishment of religion, or prohibiting the free exercise thereof; or abridging the freedom of speech, or of the press; or the right of the people peaceably to assemble, and to petition the Government for a redress of grievances.

Court cases have clarified that organizations enjoy much the same freedom of speech as do individuals. In the 1964 Supreme Court case of *New York Times v. Sullivan,* nonprofit organizations for the first time received an endorsement to use advertisements to discuss matters of public interest. In the case, *The New York Times* carried a full-page ad entitled "Heed Their Rising Voices," which made claims that Alabama state college students had been harassed by police and other state authorities. The ad was paid for by a number of African American clergy. L. B. Sullivan, a Montgomery, Alabama, city commissioner claimed that the ad libeled him. But the Supreme Court ruled for *The New York Times,* because the ad communicated information, expressed opinion, recited grievances, protested, claimed abuses, and sought financial support on behalf of a movement whose existence and objectives are matters of the highest public interest and concern.[3]

First National Bank of Boston v. Bellotti involved a for-profit organization's right of political and social free speech. When the First National Bank of Boston wanted to oppose and advertise publicly against a Massachusetts personal income tax referendum, State Attorney General Francis Bellotti said a state law barred corporations from participation in referenda that did not affect the corporation directly. First National sued the state for violating its First Amendment right to speak. In 1978 the Supreme Court ruled in favor of the bank. Today, we see full-page and electronic forms of advertisements from both for-profit and nonprofit organizations freely entering the political and social debates of our society.

In a similar case in 1980, *Consolidated Edison Company of New York v. Public Service Commission of New York,* the court reaffirmed the utility's right to discuss public issues. Consolidated Edison had spoken out to its customers using brochures and flyers included with monthly billings. Justice Powell reiterated from the *Bellotti* case: "The inherent worth of the speech in terms of its capacity for informing the public does not depend on the identity of the source."[4]

Commercial speech is another legal concept that is important to public relations programs. In 1976, *Virginia State Board of Pharmacy v. Virginia Citizens Consumer Council, Inc.* extended First Amendment protection for truthful marketing of legal products and services. At issue was whether potential purchasers of prescription medicines had the right to know the price of prescription drugs, which at that time could

Nike can be sued over its corporate policy statements, says the California Supreme Court in a 4–3 vote, according to an article in the May 3 issue of *The Recorder*—"Corporation PR Campaigns Lose Speech Protection" by Mike McKee.

The court ruled that companies can be sued for false advertising over policy statements made in public relations campaigns. Statements by the Oregon-based shoemaker denying allegations that some overseas factories are sweatshops were a form of commercial speech not protected by the First Amendment. "Because in the statements at issue here Nike was act-ing as a commercial speaker, because its intended audience was primarily the buyers of its products and because the statements consisted of factual representations about its own business operations, we conclude that the statements were commercial speech for purposes of applying state laws designed to prevent false advertising and other forms of commercial deception," wrote Justice Joyce Kennard. The court's ruling did not decide whether Nike's ads were false or misleading.

Nike appealed the ruling to the U.S. Supreme Court. The Supreme Court on June 26, 2003, dismissed the appeal and sent the case back to the California Supreme Court; however, five of the U.S. Supreme Court justices rejected the central argument that Nike's speech could be restricted as purely commercial.

Questions

1. As a public relations counsel to Nike, would you advise withdrawing the ads? Why or why not?
2. When do you think speech about corporate social responsibility is not an attempt to sell shoes?

Source: From *pr reporter,* May 27, 2002, p. 2. Also, press release from Nike, June 26, 2003.

---

vary as much as 600 percent from pharmacy to pharmacy.[5] The Supreme Court sided with the consumer's interest in the free flow of information rather than the pharmacists' claim that to discuss pricing was unprofessional conduct.

The Supreme Court decisions in these and other cases opened the door to issues-oriented advertising by corporations, associations, and special interest groups. The broadened interpretation of free speech protections resulted in increased corporate political activity through lobbying and political action committees (PACs).

Free speech is not without its limits. Most juries today interpret the First Amendment to mean that free speech should be balanced against other human values or rights. Those other rights—for example, the right to privacy, the right to a good reputation, or the right to own property—can restrict the right to free speech. Although free flow of commercial information is indispensable, public communications—news releases, company newsletters, speeches, and advertisements—are limited to the extent that they may not slander or libel an individual, invade an individual's privacy, infringe on existing copyrights or trademarks, breach contracts, or violate regulatory requirements. These protections and limitations are now being extended to a new channel of communication—the Internet.

Defamation   Defamation is speech defined as "the publication of material that would hold one up to hatred, ridicule, contempt, or spite."[6] There are two types of defamation: libel and slander. **Libel** is published defamation, by written or printed words or in some other physical form. **Slander** is defamation by spoken words, gestures, or other transitory means.[7]

Public relations practitioners have to consider that "nearly every press release, news article, or advertisement holds the potential for a libel suit."[8] At risk as well are the products and services of clients that could be disparaged in a public way. Consider Oprah Winfrey's 1996 airing of a segment on mad cow disease that implied that the U.S. beef industry lacked protections for consumers. The program resulted in immediate financial losses to the beef industry. In the subsequent lawsuit, the court eventually ruled in favor of Winfrey, stating that she had not defamed anyone. Free speech rights of corporations were questioned again in a California court ruling against Nike, as discussed in mini-case 4.1.

Libel law has two categories: criminal and civil. Although the Supreme Court has frequently overturned criminal convictions and they are rare today, individuals have been found guilty of **criminal libel** in cases of "breach of peace" or "inciting to riot."

More important to public relations practitioners is **civil libel.** For a statement to be libelous, it must contain certain elements. It must be published, it must be damaging, and it must identify the injured party. Negligence must be involved, and the statement must be defamatory. If the statement involves a public figure, another element becomes of paramount importance: It must involve **malice.**

Publication is considered to have occurred when the alleged defamation has been communicated to a third party. For example, it is "published" when the writer, the injured party, and one other person have seen or heard the remark.

Defamation deals with the words themselves or the implication behind the words. A person's reputation (not character) has been damaged, for example, by calling him or her a terrorist, a traitor, or a liar.

Damage has occurred if the remarks reflect poorly on one's reputation, impair one's ability to earn a living, or restrict one's social contacts.

Identification has occurred when readers or listeners are able to identify the person referred to, whether or not the person is specifically named.

Fault must be shown in order for the plaintiff to win a libel suit. If the wrong photograph is run with an article, if there is a typographical or mechanical error in the publication process, or if information is not carefully checked, the defendant may be found negligent.

Malice occurs when the plaintiff can prove that the defendant knew the published material was false or showed a reckless disregard for the truth. Only public figures must prove malice. Politicians, elected government officials, and CEOs of corporations are obvious public figures. So is entertainer Carol Burnett, who successfully sued *The National Enquirer* for $10 million for maliciously depicting her as a public drunk. She used her financial award to set up prizes for journalism ethics. While lawsuits are filed against media, any corporation, organization, or public relations practitioner can be guilty of defamation through written material or remarks made before any group of people.

Defenses Against Libel Charges   There are three primary defenses against libel charges—truth, qualified privilege, and fair comment. The primary legal defense is the truth. A second legal defense is **privilege.** Privilege protects materials and remarks coming from official proceedings and actions of members in executive, legislative, and judicial branches of government. The third legal defense is **fair comment.** If communication involves matters of genuine public interest, expressing critical opinions is permissible. The information must be in the public interest and supported with factual material. Examples include movie, book, and restaurant criticism, but fair comment could apply to consumer products, services, or the work of charitable organizations. For the public relations professional, all communication about employees, competitors, and campaigns must be researched and controversial material pretested, and when there is concern, legal advice must be sought.

Rights of Privacy.   Defamation concerns broadly the publication of speech that is derogatory. But even complimentary information may break the law if it invades another's **privacy rights.** Public relations practitioners disseminate many kinds of messages—about their own organizations, fellow employees, participants in special events, customers, and students on a campus. None of these messages should be created without first thinking about protecting privacy.

Legal issues are a constant concern for the public relations practitioner.

There are generally four kinds of **invasion of privacy:** appropriation, publication of private information, intrusion, and false light. **Appropriation** is the use for monetary gain of a person's name, likeness, or picture without permission. **Publication of private information** concerns information that is true but not generally known by a large number of people. Health, employment, and student records are examples of private information for which permission must be granted before it can be shared. **Intrusion** concerns videotaping, bugging, or snooping into others' private affairs. It is illegal to secretly record others' voices or actions without informing a person that the recording is being done. **False light** concerns publication of truthful information that is exaggerated or used out of context.

The best defense against invasion of privacy charges is obtaining **written consent.** Standard consent forms should be used whenever individuals' likenesses or personal information are used in public relations materials (see figure 4.1).

The **Freedom of Information Act (FOIA),** passed in 1966 and amended in 1974, generally requires that all government records—documents, press releases, and publications—are open to the public. For example, U.S. Census data and Department of Labor reports are available to all citizens.

Government agencies must tell citizens what information is available to them and how they can obtain it. These agencies even have Web sites that include descriptions of types of information and direct links to this information over the Internet. Businesses use the FOIA to obtain government statistics and other research, such as environmental impact statements and applications for government permits. Activist organizations keep track of laws and regulations under consideration by public bodies, of minutes of meetings, and proposed government plans for zoning and development changes.

Congress passed the **Sunshine Act** in 1976, which opened to the public some previously closed meetings of federal boards, commissions, and agencies, including the Securities and Exchange Commission and the Federal Trade Commission. Many state and local governments have similar statutes affecting their boards and commissions. For

---

Adult Release

In consideration of my engagement as a model, and for other good and valuable consideration herein acknowledged or received, upon the terms hereafter stated, I hereby grant _____, his legal representatives and assigns, those for whom _____ is acting, and those acting with his authority and permission, the absolute right and permission to copyright and use, reuse and publish, and republish photographic portraits or pictures of me or in which I may be included, in whole or in part, or composite or distorted in character or form, without restriction as to changes or alteration, from time to time, in conjunction with my own or a fictitious name, or reproductions thereof in color or otherwise made through any media at his studios or elsewhere for art, advertising, trade or any other purpose whatsoever.

I also consent to the use of any printed matter in conjunction therewith.
I hereby waive any right that I may have to inspect or approve the finished product or products of the advertising copy or printed matter that may be used in connection therewith or the use to which it may be applied.

I hereby release, discharge and agree to save harmless _____, his legal representatives or assigns, and all persons acting under his permission or authority or those for whom he is acting, from any liability by virtue of any blurring, distortion, alteration, optical illusion, or use in composite form, whether intentional or otherwise, that may occur or be produced in the taking of said picture or in any subsequent processing thereof, as well as any publication thereof even though it may subject me to ridicule, scandal, reproach, scorn and indignity.

I hereby warrant that I am of full age and have every right to contract in my own name in the above regard. I state further that I have read the above authorization, release and agreement, prior to its execution, and that I am fully familiar with the contents thereof.

Dated _____

Signed _____

(Address) _____

_____

(Witness) _____

FIGURE 4.1   **This use of a standard release form can protect against possible charges of invasion of privacy.**

example, local officials may be prohibited from meeting as a group unless there is public notice of such a meeting.

Organizational privacy is being contested because of the **USA Patriot Act** of 2001, which allows access to information to obstruct terrorism. Public relations professionals will have to explain opening up records against the objections of customers and clients and the confiscating of cell phones and laptops, and U.S. Customs entry.

Government Regulatory Agencies

Many federal government agencies have a watchdog role regarding business and organizational communication, such as the **Federal Trade Commission,** the **Food and Drug Administration,** the **Federal Communications Commission,** the **National Labor Relations Board,** and the **Securities and Exchange Commission.** Regulatory complaints from any of these federal agencies may originate with the agency itself, or consumers, labor leaders, or competitors may bring them to the attention of the agency. Public relations personnel should anticipate how federal laws and regulations could be broken when an organization seeks to communicate with any number of consumer, employee, or competitor publics.

The Federal Trade Commission (FTC)   The FTC governs all commercial advertising and product or service news releases, typical media for marketing communications. Advertising and news releases are illegal if they deceive or mislead the public in any way. Likewise, promotional practices are illegal unless they are literally true. The FTC requires that unsubstantiated or false claims for products be omitted from future advertising, and some advertisers may also be required to run corrective ads.

Food and Drug Administration (FDA)   The FDA regulates labeling, packaging, and sale of food, drugs, and cosmetics. The regulations govern both product safety and product advertising. Many product recalls and the prohibition of some drug products in the United States result from a failure to meet FDA safety regulations or guidelines. The FDA is responsible for the nutritional labeling on many food products. Public relations practitioners working on product introductions will have to be able to explain FDA regulations to many stakeholders, including customers and the media.

Federal Communications Commission (FCC)   The FCC regulates broadcasting, television, and radio to ensure that licensees are operating in the public interest. Of concern to political public relations practitioners are Sections 315 and 317 of the Federal Communications Act. They monitor the content of political broadcasting so that all parties have equal opportunity to be heard. A public relations practitioner for a political candidate should know the following in Section 315a:

> If any licensee shall permit any person who is a legally qualified candidate for any public office to use a broadcasting station, he shall afford equal opportunities to all other such candidates for that office in the use of such broadcasting station, provided that such licensee should have no power of censorship over the material broadcast under provisions of this section. No obligation is hereby imposed upon any licensee to allow the use of its station by any such candidate.[9]

Although Section 315 doesn't require stations to provide broadcast time, Section 312(a7) does. It requires stations to sell "reasonable amounts of time" to legally qualified candidates for federal office. Stations aren't held accountable for content, but candidates, their organizations, and their public relations practitioners are accountable.

National Labor Relations Board (NLRB)   The NLRB oversees the 1935 National Labor Relations Act, the primary law governing communications between unions and employers. The act deals with all aspects of union activities, including the right to join unions, to engage in collective bargaining, and to engage in union activities. The act also protects nonunion activities such as nonunion walkouts, working conditions, and employee discussions of compensation. All of these activities would require that managers and public relations professionals express company positions in ways that are not coercive or threatening to management-labor relationships.

Securities and Exchange Commission (SEC)   The SEC enforces laws and regulations concerning the purchase of stocks of publicly owned corporations that are listed on any of the 13 largest U.S. stock exchanges or that have assets of $1 million and 500 stockholders. It enforces the **Securities and Exchange Act of 1934** and other regulations that require that corporations "act promptly to dispel unfounded rumors which result in unusual market activity or price variations."

The Securities and Exchange Act of 1933 requires the "full and fair disclosure of the character of securities . . . and to prevent frauds in the sale thereof. The Securities and Exchange Act of 1934 supplemented the previous year's legislation and was intended to "secure, for issues publicly offered, adequate publicity for those facts necessary for an intelligent judgment of their value."

The SEC requires submission of three kinds of reports: annual reports (**Form 10-K**), quarterly reports (**Form 10-Q**), and current reports (**Form 8-K**). Although the information in these reports is produced by accountants and lawyers, these publications have strategic public relations value because they are distributed to many audiences, including stockholders, financial analysts, and potential investors.

The **Sarbanes-Oxley Act** of 2002 requires public companies to be much more "transparent" in their communication with stockholders, investors, employees, retirees, and government officials. Passed in response to the collapse of Enron, public companies must provide much more information about their officers, financial transactions, and specific codes of ethics. The Sarbanes-Oxley Act has brought new responsibilities to corporate communication officers who assist in disclosing corporate decision making to the financial media, stock analysts, and investors. See Chapter 13 for more information on this and other investor relations material.

General Business Regulations

Public relations is a practice protected by the First Amendment and regulated as a function of organizations. But public relations is also a business activity, involved in creating and protecting organizational brands and reputations. Thus, public relations practitioners need to know general business regulations, such as **copyright** law, **trademark** law, contracts, and the laws of litigation. "Public relations practitioners must understand the extent to which the general laws of business also govern their field; but they and the media are subject to the normal laws of business, such as antitrust regulations, even though their expression may be protected by the First Amendment."[10]

Copyright Law   Public relations practitioners must have legal consent to use another's creative expression or "intellectual property," such as graphic designs, music to use in videos, annual report and brochure copy, photographs, and other original artistic works fixed in any tangible form. Self-employed public relations consultants copyright their materials unless they contractually sign away that right to their clients.

Only when **fair use** is established can public relations practitioners produce or copy others' creative expression. The fair use provision of the Copyright Act allows use of others' materials with broad provisions addressing the following:

1. The purpose and character of the use, including whether such use is of a commercial nature or is for nonprofit educational purposes.

2. The nature of the copyrighted work is challenged.

3. The amount and substantiality of the portion used is verified with the copyright holder.

4. The effect of the use upon the potential market for or value of the copyrighted work is considered.

This means that in the preparation of communications, a portion of copyrighted material may be used without the author's permission

1. If it is not taken out of context.

2. If credit to the source is given.

3. If such usage does not materially affect the market for the copyrighted material.

4. If the work in which it is used is for scholastic, news, or research purposes.

5. If the material used does not exceed a certain percentage of the total work.

No percentage is given in the law; it depends on the work. One rule of thumb: Don't use any music; use only a fraction of poetry; but you can use 100 to 200 words of a book or article.

Trademark Laws   Trademark laws cover the names of businesses and business products. Just as patent laws often cover the products themselves, their names can be covered under trademarks. Organizations want exclusive rights to their brand or service names, logos, and symbols. It would be trademark infringement to market a product with a name strongly resembling or suggestive of an existing trademark or trade name.

Companies zealously protect their product brands against those who would try to use the brand without permission. They also guard against a brand name becoming generic for all of the products in its category, thus sacrificing its uniqueness and causing serious advertising and public relations problems. Think of such brands as Kleenex, Band-Aid, and Xerox that have lost their uniqueness because these trade names are used for all products in their categories.

Contracts   Copyrighted and trademarked materials may be used if permission is given by the copyright or trademark holder. Permission for use can constitute a **contract,** a legal instrument that protects the rights of two or more parties.

Public relations practitioners often must use contracts. Independent public relations professionals need contracts between themselves and the firms or individuals they represent. Special events may require contracts with hotels, musical groups, caterers, and others. Practitioners contract with outside vendors, such as publishing or printing firms, mail distribution agencies, and electronic clipping services, to do production and research work.

For a contract to be binding, it must meet certain legal criteria. For example, a contract must include the following:

1. A genuine, legal offer

2. A legally effective acceptance

3. An agreement that includes an exchange of acts or promises, which is called "consideration"[11]

Some but not all contracts must be in writing. Courts often consider oral contracts binding if all legal tests have been met in the process. If obligations set out in a contract are not fulfilled, a possible breach of contract has occurred.

Legal Considerations Surrounding the Internet

The Internet is demanding new regulation in libel, copyright, and privacy. These are important issues to public relations practitioners who have taken advantage of going directly to stakeholders with this immediate, compelling channel of communication.

Copyright and the Net   Public relations practitioners are using the Internet and online services to send and find breaking news, feature stories, speeches, photos, and information about their agencies or organizations and to receive direct inquiries and feedback from stakeholders. Even though these resources are conveniently accessible, they are still copyright protected, and public relations professionals should not use materials without permission.[12] *BusinessWeek* calls copyright violation on the Internet "highway robbery," claiming that infringement goes far beyond the copy machine violations. A digital copyright code was designed in 1995 to put a "cipher," or a code, identifying the owner into each copyrighted work on the Internet.[13]

Libel and the Net   Though there is still debate in the courts about who is responsible for libel on the Internet, public relations practitioners would be held accountable for libel should they use the Net because the practitioner controls the messages sent to the public. Common carriers such as telephone companies, however, are not responsible because they don't control the statements. A New York court decided in 1995 that an Internet provider could be held responsible if it edited electronic messages posted by subscribers. The Long Island securities investment firm Stratton Oakmont Inc. sued Prodigy for $200 million because an anonymous user of Prodigy's "Money Talk" bulletin board falsely portrayed the company as criminals involved in fraud.[14] The court said that because Prodigy marketed itself as a family-oriented online service that screened new messages on its bulletin board, it was more like a publisher than like a common carrier.

Privacy and the Net   Privacy is a "source of worry" for senders and receivers of Internet messages. Because Internet communication can be tracked and traced, and authors identified by authorities, hackers, and identity thieves, the public has a strong desire to have personal information protected as more and more of the world intrudes through e-mail and cyberspace. Organizations have varying policies on what types of information employees may exchange over the Net. E-mail addresses are being sold to vendors who want to use them for sales purposes. Public relations practitioners have to weigh the gains and hazards of this channel of communication as a means of reaching stakeholders and maintaining relationships with them.

Litigation Public Relations

Organizations must consider whether and how relationships with clients, employees, government, and the media would be affected should they find themselves in court. Media interest in an organization accused of wrongdoing or other reputation-damaging activities could be constant enough that, regardless of how the court case is resolved, the accused organization is found to be less credible and trustworthy by its constituents outside the courthouse. Dow Corning is being sued for billions of dollars by women who claim its silicone gel–filled breast implants caused them multiple ailments, pain, and suffering. This corporation found itself in litigation because of a CBS television show aired in 1990 in which Connie Chung interviewed several women who claimed

Martha Stewart seeks resolution of legal allegations against her of insider trading.

that their breast implants gave them autoimmune disease. Years later, Dow Corning was still spending thousands of dollars in time and money attempting in court to reach a bankruptcy reorganization and, at the same time, seeking means through communication to keep its employees productive and its reputation credible so that it will keep its stockholders, customers, suppliers, and successful relationships with the community, government, and the media.[15]

Public relations practitioners have to concern themselves, too, with **product liability.** This refers to the "legal responsibility of companies to compensate individuals for injuries or damages resulting from defects in products that were purchased."[16] Facing negative publicity, McDonald's settled a product liability claim filed by a woman who spilled its coffee while attempting to drive and hold the coffee cup between her legs.

THE ETHICAL ENVIRONMENT

Kant defined ethics as "a science that teaches, not how we are to achieve happiness, but how we are to become worthy of happiness."[17] What is legal is not always ethical, and what is ethical is not always legal. Laws cover only so many situations in public relations. In many situations, public relations professionals have to make judgments about "the right thing to do" to build relationships between the organization and its publics. Public relations practitioners must weigh the benefit versus the harm of their communication activities and/or have the moral resolve to say yes or no, because the long-term effects of a bad decision will offset a short-term gain.

Ethics is an area of concern for public relations for four reasons. First, practitioners are aware that, to some, public relations has a reputation for unethical behavior. Second, public relations is often the source of ethical statements from an organization and the repository of ethical and social policies for that organization. Third, practitioners have struggled to create suitable codes of ethics for themselves; and fourth, practitioners should act on behalf of their organizations as the ethical ombudsman for the publics they serve.

If public relations seeks to achieve professional status as a communication function that represents the public interest as well as the organization in business decision making, its practitioners must be held to higher standards.

Ethics as Standards of Social Conduct

Ethics is what is morally right or wrong in social conduct, usually as determined by standards of professions, organizations, and individuals. Ethical behavior is a major consideration that distinguishes the civilized from the uncivilized in society. Allen Center and Patrick Jackson argue that five factors regulate social conduct:

1. *Tradition.* Ways in which the situation has been viewed or handled in the past.
2. *Public Opinion.* Currently acceptable behavior according to the majority of one's peers.
3. *Law.* Behaviors that are permissible and those that are prohibited by legislation.
4. *Morality.* Generally, a spiritual or religious prohibition. Immorality is a charge usually leveled in issues on which religious teachings have concentrated.
5. *Ethics.* Standards set by the profession, an organization, or oneself, based on conscience—what is right or fair to others as well as to self?[18]

Individual Ethics

Ralph Waldo Emerson, an American philosopher, said, "What you are stands over you the while, and thunders so that I cannot hear what you say." This same philosophy was evident in the work of Ivy Lee, one of the early pioneers of public relations. Lee considered that public relations *actions,* not words, are more important. His 1906 Declaration of Principles was the forerunner of a **code of ethics** for public relations.

More important than ethical codes of public relations, though, is the nature of the individual, private ethics of the practitioner. When it comes right down to it, the practitioner must have a high personal standard of ethics that carries over into his or her own work. James E. Grunig, a leading proponent of public relations professionalism, argued that individual practitioners must have two basic guiding ethical principles:

1. They must have the will to be ethical, intending not to injure others, but rather to be honest and trustworthy.
2. They must make every effort to avoid actions that would have adverse consequences for others.[19]

At the heart of any discussion of ethics in public relations are some questions that are deeply troubling for the individual practitioner. For example, will she or he

- Lie for a client or employer?
- Engage in deception to collect information about another practitioner's clients?
- Help conceal a hazardous condition or illegal act?
- Present information that presents only part of the truth?
- Offer something (gift, travel, or information) to reporters or legislators that may compromise their reporting?
- Present true but misleading information in an interview or news conference that corrupts the channels of government?

John "Pat" Philbin, former director of external affairs for the Federal Emergency Management Administration (FEMA), faced an ethical issue when he accompanied his boss, Vice Admiral Harvey Johnson, to a hastily organized press conference to showcase FEMA's efforts in response to the California wildfires. FEMA staffers, and not reporters, asked the admiral questions during a broadcast on cable channels. Philbin finally stopped the press conference when he realized its misleading nature, but too late not to be caught by media listening in. The ethical issue caused a firestorm of derision.

Philbin took responsibility for the error as the top public affairs person at FEMA. The public affairs staff had failed to notify the media in time for the news conference, but a staff member made the decision to go forward with the press conference—without the media. When Philbin and Vice Admiral Johnson arrived late to the press conference, there were no reporters. They were told that the media was on the phone.

A few days after the press conference a *Washington Post* reporter contacted Philbin to talk about the "press conference." Philbin, who had resigned five days before the press conference to take another job, received this inquiry on the day he was leaving the job. Instead of responding to the *Post* report himself, he sent the inquiry on to a staff member with instructions, "You get back to him and tell him exactly what happened." The resulting *Post* article took Philbin and FEMA to task for the staged press conference.

In response to the incident, Philbin, an accredited public relations practitioner and now senior vice president for PIER Systems, Inc., said he would take responsibility again if such an incident happened because he was the leader. "I am a firm believer in . . . ethical behavior, because I think that is all you have in this business, your credibility, which is particularly troubling to me because that's what has been called into question here."

Philbin suggested the following "takeaways" from his experience:

- Know your people, their capabilities and their ethics.
- Don't hesitate to stand up and rectify things immediately.
- Be more aggressive about getting the entire story out.
- Understand your limitations.

Source: Kami Huyse, "Exclusive: Former FEMA External Affairs Head John 'Pat' Philbin Sets the Record Straight about 'Fake' Press Conference," *Communication Overtones,* January 9, 2008, retrieved at http://overtonecomm.blogspot.com/2008/01/exclusive-former-fema-external-affairs.html

---

Many public relations practitioners find themselves forced to respond to questions like these.

See mini-case 4.2 about John "Pat" Philbin. Philbin was about to change high-level government public affairs jobs and lost both his old job and his new one in the aftermath of the fake FEMA press conference.

By considering their ethical standards, practitioners can avoid difficult situations that may harm their individual reputations. Unfortunately, most ethical decisions are not black or white. When obligations to stakeholders collide over an ethical issue, the practitioner must decide whose claim is most important or entails the least harm to the fewest people. Thus, when the employer's policies are different from those of the profession or the dictates of individual conscience, which would take precedence?

Business Ethics

As controversial as the question of individual ethics is, so is the general issue of business ethics. It is relatively easy to agree in abstract terms that individual professionals have a duty to behave ethically. Unfortunately, translating abstract concepts into ethical standards for business practice in a competitive environment has not been so easy. Some practitioners have been arbitrarily fired for refusing to write news releases they thought would be false or misleading. One practitioner worked for a company that wanted him to prepare and distribute a release listing company clients before the clients had signed contracts for services. When he refused to prepare the release, this practitioner was fired and subsequently sued the company for unlawful dismissal, receiving almost $100,000 in an out-of-court settlement. Another public relations practitioner resigned after initially participating in several ethically questionable practices with a multinational fruit conglomerate. He charged the company with manipulation of press coverage as well as with political and military action involving a Latin American country in which the company was operating.

75

The increased attention of many organizations to ethical dimensions of operating can be traced back to the1968 Watergate investigation. President Richard Nixon resigned rather than face impeachment charges because of a bungled break-in at Democratic campaign headquarters and subsequent revelations of unethical campaign practices, cover-ups, and secret tapings of White House meetings.

Other indelible examples of ethical controversy that add to public skepticism of public relations include Firestone Tire, a corporation that has not yet admitted responsibility for the highway deaths linked to its tires. Coke maintains that its European distributions had no responsibility in the contamination of its product that led to schoolchildren reporting that they became ill from drinking Coke products, although Coke attempted to make amends by offering free Coke products. The American Red Cross faced negative public opinion twice after its efforts to form a September 11 liberty fund. First, the organization came under fire when it announced after 9/11 that it would hold back for future disasters donations that the American public had expected would go to the victims of the World Trade Center and Pentagon attacks. Then, when the Red Cross began to give out the money, it was criticized for being too generous.

When public relations practitioners participate in organizational decisions, they bear a heavy ethical responsibility—not only to themselves and their organizations but also to their profession and the public. They must weigh all these considerations when helping to make organizational decisions and communicate decisions once they are made.

Professional codes, corporate policy, and even law cannot ensure the ethical practice of any profession; only the application of sound personal values can guarantee ethical behavior. Nevertheless, professional codes, sound business policies, and appropriate legislation can serve as valuable guidelines for public relations practitioners who desire to maintain high ethical standards.

Establishing Standards for a Developing Profession

For any occupation to become a profession, it must meet four criteria: (1) expertise, (2) autonomy, (3) commitment, and (4) responsibility.[20] *Expertise* comprises the specialized knowledge and skill that are vital requirements for the profession to perform its function in society. *Autonomy* allows the practitioner to practice without outside interference. *Commitment,* the outcome of expertise, implies devotion to the pursuit of excellence without emphasis on the rewards of the profession. Finally, *responsibility* means the power conferred by expertise entails a trust relationship with the practitioner's stakeholder groups.

Though all four criteria are important, the last one, responsibility, is operationalized through codes of ethics, professional organizations, and licensure. Thus, to be considered fully professionalized, an occupation needs a well-developed and well-enforced code of ethics, active professional associations, and some means of controlling the practice. It is the licensure issue that continues to prevent public relations from being a fully professional occupation.

The PRSA Code

The ethics code of the Public Relations Society of America (PRSA) is the most detailed and comprehensive in the field of public relations, although it is strictly voluntary and not legally binding (see spotlight 4.1). When PRSA was founded in 1948, one of its actions was to develop a code of ethics so members would have some common behavioral guidelines, and managers would have a clear understanding of their standards. This code became the tool used to distinguish professionals in public relations from shady promoters and publicists who have been quick to appropriate the term *public relations* to describe their activities.

A Message from the PRSA Board of Ethics and Professional Standards

Our Primary Obligation

The primary obligation of membership in the Public Relations Society of America is the ethical practice of Public Relations.

The PRSA Member Code of Ethics is the way each member of our Society can daily reaffirm a commitment to ethical professional activities and decisions.

- The Code sets forth the principles and standards that guide our decisions and actions.
- The Code solidly connects our values and our ideals to the work each of us does every day.
- The Code is about what we should do, and why we should do it.

The Code is also meant to be a living, growing body of knowledge, precedent, and experience. It should stimulate our thinking and encourage us to seek guidance and clarification when we have questions about principles, practices, and standards of conduct.

Every member's involvement in preserving and enhancing ethical standards is essential to building and maintaining the respect and credibility of our profession. Using our values, principles, standards of conduct, and commitment as a foundation, and continuing to work together on ethical issues, we ensure that the Public Relations Society of America fulfills its obligation to build and maintain the framework for public dialogue that deserves the public's trust and support.

Preamble

Public Relations Society of America Member Code of Ethics 2000

- Professional Values
- Principles of Conduct
- Commitment and Compliance

This Code applies to PRSA members. The Code is designed to be a useful guide for PRSA members as they carry out their ethical responsibilities. This document is designed to anticipate and accommodate, by precedent, ethical challenges that may arise. The scenarios outlined in the Code provision are actual examples of misconduct. More will be added as experience with the Code occurs.

The Public Relations Society of America (PRSA) is committed to ethical practices. The level of public trust PRSA members seek, as we serve the public good, means we have taken on a special obligation to operate ethically.

The value of member reputation depends upon the ethical conduct of everyone affiliated with the Public Relations Society of America. Each of us sets an example for each other—as well as other professionals—by our pursuit of excellence with powerful standards of performance, professionalism, and ethical conduct.

Emphasis on enforcement of the Code has been eliminated. But the PRSA Board of Directors retains the right to bar from membership or expel from the Society any individual who has been or is sanctioned by a government agency or convicted in a court of law of an action that is in violation of this Code.

Ethical practice is the most important obligation of a PRSA member. We view the Member Code of Ethics as a model for other professions, organizations, and professionals.

PRSA Member Statement of Professional Values

This statement presents the core values of PRSA members and, more broadly, of the public relations profession. These values provide the foundation for the Member Code of Ethics and set the industry standard for the professional practice of public relations. These values are the fundamental beliefs that guide our behaviors and decision-making process. We believe our professional values are vital to the integrity of the profession as a whole.

Advocacy

- We serve the public interest by acting as responsible advocates for those we represent.
- We provide a voice in the marketplace of ideas, facts, and viewpoints to aid informed public debate.

Honesty

- We adhere to the highest standards of accuracy and truth in advancing the interests of those we represent and in communicating with the public.

Expertise

- We acquire and responsibly use specialized knowledge and experience.
- We advance the profession through continued professional development, research, and education.
- We build mutual understanding, credibility, and relationships among a wide array of institutions and audiences.

Independence

- We provide objective counsel to those we represent.
- We are accountable for our actions.

Loyalty

- We are faithful to those we represent, while honoring our obligation to serve the public interest.

Fairness

- We deal fairly with clients, employers, competitors, peers, vendors, the media, and the general public.
- We respect all opinions and support the right of free expression.

PRSA Code Provisions

Free Flow of Information

Core Principle

Protecting and advancing the free flow of accurate and truthful information is essential to serving the public interest and contributing to informed decision making in a democratic society.

Intent

- To maintain the integrity of relationships with the media, government officials, and the public.
- To aid informed decision making.

(Continued)

Guidelines

A member shall

- Preserve the integrity of the process of communication.
- Be honest and accurate in all communications.
- Act promptly to correct erroneous communications for which the practitioner is responsible.
- Preserve the free flow of unprejudiced information when giving or receiving gifts by ensuring that gifts are nominal, legal, and infrequent.

Examples of Improper Conduct Under This Provision

- A member representing a ski manufacturer gives a pair of expensive racing skis to a sports magazine columnist, to influence the columnist to write favorable articles about the product.
- A member entertains a government official beyond legal limits and/or in violation of government reporting requirements.

Competition

Core Principle

Promoting healthy and fair competition among professionals preserves an ethical climate while fostering a robust business environment.

Intent

- To promote respect and fair competition among public relations professionals.
- To serve the public interest by providing the widest choice of practitioner options.

Guidelines

A member shall

- Follow ethical hiring practices designed to respect free and open competition without deliberately undermining a competitor.
- Preserve intellectual property rights in the marketplace.

Examples of Improper Conduct Under This Provision

- A member employed by a "client organization" shares helpful information with a counseling firm that is competing with others for the organization's business.
- A member spreads malicious and unfounded rumors about a competitor in order to alienate the competitor's clients and employees in a ploy to recruit people and business.

Disclosure of Information

Core Principle

Open communication fosters informed decision making in a democratic society.

Intent

- To build trust with the public by revealing all information needed for responsible decision making.

Guidelines

A member shall

- Be honest and accurate in all communications.
- Act promptly to correct erroneous communications for which the member is responsible.
- Investigate the truthfulness and accuracy of information released on behalf of those represented.
- Reveal the sponsors for causes and interests represented.
- Disclose financial interest (such as stock ownership) in a client's organization.
- Avoid deceptive practices.

Examples of Improper Conduct Under This Provision

- Front groups: A member implements "grass roots" campaigns or letter-writing campaigns to legislators on behalf of undisclosed interest groups.
- Lying by omission: A practitioner for a corporation knowingly fails to release financial information, giving a misleading impression of the corporation's performance.
- A member discovers inaccurate information disseminated via a Web site or media kit and does not correct the information.
- A member deceives the public by employing people to pose as volunteers to speak at public hearings and participate in "grass roots" campaigns.

Safeguarding Confidences

Core Principle

Client trust requires appropriate protection of confidential and private information.

Intent

- To protect the privacy rights of clients, organizations, and individuals by safeguarding confidential information.

Guidelines

A member shall

- Safeguard the confidences and privacy rights of present, former, and prospective clients and employees.
- Protect privileged, confidential, or insider information gained from a client or organization.
- Immediately advise an appropriate authority if a member discovers that confidential information is being divulged by an employee of a client company or organization.

Examples of Improper Conduct Under This Provision

- A member changes jobs, takes confidential information, and uses that information in the new position to the detriment of the former employer.
- A member intentionally leaks proprietary information to the detriment of some other party.

Conflicts of Interest

Core Principle

Avoiding real, potential or perceived conflicts of interest builds the trust of clients, employers, and the publics.

Intent

- To earn trust and mutual respect with clients or employers.
- To build trust with the public by avoiding or ending situations that put one's personal or professional interests in conflict with society's interests.

Guidelines

A member shall

- Act in the best interests of the client or employer, even subordinating the member's personal interests.

- Avoid actions and circumstances that may appear to compromise good business judgment or create a conflict between personal and professional interests.
- Disclose promptly any existing or potential conflict of interest to affected clients or organizations.
- Encourage clients and customers to determine if a conflict exists after notifying all affected parties.

Examples of Improper Conduct Under This Provision

- The member fails to disclose that he or she has a strong financial interest in a client's chief competitor.
- The member represents a "competitor company" or a "conflicting interest" without informing a prospective client.

Enhancing the Profession

Core Principle

Public relations professionals work constantly to strengthen the public's trust in the profession.

Intent

- To build respect and credibility with the public for the profession of public relations.
- To improve, adapt, and expand professional practices.

Guidelines

A member shall

- Acknowledge that there is an obligation to protect and enhance the profession.
- Keep informed and educated about practices in the profession to ensure ethical conduct.
- Actively pursue personal professional development.
- Decline representation of clients or organizations that urge or require actions contrary to this Code.
- Accurately define what public relations activities can accomplish.
- Counsel subordinates in proper ethical decision making.

- Require that subordinates adhere to the ethical requirements of the Code.
- Report ethical violations, whether committed by PRSA members or not, to the appropriate authority.

Examples of Improper Conduct Under This Provision

- A PRSA member declares publicly that a product the client sells is safe, without disclosing evidence to the contrary.
- A member initially assigns some questionable client work to a nonmember practitioner to avoid the ethical obligation of PRSA membership.

The most recent PRSA Code revisions, approved in 2000, changed dramatically how PRSA intended to think about and educate public relations professionals about ethics. First, the PRSA Code eliminated an emphasis on enforcement of standards based on members coming forward to lodge complaints or identify others in violation of the Code, although the PRSA board of directors retained the right to bar individuals from membership or expel individuals from the society. Second, the PRSA Code focused on universal values that inspire ethical behavior or performance. Third, the PRSA Code provided illustrations to help practitioners better practice important ethical and principled business objectives.

The IABC Code

The International Association of Business Communicators (IABC), with approximately 19,000 members, also has a widely used code of ethics (see spotlight 4.2). This code differs from that of the PRSA in only a few ways. It seems to focus more on the worth of human beings in the many cultures of the world and to be sensitive to other cultural values and beliefs. It gives a more limited list of standards and does not try to spell out values that have led to the formally listed standards. Both codes are voluntary, but members are required to sign that they have read and are willing to abide by the codes.

The Question of Licensure

Some believe that codes of behavior are only part of what is needed to build professional status for the field of public relations. Controlled access is the hallmark of a

IABC Code of Ethics for Professional Communicators

Preface

Because hundreds of thousands of business communicators worldwide engage in activities that affect the lives of millions of people, and because this power carries with it significant social responsibilities, the International Association of Business Communicators developed the Code of Ethics for Professional Communicators.

The Code is based on three different yet interrelated principles of professional communication that apply throughout the world.

These principles assume that just societies are governed by a profound respect for human rights and the rule of law; that ethics, the criteria for determining what is right and wrong, can be agreed upon by members of an organization; and, that understanding matters of taste requires sensitivity to cultural norms.

These principles are essential:

Professional communication is legal.

Professional communication is ethical.

Professional communication is in good taste.

Recognizing these principles, members of IABC will engage in communication that is not only legal but also ethical and sensitive to cultural values and beliefs; engage in truthful, accurate and fair communication that facilitates respect and mutual understanding; and, adhere to the following articles of the IABC Code of Ethics for Professional Communicators.

Because conditions in the world are constantly changing, members of IABC will work to improve their individual competence and to increase the body of knowledge in the field with research and education.

Articles

1. Professional communicators uphold the credibility and dignity of their profession by practicing honest, candid and timely communication and by fostering the free flow of essential information in accord with the public interest.
2. Professional communicators disseminate accurate information and promptly correct any erroneous communication for which they may be responsible.
3. Professional communicators understand and support the principles of free speech, freedom of assembly, and access to an open marketplace of ideas; and act accordingly.
4. Professional communicators are sensitive to cultural values and beliefs and engage in fair and balanced communication activities that foster and encourage mutual understanding.
5. Professional communicators refrain from taking part in any undertaking which the communicator considers to be unethical.
6. Professional communicators obey laws and public policies governing their professional activities and are sensitive to the spirit of all laws and regulations and, should any law or public policy be violated, for whatever reason, act promptly to correct the situation.
7. Professional communicators give credit for unique expressions borrowed from others and identify the sources and purposes of all information disseminated to the public.

recognized profession. Therefore, controlled access, through **licensure,** to the title of "certified public relations counsel" is viewed as the only way to separate the frauds and flacks from legitimate practitioners. Proponents such as Edward L. Bernays, who was instrumental in formulating the modern concept of public relations, believed that licensing could protect the profession and the public from incompetent and unscrupulous practitioners.

Those who would argue for licensure see it as the only effective method of enforcing professional standards, but efforts to impose such standards are highly controversial. Even if licensure were implemented, many practitioners would probably not be affected because they work in corporate departments. There would also have to be a compelling interest on the part of state governments to regulate the practice of public relations with a state agency.

Both PRSA and IABC offer accreditation programs for experienced practitioners who pass a comprehensive examination. These programs are the closest existing approximation to licensing procedures. However, fewer than half the memberships of both associations are accredited. Despite efforts by PRSA, few people outside the profession have any notion of the accreditation process and what it means.

8. Professional communicators protect confidential information and, at the same time, comply with all legal requirements for the disclosure of information affecting the welfare of others.
9. Professional communicators do not use confidential information gained as a result of professional activities for personal benefit and do not represent conflicting or competing interests without written consent of those involved.
10. Professional communicators do not accept undisclosed gifts or payments for professional services from anyone other than a client or employer.
11. Professional communicators do not guarantee results that are beyond the power of the practitioner to deliver.
12. Professional communicators are honest not only with others but also, and most importantly, with themselves as individuals; for a professional communicator seeks the truth and speaks that truth first to the self.

Enforcement and Communication of the IABC Code for Professional Communicators

IABC fosters compliance with its Code by engaging in global communication campaigns rather than through negative sanctions. However, in keeping with the sixth article of the IABC Code, members of IABC who are found guilty by an appropriate governmental agency or judicial body of violating laws and public policies governing their professional activities may have their membership terminated by the IABC executive board following procedures set forth in the association's bylaws.

IABC encourages the widest possible communication about its Code.

The IABC Code of Ethics for Professional Communicators is published in several languages and is freely available to all: Permission is hereby granted to any individual or organization wishing to copy and incorporate all or part of the IABC Code into personal and corporate codes, with the understanding that appropriate credit be given to IABC in any publication of such codes.

The IABC Code is published in the association's annual directory, *The World Book of IABC Communicators.* The association's monthly magazine, *Communication World,* publishes periodic articles dealing with ethical issues. At least one session at the association's annual conference is devoted to ethics. The international headquarters of IABC, through its professional development activities, encourages and supports efforts by IABC student chapters, professional chapters, and districts/regions to conduct meetings and workshops devoted to the topic of ethics and the IABC Code. New and renewing members of IABC sign the following statement as part of their application: "I have reviewed and understand the IABC Code of Ethics for Professional Communicators."

As a service to communicators worldwide, inquiries about ethics and questions or comments about the IABC Code may be addressed to members of the IABC Ethics Committee. The IABC Ethics Committee is composed of at least three accredited members of IABC who serve staggered three-year terms. Other IABC members may serve on the committee with the approval of the IABC executive committee. The functions of the Ethics Committee are to assist with professional development activities dealing with ethics and to offer advice and assistance to individual communicators regarding specific ethical situations.

While discretion will be used in handling all inquiries about ethics, absolute confidentiality cannot be guaranteed. Those wishing more information about the IABC Code or specific advice about ethics are encouraged to contact IABC World Headquarters (One Hallidie Plaza, Suite 600, San Francisco, CA 94102 USA; phone, 415-544-4700; fax, 415-544-4747).

Major League Baseball and Steroids

Case Study

By Dr. Laurie Volkmann,
Dominican University

U.S. senator George Mitchell revealed in December 2007 his much-anticipated report on steroid use/abuse among Major League Baseball players. The report publicly—though not legally—indicted 86 current and retired players for "use or possession of steroids," "allegedly making purchases on the Internet of steroids," and/or "being linked to the federal case against BALCO labs."

Although the report had no disciplinary recourse, several big-name players were called out in the investigation, forcing MLB Commissioner Bud Selig to consider the public relations aspect of doing nothing. The report also came out alongside the federal indictment of All-Star and home-run king Barry Bonds for perjury charges in the BALCO steroids case. Two Cy Young Award–winning pitchers, Roger Clemens and Andy Pettitte, were called before Congress in

February 2008 to testify about their reported steroid use. Pettitte admitted to using a performance-enhancing drug, H.G.H., several times in 2004 and earlier to speed up the healing process of injuries. It was not forbidden by Major League Baseball at that time. Clemens denied any such use. The Justice Department subsequently ordered the FBI to investigate whether or not Clemens had lied under oath to Congress.

Although steroid use among professional athletes in all sports has become a larger problem in recent years, Major League Baseball has received most of the public and governmental scrutiny. This is arguably because MLB has been more lax in its own regulation and discipline of the problem, not having officially tested for steroids until 2004, despite steroids being placed on MLB's "banned substances list" in 1991 and classified by Congress in 1990 as in the same category as amphetamines, methamphetamines, opium, and morphine. Even then, the 2004 testing included only counseling for a first offense and a 15-day suspension on second offense.

In 2005, Congress subpoenaed several players, including Mark McGwire, Sammy Sosa, and Jose Conseco to testify about baseball and steroids. All three evaded questions and denied steroid use, but lawmakers scolded Commissioner Selig for such lenient penalties and lack of seriousness regarding the steroids problem. A month later, Selig asked players to agree to new penalties for a positive test—a 5-game suspension for a first offense; a 10-game ban for a second offense, and a lifetime ban for a third violation. A year later, Selig commissioned Sen. Mitchell to inquire into steroids use of Barry Bonds and others.

Government regulation of businesses or organizations is generally avoided at all costs, and your textbook authors warn public relations practitioners about convincing executives to run a tight ship to prevent necessary investigation and control. Baseball is the only professional sport so far to have government interference because of its drug use policies and disciplinary actions.

Many fans have voiced their disgust for baseball's handling of the steroids issue in the past decade, but fan support of the sport itself has not waned. Some suggest that MLB does not need to worry about a potential PR fallout over the steroids issue because fans are very forgiving and will watch the sport regardless.

Assume you work for a public relations firm that has been asked to advise Major League Baseball on its short-term and long-term public relations strategy specifically in response to recent events.

Questions

1. What do you (as a PR practitioner) say to the argument that fans don't care about the steroids problem enough to prevent them from watching/buying tickets to games? Explain why you think this.

2. Even if ticket sales and viewership do not decline, what could be long-term effects of MLB not taking drastic measures to curb its steroids use problem among players? (Consider government regulation as well as public perception.)

3. As a member of Congress, why would you be interested in the integrity of the sport of baseball?

4. In addition to increased testing and harsher penalties for steroids use, what measures should you (as MLB) take to prove to the public you consider this a major problem that should be fixed?

5. What ethical standards from either the PRSA Code of Ethics or the IABC Code would likely be tested if you were the public relations director for Major League Baseball at the time of this congressional investigation?

6. How do you think lawyers and public relations practitioners working for MLB might approach this situation differently? How might you include the "court of public opinion" in defense of your strategy?

Source: "Steroids Timeline," Associated Press, January 2008.

The issue of ethical practice in public relations is closely tied to efforts toward accreditation and licensure. By promoting professional responsibility and recognition, public relations organizations can encourage ethical behavior and awareness among their members.

Summary

For self-testing and additional chapter resources, go to the Online Learning Center at **www.mhhe.com/lattimore3e**.

Key Terms

appropriation

civil libel

code of ethics

commercial speech

contract

copyright

criminal libel

defamation

fair comment

fair use

false light

Federal Communications Commission (FCC)

Federal Trade Commission (FTC)

First Amendment

Food and Drug Administration (FDA)

Form 10-K, Form 10-Q, and Form 8-K

Freedom of Information Act (FOIA)

intrusion

invasion of privacy

libel

licensure

malice

National Labor Relations Board (NLRB)

privacy rights

privilege

product liability

publication of private information

regulations

Sarbanes-Oxley Act

Securities and Exchange Act of 1934

Securities and Exchange Commission (SEC)

slander

Sunshine Act

trademark

USA Patriot Act

written consent

Notes

1. Burt Helm, "A Google Project Pains Publishers," *BusinessWeek Online* (May 23, 2005) at www.businessweek.com/technology/content/may2005/tc20050523_9472_tc024.htm?campaign_id=search.

2. Kathy R. Fitzpatrick, "Public Relations and the Law: A Survey of Practitioners," *Public Relations Review* 22, no. 1 (1996), p. 1.

3. Roy L. Moore, Ronald T. Farrar, and Erik L. Collins, *Advertising and the Law* (Mahwah, NJ: Erlbaum, 1998), p. 50.

4. Ibid., p. 52.

5. Ibid., p. 26.

6. Kyu Ho Youm, "Libel: The Plaintiff's Case," in *Communication and the Law,* ed. W. Wat Hopkins (Northport, AL: Vision Press, 2001), p. 88.

7. Ibid.

8. Moore, Farrar, and Collins, *Advertising and the Law,* p. 189.

9. Section 315a, Federal Communications Act.

10. Greg Lisby, "Regulating the Practice of Public Relations," in *Communication and the Law,* ed. W. Wat Hopkins (Northport, AL: Vision Press, 2001), p. 167.

11. J. Edward Conrey, Gerald R. Ferrer, and Karla H. Fox, *The Legal Environment of Business* (Dubuque, IA: Wm. C. Brown, 1986), p. 197.

12. R. Penchina, "Venturing On-Line: Protecting You and Your Product in Cyberspace," *Editor and Publisher* (June 24, 1995), p. 122.

13. "Halting Highway Robbery on the Internet," *BusinessWeek,* October 17, 1994, p. 212.

14. P. H. Lewis, "Judge Allows Libel Lawsuit Against Prodigy to Proceed," *The New York Times,* May 24, 1995, p. D4.

15. "Lessons from the Ultimate Crisis: Dow Corning in the Crucible," *The Strategist* 3, no. 1 (Spring 1997), pp. 6–12.

16. Moore, Farrar, and Collins, *Advertising and the Law,* p. 174.

17. Larissa A. Grunig, "Toward a Philosophy of Public Relations," in *Rhetorical and Critical Approaches to Public Relations,* ed. Elizabeth L. Toth and Robert L. Heath (Hillsdale, NJ: Erlbaum, 1992), p. 79.

18. Allen Center and Patrick Jackson, *Public Relations Practices: Managerial Case Studies and Problems,* 5th ed. (Englewood Cliffs, NJ: Prentice-Hall, 1995), p. 476.

19. James E. Grunig and Todd Hunt, *Managing Public Relations* (New York: Holt, Rinehart & Winston, 1984), p. 72.

20. Dan Lattimore, "Professionalism and Performance: An Investigation of Colorado Daily Newsmen," Ph.D. dissertation, University of Wisconsin, 1972; and Blaine McKee, Oguz Nayman, and Dan Lattimore, "How PR People See Themselves," *Public Relations Journal* 31 (November 1975), pp. 47–60.

The Process

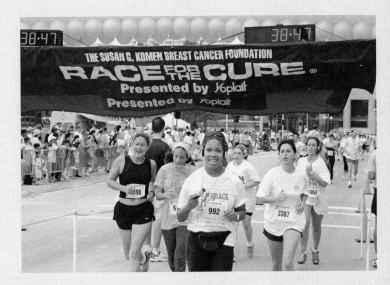

It isn't enough to know what public relations is and what purposes it serves. To practice public relations, one must understand the process by which public relations operates. As we have already discussed, public relations goes far beyond the task of producing messages. An effective public relations effort is the result of mutual understanding between an organization and its publics. The development of this understanding can be regarded as a four-step process:

1 **Research**   An initial fact-finding stage defines the problem areas and differentiates between publics.
2 **Planning**   Once the facts have been gathered from the various publics, decisions must be made regarding their importance and potential impact on the organization. After these decisions are made, strategies must be developed to enable the organization to achieve its goals.
3 **Action and Communication**   Strategies are implemented as new organizational policies and/or projects. Messages are then constructed to reach target publics.
4 **Evaluation**   Once a public relations campaign is developed and implemented, it should be followed by an evaluation of its effectiveness in meeting the criteria that were set. The results of the evaluation are used both to assess the effectiveness of the effort and to plan future action.

These four steps are essential to any effective public relations campaign. They are not, however, four independent functions. Each step overlaps the others; if any one of them is neglected, the entire process will be affected. The next four chapters discuss each of these steps in detail. To help you keep in mind the interdependence of the steps, an integrating case study will open each chapter. The case of Cedar Springs Community Hospital, presented in chapter 5 and subsequent chapters, illustrates a complete public relations project as it progresses through each stage, from research through evaluation. You may find it useful to turn back and review the previous case segments as you read through the next four chapters.

Research: Understanding Public Opinion

OUTLINE

PREVIEW

Kristen and Amy were searching for holiday outfits at the mall. Kristen looked across a rack of glittery T-shirts and raised her eyebrows at Amy, who shook her head. Everything that looked good was too expensive. The two friends left the store and went back to the mall's central aisle, where they stood fiddling with their cell phones and wondering what to do next.

"Excuse me," said a stylish-looking young woman with a pad and pen. "I'm Kara, and this is my colleague Rico. We're working with a company that wants to open a new store in the mall, and our job is to get some information from teens who are into cool clothes. Mind if we ask you some questions?"

Kristen and Amy agreed to the interview and spent the next few minutes answering Rico's and Kara's questions about their preferred style, the outfits they wore, and how they dressed for different occasions, like school, parties, and hanging out. After getting the girls' opinions on a few photographs of clothing styles, Rico and Kara thanked them and gave them a couple of coupons for free iced coffees in the food court.

THE NEED FOR RESEARCH IN PUBLIC RELATIONS

Research is a vital function in the process of public relations. It provides the initial information necessary to plan public relations action and perform the important role of evaluating its effectiveness. Management demands hard facts, not intuition or guesswork. Public relations practitioners, like their colleagues in every area of management, must be able to demonstrate convincingly their ability to "add value" in producing a product or service. The economic realities of modern organizations make it necessary for public relations to incorporate data-gathering techniques into every phase of the process. One specific major use of public relations research is in **issues management.** The process of issues management, which has become a major part of public relations practice, must be informed at every stage by research data. The early identification of issues that may impact a client or organization is most thoroughly accomplished through research methods designed to scan the environment for potential issues. Analysis to determine which issues have the greatest possible impact requires various research methods designed to determine both the strength of opinion about an issue and its perceived centrality to the client or organization. Likewise, the selection of potential methods and actions available to the researcher and the evaluation of action implementation can be determined through well-planned research activities.

The Cedar Springs Hospital case study shows how a public relations effort can utilize research in identifying and dealing with an organizational problem.

Integrating Case Study

Cedar Springs Community Hospital
Segment 1

Problem Identification

Cedar Springs Community Hospital, Inc., was formed by the merger of competing hospitals. Two years later, a new management team was brought in to help resolve concerns about the ability of the newly formed hospital to serve the needs of its patients. Soon after the new administrator and his seven assistants assumed their duties, they began to hear reports of low employee morale and declining quality in patient care. Much of this input came from physicians who felt that the changes since the merger had produced an environment that was more routine and less personal. Many doctors felt that their relationships with other hospital employees had been undermined by the new organization's attempts to eliminate duplication and build a more efficient structure. In general, the growing consensus among the physicians was that the quality of patient care had significantly declined since the merger.

Secondary Research

Because physicians are a significant public for any hospital, their concerns received immediate attention from management. The physicians had suggested mounting a campaign to make employees more aware of their responsibility for providing quality patient care. However, the public relations director thought that more information was needed in the form of secondary research (research already done by someone else) before an effective communication campaign could be planned. He began to look into the background of the merger and the relationships between hospital employees and the medical staff.

A careful review of hospital records and local newspaper files, plus conversations with several longtime employees, revealed the complexity of the situation. Not only had the hospitals formerly been competitors, but they had also originally been founded by two very different religious groups and thus had developed two distinct constituencies. Although the religious affiliations of both hospitals had been discontinued long before the merger, an atmosphere of rivalry remained. This rivalry had been most obvious when the hospitals had attempted to outdo each other in terms of benefits for physicians.

Primary Research

One important public, physicians, clearly believed the quality of patient care was not acceptable. However, employees' and patients' views were not as easily defined. The public relations department devised a primary research plan (original research) to measure the opinions of each group. A random sample of hospital employees was asked to fill out a questionnaire about various aspects of patient care. Simultaneously, a telephone survey was conducted among recently released patients to gauge their opinions on the same issues. The results were surprising.

On a scale ranging from 1 (poor) to 10 (excellent), employees rated the hospital's performance a disappointing 6.6 overall. However, the survey of former patients produced an overall rating of 8.5. Other questions related to the quality of patient care also received significantly lower marks from the employees than from the patients.

Informal Research

To understand the reasons for the low ratings given by employees, a focus group was assembled to respond to the survey findings. This 10-member focus group was composed of six representatives from nursing services and two each from ancillary support and business services. They were interviewed as a group concerning their responses to the questionnaire. The interview revealed that while employees believed that the hospital in general delivered mediocre patient care, they thought that the care in their specific areas was significantly better than in the rest of the hospital and that they, personally, were slightly above average within their departments. These employees also indicated that their co-workers sensed something was wrong in the organization but were not sure what. This led to feelings of individual helplessness and produced a high level of stress and frustration.

In the Cedar Springs case, what originally seemed like a rather straightforward employee communication problem was identified as a complex situation involving three important publics: physicians, employees, and patients. Research showed the physicians' concerns were overblown. Had the Cedar Springs management acted on the physicians' original recommendation without doing further research, the situation would have just gotten worse, increasing employee frustration and stress.

As you read about the different types of research methods public relations practitioners use, refer to this segment and notice how several of the techniques were applied. A quick comparison of the Cedar Springs case with the first step in figure 5.1 will reveal that each of the basic elements of research is present. The surprising nature of the findings in this case illustrates the need for public relations research.

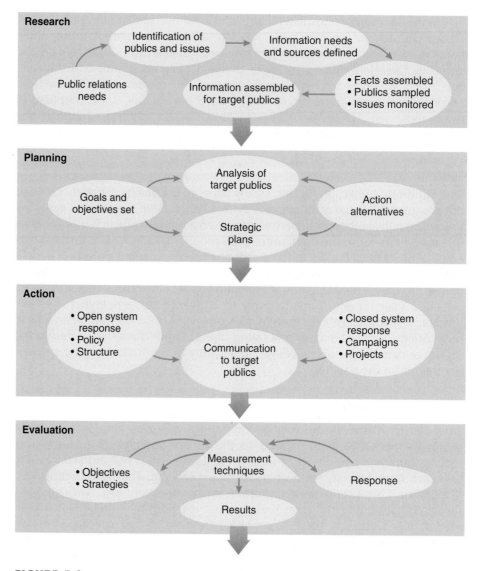

FIGURE 5.1   A Process Model of Public Relations

PROVING THE WORTH OF PUBLIC RELATIONS

Because public relations professionals have traditionally been doers rather than researchers, they often assume that others see the value of their function. That assumption places public relations necks squarely on budgetary chopping blocks. Even when economic conditions are not critical, public relations may be perceived as window dressing. Media, regulatory agencies, consumer groups, and many managers doubt that public relations has a useful purpose in American business. Typically, public relations professionals respond by claiming that they contribute to better understanding between publics and organizations, but they do not present tangible evidence of this contribution. However, the element that makes the most difference in whether a public relations campaign will be effective is research. For example, one campaign where research made a difference was the Colorado "bottle bill" referendum. In a public relations campaign to defeat a "bottle bill" where consumers could return a can or bottle for five cents to the bottler, public relations counselor Nick Del Calzo did extensive research to determine what strategies and tactics would persuade his target audiences to vote "No" on the bill.

From his research with target audiences, Mr. Del Calzo developed a campaign around the theme "Right Problem: Wrong Solution." He used Will Rogers, Jr., as his spokesman to get the message across that the best approach to the litter problem was a tough litter law, not a bottle return law. Thus, while litter was the "right problem," a bottle bill was the "wrong solution." Even though six weeks prior to the November ballot, the *Denver Post* editorialized that the bottle bill would pass 2 to 1, Mr. Del Calzo was sure his research, which showed his campaign would defeat the bill, was accurate. It was. The referendum was defeated by better than a 2 to 1 margin just as his research had indicated. As a good, ethical public relations practitioner, Mr. Del Calzo led the fight the next January in the Colorado legislature to get a tough litter law passed.[1]

Public relations practitioners must speak with authority when asked to prove their value to business and society. This authority can come only through an ability to conduct research and apply the results to public relations campaigns. Public relations professionals must maintain good media relations, produce employee publications, release financial information, and conduct community relations programs. In addition, those who succeed must also be able to measure the effects of their programs, provide sound forecasts of future needs, and account for the resources they consume. Simply counting the number of column inches of print or the number of hits on a Web site is not enough.

An independent public relations counselor was seeking a new client. "What can you do for me?" asked the client.

"I can get you exposure," explained the public relations practitioner. "I can get you speaking dates and get you in the newspaper."

"I can do that," said the client (who was rapidly becoming a less likely client). "What I need is someone to help me make money."

"That's marketing," said the public relations counselor. "I do public relations."

"You do nothing if you don't contribute to my bottom line," was the response. "All my expenditures make me money or they don't get made. No sale."

Informal or Preliminary Research Techniques

Research means gathering information, and it is typically classified as either formal or informal.[2] Research can range from looking up the names of editors of weekly newspapers in Nebraska to polling those people to discover their opinions about farm export policy. Research is not always scientific or highly structured. We begin this section by considering a few **informal,** or nonscientific, **research** methods and sources that practitioners use. Informal research is a method of gaining an in-depth understanding of an audience without the rigor of more formal, scientific research methods. It is also called *preliminary research* because it is nonscientific and often done as background research.

Record Keeping   One of the most important skills necessary to the successful practice of public relations is the ability to keep comprehensive and accurate records. Practitioners are frequently asked to produce critical information at a moment's notice for use inside and outside their organizations. Thus, when an editor or manager calls for information, the public relations practitioner must produce the needed data within a relatively short time or suffer loss of credibility. By earning a reputation as a source of valuable information, the public relations practitioner can develop a network of internal and external information contacts.

Current technology allows for the organization and storage of large amounts of information in databases. This has raised expectations about the amount of information that can be provided in a very short time frame. Public relations practitioners must be comfortable using this technology and know where to find important information, particularly from within the organization. However, the GIGO principle still applies— Garbage In, Garbage Out. Creators of these databases need to think about what information will be needed, and in what form, when the information is created and stored in the first place.

Key Contacts   Frequently, individuals who are **opinion leaders** in the community, industry, or organization act as **key contacts** for the public relations practitioner. Other people who possess special knowledge or who communicate frequently with significant publics are also good sources. For a community college, for example, key contacts would be significant business, political, student, and community leaders. Although these individuals can provide valuable information, they may not represent the majority opinion. Because they are leaders or individuals with special knowledge, they must be regarded as atypical of others in their group. Their special insight may give them a greater sensitivity to an issue than most other people would have. Therefore, the practitioner must be careful not to overreact to feedback from these sources or plan major responses based solely on such information. Key contacts are best used to provide early warning about issues that may become significant.

Special Committees   To help obtain necessary information, many public relations practitioners organize special committees. Internal and external committees of key communicators, decision makers, and opinion leaders can help identify issues before they become problems and suggest alternative courses of action. These advisory groups can be formed for a specified length of time, such as the duration of a campaign, or can be permanent boards that replace members periodically.

Focus Groups   The most widely used technique for preliminary research is the focus group. As we saw in the Cedar Springs case, a **focus group** is a small number of people who share some demographic characteristic. Group members are interviewed, using open-ended questions to encourage interaction and probe the nature of their beliefs. A focus group is generally assembled only once, and the participants' responses are recorded on videotape or observed from behind a one-way mirror. This enables researchers to consider not only what is said but also gestures, facial expressions, and other forms of nonverbal communication that may reveal depth of meaning. Although ethical and legal considerations require researchers to inform focus groups that they are being recorded or observed, experience shows that participants are seldom reluctant to discuss their feelings. Frequently, people selected for focus groups are glad someone is willing to listen to them. Sometimes the process of asking can be just as valuable as the information gained because the organization is perceived as being responsive to its publics.

Focus groups may be used as the only primary research tool. However, since you can't generalize the information to the larger group from which the focus group is drawn, it may not provide enough reliable information. Often, though, focus groups are used prior to survey research to help the researcher have enough information to ask appropriate questions in the survey questionnaire.

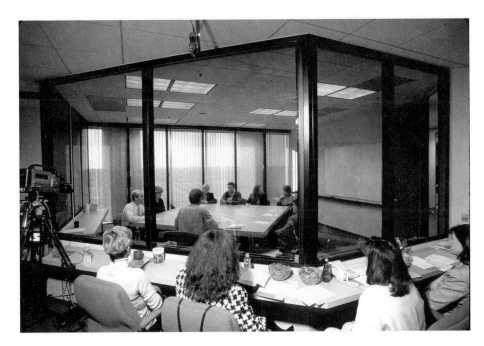

Researchers observe a focus group. It is also being videotaped for future reference.

For example, Mountain Bell used several focus groups of women ages 18 to 35 before launching its "Let's Be Friends" campaign. Three 30-second commercials had been produced. Before they were aired, they were shown to several focus groups. Two of the commercials were seen to be quite effective, but one was discarded even though the company had already spent thousands of dollars producing the spot. The campaign became one of the longest-running campaigns at Mountain Bell and later was picked up by other former AT&T companies.

In another example, Larissa A. Grunig reported on the use of focus groups to help plan a program for a county mental health department to reduce the stigma existing in the community regarding chronic mental illness. In addition to focus groups, a larger sample-size telephone survey of county residents was conducted. According to the departmental administrator, however, results of the phone survey provided fewer and more shallow responses for designing the subsequent communication campaign. Focus groups allowed researchers to discuss why residents felt the way they did, whereas the survey did not.[3]

Thus, focus groups can also be used after a survey to probe some of the issues in more depth. For instance, prior to a campaign to increase student use of off-campus sites for taking classes, a university surveyed the students currently taking off-campus classes. One demographic stood out: 75 percent of all students taking classes off campus were female, compared with the roughly 52 percent female students overall at the university. Several focus groups of female students were then asked to talk about why they chose to take the off-campus classes. With few dissenting voices, the women felt that the off-campus sites were safer than the main campus at night, so they were more willing to take an off-campus class at night than one on campus.

Casual Monitoring   Many practitioners find it helpful to systematically screen material that regularly comes through their offices. Monitoring news reports in both print and broadcast media should be done to allow consideration of the quality and quantity of coverage. The Internet must also be monitored closely. The ease and speed with which any kind of information can spread, including rumors and untruths, means that constant attention should be paid to what is being said about the organization and its industry. This includes monitoring chatrooms, newsgroups, and activist organizations' Web sites.

Carefully tracking incoming mail, telephone calls, and sales reports can also provide valuable information. Like all information collected through informal research methods, however, these techniques have built-in biases because the data are not collected from representative samples of the target publics.

The Internet, Library, and Database Sources   The Internet has revolutionized how people search for information. Some kinds of data must still be sought in books or in proprietary databases that are available only in public or company libraries, but large amounts of information are easily available via the Internet. Most companies now maintain a Web site that provides information about their business. State and city governments, as well as the federal government, maintain exhaustive databases. The same is true of the governments of many other countries. The use of a powerful search engine or directory such as Yahoo! can help locate information when the exact address is not known. Some data collections, however, are especially helpful to know about and bookmark. For example, the Federal Reserve Bank of St. Louis has a very comprehensive collection of economic data for the United States (www.stls.frb.org/research/index .html). In addition, the EDGAR database of documents filed with the SEC can provide background information on publicly owned businesses (www.sec.gov/edgar.html).

Public and private libraries are other sources of data that would be impossible for the practitioner to collect personally. Reference librarians are helpful in finding information, and many libraries now subscribe to computerized data retrieval networks that can obtain information from anywhere in the world, including data that are not available for free on the Internet. Census data and other types of public information are available at libraries that are designated as government depositories if you prefer researching hard copies instead of using a computer. In addition, a number of independent research organizations, such as the Survey Research Center at the University of Michigan, publish information that may be valuable to the public relations practitioner.

Media guides, trade and professional journals, and other reference books may prove useful in a public relations practitioner's personal library. Many valuable guides that are too large and expensive for personal libraries can be accessed at a public library. Further sources that should be noted and can be valuable in researching a future employer or competing organization include the following:

> *America's Corporate Families, The Billion Dollar Directory*
>
> *Dun and Bradstreet Million Dollar Directory*
>
> *Dun and Bradstreet Middle Market Directory*
>
> *Hoover's Handbook of World Business*
>
> *Moody's International Manual*
>
> *D & B Principal International Businesses*
>
> *Standard and Poors' Register of Corporations, Directors, and Executives*
>
> *Thomas' Register of American Manufacturers*
>
> *Fortune Magazine's "Directory of Largest Corporations"* (also available online)
>
> *Fortune Magazine's "Annual Directory Issues"*
>
> *Black Enterprise Magazine's "The Top 100"*

TABLE 5.1 Research Techniques Respondents Claimed They Used Most Frequently	
Literature searches/information retrieval	Pre- and posttests (before and after polls)
Publicity tracking	Sophisticated techniques (conjoint/factor analysis)
Telephone/mail surveys with simple cross-tabs	Psychographic analysis
Focus groups	Mall intercept/shopping center studies
PR/communications audits	Content analysis studies
Secondary analysis studies	Experimental designs
Consumer inquiry analysis	Unobtrusive measures (role-playing, observation participation)
Depth interviews with opinion leaders	
Readership/readability study	Model building

Formal, Scientific Research Techniques

The growing importance of **formal,** or scientific, **research** in public relations has prompted several studies in recent years that attempt to assess preferred research techniques among professionals. In one such study, Walter K. Lindenmann sampled 253 practitioners, among them public relations executives from Fortune 500 companies, public relations agencies, nonprofit organizations, and academia. A summary of his findings is listed in table 5.1.[4]

As you read the next section, keep in mind that secondary sources like those mentioned in the table should be exhausted before a primary research effort is planned. Researchers should review the information available to make certain the questions to be asked have not already been answered by others.

Content Analysis   **Content analysis** is a research method that allows the researcher to systematically code and thereby quantify the verbal content of written or transcribed messages. This technique provides a method of systematic observation, such as the analysis of news clippings. The content of chatrooms or newsgroups can also be analyzed for quantity and quality of coverage. Many organizations analyze the contents of the annual reports and other publications of their competitors to discover strategic plans.

Survey Research   The practice of public relations employs all types of research processes, but the survey method is by far the most common. Cedar Springs Hospital used **survey research** to answer some critical questions. Laboratory and field experiments and various types of simulations can have a place (like pretesting a message) in a public relations research effort. However, surveys are the most effective way to assess the characteristics of publics in a form that allows the data to be used in planning and evaluating public relations efforts. Surveys should provide a means of separating publics rather than lumping them all together into one amorphous mass.

The term *survey,* as it is applied in public relations research, refers to careful, detailed sample examinations of the knowledge, perception, attitudes, and opinions of members of various publics. The general purpose of a survey is to obtain a better understanding of the reactions and preferences of a specific public or publics. For public relations efforts, we divide survey data into two types: demographic and opinion. Demographic data are those characteristics (age, sex, occupation, etc.) of the people responding to the survey that help a practitioner classify them into one or more publics. Opinion data are

The Memphis PRSA research committee appointed to gather information concerning perceptions of Memphians to be used in developing its public relations plan presents this summary of its findings.

A mail survey, developed and implemented by committee members in May and June, centered on several key topics, including education, entertainment, race, health care, government, and other quality-of-life issues. A random sample of 1,900 was selected from the Shelby County phone directory. About 227 of the questionnaires were returned because of incorrect mailing addresses, but 305 usable questionnaires were completed and returned in the one-shot mail survey. The respondents were more likely to be white and more likely to not live in one of the more traditionally economically depressed areas of Memphis than is representative of the entire Shelby County area.

Key results included the following:

Overall: Almost 75 percent of those surveyed were proud to live in Memphis. The common wisdom in Memphis is that Memphians have an inferiority complex, so this number was surprising. Also, about 92 percent surveyed like their neighborhoods, and about 80 percent feel safe where they live. However, the respondents not liking the neighborhood where they lived were also the ones most likely not to be proud to live in Memphis. One thought by the committee was that perhaps the public relations plan should address strengthening and taking pride in individual neighborhoods rather than trying to promote Memphis as a whole.

More than half of the respondents do not feel safe downtown. This was not significantly different whether respondents lived in the suburbs or in midtown.

The riverfront development was thought by an overwhelming 85 percent to be a good means of attracting tourists and potential residents.

Racial Issues: Only about 30 percent of those surveyed felt that racial groups work well together in Memphis. However, 57 percent of the African American population felt they worked well together compared to 27 percent for whites, indicating it was much more an issue with the white community.

Arts, Health Care: About 90 percent felt that cultural arts make a city stronger and more attractive to newcomers. However, almost half didn't think there was enough variety in the cultural arts in Memphis and Shelby County. More than 80 percent think that the quality of health care in Memphis is good. Both are selling points and should be emphasized in selling Memphis.

Traffic: While 75 percent of the respondents felt that traffic in Memphis was much less congested than in other large cities, 67 percent did not think it is as safe to drive here as it is in other major cities.

Government: Only 23 percent of those responding felt city government was run efficiently compared to about half who think county government is efficient (still low). About 75 percent didn't trust elected officials, either city or county. So, while the city has a worse problem, it is clearly an issue that must be addressed with both levels.

Education: There was another split between city and county, with city schools getting worse marks than county schools. However, neither was great. About 90 percent felt city schools were not excellent compared to about half answering the same for the county schools. This is a major issue that must be addressed if Memphis is to attract quality business and industry.

Questions

1. Given these data, what would you emphasize in the public relations campaign?
2. Was the sample adequate to determine citizens' perceptions of Memphis?
3. How might the return rate affect the results?
4. What would you have done differently if you had been in charge of the survey?

Source: Dan Lattimore, Chair, Memphis Chapter of PRSA, Research Committee, October 2001.

---

responses to those questions a practitioner raises concerning the attitudes and perceptions of certain publics about critical issues. See mini-case 5.1.

Experimental Research **Experimental research** is generally divided into two categories: laboratory and field experiments. Laboratory experiments take place in carefully controlled environments designed to minimize outside effects. Field experiments take place in real-world settings. The trade-off between field and laboratory experiments is essentially one of authenticity versus purity.

In a field experiment, the researcher sacrifices a great deal of control over the setting to obtain reactions in a real environment. In a laboratory setting, however, the researcher can control many outside stimuli that might contaminate the results of the study. For example, a public relations practitioner might decide to pretest a particular message by inviting people into a room to view the message in several forms and then measuring their reactions. A church foundation attempting to raise funds for a chaplain in a local cancer hospital used this method to test the graphics and photographs in its brochure to avoid negative effects before publication. When the U.S. government embarked on its first funded media campaign to reduce "risky" behaviors among young adolescents, it pretested the potential effectiveness of 30 different public service announcements (PSAs) by screening them for young people. In doing so, they found that some of the PSAs actually had the opposite effect than was intended.[5]

The laboratory setting ensured that the subjects' responses were based on the message being studied and not on other stimuli that might be in a normal environment. To test the effects of a message in a more authentic setting, a field experiment such as a test-market study could be arranged, using a specific group of young people in their normal environment.

Very little public relations research is done in a controlled, laboratory setting. Other than survey research, field experiments are the second most used scientific research method along with content analysis. Before the U.S. Department of Energy launched a major energy-saving campaign, it field-tested the program over a three-month winter period in six cities, with one city as a control group (a city not given any of the campaign information like the other five cities). Each of the six cities had been surveyed with a random sample of residents prior to the campaign for awareness and use of energy-saving devices and techniques. Each was then surveyed after the three-month campaign. A small percentage increase in awareness and use occurred in the control city that was not subjected to the campaign. But a significant increase occurred in the other five cities. The difference between the control city's awareness and usage scores, then, was attributed to the public relations campaign efforts.[6]

Collecting Formal Research Data

We have described several methods of research. Next we look at ways to collect information.

Descriptive and Inferential Methods   Research information can be obtained in a variety of ways that may be classified as either descriptive or inferential. **Descriptive data** are used to describe something, such as a particular group of people (a public). If the public relations practitioner in an organization asks the personnel department to prepare a demographic profile of its employees (average age, sex breakdown, years of education, experience level, etc.), he or she is requesting descriptive data. Such studies use averages, percentages, actual numbers, or other descriptive statistics to summarize the characteristics of a group or public.

Inferential data do more than describe a particular public. Inferential data describe (infer) the characteristics of people not included in the specific group from which the information was obtained. Through sampling, which we discuss later in this section, it is possible to select a relatively small number who represent a larger population. Using inferential statistics, a public relations practitioner can infer the characteristics of a very large public, such as a consumer group, from a relatively small but representative sample of that population.

Methods for Obtaining Information   Whether research is classified as descriptive or inferential, survey or experimental, and regardless of the sampling technique employed, the three basic means for collecting public relations research data are **observations, interviews,** and **questionnaires.**

Observational techniques are easily misused in public relations research because of the informal nature of many observations used in **qualitative research** about publics. The personal observations of a practitioner are severely limited by his or her own perceptions, experiences, and sensitivity. These problems can lead to decisions based more on gut feeling than on reliable information. Personal observations are made more reliable by using structural techniques because observers are trained within established rules to systematically observe and record data, but this is normally an expensive and complex process.

Interviews can be a successful way to get information from a public. Skilled interviewers can elicit information that individuals might not otherwise volunteer. Interviews may take place in person as well as over the telephone, and they are generally classified as structured or unstructured. Structured interviews use a schedule of questions with specific response choices ranging from yes/no to multiple choice. Unstructured interviews allow subjects to respond to open-ended questions however they wish. Although interviews are frequently employed, they have disadvantages. For example, the personality, dress, speech patterns or accents, and nonverbal cues of the interviewer may bias the response. To minimize such problems, it is necessary to use expertly trained interviewers, who are often costly.

Interviewers can use the open-ended personal interviews just described, or they may use a structured questionnaire. Personal interviews can be much more in-depth than a mail or phone interview. The phone interview must be short—usually 5 to 10 minutes in length—while the mail or Web questionnaire should take no longer than 10 minutes to complete.

Questionnaires must be designed properly to gather data that are unbiased. That means questions must be simple and straightforward without being "loaded." Questionnaires are often designed using language that has emotionally charged words to influence the respondent in a certain way. Questions must also have only one answer per question.

Mail and Web questionnaires are the most common form of data collection because they are stable in presentation and inexpensive to use. Once a questionnaire is printed or posted to a Web site, each respondent is asked the same questions in exactly the same way. Questionnaires are generally designed to measure one or more of the following: knowledge, attitudes, opinions, and demographic characteristics of the sample. But they may also measure the intensity of those attitudes or opinions.

The decision about whether to use a mail or Web questionnaire or a phone or personal interview to gather data for public relations research must take into account the study's budget, purpose, subjects, and a variety of other considerations. Questionnaires can be returned by mail or the Web and may be administered to either individuals or specific groups. They provide anonymity and present a uniform stimulus to all participants. However, the response rate may be low, and those who do respond may not be representative of the larger population. Web questionnaires have become quite popular to administer to groups with specific Web access. However, the response rate is often similar to a mail questionnaire—low. On the other hand, personal or phone interviews are more flexible, get a higher percentage of responses in some situations, and can be used with relatively uneducated publics. They are also considerably more expensive to administer.

Sampling Methods   A **sample** is a subset of a population or public. Public relations researchers use samples because in most instances it is impractical to collect information from every person in the target public. There are numerous sampling techniques, but the best methods rely on the theory of probability to provide a miniature version of the target public. The theory of probability is the basis of all inferential statistics. The following sampling methods rely on the theory of probability to ensure that a sample is representative of the public from which it is drawn.

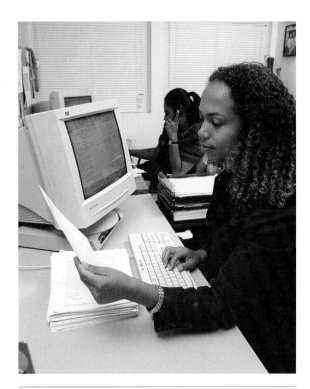

Simple random sampling is a technique that allows each member of a public an equal chance of being selected. If the sample is large enough and is selected totally at random, it will accurately reflect the characteristics of its public. For example, the Nielsen ratings use from 1,200 to 1,600 in a random sample to determine what households across the country are viewing each night.

Probably the most common example of simple random sampling is drawing a name from a hat. Assuming the names of all of the people in the target population are in the hat, and the slips of paper are mixed up adequately, each slip has an equal chance of being selected at the time of the drawing.

Systematic sampling uses a list, like a telephone directory or mailing list, to select a sample at random. Generally, a table of random numbers is used to find a starting point

Whatever the methodology, all research relies upon accurate data input. This generally requires a human interface that can be costly and subject to error.

on the list and a selection interval. For example, a researcher might randomly pick the number 293006 from a table of random numbers. Using the first three digits, the researcher could start on page 293 of the telephone directory; then, using the last three digits, he or she could select every sixth name for the sample. This method is more practical than simple random sampling in most public relations research. However, finding complete lists may be difficult for some publics. Telephone books, for instance, will not include people who have unlisted numbers or who rely strictly on cell phones.

There are other less representative sampling techniques, but pure random sampling is best to use when possible. With random sampling, a smaller sample will give more significant results than determining your sample in any other way.

Most organizational goals and objectives dealing with public relations depend to some extent on the concept of **public opinion.** Therefore, public relations research is often used to sample public opinion. It is important

MEASURING PUBLIC OPINION

to understand at the outset that an organization does not have a single indistinguishable public. The public relations practitioner who relies on so-called public opinion polls to provide insight into characteristics or opinions of his or her potential audience may be operating with erroneous data. Most polls of this type are not very useful from a public relations point of view because they actually measure **mass opinion** rather than public opinion. Before using a survey, the practitioner should be aware of the difference between measuring mass opinion and measuring public opinion.

Mass Opinion

Mass opinion represents an average taken from a group with many different opinions. However, averages tend to blur the strength of some attitudes. When substantially different opinions are averaged together, the result may be very different from the original opinions stated. For example, if we conduct a poll asking people about the image of a particular organization, we might find that 60 percent of our sample give it very high marks, while 40 percent feel very negative. Looking at the average of these responses, we might deduce that the organization in question has a moderately positive image; however, this would hide the substantial amount of negative feelings that exist.

Our hypothetical survey has actually uncovered two publics—one that has a very positive image of the organization and another that has a very negative image. In fact, no one in our sample holds the moderately positive view the average implies. To respond properly, we should construct communication strategies for two groups of people with very strong but opposite opinions. Public relations must be concerned with the strength as well as the direction of public attitudes.

Many mass opinion polls are useful for little more than predicting political elections. They do not shed much light on the complexities of public opinion that an effective public relations program must address. However, if the results of the mass opinion poll are analyzed by different demographic characteristics of those polled, the result is more nearly a public opinion poll.

Public Opinion

Public opinion polls involve carefully targeted populations. The public relations professional must break down the audience into meaningful subgroups and design specific communication strategies for each segment. Public opinion sampling is not useful unless it reflects accurately the feelings of each significant audience group and provides some insight into why these opinions are held. For example, a political opinion poll finding that middle-class, white voters think public school education is the key issue in the campaign because school funding has been cut every year for the past 10 years might give a candidate enough information to develop more commercials geared to this issue. However, if the poll had found only that this group favored one candidate over another, it would not have provided the information needed.

Identifying Publics

John Dewey, in his 1927 book *The Public and Its Problems,* defines a public as a group of people who

1. Face a similar indeterminate situation.
2. Recognize what is indeterminate in that situation.
3. Organize to do something about the problem.[7]

A public, then, is a group of people who share a common problem or goal and recognize their common interest. In the remainder of this chapter, we discuss specific methods for measuring public opinion and applying it effectively in public relations work. James Grunig proposed and tested three categories for the identification of publics based on Dewey's definition:

- **Latent public**—A group faces an indeterminate situation but does not recognize it as a problem.

- **Aware public**— The group recognizes a problem, that is, what is missing in the situation, and becomes aware.
- **Active public**— The group organizes to discuss and do something about the problem.[8]

Such categories group together people who are likely to behave in similar ways. This makes it possible for public relations practitioners to communicate with each group regarding its needs and concerns rather than attempting to communicate with a mythical "average" public. Researching public opinion in appropriate categories can help direct the public relations process. For example, it may be possible to classify the primary audience for a public relations campaign in one of the three categories listed above and develop specific messages for them. In the Cedar Springs case, physicians were an active public. However, if management had not taken care to determine the view of a latent public, the patients, costly errors could have been made.

Environmental Monitoring

Results of a survey by the Foundation for Public Relations Research and Education revealed that **environmental monitoring** is the fastest-growing category of public relations research.[9] Organizations today recognize themselves as dynamic, open systems that must react to changes in the environment, so keeping track of those changes is important.

Public relations practitioners can use formal systems for observing trends and changes in public opinion and other areas of the environment to guide many phases of organizational planning, including public relations. Issues management, discussed earlier, is one application of environmental monitoring. Another technique is scanning.

Environmental scanning is the monitoring, evaluating, and disseminating of information to key decision makers within an organization. It is an important tool for public relations because it can provide the initial link in the chain of perceptions and actions that permit an organization to adapt to its environment.

The advances in computer technology, particularly through the Internet, have made continuous scanning both more feasible and necessary. A recent study of the impact of Internet newsgroups on Intel's inability to manage the damage to its public image from a flawed Pentium chip demonstrates how quickly latent publics can become active.

The proliferation of newsgroups on the Internet has greatly increased the ability of single-issue publics to form. In the Intel case more than 130,000 people visited a newsgroup Web site in a matter of weeks, turning an obscure problem with a chip into a highly recognized problem in the minds of consumers. With the use of this technology rapidly expanding around the world, organizations need to have a regular presence in cyberspace to monitor all appearances of their corporate identity online. The Center for Association Leadership has developed a Web-based scanning service to provide access to detailed data on trends, key issues, and action planning templates 24/7.[10]

The continuous scanning model supports the strategic planning effort of organizations. For example, top executives at several government insurance pools are now engaging in environmental scanning to extract research from news stories, speeches, blogs (Web pages posted as personal journals), and various publicly accessible information sources to identify future issues and trends that may help them predict risks.[11]

Special research techniques for public relations practitioners include the public relations audit, the communication audit, and the social audit.

SPECIAL PUBLIC RELATIONS RESEARCH TECHNIQUES

The Public Relations Audit

The most frequently used mixed type of public relations research is the **audit.** The **public relations audit** is essentially a broad-scale study that examines the internal and external public relations of an organization. Many of the research techniques we have already discussed are used in public relations audits. Public relations audits provide information for planning future public relations efforts. Carl Byoir and Associates, one of the pioneers of public relations auditing, describes it: "The public relations audit, as the name implies, involves a comprehensive study of the public relations position of an organization: how it stands in the opinion of its various publics."[12] We can identify four general categories of audits in relation to organizations and their publics.

Relevant Publics   An organization prepares a list of relevant publics. A list of the organization's relevant publics is made, describing each according to its function—stockholders, employees, customers, suppliers, and the like. Also included are publics that have no direct functional relationship but are nevertheless in a position to affect the organization—for example, consumer, environmental, community, and other social action groups. The procedure is basically one of audience identification to aid in planning public relations messages.

The Organization's Standing with Publics   Each public's view of the organization is determined through various research methods, most commonly opinion studies and content analysis of newspapers, magazines, and other print media. Both of these research methods were discussed earlier in this chapter.

Issues of Concern to Publics   Environmental monitoring techniques such as those already mentioned are used to construct an issues agenda for each of the organization's relevant publics. These data identify publics according to issues of interest and their stands on those issues. The findings are then compared with the organization's own policies. This is a vital step in planning public relations campaigns for various audiences.

Power of Publics   Publics are rated according to the amount of economic and political (and therefore regulatory) influence they have. Interest groups and other activist organizations are evaluated according to the size of their membership, size of their constituency, budget size and source of income, staff size, and number of qualified specialists (lobbyists, attorneys, public relations professionals, etc.).

Public relations audits are regular components of many public relations programs. They provide input data for planning future public relations programs and help evaluate the effectiveness of previous efforts. Several public relations counseling firms offer audit services to their clients. Joyce F. Jones of the Ruder Finn Rotman Agency describes the audit process in four steps:

1. *Finding Out What "We" Think.* Interviews with key management at the top and middle strata of an organization to determine company strengths and weaknesses, relevant publics, and issues and topics to be explored.
2. *Finding Out What "They" Think.* Researching key publics to determine how closely their views match those of company management.
3. *Evaluating the Disparity Between the Two.* A public relations balance sheet of assets, liabilities, strengths, weaknesses, and so on is prepared based on an analysis of the differences found between steps 1 and 2.

4. *Recommending.* A comprehensive public relations program is planned to fill in the gap between steps 1 and 2 and to correct the deficits of the balance sheet prepared in step 3.[13]

Organizational Image Surveys

Attitude surveys that determine a public's perceptions of an organization help public relations managers obtain an overall view of the organization's image. Generally, such research seeks to measure (1) familiarity of the public with the organization, its officers, products, policies, and other facets; (2) degrees of positive and negative perceptions; and (3) characteristics various publics attribute to the organization. Frequently, organizations use such surveys as planning tools to compare existing images with desired images. Once the differences are assessed, image goals can be set, and strategic plans can be made to overcome the identified problems. For example, cities seeking to attract convention and tourist business periodically check their image as perceived by key groups, then use these data to evaluate their attraction techniques.

Although several organizations conduct their own image studies, many employ outside consultants or research organizations to supply them with data. Some major organizations that provide this type of data are Opinion Research Center, Inc.; Louis Harris and Associates; and Yankolovich, Skelly and White.[14]

Communication Audits

The **communication audit,** like the public relations audit, is applied in many different ways. An effective communication audit begins with a receiver-oriented, as opposed to a sender-focused, model. These measures assess individual satisfaction with the amount of information employees or other publics receive on a topic relative to their needs, the understandability and usefulness of the information, and overall preferences for communication modes, such as face-to-face or e-mail.

Generally, the communication audit attempts to monitor and evaluate the channels, messages, and communication climate of an organization. Sometimes audits are applied only to internal organizational communication systems; the same technique, however, can also be used to evaluate external systems. Frequently, results of a communication audit reveal problems of distortion or lack of information. See table 5.2 for a communication audit example.

Communication audits package several research methods for specific applications. The following research methods are used in appropriate combinations to audit organizational communication and investigate specific problem areas:

1. **Communication climate surveys.** These attitudinal measurements are designed to reveal how open and adequate publics perceive communication channels to be.
2. **Network analysis.** Generally done with the aid of a computer, this research method observes the frequency and importance of an interaction network, based on the most frequent linkages. These patterns can be compared with official organizational charts and communication policies to determine disparities between theory and practice.
3. **Readership surveys.** These identify which articles or sections of publications are read most frequently. Although this method is strictly quantitative, it is an excellent way to determine the reading patterns of various publics.
4. **Content analysis.** This quantitative tool, discussed earlier, can analyze the content of all types of messages. It is frequently used to describe the amount of favorable and unfavorable news coverage an organization receives.

TABLE 5.2   Example of the Second Section of a Communication Audit: Assessing Specific Informational Needs and Media Preferences

Operations (NOTE: This category is just one of many possible topics that can be assessed.): Operations information refers to information that is related to day-to-day operations, production, schedules, and use of resources.

How satisfied are you with the amount of information on operations that you receive?
(*Please circle the number that best reflects your response.*)

| Very dissatisfied | 1 | 2 | 3 | 4 | 5 | Very satisfied |

How understandable is the information on operations that you receive?
(*Please circle the number that best reflects your response.*)

| Not at all understandable | 1 | 2 | 3 | 4 | 5 | Very understandable |

In general, how would you prefer to receive information on operations?
(*Please check your desired response.*)

❏ Through written materials   ❏ Through one-on-one interactions
❏ Through group meetings   ❏ Verbally over the phone

The following section is designed to find out where you currently get information on operations and where you would prefer to get that information. Please check all of the boxes that apply and feel free to write in any sources of information that you currently use or ones that you would like to see used.

I currently get information on operations from: I would prefer to get information on operations from:

❏ The company newsletter   ❏ The company newsletter
❏ Weekly meetings   ❏ Weekly meetings
❏ Weekly status reports   ❏ Weekly status reports
❏ E-mail   ❏ E-mail
❏ Intranet   ❏ Intranet
❏ Supervisor updates   ❏ Supervisor updates
❏ Other   ❏ Other

Source: Dean Kazoleas and Alan Wright, "Improving Corporate and Organizational Communications: A New Look at Developing and Implementing the Communication Audit," in *Handbook of Public Relations,* ed. Robert L. Heath and Gabriel Vasquez (Thousand Oaks, CA: Sage, 2001), p. 477.

5. **Readability studies.** Several methods may be employed to assess how readily written messages are understood. Most of these methods are based on the number of syllables in the words and the length of the sentences used. These formulas are discussed in more detail in chapter 8 when we discuss evaluation techniques. For now, we note only that they help determine the clarity of a written message and its appropriateness to the educational level of an audience.

Usability Research

The pervasive use of the Internet requires virtually every public relations effort to include the design of Web-based materials. Because the nature of online messages is dramatically different from other visual images and printed text, online messages must be evaluated for usability in addition to other communication standards. A technique first applied to product and software development, usability research helps to assess both the objective and subjective responses of users to Web sites.[15]

Many of the research terms used in this chapter may be unfamiliar to you. Although they are defined more thoroughly throughout the chapter, and you can find the definitions in the glossary at the end of the book, you may find it helpful to study these terms both before and after reading the chapter.

Secondary research is research from sources already produced, such as books, magazines, newspapers, published opinion polls, Web articles, and other electronic records. You should read the existing research on your topic first, so the term "secondary" research is perhaps misleading.

Primary research is original research. It is needed when secondary research cannot provide the answers to the questions.

Informal research is nonscientific research or information gathering. For example, it may include phone calls to the organization as well as letters, sales reports, and informal discussions with community leaders.

Formal research is scientific research. It is done to produce results that are highly likely to be statistically accurate within a given range.

Focus groups focus or select from a certain characteristic(s) of your audience. From this select group, usually 8–12 people, a moderator asks open-ended questions to probe for the why or the in-depth answer to the question. Even though focus group research is considered informal research because the results from the group cannot be scientifically applied to the larger group or public it represents, this primary research tool has become one of the most popular of all research tools for the public relations practitioner.

Descriptive data are bits of information used to describe something, such as a particular group of people. These data often include percentages, averages, or actual numbers to summarize the characteristics of a group or public.

Inferential data are the result of systematic sampling of a population, and you can infer from the sample the characteristics of the larger group.

Sample is a subset of a population that is selected to give information from which the researcher can make inferences about the larger group. From that sample, if chosen properly, the researcher can provide a statistical degree of reliability that the sample is similar to the total population, depending on the sample size, questions asked, and type of sample.

Simple random sampling is a research gathering technique that selects a subset of the larger group with every member of the larger group having an equal chance of being selected. This type of sampling gives the best statistical chance of being accurate.

Stratified random sampling is simply random sampling within each strata or subgroup of the larger population. For instance, if you took 5 percent at random of all freshmen, then a 5 percent sample of sophomores, juniors, and seniors, you would have a sample different from a random sample of all undergraduate students. This type of sample allows you to compare the different classifications (strata).

Social Audits

The concept of the **social audit** began in the early 1960s when businesses and other organizations were challenged to recognize their obligations to society. Social audits are generally attitude and opinion surveys that measure the perceptions of various publics about an organization's social responsiveness. This technique attempts to quantify the impact an organization has on its public in much the same way that a public relations audit does. However, social audits are generally confined to issues of social responsibility.

Recent research has shown that organizations and their publics have professional, personal, and community relationships. Therefore, organizations need to be clear about the relationships they are attempting to manage with various publics. Professional relationships demand a businesslike, service-oriented approach to a public, whereas personal relationships depend on a perception of trust. Community relationships require that an organization be seen as supportive and active in improving the social and economic interests of a public. Social auditing was common in the mid- to late 1970s. In recent years, social issues have been included in other types of research, such as environmental scanning and public relations and communication audits.[16]

See spotlight 5.1 for a review of some of the terms used in this chapter.

Case Study

University Blood Drive

The local nonprofit blood bank has asked your university to prepare a public relations campaign for a university-wide blood drive next semester. The bloodmobile will be on campus for donations one week next semester. The university has asked your chapter of the Public Relations Student Society of America to do the campaign. You have been given the responsibility for conducting the research prior to the development of the campaign.

The person in charge has asked you to find answers to questions like these: Where would you find information on blood drives, blood banks, and blood donors? Who are your publics? How would you find out what they know about giving blood from experience, or what their attitudes are about donating blood? How would you find the most effective media to reach these publics? How would you decide what your message should be? What kinds of questions do you need to ask in your research? Design a formal survey research plan to answer the questions, including who you would sample, how many participants you would need, and how you would administer the survey. Write the questions for the questionnaire.

Questions

1. Who are your target audiences?
2. What preliminary research would you use?
3. What sources would you use to find out the preliminary background information?
4. What formal, or systematic, research techniques would you need to use?
5. What kind of questions do you need to ask?

Summary

For self-testing and additional chapter resources, go to the Online Learning Center at **www.mhhe.com/lattimore3e.**

Research is an important part of any public relations effort. It supplies the initial inputs to guide strategy and message development and provides a method for predicting effectiveness and assessing results. Public relations professionals must be able to measure the effects of their work and make reasonable predictions about future success if they wish to influence managerial decisions in most organizations today.

Many public opinion surveys are not useful in public relations planning and evaluation because they tend to average responses so that the relative strengths of attitudes are disguised. Good public opinion research must be sensitive enough to segment publics according to the strengths of their opinions. Four basic categories of research in public relations are sufficiently sensitive: environmental monitoring, public relations audits, communication audits, and social audits.

active public
audit
aware public
communication audit
communication climate survey
content analysis
descriptive data
environmental monitoring
environmental scanning
experimental research
focus group
formal research
inferential data
informal research
interviews
issues management
key contacts
latent public

mass opinion
network analysis
observations
opinion leaders
primary research
public opinion
public relations audit
qualitative research
questionnaires
readability study
readership survey
sample
secondary research
simple random sampling
social audit
survey research
systematic sampling

Notes

1. Nick Del Calzo, Del Calzo and Associates, video interview with Dan Lattimore.

2. Don W. Stacks, *Primer of Public Relations Research* (New York: Guilford Press, 2002).

3. Larissa A. Grunig, "Using Focus Group Research in Public Relations," *Public Relations Review* XVI (Summer 1990), pp. 36–49.

4. Walter K. Lindenmann, "Research, Evaluation and Measurement: A National Perspective," *Public Relations Review* XVI (Summer 1990), p. 10.

5. "Avoiding the Boomerang: Testing the Relative Effectiveness of Anti-Drug Public Service Announcements before a National Campaign," *American Journal of Public Health* 92, no. 2 (February 2002), p. 238.

6. Del Calzo, video interview.

7. John Dewey, *The Public and Its Problems* (Chicago: Swallow, 1927).

8. James E. Grunig, "A New Measure of Public Opinions on Corporate Social Responsibility," *Academy of Management Journal* 22 (December 1979), pp. 740–41.

9. Otto Lerbinger, "Corporate Use of Research in Public Relations," *Public Relations Review* 3 (Winter 1977), p. 11.

10. Michelle Mason, "Revolutionizing the Scan Process," *Association Management* 57 (August 2005), p. 16.

11. Dave Lenckus, "Public Entities Search Below the News Radar," *Business Insurance* 39 (June 6, 2005), pp. 11–13.

12. Lerbinger, "Corporate Use," p. 16.

13. Joyce F. Jones, "The Public Relations Audit: Its Purpose and Uses. R&F Papers," Number 3 (New York: Ruder Finn Rotman, Inc., 1975). Reprinted in *Public Relations Journal* 31 (July 1975), pp. 6–8.

14. Lerbinger, "Corporate Use," p. 12.

15. Kirk Hallahan, "Improving Public Relations Web Sites through Usability Research," *Public Relations Review* 27 (Summer 2001), pp. 223–39.

16. Cynthia E. Clark, "Differences Between Public Relations and Corporate Social Responsibility: An Analysis," *Public Relations Review* 26 (Autumn 2000), pp. 363–80.

CHAPTER 6

Strategic Planning for Public Relations Effectiveness

PREVIEW

Alessio is the public relations director of Northern State University. For the last couple of years, he and his team have been working on their plans for the celebration of the university's upcoming 100th anniversary. The theme of the celebration is "100 Years of Inspiration and Service." Now that the kickoff events are finally approaching, it's time to get down to the details. Alessio has been looking forward to seeing all his department's plans come to fruition.

Among the events to be held during the month-long celebration are the dedication of a new science building; a renaming ceremony for the athletic field—complete with a fireworks display; the installation of an outdoor sculpture to commemorate the school's founding; a black-tie dinner for faculty and administration to follow a special concert by the school's orchestra; and the placement of innumerable media stories and interviews with the university's president and other key figures. Plans for most of these, including timetables and budgets, were begun and coordinated with other departments many months ago, and Alessio has checked his staff's weekly progress reports about each event. Everything is on track.

With only a few days to go, his work is becoming ever more focused. The president's office has e-mailed with a question about the time of her upcoming interview with the local television station, and Alessio's to-do list for today includes writing the press releases announcing the opening of the new campus building.

He sits down at his computer, forwards the interview information to the president, opens his word processing program, and starts to write.

STRATEGIC PLANNING

Public relations strategic planning provides organization to the public relations process. "Strategic planning is a process of assessing what you have and where you want to go."[1] The caliber and thoroughness of thinking preceding the execution of public relations activities will determine the value of the public relations operation. Understanding how to develop a public relations plan, then, is one of the main criteria that separates entry-level positions from top management in public relations.

Planning moves public relations from a reactive activity to a **proactive** process. Public relations practitioners, like most other managers, tend to be action oriented. The constant changes that take place both inside and outside any organization produce an endless procession of public relations problems. Too often, because of the number of pressing problems, managers find themselves responding only to exceptional situations. Such situations are usually negative in that they require the practitioner to intervene after a problem has already gotten out of control.

Although putting out fires is certainly part of the public relations function, it cannot be allowed to dominate all actions. If it does, the practitioner becomes a victim of circumstances, able to react only to the situation at hand. Perhaps the most frequent complaint of public relations practitioners is that other managers ask for their services only after the problem has become unmanageable. When damage to the organization's image has already been done, the public relations manager is often directed to "fix it." This may prove to be a no-win situation both for the organization and for the practitioner who must engage in usually fruitless remedial public relations.

For a long time, public relations practitioners have been advocating preventive public relations to avoid such problems. Part of this approach involves the type of fact-finding research we discussed in chapter 5. If practitioners detect potential problems before they erupt into damaging situations, they can give management early warning and advice. Sometimes even early detection cannot forestall some negative impact. When advanced warning is coupled with adequate planning, however, negative effects can be minimized, and public relations management can provide well-designed, positive actions rather than hastily conceived reactions. As we continue the integrating case study begun in chapter 5, notice how the pitfalls of hasty reaction were avoided.

Integrating Case Study

Cedar Springs Community Hospital
Segment 2

You may remember that the physicians at Cedar Springs Hospital (chapter 5) were calling for immediate action to correct what they saw as a potentially life-threatening situation in patient care. Reaction to the problem as it appeared at the time would have generated a campaign to make employees more aware of the need for quality patient care and emphasize their responsibility for providing the best care possible. However, before taking action, the public relations director conducted some research to help him better understand the problem. The results were surprising and showed that the first action contemplated would have only made things worse. Employees already believed that the quality of patient care in the hospital was subpar and were frustrated because they felt they personally were doing a good job. In addition, research revealed that recently released patients rated the quality of care significantly better than the employees did.

The sizable difference between the ratings of employees and patients pointed to a different problem than was originally suspected. The planning process based on this research redefined the issue from one of actual care to one of perceptions about care.

Objective: The objective that grew out of the research findings was to improve employee and physician views of overall hospital performance. Obviously, since both doctors and individual employees believed they were personally providing the best care they could and patients rated their performance high, the actual quality of care was good. However, their perception of poor performance was creating a morale problem for both doctors and employees.

Planning: Two basic strategies were devised to be implemented in a yearlong campaign. The first strategy was to continually reinforce employees' feelings of worth as members of the hospital's medical team through positive feedback from management. The second strategy was to help both physicians and employees more accurately judge the overall quality of care through increased feedback from patients.

Budget: A budget of $6,000 was developed to conduct additional surveys of recent patients and communicate the message of quality care through a variety of media. Communication channels would be selected to allow both internal and external audiences to get the message that hospital employees were a quality team. Policies were changed to allow any letters with positive comments from patients to be routed first to the departments involved before being filed.

In the Cedar Springs case, research and careful planning prevented the loss of time and employee confidence that would have resulted from reacting too quickly to the first symptoms of the problem. Only through continuous advance planning can public relations practitioners avoid having to react after the damage has been done. Even though many public relations managers think they have no time to plan, the more time they spend planning based on adequate research, the less time they will need to spend putting out fires.

IMPORTANCE OF PLANNING

David M. Dozier summarized the significance of planning:

> The process of setting public relations goals and objectives in measurable form serves two purposes. First, the prudent and strategic selection of public relations goals and objectives linked to organizational survival and growth serves to justify the public relations program as a viable management activity. . . . Second, the specification of public relations goals and objectives in measurable form makes public relations accountable and makes program success or failure concrete and objective.[2]

Planning permits the development of integrated public relations efforts that support an organization's goals in a positive rather than a defensive manner. Planning provides the opportunity to involve management from other areas of the organization and to ensure their cooperation and support. When a manager from another department has input into the public relations plan, he or she is much more likely to support that effort.

Public relations efforts often fail because of communication breakdowns between practitioners and other managers within an organization. The cause of these breakdowns is frequently an imperfect alignment between the public relations planning process and planning done elsewhere in the organization. Misunderstandings can usually be prevented if public relations practitioners analyze the organizational management as carefully as they analyze any other audience.

Public relations departments must prepare messages that communicate their needs and potential contributions to other segments of the organization. Therefore, when planning, they must learn the terms and methods common to organizational management.

FUNDAMENTALS OF PUBLIC RELATIONS PLANNING

Planning is generally classified into two broad categories: strategic and tactical. **Strategic plans** are long-range plans, usually made at the upper levels of management. They involve decisions concerning major goals of an organization and policies for their implementation. Environmental scanning (chapter 5) has become a primary tool to identify and to prioritize the strategic issues upon which an organization's plans are ultimately founded.[3]

Tactical plans develop specific decisions about what will be done at every level of the organization to accomplish the strategic plans. Strategic planners typically deal with future events and must therefore rely on relatively uncertain data. The use of forecasting techniques to predict what effects economic and technical changes will have on an organization in the next five years is an example of strategic planning. Tactical planners, on the other hand, are more concerned with the day-to-day operation of an organization and its immediate future.

Public relations plans are both strategic and tactical. Decisions concerning the long-range future of an organization often take public relations into consideration. However, public relations staff members must develop tactical plans to implement and support strategic plans.

To begin the planning process, you need to look to the future, or forecast. Planning always involves the future. Predicting barriers that may exist in the future is a much more difficult job than evaluating the existing situation, yet such predictions are necessary to determine the effects of future conditions on the programs being planned. The goal of attempting to look into the future is to better understand the environment in which your publics will be forming their opinions. Such efforts are designed to help identify and categorize stakeholder groups so that their attitudes, opinions, and behaviors can be assessed and predicted with some accuracy. In addition, these efforts can help to identify target audiences, understand audience lifestyles, and identify appeals that may be successful. Some of the techniques commonly used for such analyses are discussed next. They range from the complex and quantitative to the intuitive, but each has potential to contribute to the development of a successful plan.

Public opinion surveys forecast reaction to initiative or actions contemplated by politicians, government officials, and managers. Presidents, for example, often use public opinion surveys to determine whether to support a legislative issue, a nominee for a cabinet position, or a military action; President George W. Bush looked closely at public opinion surveys in making decisions on the War on Terrorism. Predictions should also be made concerning the effects of planned public relations activities on various publics and the corresponding effects public reaction will have on the programs being planned. Often these judgments must be made by qualitative rather than quantitative means. Juries of executive opinion, sales force composites, and customer expectations are frequently employed.

Brainstorming is a group discussion technique used to generate large numbers of creative alternatives or new ideas. It has been used for some time by advertising agencies, public relations firms, and others who need to generate creative ideas. For example, brainstorming is often used to develop an appropriate theme for a public relations campaign. The basic rule of brainstorming is that no one is permitted to interject negative feedback or criticism into the discussion. As the group generates ideas, all are recorded to be critiqued later. No remark is considered too absurd or too simple because it could produce the spark necessary for a truly creative idea. Brainstorming can be effective with a group that is comfortable functioning in a freewheeling atmosphere.

Scenario construction has been used by think tanks, such as the Rand Corporation, to create very long range forecasts. A logical, hypothetical description of future events (scenario) is constructed to explore the dynamics of various alternatives. For example, if a large auto company wanted to choose one of several manufacturing plants to close, a scenario could be constructed for each case to detail possible effects on the environment, economic future of the community, availability of replacement jobs, and other positive and negative results.

With these, or other, approaches to examining the issues for the future of your organization, the planning process with its various elements can begin. Strategic plans and tactical plans combined produce either **standing** or **single-use plans.**

This hierarchy of plans is illustrated in figure 6.1. **Goals** refer to the basic direction in which an organization is heading. The purpose, mission, objectives, and strategies of an organization are all component parts of its goals. These terms are frequently used interchangeably; however, they may also be used in various combinations to indicate sublevels of planning. Since there are no universally accepted definitions for these terms, most organizations adopt their own very specific applications.[4]

ELEMENTS OF PLANNING

In the next section, we discuss the elements that are characteristic of planning, especially related to public relations campaigns. Understanding this process, along with the specifics of planning, is important to the success of the public relations effort of an organization. However, it should be noted that this is not a step-by-step or linear process. Some of the planning elements must occur simultaneously, some are ongoing, and some may occur before others in certain situations.

Campaign Plans (Single Use)

Campaigns are a frequent output of public relations planning. Because campaigns are usually designed to accomplish unique objectives, they must be planned using nonroutine procedures. Some generally accepted elements for writing the campaign-planning document include the following.

FIGURE 6.1   Hierarchy of Plans

1. Establishing Goals in Relation to the Mission Statement   In the Cedar Springs case, patient care became the goal that unified physicians, administrators, and employees. Agreeing on a goal or a set of goals must be the first step in deciding what a public relations effort will need. Frequently, in a list of possible goals, two or more are mutually exclusive. When possible goals conflict, each must be evaluated to determine the long- and short-range effects of acceptance or rejection, which is based on the organization's **mission statement.**

Resources often dictate the selection of goals. An organization may not be able (or willing) to devote the time, personnel, and capital necessary to accomplish some goals. Goals that are selected for the public relations function, however, must always relate to organizational purpose. When seeking approval for public relations goals, a manager will be more successful if he or she is able to relate them to the mission, goals, and objectives of the entire organization.

For example, Ben & Jerry's three-part mission statement provides the basis for its public relations effort:

Product Mission: To make, distribute, and sell the finest quality all-natural ice cream and related products in a wide variety of flavors made from Vermont products.

Economic Mission: To operate the company on a sound financial basis of profitable growth, increasing value for our shareholders, and creating career opportunities and financial rewards for our employees.

Social Mission: To operate the company in a way that actively recognizes the central role that business plays in the structure of society by initiating innovative ways to improve the quality of life of a broad community: local, national, or international.[5]

Many of Ben & Jerry's environmental community relations efforts have been developed to implement the social mission statement particularly. These environmental community relations initiatives have contributed significantly to making the company known throughout the country as a socially responsible, environmentally friendly organization.

Major special events, such as this Centennial of Flight celebration at the Air & Space Museum, often require their own public relations plan. Usually, though, special events are only one strategy of a plan. This event honored the 100th anniversary of the Wright brothers' flight.

2. Determining the Present Situation   In reality, it is impossible to separate planning from research because they occur almost simultaneously; thus, as a goal is considered, current data about the organization's environment must be collected and used to evaluate the likelihood that the goal can be reached. Information provided by the kind of fact-finding research discussed in chapter 5 is crucial at this point. Problem identification based on the available data should answer the following questions:

- Is this a relatively big or little problem?
- What are the larger areas of concern into which this problem may fit?
- Is this really a problem facing our publics?
- What background facts and issues from your client/organization research are relevant to this problem?
- If this is more than one problem, how should it be broken down?
- Does additional research need to be undertaken at this point to determine the extent of the problem?
- Is a public relations audit needed to understand the organization and its internal and external public relations opportunities?

Again, the Cedar Springs example demonstrates the importance of taking appropriate steps to get accurate information before a plan is begun. It is useless to set unrealistic goals or goals that have already been accomplished. Even after the goal has firmly been set, data about the current situation need to be monitored. If the situation changes, it may be necessary to alter the goal or goals. Goals must be set with a good understanding of the current situation, the available resources, and what limitations must be placed on those goals.

3. Determining Threats and Opportunities to Reaching Goals   After determining reasonable goals, a more careful investigation of the environment must take place to identify what will aid and what will hinder the attainment of goals. The resources of an organization (people, money, and equipment) are important aids for achieving any goal. On the other side of the coin, a deficiency of any of these elements is a barrier that must be overcome. Although money is frequently the first barrier to be considered, it is seldom severe enough to prevent the accomplishment of objectives. Many plans, like the one at Cedar Springs Hospital, can be carried out with relatively small budgets. Key questions to ask to define aids and barriers include Do we have the *right individuals?* (rather than enough people) and Do we have *enough* money? (rather than how much money).

The structure and policies of an organization can also be either aids or barriers to reaching goals. For example, the goal of creating a sense of unity between labor and management could be severely hindered by policies that prohibit informal communication between the company and its union. Other barriers and aids are outside the organization—from government, competitors, consumer groups, and other special interest groups.

4. Researching and Selecting Your Target Audiences   Based on preliminary research, the planning document should describe the primary target audiences, identify appeals and points of interest that will attract attention, define audience lifestyles, and determine the relative strength of each possible appeal. In selecting the audiences, you must first identify and categorize your stakeholder groups. You may divide them into primary and secondary publics. You may then analyze each group, determining which are the target audiences, or the stakeholders, you must reach if your public relations program is to be successful. Your research should also help you analyze and assess your target audiences' attitudes, opinions, and behaviors.

Audience analysis should include as thorough a description of the demographics and lifestyles of each audience as possible. It should also include identification of possible messages or other appeals that can be used to influence each audience. Once you've determined your target audiences, you can then begin to develop your objectives, strategies, and tactics to best reach those stakeholders.

Once you have identified the problems and opportunities, you must **prioritize** them. Seldom will you have the budget or the time to try to do everything at once. At this point you can develop a *problem statement* to reflect the research done to narrow the task to a manageable size. It should define the scope of the effort and recognize any special requirements of the organization, target audiences, and media. The planning document should tell how the purpose will be accomplished for the audience that has been identified. It should discuss specific tactics and alternatives, define expected outcomes, and specify communication media, activities, and channels to be used.

5. Developing a Theme for the Program or Campaign   Not every public relations plan for a program or campaign has to have a theme, but often the theme has been the creative piece that has made a public relations campaign successful. An effective theme should do three things:

- Catch the essence of the plan or campaign.
- Be short . . . around 3–5 words.
- Be something that can endure over time.

6. Developing the Objectives for the Plan or Campaign   Objectives should be the heart of the plan. They should focus on overcoming the priority problems or developing the key opportunities for the plan. Objectives for public relations plans should be written in infinitive form. Criteria for writing and selecting objectives

- Should be related to the overall goals of the organization.
- Need to be improvement oriented.
- Must be clearly defined.
- Must be specific.
- Should be measurable.
- Need to be attainable.

For example, if a community theater is relatively new to a growing town, is struggling financially because of low attendance and poor season ticket sales, and needs additional resources to produce the quality theater the community wants, its fall public relations plan might have the following objectives:

- Increase awareness of the community theater by 25 percent within the local area.
- Increase season ticket sales 10 percent.
- Raise $25,000 in endowment for the theater.
- Involve 25 new volunteers in working with the theater.

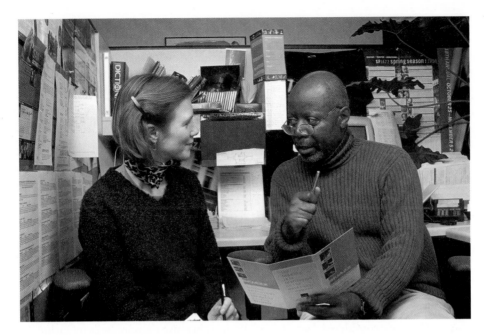

SFJAZZ volunteers examine a new brochure, one of the campaign's tactics.

7. Creating Strategies to Accomplish the Objectives   Strategies may be the most difficult of the terms to define in the planning process. Strategies can refer to the type or emphasis of a message, the way we want to approach a task, or a variety of other things. However, in this context a strategy is a way or ways you are going to accomplish your objectives.

For the community theater, some strategies to implement the first objective might include

- Developing a media campaign to publicize the theater and its upcoming season.
- Creating informational materials for the theater.
- Preparing a special event, perhaps an open house with a concert from a relatively well-known music group.

Strategies, then, are used to define means for achieving objectives more precisely, are an intermediate step between objectives and tactics, and tend to group like tactics together.

8. Developing Tactics to Implement Strategies   Tactics are the most specific, direct action that you can take in the plan. They are the most specific, concrete activity and should be related to the objectives and strategies. For the community theater, tactics for the second strategy (creating informational materials) might include these:

- Develop a brochure about the upcoming season to sell season subscriptions.
- Develop a brochure to persuade residents to become volunteers at the theater.
- Create posters for each play during the upcoming season.
- Prepare programs for the performances.
- Create a video about the theater to be used to promote the theater and its upcoming season.

9. Creating Evaluation Techniques To properly evaluate the plan, whether campaign or standing, the procedures for evaluation must be developed before implementation begins in order to have a benchmark with which to measure performance during and at the end of the program. The evaluation techniques used must evaluate each objective and should include formative as well as summative evaluation techniques. **Formative evaluation** (evaluation at various stages during the program) includes the monitoring necessary to make changes while the plan is still being implemented. **Summative evaluation** provides the summary of what went right or wrong—and why—after the campaign has ended. See chapter 8 for detailed information on the evaluation process.

10. Developing a Budget Budgets are essential to any plan. Generally, they are designed to project costs through the duration of a campaign or other period of time. **Campaign** or **project budgets** are components of plans to accomplish specific public relations activities. They provide structure and discipline in terms of time and money costs. Budgeting for specific activities is a rather straightforward process. Public relations managers prepare budgets using a simple, three-step model: (1) The required resources such as people, time, material, and equipment must be listed; (2) the extent these resources will be used is estimated; and (3) the costs of the resources are determined. These are considered "zero-based" budgets because they are built by including all specific costs needed to accomplish the project. Other budgets, such as functional and administrative ones, may need to be developed, but the zero-based budget is typically the one used for campaigns.

When Pam Smith, a public relations staff member for our community theater example, set about producing a brochure to encourage community volunteers, she first had to develop a budget for the project. Table 6.1 shows her results. The left-hand column lists resources (step 1); the center column shows estimated quantities (step 2); and the right-hand column shows costs and how they are derived (step 3).

Project and campaign budgets are the building blocks for annual public relations departmental budgets and the basis for bids submitted by independent **public relations**

TABLE 6.1   Budget for Community Theater Brochure

Resources	Quantities	Costs
1. Pam's time (interview, write, integrate photos into copy, administer project)	56 hours	$1,234.00 (based on $64,000 yearly)
2. Photographer's time (freelance) (at $125 per hour)	10 hours	$1,250.00
3. Layout (graphics dept.)	8 pages	$ 500.00 (estimate, graphics)
4. Printer (outside contractor) with halftone (estimate, printer)	1,000 copies, 2 colors	$3,000.00
5. Distribution costs (mailing and handling)	Postage for 1,000 copies Mailing lists of 500 names	$ 380.00
		$6,364.00
	10% Contingency	646.00
	Total budgeted for brochures	$7,000.00

The Rhode Island Department of Health Campaign Plan to Encourage Breast Cancer Screening

Spotlight 6.1

Duration of Campaign: November to December (13 months)

Campaign Chronology

Fourth Quarter

- Press conference introduces Breast Cancer Screening Program
- Advertisements in one (1) statewide newspaper and three (3) regional newspapers
- Talk given to American Cancer Society volunteers
- Guest appearances on four (4) television programs and four (4) radio programs

First Quarter

- Advertisements in one (1) statewide newspaper and three (3) regional newspapers

- Newspaper article on mammography
- Talk given to American Cancer Society volunteers
- Guest appearances on three (3) talk-radio programs
- Mailing to all licensed MDs

Second Quarter

- Advertisements in one (1) statewide newspaper and three (3) regional newspapers
- Public service announcement distributed to all television stations
- Posters distributed to hospitals, radiologists, and hairdressers
- Pilot mail campaign to all eligible state employees

Third and Fourth Quarters

- Repeat messages as necessary.
- Measure outcomes and evaluate campaign results with pre- and post-surveys.
  - 60% of targeted women had heard of the program.
  - 15% of women ages 40 and over received mammograms for the first time.

Source: Vicki S. Freimuth, "Mass Media Strategies and Channels: A Review of the Use of Media in Breast and Cervical Cancers Screening Programs," *Wellness Perspectives* 11 (Winter 1995), p. 79.

---

counselors. In either case, budgets become instruments in the competition for organizational resources.

11. Working Out a Timetable   A schedule of all activities for a public relations campaign should be developed. This is a process of "back-timing," or determining from what you want as a finished product how much time each step in the process will take. Various scheduling tools are available through computerized programs to provide assistance in detailing the exact time set for each of the tactics in the plan. Some organizations are small enough to use a simple calendar and denote the days needed for each activity, but whatever the means, it is essential that each individual activity or tactic be scheduled to know exactly when you need to begin in order to have it completed in time.

For example, if you need to have a **video news release** (**VNR**) for your campaign, you will need to have the concept developed and approved, script written and approved, video shot, video edited, and the final production approved before distribution can begin. You need to schedule time for each step in the process. See spotlight 6.1 for an example of a timetable.

12. Assigning Personnel   The plan must detail the human resources needed to accomplish the objectives. Thus, the plan must address which departmental personnel will be used for what activities and where the additional personnel will be found. Many times, the company's public relations agency is used for these additional personnel. Other times, freelance artists are hired, a research agency employed, or a video company contracted to provide the necessary expertise to complete the tactics required.

Although there is general agreement about the need for all the preceding steps in planning a campaign, some elements are often overlooked. A recent survey of 41 campaigns

Public relations often fails because managers do not understand what public relations people are saying and doing. Thus it is imperative that we talk in management's terms rather than trying to educate them in ours.

The Advantages of MBO

1. Communicates the way business-people think in terms of business problems and objectives.
2. Raises the importance of public relations in the corporate structure.
3. Presents a structure for implementing effective communications programs.
4. Helps keep the public relations practitioner on target in solving public relations problems.

5. Contributes to the public relations body of knowledge.

The Process

1. Get a fix on the business problem: Analyze the business problem using all available research techniques, then develop a clear, concise statement of what the problem is.
2. Translate the business problem into public relations objectives: This is the most difficult part of the process. The objectives should be stated in measurable terms.
3. Determine the audience(s): Identify to whom your message will be directed. There may be several audiences. Examples: print and broad-

cast media, company employees, customers, government officials.
4. Determine program elements: This includes exactly what vehicles will be used to effect the program. Examples: TV, news clips, news releases, institutional ads, speeches, and publicity events.
5. Determine budget: The ideal situation is to fit the budget to the need, using an objective and task approach.
6. Implement the program/campaign: Carry out the tactics of the campaign.
7. Evaluate the program: Utilize appropriate measuring instruments and techniques.

showed that 100 percent identified their target audiences, but only 63 percent specified a theme and only 62 percent documented outcomes.[6]

Management by Objectives

Once a situation has been described, aids and barriers considered, and forecasts completed, developing alternative courses of action should be relatively automatic. After listing as many alternatives as possible, the process begins, comparing alternatives in terms of costs and benefits.

The term **management by objectives (MBO),** an approach to planning that is detailed in spotlight 6.2, has become less popular in management jargon today than in the last decade. However, the basic elements are still widely used to describe management plans. MBO is an administrative planning process characterized by setting both long- and short-range objectives and then developing plans to accomplish those goals. Frequently, the process spreads to every level of an organization. Managers and their subordinates may begin the process by developing separate objectives and plans, then review one another's work and prepare a joint document as a final plan. This can occur at every level up the organization chart. Sometimes this flexible planning technique has other names. As we shall discuss in chapter 8, setting objectives prior to action is critical to the ability to demonstrate effectiveness in public relations efforts.

Standing Plans

Within all organizations, certain *programmable decisions* call for a standardized, consistent response. Standing plans provide routine responses to recurring situations. Once set, standing plans allow managers to make more efficient use of their planning time because they do not have to formulate a new plan for every similar situation. One note of caution: Overuse of standing plans may limit an organization's responsiveness to its environment, a critical issue for public relations. Nevertheless, standing plans do have a place in the public relations function. We discuss three types of standing plans: policies, procedures, and rules.

Policies   **Policies** are generally established by an organization's top management as guidelines for decision making. Those who make policy usually seek to guide decision-making activities in ways consistent with organizational objectives. Other purposes include improving effectiveness or imposing the values of top management.

Sometimes policies originate informally at lower organizational levels as a pattern of decision making occurs over a long period of time. In such cases, top management merely formalizes what is already happening. In other situations, policy may be established either as a result of recommendations from lower-level managers or as a direct result of top management's observation that a problem exists.

Outside organizations, such as governmental agencies, also set policies or at least influence them. Health and safety policies in most large organizations have changed considerably in recent years as a direct result of actions by government agencies.

Public relations departments, like all other subunits of organizations, must plan their daily operations to avoid conflict with policy. More important, public relations practitioners should be included in the strata of policymakers for any organization to ensure sensitivity to the interests of its publics. For example, policies directing that all contact with the press go through the public relations department for approval and advice should be reviewed by the public relations staff.

Procedures   Detailed guidelines for implementing policy decisions are called standard **procedures.** Standard procedures, or standard operating procedures, provide detailed instructions for performing a sequence of actions that occur regularly. Most public relations departments have standard procedures for news releases, internal publications, site tours, media interviews, and many other activities that are carried on from year to year. In addition, every organization needs a standard procedure for emergencies.

Emergencies, although infrequent, should be handled through set procedures because of the need to respond quickly and effectively. When a disaster happens, it is too late to begin a deliberate planning process that will consider every alternative before responding. See mini-case 6.1. Coordinated, deliberate, and effective response is vitally important. When an emergency situation exists, time becomes the key element in communication; plans must be made in advance so that reaction can be immediate.

Rules   Whereas policies and standard procedures serve as guidelines for decision making, rules substitute for decisions. **Rules** are statements that specify the action to be taken in a particular situation. No latitude for application is provided other than the decision to either follow or not follow the rule. Rules may be necessary when certain procedures are crucial. For example, it is often wise to have a rule requiring that signed releases be obtained before personal information or photographs are used in publicity releases.

Remember that the public relations plan is a message that must be communicated to an organization's executives. Whether that message is accepted depends on the effective execution of the planning process and how the plan is communicated to the decision makers who must understand and approve it.

The Inevitable Tragedy: NASA's Emergency Planning

The space shuttle *Columbia,* only 16 minutes from a scheduled landing at Kennedy Space Center in Florida on February 1, 2003, blew apart, spreading wreckage from Fort Worth across east Texas to Louisiana and killing all seven astronauts on board. NASA responded immediately with communication through all media, letting the world know that a disaster had occurred. While still searching for answers to the cause of the crash, NASA administrator Sean O'Keefe vowed that safety is still its top priority. President George H. W. Bush praised the space program in his message to the nation and to the families who suffered the loss.

But what was the public's response? A Gallup poll taken the day after the disaster showed 82 percent of the American public wants NASA to continue sending people into space. That was similar to the 80 percent wanting to continue the program after the *Challenger* had been lost. President Bush vowed, "America's space program will go on."

This time NASA was prepared, but years ago when the first space disaster occurred, it was not ready for a crisis situation.

No reporters or correspondents from any media were on hand at Cape Kennedy when fire broke out in the command module of *Apollo-Saturn 204,* later known as *Apollo 1,* on January 27, 1967. The three-man crew, astronauts Virgil Grissom, Edward White, and Roger Chaffee, had entered *Apollo* at 1:00 P.M. for the last simulated countdown test before to launch. A series of problems quickly arose. Two of the astronauts reported fire in the cockpit, and technicians were horrified to see flames inside the now smoke-filled *Apollo.* Despite the danger of explosion from the escape rocket, six technicians rushed to open *Apollo's* hatch. By then, all three astronauts were dead from carbon monoxide asphyxia and thermal burns. They had never even left the launch pad.

Although NASA knew within five minutes of the accident that all three astronauts were dead, the information was not released until two hours later. It was nearly midnight before UPI and AP received a NASA picture of two of the astronauts entering the capsule for the last time.

NASA claimed that withholding the facts and its issuance of misleading and wrong statements resulted from the lack of a plan for handling information in emergencies. As hard to believe as this may have been, coming as it did from an agency with a public information staff of 300, there was undoubtedly some validity to the claim.

Since then NASA's information office has maintained that an emergency plan was in effect and followed at the time of the *Apollo 1* fire.[7] NASA states that it has contingency plans for each mission. Indeed, when a fire broke out on board *Apollo 13* three years later, many thought that NASA's handling of the crisis not only saved the lives of the three astronauts but so enhanced the image of the agency that it bolstered support for the entire manned space program.[8]

On January 28, 1986, tragedy again struck the nation's space program as millions of Americans and people all over the world witnessed via live television the explosion of the space shuttle *Challenger* shortly after liftoff. In their critiques of NASA's communication on the disaster, many professional observers and news reporters commented that little seemed to have been learned from earlier experiences. Although the flight controllers knew the fate of the *Challenger* crew almost instantly, speculation about their ability to survive the accident was allowed to continue for about an hour after the explosion while technicians "gathered data."

In its most recent tragedy, NASA was once again required to put an emergency communication plan into effect. NASA moved swiftly to provide information, especially in light of the fact that debris was scattered over large portions of Texas and Louisiana. Almost immediately the NASA Web site, www.nasa.gov, provided updated information, including video streams of press conferences. But as the investigation continued, questions were raised about the effectiveness of NASA's internal communication. After *Columbia's* fatal descent, e-mails and reports surfaced that were written prior to the mission and contained warnings about the possibility of just such an explosion. Several panels looked at the tragedy.

A study comparing NASA's handling of the *Challenger* and *Columbia* disasters found substantially more positive news coverage post-*Columbia.* The differences were linked to NASA's use of specific communication behaviors along with prompt response and a constant flow of information.[9] This pattern of prompt response and a constant flow of information was repeated when foam insulation was observed falling off the fuel tank during the July 2005 launch of *Discovery.*

Questions

1. How successfully can an organization plan ahead for a disaster?
2. How would you prepare a public relations budget to cover any activities necessary after a major unexpected event?

Sources: Dianne Calhoun Bragg, graduate student at the University of Alabama, gathered the case from Charles W. Petit, "A Star-Crossed Flight," *U.S. News & World Report,* February 17, 2003, pp. 44–49; Thomas Hayden, "Landing in the NASA Hot Seat," *U.S. News & World Report,* February 17, 2003, pp. 52–53; NASA's Web site; and James Skardon, "The *Apollo* Story: What the Watchdogs Missed," *Columbia Journalism Review* 6 (Fall 1967), pp. 13–14.

Kodak Galleries

Overview

Kodak was a leader in photography and film for more than 120 years, but as film moved from analog to digital and photo from silver-based photography to digital, Kodak needed to reposition itself as a leader in the digital photography age. To help them do this, Kodak hired Ketchum Public Relations. Ketchum looked for an idea to catch the essence of the new media and Kodak. The idea was to capture all that was Kodak in one concept that could be used in many applications. Gallery was that concept.

"In 2005, Kodak launched a category breakthrough: the Kodak EasyShare-One (ESO) wireless digital camera. Together, Kodak, Ketchum and Concentric brought the Kodak transformation to life for all to experience by creating pop-up Kodak One Galleries in New York City and San Francisco during November 2005. Through a series of private events, daily seminars, media briefings and walk-in traffic, visitors experienced the ESO technology and learned about Kodak's innovations."[10] Kodak claimed the number one slot in the U.S. digital camera market for the second year in a row in 2005.

Objectives

Kodak was one of many players in the digital camera market. Because of Kodak's long tradition in silver-based photography and its slow movement into the digital world, the business community expressed great skepticism toward its digital plans. Objectives were to

1. Create opportunities for 6,000 consumers and opinion leaders to experience Kodak digital products, including the EasyShare-One.
2. Create awareness that Kodak was a leading player in the digital market.

Tactics

1. Developed "pop-up galleries" to let consumers personally experience Kodak's ability to work in the digital world.
2. Put pop-up booths in New York and San Francisco.
3. Held launch parties the evening prior to officially opening the Galleries with invitation-only attendance for about 200 professional and local photographers so that they could experience the newest Kodak products and help build buzz.
4. Used direct mail, wild postings, and street marketing to drive visitors to the Gallery.
5. Launched a Gallery photo blog to highlight the daily happenings.
6. Used podcasts of the workshop speakers by putting them on the Kodak Gallery Web site.
7. Opened the doors of the One Galleries to media outlets and various organizations, making the Galleries a "place to be."

8. Coordinated one-on-one meetings for key media at the Galleries to high-light Kodak's brand transformation and emphasize ESO as a leader in the future of digital photography.

9. Collected thousands of names and mailing addresses for Kodak's customer relationship marketing group through in-Gallery interviews and drawings.

Results

- Kodak captured the top place in the U.S. digital camera market for a second straight year, extending its lead over rivals Canon and Sony.

- The Galleries received more than 13,000 visitors, including a significant representation from the upbeat urban consumer audience.

- 1,056 site visits to the NYC One Gallery photo blog, 1,779 site visits to the San Francisco One Gallery photo blog, and 12,500 visitors to the virtual One Gallery pages on Kodak.com during the month-long event.

- "The perception of Kodak as a leading digital player is reflected in results from surveys conducted at the One Galleries: over 80% of those surveyed felt that Kodak is bringing years of picture expertise into today's digital world and nearly 70% of those surveyed agreed that Kodak offers high-tech, yet user-friendly digital photography products."[11]

- *prweek* named ESO as one of 2005's top product launches you couldn't miss.

Sources: David Westenoff, Ketchum West panel in San Jose, CA, on Ketchum Perspectives: Audio Series, 2006; also www.prfirms.org retrieved March 29, 2008.

Questions

1. What theme would you suggest for this campaign?
2. How could the objectives be made stronger and easier to evaluate?
3. What strategies did they use?
4. What additional strategies would you have suggested? Tactics?

Summary

For self-testing and additional chapter resources, go to the Online Learning Center at **www.mhhe.com/lattimore3e**.

Good public relations practice demands good planning. As exciting as they may sound, public relations actions that arise from spur-of-the-moment decisions usually produce short-term gains and long-term losses. Even emergency situations that cannot be predicted must have planned response systems. The process of planning is slow, complex, and frequently boring. However, in public relations, as in other managerial functions, careful planning increases the effectiveness and decreases the frequency of future actions. Adequate planning also establishes a system of goals that can be used to measure public relations success. This aspect of planning is expanded in chapter 8.

Planning involves a look at the future. Techniques for beginning the planning process include using existing public opinion surveys, scenario building, and brainstorming. Plans are both single-use (often public relations campaigns) and standing plans such as crisis plans.

Key Terms

brainstorming
campaign budget
formative evaluation
goals
management by objectives (MBO)
mission statement
policies
prioritize
proactive
procedures
project budget

public opinion surveys
public relations counselor
rules
scenario construction
single-use plans
standing plans
strategic plans
summative evaluation
tactical plans
video news release (VNR)

Notes

1. Fran R. Matera and Ray J. Artigue, *Public Relations Campaigns and Techniques* (Boston: Allyn & Bacon, 2000), p. 103.

2. David M. Dozier, "Planning and Evaluation in PR Practice," *Public Relations Review* (Summer 1985), pp. 21–22.

3. Don Clare and Ron Nyham, "A Grand Scan Plan," *Association Management* 53 (January 2001), pp. 73–77.

4. L. J. Garrett and M. Silver, *Production Management Analysis* (New York: Harcourt Brace Jovanovich, 1966), pp. 364–65.

5. Ben & Jerry's plant in Waterbury, Vermont, June 4, 2002.

6. Sonja L. Myhre and June A. Flora, "HIV/AIDS Communication Campaigns: Progress and Prospects," *Journal of Health Communication* (April–June 2000) (Suppl.), p. 29.

7. James Kauffman, "Adding Fuel to the Fire: NASA's Crisis Communications Regarding *Apollo 1*," *Public Relations Review* 25 (Winter 1999), p. 421.

8. James Kauffman, "A Successful Failure: NASA's Crisis Communications Regarding *Apollo 13*," *Public Relations Review* 27 (Winter 2001), pp. 437–48.

9. Ryan M. Martin and Lois A. Boynton, "From Liftoff to Landing: NASA's Crisis Communications and Resulting Media Coverage following the *Challenger* and *Columbia* Tragedies," *Public Relations Review* 31 (June 2005), pp. 57–58.

10. www.prfirms.org, retrieved March 29, 2008.

11. Ibid.

CHAPTER 7

Action and Communication

If you're a customer of Netflix, the online movie-rental company, you're probably aware of its new "Profiles" service, which allows customers to create up to five different lists of requested films with each paid subscription. That means that kids and parents can work through their own separate lists of movies to rent, a plus for many Netflix users. What you might not know is that the idea for "Profiles" came from a blogger, Mike Kaltschnee, who writes the popular Web journal *Hacking Netflix*.

Since the blog came to the company's attention, Netflix has reached out to forge a positive relationship with Kaltschnee (who was already a fan). The firm has not only adopted the "Profiles" idea but also provides Kaltschnee with timely new-product information and, in turn, mines the discussion that readers post on his blog for customer reactions to and critiques of its services. Sometimes company executives even participate in the conversations, and Netflix employees have been known to use the blog as their home page.

The beneficial relationship between Kaltschnee and Netflix could easily have foundered if Netflix had made any public relations missteps along the way. *Hacking Netflix* is just one example of the way the public relations actions required of modern organizations have grown to include channels of communication unheard of a few years ago.

Whatever the communication channel, however, public relations practitioners often use five basic steps to bring new information to their target publics: awareness, interest, evaluation, trials, and adoption. First the organization identifies the appropriate channel (which might even include a fan blog); then it can take the appropriate communication steps to relay the message.

Writing is the primary tool for constructing the message, and writing well is a critical skill for public relations practitioners. This chapter focuses on the link between action and communication and introduces ways to get the message heard.

PUBLIC RELATIONS IN ACTION

Early in the 20th century, Ivy Lee, one of the "founding fathers" of public relations, emphasized the importance of counseling management to take responsible action before beginning the communication process. The public relations practitioner, as part of the management team of an organization, must be involved in the decision-making process to ensure that management makes decisions to take positive action steps to resolve a problem or to create an opportunity. Once the organization has taken responsible actions, the public relations staff may communicate with a target audience to induce desired behavioral outcomes. For example, Standard Oil of California took immediate action to let the public know that it would spend whatever was necessary to clean up a massive oil spill in the San Francisco Bay after two of its tankers collided. The company followed up on its promise and cleaned up the bay. San Francisco papers editorialized that the "beaches had never been cleaner before."[1]

Traditionally, public relations action has included communication in some form, often a publicity release for print media. The world has changed, though, and so has the practice of public relations. Technology has impacted the types of media that practitioners must work with, requiring organizations to have a wider range of possible action alternatives from their public relations staffs. Today crisis situations, as well as many of the planned public relations programs, must make use of new technologies, such as satellite transmissions of video news releases (VNRs), video interviews and other live news transmission on the Internet, and Web sites. PepsiCo, for example, used VNRs and video interviews as a major tool in combating a crisis of national scope when a claim was made that a foreign object was found in an unopened Diet Pepsi can in Tacoma, Washington. See mini-case 7.1.

Large organizations with access to modern technology are not the only ones that require a variety of response mechanisms. Cedar Springs Community Hospital took several action steps, none of them press releases. Although much of that action involved written communication, several important steps centered on managerial decision making.

Integrating Case Study

Cedar Springs Community Hospital
Segment 3

Action Implementation

In chapter 6, goals, objectives, and basic strategies were developed for solving the hospital's problem. Next, the public relations staff turned its attention to the execution of those plans. It was clear from the patient surveys that the hospital's primary goal of quality patient care was already being achieved. Therefore, strategies were developed to try to improve employee and physician perceptions of the hospital's performance.

The two basic strategies for which action steps needed to be developed were (1) reinforcement of employee feelings of worth as members of the medical team and (2) increase in feedback from patients. Several tactics were implemented to address these needs.

Employee Team

A theme was developed to increase all employees' awareness of their value as members of the medical team at Cedar Springs Hospital. The theme "Quality People, Quality Care" was communicated to employees, physicians, and other publics through six media:

1. Theme signs were placed over the entrances to all three main buildings.
2. Mailing panels were printed for all publications.
3. Birthday cards for employees were redesigned.
4. Special employee name badges were designed for those employees who had passed the 90-day probationary period, designating them as "Quality Providers."
5. T-shirts were printed with the theme and used as gifts for participating in the personnel department's annual Benefits Fair.
6. Photos of employees who received honors were placed on the hospital's Web site with a note about the honor. Doctors were also honored on the Web with special notes from patients.

Hospital management also wanted to make a very public statement about the quality of the employees and their work. Thus, an existing program, "Employee of the Month," was revitalized. To give the recognition more visibility among patients, physicians, and the general public, a 24-inch display ad appeared in the local newspaper every month, featuring an honored employee, the "Quality People, Quality Care" theme, and a link to the hospital Web site with more information about the employee.

Patient Feedback

Three primary methods were used to increase **feedback** from patients to the hospital staff. First, the survey of recently released patients was repeated quarterly. Survey results were disseminated in various ways, such as using the hospital newsletter, table tents in the staff cafeteria, and e-mail. In addition, a contest was begun in which employees tried to guess the survey results before they were published. Second, positive letters from former patients were disseminated among the hospital employees. Third, a regular feature called "Worth Sharing" was begun in the monthly newsletter to highlight patient success stories. It was also placed on the hospital Web site.

Influencing Management Decisions

When it was first proposed that the new theme be placed over the entrances to the main buildings, many employees reacted negatively, believing that "advertising" was too commercial for a medical facility. An ad hoc committee of department managers investigated the complaints and made recommendations regarding use of the theme. The committee eventually recommended placing it above the entrances and sold the employees on the integrity of the idea. This group also suggested using the theme only on the nametags of employees who had passed the 90-day review period.

Mini·Case 7.1   The Pepsi Hoax

It began in Seattle when a TV station informed the local Pepsi franchise bottler that an 82-year-old Tacoma man had found a hypodermic needle in a can of Diet Pepsi. The report was broadcast that evening on the local news. It would be the nation's top story for the next 96 hours. Within hours another syringe turned up in a can in another locality. Soon news broadcasts from around the country had reports of people finding needles in Pepsi cans.[2] Eventually, more than 50 allegations were made in 23 states.[3]

Pepsi Cola set up a crisis management team at its corporate headquarters in Somers, New York. The team was led by Craig Weatherup, Pepsi president. Rebecca Madeira, Pepsi vice president for public affairs, directed the team's actions and coordinated the communications so the company could speak with one voice.

First, the Pepsi crisis team had to determine if the Pepsi bottlers were the problem. The crisis response plan had these key points:

- Put public safety first. Assess the problem through the public's eyes. Be clear that their needs and concerns come first.
- Find it. Fix it. Work around the clock with regulatory officials to investigate every aspect of the plant operation to identify and, if possible, correct the problem.

- Communicate quickly and frequently, using tools and timetables reporters use.
- Take responsibility for solving the crisis. Don't point fingers, assign blame, or pass the buck. Make your team accountable for a swift and sound resolution to the problem.[4]

Once Pepsi had gathered its facts and felt secure that this was not a problem caused by its bottlers, Pepsi took the offensive. President Weatherup said repeatedly through the media, "A can is the most tamper-proof packaging in food supply. We are 99.99 percent certain that this didn't happen in Pepsi plants."[5]

The crisis team decided to use VNRs to show consumers that Pepsi's canning process could not be tampered with. High-tech, high-speed equipment was shown filling Pepsi cans. Each can was turned upside down, cleaned with a powerful jet of air or water, inverted, filled, and closed—all in less than one second! Video footage of the canning process was beamed by satellite to TV stations across the country. Within 48 hours the first VNR was seen by 296 million viewers, three times the number that usually watches the Super Bowl.

The company used the video to combat the visual images of the syringes that had constantly been shown on network television since the first

instance in Seattle. Pepsi created three more VNRs within three days. By the end of the week, the president had appeared on a dozen network TV news shows and talk shows, and Pepsi spokespersons had conducted more than 2,000 interviews with newspapers, magazines, and TV and radio reporters. The strategy was to show the public that what was happening was really a hoax rather than a problem with Pepsi bottlers. The real turning point came with the third VNR. It showed a tape from an in-store surveillance camera that had filmed a shopper slipping a syringe into an open Diet Pepsi can while the cashier's back was turned. Pepsi could not release the tape, though, until the next day when an arrest was made. After the third VNR ran, viewers were overwhelmingly supportive of Pepsi. The evaluation done indicated that Pepsi's response worked. Sales for the key July 4 period were not affected adversely, which was quite important.

Questions

1. Were the communication tools used by Pepsi to solve the problem the ones you would use today?
2. Evaluate the role of the VNRs. Are they always effective?

Management decision making was again the principal action leading to the wider distribution of letters of appreciation from patients. This relatively simple action required a change in organizational policy that could have been politically explosive. A policy change of this type could have alienated both the personnel manager and the department managers if not handled carefully. The public relations manager needed a good understanding of both communication and organizational dynamics to accomplish this objective. Such letters had traditionally been routed to the personnel department and then to the manager of the department involved. This meant that for a department to get any recognition, it would have to appear to "blow its own horn." Therefore, most letters of appreciation had been handled internally, without informing the rest of the organization. The private nature of this process worked against the new objective of improving employee perceptions by sharing patient feedback. Thus, the policy was changed so that the original letter was routed first to public relations where copies were made not only for the appropriate department manager but also human resources. Some letters were featured on the hospital Web site.

Diffusing Information

Although managerial decision making was one of the public relations actions used in the Cedar Springs case, the primary action process can be described as the **diffusion of information.** More often than not, the action implemented to accomplish a public relations plan can be explained as an attempt to spread information within a target audience.

Selecting a Target Audience   The action process begins and ends with target audiences. Once each public is identified, its characteristics can be studied, and a *critical path* of influence can be planned for the issue in question.

When considering the individual characteristics of each target audience, it is helpful to categorize them as (1) primary, intervening, or moderating and as (2) latent, aware, or active. A **primary public** is the group to which the action is ultimately directed. As we have shown, however, the critical path to this group frequently requires that other audiences be addressed. Individuals in **intervening publics** have direct contact with the primary audience and can pass messages along to them. All the channels of influence except personal experience may be intervening publics. **Moderating publics** are groups that share a common goal or guiding philosophy and can make an impact on the primary public. These groups usually have high credibility with the primary public in specific topic areas.[6] Only mass media and personal experience do not have the potential to be moderating publics.

As you will recall from our discussion in chapter 5, a **latent public** is not aware of a need to change or act. An **aware public** recognizes a need but is not prone to any action, such as accepting a new idea. An **active public** is aware and ready to do something. This classification system helps determine the extent to which a given public is ready and able to respond to any planned action.

The Diffusion Process   *Diffusion* is a term used to describe *the way in which new ideas are adopted in a society.* Sociologists and communication researchers have long been fascinated by the paths that innovations follow as they make their way through a social system. Publics or target audiences are social systems that public relations practitioners seek to influence. Therefore, it is important that our knowledge about the diffusion of information be applied to the public relations process. (See chapter 3 where this theory is discussed.)

Critical Paths   Those who study the diffusion process through which new products, ideas, and technologies spread have identified five steps that describe how people are influenced to change:

1. *Awareness.* People become aware of the idea or practice, although their knowledge is limited. This awareness is often spread through the mass media.
2. *Interest.* People begin to develop an interest in the idea and seek more information about it. Again, the mass media are especially important in providing the information to large audiences in this step of the diffusion process.

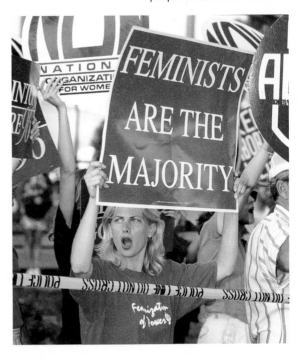

Marchers attempt to make people aware of their issues.

3. *Evaluation.* People begin to mentally apply the idea to their individual situations. Simultaneously, they obtain more information and make a decision to try the new idea.

4. *Trials.* At this point, actual application begins, usually on a small scale. Potential adopters are primarily interested in the practice, techniques, and conditions necessary for application.

5. *Adoption.* Once the idea is proven worthwhile, it is adopted by the target audiences.[7]

Channels of Influence   Researchers have tracked innovations through the adoption process and concluded that they use five basic channels of influence:

1. *Mass media.* Electronic and print media such as radio, television, newspapers, and magazines.

2. *Biased intermediaries.* Individuals or groups that stand to benefit from another's adoption (such as salespeople).

3. *Unbiased third parties.* Consumer groups, government agencies, and other groups or individuals that have credibility.

4. *Significant others.* Friends, relatives, and others who are admired by potential adopters.

5. *Personal experience.* Actual use of the innovation.

In the early stages of awareness and interest, mass media are most effective. In the critical stages of evaluation and trial, however, emphasis shifts to the influence of significant others. Finally, at the point of adoption, personal experience becomes the primary channel. The secondary, or support, path begins with significant others, moving to unbiased third parties at the evaluation and trial stages and then back again to significant others at adoption.

Facilitating the Adoption Process

The public relations practitioner can apply the critical path approach by attempting to create awareness and interest through press releases and other media coverage. From the start of the campaign, the practitioner should plan to communicate with other publics that are significant to the target audience. When the initial goals of awareness and interest are reached, public relations actions should move away from the obvious to more subtle forms of communication through significant others and unbiased third parties. After the evaluation and trial stages are passed, success can be measured by the extent to which the target public accepts the new idea.

Pressure and Special Interest Groups   Traditionally, a great deal of public relations practice has been based on a generally accepted *two-step flow of information theory.* This theory is built on the premise that certain people in our society are opinion leaders. Therefore, if those opinion leaders can be convinced to support a certain matter, they will influence others to support it also. For example, if ministers in your community strongly support a new senior center in town, as opinion leaders they are likely to have a great deal of influence on a number of their church members. The strategy, then, may be to use this two-step flow of information to convince the ministers that the senior center is good and to get them to encourage support from their membership.

Although the two-step flow theory contains a great deal of truth, both research and practice have shown that it is too simplistic. The theory allows for only two levels (leaders and followers) in any influence attempt. Further, it presumes a linear flow of information through a social system. From our discussion of systems theory and the diffusion process in chapter 3, it should be apparent that society is much more complex. Thus, some researchers now use a multi-step flow theory to describe the process.

This multi-step process is similar to the two-step flow, but instead of attempting to reach one target group who will in turn reach the ultimate audience, this theory suggests that the minister in our example might be only one opinion leader who might be used to influence other opinion leaders. He or she might influence several key church members who in turn might have more direct influence on others. Thus, the minister might influence the bankers, the doctors, the teachers, and the secretaries. In turn, these people would serve as opinion leaders for their small sphere of influence, ultimately reaching the larger target audience and convincing the community as a whole to support increased taxation for a new senior center.

When Mountain Bell decided to introduce Local Measured Service in the Phoenix area, the media devoted a great deal of coverage toward describing the advantages of the new system.[8] Because of the favorable publicity, the telephone company felt confident when the issue came up for approval by the Arizona Corporate Commission. When Mountain Bell representatives arrived at the hearing, however, they found senior citizens crowded into the chambers and other seniors picketing outside to protest the innovation. Obviously, one important public in the Phoenix area, senior citizens, had not adopted the idea. After its first request was turned down, the phone company began to work with senior citizen groups to win support from significant others and unbiased third parties. The proposal was approved without protest the next time it came before the commission. To secure the cooperation of various publics, Mountain Bell used an action strategy known as stakeholder analysis.

Stakeholder Analysis   The concept of stakeholder management provides a more realistic framework for an organization to visualize its environment. **Stakeholder analysis** is a method for differentiating among publics. **Stakeholders** are those individuals who perceive themselves as having an interest in the actions of an organization. They may be customers, shareholders, employees, or just members of society. They generally express themselves through groups that share a common purpose, such as environmental or consumer causes.

Applying the stakeholder management approach to public relations practice allows actions to be organized around an entire system of stakeholder groups. The goal is maximum overall cooperation between the stakeholders and the organization's objectives. To accomplish this, strategies are designed to deal simultaneously with issues that affect multiple groups.

The stakeholder process does not fundamentally change public relations communication or other action processes. Instead, it organizes them for more efficient use. Stakeholder management can determine *who* should be the object of an action step, *what* that action should be, *what* results should be sought, and *how* each element will fit into the overall plan.

Traditionally, many public relations activities were managed through delivery systems like news bureaus, speakers' bureaus, and complaint departments. Because these focus on a single action, they have difficulty recognizing the differences among publics. In a stakeholder management system, however, action for each public is planned *separately*. The needs and interests of a given stakeholder group determine what actions are appropriate and how they should be implemented.

When Mountain Bell managers first attempted to begin Local Measured Service, they were trying to reach all consumers through the same action strategies. Further analysis led them to realize that the task required a more complex view of their publics. Stakeholders who needed to be considered in the Local Measured Service issue included the following:

1. *Internal stakeholders.* Employees and shareholders.
2. *Residence stakeholders.* Consumer advocates, the handicapped, minorities, low-income segments, senior citizens, volunteer and service groups, educational organizations.
3. *Business stakeholders.* Those dependent on telemarketing, small businesses, large businesses.
4. *Other stakeholders.* Media, government, the Arizona Corporate Commission.[9]

Each stakeholder group was assigned to a project manager. These practitioners became familiar with the needs and interests of the groups assigned to them and worked with functional departments such as media relations, the speakers' bureau, internal publications, and others to target messages to their audiences.

Designing the Public Relations Matrix

After the appropriate channels of influence are determined and target audiences selected, messages are prepared within basic action categories. In a large organization, these functional areas, or subspecialties, within public relations are sometimes performed by different departments. Even if they are handled by one person, each action category must produce a distinct message. Frequently, different media are used as well. This creates a series of crossover or matrix relationships between target audiences and messages.

Table 7.1 illustrates the relationships between some of Mountain Bell's target audiences (stakeholders) and the action categories used to respond to the situation. In the case of Mountain Bell's response to the Local Measured Service protest, each target audience was assigned to a practitioner, while each action category was the responsibility of a functional department. For any message, at least two members of the public relations staff would be responsible for its design and implementation.

For example, a news release prepared by the press relations group could have been initiated by the residential or business consumer manager and closely reviewed by other

---

TABLE 7.1   Public Relations Matrix for Mountain Bell Target Audiences

	Media	Residential Customers	Employees	Business	Government
News Releases	Intervening	Primary	Moderating	Primary	Moderating
Speakers' Bureau	Intervening	Primary	Moderating	Primary	Moderating
Internal Publications			Primary		Moderating
External Publications	Primary	Primary	Moderating	Primary	Primary
Advocacy Advertising		Primary	Moderating	Primary	Moderating

Communication actions are on the left vertical axis, and the publics are across the top horizontally.
Source: Reprinted through courtesy of Mountain Bell.

managers for potential impact on media, employee, and government stakeholders. Under this system, messages are prepared for primary audiences and checked for their desired effect on moderating and intervening audiences. This system allows functional specialists such as writers and editors to continue performing their tasks, while project managers assume the responsibility for making sure all messages received by their publics are prepared according to the public relations plan. A single manager can be responsible for supervising contacts with several publics in more than one project. These responsibilities change as projects are completed and new ones are added.

We began this chapter by illustrating the variety of action steps possible from a single public relations plan. Although the actions that might be used are virtually limitless, one remains predominant. The ability to write effectively continues to be a primary skill demanded by those who employ public relations practitioners.[10]

THE PRACTITIONER AS A COMMUNICATOR

Just as communication is the primary action step in a public relations plan, writing is the principal tool for constructing messages. Even messages that are primarily visual, like videotape or slide presentations, generally require well-written directions or a script. Web pages also rely on the effectiveness of the written word for maximum impact. Writing for the Internet often means using keywords to drive search engines. While the use of embedded links and the compartmentalization of the screen into various messages bring different challenges, they must be met with clear, effective writing. Policies and other decisions are written as they are developed, transmitted, and preserved. Therefore, writing is a basic skill needed by all public relations professionals, regardless of the type or size of the organizations in which they work.

Principles of Effective Writing

Some people are born with an exceptional talent that cannot be explained or taught. The Ernest Hemingways of this world may not need to learn the principles of effective writing, but few of us are exceptionally gifted artists. Most people have to learn the craft of writing through study, practice, and hard work—that's the bad news.

The good news is that effective writing can be learned. People of average talent can learn to write effectively by practicing some basic principles. See spotlight 7.1 and appendix 1.

Packaging Ideas   The length of sentences in a written document is widely recognized as a key to its clarity. Many of the readability formulas use sentence length as their basis of measurement. Distinguished educator and journalist Harold Davis often tells the story of a journalist working with the American Press Institute in the late 1940s and early 1950s who helped firmly establish the link between clarity and length.

James H. Couey, Jr., of the *Birmingham News* helped conduct seminars for working journalists at Columbia University. Before a seminar began, he would ask each participant to send him a sample of his or her writing so he could test it. Couey repeated his test with dozens of articles. The results were always the same. A sentence is a package for ideas, and readers must struggle to get huge, bulky packages into their minds. By simply making the sentences shorter, he achieved large gains in understanding.

Couey continued to investigate the short sentence phenomenon and discovered some interesting facts:

The following tips can help just about everyone to effectively communicate technical and nontechnical information in letters, reports, news stories, booklets, and most other media that use the written word:

1. *Use short, simple words.* Prefer the simple to the complex. For example, write "use," not "utilize," in most situations.
2. *Use short, simple sentences and paragraphs.* Research shows the average sentence length should be 20 words or less.

3. *Write in the active, not the passive, voice.* The exception to this rule is if you need to emphasize the receiver of the action.
4. *Avoid slang and jargon.* It makes copy more difficult for a mass audience to comprehend. For example, English is a second language for many, and they, as well as others, have considerable difficulty understanding slang and jargon.
5. *Use adjectives and adverbs sparingly.*

6. *Be brief.* For example, keep most news releases to one or two typewritten pages.
7. *Be specific.* Don't communicate in generalities, but be as concrete as possible.
8. *Cite reasons for your opinions.* Support your contentions with statistics, facts, and statements from impartial sources to provide credibility.

---

1. Short sentences usually contained only one idea each.
2. A story could contain both long and short sentences for variety, as long as the average was short.
3. The optimum average for most sentences seemed to be about 17 words.[11]

Pyramid Power Couey achieved tremendous gains in understanding by simply shortening sentences, but he never taught that sentence length was the only element in effective writing. Organization is another important skill that must be mastered.

Journalists often use the inverted pyramid style of writing (figure 7.1). This method organizes a story so the most important points are covered first. The inverted pyramid is equally useful for other types of informative writing. A message should begin by answering five questions: who, what, when, where, and why? These questions are answered in the first one or two paragraphs, called the *lead*. Journalists begin with the question that is most important to the message and proceed in descending order. Each successive paragraph contains details that are less important than the previous paragraph.

Public relations practitioners must master various writing styles. To be an effective communicator it is often necessary to blend seemingly disparate styles to serve multiple purposes for multiple audiences.[12] No matter the style, however, using the inverted pyramid offers several advantages. First, it puts the most important details near the beginning, where readers who skim the message will be more likely to see them. Second, an editor may cut the story from the bottom up if necessary without losing important details. Third, a strong opening gets readers' attention and directs them into the rest of the message.

FIGURE 7.1 **Inverted Pyramid Form**

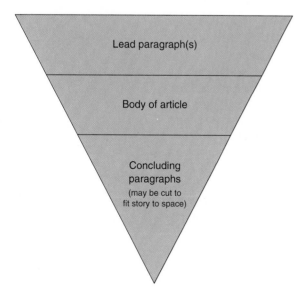

Media Selection

Various media and their audiences are discussed in detail in part 3, but it is appropriate at this point to outline a strategy for media selection. Although it is necessary to construct

Internet Writing Guidelines

1. Don't build a site for your executives; they aren't the target audience. Know the characteristics of your target audience and write for them.
2. Establish and present a logical progression of the ideas.
3. Put blocks of no more than 75 words each on initial site pages. Longer text farther into the site is fine.
4. Don't use clever headlines, but structure your articles with several levels of headlines so a reader can complete a section and continue reading or choose to move on.

5. Write 50 percent less at the beginning of an article. Most Internet users scan copy before deciding to spend time in depth to read an article.
6. Highlight keywords through hypertext links, typeface variations, or color.
7. Use bulleted lists when the copy makes this possible. The computer screen is small, and people tend to glance at key elements quickly.
8. Use inverted pyramid style for most copy with the most important information first. Don't bury your key points.

9. Use one main idea per paragraph.
10. Keep your sentences short, but on the other hand, remember that the key to a good Web site is that you have provided the answers to the questions that the reader has, so you need to be thorough.

Source: Stephen Dembner, "Web Writer Pro: In Search of a Functional Model for Effective Text on the World Wide Web," unpublished master's thesis, University of Memphis, May 2000.

---

messages carefully so they communicate the desired meaning to an audience, it is equally important to choose the proper medium to carry them. For purposes of discussion, media may be classified as controlled or uncontrolled.

The preparation of a news release is different from the preparation of an advertising message, because news depends on a third party to select and deliver the message. This is the basic difference between controlled and uncontrolled media. **Controlled media,** including internal publications, direct mail, posters, and advertising, allow the public relations practitioner to dictate what is published and how it is delivered to the primary audience. **Uncontrolled media,** for which someone else makes decisions about content, include newspapers, television, and radio.

Two controlled media have become especially important to public relations campaigns in the last few years: the World Wide Web and advertising.

The World Wide Web can be considered the first public relations mass medium because it allows managed communication to flow directly between organizations and mass audiences without the gate-keeping functions present in other mass media.[13] For this reason, writing for the Internet requires some special rules, as outlined in spotlight 7.2.

The advent of this new medium as a communication tool for public relations has spurred increased interest in relationship building through the Internet. Public relations practitioners are using the Web extensively for research, two-way communication, and many other applications.[14] Although the potential is great, the impact of public relations principles as applied to Web site design is still relatively unknown; see spotlight 7.3.

> With advertising messages, you have a "controlled" medium and can be assured your message will run as you desired.

High cholesterol comes in all shapes and sizes.

250 | Total Cholesterol | 250

Here's a tip. You can be active, thin, young or old. The truth is that high cholesterol may have as much to do with your family genes as food. So, even a strict diet may not be enough to lower it. The good news is that adding LIPITOR can help. It can lower your total cholesterol 29% to 45%.* And it can also lower your bad cholesterol 39% to 60%.* (*The average effect depends on the dose.) More than 18 million Americans have talked to their doctor about LIPITOR. Maybe you should too. Learn more. Find out if the #1 prescribed cholesterol medicine is right for you. Call us at 1-888-LIPITOR. Find us on the web at www.lipitor.com.

Important information:

LIPITOR® (atorvastatin calcium) is a prescription drug used with diet to lower cholesterol. LIPITOR is not for everyone, including those with liver disease or possible liver problems, women who are nursing, pregnant, or may become pregnant. LIPITOR has not been shown to prevent heart disease or heart attacks.

If you take LIPITOR, tell your doctor about any unusual muscle pain or weakness. This could be a sign of serious side effects. It is important to tell your doctor about any medications you are currently taking to avoid possible serious drug interactions. Your doctor may do simple blood tests to monitor liver function before and during drug treatment. The most commonly reported side effects are gas, constipation, stomach pain and indigestion. They are usually mild and tend to go away.

Please see additional important information on next page.

LIPITOR
atorvastatin calcium tablets
FOR CHOLESSTEROL®

137

Spotlight 7.3

33 Guidelines for Effective Web Sites Based upon Usability Research

Design Considerations

1. Start simple: Begin with a simple Web site design.
2. Strive for consistency: Consistency helps users find information.
3. Avoid textured and colored backgrounds: Make sure your copy is legible.
4. Use blue links: Blue hypertext links are the convention.
5. Avoid clickable links in graphic designs: Users often miss embedded links.
6. Use informative links: Describe pages so users can decide whether they should click on it or not.
7. Use narrow text columns: Column widths of 200 to 400 pixels make reading easier and faster.
8. Minimize page scrolling: Use 20- to 44-line pages.
9. Provide navigational aids: Add "Return to Home Page" and other key links.
10. Have fast download times: Keep your download times short.
11. Provide a text-only version: Not all users, or computers, are of equal ability.
12. Include key information: Be sure to identify your site and provide contact information.

13. Minimize typographical cues: Avoid overusing italics or bold type.

Other General Considerations

14. Identify your audience: Design for specific users. Take their systems into account.
15. Use the team approach: Use ideas from several people whenever possible to design your site.
16. Know your users: Ask, "What are my users like?"
17. Follow your organization's Web policy: Use the Web in an efficient, ethical, and legal manner.
18. Respect copyright guidelines: Obtain written permission to use others' work.
19. Use relative URLs: It will make site maintenance easier.
20. Include a meta tag: Help Web users and search engines find your site.
21. Test your site: Make sure your site works and will download quickly.
22. Understand cognitive processes: Communication is a cognitive activity.

Writing Considerations

23. Write in active voice: Readers understand active voice better.

24. Delete prepositional phrases: Fewer prepositions shorten sentences.
25. Delete excess clauses: Clauses add length but not meaning.
26. Write concisely: Concise sentences promote understanding.
27. Use strong verbs and release trapped verbs: Write clearly and to the point.
28. Use short words: Easy-to-understand words are better.
29. Delete unnecessary qualifiers: Qualify only when necessary.
30. Eliminate wordiness: Fewer words reduce confusion.
31. Use specific, concrete words: Make your message clear.
32. Avoid jargon: Use terms your readers understand.
33. Replace clichés: Clichés can be distracting.

Source: Kirk Hallahan, "Improving Public Relations Web Sites Through Usability Research," *Public Relations Review 27* (Summer 2001), p. 229.

Preliminary studies suggest five guidelines for building relationships with publics using Internet technology:

1. Create a dialogic loop to allow and encourage publics to query the organization sponsoring the site. This includes the availability of an adequate and well-trained staff to handle responses.

2. Make the information useful to all publics who may use the site. Even a specialized Web site should have some general use information. Make information easy to get.

3. Focus on the generation of return visits through the use of interactive strategies. Forums, question-and-answer formats, and chats with experts or corporate officers tend to build visit frequency.

4. Develop an intuitive ease to the interface. The focus of Web sites should be on the organization, product, or information located there and not on the "bells and whistles" that make it possible. Web sites with graphics that take too long to load may turn off some visitors.

5. The conservation of visitors should have priority over providing links to other sites. Too many links to other related sites too early in the design can take visitors away from your Web site before they have the chance to build a relationship.[15]

Many of these principles can also be applied to make an organization's in-house computer network or "intranet" more effective.[16]

Blogging poses both a new challenge and an opportunity for public relations practice. Many are predicting that the Web log phenomenon will forever change public relations as companies come to realize that they will be expected to engage their customers and employees in two-way conversations in real time. Already, a handful of senior executives, including Bob Luty, vice chairman of General Motors, and Jonathan Schwartz, CEO at Sun Microsystems, are active bloggers.[17]

Schwartz's blog (blogs.sun.com /jonathan) averages 400,000 hits a month and each of his posts results in dozens of comments from customers, shareholders, and others.[18]

Before launching a corporate blog,

- Determine the corporation's goal. Internal blogs serve a different purpose from public ones.
- Learn the rules. Blogging is a new form of two-way communication characterized by an informal tone, timely updates, and frank discussion.
- Make sure to devote the time and/or resources to keep the blog up-to-date.
- Study the legal ramifications of launching a blog and establish guidelines so that executives and employees understand what material is off-limits.[19]

Increasingly, the lines between public relations and advertising are blurred in an effort to communicate as effectively as possible. Public relations practitioners often use advertising as a campaign element to accomplish one or more of the following objectives:

1. Develop awareness of an organization.
2. Tie a diverse product line together.
3. Improve consumer relations.
4. Improve the organization's image.
5. Take a stand on a public issue.[20]

The three basic considerations for media selection are the audiences, the timing, and the budget available.

Audiences   Audiences must be the first consideration in any public relations effort (see chapter 5). It is necessary to identify the publics you are trying to reach and determine what will interest them. Uncontrolled media present a special problem to the public relations practitioner because publicity releases must be planned for two audiences. The primary audience, the public for whom the message is intended, is the most important; however, the editor or reporter who selects or rejects the release for publication or broadcast is the first hurdle. Thus, although the release is designed to communicate a particular message to the primary audience, it must first attract the journalistic attention of an editor.

After determining the target audience, it is next necessary to know which media are likely to be interested in particular types of information. By researching available media carefully, a public relations practitioner can become familiar with the types of stories they use and the audiences they attract. He or she may then select the best media for each release and package the information in a way that will attract the editor's attention. Chapter 9 discusses various strategies for media relations in greater detail.

Timing   The timing necessary to reach an audience is the second important factor in media selection. Once the appropriate media are chosen, the time required to reach

TABLE 7.2   Principal Media: Advantages and Disadvantages

Medium	Advantages	Disadvantages
Television	1. Combines sight, sound, and motion attributes 2. Permits physical demonstration of product 3. Believability due to immediacy of message 4. High impact of message 5. Huge audiences 6. Good product identification 7. Popular medium	1. Message limited by restricted time segments 2. No possibility for consumer referral to message 3. Availabilities sometimes difficult to arrange 4. High time costs 5. Waste coverage 6. High production costs 7. Poor color transmission
Magazines	1. Selectivity of audience 2. Reaches more affluent consumers 3. Offers prestige to an advertiser 4. Pass-along readership 5. Good color reproduction	1. Often duplicate circulation 2. Usually cannot dominate in a local market 3. Sometimes high production costs 4. Long closing dates 5. No immediacy of message
Radio	1. Selectivity of geographical markets 2. Good saturation of local markets 3. Ease of changing advertising copy 4. Relatively low cost	1. Message limited by restricted time segments 2. No possibility for consumer referral to message 3. No visual appeal 4. Waste coverage
Newspapers	1. Selectivity of geographical markets 2. Ease of changing advertising copy 3. Reaches all income groups 4. Ease of scheduling advertisements 5. Relatively low cost 6. Good medium for manufacturer/dealer advertising	1. High cost for national coverage 2. Shortness of message life 3. Waste circulation 4. Differences of sizes and formats 5. Rate differentials between local and national markets 6. Poor color reproduction
Direct Mail	1. Extremely selective 2. Message can be very personalized 3. Little competition with other advertisements 4. Easy to measure effect of advertisements 5. Provides easy means for consumer action	1. Often has poor image 2. Can be quite expensive 3. Many restrictive postal regulations 4. Problems in maintaining mailing lists
Outdoor Posters (stationary panels)	1. Selectivity of geographical markets 2. High repetitive value 3. Large physical size 4. Relatively low cost 5. Good color reproduction	1. Often has poor image 2. Message must be short 3. Waste circulation 4. National coverage is expensive 5. Few creative specialists
Point-of-Purchase Displays	1. Presents message at point of sale 2. Great flexibility for creativity 3. Ability to demonstrate product in use 4. Good color reproduction 5. Repetitive value	1. Dealer apathy in installation 2. Long production period 3. High unit cost 4. Shipping problems 5. Space problem
Transit Posters (on moving vehicles)	1. Selectivity of geographical markets 2. Captive audience 3. Very low cost 4. Good color reproduction 5. High repetitive value	1. Limited to a certain class of consumers 2. Waste circulation 3. Surroundings are disreputable 4. Few creative specialists
Movie Trailers	1. Selectivity of geographical markets 2. Captive audience 3. Large physical size 4. Good medium for manufacturer/dealer advertising	1. Cannot be employed in all theaters 2. Waste circulation 3. High production costs 4. No possibility for consumer referral to message

Medium	Advantages	Disadvantages
Advertising Specialties	1. Unique presentation 2. High repetitive value 3. Has a "gift" quality 4. Relatively long life	1. Subject to fads 2. Message must be short 3. May have relatively high unit cost 4. Effectiveness difficult to measure
Pamphlets and Booklets	1. Offer detailed message at point of sale 2. Supplement a personal sales presentation 3. Offer to potential buyers a good referral means 4. Good color reproduction	1. Dealers often fail to use 2. May have a relatively high unit cost 3. Few creative specialists 4. Effectiveness difficult to measure

Source: Reprinted by permission of Publishing Horizons, Inc., from *Advertising Campaigns, Formulations and Tactics,* by Quera, pp. 71–74.

the primary audience is critical. Some publications have backlogs of material and may not be able to get a story out in time. Therefore, the question of when the primary audience receives the message may be just as important as whether it receives the message at all.

Budgets   Budgets, the third important factor in media selection, are always limited, and frequently they, in turn, limit media selection. Usually the first decision that must be made is whether the message needs to be delivered by more than one medium. If a media mix is desirable, it may be necessary to consider cost when deciding which ones to use. Remember that while the costs of controlled media, such as advertising, are obvious, costs associated with uncontrolled media must also be counted.

Table 7.2 contrasts advantages and disadvantages of several different media. Considering these points with regard to audiences, time, and budget will help public relations practitioners select the media most appropriate to their messages.

HOW TO BE HEARD

There are times when we not only *want* to be heard, but we also *need* to be heard. Our message needs to be heard because our organizations may want to influence legislation, create goodwill among various publics, provide answers in times of crises, attract capable employees, increase sales, or raise money. There are many more reasons why we need to make sure our message is heard and acted upon, but these illustrate the variety of the reasons organizations must communicate with target audiences.

How, though, can your message be heard and acted upon? Much like passing through a funnel, the message must pass through four basic stages in which the audience may selectively decide whether to be involved with the communication:

1. Attention
2. Understanding
3. Retention
4. Action

Each of the stages must be understood and used if you are to have your message really heard.[21]

Attention (Selective Attention)

The various publics with which an organization needs to communicate attend to only a few of the messages that they are bombarded with daily. This is called **selective attention.** For your message to be heard, it must first be attended to. It is necessary to analyze the stakeholders from the stakeholders' point of view. What will attract their attention? What do we know about them that will help build rapport with them? For example, though the issues may be the same, it may take different messages to reach legislators than it does to reach newspaper editors.

Selective attention is a communication concept often overlooked by those who would rather have a "low-key" approach to public relations. However, at times it is necessary to attract attention. On those occasions it may be helpful, even essential, to have a positive image. Like it or not, every group, organization, and individual has an image. Some images are good, some are not quite so good. But images are important to getting attention. Image building involves practically every part of your organization's activities and is often what is seen as "total communication." This is a first step.

Beyond image building, getting audiences to attend to your messages involves both the mechanics and the content of your message. For example, the way you package your message to the chair of the Senate Subcommittee on Price Controls may determine whether your message is attended to. Some of the mechanical factors affecting attention to the message may include timing, setting, and authority. For instance, do you send out a news release about the importance of the independent petroleum marketers just after a price increase has gone into effect? Or would it be more effective to issue that release some months before the price increase? Do you send the release out single spaced, 12 pages in length on both sides of hot pink paper (setting)? Do you use sources (authority) that only you know are experts in their disciplines?

Understanding (Selective Perception)

The content of the message determines not only whether the message is attended to, but, to a great extent, whether it is understood. Our experiences and our role in society (or frame of reference) shape the way we perceive things. But no one has had identical experiences. Each of us is unique. So each of us perceives things slightly differently. Result: Our unconscious assumption is that the world is as we see it. We tend to believe the way we see things is "correct" and that those who don't share our perceptions are "incorrect" or have "distorted views," as shown in figure 7.2.

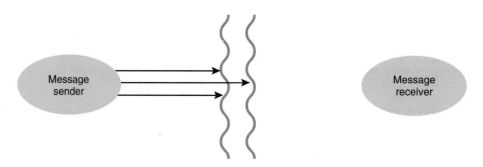

FIGURE 7.2   Communication Barrier: Difference

Thus, the major obstacles in communication are the failure to acknowledge differences and the failure to successfully negotiate those differences in perceptions. Is your experience more "true" than the experience of others? From a communication viewpoint, the perceptions of each of us are "true" because they reflect what we know and what we are. If you had someone else's frame of reference, you might see things exactly as he or she does. Consider the following cases:

1. Though messages may be sent in figure 7.3, no communication occurs (hence, no understanding) because there is no shared experience.

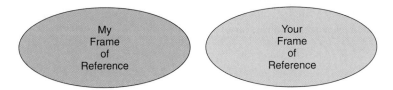

FIGURE 7.3 **No Communication**

2. Some understanding begins to occur in figure 7.4, however, because there is a common or shared frame of reference (shaded area).

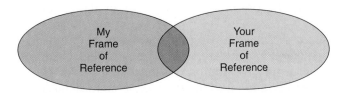

FIGURE 7.4 **Communication Occurs in the Shaded Area**

How do we find common or shared frames of reference? We must find out what other people think and why they think that way. Why? So you can attack the problem—send the message in the context of your message receiver's frame of reference (his or her knowledge, social-cultural role, attitudes, communication skills, needs, wants), not yours. The reason you are communicating is that his or her frame of reference is different from yours. The objective is to understand your receiver's perceptions—not so you can change them or criticize them, but in order to broaden them so he or she has an understanding of your **selective perceptions** and thus has a better ability to support, or at least to not obstruct, the fulfilling of your objectives. For example, look at legislative issues from the view of the legislator and other groups seeking his or her support, not from your view. You find your stakeholders' frames of references through research, both formal and informal.

Retention and Action (Selective Retention and Action)

A message may be attended to and understood, but it must still be retained in order to be acted upon. Retention and the desire to act are increased if the message receiver can answer the following questions:

1. What's in it for me?
2. Is it compatible with my values, needs, and beliefs?
3. Is it easy to remember and do? (Divide complex issues into a number of simple issues.)
4. Is it easy to try with little or no risk?
5. Can I observe the consequences of my actions?
6. Is my action positively reinforced by subsequent messages?

Even the most effective communicators don't successfully communicate all the time. Many factors of which we are unaware, or over which we have no control, may distort our messages. But by conscientiously applying the principles of communication, the percentage of success will increase.

Case Study

University Hospital

University Hospital, located in a city of about 1.2 million people, is the largest private hospital in the United States, with more than 2,000 beds and just over 50,000 patients annually. The hospital employs 6,000 persons and has a medical staff of more than 1,300 and an annual budget of more than $750 million.

Like all hospitals, University Hospital has faced tough financial challenges in the era of managed health care. As the hospital prepares for its centennial celebration, beginning in 18 months, it is looking at public relations strategies that will continue to position it as the city's leader in hospital care.

As the public relations director for University Hospital, you have been asked to assess the potential impact of contemporary demographic trends in the United States and to recommend appropriate action in relation to the upcoming centennial celebration.

Questions

1. What stakeholder groups would be involved?
2. What demographic characteristics would you expect to find in each group?
3. What responses do you want to induce in each stakeholder group?
4. What messages do you want to send to each group?
5. What channels of communication will you suggest to convey your messages to each stakeholder group?
6. What communication strategies would you expect to be most productive in this situation?

The public relations practitioner as part of the management team of an organization must be involved in the decision-making process to ensure that the organization takes positive, socially responsible actions. These actions, then, become the source of much of the organization's communication.

Often the process used to implement a public relations plan can be seen as an attempt to spread, or diffuse, information throughout the organization's primary publics. The diffusion process is how new ideas are adopted in society. The critical paths through which new ideas, products, or technologies spread include awareness, interest, evaluation, trial, and adoption. Mass media is key to the first two of these paths, while personal contact may be more important in the last three paths.

The concept of stakeholder management provides a good framework in which to visualize an organization's environment and to differentiate among the stakeholders. The goal in stakeholder management is to develop maximum overall cooperation between stakeholders and the organization's objectives.

The public relations practitioner is the key communicator within an organization. Writing remains the primary tool of the communicator, but practitioners must master a variety of writing styles. While the inverted pyramid structure is especially important because it is used by most journalists, other styles, such as writing for the Internet, are also necessary.

Another important aspect of the communication process is media selection. The three basic considerations for media selection are the needs and desires of the audiences, the optimum timing for the message, and the budget available for the medium.

Finally, if you want your message to be heard, you need to make sure you get your audiences' attention, understanding, retention, and action. Unfortunately, to be heard a message must go through a "funnel" of selective attention, selective perception, selective retention, and selective action. Therefore, the message is often lost at various stages in the process unless steps are taken to improve the likelihood that the message will be heard.

The final step in the process of public relations, measuring the effects of these messages, is discussed in chapter 9.

Summary

For self-testing and additional chapter resources, go to the Online Learning Center at **www.mhhe.com/lattimore3e.**

Key Terms

active public
aware public
controlled media
diffusion of information
feedback
intervening public
latent public

moderating public
primary public
selective attention
selective perception
stakeholder analysis
stakeholders
uncontrolled media

Notes

1. "Opinions of the Publics," Public Relations Society of America, New York, 16 mm film.

2. "The Pepsi Hoax: What Went Right?" Case study prepared by Pepsi Cola Public Affairs, Somers, NY, 1993.

3. Ray Stitle, Delta Beverage, in a speech for the Memphis Chapter of PRSA, September 13, 1995.

4. Ibid., p. 3.

5. Ibid.

6. Frank Walsh, *Public Relations Writer in a Computer Age* (Englewood Cliffs, NJ: Prentice-Hall, 1986), p. 10.

7. Herbert F. Lionberger, *Adoption of New Ideas and Practices* (Ames: Iowa State University Press, 1960), p. 32.

8. *Mountain Bell Submission,* Public Relations Society of America Silver Anvil Awards Competition, 1983.

9. Ibid.

10. Burton St. John, "Whither P.R. Writing?" *Public Relations Tactics* (April 2002).

11. Craig E. Aronoff et al., *Getting Your Message Across* (St. Paul, MN: West, 1981), pp. 28–31.

12. Cynthia M. King, "The Write Stuff: Teaching the Introductory Public Relations Writing Course," *Public Relations Review* 27 (Winter 2001), pp. 27–46.

13. Candace White and Niranjan Raman, "The World Wide Web as a Public Relations Medium: The Use of Research, Planning and Evaluation in Web Site Development," *Public Relations Review* 25 (Winter 1999), p. 405.

14. Lynne M. Sallot, Lance V. Porter, and Carolina Acosta-Alzuru, "Practitioners' Web Use and Perceptions of Their Own Roles and Power: A Qualitative Study," *Public Relations Review* 30 (September 2004), p. 269.

15. Michael L. Kent and Maureen Taylor, "Building Dialogic Relationships Through the World Wide Web," *Public Relations Review* 24 (Fall 1998), pp. 326–31.

16. Marie E. Murgolo-Poore, Leyland F. Pitt, and Michael T. Ewing, "Intranet Effectiveness: A Public Relations Paper-and-Pencil Checklist," *Public Relations Review* 28 (February 2002), p. 113.

17. Scott Morrison, "The Rise of the Corporate Blogger," *Financial Times* (July 15, 2005), p. 8.

18. "Sun CEO sees competitive advantage in blogging," www.usatoday.com. Retrieved June 25, 2006.

19. Morrison, p. 8.

20. Suzanne Sparks FitzGerald, "Tips for Using Advertising in Public Relations," *Public Relations Quarterly* 46 (Fall 2001), pp. 43–45.

21. Dan Lattimore and Derry Eynon, "How to Be Heard," presentation for the Independent Petroleum Dealers Association, Vail, CO, 1976.

CHAPTER 8

Evaluating Public Relations Effectiveness

PREVIEW

"Hi, Karen! Did you find that book I recommended to you?"

"Yes, thanks. It was in the library."

"Great! Did you get a chance to read it this weekend?"

"As a matter of fact, I read the whole thing. Well, I'll talk to you later."

Few of us would find a conversation like this very satisfying. If you recommend something to a friend and he or she follows up, you naturally want to know whether they liked it.

Likewise, public relations practitioners want to evaluate the public's attitude following a new awareness of a product or service. It is usually not enough to know simply that the audience is now informed; evaluation of results should be thorough and specific enough to tell us whether changes in attitude or behavior are likely to result.

Evaluation is an essential step practitioners take to assess the effectiveness of a public relations effort, to quantify that effectiveness for management, and to adjust tactics if necessary while the campaign is still in progress. Evaluation is all about demonstrating to management the value of public relations.

In this process, value is even more important than volume. The number of news releases sent to the media, or even the number used by the media, is no longer an acceptable measure of effectiveness. Rather, practitioners today gauge effectiveness by measuring changes in the public's behavior, attitudes, knowledge, and awareness. Some of the tools that capture these data are impact analysis, audience coverage, audience response, campaign impact, and environmental mediation.

In this chapter we talk about an open-system model for measuring public relations effectiveness; this takes into account environmental factors and before-and-after comparisons.

EVALUATION FOR PUBLIC RELATIONS PROGRAMS AND ACTIVITIES

We have divided the process of public relations into four related functions: research, planning, action and communication, and evaluation. In reality, however, the methods discussed in chapter 5 and the material in this chapter are simply different applications of the research function. For the sake of illustration and emphasis, we have separated the two chapters, but much of what we say here about evaluating public relations programs relates directly back to the research methods mentioned in chapter 5. Also, as noted earlier, the importance of the Internet and Web sites to effective public relations is widely accepted. However, early research seems to indicate that few, if any, practitioners use the basics of public relations research, planning, and evaluation of Web management.[1]

TRADITIONAL EVALUATION

Most public relations efforts in the past have not been measured, or not been measured adequately, to provide answers to key questions such as the following: Why did the campaign work or fail? What were the most effective tactics? and What would have happened had we made a change midway through the campaign? Public relations agencies and departments have often not been able to sell management or clients on the necessity of evaluation. One noted practitioner has argued that less than 5 percent of public relations programs have been effectively evaluated.[2]

Traditionally, public relations evaluation has been used to measure output, including the number of press releases used, the hits on the Web site, and the number of video clips used. This is typically the implementation phase of a public relations effort. These implementation measures of output are necessary to provide input into the evaluation, but they are not sufficient to provide an assessment of quality, cost-effectiveness, or

An Internet survey company is often used to create an online evaluation survey.

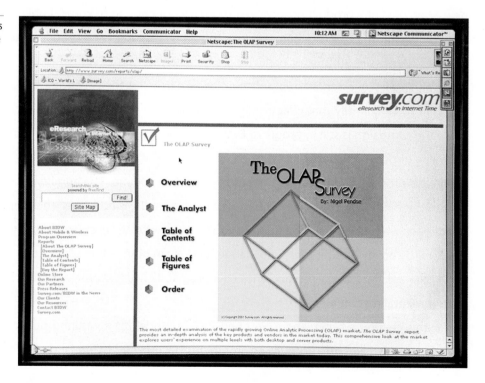

opportunities for improvement. Instead, the practitioner should be measuring changes in behavior, attitudes, knowledge, and awareness.

There are at least three levels of evaluation of public relations efforts: preparation for the public relations program, implementation of the effort, and **impact analysis** of the program.

1. *Preparation.* Evaluating preparation may involve examining the adequacy of the background information that you gathered, the appropriateness of the message content and format, and the quality of the messages.

2. *Implementation.* Evaluating implementation involves measuring the number of messages sent (distribution), the number of messages placed in the media, the number of people receiving the message, and the number of people who attend to the message.

3. *Impact.* When impact is evaluated, practitioners measure the number or percentage of the audience who learn the message content, who change their opinions, who change attitudes, and who behave in the desired fashion. They may also determine if the problem is solved or the goal is achieved.

To move toward a more successful evaluation effort, all three levels must be examined, not just the traditional implementation measures.

Although presented last, evaluation is not the final stage of the public relations process. In actual practice, **evaluation** is frequently the beginning of a new effort. The research function overlaps the planning, action, and evaluation functions. It is an interdependent process that, once set in motion, has no beginning or end.

THE NEED FOR EVALUATION RESEARCH

To help explain how evaluation can be involved in virtually every phase of a program, figure 8.1 is divided into three evaluation segments:

1. *Implementation Checking.* The central question in this start-up assessment step is, To what degree is the target audience being reached? Regardless of how complete the planning process may have been, it will still be necessary to determine the difference between *planned* and *actual* implementation. Variations from the original plan must be analyzed and explained so that a decision can be made to either modify the plan or correct the discrepancies.

2. *In-Progress Monitoring.* Periodically during the program, actions undertaken should be reviewed and, if necessary, modified. This process is often called **formative evaluation.** These reviews can be planned for regular intervals to determine the effectiveness of the program in meeting its objectives. Any unanticipated results can be assessed and factored into the evaluation. The variance between actual and anticipated progress at each point can be examined for its effect on the overall outcome. Regular monitoring helps determine why some results differ significantly from the original plan and prevents unwelcome surprises.

3. *Outcome Evaluation.* The final step is to assess the program's end results. This process is called **summative evaluation.** Once again, objectives and results are compared to determine the variance. At this point, all prior evaluations become important for explaining the context in which the program was implemented and for interpreting the results. An evaluation report transmits this information, along with any suggestions for planning future efforts, to an appropriate decision maker.

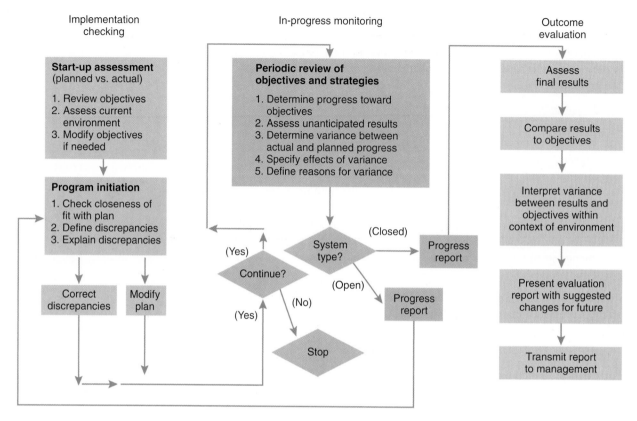

FIGURE 8.1 Components of an Evaluation Plan

Research in public relations should be continuous, constantly evaluating the process and its environment and providing new information to sustain it. Learning about the failures and successes of a public relations campaign provides information that can be used to plan more precisely for the next effort. Evaluation research is also valuable in assessing an existing campaign. This point is illustrated in the Cedar Springs Community Hospital Integrating Case Study. Research made a tremendous impact on the planning and action steps taken in the case. In this final episode, research helps determine the effectiveness of the total effort.

Integrating Case Study

Cedar Springs Community Hospital
Segment 4

Approximately one year after the program to improve the perceptions of employees regarding the quality of patient care began, follow-up research was conducted. This evaluation process began at the same point as the original research. Using the methodology of the initial employee survey, 300 names were once again chosen at random from the 1,226 employees. Each of the selected individuals received a questionnaire in the mail similar to the one used to begin the process.

Four key factors from the original survey had been selected as objectives for improvement during the preceding year. These same factors were measured again in the evaluation survey to determine how much progress had been made. The following comparisons were produced:

Factors	Average Ratings Start	Average Ratings End
1. Quality of care	6.6	7.0
2. Patients' understanding of procedures	5.7	6.2
3. Courtesy and respect shown to patients	7.4	7.8
4. Patient call lights answered <5 minutes	56%	82%

Obviously, a noticeable and positive shift in employee perceptions of the hospital's overall performance had taken place. In addition to the quantitative evidence, which showed gains in every category over the previous year, qualitative indicators also supported this conclusion. Another focus group demonstrated considerable improvement in employees' feelings about the quality of care available. This was reinforced through letters from employees and comments made during monthly employee group meetings.

Although employee perceptions did not rise to the same level as those of recently released patients in earlier surveys, the improvements were consistent and strong. Therefore, management concluded that a program to continue feedback to employees from patients would be an important part of future employee communication programs.

Another important reason evaluation research is a necessity for public relations programs is that it enhances organizational support. Public relations professionals must assume the same responsibility for effectiveness as their management colleagues do. Organizational resources are always limited, and competition for them is keen. Public relations managers must be able to demonstrate effectiveness in ways that can be measured against other competing functions, as Robert Marker, manager of press services for Armstrong Cork, reveals in mini-case 8.1.

MEASURING THE WORTH OF PUBLIC RELATIONS EFFORTS

Too many public relations programs have been eliminated or severely cut back because no "value" could be attached to them. The harsh realities of corporate existence make it necessary for public relations practitioners to demonstrate the worth of what they do. Particularly in difficult economic situations, every aspect of organizational activity is measured by its relative benefit to the firm. Public relations departments that cannot demonstrate their

Mini·Case 8.1 | The Importance of Evaluation

I remember an occasion, some years ago, which started me thinking about the need for some kind of measurement device and internal reporting system to help explain the public relations function.

I was asked by a marketing executive at Armstrong to come to his office and inform him, as succinctly as possible, just what it was he was getting for what he was spending on public relations. It really didn't bother me at the time, because we had had these inquiries before, and I was pretty sure I could handle it. I came prepared with a considerable volume of newspaper clippings, magazine features, and case histories that we had produced in support of his product line that year.

I laid all this out in front of him. . . . After an appropriate interval, I pointed out that all this publicity—if strung end to end—would reach from his office located in the west wing of the building, clear across the center wing to the east wing, down the stairs, and out into the main lobby, and there'd still be enough left over to paper one and a half walls of his office. (That was a favored "measurement" device back in those days. We used to have our secretaries total the column inches and then convert it all into linear feet of hallway space.) And then it came, the question no one had ever asked before: "But what's all this worth to us?"

I stammered for a moment and said something to the effect that I thought the material spoke for itself. After all, this was highly coveted editorial space we were talking about. . . . I said it would be difficult to attach a specific value to it.

He smiled. "My boy," he said, "I have to attach a value to everything in this operation. . . . Why don't you go back and write me a memo outlining clearly what this function does for us, and then we'll talk about your budget for next year."

Questions

1. What did Robert Marker fail to do in preparing for his interview?
2. Is it appropriate for a manager to attach a value to everything in his or her operation? Why or why not?
3. What does your answer to question 2 imply for public relations practitioners?

Source: Robert K. Marker, "The Armstrong/PR Data Management System," *Public Relations Review* 3 (Winter 1977), pp. 51–52.

---

value to the organization will not be in a position to influence the policy decisions that affect their own fate.

Measurements That Matter

The reality that everything in an organization, particularly a for-profit enterprise, must have "value" attached is the lesson of mini-case 8.1. Public relations efforts are not exempt from this reality. PR can become more influential if its results can be linked directly to things that the client organization sees as valuable. To the extent the following issues can be linked to public relations performance, these efforts will be appreciated in most corporate cultures:

- How can the PR program drive sales?
- What return on investment (ROI) does the organization get for its PR expenditures?
- To what extent can an increase in the company's share price (market capitalization) be attributed to the efforts to build a positive reputation through PR?
- How do PR efforts contribute to a positive brand image?
- How does PR work with other types of marketing communication to create value and make a marketing budget more effective?

What can be measured in public relations efforts? Of course many things about public relations efforts will remain "intangible" but many outcomes can be measured and attributed to PR. While almost anything can have some form of measurement attached to it here are some of the most common areas of PR measurement activities.

Media Coverage and Impact   While "clip counts" and "impressions" are still used as stand-alone measures of effectiveness in public relations, there is widespread recognition of the insufficiency of such metrics. However, these traditional methods can be enhanced significantly by incorporating measures that break results out by the "tone" of coverage received. The use of content analysis to determine the degree of favorableness of media impressions or clips helps to understand the results in positive or negative impact.

Event Measurement   The degree to which media coverage is increased in positive impressions due to an organization's participation in an event such as a trade show or charity benefit as well as the impact on key stakeholders who actually visited the exhibit or program.

Word-of-Mouth and Other "Social Media"   Traditional word-of-mouth recommendations and discussions are consistently cited as the most powerful influencers of public opinion. Social media, such as blogs, *myspace.com,* and *YouTube* are increasingly effective ways to reach opinion leaders. Measuring the amount and tone of coverage in these online exchanges is the purpose of Nielsen BuzzMetrics, for example.

Web-Based Messages   While number of page views and unique visitors have traditionally been a primary measure for online placement, new approaches for tracking the impact of PR Web-based initiatives are coming from services such as *Yahoo News, Google News, comScore,* and *Nielsen NetRatings.*

Corporate Reputation Enhancement   Measures of the qualitative and quantitative positive impact on an organization's reputation among various stakeholders (customers, suppliers, shareholders, employees) can be achieved through the use of marketing-mix models. These complex statistical methods can help organizations assess the relative return on investment (ROI) from various methods of communication as well as their cumulative impact.[3]

Measurement Strategies

The concept of measurement itself is not new to the practice of public relations. All public relations practitioners need to understand the following:

- Their relationship with media representatives
- The impact their messages have on publics they want to reach
- The number of people reached
- How many media use their messages
- What value their efforts have for the organization[4]

The problem, as Robert Marker discovered, is that the rest of the business world has been using different standards. Marker's measurement system was quantifiable (linear feet of hallway), and it accurately reflected the effort that had been expended. When faced with the devastating question of "worth," however, the measurement strategy could not provide any data. Because the nature of public relations is intangible, assigning a value to its activities is difficult. Often the problem leads practitioners to use erroneous measures or to incorrectly apply measures.

Like every aspect of public relations practice, evaluation needs careful planning. Ideally, the evaluation effort should be planned from the inception of the program. An evaluation attempt that is tacked on after a program is finished will produce incomplete and generally inappropriate data. When evaluation is part of the overall plan, each component can be constructed with an eye toward measuring its success later.

Measurement by Objectives   The use of management by objectives (MBO), or any similar planning process, will help alleviate the measurement problem facing public relations. Although MBO is most frequently used for evaluating individual employees, its basic elements can also be applied to programs, projects, and work groups. The object is to prepare advance statements, usually during the planning phase, concerning legitimate expectations from a given effort. These must be mutually agreed on by all those involved before the action occurs. When the set time for evaluation arrives, objectives can be compared with accomplishments to assess the degree of success. The exact process used varies among organizations, but here are the basic MBO steps:

1. *Work Group Involvement.* If more than one person will be working on the project, the entire group should be involved in setting the objectives. This is important so that no portion of the task is overlooked and each contributor feels committed to the effort.

2. *Manager-Subordinate Involvement.* Once the objectives of the group are established, each subordinate should work with the manager of the project to define a set of individual objectives. These keep the project moving by ensuring that everyone understands his or her role.

3. *Determination of Intermediate Objectives.* This step defines a series of objectives along the way toward the overall target. Setting intermediate objectives permits in-progress evaluation to be done more precisely and makes it possible to consider midcourse corrections before the project gets out of hand.

4. *Determination of Measures of Achievement.* The point when the effort will be considered complete should be specified in terms of either a time element or the achievement of a stated objective.

5. *Review, Evaluation, and Recycling.* Because no objective can be defined with absolute precision or achieved perfectly, it is important to use information gained from each evaluation process to improve the planning for the next public relations effort.

Impact Analysis   Measuring the impact or results of a public relations effort is always difficult and never totally objective. As we have discussed in this chapter, however, the more public relations practitioners can quantitatively measure the effects of their work, the better they will be able to plan future efforts and demonstrate their value to organizational decision makers. In this section, we offer four dimensions of measurement that can be applied to assess the impact of any public relations campaign, regardless of its size: *audience coverage, audience response, campaign impact,* and *environmental mediation.*

Audience Coverage   Perhaps the first point that must be documented in evaluating any public relations effort is whether the intended audiences were reached. Other questions should be answered in the initial phase: To what extent was each target audience exposed to the various messages? Which unintended audiences also received the messages?

Two basic measures are used to help answer these questions. First, accurate records must be kept of what messages were prepared and where they were sent. Second, a system must be used to keep track of which releases were used and by whom. Although the first measure is the easiest to calculate, it is worthless without the second for comparison. Massive amounts of publicity have no value unless some of it actually reaches the intended audience. Therefore, some method must be devised to accurately measure the use of publicity and the coverage of events.

Essentially, such measurement can be accomplished if the practitioner and/or other staff members keep a careful check on target media and maintain clipping files. This, of course, is easier for print than for broadcast media, but some radio and television stations give periodic reports to public relations practitioners if requested. In addition, clipping services that monitor both print and broadcast media provide regular reports for a fee. Such a service must be selected carefully, based on the recommendations of other users concerning its accuracy.

The measurement of **audience coverage** involves more than just the ratio of releases sent compared with releases used. The practitioner must also be able to specify what audiences (both intended and unintended) were reached by which media. This type of data is available from *readership surveys* and audience rating information obtainable through media advertising sales departments. Audience profiles for each publication or broadcast station can be calculated with the amount of space or time used to yield a complete measure of audience coverage. Such data can be reported in terms of total column inches (for print media), airtime per audience (for broadcast media) for each release or event, or hits for a Web page. John Pavlik, John Vastyan, and Michael Maher used a readership survey at a medical center to determine that employees who were more integrated into the organization were more likely to read a company newsletter—the newsletter could then be designed to meet the needs of this public.[5] For more of a bottom-line effect, however, many practitioners translate media time and space into dollar values based on prevailing advertising rates. Although it may be effective in illustrating a point to management, it has very little validity in determining what the effect was of that exposure on the intended audience.

Audience Response   Once it is determined that a message has reached its intended audience, the practitioner must evaluate that audience's response. Frequently, this type of information can be obtained through various message pretesting methods like those discussed in this chapter and in chapter 5. Samples of each target audience are exposed to various messages before they are released. The resulting data help predict whether the message will cause a favorable or an unfavorable reaction. It can also determine if the message attracts attention, arouses interest, or gains audience understanding. By applying good sampling techniques and questionnaire design (chapter 5), accurate predictions are possible, and problems can be corrected before messages are released. Some messages, however, such as spot news or stories written from releases, cannot be measured in advance because they are not controlled by the practitioner. Thus, it is necessary to measure audience response using the survey techniques discussed in chapter 5. Frequently, audience response can be predicted by tracking media treatment of stories in terms of favorable, neutral, and unfavorable tendencies, as we see later in this chapter.

Messages can also be pretested using *readability studies*. The basic premise of these tests is that written copy will be ineffective if it is too difficult to read. Most methods for measuring readability generate an index score that translates to an approximate educational level required for understanding the material. For example, *Time* and *Reader's Digest* are written at what is termed an 11th- or 12th-grade level. This indicates that their readers are primarily persons with at least a high school education. A great deal of controversy exists over which formula is the most accurate and what factors are necessary to compute readability. Readability tests may, however, be useful in public relations efforts to tailor writing styles toward target publications. The index score of a news release compared with the score of the publication for which it is intended should indicate whether the two are compatible.

Remember that the simplest writing is not always the best. Meaning may be lost through oversimplification as easily as through complexity. Abstract or complex concepts cannot be adequately expressed in simple, short sentences using one- and two-syllable words. The important point is to match the written message to the publication and audience for which it is intended. This textbook, for example, was written for college students who are studying public relations, not for casual readers. Frequently, editors of internal publications for highly technical organizations must avoid talking down to their readers as much as they avoid technical jargon.

Campaign Impact   In addition to considering audience response to individual messages, the practitioner must be concerned with the impact of the campaign as a whole. In this case, the whole is not equal to the sum of the parts. If a campaign is correctly researched and planned, its elements will interact to produce an effect that is much greater than the sum of the response to the individual messages. If the mix is not right, however, the elements of the campaign combined, no matter how individually excellent, may fall far short of the goal.

Therefore, it is important to measure the cumulative impact of a public relations campaign, keeping in mind the goals developed in the planning phase. This can be done only after the campaign has been in progress long enough to achieve some results. Effects are generally attitudinal, although they can also be behavioral. If one campaign goal is to maintain or increase favorable attitudes toward an organization among members of certain publics, research methods such as the organizational image surveys described in chapter 5 can be used to gauge success. Usually this calls for both pretests and posttests or for a series of surveys to track attitude trends. In addition, certain actions by members of a public can be measured, like complaints, inquiries about services, and requests for reprints.

Environmental Mediation   Practitioners must realize that the public relations campaign is not the only influence on the attitudes and behaviors of their publics. Public relations campaigns exist in an environment of social processes that can have as much or more effect on the goals of the effort as the prepared messages do. For this reason, the measured results must be interpreted in light of various other forces in operation. Failure to reach a goal may not be failure at all when unforeseen negative conditions have arisen. Likewise, a striking success may not be entirely attributable to the public relations campaign when positive environmental forces were also present at the time. Therefore, techniques such as environmental monitoring and others discussed in chapter 5 should be used to evaluate the results of a campaign.

One method used to check for environmental influences, even when the practitioner has a small budget and staff, is focus group interviewing. Focus groups are composed of individuals randomly selected from a public who meet to discuss the campaign. The group should be presented with the elements of the campaign and then directed through a discussion of its effects and the causes of those effects. A skillful interviewer will keep the discussion on the subject without disturbing candor or the free flow of ideas. Focus groups should be asked to discuss their reactions to the elements of the campaign and assess the campaign's overall effect. They can also help interpret data obtained in the campaign impact stage in relation to historical, social, and political events that may have had an effect.

These four stages of measurement can help a public relations practitioner to more completely assess the results of a campaign and plan effective future efforts. These stages of measurement also provide the same kind of real-world data that managers in other areas of an organization use to support their activities.

Sources of Measurement Error

Here are some common mistakes in the measurement of public relations effectiveness:

1. *Volume Is Not Equal to Results.* Too often, the working assumption is that if one press release is effective, three will be three times as effective. As Marker learned, a large stack or even a long chain of press clippings may be proof of effort, but results in terms of the effect of those clippings on the publics for which they were intended cannot be measured by volume. Even audience measurement devices designed to count the number of people exposed to a message do not show whether those exposed actually paid any attention or, if they did, what effect the message had on them.

2. *Estimate Is Not Measurement.* Relying on experience and intuition to gauge the effectiveness of public relations efforts is no longer acceptable as objective measurement. Experts know that appearances, even to the trained eye, can be deceiving. Guesswork has no place in a measurement system. It can be appealing and comfortable because it is easy to accomplish and flattering to the expert. However, when it comes to budget requests, managers like the one Marker encountered demand hard facts.

3. *Samples Must Be Representative.* Many wrong decisions about the future of a public relations campaign have been based on a few favorable comments that were either volunteered or collected unsystematically. Several dangers exist in doing this: Only those with positive (or negative) comments may volunteer them; some people, when asked, tend to give the response they think the interviewer wants to hear; or the selection of interviewers may be unintentionally biased. Samples must be selected scientifically and systematically to avoid such errors.

4. *Effort Is Not Knowledge.* One of the most common public relations objectives is to increase the public's knowledge about a particular subject. Sometimes practitioners assume a direct relationship between the amount of effort they expend in communicating a message and the amount of knowledge a public acquires. This erroneous assumption leads to a problem similar to the volume error discussed earlier. The study of human learning suggests that after a certain level of knowledge is reached, the rate of learning slows in most people. Therefore, in spite of any communicator's best efforts, all publics will eventually reach a knowledge level at which very little additional learning occurs.

5. *Knowledge Is Not Favorable Attitude.* Communication is often assumed successful if the public gained knowledge of the subject of the message. Even when pretest and posttest results indicate an increase in knowledge, it cannot be assumed that more favorable attitudes have also resulted. A high degree of name recall or awareness is not necessarily an indication that the public relations effort has been effective. Familiarity does not necessarily lead to positive opinion.

6. *Attitude Is Not Behavior.* Although positive public opinion may be a legitimate goal of public relations, it is incorrect to assume that favorable attitudes will result in desired behavior. When members of a particular public have favorable attitudes toward a client or an organization, they will probably not consciously oppose that person or group. On the other hand, they still may not actively support the goals of the public relations campaign. Our discussion of latent, aware, and active publics in chapter 5 emphasized this point. Practitioners must be aware of the need to predict behavior, or at least potential behavior, when measuring public opinion.

CLOSED-SYSTEM EVALUATION

Mark P. McElreath describes two models of public relations research into which most measurement efforts can be categorized: open and closed evaluation systems.[6] A **closed-system evaluation** limits its scope to the messages and events planned for the campaign and their effects on the intended publics. This is the model of public relations evaluation most frequently used. The intent of the system is to test the messages and media of a public relations campaign before they are presented to the intended publics. This pretest strategy is designed to uncover miscalculations that may have gone unnoticed in the planning stage. The posttest evaluation is conducted after the campaign has been under way long enough to produce results. Posttest data can be compared with pretest results and campaign objectives to evaluate the effectiveness of the effort. These results also provide input for planning the next campaign.

Pretest/Posttest Design

The following factors are normally considered in the standard pretest and posttest evaluation design:

1. *Productions.* An accounting is conducted of every public relations tool used in the campaign (press releases, press kits, booklets, videos, Web sites, etc.). The amount of material actually produced and the total cost of production yield important cost-effectiveness information. The amount of time and budget devoted to each segment of a public relations effort can be reassessed with this type of data.

2. *Distribution.* The evaluation design includes the channels through which the messages of the campaign are distributed. Clippings collected by professional services are often used to measure how many stories were actually printed. The number of radio and television stations that picked up the story can be important information. These kinds of data are perhaps most frequently used to evaluate public relations campaigns. Note that although these kinds of data provide a reasonable measure of the efficiency of the campaign, distribution data do not really address the issue of effectiveness.

3. *Interest.* Reader interest surveys determine what people read in various types of publications. A representative sample of the total potential reading audience is surveyed to obtain a quantitative measure of which items attract more interest. These are relatively good measures of what readers actually consume, but they do not measure comprehension or the effect of the message on the reader. Television and radio use similar survey methods to determine what programs and times people prefer.

4. *Reach.* Reader interest surveys not only provide information concerning whether a story was read but also describe the people who read it. This information can be valuable because messages frequently reach publics other than those for whom they are intended. The efficiency of a message is the extent to which it actually reaches the intended audience. A reasonably accurate measure of which audiences are being reached by which messages is imperative to any evaluation effort. Television and radio ratings services provide information concerning the characteristics of audiences at various times of the day.

5. *Understanding.* Although it is important to determine whether the target audience is being reached, it is equally important to know whether the audience can understand the message. A public relations campaign cannot be considered successful if the public does not get the point. Frequently, readability tests are applied to printed messages to measure their reading ease. As we have already discussed, readability

is measured according to sentence length and the number of syllables in the words used. Much criticism has been directed at them, but they remain standard instruments for pretest evaluation.

6. *Attitudes.* Creating and maintaining positive attitudes or changing negative ones is a central purpose of all public relations activity. Therefore, measuring attitudes, or preferably attitude change, is a highly prized form of evaluation. Frequently a pretest/posttest measurement is conducted to determine the amount of change in the attitudes of target publics that can be attributed to the public relations campaign.

Measuring attitudes is a sophisticated behavioral science technique that presents many opportunities for error. Few practitioners attempt major attitudinal studies without the help of professionals who specialize in this type of measurement. Several of the research techniques discussed in chapter 5 (e.g., the public relations audit) use some form of attitudinal measurement. Professional research organizations frequently provide attitudinal data for public relations evaluation. Many factors, ranging from the need for a scientifically selected sample to the construction of a questionnaire that will not bias results, make attitude measurement a difficult task for most practitioners.

Disadvantages of the Closed-System Method

Although closed-system evaluation is the model most widely used by public relations staffs, it has two major drawbacks. First, as we have already discussed, because a message was transmitted to the intended audience in an understandable form and produced favorable attitudes does not mean the campaign goals were reached. Second, the likelihood that desired results will occur, especially in terms of actual behavior changes, is influenced by a number of factors outside the elements of the campaign. If a public relations effort fails to achieve its goals, it may not mean that the elements or the plan of the effort were faulty. A number of environmental factors, such as economic, political, and social change, can nullify what might otherwise have been positive results.

Oil companies, caught in the grasp of an embargo that caused rapidly rising prices, shortages, and long lines at the gas pumps, experienced losses in favorable public opinion in spite of massive public relations efforts during the early 1970s. The effectiveness of their messages was eroded by events outside the control of any public relations campaign. Therefore, these events had to be considered in evaluating the public relations efforts. Even though losses rather than gains in positive public opinion were experienced, the campaigns may still have been effective. Without workable public relations plans already in place, the losses in favorable public opinion could have been even more devastating.

OPEN-SYSTEM EVALUATION

Although a pretest/posttest design may be appropriate for evaluating short-range projects, many public relations programs are too complex for simple before-and-after measures. Continuing or long-range programs, such as changes in organizational policy, require an evaluation method that can provide feedback throughout the process without waiting for end results. **Open-system evaluation** models attempt to incorporate factors outside the control of the public relations campaign when assessing its effectiveness.

The open-system model emphasizes the extent to which the public relations function is encompassed by numerous other aspects of an organization and its environment.

Factors like unintended audiences and organizational administration and effectiveness are also included.

In chapter 5, we discussed the growing use of environmental monitoring and social audits as methods of gathering information. These same techniques provide valuable data for evaluating effectiveness in public relations campaigns. The effects of public relations efforts on various environmental factors can be one useful measure of results. In turn, the environmental data can help explain the effects of a campaign. Because most of these factors are outside the organization's control, they may operate as confounding variables in a closed-system evaluation. Economic conditions, for example, can have a significant effect on the attitudes of consumers toward an organization. Thus, results from a public relations effort that do not seem positive when considered alone might really be significant when the negative effects of certain economic conditions are considered.

Internal climate data are also useful for evaluating public relations campaigns. Public relations messages should be expected to have as much effect on the managers and employees of an organization as they do on other publics. In chapter 5, we suggested that organizations research their internal climate for public relations planning information, and this is also true for evaluation. Public relations practitioners should look inside and outside their organizations to measure the effects of their efforts. Just as with environmental factors, the internal climate of an organization can help explain the effect of a public relations effort. Union activities, management perceptions, and changes in company policy can all affect the results of a campaign.

Many of the factors included in the open-system evaluation model are difficult to measure accurately. Nevertheless, recognizing these factors is itself an important step toward evaluating public relations efforts. The value of the open-system method of evaluation is that it considers public relations in the broader spectrum of overall organizational effectiveness.

The Short-Term and Continuing Approaches

Both open- and closed-system models can be used in either short-term or continuing applications. When a public relations effort does not seek to establish a dialogue with an audience or receive feedback, a short-term approach to evaluation may be appropriate. Therefore, if the objective of an effort is simply to distribute news releases to media, a short-term approach to determine their usage could be sufficient.

However, for long-term, complex programs a more flexible approach to evaluation is needed. The continuing approach allows for an iterative loop that can take into account the effects that are being created by the program as it continues over time. Therefore, the program becomes self-correcting as it processes information about its impact and redefines tactics and even strategies on a continuing basis.[7] This approach combined with an open-system model can allow public relations programs to evolve as both environments and publics change.

Evaluation methods can be further categorized as measures of either *output* or *outcome*. A recent study showed that overall output measures were used most often to evaluate public relations campaigns (see table 8.1).[8]

An Open-System Plan in Actual Practice

James F. Tirone, public relations director of American Telephone and Telegraph Company before its breakup, maintained that public relations is a managerial as well as a creative effort.[9] Tirone believed that public relations should meet the same tests of

An employee asks a question of the Qwest CEO in Denver. Qwest is trying to return to its "roots" as a regional phone provider.

TABLE 8.1 Use of Output and Outcome Evaluation Methods in Campaigns

Output Evaluation Methods	Percent Use	Outcome Evaluation Methods	Percent Use
Response rates	66.10%	Activity outcome	29.66%
Media monitoring	64.41	Surveys	22.88
Media content analysis	41.53	Unobtrusive data collection	17.80
Distribution statistics	28.81	Focus groups	4.24
Coding material	8.47	In-depth interviews	4.24
Statistical analysis	6.78	Pretests and posttests	3.39
Attitude and image studies	5.93	Quasi-experimental study	0.00
Audience analysis	4.24		
Complaint analysis	2.54		

Source: Robina Xavier, Kim Johnston, Amish Patel, Tom Watson, and Peter Simmons, "Using Evaluation Techniques and Performance Claims to Demonstrate Public Relations Impact: An Australian Perspective," *Public Relations Review* 31, no. 3 (September 2005), p. 421.

performance as other management functions. This belief is reflected in the classic measurement techniques developed by the Bell System to be uniformly applied in a wide variety of public relations situations. Although more than 20 years old, the following examples from the Bell System program still represent an excellent attempt to implement an open-system evaluation model in three areas: administrative processes, employee publications, and media relations.

Evaluating Administrative Processes   To measure the effectiveness of public relations administrative processes, Tirone used information already available from standard organization sources to make some unique comparisons. By relating public relations budgets to these standard measurements in the industry, Tirone was able to show a "return" of public relations expenditures. Taking this comparison still further, Tirone demonstrated that when compared with the increase in the consumer price index (one way to measure inflation), the general public relations budgets fell significantly behind, while the advertising budget stayed even.

Evaluating Employee Publications   The success of employee publications in the Bell System was measured against corporate objectives for them: "reach all employees, create awareness, establish a reputation for reliability, be written so the material can be understood, and be readable at an educational level appropriate to the audience."[10] These objectives were translated into the following measurement criteria: "how effectively the publication was distributed within forty-eight hours, an average estimate of reader awareness of stories, a reliability index, understanding, and readability (as measured on the Gunning scale)."[11] Table 8.2 reports the ability of a sample of employees to recall (without any help) certain stories that appeared in the company's weekly newspaper. Table 8.3 reports measures of all the components of publication efficiency as operationally defined:

Distribution. Percentage of issues delivered in a 48-hour period.

Awareness. Average of recall data.

TABLE 8.2   Top Recall by Employees of Company Newspaper Articles (Three Issues of the Publication)

Subject Matter	Unaided Recall (%)
Employment office hiring (1)	56%
Defending the company (3)	42
Pioneer circus (1)	40
Marketing/competition	36
Corporate planning seminar (3-week average)	6
Averaged recall	36%

Source: James F. Tirone, "Measuring the Bell System's Public Relations," *Public Relations Review* 3 (Winter 1977), p. 29. Reprinted by permission.

TABLE 8.3   Employee Publication Scoring

Component	Score
Distribution	67%
Awareness	36
Reliability (average)	34
Very understandable	61
Both sides/Excellent	12
Source/Excellent	30
Understanding (CPS only)	40
Readability (CPS only)	16.5 years

Source: James F. Tirone, "Measuring the Bell System's Public Relations," *Public Relations Review* 3 (Winter 1977), p. 30. Reprinted by permission.

Reliability. Average response to three questions about the newspaper: Is it very understandable? Is it excellent at presenting both sides? Is it an excellent source of information?

Understanding. Percentage of those recalling and comprehending the corporate planning seminar story.

Readability. The Gunning score for the corporate planning seminar story, which is roughly equal to the number of years of education required for comprehension.

Evaluating Media Relations   Measuring the effectiveness of an organization's relationships with media representatives is a difficult task. Tirone reported three aspects of these relationships that can be measured to some degree: "the media's views of those relationships, the consequences which follow from news release output, and the activity of our (Bell System) media representative."[12] As a first step toward accomplishing these measurement objectives, Tirone proposed a nationwide survey of news media representatives to estimate their ratings of the quality and quantity of Bell System releases. He also instigated an analysis of the media to determine what was actually being said about Bell.

To begin the second phase of the process, Bell hired PR Data Systems, Inc., to code and computerize information collected from clippings and electronic media reports. Over a long period, this type of data could help measure both access to Bell spokespersons and the quality of their relationships with media representatives. Tables 8.4 and 8.5 report the percentage of favorable, unfavorable, and neutral stories according to region of the country and media service, respectively. From these data, certain discrepancies can be discovered that are useful in pinpointing problem areas and in planning future efforts.

TABLE 8.4   Newspaper Stories by Region, *N* = 3,848

	Favorable (%)	Unfavorable (%)	Neutral (%)	Totals (%)
Northeast	14%	5%	5%	24%
South	18	5	8	31
North Central	18	3	10	31
West	9	2	3	14
	59%	15%	26%	100%

Source: James F. Tirone, "Measuring the Bell System's Public Relations," *Public Relations Review* 3 (Winter 1977), p. 34. Reprinted by permission.

TABLE 8.5   Treatment by Media Services

	Favorable (%)	Unfavorable (%)	Neutral (%)	Totals (%)
AP	61%	18%	21%	100%
UPI	19	33	48	100
Syndicates	43	22	35	100

Source: James F. Tirone, "Measuring the Bell System's Public Relations," *Public Relations Review* 3 (Winter 1977), p. 34. Reprinted by permission.

EVALUATION SOFTWARE

As public relations practitioners have seen the necessity to begin to do more systematic evaluation, many have begun to use new technology to aid them in their efforts. Several new tools have been developed to help practitioners evaluate the effectiveness of their efforts. For example, Edelman Public Relations Worldwide reports that it has developed its own Edelman Media Analysis and Planning tool, which "doesn't just tell users where the story appeared—but also who exactly read it."[13]

PRTrack by TRAKWare, Inc., is a commercially available package designed to easily calculate what the program calls "media value" by computing the equivalent value of advertising in media. While these tools can be useful, they still provide "subjective numbers" that measure only output.[14] Outcome results require more sophisticated and multivariate approaches, like those discussed in this chapter.

River City Symphony

Problem

The River City Symphony's board of directors decided to use the summer months to stimulate interest in the upcoming fall and winter concert series. They arranged for the symphony to present free open-air concerts in several area parks to give a "back-to-the-people" feeling to what had been considered a "highbrow" image.

Objectives

1. Change the image of the symphony to make ordinary people feel comfortable attending concerts.
2. Sell 25% more season tickets.
3. Increase annual fund-raising by $50,000.

To accomplish its objectives, the symphony's board planned the following.

Strategies and Tactics

1. Prepare a Media Campaign.
    a. News releases about the summer concerts
    b. PSAs for radio about the concert series
    c. PSA for TV; spot done by local university students
    d. Talk show interviews with symphony director and key members
2. Develop an Advertising Campaign.
    a. Print ads for local newspapers
    b. Radio ads for local radio stations
    c. Cable TV ads
3. Encourage Volunteer Assistance.
    a. AARP to provide ushering
    b. University music department to assist
    c. University art department to help with materials

4. Develop Informational Materials.
   a. Summer series brochures
   b. Summer series posters
   c. Video: "Summer Symphony on Tour"

Questions

1. What benchmark data would you need?
2. What would you measure in the preparation stage? The implementation phase? The impact phase?
3. How would you prepare the evaluation section for the symphony's public relations plan?

Evaluation is frequently, assumed to be the final step in the process of public relations; however, it is really best described as a new beginning. Measuring the effectiveness of a public relations effort often provides new direction and emphasis for an ongoing program. Even when the project being evaluated does not continue, the lessons learned concerning its effectiveness will be useful in numerous future activities. Knowledge gained through careful evaluation is an important payoff to any public relations effort. Evaluation of projects that are obvious failures can help prevent future mistakes. Careful measurements of successful efforts will help reproduce positive elements in future programs.

Public relations can no longer afford to ignore the question "But what's it all worth to us?" Practitioners must be ready to respond with appropriate methods, solid data, and accurate predictions.

Summary

For self-testing and additional chapter resources, go to the Online Learning Center at **www.mhhe.com/lattimore3e.**

Key Terms

audience coverage
closed-system evaluation
evaluation
formative evaluation

impact analysis
open-system evaluation
summative evaluation

Notes

1. Candace White and Niranjan Raman, "The World Wide Web as a Public Relations Medium: The Use of Research, Planning and Evaluation in Web Site Development," *Public Relations Review* 25 (Winter 1999), pp. 405–19.

2. Pat Jackson, "Measurement and Evaluation," video interview, 1998.

3. Dirk Gibson, Jerra Leigh Gonzales, and Jaclynn Castanon, "The Importance of Reputation and the Role of Public Relations," *Public Relations Quarterly* 51 (October 2006), p. 15.

4. Carole M. Howard and Wilma K. Mathews, "Measurement/ Evaluation: How to Know If Your Program Is Working," in *On Deadline: Managing Media Relations* (Prospect Heights, IL: Waveland Press, 2000), p. 272.

5. John Pavlik, John Vastyan, and Michael F. Maher, "Using Readership Research to Study Employee Views," *Public Relations Review* (Summer 1990), pp. 50–60.

6. Mark McElreath, "Public Relations Evaluative Research: Summary

Statement," *Public Relations Review* 3 (Winter 1977), p. 133.

7. Tom Watson, "Integrating Planning and Evaluation, Evaluating the Public Relations Practice and Public Relations Programs," in *Public Relations Handbook,* ed. Robert L. Heath and Gabriel Vasquez (Thousand Oaks, CA: Sage, 2001), pp. 266–68.

8. Robina Xavier, Kim Johnston, Amish Patel, Tom Watson, and Peter Simmons, "Using Evaluation Techniques and Performance Claims to Demonstrate Public Relations Impact: An Australian Perspective," *Public Relations Review* 31, no. 3 (September 2005), pp. 417–24.

9. James F. Tirone, "Measuring the Bell System's Public Relations," *Public Relations Review* 3 (Winter 1977), pp. 21–38.

10. Ibid., p. 31.

11. Ibid.

12. Ibid.

13. "Count Clips While You Make More," *PR Intelligence* 11 (January 1999), p. 4.

14. Howard and Mathews, "Measurement/ Evaluation," p. 279.

PART THREE
The Publics

A public is a group of people with certain common characteristics. A public can be large—college students, Hispanics, blue-collar workers, or even all taxpayers. It can be small—the town council, the executive council for a university, newspaper editors, or even a three-person tax appeal board. Different organizations have different publics, often called stakeholders because they have a particular interest in that organization. The publics for the auto industry are different from those for the school board. Not-for-profit organizations have publics different from profit-seeking companies. Different levels of government organizations deal with different publics.

Part III describes five general types of publics that most public relations professionals face on a regular basis. Chapter 9 discusses the media, one of the most basic publics that practitioners deal with. Chapter 10 focuses on the organization's relationship with its employees, and chapter 11 delves into the complex relationships between an organization and its community. Chapter 12 covers the importance of consumers to modern organizations. Finally, chapter 13 discusses the impact of financial markets on public relations practice.

CHAPTER 9

Media Relations

OUTLINE

Gaining support for your organization through the media is a core component of public relations practice. With the advent of the Internet, media relations work has changed dramatically for journalists and public relations practitioners as business demands instant communication on a worldwide basis.

Journalists have mixed feelings toward public relations practitioners—suspecting them of manipulation while depending on them for information. Public relations practitioners view journalists as an audience, as a medium through which to reach the broader public, and as gatekeepers representing and responding to the publics' need to know. Here are two typical media relations' scenarios.

As the public relations director for a multinational corporation, you are at the center of a national news story because members of an environmental group have been using blogs in a variety of places to criticize your corporation's handling of cleanup of a toxic waste spill at one of your major plants in the Northeast. How do you respond? Do you respond directly to the media, through blogs, or through these and other means?

You are the public affairs director for the New Orleans police department. During Hurricane Katrina reporters from all over the country and even some international reporters call to ask the police chief about the looting and crime in the aftermath of the storm. You are so busy, do you respond? If so, how?

These are only two media relations crises that occur in public relations. As more opportunities develop to respond to your audiences, more opportunities also arise to attack you or your organization. This chapter focuses on how you should deal with media relations both proactively and reactively. We outline the basic ingredients of a media relations program and give additional attention to technological changes affecting media relations. Crisis communication is also included because of the important role media relations plays in dealing with a crisis.

A journalist talks on the phone to a public relations contact.

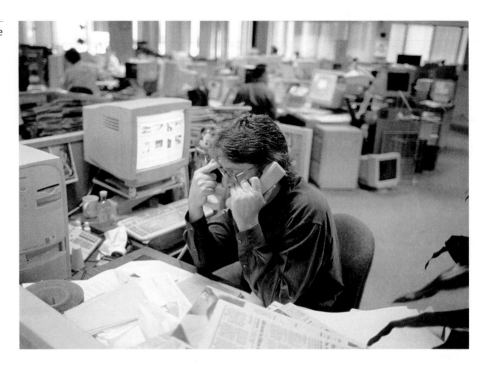

MEDIA RELATIONS

Sophisticated **media relations** and publicity work form the backbone for public relations practice. In many respects, developing and maintaining good relationships with the media continue to be hallmarks of the practice. Getting your organization's news and information printed or aired in the mass media has been the traditional means of gaining support for businesses, nonprofit organizations, and government agencies. But the mix of media is changing. The new media are still only a fraction of the media mix. The introduction of **social media** has opened an opportunity for direct interaction between an organization and its various stakeholder groups.

The media provide a relatively economical and effective method for communicating with large and dispersed publics. In this sense, the media serve as the gatekeeper or filter through which public relations practitioners reach the general public and other groups whose support they need. When the media publish or broadcast information supplied by organizations in news columns or within a news broadcast, that information seems to convey a sense of legitimacy that the organization may not get from paid advertising. This status or seal of approval that media coverage confers on an organization's news and information is called **third-party endorsement.**

THE RELATIONSHIP BETWEEN JOURNALISTS AND PR PRACTITIONERS

A basic grasp of media relations work begins with understanding the relationship between journalists and public relations practitioners. Journalists who gather and organize information for the media tend to take their responsibilities to society and the story's subject matter very seriously. They conceive of themselves as the public's eyes and ears, being watchdogs over public institutions doing the public's business. They see their jobs as seeking the truth, putting it in perspective, and publishing it so that people can conduct their affairs knowledgeably.

To the journalist, a story is a transient element in the ongoing flow of information, whereas the public relations practitioner wants the story to make a lasting impression and be seen in a positive light. The journalist is more interested in news reports that are accurate, fair, and balanced, regardless of whether the organization is seen in a negative or positive light.

Yet for all the concerns organizations manifest about how their stories are covered, the media's power does not lie so much in its ability to slant material one way or another, but rather that editors, reporters, and producers choose to cover one topic over others. The fact that some news items get published, aired, and talked about while others do not is called the *agenda-setting function* of the press. Douglas Cater, special assistant to President Lyndon Johnson and author of *The Fourth Branch of Government,* put forth the agenda-setting idea this way:

> The essential power of the press is its capacity to choose what is news. Each day in Washington tens of thousands of words are uttered which are considered important by those who utter them. Tens of dozens of events occur which are considered newsworthy by those who have staged them. The press has the power to select—to decide which events go on page one or hit the prime-time TV news and which events get ignored.[1]

Reporters resent anything and anyone they perceive as standing between them and the facts. Anyone who seeks to keep a secret is regarded with deep suspicion. Organizations of all types invite media scrutiny when they conduct themselves in ways considered less than open.

Journalists collectively maintain that they have the responsibility to provide not only information to the public but also feedback from society at large to the administrators of public institutions. As society becomes more complex and institutions have a greater impact on private lives, journalists hold that more thorough reporting and investigating provides necessary checks on possible business, governmental, and organizational excesses at the expense of the larger society.

Journalists sometimes have difficulty getting the information they need. They claim that highly placed news sources are generally overly insulated, secretive, and sensitive, recognizing neither the public's right to know nor the value of the media's role in exposing questionable practices. Another reason reporters have difficulty is that most are relatively new to their job assignments, which can change as often as every 18 months. Public relations practitioners can and do provide them with issue background information, but the reporters must learn how to ask and locate the right information and trace the issue's history in a community.

Still, working journalists echo some of the complaints registered against them by the institutions they cover. Reporters recognize that they frequently have insufficient education and experience to adequately cover complex issues and institutions. They are frustrated by the lack of time, space, and staff needed to do their jobs thoroughly, and by the profit-making requirements placed on them by their employers.

Even so, public relations practitioners and others who deal with journalists must remember that when reporters ask "nasty" questions, it is not necessarily because they are antagonistic or ignorant; they are just doing what good reporters are supposed to do. See mini-case 9.1.

The Public Relations Practitioner's View of the Journalist

From the public relations practitioner's perspective, the journalist is at once an audience, a medium through which to reach the larger public, and a gatekeeper representing and

Mini·Case 9.1   Fatal Tiger Attack at San Francisco Zoo

Laurie Volkmann, Ph.D.
Dominican University

Shortly after 5 p.m. on Christmas Day 2007, a 300-pound Siberian tiger escaped from his outdoor grotto at the San Francisco Zoo, chasing down three young men, mauling two and killing one. In the investigation that followed over the next several days, it was found that the teenage boys had taunted the tiger but also that the 12½-foot fence of the grotto was 4 feet below the standard and 7½ feet below what officials had reported the fence to be, making it possible for an agitated animal to jump over and escape. The San Francisco Zoo closed down for several days following the incident and kept the tiger exhibit closed for several months. The two injured young men filed suit against the city three months after the attack.

As the current director of public relations for the SF Zoo, consider your short-term and long-term actions in response to the crisis.

Questions

1. How do you address the media and the public about the fatality and injuries to the three young men? Draft a 200-word statement you would present at a press conference.
2. Write 10 questions you would expect the reporters to ask at your initial press conference.
3. How do you handle your communication with the families of the boys?
4. What do you do—and what is your timeline—for addressing the fencing issue?
5. Provide descriptions of three strategies for restoring the public's confidence in zoo safety and avoiding a major blow to attendance.
6. Research what was done by the zoo to deal with the media over the year following the incident, and report what you think worked and what may not have worked as well.

Sources: Steve Rubenstein, "Beloved but beleaguered zoo," *San Francisco Chronicle,* Dec. 30, 2007, A-1; Kevin Fagan, Cecilia M. Vega, Steve Rubenstein, "Wall below standard; shorter than zoo said," *San Francisco Chronicle,* Dec. 28, 2007, A-1.

---

responding to the public's need to know. Practitioners know that they must facilitate the work of journalists if they expect their organizations to get covered.

Because of this dependency, practitioners' selection and presentation of information often conforms more to journalistic standards than to the desires of their superiors in their own organizations. In a sense, both the journalist and the practitioner, in dealing with each other, are caught between the demands of the organizations they represent and the demands of the opposite party. In short, the relationship between public relations practitioners and journalists is one of mutual dependency. Public relations practitioners, as boundary spanners, are often caught in the middle between journalistic and other institutions, trying to explain each to the other.

Mutual Dependence

Although journalists like to picture themselves as reluctant to use public relations information, economic considerations force them to do otherwise. A news staff capable of ferreting information from every significant organization in a city without the assistance of representatives for those organizations would be prohibitively expensive. Through the efforts of public relations practitioners, the media receive a constant flow of free information. Facts that journalists might not have acquired otherwise become available in packaged form. The reporter or editor, as we already noted, can then decide what is newsworthy. Indeed, numerous studies have placed public relations' contribution to total news coverage between 40 and 70 percent. In one sense, the public relations practitioner makes the journalist's job much easier, saving time and effort and providing information that might otherwise be unavailable.

There's another side to this issue as well. Media scholar Oscar Gandy and others criticize the process by which public relations practitioners subsidize media costs and reporters' time by providing news releases and other information to make reporters' jobs easier. The disservice, these critics say, is that many organizations, including social movements, nonprofits, and disadvantaged groups, lack the resources to provide these "subsidies." As a result, says Gandy, the media may perpetuate information inequalities in society.[2]

Building Positive Relationships

Although much may be said about the art and craft of preparing materials for media consumption, perhaps nothing is so important to successful publicity as the relationships established between public relations practitioners and journalists. When public relations practitioners take the time and make the effort to establish good personal relations with journalists, they are much more likely to attract positive news coverage for their organizations. Good public relations begins with good personal relations. As well, mutual dependency tends to increase when public relations practitioners deal with specialized reporters who cover their industry, when the issues are more complex, and when the reporter is given enough time and space to thoroughly cover the story.

Tips for Getting Along with Journalists   As in all walks of life, it is good for public relations practitioners to get to know the people with whom they work. Sometimes the direct approach is effective. Call a journalist with whom you know you will be working. Introduce yourself. Suggest lunch or coffee. Another approach is to hand-deliver a news release to provide an opportunity for a brief introduction and meeting.

Other journalists may not want to be directly approached. With them, an indirect approach is required. Belonging to the local press club, attending meetings of the Society for Professional Journalists, or becoming involved in community activities in which journalists are also involved are ways of getting to know media counterparts. Indeed, journalists are often hired for publicity jobs not only for their writing skills but also for their network of media contacts. Encourage TV assignment editors to come to your workplace. Often good human interest stories can be developed from these visits.

Former Clinton administration press secretary James L. Fetig, now director of national media relations at Lockheed, sums it up:

> It all comes down to relationships. I trust reporters I know and I don't trust reporters I don't know. Most of us have long-standing relationships with journalists that are based on mutual trust. My advice to PR professionals is to know the journalists who cover their industry well and develop mutual credibility. This is especially true . . . given 24-hour news channels and the Internet. PR professionals have to understand the 24-hour news cycle and, when talking to any reporter, lay down the ground rules with regard to the Internet. At one time I could talk to a magazine reporter early in the week and know that my comments would not appear on the newsstands until the end of the week. Speak to a magazine reporter today, and it will likely be on the Internet tomorrow.[3]

Once relationships are established, protect and cherish them. Do not squander valuable relationships by using them for small favors or one-shot story placements. Do not ruin a relationship by expecting a reporter to always do what you want. Take no for an answer. Do not insult your relationship with inappropriate gifts because journalists, like other professionals, are sensitive to even the appearance of conflicts of interest.

Cultivate your relationships with journalistic colleagues by giving good service. Provide sufficient and timely information, stories, and pictures, when and how they are wanted. Be on call 24 hours a day to respond to reporters' needs and questions. Do not think that e-mail contact is an adequate substitute for one-on-one communication with journalists.

Nothing will destroy a relationship faster or more completely than an affront to the truth. Accuracy, integrity, openness, and completeness are the basis for trust bestowed by journalists. Once trust is broken, it can rarely be regained.

Finally, to ensure good relations with journalists, the practitioner should behave in a professional way. Live up to expectations. Don't play favorites among the media. Return phone calls promptly and with respect to deadlines. Don't beg for favors, special coverage, or removal of unfavorable publicity.

Lucy Caldwell, in an article in *Government Communications,* suggests,

> Once they (the media) trust that I actually return calls . . . the media will wait for me to confirm the information they have received from "sources" or scanners prior to releasing it themselves. It seems a simple enough task, but building these relationships requires time, patience, and the right attitude.[4]

THE ROLE OF MEDIA IN PUBLIC RELATIONS

The number of media outlets proliferates weekly, adding new challenges to the media relations function.[5] This is especially the case with cable television channels and new magazine start-ups, including trade and professional publications. There seems to be no end to segmenting audiences into smaller niches. For the public relations practitioner this means there is an ever-pressing need to tailor messages to target audiences.

Before assessing these trends in more detail, let's picture the size of the U.S. media industry, not to mention media outlets on a worldwide basis. Our emphasis here is on the news media, or what public relations practitioners call *uncontrolled media.* They're uncontrolled in the sense that public relations practitioners can send news and information to these media, but the media reporters and editors control if and how it will be used. In contrast, public relations practitioners do control the content and display of information in company publications and newsletters, e-mail, closed-circuit television, displays and exhibits, paid advertising, bulletin boards, billboards, brochures, flyers, posters, and what goes on the Web site.

Newspapers

Newspapers remain the workhorses of the public information system. That is, newspaper reporters gather most of the daily news, especially the public affairs news or news about government, social change, and economic development. Newspapers are a primary means of reaching community publics. Although no longer the primary news medium for the majority, newspapers are still a powerful force in shaping the public agenda and influencing the outcome to date. And for individuals seeking political content, survey results show that they tend to turn to newspapers. In many respects, daily newspapers offer public relations practitioners the greatest opportunities because they have more space to fill and they offer the greatest range of special sections and specialized reporters assigned to such beats as environment, health, business, science, and so on.

The number of U.S. daily newspapers has been shrinking constantly since the 1950s. There were 1,772 daily papers in 1950, for example, and only 16 fewer, or 1,756, in 1975. By 2007, there were 1,437 dailies, with losses owing to mergers and discontinued publications.[6] The average circulation of surviving dailies has increased, and adults who say they read newspapers spend an average of 28 minutes a day with their daily newspaper.

Weekly and semiweekly newspaper outlets have been holding fairly steady with 6,394 weeklies published in 2007.[7] Weeklies include suburban, rural, urban neighborhood, alternative, immigrant, and ethnic papers. Combined circulation is about 48 million. These newspapers are still an effective, direct, and intimate means of reaching the people of suburbs, small towns, and rural areas who are often the source of grassroots opinion. Readers of weekly newspapers are loyal and read their papers thoroughly. A weekly newspaper arguably exerts a far greater impact on readers' opinions than does the typical daily.

Newswires

Daily newspapers and television stations get much of their news from one or more of the newswires. Associated Press is a cooperative whose subscribers include 1,600 daily and weekly newspapers and 5,900 radio and television stations. Newspapers also subscribe to news services from *The New York Times,* the *Washington Post,* the *Los Angeles Times,* and newspaper syndicates such as King Features, National Newspaper Syndicate, News America Syndicate, United Features Syndicate, and Newspaper Enterprises Syndicate. PR Newswire distributes news releases submitted by organizations to about 1,500 major media outlets in every area of the country. PR Newswire also helps media reporters by maintaining a news release library or files of past news releases it has distributed for its clients.

Magazines

More than half of the nation's approximately 20,000 magazines are considered general interest magazines, while slightly less than half are more specialized trade and industry publications. Every possible hobby, interest, and occupation has its own magazine. Consumer magazines are fiercely competitive, with only about 1 in 10 new magazines surviving each year. The number of paid consumer magazines declined 16 percent from 2000 to 2007, but single-sales consumer magazines sold on newsstands were stable.[8]

Consumer magazines are best for production quality, placement of news near corresponding ads, reader services, and so on. In general, public relations practitioners do not make as much use of consumer magazines as they do of trade and professional publications. The "trades" reach those who work in particular industries or whose interests and information needs surpass those provided by mass media. As a result, trade magazine writers are very knowledgeable about their subject. Trade magazines are important, too, because they're read by leaders in each industry. Moreover, businesses often make their purchasing decisions based on trade magazine articles and product evaluations.

Radio

Radio is a relatively stable medium with 18,238 stations counted in 2008 in the United States and Canada.[9] Of these, 6,622 broadcast on AM frequencies and 11,616 on FM. There has been a marked shift in programming and listening patterns from AM to FM. By the 1990s, three-fourths of the radio audience tuned to FM stations. Radio is a person-to-person medium that flourishes on conversation; hence, the popularity of talk shows.

Television and Cable Television

More than 1,756 television stations broadcast almost around the clock to almost every American household.[10] Television continues to be a dominant force in children's lives and the prime source of news and entertainment for most Americans. Television viewing habits are changing as the commercial networks now attract less than 60 percent of the viewing audience, compared with more than 90 percent in the early 1960s. Video recording and such inventions as the TiVo have freed the viewer from being tied to program schedules as well. New transmission technology has expanded the channel-carrying capacity of cable networks, giving cable subscribers the choice of hundreds of program services and channels. From a media relations standpoint, television is usually best used for reaching large audiences on current news topics often involving the element of conflict. Television continues to be the principal medium for entertainment and product publicity.

About 74 percent of American homes are wired for cable, which translates into 240 million viewers.[11] Although most pay for only basic services, the sheer availability of up to 500 channels has already altered viewing patterns in many parts of the world. Beyond specialized and pay channels, cable operators offer subscribers Internet connections, ATM machine access, interactive health care, and local governmental services.

Online News Services

Major dot-com news sources include online pioneers like AOL and Yahoo; myriad traditional media with an Internet presence like NBC-TV, CNN, *USA Today, The New York Times,* and *The Wall Street Journal;* and new online media players like TheStreet.com and MarketWatch.com. To date, public relations practitioners have found that online services reach select business, consumer, investor, and professional audiences.

SOCIAL MEDIA

Social media, sometimes identified with **Web 2.0,** is an umbrella term that refers to new media that use technology to create social interaction through words and/or visual material. Key to the social media is the collaborative nature, or the sharing of information among the audiences. Social media depend on the audience to build a shared-meaning using technology as the tool.

These social media can take many forms, including wikis, podcasts, blogs, and Internet forums or discussion boards. Technologies such as e-mail, instant messaging, voice-over-Internet protocol (VoIP), and photo-sharing are the tools often used. Content can be in text, graphics, audio, or video. Examples of social media include YouTube (video-sharing and social networking), Facebook (social networking), Flickr (photo-sharing), Google (social networking and search engine), and MySpace (social networking).

Social Media Optimization (SMO) is an effort to get content disseminated across a large number of social media. This is accomplished by a Webmaster who can improve a Web site to allow social media aspects of the Web site to work. This may include links to services such as Del.icio.us to facilitate uploading of content by the users. SMO is important to public relations practitioners, advertisers, and marketers as they seek to get messages disseminated to larger audiences.

Transformation from mass media to mass collaboration is perhaps the major contribution of the personalized media. However, public relations practitioners should not neglect the traditional media. Larry Maggett, syndicated columnist for CBS News Online, New York Times Online, and other media organizations, argues that traditional media are still strong, although the trend is definitely moving in the direction of personalized media. CBS News, he says, is the third network in audience ratings for TV nightly news with about 7 million viewers, but that is still larger than all of the cable news channel audiences. And, the 25 million people that watch nightly TV news shows the strength that traditional media still have.[12]

One of the key issues in dealing with social media is how to establish Web credibility: In his research, B. J. Fogg of Stanford and founder of Yak-Pak says that it all boils down to two factors: expertise and trustworthiness.[13] Expertise can be established relatively easily by identification with an organization or through credentials. Trustworthiness is more difficult. It may evolve over time as relationships within the medium are continued. Fogg founded Yak-Pak, a company that he believes combines the emotion and trust of voice with the social interaction available on wikis. He asserts that the voice, or video, introduced into the social medium can enhance trustworthiness.[14]

Increasing percentages of Internet users are finding high degrees of reliability and accuracy on their favorite Web sites. The Digital Future Project at the University of Southern California found in its latest annual Internet survey that 83 percent of users said that most or all of the information on Web sites is reliable and accurate. They also report high levels (80 percent) of reliability and accuracy for Web pages posted by established media such as *The New York Times* or CNN.[15]

See spotlight 9.1 for a look at some of the more popular social media terms.

WORKING WITH THE MEDIA

With a basic understanding of the complex relationships between public relations practitioners and journalists, we can outline a few general principles for working with the media.

The best advice in dealing with the media is to give journalists what they need in the content, form, and language they want. For example, a public relations practitioner working with high-tech clients or start-up firms knows that reporters—especially those at trade and industry magazines—will want to verify the product claims with outside experts or analysts. Thus, the astute public relations practitioner will be prepared to give the magazine or financial reporter a list of experts and analysts to contact. This approach responds quickly and honestly to the media request. As well, public relations practitioners who work to establish a relationship of mutual trust with particular journalists can defuse many potentially antagonistic encounters.

Preparing to Meet the Media

Consider the following situations:

> You are the chief public relations official for a major company. A reporter calls your office at 9 A.M. She wants to see you for an interview at 11 A.M. She wants your company to respond to allegations made by a source that she is not at liberty to disclose. All she will say is that the charges deal with corporate finances and questionable conduct of certain corporate officials.

> As the public relations director of a major private university, you decide to hold a press conference to announce the initiation of an important fund-raising effort. A prominent alumnus has donated $5 million to kick off the campaign. You know that recent media coverage has criticized the university's budgetary problems, tuition hikes, and incursions into neighborhoods around the school that displaced poor people and eroded the community tax base.

API (Application Programming Interface) Ease of creating content and moving it into a variety of Web sites is often the result of using an open API provided by these sites.

Blog Technically a Web log. The author writes blogs like a journalist writes a column except that people can interact and post responses to the information on the blog.

Blogosphere The collective universe of bloggers.

Open Source Most commonly applied to the source code of software that is made available to the general public with relaxed or nonexistent intellectual property restrictions. This allows users to create user-generated software content through incremental individual effort or through collaboration. Open source is part of the whole Web 2.0 movement and now means more than just software. It's evolved to mean partly a group of people coming together, regardless of traditional organizational structures, to create something all benefit from but none can do alone.

Podcast Digital media files that can be audio and/or video that are distributed over the Internet for playback on portable media players or computers. The term originated with delivery to the Apple iPod combined with the term broadcast; it has much wider application now. Podcasts may be downloaded, streamed, or fed through feed formats such as RSS. The **Podcaster** is the producer or author of the podcast.

Portal A gateway. **Web portal** is a site that functions as a point of access for more information on other pages at that Web site. **Enterprise portal** is a gateway on enterprise Web software to provide a single point of access to a variety of information or tools that the organization wants you to have in one place.

Remix/Mashups An open approach to content. The "remix" society takes content, personalizes it by changing it or "mashing" it with other content to make something entirely new.

RSS (Real Simple Syndication) Feed of information to Web sites and services updated whenever something changes. Data is pushed to the user when it is new and doesn't require someone to go get it. Putting multiple RSS feeds into one feed makes viewing, organizing, and understanding vast amounts of information that is being generated much easier to understand.

Social Bookmarking Method for Web users to store, organize, search, and manage bookmarks of Web pages with the help of metadata. Users save links to Web pages privately and share with specified people or groups inside a special network or some domain. Much of the bookmarking is done informally, but others use bookmarking services. Many of the services provide ratings or comments and other social networking features.

Tagging User-generated way of describing content by adding "tags" to writing, images, videos, posts, or other social media content.

Web 2.0 Internet use that facilitates creativity and collaboration among users. It usually involves the new social media such as wikis, blogs, and social-networking sites. Rather than referring to any technical changes, it refers to changes in the ways software developers and other people make use of Web technology.

Wiki Short for a wikipedia. A wiki is a technology for creating collaborative Web sites. **Wikipedia** is now used as a term that combines "wiki" with "encyclopedia" to prove an Internet reference site begun in 2001 by Jimmy Wales and Larry Sanger.

Sources: Audrey Williams, "Best Practices and Innovation in Distance Learning: Using Web 2.0," presentation at Tennessee Alliance for Continuing Higher Education, Nashville, TN, Fall 2007; www.digitalcenter.org/, retrieved March 9, 2008; Vocus, "Five Golden Rules for Blogger Relations," Vocus White Paper, 2008; en.wikipedia.org/

You are the community relations director of the local police force. A reporter calls to request a meeting with your chief about low police morale resulting from the city's inability to meet rank-and-file demands for pay raises. When you attempt to arrange an interview for the following afternoon, the chief berates you, saying, "It's your job to keep the press off my back. Why can't you handle the guy's questions?" You convince the chief that the reporter would not talk to you because he said he was tired of the chief hiding behind his "flack." You tell him departmental integrity and morale depend on his willingness to deal with the press. You promise to help him prepare. He reluctantly agrees to the interview.

In each of these cases, a meeting with the media represents a critical challenge to the organization. Some organizations see such challenges as problems to be overcome. It is more constructive, however, to view them as opportunities. Publicity cannot replace good works or effective action, but it can gain attention for issues, ideas, or products. It can spotlight an organization's personality, policies, or performance. It can make something or someone known.

Every media contact is an opportunity to get feedback, to tell your story, to create a positive response to your organization. Of course there are dangers, but what opportunity presents itself without risk? And what opportunity can be taken without preparation?

Preparation Strategies

Before anyone in an organization meets with the media, the first step is to develop the proper set of attitudes. Meeting the media is an opportunity, not a problem; therefore, defensiveness is not appropriate. There is no need to feel intimidated, especially if your objective is worthy. In the preceding university fund-raising campaign scenario, the purpose of the press conference must be kept firmly in mind. The public relations director should refuse, in a friendly way, to be dragged by reporters' questions into subjects other than the donation and campaign.

The attitude of an interviewee toward the journalist should be one of hospitality, cooperation, and openness. At the same time, the interviewee should realize that the reporter need not be the person in control. The interviewee should decide what needs to be said and say it—no matter what the reporter's questions may be. In other words, have your own **agenda** with the points you want to make no matter what the journalist may want. A positive mental attitude is essential. Once this attitude is established among everyone in an organization who may be called on to be interviewed, it becomes much easier and less traumatic to prepare for specific interviews. After the chief of police completes one interview successfully (from the previous example), the next will be more easily handled.

Before looking further at how individuals can interact successfully with the media, we discuss how organizations can publicize themselves effectively.

Research and Planning in Media Relations

The old saying "Success is when opportunity meets preparation" is never truer than when applied to publicity. As we showed in earlier chapters, preparation indicates research and planning. In media relations, research means knowing who you are dealing with and what they are interested in. Media relations specialists deal primarily with their own management and with the media, so they must understand both parties well.

After understanding the organization, the public relations practitioner must study the specific media with which he or she will work. Research in this area consists of finding out the interests and needs of the people affiliated with the various media outlets. Media guides can provide some of this information. Effective media relations specialists also maintain their own file systems, Rolodexes, computer programs, and charts to keep track of the personal qualities and preferences of the media people with whom they work.

Most organizational news and publicity is based on a media plan. Media plans describe the circumstances with which the organization is dealing, lay out goals or objectives, identify key audiences, and specify key messages and media channels. Company information is often considered to be **publicity,** a term that refers to the publication of news about an organization or person for which time or space was not purchased. The appeal of publicity is credibility. Because publicity appears in the news media in the form of a story rather than an advertisement, it receives what amounts to a third-party endorsement from the editor. Because the editor has judged the publicity material newsworthy, the public is not likely to perceive it as an advertisement. Publicity may, therefore, reach members of an organization's publics who would be suspicious of advertising.

Publicity can be divided into two categories: spontaneous and planned. A major accident, fire, explosion, strike, or any other unplanned event creates **spontaneous publicity.** When such an event occurs, news media will be eager to find out the causes, circumstances, and people involved. While spontaneous publicity is not necessarily negative, it should be handled through standing plans such as those for emergencies.

Planned publicity, on the other hand, does not originate from an emergency situation. It is the result of a conscious effort to attract attention to an issue, event, or organization. Time is available to plan the event and how it will be communicated to the news media. If a layoff, plant expansion, change in top personnel, new product, or some other potentially newsworthy event is contemplated, the method of announcing it is a major concern. How an event is perceived by an organization's publics can determine whether publicity is "good" or "bad."

MEDIA RELATIONS PROGRAM ELEMENTS

The method by which an event is communicated can determine its impact. Three direct ways of purposefully reaching the print media are through a release, a discussion (conversation, phone call, meeting, or interview), or a news conference. The broadcast media can be reached through video news releases (VNRs), satellite interviews, or satellite media tours. Nonprofit organizations can also reach the electronic media with public service announcements (PSAs).

The most common type of publicity release is the **news release** (see figure 9.1). Any occurrence within the organization that may have local, regional, or national news value is an opportunity for publicity. Sometimes this news is not favorable to the organization. Even in these cases, however, a release is necessary. The news will always get out when something goes wrong. The role of the public relations practitioner is to be certain that the full story is told and that corrective actions are reported. Consider the following types of releases after having examined figure 9.1:

Business Features. An important form of publicity, and one highly prized by many organizations, is the feature article carried by professional, business, trade, or technical publications. Specialized periodicals that address a narrowly defined audience have increased dramatically in recent years, and these allow public relations practitioners to focus on a particular audience for maximum effectiveness. Some analysis of feature articles will provide an insight into the type and style of story editors prefer. Such publications tend to publish articles that define problems common to a particular profession or industry and describe an organization's attempts to deal with it. Unique uses of existing products, or products developed to meet old problems, are also frequent subjects. Public relations professionals often employ freelance writers who specialize in the particular field of the target publication. Most organizations have numerous other outlets for this type of publicity, including in-house technical reports, speeches discussing new technology or products, and papers prepared for professional societies.

FDA Home Page | Search FDA Site | FDA A-Z Index | Contact FDA

FDA Talk Paper

T05-29
October 3, 2005

Media Inquiries:
Susan Cruzan, 301-827-6242
Consumer Inquiries:
888-INFO-FDA

FDA Plans Public Hearing on Communication of Drug Safety Information

As part of its ongoing effort to continue to improve how it communicates information about risks and benefits of drugs, the U.S. Food and Drug Administration's Center for Drug Evaluation and Research (CDER) will convene a Public Hearing on December 7 and 8, 2005 at the National Transportation Safety Board Boardroom and Conference Center 429, L'Enfant Plaza, Washington, D.C. to discuss CDER's current risk communications and outreach strategies.

FDA believes it is critical that risk communication be timely, accurate, and easily accessible, and it must recognize health literacy limitations and include the needs of a multicultural population.

The purpose of the public hearing is to obtain public input on CDER's risk communication tools, identify stakeholders for collaboration and implementation of additional tools and obtain understanding of the strengths and weaknesses of CDER's existing risk communication.

The Part 15 public hearing will address six questions related to documents currently distributed by FDA . The questions being posed by FDA will help the agency learn which tools are effective and how these risk communications can be improved. These tools include Patient Information Sheets, Healthcare Professional Information Sheets, Public Health Advisories, Press Releases, the MedWatch Listserv Safety Updates, Patient Safety News, CDER Educational Campaigns, and the CDER Internet site. (The websites for these documents are available in the Federal Register (FR) notice.)

Examples of questions that CDER intends to ask include:

- Do these tools provide the right kind and amount of risk and other information that health care professionals need to make informed decisions about whether to prescribe drug products ?
- Do these tools provide what the public needs to make informed decisions about whether to use those products?

Those planning to participate in providing oral comments must register by November 7, 2005.

For additional information on registration, please visit CDER's webpage:
http://www.fda.gov/cder/meeting/RiskComm2005/default.htm.

Federal Register Notice of Public Meeting:
http://www.fda.gov/OHRMS/DOCKETS/98fr/05-19759.htm
http://www.fda.gov/OHRMS/DOCKETS/98fr/05-19759.pdf

Submit written or electronic notices of participation and comments to:

Division of Dockets Management (HFA-305)
Food and Drug Administration,
5630 Fishers Lane, Room 1061
Rockville, Maryland 20852
E-mail: FDADockets@oc.fda.gov
Electronic Comments

Date and Time:
December 7 and 8, 2005 from 8:00 a.m to 4:30 p.m.

Place:
National Transportation Safety Board: Board Room and Conference Center
429 L'Enfant Plaza
Washington, D.C.
Register by November 7, 2005

FIGURE 9.1   Sample News Release Prepared for Distribution over the Internet *Source:* U.S. Food and Drug Administration Web site, www.fda.gov/bbs/topics/answers/2005/ans01367.htm (Oct. 5, 2005).

Consumer Service Features. Many newspapers and magazines, as well as some television stations, publish or broadcast material designed to assist consumers. Information about almost any consumer product or service can become a vehicle for both product and institutional publicity. Stories that provide consumer-oriented information concerning food, travel, fashion, child care, books, home management, and numerous other topics are in demand by many publications. Frequently, the recipes, food photographs, travel stories, and fashion news contained in special newspaper sections are provided by public relations practitioners representing various manufacturers and industry associations.

Financial Features. Most newspapers and television stations, and some magazines and radio stations, carry financial news and feature articles, and a growing number of publications specialize in that area. Such publicity can be an especially effective tool for shareholder relations because current and potential investors assign more credibility to information when an independent editor selects it for publication. Potential sources of financial publicity include dividend announcements, mergers, profit reports, expansions, new product lines, major orders, changes in top personnel, research breakthroughs, and many other events that might be of interest to the financial community in general.

Product Features. Product publicity can frequently be newsworthy enough to be selected for use by news editors. Stories about products should be directed to periodicals, newspaper sections, and television and radio programs specializing in consumer product information. Editors and others who use this type of material are interested in information concerning the features, composition, performance, and application of products that will help consumers with their purchasing decisions. In addition to exploiting unique product features, the public relations practitioner can create newsworthy events to dramatize and illustrate product performance for media representatives.

Pictorial Features. The increasing popularity of photojournalism has made more newspapers and magazines receptive to newsworthy or unusual photographs that can communicate a message by themselves. Such photographs are often used with only a caption line and no accompanying story. Because these high-quality, unique photographs are difficult for assignment editors to plan, they provide an excellent opportunity for publicity. A public relations manager should always be alert for photographs that might be good enough for this purpose.

Many organizations employ staff photographers, and their work should constantly be examined for exceptionally good or unusual shots. Photographs taken for in-house publications, annual reports, or even advertising may present opportunities for publicity. Special events should always be planned with good publicity photographs in mind. Frequently, newspaper and television editors assign photographers to special events if they know in advance of a good possibility for getting an unusual or newsworthy photograph.

Publicity photographs should normally be printed on seven-by-nine-inch or eight-by-ten-inch paper, depending on the editor's preference. Print media prefer high-gloss photographs with a caption line attached, whereas television stations prefer slides instead of prints, but specifications should be determined in advance. Color photographs are sometimes used by newspapers and magazines, but black-and-white photos are standard. Digital photos may be preferred by some editors.

Public Service Announcements (PSAs). Nonprofit organizations are sometimes able to make use of the public service announcement. PSAs are short spots that radio and television stations may feel obliged to run to demonstrate their "public interest" commitment at license renewal time. The public relations practitioner must work with the public service director at the broadcast station to determine the particular station's requirements for a PSA. Often the station will assist the organization in actually producing the PSA. TV stations in Denver, for example, allow an organization four TV spots a year. All TV stations in Denver contribute to the production work, which is done at one station. TV spots must conform to 10-, 20-, and 30-second time frames for commercial breaks. Radio PSA's are usually done with that time frame or an additional 60-second spot, but some radio stations prefer to have their disc jockeys read the announcement and don't require specific timed copy. One problem with PSAs, though, is that they may be played at any time of day or night. Your spot may air at 6 A.M. or 2 A.M. If you're lucky, it might air during prime time.

Packaging News Releases

Packaging in the form of **media kits** can frequently increase the probability that information from a publicity release will actually be used by an editor. A media kit, sometimes called a **press kit,** includes a collection of publicity releases, fact sheets, brochures, photographs, or other information pieces enclosed in a cover or some other packaging device. Although attractive packaging can be helpful in gaining the attention of a busy editor whose desk is covered with competing releases, design is not the primary consideration in compiling a media kit. More important is that news releases, photographs, fact sheets, background information, and features are packaged in an organized and readable form to enable the editor to select the information he or she wishes to use. The strategy behind any media kit should be based on the realization that most major media will not use a release verbatim but will instead select information to be rewritten into a story unique to their publication. A media kit should be designed to help editors select the information they need.

Media kits do not need to be elaborate and costly. Releases can be packaged in simple but well-designed one- or two-color folders, as long as they are adaptable to a variety of media needs. The basic role of a press kit is to provide information to editors that would otherwise take many hours to research. Press kits can provide a service for the media by saving research time and identifying important information for consumers and others. The organization, of course, stands to gain favorable publicity. Today, many organizations distribute their media kits online from the corporate Web pages. It's too early to forecast when these online versions will replace hard copy ones. For one thing, the hard copy media kits are often distributed to people outside the media.

Distributing News Releases

News releases today are more likely to arrive by e-mail than they are by fax, regular mail, or hand-carried delivery. In fact, most releases are now either faxed or sent by e-mail directly to the editor or person targeted by the release. Broadcast fax, which is the material sent by computer to all fax machines set up on your computer to receive the material, is being used more and more often by media relations departments.

Organizing Press or News Conferences

Once considered a basic component of media relations, the press conference today takes a backseat to Internet-distributed information and accompanying multimedia components. Except for rare occasions, there is little reason for reporters to take the time to attend an organization's press conference when they can get all of the information and multimedia support materials from the company Web site. Sometimes, they can even get "exclusives" off the Web site when the organization tailors one release as an exclusive business story, another as an exclusive personality feature, and a third as a technology story. In other cases reporters use answers to e-mailed questions as the basis for their stories.

Let's assume that a press conference must be held. **Press conferences,** or **news conferences,** are structured opportunities to release news simultaneously to all media. They should be used only when the news is important and when interaction is required to promote understanding of complex or controversial topics. Do not call a news conference unless the event is extremely newsworthy and simply cannot be handled through releases or posting to the Web site or unless there is someone very newsworthy to interview.

For those rare occasions when news conferences are appropriate, the following guidelines will help ensure success:

1. *Plan the Event Carefully.* Invite all representatives of all media that may have an interest far enough in advance for editors to plan to send reporters and photographers. Select an appropriate site close to the event being covered and convenient for major media (hotel, press club, airport, boardroom—never a public relations office). Check for enough electrical outlets and telephones. Time the conference to accommodate major media deadlines. Make certain you prepare enough handout material for everyone. Prepare any visuals that may be used so that they will photograph well from any place in the room. Prepare a poster of the organization's logo or name to go over the one on the speaker's stand if you use a rented facility. Plan to phone major media the morning or afternoon before the conference as a reminder. Simple refreshments are generally a nice touch.

2. *Prepare Executives and Others to Be Interviewed.* Make certain they understand the topics that will be discussed. Help them anticipate and prepare for difficult or touchy questions. Advise them to be completely honest. If they don't know an answer, they should say so and offer to find out. If the answer to the question is considered proprietary information, they should state that it is not for public disclosure. Cultivate a pleasant, cooperative attitude among those who will be interviewed. If they are afraid of or resent the media, it will show. Advise them to avoid off-the-record comments.

   Recently, public relations practitioner Jan Harkness wrote that public relations practitioners should use the first training sessions as a stepping-stone. "Then, conduct more in-depth, one-on-one sessions for those who will serve as corporate spokespeople. Whenever possible, incorporate mock interviews into these sessions. During these interviews, think like a reporter. Ask questions to get to the heart of people and their motivations. Find out why your CEO chose his or her profession. Talk to the vice president about his or her move from human resources to information technology."[16]

3. *Coordinate the Meeting with Public Relations Practitioners Serving as Directors and Stage Managers.* Keep the meeting moving and interesting, but don't take over the job of the media representative. Try to keep relationships cordial and professional

even in the heat of questioning. Never take obvious control of the meeting unless things get out of hand.

USES OF VIDEO

Video became a major method of delivering an organization's news to the broadcast media in the 1980s. Budget cuts in TV news operations coupled with new broadcast technology have both contributed to an increasing use of video technology by public relations practitioners.

Despite the Internet, there are still four common uses of video:

1. *The video news release* is a short news package presenting the news item from the organization's viewpoint. The most popular VNR is about 90 seconds long but is accompanied by **B-roll** material (background video) with audio on separate channels. It is broadcast-quality videotape.

2. *Electronic media kits* are similar to the conventional media kit except they include VNRs, perhaps a longer version than normal and giving more background material. They also include typical background print material such as still photos, news releases, brochures, background papers, fact sheets, or other pertinent information.

3. *Satellite press conferences* provide an opportunity for TV journalists to participate in question-and-answer sessions via satellite with an organization's representatives. Often the organization makes a presentation followed by the press conference. Some participants may be in studios with interactive uplink facilities, but some watch the satellite feed and phone in questions.

4. *Satellite media tours* provide individual interviews with the guest personality in a remote studio. Each interview is exclusive, and some are carried live. Guests may appear on two or three dozen stations per day this way.

VNRs came under fire in March 2005 when a front-page story in *The New York Times* criticized the government for distributing VNRs that extolled the virtues of the Bush administration. Many of the stories ran with little or no editing, and it appeared to viewers as if they were news reports.[17]

Later in the spring of 2005 *The Wall Street Journal* reported on its front page another common public relations practice, the satellite media tour. The story revealed that some TV experts were getting paid to endorse particular products without the viewers' knowledge.[18]

The news criticism prompted Senators Frank Lautenberg and John Kerry to introduce a bill into the Senate to clearly label government-sponsored VNRs. PRSA president Judy Phair testified during a Senate committee hearing on the bill: "We must reveal the sponsors for causes and interests represented and disclose all financial interests related to the VNR," but she said that the legislation would impede the free flow of information to the public.[19] The Public Relations Society of America maintains that public relations practitioners should *voluntarily* make the disclosure as part of their ethical conduct.[20]

THE ROLE OF TECHNOLOGY IN PUBLIC RELATIONS

Today, media relations work takes on added and somewhat different importance by reaching smaller, more defined target publics or audience segments through mass, specialized, and organization-controlled media. In large part, this new media relations environment is a result of the Internet, a growing number of media outlets, and the new social media.

The Internet

The **Internet** turns every newsroom in the world into a round-the-clock operation. Writing in *PR Strategist*, Michael Lissauer describes the new media world from the vantage point of MSNBC and CNN. MSNBC.com draws five times the daily audience that its parent MSNBC cable TV news programming does. CNN.com generates approximately 2.7 million unique visitors daily, compared with 450,000 and 545,000 viewers of its 5 P.M. and 11 P.M. cable news shows, respectively.[21]

As mentioned in chapter 2, reporters get their story leads and background information from the Internet and often check the Web site while writing their stories, especially broad-based pieces. As a result, organizations work diligently, anticipating reporters' questions as a guide to what goes on the Web site and associated links. Typically, this includes basic company information such as history and background, product information, executive speeches, and news release files. Regular Web site updating is a must.

Blogs, Podcasts, and RSS Feeds

Blogs, podcasts, and videocasting are recent uses of technology that have been adopted by consumers and have led to success in public relations as tools to communicate with target audiences. Of the three, blogs have had the most use by audiences. In just a little over a year, the number of Internet users who read blogs has risen from 11 percent to more than 27 percent, according to the Pew Internet and American Life Project.[22]

Blogs   **Blogs** are simply online Web journals people use to converse about a particular subject, viewpoint, or idea. (See spotlight 9.2.) Use of a blog can be an excellent way to reach those in the target audience who are most passionate about the subject.

While blogs can be effective, they also have pitfalls. At issue in employee public relations is determining how to keep employees in line with the position of the organization. For example, when should an employee identify him- or herself with the company? Some organizations are including such policy in their employee manuals.[23]

Another issue is the legal ramifications of what you say in a blog. One columnist wrote, "Letting loose, however, is not without its risks, and this involves more than inadvertently airing your dirty laundry." He added, "Sometimes speaking freely, and publicly, about other people or organizations can get you threatened with a lawsuit if you criticize them or reveal information they don't want revealed, First Amendment or no First Amendment. Other times it can get you fired."[24]

Podcasts   Podcasts provide an audio and/or videocast of content for later use. It began mostly as a means for transferring music to mobile devices called iPods. However, the podcasts may also be delivered in other ways through the Web. For instance, the major television networks now have podcasts of their news. Most archive the podcasts for later use by consumers. This allows a user to download the audio and listen to it when he or she is ready. One drawback has been that you can't bookmark, or index, them, so you have to listen to the podcast from the beginning if you are looking for something in it. Now there are companies with products that will allow indexing for podcasts.

RSS   **Really Simple Syndication (RSS)** is a technology that lets people distribute and display content for the Web. It provides news or other information that Web site owners can access and place on their sites. The content is controlled by what the owner of that content decides to distribute. This content may be used for internal or external

The blogosphere has exploded onto the Internet recently. Technorati reports nearly 70 million Web logs (April 2007) and the number continues to grow rapidly. Perhaps more important, more and more people are starting to read Web logs. "According to the Pew Internet and American Life Project (2006), 57 million Americans currently read blogs. Just as interesting for PR pros is the increasing number of journalists who read blogs. According to a Euro RSCG Magnet and Columbia University Survey of Media (2005), 51% of journalists read blogs on a regular basis and 28% rely on them in their daily reporting."

Role of Bloggers

Many bloggers think of themselves as commentators on today's news. Many see their role as being in opposition to the mainstream media. Many bloggers are not professional writers and don't get paid for writing their blogs. Bloggers are in fact likely to be part of the audience for whom they are writing. For that reason, as a public relations professional you need to approach bloggers as you would anyone in a social situation: introduce yourself and get to know them. Blogging experts suggest,

> Bloggers are uniquely positioned for a number of reasons. First, blogs represent an unprecedented opportunity to target your message. In the past, press releases that were deemed non-newsworthy never saw the light of day. With virtually unlimited space and restrictions, blogging has opened up a new avenue for the PR professional to target their audience with a high degree of accuracy. With so many blogs, podcasts and other social media dedicated solely to niche markets, a well developed press release or pitch is sure to get through and begin its dissemination into the blogosphere.

> Bloggers also influence traditional media. Reaching journalists who are reading blogs—and more than half are—will result in coverage in the mainstream media. Reporters and editors are reading blogs for story ideas.

The blogger will also influence a search on the Web. Many links are involved in blogging and this will often influence the search rankings of other Web sites that are significant to your organization.

Five Golden Rules to Effective Blogger Relations

You can maximize your public relations opportunities and minimize your risks by following these five golden rules to effective blogger relations:

Rule #1: Do your homework. Nothing irritates bloggers more than being pitched on a story in which they clearly have no interest. If the blog is a fit for the company's news, you may already be familiar with its content. If not, familiarize yourself with the topics they care about and, more important, the perspective they have. Not only are you more likely to ensure a positive response from the blogger, but you will also protect yourself from having the blogger write negatively about your organization.

Rule #2: Join the club. The blogosphere is a community and to engage fully with it you have to take part in it. Participation in the community can take a variety of forms. Commenting on blog postings is a good first step to reaching out to bloggers. Another tactic would be to communicate directly with bloggers whom you have taken the time to familiarize yourself with, but make sure you approach them properly.

Rule #3: Bring something to the party. Do you call close friends only when you need something? If you do, chances are that you do not have many close friends who are willing to do you favors. A common downfall of PR professionals is not engaging in a true two-way relationship. You should take some time to get to know the bloggers and what topics they find interesting.

When you run across something they might like, let them know about it. It may not get you ink right then, but it will help you create a relationship with the blogger. When you do contact bloggers, they should know that you contacted them because you respect their writing and their perspective enough to want them to write about your company.

Rule #4: Honesty is the best policy. One of the most important foundations of any professional or personal relationship is honesty. Many PR professionals question whether to let bloggers know what company they are with or whether they are connected to the news that they are sharing. The answer is simple: Be transparent. Remember that bloggers often view themselves in contrast to traditional media and are highly critical of any media efforts that are not open and honest.

Rule #5: Make it a lasting relationship. Just like any relationship, good blogger relations involve a consistent and committed effort. The most successful online PR professionals have relationships with bloggers that they have been cultivating over a long time. If you have done your work properly, and engaged with the blogosphere appropriately, then you can expect a positive response when you are attempting to promote your message online.

Conclusion

Although the new world of blogging may seem unknown and risky to many PR professionals, at its core it is about the same things that good media relations has always been about: building relationships and trust. As a PR professional, whenever you deal with any writer—whether print, broadcast, or online—show him or her the courtesy of a strong, well-thought-out pitch that proves you have done your research.

Source: Vocus, "Five Golden Rules for Blogger Relations," Vocus White Paper, 2008.

communication because it provides a good way for an organization to keep its partners, customers, and employees informed about what's going on in the organization.[25]

Wikis, Intranets, Extranets, and Web Sites

No single technology application has changed media relations more than the Internet and the use of wikis, intranets, and extranets. A **wiki** is an interactive Web site that allows those with security rights to post and change content. Wikis are affecting both intranets and extranets in that wikis are interactive and intranets and extranets are not. The term **intranet** refers to computer-based systems for communicating with employees and other insiders, while the term **extranet** refers to the same process for reaching such external audiences as investors, customers, community and governmental leaders, and so on. Media relations Web sites provide a dedicated location for all kinds of information of possible interest to the media. For breaking news, this includes pointing reporters to information sources, position statements, activity calendars, press release archives, speeches, government filings, and company and executive background material.

Almost all corporate, organizational, and even social movement Web sites include a link to the media relations department. The media relations Web pages become the online newsroom for which Vocus software specialist Kay Bransford offers 10 uses and tips:

1. Link directly from your home page to the media relations site.
2. Post press releases simultaneously with distribution to the press.
3. Maintain a searchable database of press releases.
4. Offer online media kits.
5. Make it easy for reporters to reach you.
6. Include corporate and executive information.
7. Feature a searchable database of recent coverage.
8. Allow reporters to request news.
9. Provide additional tools and information.
10. List awards and recognition.[26]

Experts advise that organizations with small media relations budgets use credible spokespeople, create strong graphic identities, skip press conferences, develop exclusive story angles for different media, and, generally, generate excitement for the media site.

One reason that Internet-based media strategies have become so popular is the availability and assistance of Internet media placement and tracking services. Media Link offers clients an electronic version of such traditional public relations services as VNR Webcasting and cybermedia tours, while NetCurrents measures traffic trends to correlate public relations efforts and the impact they have on a site's success.

Beyond using the Web site to extend traditional media relations programs, public relations practitioners cultivate buzz online with postings to newsgroups, a working message board intentionally leading news to online outlets and newsletters. Media relations specialists know how to access newsgroups, respond to online inquiries, and track what's being said online about your company and its competitors.

Media relations expert Carole Howard tells public relations practitioners to invest time experimenting and innovating on the Internet. "Establish home pages. Post your organization's message on bulletin boards. Host online forums. Promote your products to online reviewers. Stage online contests. Create online update centers in crisis situations. Put your organization's spokespeople in chat rooms to tell your story firsthand and answer questions live."[27]

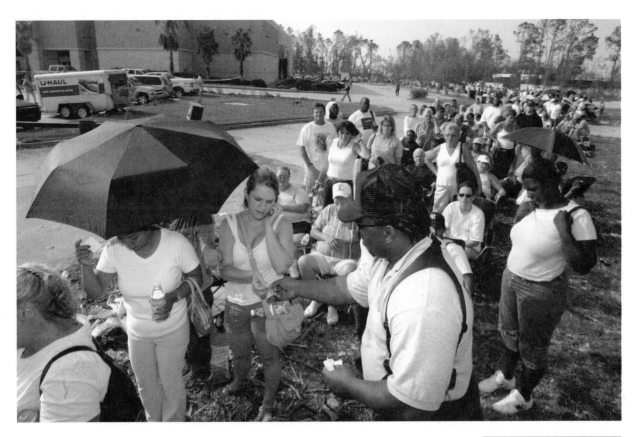

The Red Cross provides disaster relief.

Katrina Reveals Good, Bad, Ugly of Media Relations

Laurie Volkmann, Ph.D.
Dominican University

It is not often Jon Stewart praises the news media on his "fake news" program, *The Daily Show with Jon Stewart.* But when Hurricane Katrina punished the Gulf Coast in August 2005, the popular Comedy Central anchorman had no choice. It was, in fact, the news media's coverage of Katrina's aftermath that alerted the country—even the federal government—to the magnitude of the category 5 storm's destruction.

"I used to work in a bar, and there was a fat guy who just sat there and drank. One day we told him someone was stealing his car, and he ran out of the bar and beat two people with a tire iron. I thought, 'Wow, that guy can move.' That's how I feel about the news media and Katrina."

Katrina whipped through New Orleans on August 29 before ransacking Biloxi, Mississippi, and surrounding coastal towns. New Orleans appeared to escape the predicted devastation until flooding on August 30 crumbled levees that protected the jazz city's precarious position below sea level.

Tens of thousands of stranded New Orleans citizens were stuck in a city with waist-high standing water, no power, no water, and no way out of town. Many spent days on their rooftops waiting to be rescued by local, state, or federal officials. More than 20,000 displaced citizens crowded into the New Orleans Superdome for protection from floodwaters, despite the building having no power, air conditioning, or running water.

News video showed angry, dying citizens waiting for days to be rescued. What started as another disaster story turned into a news media cry for government help.

Volunteers from southeastern cities tried desperately to get supplies to citizens in Louisiana and Mississippi, often being turned away by officials unsure of proper protocol during a disaster.

In an interview with CNN's Paula Zahn, then Federal Emergency Management Agency director Michael Brown admitted FEMA was not aware of how bad the situation was in New Orleans and that they had only just learned that so many people were stranded at the dome.

The White House's lack of response to the hurricane quickly became a major source of criticism, forcing President George W. Bush more than a week after the storm hit to take the blame for inadequate federal assistance.

Internet Provides Outlet in Chaos

Katrina exposed the nation's vulnerability and disorganization at various levels, but it also revealed a general lack of crisis preparedness at the local level. Destroyed phone lines and cell towers prevented basic communication for weeks. People had scattered in a panic, and it was impossible for friends and relatives to locate each other with traditional methods.

Suddenly, communication via the Internet was not just useful, it was critical. Craigslist.org, a popular San Francisco–based Web site known for giving people a forum to buy, sell, find a date, or just rant, became an electronic SOS. After the hurricane, founder Craig Newmark added "Katrina relief" to the site's options. People could search for missing persons, seek housing options, look for jobs, donate to relief organizations, or volunteer to help.

The *New Orleans Times-Picayune* published online-editions-only for days as reporters worked from remote locations to produce content for the Web. For several days after the disaster, the *Times-Picayune* devoted its entire coverage to the hurricane and its aftermath. Reporters even started their own blog, detailing their experiences in the harrowing moments during and after the flooding.

In fact, blogs became the method of choice for posting messages to find people and locate pets, request assistance, relay whereabouts, or vent about the lack of help and disorganized responses.

Organizations Respond to Crisis

While President Bush and his administration frantically mobilized local, state, and federal officials to evacuate residents, emergency response organizations from Baton Rouge to Houston to Memphis to Atlanta prepared for an onslaught of hurricane victims in search of shelter.

Federal law states the American Red Cross is the first responder in any national catastrophe, but Red Cross volunteers in major Southeast cities were overwhelmed quickly as tens of thousands of evacuees poured into these cities seeking shelter, clothing, food, and water.

Houston officials worked with Louisiana to transport stranded residents to its Astrodome. Hospitals in Memphis and Atlanta accepted hundreds of critical patients and worked to open temporary medical facilities. Colleges and universities around the South worked with New Orleans students to enroll them for fall and spring semesters. Public school systems integrated thousands of students to help transient families adjust during uncertain times.

United Way of Metropolitan Atlanta Mobilizes City Response

In the midst of trying to meet short-term needs, United Way of Metropolitan Atlanta (UWMA) recognized the long-term implications of hurricane victims in the city. The nonprofit responsible for providing funding to dozens of local charities called in a crisis response team and immediately began working on housing, employment, and transportation solutions. "This crisis is moving whether we are ready or not," said UWMA president Mark O'Connell during a media briefing September 13. "The public is still focused on the emergency, which is real and urgent, but we've got to focus on the second phase—resettling."

UWMA took the lead in mobilizing groups interested in helping with resettlement. Its first step in the crisis plan was appointing the former CEO of Bell South Georgia as chairman of "Operation Helping Hand"—a coalition of nonprofit, business, government, and faith leaders—to develop a coordinated response. The coalition later changed its name to Neighbors Helping Neighbors to signify the partnership with those affected.

UWMA also maintained a leading role in other major areas:

- Created a consolidated information sharing network for all participating agencies through its Web site.
- Tracked donations and placements within the network.
- Provided information to local and national news media.

Using the News Media to Inform

Neighbors Helping Neighbors identified five priority actions for resettling hurricane victims and set these goals:

- Housing—helping 1,500 households find permanent housing.
- Employment—providing resources for 4,000 evacuees to find work.
- Food/immediate needs—$500,000 to Atlanta Food Bank; quality care to 500 children and 900 youth; support for 700 older adults and those with disabilities.
- Community education—training 500 advocates how to assist evacuees; finding host families for 500 more evacuees.
- 211 Call Center—adding resources to UWMA's hotline for finding housing and job opportunities in the city to handle 600 to 800 more calls per day, double what it was used to handling.

Within two weeks of creating the coalition, United Way of Metropolitan Atlanta sponsored a job fair that featured more than 300 Georgia businesses and corporations at the downtown World Congress Center. The event attracted national network and cable news coverage with just one press release and one story pitch. "What was extraordinary was that the requests for more information came from the news media," said Erin Steele, public relations manager for UWMA. "During the first couple of weeks, the media came to us, which is very unusual in nonprofit."

United Way capitalized on that media interest, sending dozens of press releases in September and October to local and national media outlets to help make the city aware of its efforts and keep the community focused on the problem. Press releases included news about major corporate donations and information about fund distribution to organizations helping Katrina victims with child care assistance, housing resettlement, food and clothing, job training, medical services, school supplies, transportation, and other needs. "There is nothing we can do better without you," O'Connell told media representatives during the September 13 briefing. "The key is communication."

Nonprofit Challenges During a Disaster

One of UWMA's biggest challenges for the Katrina effort was simultaneously raising money for the hurricane fund while kicking off its annual fall fundraising campaign. It was funding from the previous year's campaign that allowed the United Way to help local groups provide emergency assistance as quickly as it had after Katrina. But the Atlanta nonprofit wanted to avoid the situation it found itself in after September 11, 2001—people responded so generously in donating to 9/11 relief funds that they did not give regular contributions to other nonprofits.

UWMA had announced a 2005 campaign goal of $76.5 million just after the hurricane hit. In light of the emergency needs, the organization added a separate $10 million goal specifically for hurricane relief in Atlanta. "We have to make people recognize we have an enormous size challenge," O'Connell said.

Sources: Mark O'Connell, president of United Way of Metropolitan Atlanta, personal interview, September 13, 2005; UWMA press releases; *Atlanta-Journal Constitution,* August 31, September 1, 7, 15, 2005; *The New York Times,* September 14, 2005; National Public Radio, September 13, 2005; www.craigslist.com (September 2005); and www.nola.com (September 2005).

Drew Jubera and Mike Williams, "Gulf Coast Walloped; Storm Leaves Trail of Death, Destruction," *Atlanta Journal-Constitution,* August 30, 2005, p. A1.

Patricia Guthrie, "Atlanta Hospitals Brace for Influx. Already Taxed Facilities Worry about Resources," *Atlanta Journal-Constitution,* September 1, 2005, p. A7.

Charles Yoo, "Red Cross Atlanta Swamped by Influx," *Atlanta Journal-Constitution,* September 7, 2005, p. A1."Warring Officials Turn Disaster to Anarchy," *The New York Times,* September 11, 2005.

Jon Stewart, *The Daily Show,* September 12, 2005.

Mark O'Connell, president, United Way of Metropolitan Atlanta, briefing, September 13, 2005.

Elisabeth Bumiller and Richard W. Stevenson, "President Says He's Responsible in Storm Lapses," *The New York Times,* September 14, 2005.

Barbara Bradley Hagerty, "Charities Concerned about Red Cross Dominance," National Public Radio *Morning Edition,* September 13, 2005.

"Key Areas of Focus for Resettlement of Katrina Evacuees," United Way of Metropolitan Atlanta press release, September 13, 2005.

M.A.J. McKenna, "Medical System Strains to Cope in Louisiana," *Atlanta Journal-Constitution,* September 15, 2005, p. B1.

"United Way Giving Opportunities Following Hurricane Katrina," United Way of Metropolitan Atlanta press release, September 19, 2005.

"Neighbors Helping Neighbors: Find a Job Now," United Way of Metropolitan Atlanta press release, September 19, 2005.

"United Way Helps Georgians Come Together to Respond to Longer-Term Needs of Katrina Evacuees," United Way of Metropolitan Atlanta press release, September 19, 2005.

"United Way Announces First Round of Grants to Support Relief," United Way of Metropolitan Atlanta press release, September 29, 2005.

Questions

1. Why is the news media crucial to the coordination of disaster relief efforts? What can it do that others, even government, cannot?
2. Why would a good relationship with local news media be crucial for an emergency response organization in the wake of a disaster?
3. How can groups not as well known as United Way or the American Red Cross establish good relationships with the news media?
4. What would be major challenges to an organization such as UWMA trying to coordinate all the response efforts to a disaster?
5. What would be necessary for an organization to be able to coordinate such a massive undertaking?
6. Think of a likely crisis that could affect your city or university. As the leader of the crisis response effort: Who would you need to be involved? What would be the top 5 major issues you would need to handle? How would the news media be of help to your efforts? What kind of preparation before the crisis would be helpful? Necessary?

Summary

Media relations and publicity work are essential ingredients of public relations practice. In recent years the whole framework for media relations work has changed based on the growth and multiple uses of the Internet, global communication demands, and proliferating communication channels. The mass media offer an economical method for communicating with large and dispersed stakeholders, while the specialized press and online newsrooms are more useful in reaching more narrowly defined audience segments and stakeholders, including customers, investors, employees, the business press, and so on. Social media have inserted a new dimension into media relations with the technology making interaction possible between organizations and their stakeholders without going through the traditional media.

For self-testing and additional chapter resources, go to the Online Learning Center at **www.mhhe.com/lattimore3e.**

The relationship between journalists and public relations practitioners is a difficult one. If practitioners understand the media and the reporter's role, however, positive relationships can be developed that are beneficial to all.

Specific techniques for communicating with the media include publicity releases, news kits, news conferences, video releases, and news posted to Web pages. All of these approaches must be used judiciously—for publicity may backfire. Inappropriate publicity efforts can injure the relations that have been built over time with the media and the public. Electronic media have become especially important, with VNRs, electronic media kits, satellite press conferences, and satellite media tours leading the way. Public service announcements provide a means for nonprofits to communicate through radio and television. New technology has introduced social media such as blogs, wikis, and iPods into the media relations mix.

Key Terms

agenda
B-roll
blog
extranet
Internet
intranet
media kit
media relations
news conference
news release

planned publicity
press conference
press kit
publicity
Really Simple Syndication (RSS)
social media
spontaneous publicity
third-party endorsement
Web 2.0
wiki

Notes

1. Douglas Cater, *Press, Politics and Popular Government* (Washington, DC: American Enterprise Institute, 1972), pp. 83–84.

2. Cliff Webb quoted in Lucy Caldwell, "Maintaining Media Relations: One Perspective with Tips for Radio, Print and TV Personalities," *Government Communications* (July 1995), p. 16.

3. James L. Fetig, APR, in "Views on Media Relations from Both Sides of the Fence," Special Report, Public Relations, *PR Tactics* (December 1999). Online-1.

4. Caldwell, pp. 15–16.

5. "Future Perfect? Agency Leaders Reflect on the 1990s and Beyond," *Public Relations Strategist* (Summer 2001), p. 11.

6. *Editor & Publisher International Yearbook, Part I, Dailies* (New York: 2007), p. vi.

7. *Editor & Publisher International Yearbook, Part II, Weeklies* (New York: 2007), p. viii.

8. Baird Davis, "Why Consumer Magazine Circulation Levels Are Still Bloated, *Folio Magazine,* www.foliomag.com/2008, retrieved Aug. 5, 2008.

9. Harry A. Jessell, ed., *Broadcasting & Cable Yearbook 2005* (New York: Reed Business Information, 2008), pp. D-729–730.

10. Ibid., p. A-14.

11. Baran, p. 227.

12. Larry Maggett, "New Media: Evolution or Revolution," panel discussion at the Tech Museum of Innovation in San Jose, CA, convened by Ketchum Public Relations in April 2006.

13. B. J. Fogg, "New Media: Evolution or Revolution," panel discussion at the Tech Museum of Innovation in San Jose, CA, convened by Ketchum Public Relations in April 2006.

14. Ibid.

15. 2008 Digital Media Future Project, University of Southern California.

16. Jan Sokoloff Harkness, "Media Relations Training: Make It Work for You," *PR Tactics,* December 1999. Online-1.

17. Katie Sweeney, "Fuzzy Picture for VNRs, SMTs," *Public Relations Tactics* 12, no. 6 (June 2005), p. 18.

18. Ibid.

19. "Phair Testifies During Senate Committee Hearing on Pending VNR Legislation," *Public Relations Tactics* 12, no. 6 (June 2005), p. 19.

20. Ibid.

21. Michael Lissauer, "Online Media Strategy: Reaching Dot-com Newsrooms," *Public Relations Strategist* (Fall 2000), p. 26.

22. Nick Galifianakis, "Blog Growth," Infomatic, *Public Relations Tactics* 12, no. 3 (March 2005), p. 1.

23. Diane P. Burley, "Get the Conversation Started with Blogs," *Public Relations Tactics* 12, no. 8 (August 2005), p. 10.

24. Reid Goldsborough, "Blogging and the Law: Letting Loose Is Not Without Its Risks," *Public Relations Tactics* 12, no. 8 (August 2005), p. 11.

25. Elizabeth Albrycht, "Ten Ideas for Corporate RSS Feeds," *Public Relations Tactics* 12, no. 6 (June 2005), p. 15.

26. Kay Bransford, *Better Access, Better Information, Better News: The Ten Essential Elements of an Online Newsroom* (Lanham, MD: Vocus, 2001).

27. Carole M. Howard, "Technology and Tabloids: How the New Media World Is Changing Our Jobs," *Public Relations Quarterly* (Spring 2000), p. 11.

CHAPTER 10

Employee Communication

PREVIEW

Michael H. Mescon, a management professor and consultant, tells the story of an experience aboard a Delta Air Lines jet:

> I was just settling into my seat when I casually remarked to the fellow sitting next to me about the skyrocketing cost of airline tickets. The fellow didn't take my remark very casually. "Do you know why that ticket costs what it does?" he asked.
>
> No," I said, "And I don't really care."
>
> "Well, you ought to care," he said. "Because what that ticket pays for is your safety, comfort, and convenience."
>
> Well, by now I knew I was in for it. The guy told me what the carpet on the floor cost and why that particular kind of carpet had to be used. He explained the construction of the seat I was sitting in. He talked about support personnel on the ground for every plane in the air, and, of course, he dealt with the costs of jet fuel.
>
> Finally, I stopped him. "I know the president and several of Delta's vice presidents," I said. "You must be one of the vice presidents I don't know."
>
> "No," the fellow said, "I work in the upholstery shop."
>
> "Well, how do you know so much about Delta's operations?"
>
> "The company keeps us informed."

When organizations achieve effective employee communication, the results include more satisfied and productive employees, improved achievement of organizational goals, and improved customer, community, and investor relations.

Employees work in organizations with specific cultures. Effective employee communication depends on the establishment of a positive organizational culture, through clear communication policies, programs, and assistance with organizational change.

Employee communication will help employees become well informed about their organizations and encourage them to express their views to management.

Well-informed employees are usually satisfied employees. They are better, more productive workers who get more out of their work and do a better job for the organization. As the first spokespersons for their organization outside of work, well-informed employees interacting with an organization's stakeholders will have significant positive influence on relations with customers, the community, investors, and the media, to name a few important groups. In a nutshell, when lines of communication are open between employers and employees, organizational goals are more likely to be achieved.

Achieving successful communication within an organization is no simple task. Amid the corporate changes of the last few years, including corporate takeovers and mergers, downsizing, scandals, cost cutting, and technological changes, organizations face challenges to keep good employees and to hire new ones.

When hiring new employees, given the following labor force projections for 2010, employers will have to throw out old thinking about what workers want and need on the job:

1. Women will account for 48 percent of the labor force.
2. The baby-boom cohort (ages 46 to 62) will show significant growth.
3. The Asian labor force will be higher than average.
4. The Hispanic labor force will be larger than the black labor force.
5. The youth labor force (ages 16 to 24) will grow more rapidly than the overall labor force.[1]

Each of these demographic groups will bring very different expectations to their places of work and will require different strategic public relations thinking about their communication needs. Already, hiring and keeping productive employees means creating family-friendly policies, flexible scheduling, domestic partner benefits, sick days for dependent care, health club memberships, and time off for volunteer activities. See minicase 10.1 as an example of how employee demographics mean different thinking about employee retention.

Public relations practitioners look at plans for the employee Web site.

Employee Retention: It's the Employer Who's on Probation

Mini·Case 10.1

Remember ARCNET, the New Jersey engineering firm that gave each of its employees new BMWs as part of their benefits package (*pr reporter*, 9/20/99)? Nice touch and it worked. But a new study from O'Connor Kenny Partners (Memphis) says employers need not be so dramatic in efforts to retain employees. "Before doling out bonuses and cars, an organization should first study the demographics of its workforce to determine how little it may take to keep employees onboard," says director of communications Christine Luporter.

Luporter advises employers to take a look at their staffs and consider their true needs. She points to a case study of a midsized retailer with 2,000 stores. The retailer's workforce is 94 percent composed of female 20-something part-timers. The turnover rate is 1,170 percent, costing the retailer $1.3 million a year. The company estimates it takes 30 days for an employee to decide to stay with the company. "It used to be employees were the ones on probation. Today it's the employees who look at the company to determine if they will stay." This new strategy was devised:

- Look at the demographics. "For 20-somethings, it's about friendships and relationships," the retailer's human resource vice president finds. "They want to feel they belong, fit in, and want to make friends at work."

- During this 30-day time period, managers were told to implement "critical care"—essentially, a buddy program with a twist. Each new employee is assigned a buddy with a list of skills to be learned and goals to be met within the first 30 days. If the new hire stays past the 30 days and meets the goals, the buddy receives the financial incentive.

This pilot program slowed the turnover rate 20 percent last year. "The cost of that improvement is far less than a new fleet of cars," notes Luporter. "Essentially, employers should look at the root cause of the retention program. I'll bet they will find they can come up with a communications solution that is a lot cheaper than a new car or a huge bonus."

Questions

1. Why was the buddy program so successful? What is the thinking behind it?
2. How else would you advise employers who have high turnover rates to retain employees?

Source: pr reporter, January 31, 2000, p. 4.

Employee communication is a specialization of public relations concerned with "how public relations professionals in corporations, counseling firms, and nonprofit organizations help promote effective communication among employees and between line employees and top management."[2] Employee communication efforts begin before an employee is hired and carry on past the employee's departure from the organization. Thus, from recruitment to beyond separation, public relations has a major role to play in an employee's work experience.

THE ROLE OF EMPLOYEE COMMUNICATION

Employee communication, also called **internal communication** or **employee relations,** creates and maintains internal systems of communication between employers and employees. Communication lines are two-way, so that all employees participate freely in an exchange of information.

"Experts doubt that we'll ever return to the pre-boom era of 'company knows best.' In fact, as the economy continues to struggle, solid employee relations will play a key role in overall success," said Bernard Charland, senior vice president for Golin Harris, an international public relations firm.[3] To understand the process by which it is accomplished and the role of public relations in that process, we must first discuss the concept of organizational culture.

Organizational culture refers to the character of an organization, "its history, its approach to decision making, its way of treating employees, and its way of dealing with the world outside."[4] Another definition describes organizational culture as "the sum total of shared values, symbols,

THE CONCEPT OF ORGANIZATIONAL CULTURE

meanings, beliefs, assumptions, and expectations that organize and integrate a group of people who work together."[5]

The groundbreaking study *Excellence in Public Relations and Communication Management* identified two types of organizational culture—authoritarian and participative. **Authoritarian cultures** feature centralized decision making by the CEO and a few high-level managers. Departments have different agendas, sometimes in conflict with each other. Employees do not perceive rewards for innovation, but for following orders. They believe that their supervisors are interested in them only as workers and not as people. Authoritarian cultures are closed and resistant to change from outside the organization.[6]

Organizations with **participative cultures** feature the common value of teamwork. Employees feel empowered to make decisions rather than to wait for orders from those in power. The departments work together "like a well-oiled machine."[7] Department goals match overall organizational goals. Workers feel valued as people, not just as employees. Participative organizational cultures are open to new ideas from inside and outside the organization.[8]

The primary responsibility for organizational culture belongs to management—the decision makers of the organization. Successful managers seek a workplace culture that supports the goals of the organization. For example, General Motor's management has acknowledged the influence on its productivity of the labor strife of the automotive industry in recent decades by attempting to change its culture. GM management is attempting to move away from employees as cogs to employees as "a potential resource."[9] "We want them (employees) developing an actionable plan about what they can do themselves to make GM a more successful company," according to GM's vice president of communication.[10]

Public relations professionals can make three contributions to a productive workplace culture: (1) They can establish organizational communication policy based on a goal-oriented approach, (2) they can help in designing and implementing organizational change programs, and, most important, (3) they can provide expertise as employee communicators.

Establishing Communication Policy

An important factor in improving organizational culture is the establishment of communication policy. According to communication expert Norman Sigband, top management generally recognizes the need for and sincerely desires two-way communication.[11] The bottleneck in corporate communication is usually found in the middle of the corporate hierarchy. Breakdown in the communication process is most often at the first-line supervisor level.

Public relations managers can facilitate cultural change by convincing top management that communication, like finance, personnel, marketing, promotion, and almost every other area of organizational activity, should have established, clearly stated policies. Unstated policies leave dangerous vacuums that rumor, confusion, and misinformation rapidly fill.

Communication policies must be goal oriented rather than event oriented. In other words, rather than addressing specific issues or topics, policies should help employees understand, contribute to, and identify with organizational objectives and problems. Successful communication policies should reflect management's desire to do the following:

1. Keep employees informed of organizational goals, objectives, and plans.
2. Inform employees of organizational activities, problems, and accomplishments or any subject they consider important.

TABLE 10.1   Workers' Preferred Information Sources

1. Immediate supervisor
2. Small group meetings
3. Top executive
4. Annual report to employees
5. Employee handbook/other booklets
6. Orientation program
7. Regular local employee publication
8. Regular general employee publication
9. Bulletin board
10. Upward communication programs
11. Mass meetings
12. Audiovisual programs
13. Unions
14. Grapevine
15. Mass media

Source: IABC Study, quoted in Allen Center and Patrick Jackson, *Public Relations Practices,* 5th ed. (Englewood Cliffs, NJ: Longman, 1995), p. 40.

3. Encourage employees to provide input, information, and feedback to management based on their experience, insights, feelings, creativity, and reason.

4. Level with employees about negative, sensitive, or controversial issues.

5. Encourage frequent, honest, job-related, two-way communication among managers and their subordinates.

6. Communicate important events and decisions as quickly as possible to all employees, especially before they learn from media. They must be told first.

7. Establish a culture where innovation and creativity are encouraged.

8. Urge every manager and supervisor to discuss with each subordinate the latter's progress and position in the firm.

Employees want information first from their immediate supervisors, as shown in table 10.1. The last place they want to hear the company news is in the media.

Organizational Change

Employee communication expert Gary Grates believes that organizations of the future will be structured to accommodate change, and employee communication will have an integral role. This role should include forecasting and monitoring relationships with key audiences and planning flexible communication structures so that employees will understand and support new situations and organizational environments. Grates shared these lessons with the PRSA counselors:

1. Planning for communications replaces a communications plan.
2. Lead people through dialogue, discussion, and dissent.
3. Think externally to legitimize internal actions.
4. Become conversant and knowledgeable about the goals and priorities of the organization.
5. Accept the fact that real change is about uncertainty.

6. Help management turn complex business initiatives into simple, easily understood concepts so employees can comprehend them and contribute to their successful implementation.

7. Understand what managers and employees understand.

8. Don't underestimate people's desire for relevant information.

9. Communications must be integrated into change by organizational leaders.

10. It is how you think, not what you do.

11. Become a teacher.

12. Define communication as information exchanged between and among human beings.[12]

Employee values have shifted. If employers want to count on a productive workforce in changing times, they have to understand why employees will work for an organization and the commitment they desire.

THE IMPORTANCE OF EMPLOYEE COMMUNICATION

Four realities of employee communication establish its importance for organizational success. First, employees want information about their companies and they crave communication, especially from their leaders. Second, there is a link between open communication and manager satisfaction with their roles. A study by the Institute of Excellence in Employee Management Communications reported that "more than 90 percent of managers who felt they had the ability to offer ideas and question management decisions were also highly satisfied and engaged in their jobs."[13] Third, effective two-way communication is key to addressing new business challenges because employees are more confident that they can help move their businesses forward.[14] Fourth, employee communications can be critical to maintaining good customer experiences. Employees convey the brand, according to Bill Margaritis, senior vice president of FedEx corporate communications:

> We like our employees to know what our brand attributes are, including the vision and values of the company. So, when we made some acquisitions and the new employees started wearing the FedEx uniform and selling the FedEx service, it was important that we made sure they understood the value of the culture and the value of the brand. We didn't want any gaps in what we promised and what we delivered.[15]

Employee communication has become a distinctive specialization of public relations, involving ongoing programs of communication, communicating with labor unions in collective bargaining and strike situations, and explaining employee benefits. Employee communication has its own theories and practices, including controlled specialized media.

Special Employee Communication Situations

One of the special employee situations involves communication with employees who are union members.

Unions in the Workforce Environment   Unions are powerful organizations. They are active in the political arena. Sometimes in conjunction with business and sometimes in opposition to business, they exert a powerful influence on the government's

FedEx employee communication is spread worldwide and must make use of technology to keep them informed and to get their feedback.

role in the economy. Workers join unions to gain the power necessary to better pursue their needs and goals. Increased pay, shorter hours, and improved working conditions are common reasons for unionizing.

Many organizations attempt to use effective employee communications to ward off union efforts to organize their labor force. The threat of unionization, in effect, scares management into instituting communication policies and programs that should have existed in the first place. Unfortunately, the timing and motivation of efforts to establish the proper communication climate and facilitate upward communication have sometimes caused employers to be perceived as anti-union. Unionization of an organization's workforce places employee communication and public relations in a slightly different light, but basic practices of effective employee communication still hold.

Public Relations in Collective Bargaining   When union representation has been established, management is required to bargain in good faith with its representatives. All matters relating to a previously established set of issues are resolved through a process known as **collective bargaining,** which Harold Davey defines this way:

> A continuing institutional relationship between an employer . . . and a labor organization . . . concerned with the negotiation, administration, interpretation, and enforcement of written agreements covering joint understandings as to wages or salaries, rates of pay, hours of work, and other conditions of employment.[16]

Davey's phrase "continuing institutional relationship" is an important one. The general public has a poor understanding of collective bargaining, associating the process with strikes, labor unrest, or protracted negotiations. In fact, these are exceptional circumstances. In 98 percent of negotiations, contracts are agreed on without resorting to strikes or lockouts.

Contract negotiations and strikes often draw intense public scrutiny. At such times, the public relations function becomes very important, and practitioners really earn their pay. Part of the challenge is the sensitive nature of the negotiations under way. Management and labor usually agree that public disclosure of the negotiating process would result in miscommunication at best and would lead to disruption and intransigence at worst.

When negotiations are successfully concluded, the public relations spokesperson should tell the story of that success and explain the contract terms to the public. The contract and its impact on the local or national economy are matters of critical public interest and importance. Even after a strike, when the ending of conflict seems to be the main story, information concerning these factors has to be spelled out clearly in organizational and mass media.

Communicating Employee Benefits   "Too often, we dismissed functions like internal communications or benefits communications as necessary but not too interesting. Well, get ready. Because of Enron, internal communication is about to take center stage,"[17] writes specialist Jody Buffington Aud.

Employee benefits are services an organization provides as part of employees' compensation. Benefits may include health and life insurance programs, sick leave, vacations, employer-paid social security, retirement programs such as Enron's 405(k) plan, and a variety of other services ranging from day care to prepaid legal advice to physical fitness programs. Benefits attract and motivate employees and promote employee productivity.

In relation to employee benefits, managers often claim employees "just don't appreciate what they have." Often this lack of appreciation is the result of poor communication on the part of management, as the following episode illustrates:

> Workers at a corporation had just voted for union representation, and one of the strongest appeals the union offered was its benefits package. Management could not understand what had made the package so attractive to employees. "Those benefits offer no substantial improvements over the package we already had," complained one executive. Closer examination, however, revealed that the company had never prepared publications to explain its package. Employee meetings to discuss benefits were irregular, almost nonexistent. No employee handbook or guide had been published; no orientation program for new employees had been established. There is little doubt that when the employees cast their ballots for the union, they were not voting for better benefits but for communication and a plan they understood.

Some organizations have become highly creative in benefits communication. United Technologies developed a 17-minute film/video featuring a popular comedian to discuss six benefit areas: retirement, health care, disability, life insurance, dental care, and savings plans. Bankers Land Company of Palm Beach Gardens, Florida, devised a game board to explain health benefits. Exxon Coal USA put together its 81-page *Guide to Your Employee Benefits* in the style of a magazine or annual report. Golin Harris used the theme "GH Lifeworks" to capture the idea of its employee benefits package.

The role of corporate communicators in dealing with employee benefits can be vitally significant. Public relations practitioners working in this area do not merely disseminate information about existing programs. Perhaps more important, they can serve

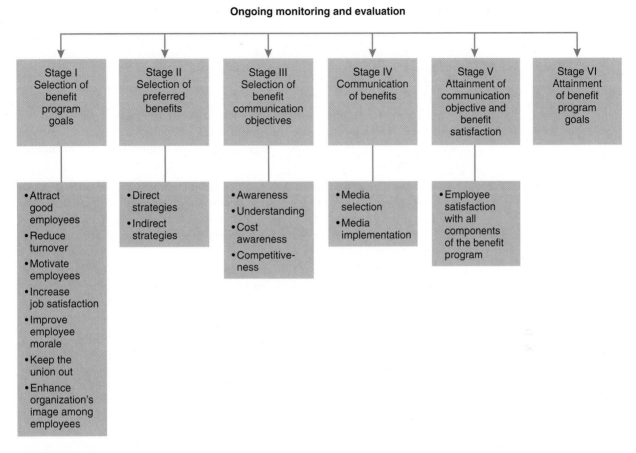

FIGURE 10.1   A Model of Benefits Communication

as conduits for the expression of employees' needs and desires, and thus play a significant role in determining and evaluating benefit programs. Figure 10.1 is a model of the benefit communication process, demonstrating the various points at which corporate communicators can be useful.

In the first part of this chapter, we took a general approach to employee communication. We discussed a positive organizational culture supported by appropriate communication policies as prerequisites for effective employee communication. We also discussed employee communication under special circumstances and for special purposes.

THE MEDIA OF EMPLOYEE COMMUNICATION

This section is devoted to the technical aspects of employee communication media—how to get your message across. Internal media, video, and new media are means of reaching large numbers of employees on an ongoing basis. Personnel and resources devoted to these media have increased markedly in the past decade. This is the fastest growing aspect of the overall public relations effort. It is also the effort over which we have the most control. That's why **internal media** are often called "controlled media."

Objectives of Internal Media

In a broad sense, the goal of internal media is the improvement of relationships between employees and management. Setting policy and defining more specific objectives for such internal media is a complicated undertaking. Without specific guidelines, however, it is hard for an in-house medium to be successful, and it is even harder to measure its success.

As we have said, in-house media must fulfill the needs of both the organization and its employees. Employee audiences must see the information in the medium as useful and meaningful. Following are some broad topics that are frequently chosen by successful internal media:

1. *Employees' Understanding of Their Role in the Organization.* Internal media can stress the importance of each worker's job in meeting organizational goals. Information about the eventual use of products illustrates the importance of everyone's part in the process. Internal publications should support the idea that each employee is a representative for the organization.

2. *Clarification of Management Policies.* Consider the point of view of both management and employees. Employees must be accurately informed about business activities if management expects them to support its programs. Understanding can be helped by explaining policies and rules, which builds confidence in management, and by combating rumors and misunderstandings.

3. *Employee Well-Being and Safety.* This is explained through information on safety practices, rules, and procedures. Worker safety is always an appropriate area of concern for management and employees. In some organizations, this involves little more than ensuring that everyone knows the location of fire exits. In others, however, the success of the operation, and indeed the operation itself, may depend on adherence to safety procedures.

   There is a continuing need to explain benefits, vacations, holidays, taxes, workers' compensation, affirmative action, and equal employment opportunity policies. Employees want to know about community issues and educational and training opportunities.

4. *Recognition of Employee Achievements.* This should occur both on the job and in the community, to encourage internal cooperation by helping management and employees become better acquainted with other members of the organization. Social activities can also be recognized but should not take precedence over job-related and community-service accomplishments.

An in-house medium can accomplish these objectives if it meets the needs of employees, says something that employees want to think about and talk about, and is attractive and easy to read.

What type of media does your organization need? An organization must decide what kinds of internal media will best meet its needs: a newsletter, a tabloid newspaper, a magazine, a home page, video news, an intranet, or some other format. Sometimes communication needs change. Frequency of publication and methods of distribution should also be decided based on the preferences of the employee audiences. Most in-house publications are published monthly, but some appear quarterly or even weekly. The easiest, cheapest, and simplest method of distribution is to make them available for pickup around work areas. To get wider distribution, some organizations hand print materials directly to employees, use the in-house mail, or send them to employees' homes. All of these matters are interdependent. The format (size and shape) may limit the possibilities for distribution.

However, it is too easy to fall back on print media as the preferred choice. They are the most traditional forms used in organizations, but consider how best to communicate emergency information. It might be easy to send messages electronically to an established listserv, but what if there is no electricity? How about a cell phone chain? Our technology permits us to communicate rapidly, which we need to do internally when a crisis occurs, but face-to-face delivery of messages is still the most preferred and might be the most effective in crisis situations.

Other considerations in determining the number and kinds of media are budget and researching what employees want to know. Once a budget for the medium is established, information about employee needs must be gathered. Interviews and questionnaires can tell a great deal about content, frequency, and distribution needs. To help select a format, many companies ask employee panels or focus groups to review sample media from other organizations. The panel can also evaluate data obtained in the interviews and questionnaires. The results of such planning efforts help set objectives and evaluation measures for which communication media will be used.

Starting Internal Media

Producing an internal medium takes organization and coordination. It must appear at regularly scheduled intervals. Such consistency requires budget and staff. Putting out a medium on a shoestring may be worse than doing nothing at all. A medium, such as a Web site, that cannot be properly maintained creates negative attitudes by building expectations it cannot fulfill. Therefore, organizing the details of production is key to to its effectiveness.

What is news? The content of an internal medium varies from one organization to another. Remember, company information must satisfy the needs of its employees, not just those of management. Topics of most importance to employees in an IABC study are shown in order of importance in table 10.2. There is an increasing employee concern

TABLE 10.2	Subjects of Interest to Employees	
Rank	**Subject**	**Scale (1–10)**
1	Organizational plans for the future	8
2	Job advancement opportunities	7
3	Job-related "how-to" information	7
4	Productivity improvement	6
5	Personnel policies and practices	6
6	How we're doing vs. the competition	6
7	How my job fits into the organization	6
8	How external events affect my job	5
9	How profits are used	5
10	Financial results	4
11	Advertising and promotional plans	4
12	Operations outside of my department or division	4
13	Organizational stand on current issues	4
14	Personnel changes and promotions	4
15	Organizational community involvement	4
16	Human interest stories about other employees	2
17	Personal news (birthdays, anniversaries, etc.)	2

Source: Allen Center, Patrick Jackson, Stacy Smith, and Frank R. Stansberry, *Public Relations Practices,* 7th ed. (Upper Saddle River, NJ: Pearson/Prentice-Hall, 2008), p. 26.

for job security, which is evident in the top item of importance, "organizational plans for the future." The wishes of workers are clear: They want to know where the organization is headed, what its plans are for getting there, and what that means to them.

Set and maintain strict policies about what will be published in-house. The following criteria can help evaluate a topic's newsworthiness:

1. *Timeliness.* Is the topic timely enough to interest most of the readers?
2. *Scope.* Does it affect enough people directly or indirectly?
3. *Noteworthiness.* Is something or someone important or well known involved?
4. *Human Interest.* Does it deal with things vital to the interests of the readers or those involved?

Objectivity is an important goal of internal media, but in-house media should have a more personal tone than public newspapers or magazines. They should reflect a sense of closeness and common interest that says to the reader, "We're all in this together."

Controlling Internal Media

Every medium should periodically evaluate its progress toward its objectives. Purpose, content, and frequency of publication should all be examined in terms of the needs of the target audience. The panel that originally identified the target audience can be used again to evaluate progress. Surveys and questionnaires also give useful information about how well a medium fulfills expectations. National magazines have found that even simple surveys can provide excellent insight into the interests of readers. To pretest the potential readership of planned articles, for example, a questionnaire can be prepared that lists various headlines and asks a sample of the intended audience which articles they would read. An editor can thus get feedback about the probable success of certain stories.

Occasional and Special Media

Most organizations prepare publications on miscellaneous topics at irregular intervals. Forms range from mimeographed one-sheet leaflets to books by professional writers. Responsibility for these is often with human resources personnel because of legal requirements, government regulations, or company policy. But in smaller organizations, public relations people may also become involved. These publications can generally be divided into three categories, according to purpose:

1. *Orientation literature* explains organizational policies to new members. It can help a new employee get off to a good start by setting forth the ground rules. Goals and objectives of the organization are often included to give a sense of where the company is going and the employee's role in achieving that objective.
2. *Reference material* is designed to be kept for future use. Because of the nature of these publications, it is unlikely that anyone will ever read them from cover to cover; therefore, they must give fast and easy answers. Because this information sometimes changes, publications should be designed so that supplements or other materials can be added later. Reference materials deal with subjects like benefits, insurance, and recreation programs.
3. *Position or special-topic publications* are put out only once. They deal with a specific subject or occasion the organization feels it should discuss. The free enterprise system, charitable and social commitments, history, awards, and scientific or technological developments are among the most frequently treated subjects. Occasional

publications have more impact than regularly scheduled newsletters and give an organization the chance to convey a specific message. The same requirements of credibility and interest that apply to newsletters must be followed if special-topic publications are to state their message effectively.

Leaflets, Inserts, and Enclosures   Inexpensive publications that may be read and thrown away are often printed on a single sheet that can be folded to produce any of several formats. Leaflets or handbills duplicated on a copying machine are inexpensive and fast to prepare. With a little more effort, single-sheet publications can be folded into brochures for information racks, in-house distribution, or direct mail. Many organizations use them as inserts in pay envelopes.

Booklets and Manuals   Because of their expense, booklets and manuals are made to be read and saved for reference. Their greatest shortcoming is that they can be hard to read and use if not designed properly. Employee orientation manuals or insurance plan booklets need indexes, and their information can be more accessible if tabs or color-coded pages are supplied.

Booklets and manuals can be used successfully to do the following:

1. Orient new employees.
2. Convey information in jargon-free, non-technical language.
3. Explain the safety regulations as they comply with Occupational Safety and Health Administration (OSHA) standards.
4. Explain the benefit plan and its value to the employee.
5. Explain company policies and their compliance with government regulations.
6. Explain the costs and benefits of the organization's insurance package.
7. Explain the company retirement plan and its requirements.
8. Give information helpful to the employee in his or her job.
9. Give information about social or community issues.
10. Explain organizational compliance with environmental standards.

Printed Speeches and Reprints   Speeches and reprints are sometimes distributed as publications. When organization officials speak to professional, community, or other groups concerning topics of interest to employees, it may be useful to print them for distribution within the organization. Reprints of magazine articles of concern to the organization and its employees can be bought inexpensively. Magazine reprints have the advantage of outside credibility.

Message Displays   A growing number of laws and regulations require that notices be posted where employees can see them, and many organizations find this a quick, inexpensive way to reach large numbers of people. Message displays include posters, kiosks, electronic and standard bulletin boards, information racks, and exhibits.

Bulletin Boards   The bulletin board displays messages in regular locations with minimum effort and expense. The board remains a much-used and effective means of communication within organizations. Notices that have been mailed or given out to employees can also be posted as reminders. Details of announcements already made in meetings or in the house publication can be posted for those who wish more information. Further, bulletin boards are an appropriate location for information that the law requires to be posted.

To ensure credibility and readability, bulletin boards must be carefully planned and kept current. In electronic form through intranets, listservs, and special Web sites, they can provide time-sensitive information as well.

Posters and Billboards   Like bulletin boards, posters and billboards offer fast, effective communication. They are most appropriately used to give emphasis to an idea and provide messages that can be grasped quickly. Posters and billboards should be placed in high-traffic areas where they can easily be seen by most employees.

Information Racks   Information racks are designed to invite the reader to take the brochures or booklets displayed. Racks should provide information that cannot be handled in short messages, such as manuals, booklets, printed speeches, and reprints. Because the materials are selected by readers without pressure from management, interest is likely to be higher. The economic advantage to information racks is that only interested employees are likely to take material.

Information racks work best in areas where employees can look at the material in a leisurely way, such as cafeterias and lounges. Empty information racks suggest that management is uninterested, so regular maintenance is needed.

Exhibits, Banners, and Displays   Exhibits, banners, and displays rely primarily on visual messages. Their effectiveness is in showing a sample or model of what is being discussed. Many organizations recognize the value of exhibits and displays at industrial meetings or in sales-related contexts, but they are equally valuable in employee communication. Exhibits and displays can show how production facilities work, display products, honor those who receive awards, or depict the history of the organization. Banners announce and celebrate special events and occasions.

Electronic Media   New technology has led to at least four major electronic approaches to employee communication. Electronic-mail communication, through organizational intranets, computer home pages, internal video, and Web blogs, or social media are fast becoming the media of choice by employers and employees alike. IBM offers employees blogging tools to keeping one another informed about the organization, for town meetings and brainstorming sessions (called Innovative Jams), and to receive input of employees and to encourage employee exchange of concerns and opinions.[18]

> *E-mail.* Because of its immediacy, ease of distribution, and virtually no added cost, electronic mail has become a major employee communication tool. It's even relatively inexpensive for organizations that are spread throughout the world to maintain their own controlled intranets.
>
> *Home Pages.* A fast-growing, controlled media is the computer home page. With graphic and sound capability coupled with the advantages of e-mail, this medium may soon replace the company newsletter as the employee communication tool of choice.
>
> *Internal Video.* For the past 20 years, larger companies, especially those spread over several distant locations, have turned to internal video to keep employees informed about the organization.

We'll soon be starting a feature on this blog [see Source below] that contains a regularly updated list of important blogs that I think those of us involved in employee engagement and communications should be reading. In the meantime, here are a few to get you started. Don't see your favorite one? Please comment on it, and we'll add it to our master list.

A Shel of My Former Self (http://blog.holtz.com). Run by Shel Holtz, principle of Holtz Communication and Technology, it contains one of the best lists of hot blogs for communicators, as well as a weekly podcast on communications issues that he co-produces with Neville Hobson of the Nev On blog referenced in this list.

BNET (www.bnet.com). A compelling collection of blog links, white papers, and perspectives on business issues. Content is organized by interest to particular job function or industry.

CorporatePR (http://ringblog.typepad.com/corporatepr). Covers a wide variety of communications issues as surfaced by Elizabeth Albrycht, a 15-year veteran of high-technology public relations.

Diva Marketing (http://bloomberg marketing.blogs.com). Authored by Toby Bloomberg of Bloomberg Marketing, it contains a rich mix of links to other blogs and insights into how high-profile blogs were created and are maintained.

Elanceur (http://elanceur.weblogger.com). Written by Christophe Ducamp and focused on wikis, cooperation, e-talking, e-writing, tribal marketing, e-influence, and online communities. Ducamp is co-author of the book *Les Blog* and co-founder of CraoWiki, one of the most influential French wikicommunities.

Micropersuasion (www.micropersuasion.com). Run by Steve Rubel, a vice president at Cooper Katz in New York City, this blog offers commentary and how-to resources for marketers, advertisers, and communications professionals.

Musings from POP! Public Relations (http://pop-pr.blogspot.com). A collection of insights, photos, and interesting links from Jeremy Pepper, principle of POP! Public Relations.

Nev On (http://nevon.typepad.com/nevon/investor relations). Neville Hobson is an independent communicator based in the Netherlands who offers insights, links, and commentary about a variety of business issues and who has a special interest in business communications and technology.

Source: www.edelman.com/speak_up/empeng/archives/2005/06/mustread_blogs.html (Feb. 21, 2006).

Blogs. Public relations people can learn how well their organizations are communicating with employees by reading employee blogs. Spotlight 10.1 is a blog by a public relations agency head providing information on employee engagement.

Maintaining Employee Relationships in a Tragedy

Case Study

Company in Crisis

West Pharmaceutical Services, Inc. (NYSE:WST) is a global drug delivery technology company. When an explosion ripped through its Kinston, North Carolina, factory, leaving death and injury in its wake, West Pharmaceutical Services became an immediate lightning rod for media coverage and controversy that had very real potential to harm the health of this $500 million public corporation.

Communications Objectives

Schwartz Communications helped West navigate the crisis by

- Building awareness that concern for human life is always West's top priority and that West's top decision makers were fully engaged with the crisis. Within the first 24 hours, Schwartz immediately established itself as a reliable and responsive source of information with the media and worked with West to implement processes for information gathering, decision making, and rapid response.

- Diffusing media speculation linking West's OSHA safety violations with the explosion. It was critical to build awareness that West was cooperating with public officials and to reassure West employees that working conditions in other locations were safe.

- Building public awareness of West's commitment to affected employees and their families and, on the business side, awareness of West's continued ability to fulfill customer product needs.

- Communicating West's desire and intention to rebuild the plant. Schwartz began to implement its government relations initiatives at this time in order to build partnerships with public officials so as to explore options for recovery assistance.

Public Relations Approach

- Schwartz convened a crisis team representing PR, operations, finance, legal and human resources.

- Schwartz developed and issued a press statement, preparing the CEO to be spokesperson and dispatching him to North Carolina, and secured timely interviews with the Associated Press, CBS News, ABC News, and local media.

- With investigations from the U.S. Chemical Safety Board, FBI, and ATF under way, Schwartz organized a news conference at a local airport, where CEO Don Morel confirmed that criminal activity had been ruled out, that the explosion's cause remained unknown, and that West was fully cooperating with government agencies and also conducting its own investigation.

- Through CEO Morel, Schwartz issued press statements to communicate West's actions regarding grief counseling and future intentions for disaster relief. Schwartz wrote and placed a series of corporate advertisements from West to thank all rescue and recovery workers and doctors for their efforts.

- To soothe community- and companywide grief, Schwartz planned, produced, and promoted a memorial service and drafted written remarks for all presenters. Schwartz produced the event as a live broadcast, providing an external line to regional television stations so they could cover it live without disrupting the proceedings. Schwartz secured the attendance of key governmental officials to set a tone of importance.

- When Schwartz was asked by West to announce official layoffs at the point that extended salary benefits were ending for plant employees, Schwartz used the opportunity to restate that West had offered employment, via relocation, to nearly 100 percent of all Kinston plant workers.

- Sensitive to the interests of elected government officials, Schwartz initiated meetings for West with Governor Mike Easley, Senator Elizabeth Dole, Senator John Edwards, and Congressman Frank Ballance. Schwartz also organized a Kinston economic recovery summit in Washington, D.C., for West's CEO and government officials.

Results

All media coverage positively conveyed the steps that West was taking to address the financial, medical, and emotional needs of employees and their families.

Offers of economic recovery relief have been privately tendered, including land, $2 million in environmental cleanup, and grants for emergency services equipment damaged in recovery efforts. In May 2003, West received an economic incentive package from the local Lenoir County Board of Commissioners, who also approved the sale of a community-owned building to West. In addition, the governor of North Carolina granted West, through a state fund, $250,000 for the relocation of the Kinston plant that was destroyed less than four months earlier.

Two months after the disaster, West's stock price was virtually unchanged from where it was at the point and immediate aftermath of the Kinston event.

Source: Adapted from http://schwartz-pr.com/case_studies_pages.php?ind=9&id=39 (Feb. 21, 2006).

Questions

1. What did Schwartz PR do to maintain West's relationships with employees?
2. What types of controlled media are indicated in this case?
3. Do you agree or disagree with the Schwartz PR's employee communication strategy? Why or why not?

Summary

For self-testing and additional chapter resources, go to the Online Learning Center at www.mhhe.com/lattimore3e.

Employee communication is a large and complex aspect of public relations practice. Many different topics and issues confront practitioners working in this area. In this chapter, we discussed the importance of keeping employees informed, creating the proper organizational culture to facilitate proper communication, establishing communication policy, and building employee communication programs. We also considered the special issues of employer communication with a unionized workforce and communication of employee benefits. Finally, we detailed production of employee newsletters and other media. Armed with this knowledge and these tools, public relations practitioners can make great contributions to their organizations' success.

Key Terms

authoritarian cultures
collective bargaining
communication policies
employee benefits
employee communication

employee relations
internal communication
internal media
organizational culture
participative cultures

Notes

1. www.diversityrescoures.com/nas/labor_force_proj.htm, accessed on March 27, 2008. Excerpt from Howard N. Fullerton, Jr., and Mitra Toossi, "Labor Force Projections to 2010: Steady Growth and Changing Composition," *Monthly Labor Review* (November 2001).

2. Employee Communications. www.prsa.org/empcom.

3. Bernard Charland, "Commentary: Employee Relations—Back to the Future?" Accessed at www. golinharris.com.

4. David M. Dozier, Larissa A. Grunig, and James E. Grunig, *The Manager's Guide to Excellence in Public Relations and Communication Management* (Mahwah, NJ: Erlbaum, 1995), p. 17.

5. K. Sriramesh, James E. Grunig, and Jody Buffington, "Corporate Culture and Public Relations," in *Excellence in Public Relations and Communication Management,* ed. James E. Grunig (Hillsdale, NJ: Erlbaum, 1992), p. 591.

6. Larissa A. Grunig, James E. Grunig, and David M. Dozier, *Excellent Public Relations and Effective Organizations: A Study of Communication Management in Three Countries* (Mahwah, NJ: Erlbaum, 2002), pp. 482–83.

7. Ibid.

8. Ibid., p. 482.

9. "Working with the Workers," *PR Week,* July 1, 2002, p. 15.

10. Ibid.

11. This discussion is based on Norman B. Sigband, "What's Happening to Employee Commitment?" *Personnel Journal* (February 1974), pp. 133–35.

12. Gary F. Grates, "Ten Tumultuous Years: Examining a Decade of Change (A Peek at the Future)." www.prsa_counselors.org, retrieved March 10, 2002.

13. "Managers Want to Be More Than a Channel of Communication," *Holmes Report.* www.holmesreport.com/holmestemp/story, retrieved July 18, 2002.

14. Ibid.

15. "Working with the Workers," p. 15.

16. Quoted in Donal P. Crane, *Personnel: The Management of Human Resources,* 2nd ed. (Belmont, CA: Wadsworth, 1979), p. 79.

17. Jody Buffington Aud, "What Internal Communicators Can Learn from Enron," *The Public Relations Strategist* 9 (Spring 2002), p. 12.

18. Gary F. Grates, "Why Don't I Know?" *Perspective* 1 (3), p. 5.

CHAPTER 11

Community Relations

Businesses should want to be integral to the lives of those who live in the cities and neighborhoods where they operate. A well-planned community relations program can have a positive effect on many areas, including recruitment, employee relations, and economic success. All businesses, regardless of size or type, can benefit from such a program, as the following example illustrates.

Billie found herself frequently explaining to her friends what she did as a summer intern at her local newspaper. No, she didn't cover stories or sell ads. She worked in community relations. Billie had to admit that until a month ago, she, too, didn't know that newspapers even did community relations. Now she realizes that newspapers and media outlets are like any other business that wants to give back to its local community.

Her days were packed. One of Billie's first activities of the day was to review and edit the calendar item submissions received from the paper's Web site. Sometimes the person who submitted the item had a question, so Billie would follow up with an e-mail or phone call. She also collected applications for grants. Her paper would provide funding—between $10,000 and $40,000—to agencies and organizations in the area served by the paper. The community could point to many wonderful results of this investment as the money often addressed problems in the areas of literacy and education, domestic violence, and arts and culture. Unfortunately there were more requests than there was money, and Billie knew her boss and the citizens who served on the selection committee had difficult decisions to make.

Billie tried to devote several hours each day to planning for the annual holiday fund-raising drive. The newspaper worked with health and human services agencies throughout the area to raise money for worthwhile projects. She was gathering information about projects and programs that would be highlighted in the integrated campaign, including advertising, editorial,

Internet, and direct mail. The Web site needed to be updated to reflect the current campaign. Billie also needed to think about the number of volunteers that would be needed and what their responsibilities would be. She was thankful for all of the materials that were available from the previous year, even though most needed to be reviewed and updated. Every penny of the millions raised could go to a worthwhile cause because her paper absorbed the administrative costs through her department.

Billie hoped that she would be able to land a community relations position after graduation. She loved being a part of what was being developed and planned for the local area. It was satisfying to see people benefit from what her department and other citizen leaders did. But for now, Billie turned her attention to the first item on her ever-growing to-do list.

THE IMPORTANCE OF COMMUNITY RELATIONS

The headlines tell of global mergers and acquisitions, spin-offs, initial public offerings, and corporate earnings that are lower or higher than expected. Marketing, technology, resource acquisition, and management are increasingly international in scope, and the federal government is the most conspicuous aspect of many organizations' operating environments.

In this large-scale environment, concern for community seems almost small and old-fashioned. But appearances are deceiving. As the following two examples illustrate, citizens care deeply about what happens in their communities. It's where they live and work, raise their families, educate their children, and spend most of their time.

Residents living near Pier 40 in the Hudson River Park of Manhattan, New York, said no to a $625-million entertainment complex that would house Cirque du Soleil and other visitor attractions. Noted one concerned citizen: "The life of a neighborhood is at stake." Board members of the park's trust struggle with how to address the desires of those who live nearby with the need to raise funds for the area's upkeep.[1]

Representatives of British business and tourism organizations and the English government's transport secretary are going head-to-head with environmentalists and some government officials over the need to expand Heathrow, the world's busiest airport. Long lines, congestion, and increased travel times threaten to divert travelers to other facilities, endangering jobs, exports, and the airport's reputation as Europe's main gateway, say supporters. Opponents fear increased noise and pollution and damage to the environment. Up to 700 homes may need to be demolished in the process. The public stands to both win and lose.[2]

Countless other examples demonstrate how neighbors are banding together to improve their schools, security, and community services and how corporations and other organizations are reaching out to their communities. Back-to-the-city movements are repopulating many metropolitan areas; downtown businesses are reviving after years of inactivity; people are interested in family and community roots. As Detroit Mayor Kwame F. Kilpatrick noted, "If you don't have community pride, if you don't have a safe, clean city, you don't have a world-class city."[3]

The lesson for organizations is simple: Regional, national, and international concerns may preoccupy you, but don't forget the folks next door. In the past, constructive community relations programs were characterized by phrases like "corporate citizenship" or "good neighbor." Now the concept is one of selection, with communities and corporations choosing each other for mutually beneficial purposes.

Today's corporations must cooperate as well as compete to succeed. An organization becomes part of the community, creating win-win solutions that result in a healthier bottom line and in benefits for stakeholders and for society as a whole. The key to any effective community relations program is positive, socially responsible *action* to help the community on the part of the organization.

Effective community relations depend on recognizing the interdependence of institutions with their communities. The cycle begins with people wanting to live in good communities and bringing their talents and skills to the local labor market. Corporations hire those employees who help the organization make a profit. A corporation then uses its resources to address needs and to make the community an even better place to live.

Ford Motor Company is just one example of this interdependence. The company's 2001 corporate citizenship report notes that the same employees who are the lifeblood of its organization are also the lifeblood of their communities. They live in the same communities in which the company operates, and many are investors in Ford. The car company's customers include employees, investors, business partners, and members of local communities and society more broadly. Ford considers this interdependence as an advantage: The steps they take to build deeper relationships with one stakeholder group may result in greater knowledge of another stakeholder group.[4]

All types of organizations practice community relations. Schools, churches, hospitals, museums, and groups like the Red Cross and the Boy Scouts depend on community relations the way businesses depend on marketing—as the primary means by which "customers" are attracted. Prisons, military bases, and universities must strive for community acceptance. Except for corporate philanthropy, however, the process of community relations is the same whether or not the organization seeks financial profit.

Every community has a vital stake in the economic health and prosperity of its institutions. Every organization has a vital stake in the health and prosperity of the community it inhabits. Quite naturally, therefore, organizations and their communities develop a mutual interest in each other's successful and effective operation. Spotlight 11.1 outlines the scope of Kodak's involvement in the global communities in which it does business. More than half of the company's sales come from outside the United States, and its community relations practices support initiatives in quality of life, diversity and inclusion, technology access, and education in those locales.

At the very least, organizations expect communities to provide adequate municipal services, fair taxation, good living conditions for employees, a good labor supply, and a reasonable degree of support for the plant and its products. In addition to employment, wages, and taxes, communities expect from their institutions an attractive appearance, support of community institutions, economic stability, and a focus on hometown pride.

Good community relations aids in securing what the organization needs from the community and in providing what the community expects. Moreover, it helps to protect organizational investments, increase sales of products and stock, improve the general operating climate, and reduce costs of dealing with government agencies. Positive community relations can affect worker productivity when organizations sponsor community health and education programs. Also, favorable community attitudes may influence worker attitudes toward the organization. The best community relations programs are those that flow naturally from the organization's resources.

Spotlight 11.1 | Kodak's Commitment to Community during Transformation

As a leader in corporate citizenship, Kodak has maintained a commitment to the communities in which it does business. The company prioritizes four key areas:

- Community quality of life
- Diversity and inclusion
- Technology access
- Education

At the heart of this commitment is continuous improvement in everything it does. In 2007, Kodak completed a four-year transformation to become a leader in digital imaging technologies. This encompassed a global reduction in its physical facilities, as well as a reduction of some 30,000 employees. Yet, the company honored its community commitments.

Environment

During this transition, Kodak continued its progress to reduce the environmental impacts associated with its traditional business. In 2003, Kodak enacted a second set of five-year Health, Safety, and Environment (HSE) goals to reduce emissions, conserve resources, and enhance the company's product stewardship and employee safety. In 2005, Kodak met or surpassed all of its manufacturing-focused HSE goals. These goals were achieved well ahead of schedule by implementing lean manufacturing practices and reducing manufacturing assets ahead of the decline of traditional photographic products. For its continued environmental focus, Kodak was again named to the Dow Jones Sustainability Index, the FTSE4Good Index, and the "Global 100—Most Sustainable Corporations in the World" listing.

Recycling

Even in a digital world, 35mm one-time-use cameras remain hugely popular. Kodak has recycled more than 1 billion one-time cameras, with components recycled or reused in the manufacture of new cameras and related products.

Junior Achievement

Kodak employees volunteer as tutors and mentors in Rochester [New York]-area school enrichment programs.

Arts, Culture, and Education

Kodak is a leading contributor to museums and science centers in Rochester, as well as art galleries and the Rochester Philharmonic Orchestra. In addition, Kodak provides support for several area universities, including Rochester Institute of Technology and the University of Rochester.

Local Contributions

Kodak provides the largest single corporate gift to the annual campaign of the United Way/Red Cross of Greater Rochester, a $1 million donation. This is in addition to funds donated by thousands of Kodak employees. Additional grants support other area organizations and initiatives, such as children's centers, women's foundations, and charities that support education initiatives in communities where Kodak people live and work.

_____

Source: Kodak Community Affairs, February 2008.

THE COMMUNITY RELATIONS PROCESS

The clarity of the mutual interest of organizations and their communities, however, does not imply that community relations can be practiced without careful planning and execution. Effective community relations does not just happen, nor is it an inevitable by-product of a well-run, civic-minded organization. Like all aspects of public relations, successful community relations programs must be built into the structure and culture of an organization. Community relations is not based on pure altruism; it looks to the organization's self-interest. W. J. Peak offers the best definition of **community relations** we have seen:

> Community relations, as a public relations function, is an institution's planned, active, and continuing participation with and within a community to maintain and enhance its environment to the benefit of both the institution and the community.[5]

Good community relations is a mutually beneficial partnership, going far beyond, say, a generous financial donation to fund a civic project. Ideally an institution will garner its resources—the product and services the company provides, customer relations, recruitment, employee relations, production processes, marketing and advertising strategies, design of the organization's building and facilities—and use them to better the community and to shape the environment in which it exists. As Stanford University professor David P. Baron notes,

Expedia employees volunteered to quickly build the framework for a Habitat for Humanity house that was shipped to the Katrina-devastated Gulf Coast for a family in need.

For many companies, market success depends not just on their products and services, the efficiency of their organizations, their internal organization, and the organization of their supply chains, distribution channels and alliance networks. Success also depends on how effectively they deal with governments, interest groups, activists and the public. The forces these parties generate can foreclose entry into new markets, limit price increases and raise the costs of competing. They can also unlock markets, reduce regulation, handicap rivals and generate competitive advantage. These forces are manifested outside of markets but often work in conjunction with them.[6]

Arguably, community relations is an organizational attitude or state of mind, rather than any specific process or practice. Coca-Cola's Rob Baskin notes that building relationships in communities is "the best PR" and that it's "the kind of work that can never be abated."[7]

Determining Objectives

Companies are engaging their employees when planning and implementing their community relations activities. The needs of the local community and the concerns of their employees are the two most important criteria in determining which causes to support. These employees participate in the selected activities, bringing their social commitments to life and creating a team of ambassadors for the company in the community.[8]

General objectives, however, do not suffice. Companies should have a written strategic plan for community relations that defines management's view of its obligation to the community so that efforts can be coordinated and concentrated. Specific community relations objectives should be spelled out. Failure to do this kills too many community relations programs before they get started.

Knowing the Community

Community relations policies and objectives are not determined according to idealistic principles. They come about by assessing organizational needs, resources, and expertise on the one hand and community needs and expectations on the other. Before meaningful policies and objectives can be developed, the organization must know its community.

Although community relations usually stresses communication from the organization to the community, the success of such efforts rests on the communicator's knowledge of the audience. Each community defines its publics, and no two are exactly alike. For example, the greater Detroit, Michigan, area has the largest Arab American population in the United States.[9] Many technology workers who live in San Francisco are Asian, and one estimate notes that more than 50 percent of all first graders in the Texas public school system are Hispanic.

Real knowledge of the community, however, goes beyond the standard demographic, ethnic, historical, geographic, and economic data. "To build a community you have to participate in communities," notes Annie Heckenberger of GPTMC, the Greater Philadelphia Tourism Marketing Corporation. GPTMC opted to use a blog called "uwishunu" (You Wish You Knew) instead of a Web site to encourage local conversations about the city's restaurants, nightlife, arts, music, and other activities.[10]

A solid community relations program must be built on the answers to questions like these:

1. *How is the community structured?*
   Is the population homogeneous or heterogeneous?
   What are its formal and informal leadership structures?
   What are the prevailing value structures?
   How are its communication channels structured?

2. *What are the community's strengths and weaknesses?*
   What are the particular problems of the community?
   What is the local economic situation?
   What is the local political situation?
   What are the unique resources (human, cultural, natural) possessed by the community?

3. *What does the community know and feel about the organization?*
   Do its neighbors understand the organization's products, services, practices, and policies?
   What are the community's feelings about the organization?
   Do misunderstandings about the organization exist?
   What are the community's expectations regarding the organization's activities?

The answers to such questions are not necessarily easy to get. Moreover, answers change over time and thus require frequent monitoring. Good information can be acquired in several ways. The U.S. Census report contains a wealth of information about communities and the people who live there. Many organizations engage in survey research to determine community knowledge, attitudes, and perceptions. Professional polling organizations are often employed to provide such services. Close contact with community leaders is an extremely important source of information. Professional, civic, religious, or fraternal leaders; political officials; and media editors can generally be reached through membership in local organizations or through face-to-face meetings on a variety of subjects. Some organizations formalize such input by including community leaders on their task forces or committees that deal with important community issues.

Guidelines for Effective Community Relations Programs

Having established the means for ongoing community inputs, the following guidelines should be used to establish an effective community relations program:

1. Careful effort should be made to establish the objectives top management wishes to achieve. The organization may seek many objectives—reputation, experience with a potential future payoff, stability of environment, and so on—but whatever it seeks ought to be established in realistic and concrete terms.

2. Alternative strategies should be explored and choices made. If an organization wishes to improve housing conditions in a city in which it operates, for instance, possibilities for action range from partially funding research into new ways to build low-cost housing to actually building low-cost housing.

3. Impacts of community relations programs on the organization and the community should be anticipated. Offering training for jobs that will not exist when the training is concluded helps no one.

4. Attention should be paid to the likely total costs of a nonprofit action and to the volume of the organization's resources that may legitimately be allocated to community relations. It is not advantageous to either the organization or the community if the organization suddenly discovers a given program is costing too much and abruptly stops all community service.

5. Many managers have found that certain types of involvement in urban affairs require knowledge and understanding that go beyond the usual managerial and technical business talents. Political skills, deep understanding of community problems, and the ability to settle problems in an unfamiliar cultural setting are requisites for some activities. Special expertise may have to be acquired.[11]

Communicating with Communities

Community communication has no single audience. Corporations must be open to a variety of communication tactics if they are to reach important publics. One of the most significant ways to reach the community is through employee communication. For example, Home Depot employees usually live in the local community. These employees can share the company's messages with neighbors and friends at the high school football game, while shopping for groceries, when picking up children at school, while attending church, and at many other places.[12]

Other important communication channels consist of a community's opinion leaders: teachers, clergy, public officials, professionals and executives, bankers, union leaders, and ethnic and neighborhood leaders.

Local organizations are also important vehicles of communication in communities. Fraternal, civic, service, and social clubs; cultural, political, veterans, and religious organizations; and youth groups all provide platforms for institutional messages and ample opportunities for informal communication. Organizational managers should be encouraged to belong to such groups and should be available to make public speeches to them as well.

Channels of Communication

The communication channels through which audiences are reached may range from an informal chat over lunch at a Rotary or Kiwanis Club meeting to advertisements in local mass media such as newspapers, radio, and television. In-house publications, brochures, and annual reports can easily be shared with community leaders. Some organizations even create newsletters specifically for their neighbors.

A uniquely community-oriented method of organizational communication is the open house. Successful open houses provide small group tours of organizational facilities with knowledgeable guides. They include films, displays, and brochures and usually provide product samples or mementos for participants to take home. The major message of such activities, of course, is the interdependence between the institution and the community.

In some cases, industrial or company tours become major tourist attractions. The General Motors Corvette assembly plant in Bowling Green, Kentucky, and the Callaway Golf plant in Carlsbad, California, are two examples. It may be necessary for organizations to limit, cancel, or restrict tours, however, because of staffing, industrial espionage concerns, world affairs, and many other reasons. Visitors at the Corvette plant are not allowed to take photographs. The city of San Jose, California, canceled tours of its water pollution control plant after the events of September 11, 2001, because the city was in an enhanced state of emergency readiness. The *Seattle Times* printing facility limits tours to its North Creek location, and an appointment is required.[13]

SPECIFIC FUNCTIONS OF COMMUNITY RELATIONS

Community relations managers would like to spend most of their time identifying and building relationships and networks with community leaders, organizations, and government officials (91 percent); developing and managing plans to meet community concerns, needs, and issues (85 percent); and developing and managing partnerships with organizations in the community (85 percent), according to the Center for Corporate Citizenship.[14] Although considerable time is spent on these activities, community relations managers also attend community relations meetings with colleagues, assist other departments with their community relations plans, assist with recognition ceremonies, speak before community groups, review requests for contributions, and conduct community events and programs.[15]

The average number of employees in a community relations department is about five, and the average number of employees per company is about 4,000, according to the Center for Corporate Citizenship.[16]

When an Organization Moves

Community relations is particularly critical when an organization moves into a new community or leaves an old one. Communities now ask questions before they accept new businesses, industries, or even nonprofit undertakings. Community response to an organization should be an important factor in the location decision.

Once the decision to move into a particular community is made, it is essential to provide local media with factual information on the timing of the move, the hiring of new employees, the opening of the plant, and other similar activities. The goal is to familiarize key groups with the organization and its products, activities, policies, and people, using all available media and methods.

The dependence of a community on its organizations is never clearer than when a plant or facility leaves town. Winn-Dixie announced that 22,000 people, roughly 28 percent of its workforce, would lose their jobs in its attempt to emerge from bankruptcy.[17] The shutdown of Texas Instruments' Santa Cruz, California, plant left 600 workers feeling afraid and uncertain and city officials wondering how they would fund redevelopment activities such as downtown revitalization and street widening.[18]

Beyond the economic implications, plant shutdowns may affect communities in many other ways, such as raising levels of psychological depression, alcoholism, drug abuse, marital stress, child abuse, and even suicide among former employees. A plant closing can have wide-ranging effects, and companies need to prepare appropriately if it becomes necessary to depart from a community.

Criteria for Community Relations Activities

In Philip Lesly's *Handbook of Public Relations,* several criteria are suggested that organizations must apply to community relations activities. These criteria are presented here with a case example of how organizations have used each criterion to establish a community relations program.[19]

1. *Creating Something Needed That Did Not Exist Before.* Intel is harnessing spare processing power of personal computers to fight cancer. Based on the theory behind Napster, the Philanthropic Peer-to-Peer Program allows researchers to receive information from as many as 6 million people and could reduce the amount of time to develop new drugs from 12 years to as few as 5 years.[20]

2. *Eliminating Something That Is a Community Problem.* The Birmingham Summit, a national town meeting that focused on race relations, was sponsored by MSNBC and *Newsweek* magazine. Subtitled "The Challenge for America in the 21st Century," the two-day event featured an all-day conference and a panel discussion. It was the first such collaboration between two media giants.[21]

3. *Developing a Means of Self-Determination.* Kinko's uses its branches in the numerous communities it operates in as a way to heighten knowledge about environmental issues and to identify what can be done to improve and protect the community.

4. *Broadening Use of Something That Exists to Include "Have-nots."* Hotelier Marriott provides day care for service-industry workers in Washington, DC, and Atlanta.

5. *Sharing Equipment, Facilities, and Professional Expertise.* McDonald's lets groups use its juice machine for parties, many banks let groups use their seminar rooms for meetings, and professional groups such as the American Bar Association provide free professional advice to the poor or elderly. Local CPA groups often provide free tax consulting to the elderly at tax time.

6. *Reconstituting, Repairing, and Dressing Up.* Lowe's has made a five-year $10 million commitment to be the national underwriter of Habitat for Humanity International's "Women Build" program.

7. *Tutoring, Counseling, and Training.* Many corporations encourage their employees to teach classes and guest lecture in grades from kindergarten to college and to counsel start-up businesses in their area of expertise.

8. *Activating Others.* St. Jude's Children's Research Hospital has worked with FedEx in Memphis to host the FedEx–St. Jude PGA Golf Tournament. A total of more than $14.7 million has been donated to St. Jude over the past 30 years, most of which has been raised since FedEx began its sponsorship in 1986.[22]

Typical community relations activities include open houses, speakers' bureaus, community service by employees on nonprofit boards of directors, and monetary support and volunteer support of community events. Community relations activities also include making facilities available, sponsoring social projects to attack major community problems, and creating employee volunteer programs. Publicity and promotion in all these community relations programs must be seen as tools in support of the actual programs, not as substitutes for them.

Local Government and Political Action

Community relations goes beyond mere communication. It requires action by organizations in relation to community health and welfare, education, government, culture, recreation, and other areas.

Business–government relations are discussed in much greater depth in another chapter of this book, but community relations and governmental relations clearly overlap in local government and politics. In fact, the term *public affairs* is usually defined in public relations as two related activities—government relations and community relations.

As stated earlier, local political officials can supply invaluable input to corporate community relations programs. Corporations have a great stake in effective local government because they are major taxpayers and users of municipal services. Part of the community relations effort, therefore, must be devoted to building solid relations with city officials, county commissions, and other agencies of local government. This is accomplished, in part, by making organizational expertise available to governments through loans of managerial personnel or through service on panels, commissions, or committees established by or for local government.

All institutions must mobilize on the local level those who recognize the importance of their contribution to the health and prosperity of the community and those who will speak out for policies in the best interests of their community and its institutions. The United Way Loaned Executive Program is one such example. Businesses lend key personnel to their local United Way during the fall fund-raising campaign. Through presentations and individual meetings at community-based businesses, these executives raise the awareness of and make a case for supporting United Way. Similarly, political experts now recognize that strength in Washington is derived from organized, localized grassroots support. In an era when virtually all members of Congress are looking out for their own districts and careers, local people making local demands and representing local interests are far more effective than Washington-based lobbyists. In this regard, community relations may be not only an end in itself but also an integral part of national efforts.

Corporate Social Responsibility and Philanthropy

Corporations want to be seen as good neighbors, working alongside government agencies and other organizations to address social problems. Philanthropic support is usually provided in three ways: cash donations, in-kind donations, and employee volunteering.[23] Almost three-fourths of corporate executives say that corporate citizenship needs to be a priority, and nearly as many say that the public has a right to expect good corporate citizenship.[24]

Meeting the needs, however, is not a simple matter. Here are some of the challenges that corporations face in being good citizens:

1. *The issues are not static.* As figure 11.1 illustrates, public education is one of the issues Americans feel businesses should work the hardest to solve. This graphic also illustrates how priorities shift over time as Americans focus on issues that have a direct impact on their own well-being in their communities. In 1993, crime and homelessness were among the top issues. Education, health, and the environment are now at the forefront.[25]

2. *The priorities vary among publics.* figure 11.2 shows the difference in how different groups of multicultural consumers prioritize issues. Almost all of the 15 concerns identified are unique or express varying shades of interpretation. In an AARP study, adults age 50-plus said that government competence, Social Security, and rising health costs were the issues the president should focus on.[26]

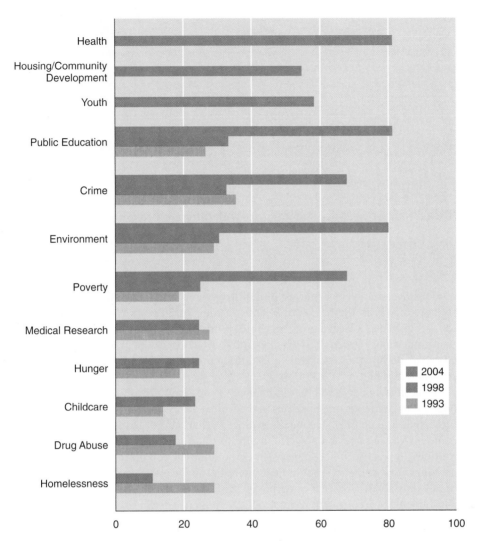

FIGURE 11.1 **Important Issues to Americans** *Sources:* "First Time Research Finds That Nonprofit and Corporate Partnerships Result in Reputation and Financial Gains for the Nonprofit," 2004 Cone Corporate Citizenship Study; and 1999 Cone, Inc., and Roper Starch Worldwide Cause-Related Trends Report.

3. *The problems are complex and not easily solved.* The state of the economy was the top concern voiced by respondents in a February 2008 *New York Times*/CBS News poll.[27] While business plays an obvious and critical role in keeping the economy afloat, other factors influence the nation's financial health, including world markets, regulatory policies, weather, and war.

4. *It can be difficult to satisfy the public's expectations.* Perception gaps exist regarding large companies' involvement in solving social problems. In one study, 80 percent of those polled said that corporations should be held responsible for ensuring that all of their products have been produced in socially and environmentally responsible manner, with only 55 percent of executives feeling the same way. Sixty percent of the public felt that business should improve education and skills in communities where they operate, an expectation shared by only 41 percent of the executives.[28]

	African American	Asian	Hispanic
1	Education	Green/sustainability	Education
2	Health issues such as HIV/AIDS, hypertension, diabetes, and heart disease	Inclusion/diversity	Healthcare
3	Employment	Quality of life	Financial literacy
4	Diversity in terms of recruitment and retention	Affinity	Economics
5	Economic development (home ownership/financial literacy)	Leadership	Political empowerment

FIGURE 11.2 Five Issues that Resonate with Different Groups of Multicultural Consumers *Source:* Michael Bush, "A Genuine Connection," *PRWeek,* May 14, 2007, p. 29.

Controversies over **corporate philanthropy** and social responsibility will probably not go away in the near future. Only in the past 50 years has corporate charity been recognized as a legal use of stockholders' funds. Even after having established its legality, questions remain as to whether and to what extent the practice is appropriate and useful. Beyond these issues are questions of proper motivations, goals, and criteria for corporate giving.

Small stockholders and other individuals are responsible for 75 to 80 percent of all donations to charitable organizations in the United States. By law, corporations are permitted to donate up to 10 percent of earnings to charitable organizations. Government tax incentives can serve as a powerful motivator for businesses to make charitable contributions. In practice, however, very few corporations give to the limit, perhaps because they believe that doing so is not in their interest or in the interests of their stockholders. Overall, only about 1 percent of corporate profits is actually given away. In 2006, total contributions from corporations totaled $12.72 billion, a decline of 7.6 percent from the previous year. The decrease is attributed to extraordinary giving for disaster relief in 2005 for Hurricane Katrina and a slowdown in the economy.[29] Figure 11.3 identifies the source of contributions.

In developing a coherent approach to corporate giving, several factors should be considered:

1. *Do No Harm.* Contributions should not be made to any cause that may be contrary to the best interests of the donor or the recipient.

2. *Communicate with the Recipient.* Effective grant-making requires a close partnership between donor and recipient.

3. *Target Contributions toward Specific Areas.* Gifts should achieve maximum impact on the community and maximum benefits for the donor. In this regard, donations should go to areas where individual corporations have unique expertise not available in the voluntary, nonprofit sector.

4. *Make Contributions According to Statements of Corporate Policy.* Fully developed policies of this nature should include the charitable aims and beliefs of the company, the criteria to be used in evaluating requests for funds, the kinds of organizations and causes that will and will not be supported, and the methods by which grants will be administered.

5. *Plan within the Budget.* Corporate giving should be tied to set percentages of net earnings.

6. *Inform All Persons Concerned.* Employees and the community at large should be fully aware of corporate activities.

7. *Do a Later Follow-Up.* The corporation does a valuable service by demanding of recipients high levels of performance and proper financial accounting.

8. *Remember That More Than Money May Be Needed.* An effective corporate contribution requires more than checkbook charity. Volunteer workers, managerial expertise, and corporate leadership are essential elements of an effective program.

Two trends in corporate giving hold the promise of making such philanthropic and social programs more effective. Rather than reacting to public issues and public pressures, more firms, particularly the larger ones, are taking greater initiative in channeling dollars and corporate talent into problem areas they deem significant and in which they wish to make an impact. Mini-case 11.1 highlights how Deloitte Touche Tohmatsu employees worldwide contribute to their communities. In another example, Larry Ellison, founder and chief executive officer of Oracle, endowed the Ellison Medical Foundation, a philanthropic institution that provides vaccines to combat infectious diseases in the Third World. This center also funds research into finding cures for diseases of the elderly. Ellison rationalizes his commitment to funding research in a *Fortune* magazine article, noting, "What do you think is cooler: being the richest guy on earth or helping find the cure for cancer?"[30]

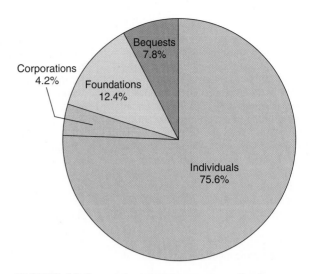

FIGURE 11.3 **2006 Philanthropic Contributions: $295.02 billion by source of contributions** *Source:* Giving USA, a publication of Giving USA Foundation™, researched and written by the Center on Philanthropy at Indiana University.

A second trend in corporate giving is what might be called "venture philanthropy." Pierre Omidyar, the founder of eBay, gives money to charities that follow solid business plans and can create income streams to support the nonprofit work. Omidyar also fosters a network of "social entrepreneurs," one example of which is New Profit Inc. This Boston nonprofit funds causes such as early reading and public health clinics by identifying the winning elements of successful programs. One example is an after-school program that keeps kids out of trouble by pairing them with volunteers from the working world.[31]

Many corporations match employee contributions to educational institutions, museums, orchestras, public TV, hospitals, and ballet, thus, in effect, permitting their contributions to reflect those of their employees. In these ways, employees can be the motivating force behind their companies' charitable donations. In addition to cash contributions, corporate giving also includes sponsoring events, pro bono work, in-kind contributions, and cause-related marketing.

It should come as no surprise that the largest portion of corporate philanthropy supports education. The Bill and Melinda Gates Foundation is the richest philanthropic organization in the world and disbursed $1.2 billion in 2004, with 60 percent going to education. Coca-Cola founded the Council for Corporate & School Partnerships in 2001, as a way to exchange information, expertise, and ideas to ensure that partnerships between schools and businesses achieve their full potential for meeting key educational objectives. Grades, test scores, attendance, reading abilities, and related areas have improved as a result.[32]

Thousands of Deloitte Professionals Worldwide Take Part in IMPACT Day

To celebrate and renew commitments to community investment activities, many Deloitte member firms choose to set aside a day each year called IMPACT Day. Since its inception, member firms' participation in IMPACT Day has spread widely across the globe. Their participation went from 6 countries in 2004 to 43 countries three years later. In 2007, 31 percent of the approximately 150,000 people of Deloitte member firms volunteered their time and services during IMPACT Day events.

Goals

Here are some of the many goals of IMPACT Day:

- Raise visibility of Deloitte member firms' overall commitment to their local communities.
- Enhance the Deloitte brand.
- Reinforce Deloitte's position as a leader in community investment.
- Reinforce Deloitte's Global Shared Values, especially "commitment to each other," to its employees.
- Receive recognition of Deloitte's community investment initiatives through increased media coverage.

Implementation

As community involvement takes on different forms around the world, IMPACT Day activities have been as diverse as the member firms taking part. The following is a recap of IMPACT Day activities from 2007.

- **Brazil** Almost 1,000 volunteers from the Deloitte Brazil offices took part in IMPACT Day activities on 1 June 2007. Deloitte Brazil employees dedicated that day to show their commitment to the development of a better society. IMPACT Day activities included blood drives, collecting winter clothes and food, as well as giving presentations about environment and sustainability. Member firm employees were also involved in fun activities with community associations and public schools, such as contests, workshops, and presentations, providing entertainment for hundreds of children and for the Deloitte Brazil member firm volunteers as well.

- **Peru** On IMPACT Day, Deloitte Peru helped a local community build a new medical center and a house for children, in addition to donating children's toys and improving the village kindergarten. More than 130 member firm employees participated in IMPACT Day, with over 200 member firm employees making donations to enable the Deloitte Peru member firm to buy construction materials. The Municipality of San Juan de Miraflores also supported Deloitte Peru with construction vehicles. The commitment went beyond IMPACT Day—everyone participated actively in all construction activities for almost three weeks, including weekends.

- **United States** From coast to coast, IMPACT Day t-shirts created a sea of blue in U.S. cities as people participated in IMPACT Day. Deloitte U.S. employees worked together on more than 500 projects throughout the United States and through the Deloitte U.S. firms located in India. In addition to painting, gardening, and cleaning, activities included skills-based projects, such as those for Junior Achievement, a nonprofit organization dedicated to teaching students about the importance of business, economics, and the free enterprise system. Deloitte U.S. employees who volunteered for Junior Achievement activities brought their business expertise to the classroom, teaching career-based curriculum to students.

- **Australia** "Red Nose Day" is Deloitte Australia's annual national fundraiser, with funds donated to research on Sudden Infant Death Syndrome (SIDS). On IMPACT Day 2007, more than AU$77,000 (approximately US$68,000) was raised. All money raised from sales of merchandise during the Red Nose Day campaign is used to provide bereavement support to families whose children have died, to provide safe sleeping education to the community, and to fund research.

- **Singapore** On 27 July 2007, more than 200 of Deloitte Singapore's people made their way to the Boys' Town Home in Upper Bukit Timah, where they spent the day improving the premises by cleaning, painting, and redecorating certain parts of the home. Chaly Mah, CEO, Deloitte Singapore, said, "This was indeed a meaningful project for our IMPACT Day. By contributing our time and resources, we were able to make a direct impact on the lives of the youths who live there. At the same time, this makeover will raise awareness about this home with staff, and it kicks off our community partnership with Boys' Town Home for the next 12 months."

- **Hungary** On this year's IMPACT Day, Deloitte Central Europe's offices in Hungary worked at four locations. Deloitte Central Europe's offices in Hungary have been supporting the Camp of Courage Foundation for years. The main task of this year's IMPACT Day was to tidy up the foundation's camp in Hatvan, a small town located one hour outside of Budapest. In the office of the Camp of Courage, a charitable organization, the Deloitte team was involved in administrative support (data capturing, printing, filing, and registration) as well as in preparing necklaces and bracelets for the kids. For the second year, the Institute of the Blind welcomed the firm to tidy up the yard of the kindergartners. The Deloitte team cleaned and renovated the playground; they chiseled, painted, and also did some gardening. At Vörösmarty Primary School, this year once again the Deloitte team held some fun lessons, including, among others, the "Chocolate Exchange," always a favorite with the children.

- **Commonwealth of Independent States (CIS)** Deloitte CIS marked IMPACT Day officially for the first time in 2007 with four events taking place in the region during June and July 2007, including an adventure race in May, which raised US$2,000 through personal sponsorship for the newly established Deloitte Foundation; participation in an urban race in St. Petersburg where proceeds were donated to Fund Parent Bridge and EveryChild, helping to finance a summer camp for adopted children and their parents, and a rehabilitation center for handicapped children; a training workshop for EveryChild, a charity that works toward giving vulnerable children a chance to grow up in a loving family with a secure future, where children aged 12–14 were given up-to-date information on universities and colleges, exams, resumes, and possible job placements; and a second Extra Mile Moscow, which took place on the last weekend of July 2007. Nearly 150 people ran, cycled, rafted, and orienteered their way over a challenging course, raising more than US$25,000 through personal sponsorship for DownsideUp, a local charity that works to improve the quality of life for children with Down syndrome.
- **Finland** Deloitte Finland worked with the local branch of the International Youth Foundation to create a booklet called "Edge," which enhances young people's understanding, appreciation, and acceptance of diversity. The booklet has been sent to all upper level schools in Finland (7th–9th grade), and it fulfills a gap in the material available for Finnish schools, handling issues like diversity and multiculturalism. On IMPACT Day, Deloitte Finland invited 50 children to Kiasma, the Museum of Contemporary Art, to hear the Edge spokesperson and Idols host Jani Toivola speak about diversity. Later they enjoyed the Kiasma Landscape exhibition, which showed that you can see things in many different ways. "We wanted to seek ways to support a positive attitude toward diversity in the community, especially among young people. The Edge theme booklet and IMPACT Day were concrete ways for us to share our value 'Strength from Cultural Diversity' with our surrounding community, and we are very proud of the outcome," says Teppo Rantanen, Deloitte Finland Managing Partner.
- **Southern Africa** On 15 June 2007, the partners and staff of Deloitte Southern Africa's offices in Malawi spent the day celebrating and renewing their commitment to the communities around the cities of Blantyre and Lilongwe. The Blantyre and Lilongwe offices' staff divided themselves into five subgroups and donated over 450 blankets to orphans and the elderly in the following venues: Tabvi Association for the blind; Stevens and Boyd villages in Blantyre; and the Lilongwe crew visited orphans and elderly at Mitundu and Kauma. The blankets were bought using funds donated by the Malawi offices coupled with the generous contributions by their staff. The main event for the day took place at Steven's Village in Chileka where 140 blankets were distributed to orphans, the elderly, and other vulnerable people in the village.
- **United Kingdom** Rather than IMPACT Day, the U.K. firm participates in Community Days, which provide an opportunity for teams of Deloitte U.K. people to get involved in their local community for a day on the member firm's time. This year over 1,500 people from Deloitte U.K. undertook a variety of rewarding indoor and outdoor community and environment projects such as painting and decorating a youth center, clearing and planting within a woodland area, taking on gardening projects for a senior citizen's home, and painting murals in a school classroom. Deloitte U.K.'s involvement with Community Days benefits a variety of local charities and community organizations.

Media Coverage

Media coverage of these activities might include the following:

- Profiling employees who attribute part of their professional success to volunteering.
- Inviting a reporter to join Deloitte employees as they carry out their IMPACT Day activities.
- Pitching an opinion piece that shares how volunteerism has a positive effect on the morale of the corporate environment and on professional leadership development of individuals.
- Releasing a research study on community involvement in conjunction with the volunteerism efforts.

Evaluation

Since implementing IMPACT Day, Deloitte's community investment efforts were positively presented in papers across the United States, including the *Dallas Morning News* and the *San Francisco Chronicle.* Television and radio coverage included mentions and interviews on the *CBS Morning Show* as well as leading stations in St. Louis, Los Angeles, and Detroit. Online media, including those dedicated to nonprofits, posted features about IMPACT Day. Similar results were realized with international media.

Questions

1. Why is it important for an organization to get credit for its community investment efforts?
2. What are some of the publicity challenges faced by the Deloitte organization in branding IMPACT Day on an international level? How does this compare to the challenges faced on the regional or local level?
3. What research would you do to measure the effectiveness of IMPACT Day from a public relations perspective?

Source: Karen Frankola, Deloitte Touche Tohmatsu, August 2005; updated in 2007 by Rachel Flanagan, Deloitte Touche Tohmatsu, February 2008.

Education, though, is an area in which corporate support calls for more than money. With school budgets stretched to the breaking point, donations of classroom and recreational materials are extremely important. Examples of contributions include pencils and pads, printing of high school newspapers, automobiles for driver training, and sophisticated computers and equipment for advanced research. Businesses can also provide plant tours for student field trips, speakers for classes and assemblies, internships for high school and college students, and managerial and financial expertise for school administrators. Bridges built between the corporation and the classroom are among the most important relationships in any community.

Health and Human Services   The self-interest of corporations in their philanthropic efforts is perhaps most obvious in the community health and welfare area. In fact, the personal experiences of corporate executives can provide an impetus for giving. The then-girlfriend of Sidney Kimmel, the billionaire head of Jones Apparel Group, had a cancer scare, and later Kimmel watched as the young daughter of a longtime friend died of the disease. The result was several multimillion-dollar gifts to cancer centers that provide research and treatment under one roof.[33]

Medical equipment manufacturer Agilent donated $1 million of equipment featuring Agilent components to the Flying Hospital, an international nonprofit organization based in Virginia Beach, Virginia. The Flying Hospital is a fully equipped surgical hospital constructed inside an aircraft.[34] A celebrity golf tournament raises funds for pediatric eye cancer at the Children's Center for Cancer and Blood Diseases at Children's Hospital in Los Angeles.[35]

Urban Renewal   Major problems have haunted our large cities since the 1960s, and most of them can be traced to poverty in one way or another. Minority groups are disproportionately represented. The inner areas are frequently centers of poverty, unemployment, pollution, and crime. In addition, civic functions such as sanitation, police and fire protection, and transportation are often inadequate.

Many of the efforts to improve conditions for those who live in the inner cities have been conceived and initiated by concerned business leaders who feel their organizations have certain responsibilities to the society in which they exist. Notes philanthropist Ann Lurie, "I focus on organizations that have a proven ability to do well in their field—not to transform the mediocre but to help a few agencies improve their services." On this basis Lurie's foundation gave money to the Greater Chicago Food Depository, which supplies hot meals to the homeless.[36]

Business contributes to urban renewal in a variety of ways, including monetary donations for rebuilding and providing expertise and talent to address concerns. Beyond immediate problems, corporations are trying to equip residents with the knowledge and skills they need to improve their lives. Programs like the National Foundation for Teaching Entrepreneurship (NFTE) have helped more than 100,000 children from low-income communities in 45 states and 16 countries to become economically productive. Research indicates that graduates of the NFTE program are more likely to stay in school and start their own businesses than those who have not participated. The Goldman Sachs Foundation has worked with the NFTE students for more than 18 years and has contributed to its $8 million annual budget.[37]

Some programs are intended to address immediate needs. Mort Meyerson had just started his job as chief executive officer of Perot Systems when he realized that the company holiday party was going to cost $360,000. Shocked by the amount and seeing no return on the investment, Meyerson canceled the party. Instead he used the monies to buy toys, food, and clothes. Employees volunteered to personally deliver the items to needy folks in the inner-city of Dallas.[38]

The Arts   The connection between community relations and arts patronage is very clear. "Successful businesses do more than simply pass through a community. We have a vested interest in living where the quality of life attracts the very best employees, customers, suppliers and government, academic and civic leaders. It is inconceivable that such a quality can exist where the arts are silent," notes A. Thomas Young, former executive vice president of Lockheed Martin Corporation.[39] Former Philip Morris chairman George Weissman made his company one of the nation's most generous arts patrons by observing, "More people go to museums than to ball games."

Judith A. Jedlicka, president of the Business Committee for the Arts, defines the arts as "everything from A to Z—arboretums to zoos."[40] However they are defined, business continues to increase its commitment to arts activities. Overall financial support reached a record $3.32 billion in 2003, compared with $22 million in 1967.[41] Nonprofit arts organizations annually multiply this support to generate income for the arts, creating, on a national level, $37 billion for communities and accounting for 6 percent of the gross national product. More than 3.2 million Americans, or 2.7 percent, are employed in some aspect of the arts.[42]

Beyond the financial benefits, business-art partnerships create long-range success stories in other areas, such as economic development. Like many cities, Greenville, South Carolina, was faced with revitalizing its downtown area. Trying to encourage development in an area with vacant buildings and few people was difficult. Over a period of 30 to 35 years, beginning in the 1970s, Greenville developed and implemented a master plan that made its once stagnant downtown into a vibrant community. In addition to public-private partnerships that built parks, plazas, and commercial assets, Greenville created a performing arts complex that incorporated historically significant buildings and a Governor's School for the Arts.[43]

Citizens who participate in the arts are more than two and a half times more likely to volunteer in their communities, 51 percent versus 19 percent, according to a National Endowment for the Arts study.[44]

Commitment to the arts can sustain a business through tough times. Houston jeweler I. W. Marks believes that its support of the city's opera and symphony helped develop customer loyalty. It was this loyalty that helped the jeweler ride out the recession of the 1990s when many of its competitors closed their doors.[45]

Whether consciously or not, corporations routinely act as arts patrons whenever they engage the services of an architect. The community relations aspect of architectural decisions should not be overlooked. Cummins Engine has transformed Columbus, Indiana, into an oasis of architectural excellence by paying top architects to design new buildings and restore old ones in the town. Included are 12 schools, two churches, a fire station, a library, a golf course and

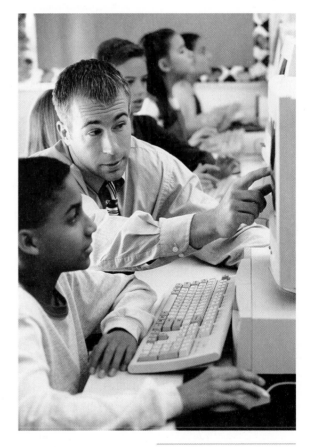

An engineer volunteers to help students after school.

clubhouse, newspaper and telephone company offices, a mental health clinic, city hall, and more.

To encourage participation by business in the arts, more than 160 top business leaders in the United States have established the Business Committee for the Arts. The committee assists companies of all sizes in their efforts to establish arts programs that can enhance a company's image, benefit employees, or provide tax breaks.

Typically art organizations approach corporations about sponsorships, and corporations usually have to make choices among the many options. But it can work the other way, with a corporation having a specific philanthropy in mind. Regardless of how the project is initiated, it's important that the gift supports community needs. For example, a man in Wisconsin gave a $100 million gift to build an arts center that only he wanted. Others thought the funds would be better spent elsewhere.[46] When reviewing the proposals, corporations are looking for compatibility between their goals and those of the arts organization. Here are some points to consider:

1. Why does the corporation want to invest?
   - Network with others in the local community.
   - Heighten awareness of the company and its products and services.
   - Attract employees and increase job satisfaction.
   - Enhance relationships with existing and future customers.
   - Set the company apart from competitors.
   - Increase the bottom line.
2. Which arts organizations will reach present and future employees?
3. Which type of partnership is desired?
   - Donated services and products.
   - Volunteer initiative.
   - Marketing, advertising, and public relations tie-in.
   - Financial assistance.[47]

The extent of corporate arts activities sometimes requires outside public relations counsel. Ruder Finn Public Relations established an innovative and revolutionary business and the arts consulting program when it opened its agency in 1948. Today, Ruder Finn advises corporations on cultural support programs. The firm develops and implements corporate public relations programming keyed to cultural activities. The organization assists in managing corporate-sponsored museum exhibitions, jazz festivals, corporate history books, an entertainment marketing CD-ROM game, performing arts presentations, symphony tours, and other arts-related activities.

Every company can make an important contribution to its local community by investing in the arts.

Cause-Related Marketing   Cause-related marketing ties a company and its products to a cause. It's an area that has experienced huge growth in recent years because of its ability to sell products, enhance image, and motivate employees. Today's consumers expect businesses to use their resources to address community concerns. When corporations contribute to the communities they serve, they make a powerful connection by sharing their customers' and employees' values. Cause-related marketing is *not* philanthropy.[48]

The *2001 Best Practices in Corporate Communication* identifies three primary benefits for sponsors and corporations of cause-related marketing efforts.[49]

1. *Cause-Related Marketing Increases Sales.* Corporate citizenship is more effective than coupons, rebates, and discounting when it comes to attracting customers. Retailers from New York to Los Angeles attest to the power of partnering with a charity in boosting the bottom line.[50] According to a 2004 Cone study, Americans will reward companies who meet their expectations:

   - Seventy-two percent say it is acceptable for companies to include a cause or issue in their marketing.
   - Eighty-six percent say they are very/somewhat likely to switch brands if one is associated with a cause.
   - Eighty-five percent say they want to see what social issues businesses are supporting in their local communities.
   - Eighty-one percent say a company's social commitment will influence where they work.
   - Seventy-four percent say a company's social commitment will influence what products and services they recommend to others.
   - Seventy percent say a company's social commitment will influence what stocks or mutual funds to invest in.
   - Eighty percent can name companies who stand out as strong corporate citizens.[51]

2. *Cause-Related Marketing Enhances Image.* Supporting good causes can benefit corporations with an enhanced image as a good corporate citizen, a greater sense of integrity and dependability for its products, and more favorable media coverage as community needs are addressed.[52] LensCrafters has helped more than 1.3 million people worldwide through its Give the Gift of Sight program that helps needy people see more clearly.[53] In addition, the program also responds to those affected by disasters. The Gift of Sight twin Vision Vans, Seemore and Iris, drove to areas that had large concentrations of Hurricane Katrina evacuees and delivered thousands of free exams and glasses to people in need.[54] Mervyn's California, a division of Target Corporation, sponsors ChildSpree, a back-to-school shopping spree for new clothes and shoes for 10,000 underprivileged children annually. Mervyn's and various nonprofit partners have contributed more than $17 million and served more than 170,000 children since 1992.[55]

3. *Cause-Related Marketing Benefits Properties and Sponsors.* Charities and other worthwhile causes on the receiving end typically enjoy more visibility that can lead to increased donations. The nonprofit that lends its name to a corporation can receive a rights fee or a cut of the purchase price of a product on top or in lieu of a rights fee. In spite of the many benefits, cause-related marketing does have some downfalls:

   - Nonprofits and corporations have different objectives. Alliances fail if the corporation is looking to mend its public image or if the nonprofit feels it is being used as the company's promotion agency.
   - Size can bring about problems. Many nonprofits are small and entrepreneurial, the opposite of a large and well-established corporation. The decision-making and approval processes and accounting procedures of a global organization can seem slow and unwieldy when compared with a nonprofit office employing a handful of people.

■ The public is finding it increasingly more difficult to distinguish between cause-related marketing and traditional philanthropy. Consumers may feel that they have already contributed by buying the product, and the nonprofit suffers from reduced donations. And it's often hard for consumers to know how much money a corporation is actually giving to charity.[56]

As with any other strategic initiative, a corporation should evaluate its cause-related marketing efforts from time to time to ensure the activities support the corporate mission and business objectives. For example, although Sprint has always supported initiatives in the communities where it has a presence, there was little continuity to what was being supported in different cities. In one city, Sprint would sponsor a walk or run for muscular dystrophy; in others, it might be participating in the local United Way, fundraising for breast cancer research, or building a playground. The company conducted consumer research to determine if it should continue community-specific programs or if it should be recognized for a universal cause. The result is that Sprint now focuses its community relations efforts on helping those with disabilities, one part of which is to enhance lives through wireless communication.

THE EMERGING CHALLENGE OF COMMUNITY ACTIVISM

Particular societal and community circumstances give rise to special challenges and opportunities for community relations efforts. Community activism is one such example.

Activism is intensifying in the 21st century. Organizations must be prepared to deal with the increased media scrutiny, potential disruptions to normal operations, and the fear and embarrassment that can occur with activist activity. Corporations are vulnerable to many different types of activists, including shareholders and disgruntled employees, on many different kinds of issues, such as human rights, the environment, health, biotechnology, and discrimination.

To be sure, organizations that are misusing, abusing, sidestepping, or violating laws and other commonly accepted practices should be held publicly accountable for their actions. But the kind of activism discussed in this section is more of a power struggle or a strong difference of opinion with an organization that is within compliance.

Problems with activism can arise in spite of an organization's best efforts to cooperate with its community. Community activists can exert undue pressure and unreasonable influence in attempting to raise public consciousness about issues and concerns that are more often based on emotion than scientific facts. These groups not only create opportunities to share their perspectives but also use national and local activities and problems to gain a voice.

In early 2000, telecommunication companies in many towns and cities experienced the wrath of community activists when they tried to construct towers to support the growing demand for wireless and digital communication. The result is that zoning requests were denied, health scares were initiated, and distrust of corporate entities was promoted. In turn, this upset customers who wanted better cell phone reception or who couldn't purchase additional phone numbers or other services due to lack of availability.

Activists use a variety of tactics, including e-mail, the Internet, signage, media interviews, lawsuits, and pickets, and they have been known to resort to violence, destruction, and terrorism. The attacks on the World Trade Center and the Pentagon in September 2001, which claimed thousands of innocent lives and disrupted many communities, are the most extreme terrorist acts to have ever occurred in the United States.

Counteracting Predictable Patterns of Activist Attacks	
Attack (They will . . .)	**Counter attack (You will . . .)**
1. Polarize the issue. No matter what, you're 120 percent wrong.	1. Point out the exaggeration; admit errors; outline action steps.
2. Build a base on the Web; use e-mail lists; post to bulletin boards to create support for their cause.	2. Assess the actual damage; estimate potential damage; determine need for preemptive action.
3. Trivialize, emotionalize, insult, and humiliate; pick a Web address like "companysucks.com."	3. Create a neat, clean, corporate-looking response site; contrast your legitimacy with their juvenile, trivial approach.
4. Anger, irritate, debilitate, violate trademarks, and misinterpret every response; force your hand by intentionally provoking a legal response to showcase their site.	4. Choose your battles carefully; respond calmly, deliberately, succinctly, competently, incrementally. Stay focused; use appropriate language for the medium and key themes.
5. Use ultimatums: bombard the company with "last chances" to correct allegations, charges, and "testimony" before "going live" and staging demonstrations.	5. Respond carefully, positively, candidly, politely. If in the wrong, correct the problem. Point out errors; point out emotionalism; insist on independent, unbiased proof.
6. Register their site on search engines— in your corporate section, if possible.	6. Register your site in the same manner; when resolved, remove listings.
7. Post messages on electronic bulletin boards to promote their cause; promote their site; locate others suffering from the same problems; find disgruntled employees willing to help.	7. Monitor the Internet; assess actual impact. Discourage local employees from responding on your behalf; respond only if necessary. Have erroneous posts removed from search engines.
8. Work the news media; target specific journalists who cover your company or industry. The media never tire of finding ways to attack business.	8. Direct journalists to your response site. Point out the exaggeration; admit errors; outline action steps. Avoid whining.

FIGURE 11.4   Counteracting Predictable Patterns of Activist Attacks

Much less severe, but no less frightening, is when an environmental group opposed to the expansion of the Vail, Colorado, ski area claimed responsibility for burning the resort's multimillion-dollar Two Elk Lodge.

Activists tend to use the same techniques when trying to gain media attention or gain supporters for their cause. Figure 11.4 identifies some of these predictable patterns of attack and how organizations can counterattack.

Companies should take a proactive stance when dealing with community activism and follow what practitioner David Schultz calls a "3-P" approach—planning, practice, and precision.[57] Phillips-Van Heusen Corporation's proactive stance helps the global garment manufacturer anticipate and avoid many problems. As one of the few American companies that has a vice president for human rights, it addresses on an ongoing basis issues such as wages, factory conditions, hours worked, and freedom from harassment and association for its employees. Like Phillips-Van Heusen's employees, its suppliers and vendors are expected to participate in human rights training and to adhere to the company's code of conduct.[58]

Yet even the most socially diligent companies can come under attack. The following are some of the ways that companies can handle situations involving community activists:

- Identify what kind of protest groups you're dealing with. Some just want to damage the company, whereas others truly desire to effect mutually beneficial changes.
- Speak the truth and be open and accessible. Provide information.
- Keep your cool and don't become overly confrontational. Adopt a friendly tone.
- Know the strengths and weaknesses of your activist groups. Determine if they should become strategic partners.
- Consider policy changes to neutralize or placate hostile organizations.
- Provide employees with the facts, to allay fears and to be ambassadors for the organization.
- Don't underestimate the power of an activist group to damage an organization.[59]

Liz Claiborne Inc. Launches Innovative High School Curriculum for "Love Is Not Abuse" Campaign

Background

For the last 14 years, Liz Claiborne Inc. has worked to raise awareness about domestic and relationship violence through its "Love Is Not Abuse" program. When the company decided it needed a fresh perspective, it turned to the Global Issues Communications group based out of Ruder Finn/New York in February 2005. RF GlobeComm and Liz Claiborne agreed that the first step was to commission a study about violence and abuse among teenagers (13 to 18 years) in dating relationships.

Research

Liz Claiborne Inc. commissioned Teenage Research Unlimited to conduct a survey to evaluate verbal, physical, and sexual abuse among teens in dating relationships. Teens surveyed ranged in age from 13 to 18 years. Reports of abuse extended across suburbs, cities, regions, and all ethnic groups. The findings conveyed a compelling call for help from an overwhelming majority of teens who stated that physical and verbal abuse is a serious issue for them.

Key Findings

- 1 in 3 teenagers reported knowing friends or peers who have been hit, punched, kicked, slapped, choked, or physically hurt by their partner.
- Nearly 1 in 5 teenage girls who have been in a relationship said a boyfriend had threatened violence or self-harm if presented with a breakup.
- 13 percent of teenage girls who said they have been in a relationship report being physically hurt or hit.
- 1 in 4 teenage girls who have been in relationships revealed they have been pressured to perform oral sex or engage in intercourse.

- More than 1 in 4 teenage girls in a relationship (26 percent) reported enduring repeated verbal abuse.
- 80 percent of teens regarded verbal abuse as a "serious issue" for their age group.
- If trapped in an abusive relationship, 73 percent said they would turn to a friend for help; but only 33 percent who have been in or known about an abusive relationship said they have told anyone about it.

Planning

Using these new data, RF GlobeComm and Liz Claiborne set up a national advisory board on teen dating abuse and organized the development of a high school curriculum, targeted to ninth grade students (ages 14 to 15), to help teens prevent and deal with the growing incidences of physical and verbal abuse and sexual pressure.

The goals of this "Love Is Not Abuse" curriculum are to

- Increase students' awareness and understanding of teenage dating violence.
- Enable students to challenge beliefs that support teenage dating violence.
- Increase help-seeking behavior among students involved in dating relationships that include violence.

Assisting RF GlobeComm and the Liz Claiborne advisory board, the Education Development Center, Inc. (EDC), developed the three-lesson teenage dating violence curriculum. The lessons are designed for health education and/or English language arts classes, drawing on brief, engaging literary texts (e.g., poetry, short stories) to build awareness of how to make healthy choices in relationships.

The curriculum contains detailed background information for teachers on the scope of the teenage dating violence problem and strategies for responding to students who disclose being in an abusive situation. Break the Cycle, a nonprofit organization whose mission is to engage, educate, and empower youth to build lives and communities free from dating and domestic violence, also worked closely with EDC in helping to shape the curriculum and acting as a resource for students or teachers who are themselves dealing with an abusive situation or need advice on how to help a friend/student.

Implementation

To announce both the survey results and the curriculum, RF GlobeComm designed a press conference in June 2005 at the National Press Club in Washington, DC. The objectives were twofold: to create strong awareness about this prevalent issue in the mainstream press, and to provide clear visibility for Liz Claiborne as a private sector leader in developing and supporting domestic and relationship abuse programs. To help generate preconference publicity, the group offered an exclusive to NBC's *Today* show. The tactic worked; the six-minute piece aired the morning of the announcement and help set the tone for the day's news.

The press conference and prepublicity had widespread impact, reaching far beyond the client's expectations. In addition to the *Today* show, broadcast coverage highlights included segments on CNN's *NewsNight with Aaron Brown* and *American Morning* shows, MSNBC's *Live with Lester Holt,* BET, and Univision, and in 12 out of the top 15 markets. Overall, there were more than 135 television media hits across the country and more than 60 print and online articles, including major dailies such as the *Dallas Morning News,* the *Washington Times, Boston Herald,* and the *San Diego Union-Tribune.* Most of the major wires—AP, Reuters, and Knight-Ridder/Tribune—all ran stories, which were picked up by many midsize to smaller daily newspapers.

The "Love Is Not Abuse" curriculum was piloted in 16 schools during the fall of 2005. The schools were chosen based on previous relationships with EDC and past experience in piloting new educational programs, while other schools were selected by RF GlobeComm based on the size of the media markets.

- Forest Park High School, Ferdinand, IN
- Jasper High School, Jasper, IN
- Southridge High School, Huntingburg, IN
- West High School, Sioux City, IA
- Woodbury Central High School, Tacoma, Moville, IA
- West Hills High School, Santee, CA
- Horace Howard Furness High School, Philadelphia, PA
- Wilson High School, Tacoma, WA
- Lakes High School, Lakewood, WA
- Sentinel High School, Pueblo, CO
- Central High School, Pueblo, CO
- South High School, Pueblo, CO
- Newton North High School, Newton, MA
- Cambridge Rindge and Latin School, Cambridge, MA
- Sebring High School, Sebring, FL
- Lee High School, Huntsville, AL

In addition to the curriculum, Liz Claiborne supplemented the campaign with handbooks, public service announcements, and other communications materials developed earlier to help schools and communities deal with the broader issue of domestic violence.

Evaluation

Since this is a pilot program, the curriculum will evolve based on feedback through a survey of the teachers after they've implemented the program. Until domestic violence is stopped, the "Love Is Not Abuse" campaign will continue. Liz Claiborne is committed to raising awareness and providing tools to educate citizens about the problem. In the meantime, the hope is that no one will suffer at the hands of another.

Source: Christie Ly, Ruder Finn, August 2005.

Questions

1. As a publicist, how do you convince a teacher or school to work with you in speaking with the press about such a sensitive, oftentimes secretive, topic?
2. How do you communicate or raise awareness about such a prevalent problem when it's a sensitive issue that deals with minors?

3. What other strategies or tactics could have been implemented to raise awareness about the issue and the curriculum?
4. What are some ideas you would pursue to sustain visibility about the issue and program?

Summary

Although community relations as an organizational activity is as diverse as are the communities in which organizations operate, the key to effective community relations is positive, socially responsible action to help the community on the part of the organization. Depending on the organization, community relations may be carried out by an officially designated community relations staff, by a general public relations staff, or by various departments throughout the organization.

Many companies are focusing their philanthropy programs on issues in which they would like to make an impact. Cause-related marketing ties a company and its products to a cause. It can sell products, enhance image, and motivate employees.

Activists are demanding a larger voice in decisions made by institutions, highlighting an increasing need for community relations efforts.

For self-testing and additional chapter resources, go to the Online Learning Center at **www.mhhe.com/lattimore3e.**

Key Terms

community relations
corporate philanthropy

Notes

1. Karen Matthews, The Associated Press, "Cirque du Soleil on NYC Pier? Community Says No," newsday.com, February 17, 2008.
2. Dan Milmo, "Kelly launches fight for Heathrow expansion," *The Guardian,* November 22, 2007.
3. Kwame F. Kilpatrick, as quoted by Jodi Wilgoren, "Detroit Urban Renewal without the Renewal," *The New York Times on the Web,* July 7, 2002.
4. "Connecting with Society," Ford Motor Company Corporate Citizenship Report, 2001, p. 28.
5. W. J. Peak, "Community Relations," in *Lesly's Handbook of Public Relations and Communications,* 4th ed., ed. Philip Lesly (New York: AMACOM, 1991), p. 117.
6. David P. Baron, "The Nonmarket Strategy System," *Sloan Management Review* (Fall 1995).
7. John Frank, "In-house PR Stretches Its Dollars in Slowdown," *PRWeek,* March 19, 2001, p. 13.
8. 2000 Cone/Roper Executive Study.
9. The Arab Population 2000, Census 2000 Brief, U.S. Census Bureau, p. 4.
10. Tanya Lewis, "Tourist Attraction," *PRWeek,* March 17, 2008, p. 12.
11. Adapted from Jules Cohen, "Is Business Meeting the Challenge of Urban Affairs?" *Harvard Business Review* (March–April 1970), pp. 81–82. Reprinted by permission of the *Harvard Business Review.* Copyright 1970 by the President and Fellows of Harvard College. All rights reserved.
12. Gloria Smith, "Doing Community Relations When You're the New Kid on the Block," *PRWeek,* July 16, 2000, p. 22.
13. "Printing Plant Tours," Seattle Times Co., www.seattletimes company.com/operations/tours.htm, June 21, 2000.
14. Platon Coutsoukis, assistant director of research, and Leslie Carbone, research analyst, "2001 Community Relations Index," Center for Corporate Citizenship at Boston College, pp. 8–9.

15 Ibid.

16. Ibid, p. 2.

17. Associated Press, "Winn-Dixie to Close 35 Percent of Its Stores," *Jefferson City Post-Tribune,* June 22, 2005, p. 31.

18. Ken McLaughlin, "TI's Santa Cruz Employees Ponder Life After Plant Closing," *San Jose Mercury News,* mercurynews.com, March 15, 2001.

19. Peak, "Community Relations," p. 130.

20. Associated Press, "Program Links Personal Computers to Fight Cancer," *Jefferson City News Tribune,* May 12, 2001, p. 7.

21. Craig McGuire, "Even News Media Like to Make News," *PRWeek,* December 11, 2000, p. 32.

22. Facts and Figures, FedEx–St. Jude Classic Web site, www.hushyall.com, 2005.

23. Boston College Center for Corporate Citizenship and The Hitachi Foundation, The State of Corporate Citizenship 2007, "Time to Get Real: Closing the Gap Between Rhetoric and Reality," pp. 6–7.

24. Ibid.

25. Mindy Gomes-Casseres, "First-time Research Finds That Nonprofit and Corporate Partnerships Result in Reputation and Financial Gains for the Nonprofit," 2004 Cone Corporate Citizenship Study, www.coneinc.com, May 25, 2005.

26. Important issues in choosing whom to vote for in the presidential election (percentage responding "very important"), *AARP Bulletin,* March 2008, www.aarp.org/bulletin/yourlife/the_bulletin_poll_top_voter_issues.html

27. *The New York Times* and CBS News Poll, February 20–24, 2008, http://graphics8.nytimes.com/packages/pdf/politics/20090226poll.pdf#page=3

28. Boston College Center for Corporate Citizenship, p. 7.

29. Press Release, "U.S. Charitable Giving Reaches $295.02 Billion in 2006," Giving USA Foundation, June 25, 2007.

30. Brent Schlender, "The Playboy Philanthropist," *Fortune,* September 3, 2001, pp. 163–66.

31. Quentin Hardy, "The Radical Philanthropist," *Forbes,* May 1, 2000, pp. 114–21.

32. Southard Davis, "Six School-Business Partnerships Set Standard for Improving Student Experience," The Council for Corporate & Social Partnerships, www.corpschoolpartners.org, June 21, 2005.

33. William P. Barrett, "I Don't Like Making Mistakes," *Forbes,* October 11, 1999, pp. 158–60.

34. www.forbes.com, September 9, 2001.

35. Heather Lindsey, "Golf Event Covered Despite No-Shows," *PRWeek,* April 2, 2001, p. 22.

36. Ann Lurie as quoted by Susan Adams, "Life After Death," *Forbes,* September 20, 1999, p. 166.

37. Tom Phillips, "100,000 Students Served! NFTE Program Turns Hardship into Triumph," NFTE press release, www.nfte.com, October 26, 2004.

38. Geoffrey Colvin, "Think About This as You Don Your Tuxedo," *Fortune,* December 18, 2000, p. 74.

39. A. Thomas Young, former executive vice president of Lockheed Martin Corporation, as quoted in Best Practices in Event Marketing and Corporate Sponsorships, *2001 Best Practices in Corporate Communications,* p. 79.

40. Judith A. Jedlicka, Business-Arts Partnerships That Achieve Real Results, a speech posted at www.bcainc.org, October 22, 2001.

41. 1998 National Survey of Business Support to the Arts, www.bcainc.org, October 22, 2001, and August 2005.

42. "Why Business Invests in the Arts," Business Committee for the Arts, Inc., www.bcainc.org, October 25, 2001.

43. The official Web director of Greenville, SC, USA, www.greatergreenville.com, 2005.

44. 2002 Survey of Public Participation in the Arts, National Endowment for the Arts, March 2004.

45. Judith A. Jedlicka, Business-Arts Partnerships.

46. Dale DeGroff, Bill Downes, Rebecca Ascher-Walsh, Joan Hoffman, et al., "Reward Yourself," *Fortune,* September 18, 2000, p. 376.

47. "8 Easy Steps," Business Committee for the Arts, Inc., www.bcainc.org/company.asp.html.

48. "Cause-Related Marketing," Event Marketing and Sponsorship Report, *2001 Best Practices in Corporate Communication,* p. 93.

49. "Cause-Related Marketing," p. 97.

50. Ann Zimmerman, "Promotional Ties to Charitable Causes Help Stores Lure Customers," *The Wall Street Journal,* December 4, 2000.

51. "Multi-Year Study Finds 21 Percent Increase in Americans Who Say Corporate Support of Social Issues Is Important in Building Trust," Cone, Inc., www.coneinc.com, December 8, 2004.

52. Joseph J. Ptacek and Gina Salazar, "Enlightened Self-interest: Selling Business on the Benefits of Cause-Related Marketing," *Non-Profit World,* July 7, 1997.

53. "Doing Their Part," *Chain Store Age: The Newsmagazine for Retail Executives,* August 2000, p. 44.

54. "Gift of Sight Supports the Victims of Hurricane Katrina," LensCrafters corporate Web site, www.lenscrafters. com, 2005.

55. Mervyn's 13th Annual ChildSpree Provides $1 Million in Clothes to 10,000 Deserving Children Nationwide," Mervyn's corporate Web site, www. mervyns.com, July 26, 2005.

56. "Cause-Related Marketing," pp. 100–101.

57. David L. Schultz, "Strategic Survival in the Face of Community Activism," *Public Relations Strategist* 7, no. 2 (Spring 2001), pp. 37–38.

58. Elizabeth Howard, "Vice President for Human Rights," *Public Relations Strategist* 2, no. 7 (Spring 2001), pp. 23–26.

59. Douglas Quenqua, "When Activists Attack," *PRWeek,* June 11, 2001, p. 15.

CHAPTER 12

Consumer Relations and Marketing

PREVIEW

Consumer relations and marketing are playing a more prominent role than ever before in public relations practice. Sophisticated techniques must be applied to understand the needs of consumers, solicit their comments, and attract their attention, as the following example illustrates.

Robyn munches on her morning bagel as her taxi zips through the early morning New York traffic. Today is the day she and others on the Lay's project team will learn if their months of planning will generate the desired level of media coverage and drive sales for the brand's new Lay's STAX, stacked potato crisps in a portable, resealable, crush-resistant container. Frito-Lay gave the assignment to the Entertainment Marketing division of Ketchum, one of the world's leading public relations agencies, in hopes of ensuring that the product would "stack up" against the competition.

The assignment was not without some pressure. Only public relations would serve as the primary sales driver for the brand. The national advertising rotation would not begin for two weeks.

The taxi arrives in Times Square, and Robyn surveys the scene as she pays the driver and exits the car. The 120-foot tall, 84-foot wide—roughly seven stories high—Lay's STAX container by the NASDAQ Tower is definitely catching the attention of passersby. She eyes the stage area and thinks the "Lay's STAX Challenge" banner will show up well in photographs. One of Robyn's early assignments was to secure the permits and city permission needed to utilize a designated area in the center of Times Square. Robyn waves at other Ketchum colleagues who are visiting with representatives of their launch partner, Speed Stacks. The sport of cup stacking was considered a perfect fit for the stacked snack because it involved the brand's youth target while bringing the broad appeal of Lay's to a wide consumer audience.

Robyn takes her place by the press table and spends the next two hours handing out media kits to members of the media as they arrive. A large crowd starts to gather. Finally the big moment arrives. Speed Stacking World Record–holder Emily Post steps onto the stage, and as hundreds of New Yorkers cheer her on, breaks the world's record in 8.42 seconds. The departing crowd accepts product samples from street teams of Lay's STAX ambassadors.

But Robyn's day is not over. She will escort Emily to interviews, field other media requests, and generally assist the project team as needed to help ensure the desired results. It would be several weeks before Robyn learns that the event generated more than 33 million media impressions with a media equivalency of more than $4.4 million and that sales projections for the public relations activities were met.

TEAMING PUBLIC RELATIONS WITH MARKETING

Though it is wrong to view public relations as simply another method of product or service promotion, promotion is one of the most powerful ingredients in any organization's marketing mix. Public relations and marketing functions have some fundamental differences, but they share one significant goal. Both attempt to help an organization respond to a very significant public: the consumers of its products and services. Figure 12.1 compares old marketing practices with today's newer approaches.

For those desiring to work in the arena of consumer relations and marketing, the following examples of how public relations is involved in the marketing process makes certain things clear: anticipate a blistering pace, a constant turnover of products, and an ongoing search for "the next big thing"—oh, and a job that never leaves you bored.

Reinvigorating an Older Brand

Older brands often face the task of staying fresh and current in the face of increasing competition (see mini-case 12.1). Procter & Gamble's Tide brand, introduced in 1946 and the world's best-selling detergent, faced such a challenge. To reposition itself, the company developed the energy-efficient Tide Coldwater. P&G aligned with the Alliance to Save Energy, and the two partners challenged attendees at the U.S. Conference of Mayors to encourage their citizens to wash their clothes in cold water—and save an average of $63 a year in the process.[1] Tide Coldwater also donated $100,000 to the National Fuel Funds Network, a charitable energy assistance program. Kosher-food maker Manischewitz pitched *Cooking Light* and *Gourmet* magazines in looking at Jewish food as another interesting cuisine, not just an option for holidays.[2]

Exporting an Established Brand to New Markets

Martinique, an island in the French Caribbean, is not well known to U.S. travelers. To encourage tourism, the French Government Tourist Office invited people, especially influential travel bloggers, to share their stories and possibly win a one-week trip for two to the island. The word-of-mouth campaign was supported by traditional media

	Old Marketing	New Marketing
Marketing mind-set	One-way, one-sided communications to tell a brand story	Nurture talks/relationships more up-front and trust; build credibility
Brand equity	Brand recall is paramount	Brand value of consumers. How likely are consumers to recommend a product or service
Targeting	Based on demographics	Based on behavior
Segmentation	Based on demographics	Groups by attitudes, interests, behavioral patterns
Content	Professionally created and distributed	A combination of consumer and professionally created
Reviews	Provided by experts	Provided by experts and users
Communication	Messages are pushed to consumers who soak up the messages	Interaction of personal search and query, reviews, comments, dialogue
Hierarchy	Content structured by channels, categories for marketers	Content is customized and available on demand
Payment	Cost per thousand, emphasis on cost use share of voice and share of market as metrics	Emphasis on return on investment and accountability

FIGURE 12.1   **Old Marketing Practices vs. New Practices** *Source:* Horizon Media

outreach and trips for travel journalists.[3] Kia Motors has a 61-year history of innovation in automobile manufacturing in Korea. The company produced a number of firsts for the country: its first gasoline engine, passenger car, exported car, and diesel engine.[4] But in America, the brand has been almost forgotten among imports. To establish the make in the United States, Kia is reaching out to its key publics through public relations. Efforts include a clear-cut "young at heart" positioning of the brand, an aggressive media relations program, enhanced relationships with dealers and employees, a new community relations function, and improved corporate communications. An additional challenge for the U.S.-based public relations office is to teach its Korean colleagues that American news about the company and its products may not always be completely positive.[5]

Reinforcing a Brand Positioning

Subway was well positioned menu-wise when the company received a letter from Jared Fogle's mother. She wrote that her son had lost 245 pounds in one year on a steady diet of Subway food. This testimonial gave a face to Subway's desire to position itself as healthy fast food. Using Fogle as spokesperson, the company launched a heathy-eating campaign that has included guest appearances by Fogle on television talk shows, the launch of the Feel Responsible, Energized, Satisfied, and Happy (FRESH) Steps program, and sponsorship of the American Heart Association's Jump Rope for Heart program and a nationwide "Jared and Friends" school tour to promote a healthy lifestyle to young children.[6]

Situation Analysis and Research

Americans know Kleenex® Facial Tissue. In fact, the brand enjoys 98 percent awareness among consumers. However, a successful brand constantly finds new ways to keep itself relevant and influence purchase behavior by connecting emotionally with its target audience. For Kleenex® Facial Tissue, the 2004 Olympic Games in Athens offered such an opportunity through the brand's role as an official supplier of the U.S. Olympic team. The brand charged Ketchum Public Relations with developing a high-profile campaign that would attract national media attention and entice the Kleenex® Facial Tissue audience, mothers ages 25 to 54.

Research data determined several significant findings:

- Couples tend to watch the Olympic Games together, so messaging should appeal to both male and female audiences.
- Mothers ages 25 to 54 prefer human-interest stories to sports statistics, so programming should focus on the moments, not the medals.
- The target audience enjoys replaying emotional moments, so

execution should feature an engaging, interactive call-to-action.

In response, Kleenex® Facial Tissue and Ketchum PR developed a brand-defining idea called Kleenex Moments™, which celebrated unforgettable emotional moments of the Olympic Games—both past and present.

The campaign's launch faced several critical considerations. First, the media initially focused on terrorism and security issues. Second, the U.S. Olympic Committee (USOC) had to approve all program activities to ensure they coincided with the value of the U.S. Olympic team and didn't violate athlete eligibility regulations. Third, the Olympic Games and on-site Kleenex Moments™ activities occurred eight hours ahead of Eastern Standard Time, and NBC instituted a 48-hour tape delay for several athletic competitions occurring in Athens.

Strategy and Execution

The Kleenex Moments™ campaign was executed in three phases. Phase 1 included participation in the U.S. Olympic Media Summit, a virtual who's who of accredited journalists. Having a presence at the summit enabled the Kleenex® Facial Tissue brand a chance to align

itself with larger worldwide sponsors. Summit participation also served as the first step toward seeding the term "Kleenex Moments™" among key audiences like athletes, USOC members, and accredited journalists.

Phase 2 involved the 2004 U.S. Olympic Hall of Fame induction ceremony. This was the first induction ceremony held in 12 years due to lack of funding, and the Kleenex® Brand was an associate sponsor. The event provided the ideal environment to honor Kleenex Moments™ of past Olympic Games. To celebrate them, the Kleenex® Brand produced vignettes for each of the inductees, during which they discussed their most emotional Kleenex Moments™. These vignettes were played during the broadcast. A satellite media tour was also conducted with two new Hall of Fame inductees.

Phase 3 served as the climax of the Kleenex Moments™ program on-site in Athens. Each day, the Kleenex® Brand and NBCOlympics.com selected three unforgettable Kleenex Moments™ and invited consumers to vote for their favorites online. These moments were also edited into vignettes and played daily at the USA

Getting an Image Makeover

Vodka and rap music are not usually associated with one another, a situation that Smirnoff vodka wanted to change. The brand paired three old-school rappers with contemporary musicians to create three new versions of iconic hip-hop songs and matching drinks. The songs and their corresponding videos plus behind-the-scenes production video were made available on a special Web site created by Smirnoff.[7]

Anticipating What's Next

A subhead in *The Wall Street Journal* reads, "It takes a lot of marketing to convince consumers what they're lacking."[8] Manufacturers pay big bucks to discover and create what the article calls "unmet needs." Such research led Procter & Gamble to create a CD-like player that spreads scents in a room. A pourable Betty Crocker cake frosting was one of 92 new products rolled out by General Mills in 2004. Some competitors let others do the R&D and then quickly replicate successes with products of their own. "You might be able to hold on to an innovation for 6 months, maybe 12 if you're really strong," says Bart Becht, house—home base of operations for the U.S. Olympic Committee. Live television and radio remotes were conducted from Athens with the athletes featured online, all of which included Kleenex Moments™ messaging and an invitation to consumers to vote online for their favorite Kleenex Moments™ of the Day.

Measurement and Evaluation

After the 2004 Olympic Games, Ketchum PR conducted a comprehensive survey of 1,000+ Americans (33 percent Kleenex® Brand target audience) to assess awareness, understanding, attitudes, and behavior toward the Kleenex Moments™ program.

Awareness: Twenty-one percent of those surveyed were aware of the Kleenex Moments™ program. These numbers increased dramatically if the audience also visited NBCOlympics.com to vote for their favorite Kleenex Moments™ of the Day (33 and 19 percent, respectively).

Understanding: Fifty-two percent recalled emotional moments in Athens, which means the target audience comprehended the role of emotion in the Olympic Games.

This number increased when the audience visited NBCOlympics .com (80 percent), or was aware of the sponsorship (64 percent).

Attitude: Sixty-three percent believed it was natural for the Kleenex® Brand to be linked to the emotional moments of the Olympic Games. Thirty-seven percent thought more favorably of the Kleenex® Brand because of this. These numbers increased when the audience visited NBCOlympics.com (80 and 61 percent, respectively).

Behavior: Seventy-nine percent of those aware of the sponsorship and those who had heard of Kleenex Moments™ were much more likely to purchase Kleenex® Facial Tissue next time. Among those who plan to purchase Kleenex® Facial Tissue in the future, 7 percent are buyers of other facial tissue brands.

Additional Measures

- Media outreach generated 1,716 news stories (goal was 850) for a total of 134,981,869 media impressions (goal was 100,525,000). Placements included *Fortune* magazine, *BRANDWEEK, USA TODAY, Reuters, Chicago Tribune, Pittsburgh Post-Gazette, Rocky Mountain News, Philadelphia Daily News*, WGN-TV, FOX News (national), FOX & Friends (national), Good Day Live, MSNBC, CNBC, ABC Radio Network ("Satellite Sisters" radio program three times), Westwood One (syndicated nationally), and USA Radio Network (nationally syndicated).
- NBCOlympics.com reported a total of 70,923 votes for the Kleenex Moments™ of the Day. The Kleenex Moments™ Web page received the second highest traffic and garnered nearly a quarter of all sponsored page views (373,435 page views).

Questions

1. What elements of the Kleenex Moments™ campaign contributed to its success?
2. How did the campaign ensure that its message would appeal to both males and females in the Olympic viewing audience?
3. Which strategies in this campaign could effectively be used by other marketers?

Source: Kimberly-Clark Corporation and Courtney Leddy, Ketchum Public Relations, September 2005.

chief executive of Reckitt Benckiser PLC. Pfizer's Listerine PocketPaks is one such example. The thin mouthwash strip caught on quickly with teens when introduced in 2001, but the plant where the strips were made closed in 2004 due to declining demand.[9]

Establishing Your Company as a Good Corporate Citizen

The most effective corporate social responsibility efforts are those that are seamlessly integrated into every aspect of a company, including the marketing platform. When founder Henry Heinz founded H. J. Heinz in 1869, he advocated pure food and corporate transparency. Today Heinz supports four CSR initiatives: a micronutrient program that provides nutritional supplements to undernourished children in countries where Heinz does business, health and wellness initiatives, sustainable agriculture, and eco-friendly packaging. While the company has traditionally communicated its CSR updates with internal audiences, Heinz issued its first annual report in 2006 and will utilize other methods to share the story with external publics. It is hoped that the report will encourage other stakeholders and companies to engage in CSR. [10]

Each of the following concepts describes a facet of how public relations and marketing can work together to build customer trust and loyalty while selling the product:

- **Public relations** focuses on the long-term goals of building positive relationships with consumers, suppliers, competitors, and other publics. Its primary goal is to "build and maintain a hospitable environment for an organization."[11] Customers want to be served, not sold. Public relations can help an organization's corporate climate to be conducive to customer service.

- **Relationship marketing** is a long-term process, as the goal is to build trust that enhances the selling of products or services. "You can earn trust over a number of years, but you must work every hour, every day to keep it," says a Heinz executive.[12] Relationship marketing in action is when a customer buys the same laundry detergent year after year. The consumer has learned that this product does a satisfactory job of cleaning clothes and, as a result, does not feel the need to try other products.

- **Marketing communications** refers to all activities—research, strategies, or tactics— that support the selling of products and services.

- **Integrated communications** is a truncated way of referring to **integrated marketing communications.** Marketers use a variety of tactics such as advertising, public relations, sponsorships, and the like to reach consumers.

- **Corporate social responsibility** is a demonstration of a company's commitment to its neighbors, consumers, and others to be a good citizen.

Public relations and marketing are similar in that they do extensive research, identify target publics, and develop communication action plans. Because public relations is integrated completely into the marketing process, it is easy to understand why the distinction between the two functions is difficult for many to grasp.

Public relations addresses the following elements not associated with marketing:

- Internal publics such as employees, stockholders, and management
- Reputation, or image building
- External publics (other than consumers) such as government and suppliers
- Crisis management
- Public opinion change and social issues
- Issues management

The Ford/Firestone tire crisis in 2000 is a key example of how quickly consumers respond to negative information about a product. The tread separated on some models of Firestone tires that were mounted as standard equipment on certain Ford vehicles, resulting in numerous injuries and fatalities. More than advertising and other traditional marketing tools are needed to restore customer confidence and sales in such situations. Firestone replaced millions of tires. Ford took the bold step of severing its more-than-century-old relationship with Firestone. This decision had not only business ramifications but also personal ones. Likewise, product publicity can augment advertising efforts and make other marketing techniques more effective.

The positive relationships a company develops through public relations with its consumers and other publics are a means to an end: sales and profits that can be strengthened quarter after quarter, year after year. In many organizations the structure of departments and divisions blurs the relationships between public relations and marketing to the point that the two are almost always linked. Mergers of public relations firms and advertising agencies have further clouded this issue in the minds of many managers and others.

It's important to point out that consumer relations and marketing must be integrated into the overall communications planning process. One obvious reason for this is to ensure that a problem can actually be addressed by communicating. No amount of public relations activity can make up for an inadequate distribution system, a food that doesn't taste good, or a poorly designed product.

In a column in *The New York Times,* David Pogue talks about his research for a book he's writing on the backstage story of Palm, Handspring, and the palmtop craze. He noted that in the early days, Palm's vice president of marketing had a favorite saying: "Delight the customer." Pogue thought the saying sounded not only obvious but hackneyed. No company sets out to disappoint the customer, he felt. Pogue's co-author, who was one of the original Palm employees, responded by saying that that wasn't the point:

> In the technology industry, you'd be surprised how much "Delight the customer" ISN'T the point. The alternative isn't "Disappoint the customer," but "What can we do with this neat technology?" The customer doesn't even come up in the product designers' thoughts. . . . When you think of delighting the customer as a guiding light in making choices, it explains a lot why the Pilot ended up being a product people loved, and are so emotionally attached to.[13]

All companies have probably been guilty, to some degree, of overlooking, disregarding, or ignoring the needs of their customers. McDonald's focus on itself may have been part of the reason for years of declining sales. Theme lines such as "We do it all for you," "We love it when you love it," and "We love to see you smile," were indicative of the problem, says the company's marketing chief. "We took our eyes off the consumer and we lost consumer relevance," he said.[14] The difference is that smart, thriving companies constantly *listen* to their customers and act on what they hear.

Imagination is the limit when it comes to applying public relations techniques to marketing. When Hewlett-Packard wanted to send the message that it is a "total solutions provider" and an "innovative technology leader," the company thought that the Formula One

motor sport racing at the Indianapolis Grand Prix provided the right kind of environment for this message.[15] Hasbro, maker of the Monopoly board game, had the public pick the first new game piece in 40 years and created a world championship as a way to keep up interest in the game.[16] Using a collection of pantomime-like cows, Chick-fil-A formed a political party called the Cow Preservation Party with a platform of promoting chicken consumption.[17] A social media campaign helped Chick-fil-A find its most passionate fans during its 40th anniversary celebration. The restaurant chain leveraged media coverage and its corporate Web site to encourage fans to submit an up-to-one-minute creative video showing why they were the brand's biggest fan. The public weighed in on their favorite entries, helping a set of twins win 40 months of free combo meals, a trip to Atlanta to visit the corporate headquarters, and other Chick-fil-A merchandise.

Product and Service Design

Because public relations practitioners keep in constant touch with the various publics of an organization, they can provide valuable insight into consumer behavior issues. This type of informal research can be an important check on other data used in the design of products and services. The frequent monitoring of mass media, the use of

Anniversary promotion gives online voice to brand's devotees.

social forecasting services, and other forms of environmental surveillance discussed in chapter 6 make public relations practitioners important sources of information in the marketing process.

All products and services have life cycles that must be a part of the marketing plan. The product life cycle starts with the development of new products and services, which are then introduced to a market. As industry sales increase during the market growth stage, so does competition. This often results in higher promotional costs and lower profits. The intense competitive environment of the third stage, that of market maturity, is usually marked with a decrease in sales and profits. The product life cycle begins to repeat itself during the final sales decline stage, as new products and services replace old ones.

Public relations can help extend the life cycle of a product or service at several stages by developing events to support product introduction and sales and by generating positive news coverage of products and services. When a new product is launched, special events and publicity can help develop a positive reception. Schick Shave Shack, a mobile karaoke competition born from the idea of people singing and shaving in the shower, promoted the company's entire product line and attracted more than 100 million media impressions.[18] Publicity can help increase consumer awareness during the growth stage of a product. Not only has Tiger Woods attracted more people of all ages and ethnicities to the sport of golf, but he has also prompted increased coverage of products he endorses.[19] When a mature product has achieved almost universal name recognition, it often gets taken for granted and needs help in maintaining its visibility. For example, in spite of the high brand awareness that the Red Cross has developed in its 100+ years, public relations and other marketing activities are needed on an ongoing basis to maintain the nation's blood supply.[20]

The public relations information base regarding a wide range of publics, including but not limited to consumers, can be instrumental in naming, style, and packaging. Marketing texts are filled with examples of ill-chosen names that doomed or delayed the success of a perfectly good product. The Chevrolet Nova ("doesn't go" in Spanish) is one of the most famous of these legends. Names need to reflect the organization's core mission and values, be easy to say and find online, and be easily represented with a logo and other brand identity elements.[21] Beyond the name, consumers view products and services as a bundle of utilities or a collection of attributes that hold value. Packaging and style must add to that perception. Because of their skill in communication and understanding of publics, public relations practitioners can contribute to the selection of proper styling and packaging for products and services.

Corporate Social Responsibility

Successful brands today need to stand for something beyond the actual product or service, and the Internet makes it possible for these efforts to be made on a large scale. "Teens for Jeans," an initiative of the company Aéropostale and the group Do Something, wanted to collect 100,000 pairs of jeans to donate to homeless teens. To reach its consumers the campaign utilized a multifaceted communications strategy, which included a teensforjeans.com Web site, celebrity endorsement, a public service announcement that was shown on various social networking sites such as Facebook and MySpace, media outreach plus events and programs of interest to teens.[22]

Distribution

Public relations practitioners, and the information they provide, can assist marketing in making decisions about how and where a product or service will be offered to the consumer. Issues of logistics related to location and time availability must be thoroughly analyzed for target markets before a product or service is released.

Johnson & Johnson made a marketing decision to merge the sales forces for its German pharmacy and retail trades. German pharmacies did not carry feminine hygiene products before the merger, but they now carry J&J women's hygiene products o.b. tampons and Carefree protection shields, as well as baby-care Penaten products. Nonpharmacy retail outlets sell Neutrogena hand cream for the first time, a product previously available only in pharmacies. The integration saves customers money, as products are less expensive in nonpharmacy stores. J&J promoted the new product distribution with a combination of advertising and public relations activities, including television and cinema commercials, print ads, and event marketing.[23]

Banks learned that automated teller machines must be safe to use as well as near to their customers' homes and workplaces. Today, these machines are found in most supermarkets and convenience stores in addition to after hours at banks. Wireless technology addresses the desire of consumers to receive their e-mail, access the Web, and perform a host of other communication activities from anywhere in the world. Again, communication and promotion about product and service availability are important for success.

Communication

Today's marketers know they can't live by advertising alone. Lois Raimondo, the vice president of marketing for Times Square Alliance, which coordinates the dropping of the ball at midnight on New Year's Eve, says, "Our advertising was minor. It was our PR efforts that got us the coverage that we got."[24]

As part of an integrated marketing campaign, 1-800-Flowers partnered with Google and YouTube to find the "World's Greatest Love Stories." The Valentine Day contest invited users to submit videos sharing how they fell in love with their partner or their marriage proposal. *The New York Times* was granted an exclusive news scoop about the promotion, and marketers also utilized blogs and online word-of-mouth to generate submissions.[25]

Allure magazine, cosmetic retailer Sephora, and trade association Cosmetic Executive Women invite readers, customers, and members to vote on their favorite beauty products. Winning brands use the endorsements in ad campaigns, in-store promotions, Web sites and packaging. The contest sponsors also benefit with additional exposure, advertising and sales.[26]

When *Pearl Harbor,* a movie about the 1941 Japanese attack that drew America into World War II, made its debut, the Walt Disney Corporation and U.S. Navy spent a reported $5 million on events in an effort to create box office buzz. Their efforts earned the front cover and extensive coverage in *Newsweek,* the major wire services, and entertainment television shows. The navy sent almost 40 navy reserve information officers to Hawaii to handle prerelease activities. The film screening for journalists was held outdoors on the flight deck of the USS *Stennis,* a working navy ship. The public relations endeavors paid off with to-die-for endorsements and being rated in polls as the summer's most anticipated movie.[27]

As you can see, public relations plays a natural role in supporting a variety of marketing activities. This makes it easy to overlook the critical role public relations can have in the company's larger environment of image and reputation management and handling whatever crises may occur.

Your CEO as the Marketing Spokesperson

The chief executive officer is usually the ideal spokesperson during a crisis. Does the same hold true for marketing activities? When the late Victor Kiam acquired Remington Product's shavers, the company was ailing. A positive bottom line one year later was the result of staff cuts, product line changes, and Kiam starring in Remington's aggressive television advertising campaign. "I liked it so much, I bought the company," confirmed Kiam's commitment to the brand in the ads.[28] David Oreck promotes the virtues of the eight-pound Oreck XL vacuum sweeper. The late Dave Thomas appeared in ads for his daughter's namesake restaurant, Wendy's. The spokesduo for Bush's Baked Beans, Jay Bush and his dog, Duke, credit the brand's great taste to a secret family recipe.

Bill Gates used television ads and personal appearances on talk shows to present Microsoft's side of the story in its antitrust battle with the U.S. Department of Justice. Lee Iacocca, former CEO of Chrysler, spoke to the American public about his personal pledge to quality when the company was experiencing credibility problems.

Merrie Spaeth, president of Spaeth Communications, Inc., Dallas, Texas, provides the following guidelines for using company CEOs in their own ads:

1. The CEO who is an owner or part of the family who has owned the company for several generations can communicate a personal commitment to the brand.
2. The copy should sound like the CEO actually talks in real life.
3. Delivery skills are important but should not be the only criteria for determining if your CEO is suitable for the job. Message and audience should also be considered.
4. Charisma counts, as it lends credibility to the message. The listener or viewer needs to believe that the speaker believes what he's saying.
5. Reasons not to use your CEO include diction problems that probably can't be overcome or a top executive who doesn't look the part.[29]

Although some CEOs enjoy being in the limelight, and not having to pay for talent saves money, practitioners need to understand the strategy before selecting a CEO spokesperson over a celebrity endorser. For example, the accomplishments of major sports figures can influence buying decisions for athletic brands such as Nike, Reebok, and L.A. Gear in a manner that would be difficult for a CEO. Similarly, glamorous models and famous actresses build and refresh cosmetic brands. Movie, television, and rock stars can capture the attention of their fans as they try to increase awareness of a product or service. Britney Spears, for example, appeared in Pepsi commercials.

What matters in selecting a spokesperson, CEO, or celebrity is the ability of that individual to add value to the brand. Consumers' perception of the qualities of the spokesperson must match the messages that need to be communicated to the target audiences. Spokespersons must be able to transfer their values.

Integrating Disciplines and Technology

Unbelievable as it may seem, terms like **podcasting, blogs, DVR / TiVo, satellite radio, advergaming, RSS,** wireless, **advertainment,** and **VOD** weren't part of our vocabulary until the early 2000s. Even though technology is expanding the opportunity for consumer contact, traditional print and electronic mainstays still have a role in today's communication mix.

"The traditional marketing model we all grew up with is obsolete," says James R. Stengel, global marketing officer of Procter & Gamble, the world's largest advertiser.[30] He warned marketers who are using only TV, newspapers, and magazines that "they must become more accountable, innovative and creative or be doomed to failure."[31] Says Marian Salzman of J. Walter Thompson, "It's all about your gut now. The Internet has changed everything."[32]

Today's elusive consumers are moving targets and not limited by traditional marketing channels. Figures 12.2 and 12.3 compare the media landscapes of 1980 and 2007.

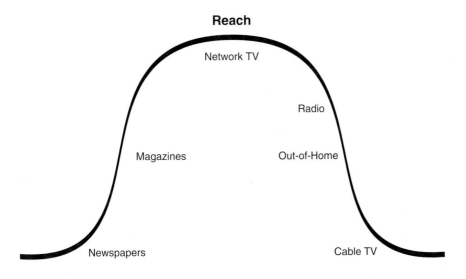

FIGURE 12.2   **Media Landscape 1980** *Source:* Horizon Media

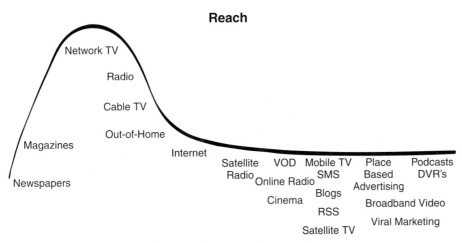

FIGURE 12.3   **Media Landscape 2007** *Source:* Horizon Media

While network television still enjoys the most reach, the number of communication channels has at least tripled. This creates many more opportunities and methods in which to reach publics.

Beyond technology, though, here are four other reasons why organizations have moved to an integrated approach. One is that an increasing concern for the bottom line has caused management to look at ways to reduce expenses. A second factor is that public relations firms and advertising agencies are merging with and acquiring one another. This has created a natural tendency to consolidate functions that overlap among advertising, marketing, and public relations. A third reason for integration is an increased emphasis on relationship marketing and one-to-one marketing, both of which require development of a good reputation, or image building, which is a public relations activity. A fourth motivation for integration is the importance of good governmental public relations. Influencing laws and regulations at the local, state, and federal levels often affect a firm's sales and marketing aspects.

Given the stealth speed with which new techniques develop and blend with current practice, the following list is intended to serve only as an overview of integrated marketing techniques.

Multitasking Portable Gadgets   Cell phones, Blackberrys, iPods, DVDs, wireless broadband-enabled laptops, and other multitasking portable gadgets signal a major shift from mass production, mass marketing, and mass merchandising to an era of customized products and services.[33] It is estimated that more than 250 million Americans subscribe to a mobile phone service, placing the penetration rate at approximately 81 percent.[34] Worldwide the rate stands at approximately 50 percent, a number that promises to continue to grow given that mobile networks now cover 90 percent of the global population.[35] Users are able to use their phones to keep a calendar, download ringtone, play games, instant message, take pictures, send and receive e-mails, access the Internet, and make phone calls. They allow clients "to go right to the behavior" and are "a technology-enabled form of measurement," according to Mark Weiner of Ketchum Research.[36] For example, Ketchum's overseas agency, Mobile One2One, created individualized bus routes for a Spanish company with recruitment problems. The maps proved to be a win-win situation as hiring improved, and the client was able to learn which geographic areas yielded the best results.[37]

Product Placement   Personal video recorders like TiVo enable consumers to skip commercials altogether. Soft drink companies, computer manufacturers, cell phone makers, and others are using **product placement** to raise the visibility of their products in videogames and other electronic programming options as well as traditional channels; for example,

- CBS digitally embedded the logo of the new Chevrolet Impala in five of the network's prime-time shows during premiere week of its new fall 2005 schedule and gave away one car each night of the promotion.[38]
- In the *Meet Mister Mom* reality show, dads drive Nissans, use Clorox to clean, and shop for their families at JCPenney.[39]

The industry continues to debate how much product placement should cost and whether it is really effective. For example, Procter & Gamble's Crest toothpaste appeared in *The Apprentice* show. Tracking indicated that the placement was equal to 10.8 thirty-second commercials, which would cost $4.2 million. But, says the senior vice president for Mitsubishi Motors, "I will not do it [product placement] unless there is some quantifiable measure of what we are going to get out of it."[40]

Product placement can have public relations implications beyond those for marketing purposes. Germany's Linux Association protested against "product placement in informational and news broadcasts" when the country's ARD, the public Channel One station, displayed Microsoft's logo on election reports. The association's executive director explains, "News reports on public television lose credibility and authenticity when they are mixed with advertising."[41]

Web Sites   Web sites are an integral part of almost every integrated communications plan. Food brands offer recipes, promotional booklets, screen savers, meal planners, and dozens of other features to strengthen their ties to the consumer. Fast-food restaurants provide nutrition information about their menu items, entice users to participate in their sweepstakes, and identify their locations. They also might create, as Burger King did, a "Subservient Chicken" Web site where you could give orders to a garter-clad hen in a dingy motel room.[42] A campaign for Procter & Gamble's Tide included a Web site where consumers could see how many people in their area tried the product.[43] **Branded news** is live, Internet-based newscasting, narrowly focused on news about the product or service category of that organization that is providing the newscast. One example of a branded news Web site is NRANews.com (see the end of chapter 15).

Web sites, though, are more than a tactical tool for the marketers. They are also products. When launching the beta version of Brilliant Shopper, a site that helps consumers do comparison shopping, the company's CEO tapped into blogs to reach the target market. Research indicated that a "hub and spoke" approach would help maximize their $25,000 public relations budget. The goal was to focus on the most prominent bloggers (hubs), whose work was often picked up by others (spokes). The campaign also allowed bloggers to break the news before traditional media. Page views increased about 250 percent as a result.

Search Engine Marketing   With so many consumers using the Web for product information and cost comparisons, the ability of a company to come up at the top of a search is critical. Search engine marketing is a tool that companies can use to increase the possibility that their listings and brands will appear when one searches for a particular term.[44] Research is important to identify the terms and language used by consumers for goods and services. Still, even the best keywords are of no use unless the copy is well written and appeals to your users.[45]

Guerilla Tactics   When budgets are small, time is tight, and the product isn't the category leader, practitioners often turn to **guerilla tactics.** These nontraditional communication vehicles attempt to highlight a brand in an unexpected way.

Caution must be exercised, though, when utilizing guerilla tactics. The search for a coin worth $10,000 in a Dr Pepper promotion led Boston treasure hunters to a cemetery. Fortunately the gates to the Granary Burying Ground were locked due to icy conditions, and participants were unable to enter. Dr Pepper apologized for potentially desecrating a hallowed site and donated $10,000 to the cemetery.[46]

Nobody was laughing when the Cartoon Network placed electronic light boards around Boston and nine other cities to promote the late-night Adult Swim cartoon "Aqua Teen Hunger Force." The devices were assumed to be potentially dangerous, and law enforcement efforts disrupted city services for hours. The tactic was called "unconscionable" and "outrageous."[47] Boston's mayor estimated that the incident cost the city about $500,000.[48] The president of the Cartoon Network resigned soon afterward, and the fiasco cost the parent company, Turner Broadcasting System, $2 million.[49]

Viral Marketing   **Viral marketing** is a social media phenomenon in which citizens share experiences, knowledge, and feelings about a brand. Book reviews, restaurant recommendations, product evaluations, customer service horror stories, and more are available on YouTube, Facebook, MySpace, numerous blogs, discussion boards, and Web sites. Viral marketing creates huge opportunities to extend the efforts beyond what might originally have been thought possible.

When Sarah Jessica Parker launched the brand Bitten at Steve & Barry's stores, her agency did so using viral documentary-type video and other public relations tactics. Selected clips were put on YouTube, and these were supplemented with articles in *Glamour* and *O, The Oprah Magazine* and with appearances by Parker on *The Oprah Winfrey Show*. The agency incorporated a local news angle through the "First in Line" program. Parker called the first ten people who got in line in ten select cities, generating publicity about those receiving the calls. Most important, the public relations efforts significantly increased sales in locations throughout the country.[50]

Contests and Sweepstakes   Contests and sweepstakes can be a fast way for companies to have direct contact with their current and prospective consumers. Many vied for an opportunity to have a brown-bag lunch with Duchess of York Sarah Ferguson when French's GourMayo Flavored Light Mayonnaise brand staged a contest.[51] Contests and sweepstakes to win new furniture; home makeovers; backstage meetings with rock stars; trips to Disney, Bangkok, and other cities; home entertainment systems; and tons of other products and services are offered online, in print, at point-of-purchase locations, at events, and the like. Winners are announced daily, weekly, monthly. For the marketer, contests and sweepstakes can be an inexpensive way to gain valuable information about its customers and to reach them with news and information of interest.

Some truisms, though, apply regardless of all that technology has to offer: Never put anything in writing that you don't want someone else to see; and, there is no substitute for old-fashioned face-to-face communication. The head of Sears public relations learned this when he inadvertently sent an uncomplimentary e-mail about a columnist—to the journalist himself. While not surprised, given what he had written about Sears, the columnist wished that the executive had talked to him directly: "I would like to see PR people, if they have issues, put them on the table."[52] See spotlight 12.1 for some helpful tips on supporting consumer relations.

CONSUMER RELATIONS BRIDGES THE CORPORATION AND THE CONSUMER

Consumer relations is the bridge between the consumer and the manufacturer. When unexpected shipping charges are added to a mail order, when the quality is poor, when a warranty is not honored, when local branches are unresponsive to requests for help, when products are not safe, when the advertising is misleading, when repair people don't fix the problem, when information is desired, when

Public Relations Tactics to Support Consumer Relations and Marketing Efforts

As a public relations practitioner, you can blend traditional and nontraditional tactics you use to reach your objectives. The list below shows some, but certainly not all, the ways you could use some of these tools.

Media relations: News releases, pitch letters, backgrounders, biographies, fact sheets, desk-side visits, media advisories, media tours, press conferences, photographs.

Publicity: Press conferences, research results, satellite media tours, autograph parties, announcements, speeches, talk show appearances, video news releases.

Collateral material: Brochures, downloadable pdf handouts, fact sheets, product specifications, photographs, and other graphic images.

Special events: Anniversary and other commemorative activities, celebrations, conferences, time capsules.

Corporate relations: Identity programs, position papers, letters to the editor, advertorials, spokesperson training, policy statements, vodcasts.

Corporate social responsibility: Initiatives and programs that demonstrate a commitment to better the world through relevant activities.

Integrated marketing communications: Podcasts, Web sites, handbooks, sponsorships, brochures, grassroots campaigns, instruction manuals, pamphlets, article reprints, direct mail, demonstrations, sales promotions (POP, coupons), mass advertising (radio, TV, print,

outdoor), targeted direct marketing (Internet, kiosks), sweepstakes.

Awards/recognitions: Achievement awards, commemorative events, certificates.

Community relations: Advisory boards, open houses, speakers' bureaus, presentations, public service announcements, exhibits.

Employee/dealer relations: Intranet, e-mail, conferences, memorandums, training aids, contests, gifts.

Online word of mouth: Consumer-to-consumer e-mails, postings on public Internet discussion boards and forums, consumer ratings Web sites, blogs, moblogs where digital images, photos, and movies are posted.

---

a multitude of things can and do go wrong, consumer relations is there to respond. And for good reason. What companies do and how they do it are under scrutiny like never before. Consumer relations helps a corporation cope and thrive under this analysis.

The Challenges of Consumer Relations

Nothing is perfect, of course. People have bad days. Products can be defective in spite of rigorous testing. As noted earlier in this chapter, smart organizations constantly *listen* to their customers and act on what they hear. When the Hedstrom Corporation, of Bedford, Pennsylvania, received reports about the seats on its backyard swings falling off, causing children to drop to the ground, it asked consumers to stop using the swings immediately and to detach them from the gym set. The company made a free repair kit available through a toll-free number.[53] The manner in which Hedstrom resolved this problem works well with the customer complaint process discussed later in this chapter.

At the same time, some consumers have not demonstrated common sense when using some products. One woman sued a fast-food company when she was burned after putting a hot cup of coffee between her legs while she was driving. Although parents should know better than to leave their infants alone in a baby bath seat in a filled tub, some want the product banned because some babies died when left alone in the seats. Consumers are often quick to blame others for their own lack of judgment or failure to follow directions. Unfortunately there's little a manufacturer can do when consumers choose to ignore safety guidelines, printed warnings, and other measures that spell out the safe use of a product or service.

Trust is at the heart of these issues, and there are no easy answers. What is certain, though, is that these issues aren't new and they won't go away. Finger-pointing and not taking responsibility for one's actions aren't just 21st-century phenomena. History provides abundant examples. Today's business environment requires both corporations and consumers to be much more diligent and proactive than ever before. Consumers demand a greater emphasis on product performance, quality, and safety than ever before. They're more aware of their rights and more responsive to political and legal initiatives to protect those rights.

Consumer relations is a direct reflection of a corporation's values about its business in general. The Palm example presented earlier in this chapter discussed how the company's desire to "delight the customer" drove the product from its development stage. August A. Busch III, president of Anheuser-Busch, has a saying: "Making friends is our business." A-B makes friends by encouraging responsible consumption of its products by adults of legal drinking age and by investing in communities through education, disaster relief, and environmental and numerous other areas.[54] This consumer relations viewpoint is nothing new. Thomas Carlyle is just one of many famous philosophers through the centuries to observe, "Thought is the parent of deed."

The bottom line is that consumer relations should be more than a toll-free hotline to the company. It's how an organization fulfills its promise to serve its key publics.

Know Your Consumer

Good consumer relations begins with an organization's knowledge of its key publics. It's hard to identify an area that isn't affected by this knowledge in some way, from the product itself and its packaging to how the product is described and the selection of communication tactics. However, knowing your customer isn't always as easy as it first might seem. For example,

- *Your consumer might change traditional consumption patterns.* Fast-food chains used to ignore the late-night eaters, those wanting a burger or pizza or other munchies between 10 P.M. and 5 A.M. No more. Denny's and Taco Bell restaurant chains say the late-night segment accounts for about one-fourth of their annual sales. Wendy's saw a significant 30 percent growth in purchases after 10 P.M. in 1999.[55]
- *Economic and social shifts might open up new audiences.* Many states are recording an increase in consumers of Hispanic, Asian, and other ethnic origins. Reaching them might necessitate additional consumer research, marketing in languages other than English, adapting products, and using nontraditional communication vehicles. This trend affects global markets as well. By targeting distinct ethnicities in Brazil, manufacturers found 160 million new consumers who wanted to purchase clothes, cosmetics, soft drinks, toys, and a host of other personal and household products and services.[56]
- *Your brand may no longer resonate with your consumer.* Nike's consumers started to switch to leather shoes from athletic shoes in 1997, and the company didn't produce this type of footwear. Competitors lured Nike's customers away with new products and aggressive marketing campaigns. Nike hopes the innovative technology in the recently introduced Shox will allow it to reestablish itself as a market leader.[57]

The preceding illustrations highlight that shifting demographics, converging technologies, and changes in customer expectations all reinforce the point that your consumer group isn't static and often isn't satisfied. Thus, consumer relations programs must be proactive to ensure that they are meeting the needs of those they serve. This might mean extending the hours of customer service phone lines, initiating new research projects, exploring alternative communication outlets, repositioning a brand, creating new packaging, and a host of other considerations.

In the past three decades, consumer affairs units have become fixtures in most organizations that have direct links to consumers. A variety of names describe this function: public affairs, customer relations, consumer relations, consumer advocate, or public relations. Whatever the title, these staff members usually

work both inside and outside the organization. The staffing of consumer affairs units varies tremendously, with smaller organizations having only one consumer affairs specialist and larger ones having more than a hundred. Organizations frequently staff their consumer affairs units with employees who have enough prior experience in the company to handle complaints and investigate problems effectively.[58] Frequently, the staff is divided into groups responsible for certain functions, such as complaint handling, publications, consumer education, and the like.

The goal of consumer affairs is to improve the organization's relationships and communication with consumers by investigating consumer issues and conveying the results to management. Responsibilities of the consumer relations unit may include resolving customer complaints, disseminating consumer information, advising management on consumer opinion, and dealing with outside consumer advocate groups.

Frequently, the consumer relations unit is linked to the public relations department of an organization. This connection is natural, since consumers are one of the publics that public relations practitioners have traditionally served. The exact placement and design of consumer relations units vary, depending on the size and nature of the organization and the diversity of its products or services. One common characteristic does appear among the different approaches: The vast majority of consumer relations units report directly to top management. This provides the necessary autonomy to investigate issues and identify problems early with easy access to those who make policy decisions.

Consumer Information and Education

The major tenet of consumer advocacy is that consumers lack adequate information for making purchasing decisions. The complexity of the business system and the proliferation of products contribute to this difficulty, but many consumer problems result from product misuse or improper maintenance. A satisfied customer may tell another 5 to 8 people, but dissatisfied and angry customers are taking their complaints to public forums like Web sites, talk shows, and other media outlets, in addition to telling 10 to 16 of their friends and acquaintances. Consumer relations units have responded to the need for fuller and clearer information by providing simplified warranties, clarified product use instructions, and educational programs to help consumers select the right products for their needs and use them properly.

Toll-free numbers, e-mail, and Web sites are among the ways that consumers can reach companies with their complaints, questions, and suggestions. It is important that companies actually follow through and reply to customer complaints and inquiries. Some research suggests that corporations are failing miserably in responding to the feedback they have received or are not communicating to consumers the actions that have been taken to rectify the problems. As noted earlier, the kinds of organizations that gain the most from their marketing and consumer relations activities are those that constantly listen to their customers and act on what they hear.

Consumers usually value a message more if it comes from the media than from company representatives. Recognizing that, managements work with their consumer and public relations staffs to schedule new product releases and major announcements for times when they will gain the most publicity possible. General Nutrition Centers rolled out its newest supplement, the Officially Licensed NASCAR® Kids Multi-Vitamin, for instance, at the Milwaukee Mile. The chewable vitamins come in three dimensional race-car shapes, and the company included a free die-cast replica of the No. 36 GNC Live Well race car with purchase.[59]

When audiences are difficult to reach through traditional media, organizations must be extra creative.

Generally Satisfied But Not Always Served

A 1999 Harris Interactive poll found most people believe that computer hardware and software companies, airlines, hospitals, car manufacturers, banks, telephone companies, and pharmaceutical companies are generally doing a good job in serving their customers and would do the right thing if they had a serious problem with one of their products or services. Although this is encouraging news, there are two other sides to the story. One is that this overall degree of satisfaction has been falling since 1997, from 67 percent to 55 percent.[60] The other is that developing a consumer-lifestyle philosophy for new product development can be risky for business. Notes Gerard Kleisterlee, CEO of consumer electronics giant Philips, "It's a huge decision. Organize however you like: around product lines, manufacturing, markets, geography, customers, etc. But get it wrong, and your company will wobble in the wrong orbit for years."[61]

Thus, the potential for problems often begins with the products and services themselves. Mass-produced products don't work and behave like those that are custom designed. This can be a breeding ground for consumer frustration and disappointment.

Unfair and Deceptive Practices

Damage to the buyer-seller relationship occurs when products and services are promoted using unfair or deceptive means. Although only a small percentage of goods do not live up to their advertising, enough consumers have had bad experiences with products in general to believe the worst and be suspicious of claims and promises.

Voluntary self-regulation is the primary reason why unsubstantiated claims are not allowed to proliferate in advertising. The National Advertising Division (NAD) and the Children's Advertising Review Unit, both part of the Council of Better Business Bureaus, are the investigative arms of the industry's program. Competitive challenges come from other advertisers and also from self-monitoring traditional and new media and consumers.

For example, a review board determined that AT&T had a reasonable basis to substantiate that its 1-800-CALL-ATT collect calling service "always costs less than MCI's 1-800-COLLECT."[62] A concerned consumer questioned whether M&M Mars's "NEW" Peanut Butter Twix bar could be described as "new" since it had been on the market before being discontinued in 1997. The panel found that the "new" version of Peanut Butter Twix was materially different from its earlier version and that the "new" claim was truthful and nonmisleading.[63] Unilever was asked to modify certain advertising claims for its Thermasilk line of shampoos and conditioners. While it was found that Thermasilk products help protect hair from damage caused by heat, there was inadequate evidence to support the claim that heat styling with the brand will make hair healthier.[64] The voluntary self-regulation system works. There is about a 96 percent compliance rate in the more than 3,750 cases reviewed since NAD's founding in 1971, with only about 4 percent referred to government agencies for further action.

Public relations practitioners need to be careful not to mislead or dupe the gate-keepers to the consumer: the media. When dot-coms were closing and agencies were handing out pink slips, *PRWeek* received a press release about a "Seattle Company Up-sizing." It turned out the Internet and marketing firm in question had hired an art direc-tor. Future news releases from the company probably won't receive much attention.[65]

Handling Consumer Complaints

Although they are hard to quantify, probably the overwhelming majority of consumer inquiries and complaints are handled in a routine manner. The item is replaced or re-paired, the purchase price is refunded, instructions are given, or some other appropriate action is taken. Companies of all sizes realize the critical importance of consumer rela-tions and want to be responsive. Some companies, such as L.L. Bean, Lands' End, and Nordstrom, have service reputations that are legendary in the retail business.

The Council of Better Business Bureaus expanded its 2003 annual complaint sur-vey to include Canada because e-commerce and cross-country shopping makes it easy for buyers to do business with merchants anywhere in the world. Automobile dealers topped the list of the most-complained-about industries. Cell phone and credit card companies came in second and third. Others in rank order were Internet services, credit collection agencies, mortgage and escrow companies, computer sales, home furnishing stores, telephone companies, and banks.[66]

The more expensive the item, the more likely the consumer will complain, according to *Consumer Reports*. This is why household goods like computers, electronics, appliances, and furniture receive so many complaints. Consumers gripe about defective products, deceptive advertising, and manufacturers that don't honor warranties and refunds.[67]

Of course, not all complaints are routine. Azza Basarudin found profanity and racial slurs written in the used copy of the Quran that she had ordered from Bellwether Books through the "Marketplace" section of Amazon.com. Both Amazon and Bellwether is-sued apologies and gift certificates to the Los Angeles graduate student, recognizing that the book was used, not new, and that such books can contain comments written by the previous owner. The incident made national headlines.[68]

Technology and Complaints

Many opinions and complaints are never sent directly to the manufacturer or company. Instead, technology has made it possible for consumers to share their honest assessment about any or all aspects of a product or service with each other. The much-hyped *Harry Potter* Book 6 received more than 2,600 comments—and four out of five stars—from readers on Amazon.com. Buyers on eBay rate the sellers on everything from honest pre-sentation of the product to customer service.

Little gets by today's bloggers or those who use consumer-generated media. They check out facts, provide the inside scoop about what's going on in companies, and share personal experiences. Puffery, dishonesty, misleading statements, and the like are ex-posed for what they are. There is no room to hide. Blogger B. L. Ochman called Daim-lerChrysler "clueless" for limiting its "journalist-only" blog to those who work for a known or established media organization, which apparently doesn't include blogs.[69]

Marketing and Complaints

One way companies handle consumer complaints is through advertising. In the debate as to who's responsible for the nation's obesity problem, especially in children, General Mills launched an advertising campaign that touted the healthy benefits of eating its sugary cereals in the morning. The idea is that eating breakfast is a healthy behavior, and while nutritionists may cringe at the products' high sugar content, they agree that the approach is better than no breakfast at all.[70]

The Corporate Liaison

The consumer affairs role within corporations has become that of consumer spokesperson to management. Most consumer affairs specialists see it as part of their jobs to take an active role in decision making by speaking out for the consumer. They actively solicit consumer opinion and make management aware of the effects various decisions will have on consumers. The in-house ombudsman must balance the needs of the actual customers, the demands of consumer activists, and the goals of the organization. This role of liaison has always been the highest calling for public relations professionals.

Those who understand the purpose of public relations realize that the practitioner must do more than echo the company line. Public relations professionals should help senior managers stay in touch with their various publics. Doing so is especially critical in emergencies, when public relations professionals must serve as management's bridge to the media and the public. As Mark Rockefeller, founder and CEO of Sponsor Direct, says, In an *increasingly competitive* and *mature environment* where the quality of products and services are consistently high and differences are less recognizable, it is going to be *less and less* about telling and *more about* showing target customers *who you are* (associations) and *what you care about* (actions).[71]

Operation Geek Squad

Case Study

Overview

When it comes to computers, most users want nothing more than a machine that works day in and day out. Setup, software and hardware installation, repairs, anti-virus and anti-spyware security, and whatever else is needed to maintain computer health—and the owner's sanity—are best left to an expert. This is where Geek Squad's task force of highly skilled computer support Agents triumph.

When electronics retailer Best Buy purchased Minneapolis-based Geek Squad in 2002, they had an opportunity to differentiate themselves by expanding this small, local, elite technical service nationwide. No other electronics/computer retailer could offer consumers nationwide multichannel computer setup, repair, and education (i.e., in-home, in-store, Web site, and 800 number).

In 2004, Best Buy was ready to launch Geek Squad in all its stores, and they turned to Ketchum for help in developing the public relations campaign. This campaign would receive no advertising support, relying solely on public relations to attain Best Buy's business goal. The business goal was to increase the number of consumers who accessed in-home and in-store Geek Squad service in the 45 launch markets across the country. To accomplish this, Ketchum and Best Buy identified three communications objectives:

- Raise Geek Squad awareness.
- Protect the established brand identity of Geek Squad while introducing it as a new customer service unit of Best Buy.
- Differentiate Geek Squad from its technical support service competitors.

Research and Planning

A Best Buy–commissioned survey of Minneapolis residents established awareness benchmarks for future Geek Squad markets. National and local competitive analyses were conducted by Ketchum to verify differentiating Geek Squad factors and existing service availability. Finally, a national survey helped determine the current mind-set of consumers' technology fears and frustrations. Basic findings showed that, generally, consumers were ready for someone or some company to help them understand technology at their own pace.

The following tactical elements of the plan initially focused on anyone owning or using a computer, executed through nine launch waves, infiltrating each of the 45 markets:

- Pitch print exclusives to media where Geek Squad brand identity and story could best be showcased.
- Execute guerilla-marketing tactics that reflected the brand's quirkiness while sparking customer curiosity.
- Find potential influential users and recommenders of Geek Squad services in every market to drive trial and generate word-of-mouth buzz.

After the story of Geek Squad was released in seven of the nine launch waves, the team shifted its focus from local to national, riding the building momentum from the local media placements.

Execution

A three-pronged approach to drive trial in a calculated manner included local/national media strategy, local/national events, and "influencer" outreach.

Offbeat local and national events to drive consumer curiosity included using a live Agent working on a laptop inside a giant glass box that read, "In Case of Technical Catastrophe, Break Glass," and swarms of 8 to 12 Geek Squad's signature Geekmobiles weaving down heavily traveled roadways and downtown business districts. The ringing of the New York Stock Exchange's closing bell and a celebrity bash at Los Angeles' Cineramadome offered further visibility for Geek Squad's launch.

To seed markets with advocates of Geek Squad services prelaunch, influencer kits containing "Advance Reconnaissance Offers" of free Geek Squad services were made available to individuals deemed "influential" in each market.

Evaluation

Geek Squad's national launch campaign exceeded Best Buy's desired business results and unaided awareness goals. A Geek Squad feature story was secured in all 45 of the launch markets. An analysis of the media content revealed that in three of every five stories, Geek Squad Agents were positioned as tech experts; 89 percent of Geek Squad coverage included key messages; in nearly all coverage, Geek Squad was mentioned more than competitors or competitors were mentioned not at all, clearly differentiating the brand from its technical support service competitors.

Source: Robyn Massey and Sara Wingert, Ketchum, February 2008.

Questions

1. What are the benefits of a multifaceted public relations plan, not just media?
2. How could a marketing mix have added to the results?
3. Why is it important to reach out to influencers?
4. Why is it important to stay within or protect a mass retailer's brand's image?
5. Why was it important to "go national" at the point in this campaign when Ketchum did?
6. What other nontraditional media could Ketchum have considered?
7. What was the importance of media training?
8. What guidelines should be considered when considering a guerilla-marketing strategy?
9. What questions might have been asked in the research to determine awareness levels, competitive positioning, and consumer mind-sets regarding Geek Squad?

Summary

For self-testing and additional chapter resources, go to the Online Learning Center at **www.mhhe.com/lattimore3e.**

Public relations and marketing can work together to build customer trust and loyalty while selling the product or service. The kinds of organizations that gain the most from their marketing and consumer relations activities are those that constantly listen to their customers and act on what they hear.

A multitude of communication tools is available for marketing and consumer relations activities, to be used singularly or in a multitiered effort, or to synthesize into new cross-discipline vehicles.

An organization fulfills its promise to serve its key publics through trust. Consumer affairs improves an organization's relationship and communication with consumers by investigating and resolving consumer issues and concerns.

Key Terms

advergaming

advertisement

blogs

branded news

consumer relations

corporate social responsibility

DVR / TiVo

guerrilla tactics

integrated communications

integrated marketing
   communications

marketing communications

podcasting

product placement

public relations

relationship marketing

RSS

satellite radio

viral marketing

VOD

1. Procter & Gamble, "Take the Plunge! Alliance to Save Energy and Tide Coldwater Issue Joint Challenge: Switch to Cold Water Washing to Save Money and Reduce Energy Usage," www.pg.com, January 18, 2005.

2. David Ward, "Teaching an Old Brand New Tricks," *PRWeek*, August 15, 2005, p. 15.

3. Adrian Brune, "Martinique Focuses on Blogs in Tourism Drive," *PRWeek*, February 25, 2008, p. 4.

4. Kia Motors Web site, "Company at a Glance," www.kia.com, August 2005.

5. John N. Frank, "Custer Helps Kia Stake Out a 'Young at Heart' Image," *PRWeek*, August 8, 2005, p. 11.

6. Erica Iacono, "Subway Positions Itself as Healthy Fast-Food Option," *PRWeek*, January 24, 2005, p. 10.

7. Adrian Brune, "Smirnoff Adds Hip-Hop Flavor to New Initiative," *PRWeek*, February 25, 2008, p. 5.

8. Deborah Ball, Sarah Ellison, and Janet Adamy, "Just What You Need!" *The Wall Street Journal*, October 28, 2004, p. B1.

9. Ibid.

10. Tanya Lewis, "A Clear Mission," *PRWeek*, July 16, 2007, p. 12.

11. Glen M. Broom and Kerry Tucker, "An Essential Double Helix," *Public Relations Journal* (November 1989), pp. 40–41.

12. Douglas Quenqua, "The Trust Timeline," *PRWeek*, June 13, 2005, p. 11.

13. David Pogue, "From the Desk of David Pogue: The Dumb and the Delightful," *The New York Times Online*, www.nytimes.com, June 7, 2001.

14. Stuart Elliott, "Consumer Advice for Advertisers," *The New York Times Online*, www.nytimes.com, October 11, 2004.

15. David Rovella, "WSW Finds Formula to Tout PR Products," *PRWeek*, April 9, 2001, p. 22.

16. Thom Weidlich, "Monopoly: Entire World Is on Board," *PRWeek*, April 2, 2001, p. 22.

17. Kris Oser, "Cows Campaign in DC," *PRWeek*, October 23, 2000, p. 38.

18. Colin Nash, "A Shave and a Song," *PRWeek*, October 16, 2000, p. 24.

19. David Ward, "Woods Appeal Taking Golf Mainstream," *PRWeek*, February 11, 2008, p. 11.

20. "The Red Cross Faces Disaster Undaunted," *PRWeek*, November 13, 2000, p. 10.

21. Ted McKenna, "New Name Must Be More Than Just a Moniker," *PRWeek*, January 14, 2008, p. 9.

22. Irene Chang, "Campaigns with Style," *PRWeek*, February 11, 2008, p. 13.

23. Dagmar Mussey, "J&J Increases German Ad Spending behind Key Brands," www.AdAge.com, June 5, 2001.

24. Matthew McGevna, "TSA's Raimondo Helps World Ring in New Year," *PRWeek*, January 24, 2008, p. 8.

25. Aarti Shah, "1-800-Flowers Hooks Up with YouTube, Google in New Effort," *PRWeek*, January 14, 2008, p. 3.

26. Ellen Byron, "Awards Promote Beauty Contest," *The Wall Street Journal*, March 4, 2008, p. B4.

27. Robin Londner, "Film PR Blitz Leaves Nothing in Reserve," *PRWeek*, May 21, 2001, p. 2.

28. Laura Q. Hughes, "Never to Shave Again: Remington's Victor Kiam Dies," www.AdAge.com, June 4, 2001.

29. Merrie Spaeth, *Marketplace Communication* (New York: Mastermedia Limited, 1996), pp. 77–78.

30. Stuart Elliott, "Consumer Advice for Advertisers," *The New York Times Online*, www.nytimes.com, October 11, 2004.

31. Ibid.

32. Andrew Gordon, "The Futures Market," *PRWeek*, August 15, 2005, p. 11.

33. Devin Leonard, "Nightmare on Madison Avenue," *Fortune*, June 28, 2004, p. 94.

34. Industry information, wireless quick facts, CTIA The Wireless Association, www.ctia.org, February 24, 2008.

35. Patrick S. Campbell, "Global Mobile Penetration Rate Reaches 50% Mark," *Lexology*, www.lexology.com, November 30, 2007.

36. Tonya Garcia, "Mobile Campaigns Offer Innovative Avenue for Outreach," *PRWeek*, January 14, 2008, p. 15.

37. Ibid.

38. Jeff Greenfield, "Impala Product Placement," *Hollywood Product Placement News*, www.productplacement.biz, September 14, 2005.

39. Ibid.

Notes

40. Brian Steinberg, "Product Placement Pricing Debated," *The Wall Street Journal,* November 19, 2004, p. B3.

41. "Linux Association Protests against 'Product Placement' for Microsoft on German TV," heise online, www.heise.de.english, September 9, 2005.

42. Devin Leonard, "Nightmare on Madison Avenue."

43. John N. Frank and Beth Herskovits, "P&G, Bristol-Myers Squibb Swap Ads for Subtler Tactics," *PRWeek,* June 20, 2005, p. 1.

44. Ed Schipul, "Search Engine Marketing Allows Targeted Outreach," *PRWeek,* August 8, 2005, p. 6.

45. Chris Sherman, "An Experts' Guide to Keyword Research," *SearchEngineWatch,* searchenginewatch.com, September 20, 2005.

46. Katie Zezima, "Soda Promotion Backfires in Boston," *The New York Times,* February 24, 2007, p. A13.

47. Dan Lothian and Deborah Feyerick, "Two Held after Ad Campaign Triggers Boston Bomb Scare," cnn.com, February 1, 2007.

48. Mark Starr and Nick Summers, "A Viral TV Blunder," *Newsweek,* February 12, 2007, p. 12.

49. Katy Byron and Rob Kelley, "Cartoon Network Boss Quits Over Bomb Scare," cnnmoney.com, February 9, 2007.

50. Michael Bush, "Steve & Barry's Caters to Expanded Audience," *PRWeek,* June 18, 2007, p. 9.

51. David Ward, "Designing a Contest to Win Media Attention," *PRWeek,* June 6, 2005, p. 20.

52. John N. Frank, "E-mail Negligence Turns into Bad Press for Sears," *PRWeek,* August 29, 2005, p. 5.

53. Associated Press, "Backyard Gym Swings Recalled," *Jefferson City Post-Tribune,* June 6, 2001, p. 11.

54. "Making Friends. Making a Difference," Anheuser-Busch corporate brochure, 2001.

55. Suzanne Vranica, "Wendy's Feeds Off of Nighttime Cravings with Launch of New TV Ad Campaign," *The Wall Street Journal Online,* www.wsj.com, June 13, 2001.

56. Miriam Jordan, "Marketers Are Beginning to Target Blacks in Brazil as Consumer Group," *The Wall Street Journal Online,* www.wsj.com, November 24, 2000.

57. Judith Berck, "Has Nike Found the Springs Missing from Its Step?" *The New York Times Online,* www.nytimes.com, November 12, 2000.

58. E. P. McGuire, *The Consumer Affairs Department: Organization and Functions, Report No. 609* (New York: The Conference Board, 1973).

59. "GNC Launches New Children's Multiple Vitamin; NASCAR Kids Multi Rolls Out During GNC Live Well Milwaukee Mile," www.individual.com, June 29, 2001.

60. Humphrey Taylor, "Public Sees Huge Difference Between Industries on 'Serving Their Consumers' and 'Doing the Right Thing,'" www.harrisinteractive.com, April 28, 1999.

61. Adam Smith, "The Complex Task of Simplicity," *Time,* www.time.com, February 21, 2008.

62. "National Advertising Review Board Panel Finds Advertising for 1-800-CALLATT Substantiated," The Better Business Bureau, www.bbb.org, July 2, 2001.

63. "M&M Mars, Inc. Substantiates Claims for 'New' Peanut Butter Twix," www.nadreview.org, July 2, 2001.

64. "Unilever & P&G Participates in Advertising Self-Regulatory Process," www.nadreview.org, July 2, 2001.

65. "Firm's Growth Nearly Slips by Undetected," *PRWeek,* February 19, 2001, p. 32.

66. Sheila Adkins, "BBB Services Nationwide Surged in 2003; Businesses Ranked by Inquiries and Complaints," The Better Business Bureau, www.bbb.org, May 4, 2004.

67. "Your Top Gripes," *Consumer Reports,* www.consumerreports.org, February 2001.

68. Associated Press, "Mail-order Quran Arrives with Slurs," MSNBC, www.msnbc.com, May 18, 2005.

69. B. L. Ochman, "DaimlerChrysler Launches Media Only Blog and Locks Out Bloggers," www.whatsnextblog.com, September 15, 2005.

70. Janet Adamy, "General Mills Touts Sugary Cereal as Healthy Kids Breakfast," *The Wall Street Journal,* June 22, 2005, p. B1.

71. Mark F. Rockefeller, founder and chief executive officer, Sponsor Direct, in remarks to sports marketing professionals, September 24, 2007.

CHAPTER 13

Investor Relations

PREVIEW

Effective investor public relations creates and maintains investor confidence. It builds positive relationships with the financial community by providing corporate information. Increased interest in investor relations following the *Texas Gulf Sulphur Co.* case has greatly increased public relations involvement in the financial reporting of corporate information. With Enron's bankruptcy amid criminal charges against its accounting and financial advising firm, Arthur Andersen, the spotlight was again placed on the need for accurate, current financial reporting.

Strong financial relations programs, characterized by responsiveness, openness, and regular communications, help lower the cost of capital for businesses. A key function of financial relations is to provide prompt disclosure of corporate news that is significant to the financial community.

Hostile takeover attempts through tender offers or management takeover through a proxy fight are two key financial public relations crises that management of a corporation may face. Public relations professionals must become intimately involved in the battle for control when these crises occur.

Audiences for financial relations include individual stockholders, financial analysts, and the financial media. Major tools of financial relations to reach these key audiences include annual reports and annual stockholder meetings. But with many new technologies, the company's financial reporting also includes use of cable or satellite television, placement on the Web, or discussions with key stakeholders through video conference calls.

Effective financial relations gives a business increased support for its management, higher stock prices, and greater ease in attracting new capital.

Consider the following scenario. You have just been hired by a public corporation to join its investor relations area. As an entry-level employee, you've been assigned the task of working with the printed annual report to turn it into an electronic report. It won't replace the printed report this year, but it will provide an accessible version for those stockholders and related audiences who prefer to receive their reports in electronic form. Your first task is to find out the regulations for electronic reporting required annual information for the Securities and Exchange Commission.

What else is important to your assignment, and what pitfalls do you need to avoid?

DEFINING EVENTS

Two defining events highlight the essential function of financial relations in corporate America—a case settled by the U.S. Supreme Court in 1968, and the Enron case, coming to the forefront in October 2001. The 1968 landmark case *SEC v. Texas Gulf Sulphur Co.*, 401 F.2d 833 (2nd E.r. 1968), underlined the essential nature of timely and full disclosure of information in avoiding "insider trading" charges against a publicly held company. The Enron situation, with lawsuits and appeals that may not be settled for some years, emphasized both to investors and to the business community the necessity for accurate financial accounting and for reporting that financial condition through a company's investor relations materials.

Ultimately the success of any organization depends on its ability to attract resources from its environment. Among the most important of these resources is capital—the money with which other resources can be purchased. Corporations raise money in a variety of ways, including selling stock, issuing bonds, and securing loans from financial institutions. In all cases, a company can attract capital only if investors have confidence in the business and its management. Without accurate, honest financial reporting the investing public cannot have this confidence. Investor relations has developed in the last 30 years as a specialized public relations function "to build and maintain relationships with financial audiences, primarily institutional investors, analysts, and individual stockholders."[1]

Bond ratings, interest rates, and stock prices are not just a matter of negotiation between a corporation's financial officers and its bankers or brokers. Such negotiations are preceded by and based on the business's current performance and future prospects. These facts must be persuasively communicated, and that is where public relations is essential.

GROWING INTEREST IN INVESTOR RELATIONS

Since 1968 when the *Texas Gulf Sulphur* case was decided by the Supreme Court, business has had an increased interest in improved investor relations. Company executives were fined, and some served time in jail in the first major case of insider trading since the **Securities and Exchange Commission (SEC)** had been formed in 1934. That landmark decision was the wake-up call to American corporations

Internal Public Relations Lessons Learned from Enron Inc.

Spotlight 13.1

The collapse of Enron, a leading energy company headquartered in Houston, Texas, sent shockwaves through the financial marketplace in late 2001 and early 2002. The congressional hearings, court cases, and other investigations may go on for years, but the immediate impact on financial reporting no doubt will be far-reaching. Included is the internal impact that it is likely to have for financial public relations practitioners.

Here are some of the internal public relations lessons learned from the debacle:

1. *Share the bad news as well as the good news.* Although not a new concept to public relations, sharing bad news as well as good news is emphasized in this case because employees were heavily invested in the company through their retirement plan. The hardest time to convince a CEO to share bad news with employees is when things seem good and morale is high. But, to keep morale high, management needs to build long-term credibility by sharing the bad as well as the good with its employees before it becomes known outside, and especially before it is reported in the media.

2. *Treat all investors equally.* Often the largest number of investors comes from employees (although not usually the most total dollars). In Enron's case this was especially true because of the retirement funds being invested in Enron stock. SEC guidelines require disclosure of any information that would make a significant difference in the financial results of a publicly held company. Thus, employees who are stockholders should receive that same information. Investors must be given the potential downside as well as the upside of a company's performance, whether they are external investors or employee investors.

3. *Give internal communication center stage.* Some of Enron's problems might have been mitigated with better communication; some will require new legislation. The question of how much investor information should go to employees will become an issue in the next several years. Congress is studying potential legislation to require certain disclosure to employees in regard to their stock. Another similar issue is that Enron employees were kept from selling their stock for a period of time when the stock was dropping in value rapidly. Today, these "lockdowns" are legal. Congress may change that, or at least it may require certain notice to employees about any such lockdowns. Companies must have good internal channels of communication to deal with these issues.

4. *Know the difference between motivating and misleading.* Enron's communication from its CEO was overly optimistic. A company should refrain from being misleading in its optimism. If you have knowledge that something is wrong, it is misleading to say everything is great.

Source: Judy Buffington Aud, APR, "What Internal Communicators Can Learn from Enron," *Public Relations Strategist* 8, no. 2 (Spring 2002), pp. 11–12.

that the SEC meant business with its insider trading and related disclosure of information rules.

Enron, and its connection with Arthur Andersen as its accounting and financial reporting firm, has put financial reporting in the limelight. With a major public company going into bankruptcy and the inaccurate reporting of financial information that misled investors, analysts, and everyone else, financial reporting has suddenly undergone intense scrutiny by the press, the government, and investors (see spotlight 13.1 for lessons learned from Enron).

In 2002, WorldCom followed the Enron scandal with one of its own when it filed the largest bankruptcy in U.S. history (see the case study at the end of this chapter). Six former WorldCom officials have since been found guilty and sentenced to varying prison terms for their part in the corporate fraud case, including ex-WorldCom CEO Bernard Ebbers, who was sentenced to 25 years in prison. Ebbers resigned as CEO two months prior to the bankruptcy scandal. WorldCom investors, however, are expected to recover more than $6 billion of the $11 billion cited in the accounting fraud case.[2]

Other catalysts have vaulted investor relations into a multibillion-dollar-a-year operation. Among these factors have been a growing number of companies "going public" in the last three decades, high visibility of corporate mergers and acquisitions, efforts to stop hostile takeovers of companies, and much tougher requirements for disclosure by the SEC and the stock exchanges. In addition, the expanding importance of global financial markets and the growing understanding of the need for expert public relations guidance in view of court cases such as the *Texas Gulf Sulphur* case have increased management's interest in financial public relations.[3]

In the following sections of this chapter we examine the tasks of financial public relations, then look at disclosure of information and at the major issues facing the financial public relations practitioner. We also discuss the role of financial public relations practitioners, their audiences, and communication strategies, including the annual meeting and the annual report.

MAINTAINING INVESTOR CONFIDENCE

The first task of **financial public relations** is to create and maintain investor confidence, building positive relationships with the financial community through the dissemination of corporate information. Executives who fail to do this may be unable to attract capital investment. They may lose control over their organizations and even lose their jobs. Financial public relations is much easier to relate to the proverbial bottom line than are other kinds of public relations. Relative stock prices, bond ratings, and interest rates charged for loans are direct measures of confidence in a company. When confidence is high, stocks are worth more, and bonds and borrowing cost less. When confidence is low, stock is worth less, and higher interest is demanded by those who loan funds to the business. Most corporations consider their financial relations programs effective if they have been able to reduce the cost of funds or obtain the best cost of capital. (See mini-case 13.1.)

"The pace of communications and change in today's global marketplace, along with the thousands of institutions and millions of individuals around the world investing in equities has become increasingly complex, with thousands and thousands of investment alternatives," according to Mark Begor, executive vice president and chief financial officer for NBC. He also noted that "communicating a clear, concise and meaningful message to those investors is critical."[4]

Characteristics of a Corporate Communications Strategy

Peter Anastas, financial analyst, suggests that a corporate communications strategy has three major characteristics: consistency, credibility, and clarity. There needs to be consistency not only in the style and culture of the annual report but also in what the company says it is going to do compared with what it actually does. Credibility is increased when the company uses a candid and straightforward approach to describe its operations with a minimum of hype and a maximum of information. Clarity needs to be the focus of the communication—be understandable, not obtuse.[5]

Specific Objectives for Practitioners

The practice of financial public relations touches on diverse areas like finance, accounting, law, public affairs, community relations, marketing, and employee relations. Consequently, its list of objectives is a lengthy one. Practitioners are charged with doing the following:

Building interest in the company

Creating understanding of the company

Selling company products

TurboBoosting Scios Inc.'s Reputation and Shareholder Value

Mini•Case 13.1

Overview

A *Forbes* account of Scios Inc., a bio-tech company, was not what the company management wanted to read. It depicted the 18-year-old company as "the oldest biotech company in the world without an approved product." This came just before an FDA report that rejected the drug Natrecor, a product to combat heart failure, said more research was needed to show the drug was as good as intravenous nitroglycerin. With that announcement Scios stock dropped from $6 a share to $3.84 per share.

However, within a year and a half, Scios was described by the *San Jose Mercury News* as being "like a phoenix that has risen from the ashes," as the stock had risen to $20 per share. Scios had been the beneficiary of a carefully executed and integrated communications program that focused on all key influencers in the health care, financial, and biotech industries.

Edelman Public Relations Worldwide, assisting Scios with a campaign entitled "Project TurboBoost," used select news media, analyst sessions, and medical meetings as communication tactics to reach target audiences with strategic information on the restructuring of Scios and highly persuasive new Natrecor clinical trials that Scios thought would have positive results.

Goals

Three goals were set:
1. Unlock the value of Scios's assets.
2. Position the company as a capable player within the biotech industry.
3. Narrow the perception gap between what the company desired and what its target audiences perceived.

Strategies

Five basic communication strategies were used:
1. Relaunch Scios as a completely new company to new audiences.
2. Exploit business milestone achievement vigorously.
3. Plant the first seeds of milestone achievement with key national media and stimulate broad-base support from other media.
4. Use third parties such as analysts and physician investigators to validate the Scios story.
5. Leverage value for all Scios pipeline activities and progress beyond Natrecor.

Questions

1. What is the value of its NASDAQ stock price today (NASDAQ: Scio)?
2. What would the value suggest about the long-term sustainability of the public relations effort by Edelman Worldwide?
3. Check the Scios Inc. Web page at www.sciosinc.com to find out more information on Scios. What effect, if any, do you think Project Turbo-Boost had on the FDA?
4. What evaluation techniques would you suggest for this campaign that was measured only in terms of increase of its stock price?
5. What public relations goals would you suggest at this point?

Source: PRSA Silver Anvil competition, 2001, Investor Relations.

Broadening the stockholder base by attracting new investors

Stabilizing stock prices

Winning stockholder approval for management

Increasing the company's prestige

Creating favorable attitudes in the financial community

Developing political sensitivities of stockholders for issues relating to the company

Improving employee relations

Building loyalty of stockholders

Arthur Roalman sums up the purpose and rationale for financial public relations:

An individual is not likely to invest money . . . in a corporation's stocks, bonds, commercial paper, or other financial pledges unless he believes strongly that he understands fully what is likely to happen to that corporation in the future . . . most investors' willingness to invest in a corporation is influenced by their trust in its management. Trust isn't built overnight. It is the result of long-term actions by the corporation to provide factual financial information in proper perspective.[6]

Investor relations changed considerably in the last decade of the 20th century as it moved into the 21st century. It had been primarily a passive carrier of information delivered mostly to the financial community. Today it has become much more proactive. "Investor relations has moved from a primarily passive role to an active, indeed interactive, marketing function. In this evolving marketing role, investor relations serves as a link between the company and the investment community, responding to the needs of both."[7]

PROVIDING PUBLIC INFORMATION

Investors bet fortunes on what they believe to be true about a particular enterprise. Fraud and deception can part uninformed investors from their funds. These dangers have been reduced by government law and regulation, stock exchange policies, and the voluntary disclosures of corporate management. But, the recent cases with Enron and Tyco have illustrated the problems that can occur when these laws and regulations are ignored. For example, in September 2005 the former CEO and the finance chief at Tyco were each sentenced to eight and a half years in prison, fined $134 million, and required to pay back $105 million for their part in the fraudulent use of funds and stock manipulation.[8] The importance of corporate information to investor decisions, however, points out the second major function of financial public relations: prompt provision of public information required by law, regulation, and policy.

SEC Regulations

Many aspects of financial public relations are affected by laws and regulations. The Securities Act of 1933 was passed "to provide full and fair disclosure of the character of securities . . . and to prevent frauds in the sale thereof." The Securities Exchange Act of 1934 supplemented the act of the previous year and was intended "to secure for issues publicly offered, adequate publicity for those facts necessary for an intelligent judgment of their value." These and other SEC regulations apply to all companies listed on any of the 13 largest U.S. stock exchanges, or with assets of $1 million and at least 500 stockholders. Other regulations require that corporations "act promptly to dispel unfounded rumors which result in unusual market activity or price variations."

SEC regulations are copious and subject to frequent changes. It is therefore impractical to present them all here. The commission routinely requires submission of three kinds of reports: annual reports (**Form 10-K**), quarterly reports (**Form 10-Q**), and current reports (**Form 8-K**). Form 10-K asks for descriptions of a corporation's principal products and services; assessment of competitive conditions in its industry; the dollar amount of order backlog; source and availability of raw materials; all material patents, licenses, franchises, and concessions; and the estimated dollar amount spent on research.

All of the information required by Form 10-K must be accompanied by corporate financial statements prepared in accordance with SEC accounting rules and certified by an independent public accountant. Moreover, the entire form must be submitted to the commission no later than 90 days from the close of the fiscal year. It must be submitted electronically through EDGAR (Electronic Data Gathering, Analysis, and Retrieval). EDGAR is the SEC's computer system for the collection, validation, indexing, acceptance, and dissemination of documents submitted in electronic format to the SEC. Finally, 10-K must be available free of charge to anyone upon request.[9]

The 10-Q quarterly report is much less detailed. It asks primarily for the corporation's summarized profit and loss statement, capitalization, stockholders' equity at the end of the quarter, and the sale of any unregistered securities.

In its effort to gather all relevant investment-related information on a continuous basis, the SEC also requires filing of Form 8-K, the current report. Filing this document is required when an unusual event of immediate interest to investors occurs, such as the acquisition or sale of significant assets or changes in the amount of securities outstanding.

These documents are prepared largely by accountants and lawyers. They are described here, however, because public relations professionals should (1) recognize the extent to which SEC-regulated corporations must share information, (2) understand the kinds of information deemed significant by investors, (3) realize the extent of federal regulation in this aspect of business, and (4) avail themselves of the information contained in these forms.

In an effort to help restore investor confidence, the National Investor Relations Institute (NIRI) approved a 10-point program aimed at disclosure actions that would help the investor better understand what was in these reports. The first point of the 10 suggests that companies should use a two-tier system in information disclosure. The first tier would be a plain English summary, or executive summary, of information contained in these various required reports in order to help an investor better understand significant trends that would likely affect a company's performance. This summary, the NIRI suggests, should be placed on the company's Web site as well as in the annual report. The second tier would be the information required by the SEC and accounting requirements.[10]

Public relations should be involved in the preparation of the executive summary, as well as other parts of the reports. A 1998 SEC regulation requires that certain parts of disclosure documents be written in plain English: "The cover page, summary, and risk factor sections of prospectuses must be clear, concise, and understandable, according to the new SEC regulations."[11] The SEC has prepared a handbook entitled *A Plain English Handbook: How to Create Clear SEC Disclosure Documents,* which is available online at the SEC Web site or can be obtained in hard copy from the commission.[12]

Sarbanes-Oxley Act

In the wake of corporate scandals involving companies such as Enron and WorldCom, Paul Sarbanes (D-MD) and Michael Oxley (R-OH) sponsored the Sarbanes-Oxley Act of 2002, which many have said to be one of the most significant changes to federal security laws since President Roosevelt's "New Deal" legislation of the 1930s. The act, which was signed into law by President George W. Bush on July 30, 2002, is directed toward public companies and establishes a more rigorous standard for accounting practices. The congressional intent of the act was to bolster public confidence in the corporate arena and place duties and responsibilities on not just the company but also the executives, accountants, attorneys, and auditors who manage these companies. Although public outcry for federal reform of corporate management led to its creation, the Sarbanes-Oxley Act has fallen heavily on small companies and created substantial financial burdens with large companies who are trying to comply with the new standards.

The Sarbanes-Oxley Act, officially the Public Company Accounting Reform and Investor Protection Act of 2002, has some key provisions:

- Reporting of stock trades by company insiders
- Creation of an independent accounting oversight board, overseen by the SEC
- Public reporting of CEO and CFO compensation packages
- Larger fines, along with criminal penalties, for security violations
- CEOs being held responsible for internal information technology security measures

Along with establishing new standards of accounting practices, the Sarbanes-Oxley Act works toward corporate responsibility by requiring detailed accounting, increased independent auditing controls, corporate fraud accountability, and increased financial disclosures, all of which can drain company resources and finances. The cost of maintaining compliance with the act varies with the size of the business, and according to 2004 auditing reports done by University of Nebraska at Omaha researchers and accounting professors Susan Eldridge and Burch Kealey, auditing costs of large Fortune 1000 companies have seen auditing costs increase by $1.4 billion.[13] The same research shows differing audit fee increases for differing industries, all of which range from the banking industry's audit fee increase of 65 percent to the retail industry's increase of 180 percent. The high costs of implementing Sarbanes-Oxley have left some to wonder if the cure is better than the disease.

While the Sarbanes-Oxley Act is beneficial to the general public who invests in these public companies, it places a formidable task on all companies to ensure compliance with these new standards. Whether a small company, or a large multibillion-dollar corporation, implementation of Sarbanes-Oxley means that management will be forced to reallocate critical assets and dedicate time and resources toward compliance with it.

Stock Exchange Policies

Policies of various stock exchanges also influence the task of financial public relations. The New York Stock Exchange states, for example, that news on matters of corporate significance should be given national distribution.[14] What is significant is a matter of some debate. The American Stock Exchange considers the following kinds of news likely to require prompt disclosure and announcements:

(a) joint venture, merger or acquisition;

(b) the declaration or omission of dividends or the determination of earnings;

(c) a stock split or stock dividend;

(d) the acquisition or loss of a significant contract;

(e) a significant new product or discovery;

(f) a change in control or a significant change in management;

(g) a call of securities for redemption;

(h) the borrowing of a significant amount of funds;

(i) the public or private sale of a significant amount of additional securities;

(j) significant litigation;

(k) the purchase or sale of a significant asset;

(l) a significant change in capital investment plans;

(m) a significant labor dispute or disputes with contractors or suppliers;

(n) an event requiring the filing of a current report under the Securities Exchange Act;

(o) establishment of a program to make purchases of the company's own shares;

(p) a tender offer for another company's securities; and

(q) an event of technical default or default on interest and/or principal payments.[15]

To facilitate *timely* national disclosure, financial relations practitioners use several newswire networks and the World Wide Web. The Associated Press (AP) is the major general newswire service. Dow Jones and Reuters Economic Service specialize in business and financial news. PR News Wire and Business Wire charge a fee for their services but guarantee that corporate news is carried promptly. The key issue is that the disclosure of information must be made at the same time to all audiences.

The Disclosure Issue

One other SEC regulation of particular interest to the public relations practitioner is Rule 10B-5, which makes it unlawful "to make any untrue statement of a material fact or to omit to state a material fact . . . in connection with the purchase or sale of any security." In the landmark *Texas Gulf Sulphur Co.* case, this regulation was applied to press releases.[16] In subsequent suits, public relations counsel has been named as a defendant when press releases and other materials "contained false and misleading statements and omitted to state material fact."[17]

Two later cases focused sharply on the disclosure issue, although financial relations officers were confused by their outcomes. One involved the 1984 merger between food giants Nestlé and Carnation. The other involved Chrysler Corporation's struggle to survive in the early 1980s.

Nestlé was secretly bidding for Carnation. Rumors were flying, and Carnation stock rose nearly 50 percent before Nestlé announced the purchase for $83 per share. Throughout the negotiations, Carnation's spokesperson refused to comment. A year after the merger, the SEC ruled that by saying no comment during negotiations, Carnation had been "materially false and misleading." Because the company no longer existed, however, the SEC took no action to back its ruling.

Chrysler was saved by an unissued press release. One day in early 1981, Chrysler was down to $8 million in liquid assets. Company lawyers held that Chrysler must issue a press release to disclose its near insolvency, but company officials risked being charged by the SEC rather than destroy what little confidence their creditors and customers had left. The release went unissued and the company survived, its potential insolvency made a moot point by its renewed financial health.

No simple formula provides guidance in disclosure situations. Although the Chrysler example is unusual, it shows that judgment must be used. In general, however, disclosure is both required and desirable. "The bottom line: The moment you have information that will make a material difference in the outcome of your financial results, you should be preparing and disseminating a statement to disclose that information."[18]

CRISIS ISSUES IN INVESTOR RELATIONS

Several issues may come up in the life of a corporation that are crises in its effort to survive. In the last decade we have seen mergers and acquisitions that have often been hostile takeovers. In an effort to thwart hostile takeover attempts, bitter proxy fights have often ensued. Win or lose, the company is often left with considerable debt and, if it can survive, may have to spin off some of its assets.

Eugene Miller, executive vice president of United States Gypsum Company, says "the most stressful and crucial element of investor relations is in forestalling and defending against efforts of outside interests to take over the company."[19]

Takeover attempts come in two fundamental forms: the proxy fight and the tender offer. Both attempt to persuade shareholders, but in different ways and perhaps for different reasons.

The Tender Offer

Money is the key factor in a tender offer. The **tender offer** is one that is enough above the market price of the stock to entice the shareholder to sell despite his or her loyalty to the company or desire to keep the stock. For example, if the shareholder had bought stock at $20 per share and it was now selling for $25 on the stock exchange, the person might be given a tender offer of $35 per share to sell to whomever wanted to get control of the company. Because of the financial gain that the shareholder would make, this is a tough fight by management to keep control of the company.

The Proxy Fight

In a **proxy** fight, the two (or more) contestants striving for control of management (or an issue) seek to get the shareholders to let them cast their vote for them. Thus, shareholders are requested to give their "proxy," or absentee voting rights, to one side or the other. In this case, though, the shareholder does not sell his or her stock.

Public relations for the management of the company under siege in a proxy fight can do several things to defend itself. Primary, of course, is focusing on providing information to stockholders, the financial press, and investors about the current management's operation and strategic plans for the future compared with what the competing group is suggesting.[20]

Laura Johnston, investor relations specialist at Citigate Communications, suggests that public relations practitioners in the financial arena need to be prepared as soon as possible. If you know you are going to have a tough fight ahead in the next year, begin now to prepare. She suggests these four strategies in the preparation stage:

1. *Don't procrastinate.* Start planning your investor relations strategy early.
2. *Begin by managing your shareholder's expectations.* Pave the way for the proposal by informing shareholders about management's general line of thinking on that particular issue well before a proxy statement is produced.
3. *Involve investor relations people in drafting the proxy statement.*
4. *Hire a proxy solicitor* who will get down in the trenches and fight for every vote.[21]

Once the fight is under way, you can take a number of tactics to help you win. You should use every means at your disposal to reach your shareholders. You may need to go online or set up a World Wide Web page. Use all the communication tools at your disposal. A key element is also to target your message to a few key ideas and repeat them throughout the proxy campaign. Your theme should be recognized quickly by your shareholders. Rally your past supporters and don't be afraid to use the endorsements of the media or other credible third-party sources to your advantage.[22]

FINANCIAL RELATIONS PROFESSIONALS

Financial relations professionals must have a broad base of knowledge and skills to deal effectively with their many-faceted responsibilities. A survey of 300 senior financial relations officers in leading corporations showed that a broad financial background combined with marketing communication skills is considered the best preparation for the field.[23] The survey indicated that although financial and security analysts may go into financial relations, their lack of marketing and communication backgrounds often impedes their success. Knowledge of finance, marketing, law, and public relations skills are all important for those considering financial relations careers.

In addition to the SEC, those interested in a corporation's financial information include stock exchange firms, investment counselors, financial writers, brokers, dealers, mutual fund houses, investment banks, commercial banks, institutional buyers, employees, and both current and future stockholders. For the purposes of discussion, however, these categories can be lumped into three broad audiences:

individual stockholders, financial analysts, and the financial press. Following is an examination of each group, their informational needs, the means by which they may be reached, and the best ways to secure positive relations with them.

Individual Stockholders

Some corporations consider their stockholders a vast untapped resource of potential customers and grassroots support on political and financial issues. Harrison T. Beardsley recommends that financial relations efforts, particularly of smaller companies, concentrate on stockholders rather than on financial analysts.[24]

As discussed earlier, the SEC requires companies to keep their investors fully informed. Management has learned the hard way that uninterested stockholders may be quick to sell their shares to even the most unfriendly entity attempting takeover. Moreover, stockholders themselves have become more vocal and active—initiating proxy fights or raising financial, social, and ethical questions in relation to environmental issues, sex discrimination, corporate political activities at home and abroad, labor relations, and many other issues.

Most corporations now recognize that "a company's foremost responsibility is to communicate fully anything that can have a bearing on the owner's investment."[25] The extent and quality of their efforts vary widely, however. Informative annual and quarterly reports, dynamic Web pages, and well-organized annual meetings with follow-up reports are the basic tools of stockholder relations.

Sound stockholder relations are built on three principles: (1) learn as much as possible about your stockholders, (2) treat them as you would your important customers, and (3) encourage investor interest from people who are predisposed toward your company. A basic principle of communication is to know your audience. Consequently, learning as much as possible about stockholders makes excellent sense from a communications perspective. The stockholder survey, which asks for demographic and attitudinal information, is a readily available tool, but too few actually use it.

Treating stockholders as important customers has a number of implications for financial relations officers. Communicating in readable, nontechnical language is a must. Welcoming new stockholders and writing to express regret when stockholders are lost is good business practice. Prompt and appropriate response to stockholder correspondence or e-mails also helps maintain positive relations.

Sun Company follows a comprehensive stockholder relations plan. The company believes, "Shareholders are our business partners. It's helpful to us if management gets an insight on what they think of us." Each new Sun stockholder receives a welcoming note from the company's chairman. A very readable newsletter goes out with every dividend check. About 100 shareholders are selected at random six or eight times a year and invited to a dinner at which a top company executive speaks. Sun also maintains a toll-free telephone line to make corporate news available to stockholders and invites them to call collect to the shareholder relations department with questions or complaints.

Finally, just as a company should seek new customers among the most likely segments of the population, it should seek stockholders from those predisposed toward buying stock. Employees, suppliers, dealers, and members of communities where the corporation is located are the most likely prospects. They should receive annual reports and other materials that encourage investment.

Financial Analysts

Financial analysts include investment counselors, fund managers, brokers, dealers, and institutional buyers—in other words, the professionals in the investment business. Their basic function is to gather information concerning various companies, to develop expectations in terms of sales, profits, and a range of other operating and financial results, and to make judgments about how securities markets will evaluate these factors. They gather quantitative and qualitative information on companies, compare their findings to statistics from other companies, assess opportunities and risks, and then advise their clients. Corporate financial relations assists analysts by providing information and, in doing so, may positively influence expectations and judgments.

To maintain relations with financial analysts, the basic method is to identify the prospects, meet them, establish interest and understanding, and then maintain the relationship. All dealings with professional analysts should be characterized by responsiveness, openness, and regular communication, but care should be taken not to overcommunicate.

"Fluff and puff" will quickly sour an analyst's view of a corporation. When analysts become overly enthusiastic based on what they have been told by a company's financial relations staff, and corporate performance fails to live up to their expectations, the results can be disastrous. When Toys "R" Us Inc. announced that its Christmas sales were up 17 percent, its stock dropped 20 percent. Based on discussions with the company, analysts had expected a sales gain of 30 percent and thus were disappointed.

The shoe manufacturer Nike Inc. lost half its value when it earned 88 cents per share rather than the anticipated $2. Rather than informing the financial community when it realized profits would be lower than expected, Nike management tried harder to live up to the inflated figures. The next year the company set aside more time for communicating with financial analysts.[26]

Analysts want to know the company's background; that is, the nature of the business, primary factors affecting the business, current operating conditions, and estimates of future outlooks. Analysts are also vitally interested in management forecasts, pricing data, capital expenditures, financial data, labor relations, research and development, and any other information that may materially influence the quality of an investment. Annual reports provide much of the needed information. A survey of institutional investors showed annual reports as the most useful and informative source of information within a company's financial relations program.[27] Annual reports are discussed in detail later in the chapter.

A primary way to reach financial analysts is through **investment conferences,** which are meetings that investment professionals attend specifically to hear company presentations or discuss corporate issues. These programs contain information on a company's performance and provide persuasive arguments for buying its stock. Although such presentations center on speeches by company executives, they usually provide slick publications and audiovisual support materials as well.

A more popular conference in recent years has been the **conference call,** rather than an actual meeting. In some cases it is a video conference, and in other cases it is a phone conference. The conference call has become a quarterly ritual for many companies. The call is held the day after the quarterly report comes out. The CEO and CFO sit in front of

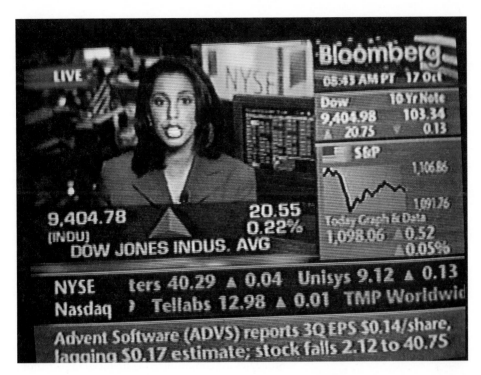

LIVE

NYSE

Bloomberg

08:43 AM PT   17 Oct

Dow   10 Yr Note
9,404.98   103.34
▲ 20.75   ▼ 0.13

S&P
                        1,106.86

                        1,091.76

9,404.78   20.55   Today Graph & Data
(INDU)   0.22%   1,098.06 ▲0.52
DOW JONES INDUS. AVG   ▲0.05%

NYSE   ters 40.29 ▲ 0.04 Unisys 9.12 ▲ 0.13
Nasdaq ⟩ Tellabs 12.98 ▲ 0.01 TMP Worldwid

Advent Software (ADVS) reports 3Q EPS $0.14/share,
lagging $0.17 estimate; stock falls 2.12 to 40.75

Bloomberg Television provides 24-hour business and financial news. Bloomberg's Web site is among the top five sites in the United States for financial news and information.

a speakerphone or video camera and brief analysts, financial reporters, and other members of the investment community on the meaning behind the numbers. These calls provide the same story and interpretation for all the interested audiences at one time. A recent NIRI survey reported 73 percent of the responding companies held quarterly conference calls.[28]

Relationships with financial analysts are not all one-way. Analysts can provide valuable information to companies as well. When communicating with financial analysts, first be prepared to listen. They can give significant feedback about a financial relations program in terms of its adequacy, credibility, and sufficiency of information. Perhaps even more important, this is an opportunity for the company to understand how the market perceives its strengths and weaknesses and the behavior of the business as a whole.

The Financial Press

The third major audience for financial relations is the **financial press.** "The financial press provides a foundation and backdrop for any corporation's financial communications program," says Hill and Knowlton executive Stan Sauerhaft. "It develops credibility and it can add impressive third-party endorsement."[29]

Financial public relations practitioners deal with media much as other public relations specialists do. The major difference lies in the specialized nature of the financial media. Major daily newspapers carry financial items of local, regional, or national interest. Weekly newspapers generally carry items of local interest. The business press includes *The Wall Street Journal, Forbes, Barron's, BusinessWeek, Fortune,* and other national publications as well as various local business-oriented publications (for example, the *Business Chronicle* in Houston, Atlanta, Los Angeles, San Francisco, and other cities).

These are primary outlets for financial news, but they are deluged with information, so their channels of communication should not be cluttered with trivia or fluff.

Do not overlook the financial columnists. They carry considerable influence and can offer unique perspectives on particular companies. Trade magazines, usually devoted to particular industries, occupations, or professions, are also important outlets. They may reach such likely prospects as suppliers and producers.

Cable television is now a major outlet for financial news. Several cable or satellite channels are devoted exclusively to business news. With additional stations made possible through direct satellite transmission to homes or through fiber-optic cable systems, this is likely to increase several-fold. Certain local and network programs are devoted specifically to business. Bloomberg Television, Public Broadcasting's *Wall Street Week,* Cable News Network's financial programs, and Associated Press Radio's *Business Barometer* are examples of such programs. Network or local major market news operations should generally be approached only if the information has news value that affects the community at large.

Finally, specialized financial media are extremely interested in company news. Market newsletters (often published by brokerage firms), investment advisory services, and statistical services (like Standard and Poor's, Value Line, or Moody's) frequently carry the greatest weight with potential investors.

COMMUNICATION STRATEGIES IN INVESTOR RELATIONS

Strategies for communicating financial information, like those for implementing other plans (see chapter 6), must grow out of management's long-term view of the corporation. Communication strategy is a plan for getting from where you are to where you want to be. Thus, the perception of the company by its relevant publics should be compared with how it hopes to be perceived in the future.

The methods available for implementing strategy include personal meetings, financial literature (correspondence, quarterly and annual reports, dividend enclosures), financial news releases, and annual meetings. But with unprecedented advances in communication technology, the mode of communicating these strategies has also been changing rapidly. Videoconference calls, e-mail, cable business news shows, and the World Wide Web all provide the potential for more timely, specific information. These new technologies also increase the possibility for interactive communication with key stakeholders such as financial analysts, investors, and company employees.[30]

Whatever a corporation's current status or ultimate objectives, its financial relations communication strategy must be characterized by responsiveness, regularity, and openness. Communication should never be evasive and must include bad news as well as good. "Telling employees bad news seems to be the hardest thing for senior management to do."[31] But this is essential to building credibility with your employees. Credibility is the key to a strong financial relations program.

Annual Meetings

Annual meetings are a kind of mandated ritual in which the actual owners of a business consider and vote on the effectiveness of management. In theory, stockholders have the power to do what they please (within the law) with their company. But in practice, issues are rarely discussed and even more rarely voted on because management collects proxies in advance to support its positions, appointments, and decisions.

Views on the annual meeting ritual are widely divergent. Whatever the case, the annual meeting presents certain opportunities and entails genuine risks; thus, careful planning and orchestration are essential. Most major public accounting firms publish guides for corporate executives facing annual meetings.

Besides trying to attract, inform, and involve the audience of stockholders, the annual meeting has other functions. It enables corporate management to reach all stockholders through pre- and post-meeting communication. It provides a showcase and a focus for corporate publicity. It permits personal contact between executives and stockholders through which actions can be explained, accomplishments recognized, and feedback offered. It is a marketing tool when products are displayed in their best light.

The annual meeting is also a safety valve by which stockholders can let off steam. The democratic nature of the annual meeting makes the company vulnerable, and organized dissent is possible from stockholders who have bought a few shares of stock just to gain a platform. Such individuals may intervene or disrupt—confronting management with embarrassing questions and drawing the attention of the news media. For example, Chrysler Corporation, the third-largest U.S. automaker, was confronted with the possibility of hostility at its 1995 annual meeting when Kirk Kerkorian, who held a large block of Chrysler stock, was unhappy with the performance of the stock. His concern led to actions by the Chrysler board to improve the stock price. G. A. Marken suggests doing the following to improve the chances for an effective, successful meeting:

- Ensure the CEO is well prepared for the presentation.
- Provide displays highlighting company products, services, and financial results.
- Invite the media and representatives from the financial community.
- Prepare an advance news release for the media to highlight the CEO's presentation at the meeting.
- Have handouts such as annual reports, product literature, CD-ROMs, and videos available.
- Consider the meeting environment and amenities carefully (invitations, name badges, refreshments, tours, favors or specialty advertising gifts, etc.).
- Develop an executive summary or digest of the meeting, if it is particularly unusual or controversial.[32]

Commenting on such annual meetings, former Atlanta newspaper business editor Tom Walker observed tongue-in-cheek that corporations should retain consulting sociologists, "especially during the annual meeting season when managements are forced to line up before their shareholders and give an account of themselves."[33] Financial relations actually plays the role that Walker would give to sociologists. By anticipating the concerns, the issues, and even the mood of stockholders—based on continuous interaction—financial public relations should be able to prepare management for most situations that could arise. With careful planning, the positive potentials of annual meetings may even be realized.

Annual Reports

Annual reports are prepared not only to publish the required SEC information but also to perform a public relations and marketing function. Reports are usually released in March about six weeks before the company's annual meeting, which is often held in April or May. The trend in annual report preparation is for more CEOs to write their own letters to shareholders, to include the bad news up front, and to contract out the production of the annual report to consulting firms.

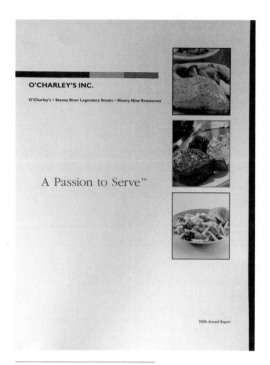

O'Charley's restaurant chain from Nashville, Tennessee, produces effective annual reports with excellent graphics, photos, and content.

Annual reports come in a variety of shapes and styles. They are, on average, 44 pages long, according to Sid Cato, whose annual report newsletter office is in Kalamazoo, Michigan. Some reports, he says, "are spectacular, with glossy covers, creative art design, terrific color photographs and graphics, superior paper stock and easy to understand explanations of company performance."[34] Some reports are produced on CD-ROM and some on video; most are available on Web pages, while others may be done as newspaper supplements. However, some companies produce only the 10-K report in black and white that is required by the SEC.

Oscar Beveridge calls the annual report "unquestionably the single most important public document issued by a publicly held corporation."[35] Writing in *Fortune,* Herbert Meyer states, "Out of all the documents published by a Fortune 500 corporation, none involves so much fussing, so much anguish—and often so much pride of authorship—as the annual report to shareholders."[36] In short, the annual report can be considered the keystone of a company's financial relations program.

The Purpose of Annual Reports Fundamentally, the annual report fulfills the legal requirements of reporting to a company's stockholders. As such, it becomes the primary source of information about the company for current and potential stockholders, providing comprehensive information on the condition of the company and its progress (or lack thereof) during the previous year.

Some companies leave it at that. But nearly all major companies carry their annual reports considerably further, taking the opportunity to reinforce their credibility, establish their distinct identity, and build investor confidence, support, and allegiance. In this sense, the annual report becomes the company's calling card, a summary of what the company has done and what it stands for. By accident or by design, the report usually conveys much about the personality and quality of the corporation's management.

Some companies get further service from their annual reports by using them for marketing, public relations, and employee recruitment and orientation purposes. Most are on the World Wide Web for all the constituencies, from investors to reporters, that want to examine them. A report may also serve as an informational resource for financial advisers, a "backgrounder" for business editors, or even an educational tool for teachers, librarians, and students. General Motors uses its report to advertise its products. Goodyear produces a special edition for classroom use. Increasing numbers of companies produce special editions for employees to gain their loyalty and support, build morale by stressing their contributions, and improve their understanding of company operations.

Although accountants may decry verbal and pictorial embellishment of their ciphers, the communication opportunity presented by annual reports is too important to pass up. A few companies have toned down their documents, but annual reports are not likely to return to the minimum level of information required by the government.

Contents of Annual Reports The typical annual report consists of a cover; a president's letter; financial and nonfinancial highlights; a balance sheet and an income statement; a description of the business (products and services); names and titles of corporate officers; names and affiliations of outside directors; location of plants, offices, and representatives; the address and telephone number of corporate headquarters; and reference to stock exchanges on which company stock is traded. The report may also include

FIGURE 13.1   Annual reports come in a variety of styles.

the company's history (particularly in anniversary issues), discussion of company policies, request for support of the company's stance on a political issue, results of stockholder surveys, and other reports or features. Figure 13.1 shows a sample of some annual reports.

Annual reports should always put corporate earnings in perspective and spell out prospects for the next year. They should answer these questions:

What is the major thrust of our company?

Where do we excel?

What are our weaknesses?

Why has the company performed as it has?

What are we doing about the future?

Financial highlights are a well-read aspect of annual reports. They generally include figures representing net sales, earnings before taxes, earnings after taxes, net earnings per common share, dividends per common share, stockholders' equity per common share, net working capital, ratio of current assets to current liabilities, number of common shares outstanding, and number of common stockholders. Other highlights include profit margin, percent return on stockholders' equity, long-term debt, and the number of employees. Report designers are concerned not just with the numbers but also with how they look. Financial data are most often integrated into the entire report and presented in interesting or unusual ways.

Herbert Rosenthal and Frank Pagani list eight elements of what they call "big league annual reports":

1. A meaningful or provocative pictorial cover
2. A well-designed format
3. Complete and understandable graphics
4. Unstilted photographs and artwork
5. Comprehensive text
6. Comparative figures
7. Tasteful presentation of products
8. Stylish printing[37]

Electronic Annual Reports   Form 10-K is the SEC report that must be filed electronically. However, most companies prepare an annual report for stockholders in addition to the Form 10-K. The SEC allows information from one report to be used in another. Thus, the principal information from the 10-K is often included in the annual report to stockholders. A 2002 NIRI survey found that 89 percent of companies post their annual reports online, up from 31 percent in 1996.[38] A few companies produce no printed report at all but rely only on the electronic reports. The NIRI survey, though, found only 6 percent of its companies planned to discontinue the printed report. Of the 500 companies surveyed, 473 (95 percent) included the annual report to shareholders for at least one year on their corporate Web site.[39]

WorldCom Scandal

Overview

In 2002, WorldCom filed the largest bankruptcy in U.S. history. Bernard Ebbers resigned as CEO in April 2002, two months before the bankruptcy scandal. Six former WorldCom officials have since been sentenced to varying prison terms for their part in the corporate fraud case, and Ebbers was sentenced to 25 years. Employees were devastated, many investors ruined, the story ran in media all over the world, and the company's future was in doubt.

Unlike Enron, however, WorldCom came back. It hired as its new CEO a battle-tested "crisis junkie" in November 2002. Michael Capellas came to WorldCom from his position as president of Hewlett-Packard. Here are some of the many business challenges Capellas faced at WorldCom:

1. Retain key employees and customers.
2. Establish a new board of directors.
3. Rebuild the management team.
4. Work with the corporate monitor.
5. Bring closure to the government investigations.
6. Create a culture of ethics and good corporate governance.
7. Rebuild the finance department.

8. Complete the largest financial restatement in history.
9. Emerge from Chapter 11 bankruptcy.
10. Relist the company on NASDAQ.

In addition, the communication challenges faced by the company were huge.

Strategy

Capellas's strategy to rebuild the company was based on a four-pronged approach:

1. Recognize an outrageous sense of urgency.
2. Emphasize commitment to ethics.
3. Use the CEO as chief communicator.
4. Focus on the three highest priorities: customers, customers, customers.

With a keen sense of urgency, the company installed a new board and management team. Capellas rebuilt the management team by bringing in several key players from Silicon Valley, including the senior vice president for communications and chief of staff Grace Chen Trent. The company launched a 100-day Plan for creditor approval and rallied the employees around the new plan by overcommunicating. On the 100th day the company rebranded itself by changing its name back to MCI and by filing a plan of reorganization with the bankruptcy court.

To emphasize ethics, the company introduced the MCI Guiding Principles that were written by the CEO. They also revitalized the corporate ethics office and instituted ethics training for all 50,000 employees.

MCI used the CEO as its chief communicator by having him speak at 25 employee town meetings, 7 all-employee worldwide Webcasts, 8 all-employee conference calls, 26 all-employee e-mails, and 4 employee voice-mails in those first 100 days.

To communicate with customers, the company had a high-touch retention effort that included customer advisory boards, an executive outreach program to the top 100 accounts, direct customer communications, and emphasized customer service quality for all its employees.

Outcome

MCI emerged from Chapter 11 bankruptcy in April 2004 and was relisted on the NASDAQ in July 2004. U.S. District Judge Jed Rakoff of New York said, "The Court is aware of no large company accused of fraud that has so completely divorced itself from the misdeeds of the immediate past and undertaken such extraordinary steps to prevent such misdeeds in the future." CEO Michael Capellas gave credit to his employees: "MCI's emergence is really about the triumph of the human spirit and a testimony to our 50,000 employees."

After its emergence from bankruptcy, MCI merged with Verizon following a bidding war between Quest Communications and Verizon. Verizon paid $8.44 billion in cash and stock in a deal agreed upon February 14, 2005, and approved by the government for closing on January 6, 2006.

Sources: Grace Trent and Brad Burns, "The Role of Communications in Restoring Trust and Credibility at MCI," presentation at the Public Relations Society of America national convention, New York, October 2004; Marguerite Reardon, "Verizon closes book on MCI merger," Jan. 6, 2006. http/News.zdnet.com/2100-1035_22-146119.html, retrieved Aug. 17, 2008.

Questions

1. What should the communications role of a CEO be in a financial crisis such as this one?
2. What are the lessons that can be learned from communication in this crisis?
3. Find the company press release of September 1, 2005, about the decision by the U.S. attorney in New York. What did he decide about the company in regard to the WorldCom era scandal?
4. MCI has now merged with Verizon. How was the merger communicated to investors? Did MCI seek to get stockholders' proxies?
5. Check the Web site to see what changes have resulted since the merger. Financial reporting has never been more important than it is today. This has been highlighted by the collapse of Enron and its lack of accurate financial information provided to the investing public and its employees.

Summary

For self-testing and additional chapter resources, go to the Online Learning Center at **www.mhhe.com/lattimore3e.**

Effective financial public relations is necessary to develop and maintain investor confidence. Relationships with the financial community are developed by strategically planning investor relations.

Well-planned financial relations programs help lower the cost of capital for businesses. To meet the legal guidelines of the SEC, the company must provide prompt disclosure of corporate news that is significant to the financial community. But the corporation should go far beyond the minimum requirements. Good investor relations can help a company deal with hostile takeover attempts through tender offers or a proxy fight.

New technologies have provided an increasing array of tools for the financial public relations practitioner to communicate with key audiences such as stockholders, financial analysts, and the financial media. Annual reports and annual stockholder meetings remain important investor relations functions, but additional tools including cable television, the Web, satellite interviews, and e-mail are becoming increasingly essential to have an effective financial relations effort. This effort gives a business increased support for its management, higher stock prices, and greater ease in attracting new capital.

Key Terms

annual meetings	Form 10-Q
annual reports	Form 8-K
conference call	investment conferences
financial analysts	proxy
financial press	Securities and Exchange Commission (SEC)
financial public relations	
Form 10-K	tender offer

1. Madeline Turnock, APR, "IR and PR Come Together," *Public Relations Strategist* 8, no. 2 (Spring 2002), pp. 13–14.

2. "WorldCom Investors to get $6.13 Billion," *Commercial Appeal,* September 22, 2005, p. C2.

3. Eugene Miller, "Investor Relations," in *Lesly's Handbook of Public Relations and Communications,* 4th ed., ed. Philip Lesly (New York: AMACOM, 1991), pp. 164–65.

4. Richard Higgins, *Best Practices in Global Investor Relations* (Westport, CT: Quorum Books, 2000), p. xii.

5. Ibid., p. 15.

6. Arthur R. Roalman, ed., *Investor Relations Handbook* (New York: AMACOM, 1974), p. iii.

7. Higgins, p. 26.

8. Samuel Maull, "Jail Time for 2 Former Tyco Execs," *Commercial Appeal,* September 20, 2005, p. A4.

9. Luke Hill, Interview with Jacob Fien-Helman, SEC, September 2005.

10. National Investor Relations Institute, "NIRI Ten Point Program to Help Restore Investor Confidence," NIRI Executive Alert press release, April 9, 2002, p. 1.

11. James B. Strenski, "The New SEC Regulations: Write in Plain English," *PR Tactics,* April 1998, p. 4.

12. Securities and Exchange Commission, *A Plain English Handbook: How to Create Clear SEC Disclosure Documents,* www.sec.gov/pdf/handbook.pdf, June 9, 2002.

13. Higgins, p. xii.

14. NYSE Company Manual, August 1, 1977.

15. American Stock Exchange, "Part 4. Disclosure Policies" (last updated November 2000), www.amex.com, June 9, 2002.

16. Henry Rockwell, "A Press Release Goes to Court," *Public Relations Journal* (October 1968).

17. G. Christman Hill, "Financial Public Relations Men Are Warned They're Liable for Clients' Puffery," *The Wall Street Journal,* March 16, 1972, p. 30.

18. Jody Buffington Aud, "What Internal Communicators Can Learn from Enron," *Public Relations Strategist* 8, no. 2 (Spring 2002), p. 11.

19. Miller, p. 196.

20. Ibid.

21. Laura Johnston, "How to Succeed in a Close Proxy Vote," *Public Relations Quarterly* (Spring 1994), pp. 35–36.

22. Ibid.

23. "Investor Relations Pros Downplay PR Skills," *Communication World,* May 1983, p. 15.

24. Harrison T. Beardsley, "Problem-Solving in Corporate Financial Relations," *Public Relations Journal* (April 1978), p. 23.

25. Oscar M. Beveridge, *Financial Public Relations* (New York: McGraw-Hill, 1963), p. 68.

26. Stuart Weiss, "Hell Hath No Fury Like a Surprised Stock Analyst," *BusinessWeek,* January 21, 1985, p. 98.

27. Holly Hutchins, "Annual Reports: Earning Surprising Respect from Institutional Investors," *Public Relations Review* (Winter 1994), p. 311.

28. Charles Nekvasil, "Getting the Most Out of Your Investor Relations Conference Calls," *PR Tactics,* August 1999, p. 10.

29. Stan Sauerhaft, "Won't Anybody Listen?" in Hill and Knowlton Executives, *Critical Issues in Public Relations* (Englewood Cliffs, NJ: Prentice-Hall, 1975), p. 37.

30. Higgins, p. 47.

31. Aud, p. 11.

32. G. A. Marken, "There's More to Being Public Than Being Listed," *Public Relations Quarterly* (Fall 1993), pp. 44–45.

33. Tom Walker, "J. P. Stevens Fights Catholics' Proposal," *Atlanta Journal and Constitution,* March 2, 1980, p. 10.

34. Ibid.

35. Beveridge, p. 137.

36. Herbert E. Meyer, "Annual Reports Get an Editor in Washington," *Fortune,* May 7, 1979, p. 219.

37. Herbert C. Rosenthal and Frank Pagani, "Rating Your Annual Report," *Public Relations Journal* (August 1978), p. 12.

38. *Journal of Business and Finance Leadership,* www.haworthpressinc.com, September 9, 2005.

39. Ibid.

PART FOUR
The Practice

Public relations serves all types of organizations. Governmental organizations and agencies, nonprofit organizations, and corporations have embraced public relations and set it to work, recognizing it as a means of increasing organizational effectiveness in a complex and changing environment.

To operate effectively within these organizations, public relations practitioners must be thoroughly aware of all we have discussed to this point: the process of communication, the role of public relations in organizational decision making, the four-step public relations process, and the primary publics of public relations. Practitioners must also recognize the problems and publics that are specific to public relations in each organizational type.

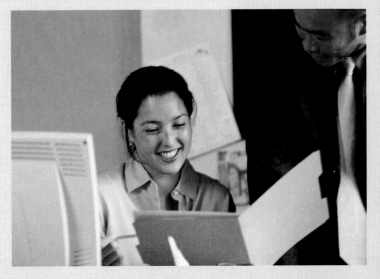

In this section, we look first at the practice of public relations in three distinct types of organizations: chapter 14, government; chapter 15, nonprofit organizations; and chapter 16, corporations. We conclude in chapter 17 with a realistic look at emerging trends in public relations.

Public Affairs: Relations with Government

PREVIEW

Nickelodeon, the children's cable television network, wants kids to go out and play. In fact, it wants them to play so much that as part of its annual fall "Worldwide Day of Play," the network goes off the air for three hours, leaving the screen dark with only a "Let's Just Play" logo.

Nickelodeon's public affairs department has developed an elaborate program to support the Day of Play, including media advertising, public service announcements, health and wellness messages shown during the broadcast day, special appearances by the stars of its shows, and a yearlong giveaway of more than $1 million in grants to help kids encourage healthier lifestyles by improving play facilities in their communities.

Nickelodeon's goal is to combat the often-documented trend among kids to become overscheduled and sedentary. The bottom-line message of the campaign: Get up, get moving, be active, be healthy, and play.

Public affairs units like Nickelodeon's help organizations anticipate and respond to issues that affect their publics and their environment. Public affairs functions also include responding to government activity by, for instance, lobbying public officials, building grassroots campaigns, and helping to shape public policy.

The government itself has a public relations role in keeping the public informed about issues, problems, and actions taken or contemplated at all levels of government. Government public information officers seek citizen approval of government programs, help explain what citizens want from government, and strive to make government responsive to citizens' wishes, and understand and affect public opinion. Public relations also plays a central role in political campaigns. This chapter introduces public affairs by touching on all these functions.

PUBLIC AFFAIRS

State revenues go down and universities suffer. A county budget passes, giving libraries and cultural centers a shot in the arm. A zoning hearing opens the way for a major new development. A tariff is enacted, helping an industry to thrive. Changes in the federal tax code shift $100 billion in liabilities from wage earners to corporations. A local ordinance bans smoking in the workplace. The unwillingness of a local government to promote a bond issue makes a proposed museum seek another city in which to locate. A regulation is changed, and a manufacturer goes out of business.

The list goes on and on. When organizations review the external forces that affect their operations, governmental bodies should be at the top of the list. Indeed, public opinion and media, employee, and community relations are considered important in part because of their potential influence on governmental action or inaction.

In this chapter we first examine the public affairs function of business and other organizations in their relationships with local, state, and federal government at all levels. Then we look at the public affairs function from the point of view of governmental bodies with obligations to provide public information to many constituencies.

WHAT IS PUBLIC AFFAIRS?

Public affairs, a term sometimes used as a synonym for all of public relations, more often describes the aspect of public relations that deals with the political environment of organizations. Sometimes it is called *governmental relations.* Public affairs is related to issues management because through its relationship building it helps organizations anticipate or respond to issues affecting their activities. Public affairs efforts include seeking to shape public opinion and legislation, developing effective responses to matters of public concern, and helping the organization adapt to public expectations. Specifically, public affairs may be involved in monitoring public policy, providing political education for employees or other constituents, maintaining liaisons with various governmental units, and encouraging political participation. "Access to lawmakers and their staffs is without a doubt the most important aspect of public affairs work in Washington. Without access your message will not be heard."[1] As shown in figure 14.1, public affairs practitioners facilitate the two-way flow of information between an organization and its political environment.

Public affairs is a specialization of public relations that concerns building public policy relationships between organizations. To be successful, all organizations—businesses, nonprofits, and governments—must build governmental relationships and actively collaborate with those government contacts to influence public policies. The most prominent professional association of public affairs officers, the Public Affairs Council, defines public affairs as "used variously as a synonym for external affairs, government relations, and corporate communications. Most practitioners use public affairs as the name for the integrated department combining all, or virtually all, external noncommercial activities of the business world."[2]

Definitions of public affairs focus this specialization on the building of relationships in the public policy arena. John Paluszek, former president of Ketchum public relations, defines public affairs as addressing public policy:

> Public affairs helps an organization develop and maintain quality relationships with the various groups of people ("publics") who can influence the future. Public affairs is the public relations practice that addresses public policy and the publics who influence such policy.[3]

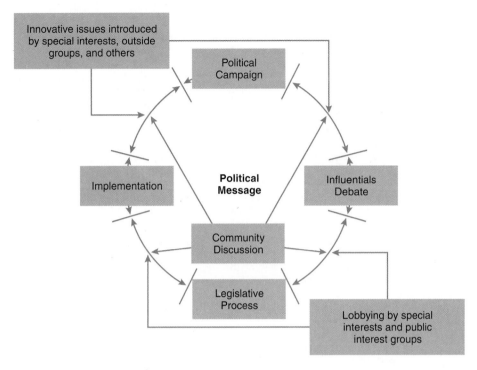

FIGURE 14.1   **Flow of Campaign Messages** *Source:* L. Powell and J. Cowart, *Political Campaign Communication: Inside and Out* (Boston: Pearson Education, Inc., 2003)

Unions, schools, hospitals, libraries, cultural organizations, foundations, businesses, and other organizations have both the problem and the opportunity of dealing with government. All want to improve communication with governmental agencies and employees, monitor and influence legislative and regulatory actions, encourage constituent participation, and expand the awareness and understanding of people in power.

PUBLIC AFFAIRS FOR NOT-FOR-PROFIT ORGANIZATIONS

These organizations realize that they can no longer even pretend to be above the political fray. Fundamentally, ours is a pluralistic society in which various interests compete in the political arena. Under these circumstances, nonprofit organizations recognize that their interests, indeed sometimes their survival, require political acumen and effort.

PUBLIC AFFAIRS IN BUSINESS

Because business practices public affairs most ardently and extensively, a deeper understanding of that function will give insight into how public affairs applies in all organizations. In relation to business and the economy, government now plays a variety of roles: stimulant, referee, rule maker, engineer, pursuer of social goals, defender, provider, customer, and controller. To be successful, business must be prepared to deal with government in any of these roles. That is the critical importance of governmental

Although public diplomacy has traditionally meant formal government communication with foreign governments, the war-torn post-9/11 world is now focused on other means of bridging differences between nations. Seong-HunYun, Kansas State University, and Elizabeth L. Toth, University of Maryland, in a forthcoming article in the *American Behavioral Scientist*, argue that there are three different views of public diplomacy at play: realism, international liberalism, and sociological globalism.

Realism is a "hard power" form of public diplomacy focused on power politics and national security. War is the purist form of power politics. American realist public diplomacy has pursued strategic political, military, and economic aid and trade interests.

Realist public diplomacy used persuasive messages to "win the hearts and minds" of peoples in adversarial nations so that they would influence their governments.

International liberalism is a view of the world beyond the state to the interconnectedness of many partners, such as foreign citizens, nongovernmental organizations (NGOs), as well as states. Liberalists use "soft" power, such as attraction to a country's culture, ideals, and policies—for example, sending the New York Symphony to perform in North Korea. Countries are "branding" themselves to attract tourism, export, and inward investments. Countries seek to build credibility and legitimacy with policy communication in such global issues as sustainability and human rights.

Sociological globalism is a view of the world through the perspective of the flow of peoples through migration. Migrants are now mediators of the cultures in which they live and their home countries, through the ease and rapidity of the Internet and cell phones. Millions of people are on the move either for a better economic life or because wartime conditions have pushed them beyond borders. The living experiences of migrants make them the most credible reporters of the destination country's reputation. They represent word-of-mouth, interpersonal networks, and their power is much stronger than managed "soft power" communication. In sociological globalism, relationship building will have to rely on substantial channels of communication but could provide the greatest benefit to global understanding.

Questions

1. Can you give an example of realist, liberalist, and sociological globalism public diplomacy that happened in the United States?
2. What would be the role of public affairs in each of these public diplomacy perspectives?
3. What kinds of skills and knowledge would a public affairs professional need to carry out sociological globalism public diplomacy?

---

relations and why public affairs has become, in the last 20 years, a crucial dimension of public relations.

Government's enormous power and ability to take an active hand in business management are further pressures for corporate involvement. There are shifts in power from government to business, from business to activist groups, and back to government. Public affairs specialists assess and anticipate the possible interests that government will have on corporate activities. Sheila Tate, former press secretary in the George H. W. Bush administration, said,

> I recognized the shift in power 10 or 15 years ago when a merger was about to take place. All the two companies cared about was Wall Street. Then, at the end of the 1980s, and at the beginning of the 1990s, what happened was that Capitol Hill and the Departments of Commerce, Justice and State became just as important and could derail a deal more quickly than Wall Street could.[4]

Not only does business have to detect shifts in public opinion and politics, it has to act quickly. At one time business merely reacted to the threat of government action, whether that action took the form of taxation, regulation, legislation, or the opposing efforts of labor and public interest groups. However, corporate public affairs is called upon now to "run faster and jump higher," according to Doug Pinkham, head of the Public Affairs Council. Pinkham cites trends, such as the emergence of the Internet and other sophisticated communication tools that make business activities increasingly transparent. He cites the globalization of business, presenting such new public affairs issues as national differences in laws, customs, and political structures. See mini-case 14.1 as an example of proactive public affairs on the part of global chocolate manufacturers. Public affairs must also contend with public cynicism and mistrust of the business community.[5]

Business has realized the value of developing continuing relationships with government at all levels that permit early involvement in issues, policies, regulations, and legislation. Joseph Gleason, managing director of Manning Selvage & Lee in Washington, says, "It's also important to develop relationships with policy-makers, many who know little about your client or organization prior to initial communication."[6] Advance notice can be a critical factor in political effectiveness. Moreover, early involvement makes provisions for crisis management less necessary when a critical bill comes to a vote later on.

The increasing importance of business public affairs and political activities has had substantial impact on management in general and public relations in particular. Because the issue is one of corporate control, top corporate leaders take an active role in public affairs efforts. Former congressman Donald G. Brotzman, past president of the Washington-based Rubber Manufacturers Association, explains: "Involvement of top management is a most important principle. The chief executive officer and all top managers must be active participants. The direct and indirect influence of government action on business changes the kinds and mix of skills that one needs to succeed as a manager."[7] The effect on top management, he feels, is even more pronounced: "Top managers must now be as concerned about public policy as they are about anything else they do."[8]

PUBLIC AFFAIRS TASKS

Today, no public relations program is complete unless it includes provisions for dealing with the government. This job is, in part, a complex sequence of information acquisition, processing, and dissemination. Fact-finding and serving as a listening post may be the most important aspects of governmental relations.

After gathering information, governmental relations specialists weigh and evaluate its potential impact on the company or industry. Information is then disseminated to corporate decision makers, employees, stockholders, and the public. Indeed, public affairs has its greatest impact on an organization when it aids corporate planning. At the same time, government relations staffs convey information to legislators, regulators, congressional staffers, potential political allies, and the public.

Public affairs is also sometimes called on to fight fire with fire on the governmental relations front. Investigation and publicity lack the force of law but are clearly among the weapons government uses to influence business. Leaks to the media by "high-level sources," visits to the sites of supposed infractions, staged public hearings, and the like may be used against business by government officials. Businesses' public affairs efforts must sometimes respond in kind. Their public affairs specialists must compete with the public forums of government and the public affairs operations of a variety of special interests. Honesty and forceful public communication is a crucial aspect of the government relations process.

UNDERSTANDING THE POLITICAL SYSTEM

To operate effectively, public affairs professionals must thoroughly understand the United States political process. In a general sense, political activities fall into three broad categories: electoral, legislative, and regulatory. Electoral activities involve the election of

Anti–World Trade Organization protesters march in
downtown Seattle.

candidates favorable to an organization's interests and the development of plans for
financially supporting selected political campaigns. Political action committees are the
major vehicles for fund-raising efforts.

Legislative activities work to create or gain support for favorable legislation and
build opposition against unfavorable activities. Lobbying is the major avenue for legislative activities.

Public affairs officers seek to influence government regulators who must interpret
new laws by writing policies and regulations by which to carry them out. For example,
if a new law says "no building within 120 feet of the ocean," the regulators must decide
how land developers are going to have to apply for oceanfront permits and prove that
their plans meet the new law. Government regulators are more difficult to lobby because
they are rarely elected officials. Nonetheless, many public affairs efforts related to regulatory activity take a form quite similar to lobbying.

Electoral Activities

A few wealthy cattle ranchers, logging companies, and mining companies have used federal lands for tremendous gain while paying little to the government. Critics claim this
usage has damaged the environment and cost the taxpaying public billions of dollars.
When President Bill Clinton sent a bill to Congress in early 1993 to raise the rent for
using federal lands, many people thought it would pass easily. Not so. It was defeated
soundly. Critics said this defeat was directly attributable to the $7 million contributed to
key congressmen by **political action committees (PACs)**.[9]

A PAC is a group of people who raise or spend at least $1,000 in connection with
a federal election. The people belonging to a PAC usually have some common political
concern, interest, or cause. To pool resources in support of favored candidates, PACs
have been formed by unions, businesses, industry groups, church groups, professionals,
and many others.

In 1974, the Federal Election Campaign Act legitimized the role of corporations and business-related groups in federal elections, greatly improving their position vis-à-vis labor and other special interests.[10]

The objective of legislation allowing PACs was to reform campaign financing. Legal limits on and full disclosure of contributions are supposed to ensure fairness in the electoral process. However, numerous loopholes exist and have caused the concern that PACs may promote corruption or tip the political scales in favor of special interests. Some critics maintain that PACs are costly, time-consuming, and demeaning to candidates. Others say that since PACs multiply and therefore tend to neutralize one another, they should be abolished.

Supporters maintain that PACs are an example of citizens' rights to free speech, that they promote political awareness and involvement, and that they have brought campaign financing into the light. Table 14.1 shows the PACs that made the largest contributions in 2007.

Corporate PACs get their money from their employees or stockholders. Other PACs get funds from their members or constituencies. Thus, if a PAC is to be effective, it "must first educate its people and motivate them to participate."[11]

TABLE 14.1 Top 20 PACs by Total Expenditures, 2007*	
PAC Name	Total Expenditures (millions US$)
Service Employees International Union	$18.4
EMILY's List	18.4
ActBlue	15.8
Moveon.org	9.7
American Federation of State/County/Municipal Employees	8.7
International Brotherhood of Electrical Workers	7.6
American Federation of Teachers	6.7
Laborers Union	6.4
Teamsters Union	5.9
Operating Engineers Union	4.7
Plumbers/Pipefitters Union	4.1
National Association of Realtors	4.1
AT&T Inc	4.0
American Postal Union	3.5
American Bankers Association	3.5
National Rifle Association	3.5
Lyndon LaRouche PAC	3.5
American Association for Justice	3.3
United Food & Commercial Workers Union	3.2
Communications Workers of America	2.9

*Totals include subsidiaries and affiliated PACs, if any. Data released by FEC March 25, 2008.
Source: www.opensecrets.org/pacs/topacs.asp?cycle=2008&Type=E, accessed March 28, 2008.

Some have charged that PACs attempt to "buy" political officials or unduly influence legislators in relation to pet issues. Senator Edward Kennedy (D-MA) has claimed that PACs "are doing their best to buy every senator, every representative, and every issue in sight."[12] Typically, PACs contribute to candidates whose philosophies are consistent with their own. One PAC official explained that his group has two tests for campaign contributions: Is the candidate someone we agree with, and is it someone in the area of government that relates to how we do business? Consequently, a senator on the banking committee gets contributions from bank PACs, and one on the agriculture committee receives funds from the Associated Milk Producers.

What PACs typically seek is access. That is why funds more often flow to incumbents. PACs are so eager to back winners, they often do so retroactively—making contributions after the election is over. Funds contributed after the election are called "hundred percent money," meaning none is wasted on losers. Many PACs switch sides after the votes are counted. When Senator Charles Hecht (R-NV) upset incumbent Howard Cannon, post-election contributions came from former opponents, including the American Dental Association, the American Bankers Association, and McDonald's Corporation. The National Association of Realtors kicked into Hecht's campaign chest after opposing him in the primary and the general election. In many cases, PAC funds are used to keep from making enemies.

Because a PAC contribution may be as much as $10,000 per election, the gift generally helps open the door to a legislator's office. Indeed, the most important outcome of electoral contributions is to obtain access to legislators and gain influence on legislative activities.

Legislative Activities

Most political decisions important to organizations are made long after elections are over. Consequently, business firms and other organizations concentrate their efforts on affecting legislation and regulation in relevant areas. These activities are known as **lobbying.**

Lobbying has been defined as "the practice of trying to influence governmental decisions, particularly legislative votes, by agents who serve interest groups."[13] Lobbying is an extensive and expensive activity. Although the term has acquired an unsavory connotation of graft and influence peddling, lobbying has long been recognized as a legitimate practice. James Madison, writing in 1788, held that an essential characteristic of a representative democracy is that the various interest groups in society are permitted to compete for the attention of government officials.

Today, lobbyists are likely to be very carefully selected professionals who have business acumen, a thorough grasp of sometimes highly technical information, and lots of political savvy. Henry Ford II sums up the new attitude: "The problem with 'lobbying' activities is not to conceal their existence, nor to apologize for them, but to make sure they are adequate, effective and impeccably correct in conduct."[14]

What do lobbyists do? They inform corporate executives about developments in legislation, report on the introduction and progress of specific bills, offer or arrange testimony to congressional committees, file statements, communicate with legislators, analyze policies and legislation, inform legislators about the potential effect of legislation, educate legislators about business and economics, help draft laws, publicize testimony, and develop strategy to support or oppose specific legislation.

Lobbyists gather information from studies, surveys, experts, and records, then prepare positions for corporate executives, persuade government officials, promote or oppose legislation or other governmental action, and seek governmental cooperation. Lobbyists devote much time to creating contacts and programs that will improve communication with government officals and to monitoring legislators' activities regarding statutes and laws.

Lobbyists involve themselves in the earliest stages of the legislative process. Recognizing that lobbying can work only while the legislator is still in the decision-making stage, lobbyists provide information before bills are drawn up. Their emphasis is on information and advocacy, not pressure. Lobbyists seek to define issues in terms of the legislators' constituencies and the public interest, providing briefly stated, neatly organized facts that answer questions. Often, they must communicate through a legislator's staff or assistants.

Facts must be presented in a truthful, straightforward, and helpful fashion. Honesty is essential because credibility is the lobbyist's most important asset. Lobbyists who have achieved credibility are relied on by senators, representatives, and their staffs. When such relationships are established, the lobbyist is in a position to suggest legislation, prepare speeches, line up witnesses for congressional hearings, and provide research and position papers. Under such circumstances, it is difficult to tell where the legislator leaves off and the lobbyist begins.

Perhaps an even more important role of lobbyists is to provide expert advice on which issues to address. Legislative battles must be carefully chosen and related to the overall objectives of the corporation.

Politicking from the Grass Roots

In a democracy, the attempt to influence government occurs in the context of public opinion and requires dealing with an audience much broader than political officials. This broader audience is reached through **grassroots lobbying** and issue advertising. As we have mentioned in other chapters, businesses increasingly seek to organize employees, stockholders, community leaders, and others as potent weapons in the political arena. Washington lobbyists must demonstrate that their positions are those of the congressman's or congresswoman's constituents. To accomplish this, the constituents must be organized to make their voices heard.

According to *BusinessWeek,* "The wedding of lobbying and PR makes sense . . . because of the increasing need to win public support for their causes."[15] Top lobbyist Charles E. Walker maintains, "Lobbying has come to require strong grassroots efforts. . . . I go to a congressman and he tells me 'You can sell me if you can sell my constituents.'"[16]

Different constituents can be mobilized to communicate in a variety of ways. The grassroots approach may consist of asking local groups to partner on a corporate issue by sending messages to legislators, flooding Congress with mail, or getting the right people to call their representatives. Grassroots lobbying means establishing an organization at the local level by which support can be activated when needed. The Associated General Contractors, for instance, maintain a legislative network among their 113 chapters across the country. At least one person in each chapter personally knows his or her senator or representative. On one occasion, this network was invaluable in defeating a labor law reform bill.

The American Bankers Association (ABA) asks legislators which bankers they want to hear from. Then the ABA asks those bankers to transmit the ABA's position on specific legislation. The ABA has 1,200 designated contact bankers, many of whom know members of Congress, have served as campaign treasurers, or have worked on campaigns.

Issue advertising (or **advocacy advertising**) is a way of taking an organization's position straight to the people, with the anticipation that they will support it politically. This kind of advertising is not new. Organized labor, private voluntary groups, governmental agencies, and others have long used advertising to support their positions on public issues. Mobil Corporation is perhaps the nation's leading issue advertiser. Under its former vice president of public affairs, Herbert Schmertz, Mobil pioneered corporate advocacy.

Regulatory Activities

In an era of governmental growth, government regulation is the area in which the most dramatic expansion has occurred. During the 1970s, the years of greatest growth in government regulations, 22 new regulatory agencies were created, including the powerful Environmental Protection Agency (EPA), the Consumer Product Safety Commission (CPSC), and the Occupational Safety and Health Administration (OSHA). A total of 120 major regulatory laws were passed during the decade.

"We have become a government, not of laws passed by elected officials . . . but a government of regulation," claimed former congressman Elliott H. Levitas (D-GA). "A Congress . . . will enact 500 laws during its two-year tenure. During that . . . time, the bureaucracies will issue 10,000 rules and regulations."[17]

Almost every facet of business activity is subject to the rules, standards, or other controls of one or more federal agencies that have the power to review, inspect, modify, or even reject the work of private industry.

State and Local Public Affairs

Traditionally, most attention has been paid to interaction with government at the federal level, but the relative importance of local and state governments has recently increased for organizations of many types. Although builders and developers have long sought to influence local zoning decisions, for example, the players in local and state government affairs are now more numerous and more intense.

Deregulation, federal budget cutbacks, and the Reagan administration's determination to return government to the people have forced state and local governments to pick up the slack. As a result, state officials are now dealing more extensively with environmental sustainability issues, social services, labor legislation, bank deregulation, and international trade. Moreover, state and local funding in the areas of the arts, transportation programs, health care, education, and others has become more critical. Naturally, both profit-seeking and not-for-profit organizations have increasingly focused on the 50 state capitals, in addition to Washington, D.C.

Covering 50 cities is more difficult, complex, and expensive than merely focusing on Washington. "In a two-year period almost 250,000 bills are introduced in the various state legislatures. For a company with nationwide interests, this volume appears to create an insurmountable obstacle."[18] To deal with multiple governments at any one time, some companies have established their own networks of private legislative information in all 50 state capitals. Others have monitored only those states where they have a major interest. Another approach has been to rely on the industry's association to do its political scanning and research and lobbying efforts for them. Often companies use a combination of all of these efforts.

When national organizations seek to influence local affairs, they must understand local politics and culture. A major New York corporation dealing with a tax problem in a southern state got an audience with the chairman of the state senate's tax writing committee. After an informative and persuasive 30-minute presentation, the senator asked, "Y'all aren't from around here, are you?"[19]

Staying on top of issues, tracking bills, knowing the right people, knowing which PACs to contribute to, cultivating the right media contacts, and all the other necessary lobbying activities may be approached in a variety of ways. Generally, goals and objectives, the scope of the effort, and key states must be identified. The corporation or association may then set up its own in-house operation, employ outside lobbyists or consultants on a retainer basis, or depend on industry or state business associations. The national interests, which prevailed, used a combination of in-house lobbyists and an industry association.

Internal Political Communication

We have already discussed PACs as a means of promoting employee and shareholder awareness and involvement. Beyond PAC activities, however, a public affairs practitioner whose position requires monitoring government relations can also use in-house publications and other media to provide political education, increase employee awareness of political issues, and encourage employee political involvement.

Organizations can stimulate employees' political awareness in many ways. Bliss and Laughlin Industries of Oak Brook, Illinois, provides worksheets with employees' W-2 forms so employees can calculate how much of their wages have gone to taxes, what percentage of income goes to taxes, and how long each must work to support the cost of government. The employees have learned that their biggest expense is not shelter or food, but taxes.

Dow Chemical maintains an extensive public affairs program for employees. The program rests on four objectives:

1. Informing employees about national and local issues that potentially affect the firm.
2. Making employees aware of governmental processes and legislative procedures.
3. Encouraging employees to take part in the political process and giving specific examples of approaches they might use.
4. Advising employees of the value of political contributions and providing the opportunity to do so through political action committees.

Budd Company gives its managers a "discretionary bonus" of up to several thousand dollars based on evaluation in 11 categories, including "involvement in government affairs." Managers are judged on their ability to get their people involved in political campaigns, their willingness to write to government officials on issues affecting the company, and their ability to organize in-plant political education committees. All of these companies recognize that if business intends to remain a viable part of society, its leaders must encourage employee participation in the political process.

On the other side of public affairs efforts by nonprofits and businesses is the public information function of government itself. While the practitioners who deal with government are most likely to be called public affairs specialists, the governmental public affairs or public relations personnel are most likely to be called public information officers. In the remainder of the chapter we look at the task of the public information practitioner for government itself.

GOVERNMENTAL PUBLIC AFFAIRS

The framers of the U.S. Constitution believed that the American people were capable of governing themselves. To do so, however, citizens needed to be fully informed about issues and problems confronting them and actions taken by their government. Despite their belief, the founding fathers provided no specific means to disseminate information or any assurance that citizens would be kept informed. It was assumed that government would maintain open communications channels with the public and provide sufficient information to enable citizens to make intelligent decisions about its policies and activities.

To a certain extent, these ideals have been realized through a system that evolved in response to public needs. The mass media struggle to serve our right to know. In providing information to the public about governmental affairs, they draw on the public relations arm of government—local, state, and federal—that offers the media a constant flow of information.

Governmental public relations practitioners are often called **public information officers (PIOs),** suggesting that they simply transmit information in an objective and neutral fashion. In fact, they are no more neutral or objective than public relations professionals working in the private sector.

Because the success and stability of democratic governments are ultimately determined by continuous citizen approval, PIOs seek to ensure such approval. The democratic system implies that government will respond to the wishes of the governed, so PIOs work to determine those wishes, then strive to make government responsive to them. Because public opinion provides the climate in which public officials, agencies, and institutions succeed or fail, PIOs try to understand and affect public opinion. A multitude of institutional interests coexists in any society, so public relations practitioners both inside and outside government represent a similar variety of perspectives. As a consequence, much of the significant dialogue needed to ensure democracy's proper functioning is generated, molded, and enunciated by public relations practitioners.

In short, in government—as in any other organization—public relations is a management function that helps define objectives and philosophies while also helping the organization adapt to the demands of its constituencies and environments. Public relations practitioners, whether referred to as PIOs, **public affairs officers (PAOs),** press secretaries, or just plain administrative aides, still communicate with all relevant internal and external publics to make organizational goals and societal expectations consistent. Public information officers, like their counterparts in business and industry, develop, execute, and evaluate programs that promote the exchange of influence and understanding among an organization's constituent parts and publics.

Of course, because they work in a different context with different constraints and problems, government public relations specialists operate somewhat differently from their private sector counterparts. Public information officers face unique problems. Their mission and legitimacy are questioned more extensively. Their constituents are forced to provide financial support through taxation. Red tape, internal bureaucratic situations, and political pressures hinder their efforts. Career development opportunities are limited.

Background of Public Relations in American Government

In 1913 the U.S. Civil Service Commission announced an examination for a "Publicity Expert." On October 22 of that year, Congress passed the Gillett Amendment

(38 U.S.C. 3107), which stated, "No money appropriated by any act shall be used for the compensation of any publicity expert unless specifically appropriated for that purpose."

Despite the law, the governmental public relations function continued. Most notable among government's early public relations endeavors was George Creel's World War I Committee on Public Information.

Public relations in the federal government came of age during the New Deal, when the creation of the so-called alphabet agencies "precipitated a flood tide of publicists into the channels of government."[20] The Office of War Information, created during World War II, gave further federal support to the profession. When the war was over, it became the United States Information Agency. During the late 1940s, public relations activity was increasingly evident in state and local government. By 1949 nearly every state had established a state-supported public relations program to attract both tourism and industry. Since 1970 at least 20 new federal regulatory agencies have been created. All of them have extensive public information programs.

U.S. Secretary of State Condoleezza Rice is accompanied by officials on a visit to quake-torn southwest China's Sichuan province. She praised China's post-earthquake recovery efforts.

Importance and Scope of Governmental Public Relations

Despite the limits placed on public relations activity by Congress, government publicity has always been necessary, if for no other reason than to tell citizens what services are available and how to use them. With the developing complexity of government has come a corresponding increase in publicity.[21]

Ron Levy, counselor to government communicators, argues that government needs to do a better job giving the public more information about what government literature is available, what services are available, and where to write for specific government information materials. He says government communicators also should give wider dissemination of speeches by government leaders.[22]

It is impossible to estimate the number of people involved or the money spent in governmental public relations. As William Gilbert states, "If you are in government, you are in public relations. . . . [There is a] public relations element in all the things . . . government . . . does."[23]

Governmental public information or relations became increasingly important after the terrorist attacks of September 11, 2001. Victoria Clarke, former assistant secretary of defense for public affairs, has led the change from a public information service to working strategically to build alliances and relationships, seeking to engage not only the media but also religious leaders, education leaders, and communities—a wider range of audiences. She states,

> If you are going to do public affairs in the 21st century, you've got to do more than react to the 10,000 media hits every day. That's largely what I did. . . . That, in and of itself, is a high challenge. But, my challenge is to transform the public affairs department overall. . . . If you want support for a strong defense or a different defense, if you want support over the long haul, you're going to have to engage a wider range of audiences.[24]

Function of Governmental Public Relations

Governmental PIOs, like any other public relations practitioners, seek to achieve mutual understanding between their agencies and publics by following a strategic public relations process. They must gauge public opinion, plan and organize for public relations effectiveness, construct messages for internal and external audiences, and measure the effectiveness of the entire process.

Like all organizational boundary spanners, PIOs jointly serve two masters—their publics and their employers. On the one hand, they provide the public with complete, candid, and continuous reporting of government information and accessible channels for citizen inputs. On the other hand, the late public relations educator Scott Cutlip maintained that governmental administrators believe the primary purpose of the public information function is to advance the policies of the incumbent administration.[25]

Public information officers serve neither master very well, as evidenced by millions of Americans viewing their "government as distant and unresponsive, if not hostile."[26] Both the public and the politicians might be better served if PIOs could provide more active input to governmental decision makers. In his seminal 1947 report, *Government and Mass Communication*, Zachariah Chafee, Jr., held that

> Government information can play a vital role in the cause of good administration by exploring the impact of new social forces, discovering strains and tensions before they become acute, and encouraging a positive sense of unity and national direction.[27]

The most basic functions of governmental public relations are to help define and achieve government program goals, enhance the government's responsiveness and service, and provide the public with sufficient information to permit self-government. The goal of PIOs is to promote cooperation and confidence between citizens and their government. This, in turn, requires governmental accessibility, accountability, consistency, and integrity.

Practice of Governmental Public Relations

The practice of public relations in government is much like that in other institutions, but governmental PIOs do face some difficulties unique to their area. Because they are paid with public funds, their mission and legitimacy are questioned more than in private organizations. Gilbert points out that "the citizenry . . . regards government public information activities as wasteful of the taxpayers' money and essentially propagandistic."[28] This is why the Gillett Amendment has never been repealed and why governmental public relations practitioners ply their trade under euphemisms like "information officer," "public affairs officer," or "education officer."

Unlike the customers of corporations, the constituents of governmental entities are forced to support those entities financially through taxes. Thus, while government may be responsive to political forces, it is not directly responsive to market forces.

"Government red tape" has become a sadly accurate cliché and a serious public relations problem.

David Brown points out other problems of PIOs: internal bureaucratic situations that hinder professional efforts, weak job standards, political pressure, and little career development or recognition. Moreover, he states, government public relations specialists are considered "after-the-fact operators, expected to put out fires started by others or to implement information about programs that we strongly feel will not stand the muster of the media."[29] Increases in the complexity of government policies, rules, and practices; the widening chasm between citizens and their government; and the escalation of demands made by citizens without understanding the political, legal, and financial constraints placed on government are additional difficulties PIOs face.

To deal with these problems, PIOs may adopt several strategies. First, they should strive to be generalists in both public relations and management skills while becoming expert in the language and discipline of particular fields within government (health, education, transportation, welfare, defense, etc.).

Second, PIOs should practice preventative maintenance, providing policy guidance before programs are approved. This requires them to enter government's management mainstream. Third, governmental PIOs must develop a service orientation—responding to a public composed of consumers of government services. Moreover, public relations should foster this perspective in all government employees, using established channels of internal communication.

Fourth, governmental PIOs should concentrate on inputs as much as outputs. This calls for getting direct feedback through citizen participation, surveys and questionnaires, and community meetings that will be used to adjust programs, messages, and media.

Finally, as the downfall of the Nixon administration so aptly demonstrated, great hazards confront governmental attempts to hide failures, ineptitude, or mistakes. Openness is essential to effective governmental public relations.

Using the Internet

Using technology to communicate with the public has become popular with government public relations because it is a relatively inexpensive two-way communication tool that can be used on low operating budgets prevalent in governmental public relations.

Government agency home pages often contain full-color photos or graphics and text that can be designed like a brochure or newsletter. They also provide an alternative to printing large documents. For example, census data can be downloaded from the U.S. Census Bureau's Web site immediately without having to order a publication, pay for it, and wait weeks for it to arrive. Government Web sites range from the White House to local city and county ones, such as one in Hennepin County, Minnesota. Almost all city governments from large to small cities have Web sites serving a public information function.

Web sites can accomplish several objectives:

1. *Communicating with the Public.* With the Web you can bypass the media. The Web site can supplement your media relations efforts and may eventually replace much of the media effort.

2. *Communicating with Researchers, Activists, Specialists, and Journalists.* People will use your site for information they need.

3. *Distributing Large Volumes of Information.* The Web user can pick and choose what he or she wants from the information provided. A good Web site, though, routes users to information that interests them.

4. *Publicizing Anything from a New Policy to an Upcoming Event.* A Web site is accessible all over the world, and it can be updated easily. You can also use other forms to invite the public to your Web site.

5. *Soliciting Public Comment.* The Web provides a two-way communication medium. You can build in an e-mail option with a click of the mouse.[30]

Public Relations and Political Campaigns

Government really cannot be discussed without recognizing its political context. While it provides many and diverse services to its constituents, government's policies are guided by politics. The political campaign is the most overt expression of politics. Public relations activity on behalf of political candidates is practically synonymous with the campaign itself.

Political campaigning is a nonstop industry, raising hundreds of millions of dollars from PACs and spending that money to attract votes. Public relations plays a critical role in both raising and spending those funds.

The public relations practitioner in the political campaign is not just a spokesperson to the media but is usually also a trusted adviser who helps formulate campaign strategy and positions on issues. Gaining votes first requires gaining funds, media exposure, and volunteers. Public relations practitioners work hard to attract all three. These resources must then be converted into political support. All of this activity is designed to get the candidate elected so that he or she can become a part of the governing process. Campaign press aides to successful candidates often become PIOs for the successful candidate.

Go Direct® Campaign

U.S. Department of Treasury with Weber Shandwick

Case Study

Problem

Americans say direct deposit tops both ATM cards and checkbooks as their most important tool for managing personal finances. Yet approximately one in three Americans still do not use direct deposit, including nearly 10.5 million Social Security recipients, despite the widespread opinion that direct deposit is reliable and safe.

The national survey was sponsored by the U.S. Department of the Treasury's *Go Direct* campaign, which encourages people who receive Social Security and other federal benefits by paper check to switch to direct deposit. The survey findings were released in February 2008.

Overview

Go Direct is an ongoing public relations program begun in 2005 when the U.S. Treasury Department hired Weber Shandwick to create a direct deposit campaign to encourage Americans who receive Social Security or other federal benefits to use the convenience and safety of direct deposit. While most recipients use direct deposit, those that don't cost taxpayers about $120 million in printing and postage costs. The research indicates that those who still receive checks are a diverse and disbursed audience of "hard-to-reach or difficult-to-persuade individuals." Go Direct began nationally in September 2005 after a six-month successful pilot program. The campaign's goal was to reduce significantly the number of paper checks issued by the federal government each month.

Research

WirthlinWorldwide, now Harris Interactive, was hired in 2003 by the Treasury and the Federal Reserve Banks to study attitudes toward direct deposit by the stakeholder group. The study found that awareness of direct deposit was already high; therefore, an awareness campaign would likely do little to move this group to do direct deposit.

Another study was conducted in 2004 by KRC Research "to test key messages Weber Shandwick developed based on the earlier research. It included both phone surveys and focus groups with English- and Spanish-speaking individuals. Subsequent research by KRC included testing the effectiveness of campaign-designed television ads and Social Security check inserts."

Planning Strategies

Weber Shandwick developed the Go Direct campaign to provide the target group with information, endorsement, and reinforcement for choosing direct deposit. Repetition with credible, personally relevant messages from trusted sources was a major element of the campaign. Key elements included

- Develop an aggressive effort to change behavior among target audience members by building partnerships with trusted community organizations, social service agencies, and faith-based groups.
- Work with national, regional, and local banks and credit unions to help them "with necessary training and materials to encourage check recipients to opt for direct deposit and help them sign up."
- Create multicultural information and work with trusted groups within the Hispanic community. There was a "Hispanic-focused parallel campaign named Directo A Su Cuenta featuring a Spanish-language Web site and campaign materials."
- Use messages that the target audience understood and related to with credible spokespersons to not only deliver the message but also help create personal interaction among the audience with the spread of that information.
- Support the grassroots efforts with media relations efforts, national advertising, and direct mail to tell the benefits of direct deposit, a toll-free enrollment number, and the Go Direct Web sites.

Tactics

- *Grassroots outreach.* Partnerships were developed with banks and credit unions, community and faith-based organizations, human service agencies, and advocacy groups nationwide. (messages and materials provided)

- *Turnkey materials.* Brochures, posters, videos, and program materials were created.
- *Media relations.* News release, satellite media tour, radio media tour, and video B-roll feed kicked off Go Direct on September 27, 2005. Also included were partnering groups writing op-ed pieces, letters to the editor, and other news releases promoting the campaign.
- *Advertising.* National TV advertising with a "call to action" for target audience members to sign up through a dedicated toll-free number.
- *Toll-free numbers.* Go Direct created helplines in both English and Spanish to facilitate direct deposit sign-up.
- *Direct mail.* Inserts were mailed along with federal government checks to benefit recipients.
- *Web sites.* English and Spanish Web sites (www.GoDirect.org and www.DirectoASuCuenta.org) were created.

Results

- *Direct deposit enrollments.* By June 2006, 600,000 Americans had converted to direct deposit through the Go Direct call center. Other avenues for sign-up were available, so this is not the total number of new enrollments.
- *Media coverage.* Media exceeded expectations. Estimated audience for this media exceeded 250 million possible impressions.
- *Partnerships.* The campaign had more than 450 active partner organizations.
- *Other.* Web hits exceeded 18 million on www.GoDirect.org, and the campaign has "distributed more than 1.8 million brochures, 28,000 posters, 44,000 table tents, and 42,000 'Ask me about Go Direct' buttons."

Sources: Council of Public Relations Firms, "U.S. Treasury's Go Direct Program with Weber Shandwick. Retrieved at www.prfirms.org/index.cfm?fuseaction=page.viewpage&pageid=635 and www.godirect.org/ on March 31, 2008.

Questions

1. What other evaluation research should be done?
2. Why is it no longer possible for the federal government "to assume" that its constituent groups will seek out information, even when it seems to be in their best interest to do so?
3. Why shouldn't the U.S. Congress appeal the Gillett Amendment?
4. What are the biggest challenges of communicating with multicultural audiences faced by the U.S. Treasury?
5. Go to the campaign's Web site at www.godirect.org and check the upcoming events. Write a one-page news release announcing the event using some of the research results on the Web site as part of your message about the upcoming event.

The public affairs function of business and nonprofit organizations has increased in importance at the start of the new century. Whether it be corporations listed on the New York Stock Exchange or the American Red Cross, their employees, volunteers, and communities are demanding government intervention and leadership. Businesses and nonprofits seek to reach global markets and supporters, requiring increased knowledge of how to build relationships with different governmental laws, customs, and regulations.

Public relations has become as critical to governmental organizations as it is to other institutions. Governmental activities depend on public opinion that is informed and involved in public policy. Citizens still have to understand the strategic role of governmental public affairs and information. Governmental public relations specialists can help to build support for this role by establishing their own professional practices and standards.

Summary

For self-testing and additional chapter resources, go to the Online Learning Center at **www.mhhe.com/lattimore3e.**

Key Terms

grassroots lobbying
issue advertising (advocacy
    advertising)
lobbying
political action committees (PACs)

public affairs
public information officers/
    public affairs officers (PIOs/
    PAOs)

Notes

1. "Winning in Washington Takes Luck as Well as Skill," *Public Relations Journal* (February 1994), p. 6.

2. "Public Affairs: Its Origin, Its Present, and Its Trends," Public Affairs Council, www.pac.org/whatis/index.htm, 2001.

3. John L. Paluszek, "Editorial Note: Defining Terms," in *Practical Public Affairs in an Era of Change: A Communications Guide for Business, Government, and College,* ed. Lloyd B. Dennis (Lanham, MD: University Press of America), p. xvii.

4. Sheila Tate, as quoted in Elizabeth Howard, "Capital Gains: Public Relations Inside the Beltway," *The Strategist* (Summer 2002), p. 7.

5. Douglas G. Pinkham, "Corporate Public Affairs: Running Faster, Jumping Higher," *Public Affairs Quarterly* 43, no. 2 (Summer 1998), p. 33.

6. "Winning in Washington Takes Luck as Well as Skill."

7. Grover Starling, *Changing Environment of Business,* 2nd ed. (Boston: Kent, 1984), p. 96.

8. Ibid., p. 516.

9. Herbert Buchsbaum, "Money Talks, Lobbying in Congress," *Scholastic Update,* November 5, 1993, p. 10.

10. Edward M. Epstein, "An Irony of Electoral Reform," *Regulation,* May/June, 1979.

11. Edie Fraser, *PACs: The Political Awakening of Business* (Washington, DC: Fraser & Associates, 1980), p. 2.

12. Ibid., p. 15.

13. Starling, p. 531.

14. "The Swarming Lobbyists," *Time,* August 7, 1978, p. 17.

15. Christine Dugas, "Now, Madison Avenue Runs Straight to Capitol Hill," *BusinessWeek,* August 4, 1986, pp. 27–28.

16. Ibid., p. 28.

17. Elliot H. Levitas, "Bureaucracy Stifling America's Right to Self-Govern," *Atlanta Business Chronicle,* June 9, 1980, p. 4.

18. Richard A. Armstrong, "Working with State Government," in *Lesly's Handbook of Public Relations and Communication,* 4th ed., ed. Philip Lesly (New York: AMACOM, 1991), p. 99.

19. *Parade* magazine, November 9, 1986, p. 8.

20. Wlliam H. Gilbert, ed., *Public Relations in Local Government* (Washington, DC: International City Management Association, 1975), p. 9.

21. Ibid., p. 8.

22. Ronald Levy, "New Realities in Government Communications," *Government Communication*, November 1995, pp. 8–9.

23. Ibid., p. 5.

24. Victoria Clarke, "Life at the Pentagon," *The Strategist* 8, no. 3 (Summer 2002), p. 23.

25. Scott Cutlip, Allen Center, and Glen Broom, *Effective Public Relations,* 8th ed. (Upper Saddle River, NJ: Prentice-Hall, 2000), pp. 488–502.

26. Final Report of the 32nd American Assembly, Columbia University. www .americanassembly.org

27. Zachariah Chafee, Jr., *Government and Mass Communication*, 2 vols. (Chicago: University of Chicago Press, 1947), chap. 2, p. 736.

28. Gilbert, p. 11.

29. D. H. Brown, "Information Officers and Reporters: Friends or Foes?" *Public Relations Review* (Summer 1976), p. 33.

30. Cliff Majersik, "Deciding Whether to Build a World Wide Web Site," *Government Communications*, September 1995, pp. 7–8.

Public Relations in Nonprofit Organizations

OUTLINE

PREVIEW

The scope of nonprofit organizations goes far beyond small, well-intentioned community-based programs. Today's nonprofits are business oriented and expect public relations to contribute to the bottom line. The lines between nonprofit, for-profit, and government are increasingly blurred.

Success factors in nonprofit public relations are similar to those in for-profits. They include a focus on mission, strong internal and external communication, active board participation, and simple messages. The following example illustrates how some of these factors are implemented on a daily basis.

Mindy made a few notes as she concluded her phone interview with a newspaper reporter. The children's museum where she worked was opening a new exhibit, and she was pitching story ideas for the paper's feature section. From her college studies Mindy knew that media relations was a key component of most public relations efforts, but she was somewhat surprised to learn how important media impressions were to her nonprofit's fund-raisers. Good press, especially when accompanied by increased memberships, attendance, and community interest, told donors that their investment in the museum was appreciated and valued. No problem there, she thought. They were serving twice as many people as the facility was intended to serve.

Mindy was also amazed at the competitive level of the work. When participating in her sorority's philanthropic activities during her undergraduate years, she hadn't really thought about the business side of nonprofits. The focus on helping people had made nonprofits seem less cutthroat than companies that have to deliver bottom-line results to shareholders. Yet, here she was a year later trying to out-think and out-deliver the local aquarium, the science center, and others as they garnered press coverage and financial support for their children's programs. Unlike the museum where she worked, some of these other organizations had big advertising budgets that allowed them to pay for eye-catching billboards in heavy traffic areas and run creative television and print ads.

It wasn't only the competition that kept Mindy's two-person department on its toes. The general public seemed to have an insatiable appetite for more programming and more ways to learn about it. The museum recently responded by introducing bilingual offerings, off-site exhibits, and contests. Mindy always wished she had more time to think of better media hooks and to develop her promotional activities. Maybe next year, she thought.

Suddenly an idea popped into Mindy's head. What if a local television reporter did an afternoon segment on nutrition at the museum's café? Mindy made a few notes, picked up the phone, and dialed the station's number.[1]

FOR-PROFIT VERSUS NONPROFIT ORGANIZATIONS

It's not a simple task to define what a modern-day nonprofit organization actually is. For-profits are operating nonprofits, and nonprofits are operating for-profits. To make matters even more confusing, the government not only purchases services from both for-profits and nonprofits, but it also provides some of the same services. Consider the following examples.

When Procter & Gamble launched its Tide Coldwater laundry detergent, it formed a partnership with the Alliance to Save Energy and donated $100,000 to the National Fuel Funds Network, a group that works with fuel assistance programs across the United States. In keeping with the energy-saving theme, Tide created a consumer challenge to try the new product in cold water, and both the Alliance and NFFN promoted it on their own Web sites.[2]

The National Crime Prevention Council, best known for its McGruff the Crime Dog public service announcements, works with communications services firm Global-Fluency to form private–public partnerships that will underwrite anticrime campaigns. The grassroots efforts will concentrate on high-risk communities, giving corporations an opportunity to demonstrate their commitment to being socially responsible.[3]

3M Post-It notes formed a partnership with City of Hope, a cancer research and treatment center in the Los Angeles area. Post-It notes imprinted with a pink ribbon to commemorate Breast Cancer Awareness Month reminded women to be checked. The Post-It Web site attracted more than three million people, and sales expectations exceeded 80 percent, allowing 3M to donate $300,000 to the City of Hope.[4]

"Alliances between for-profit companies and nonprofit groups that do research are the 'new economic model,'" says former Pennsylvania governor Mark Schweiker.[5]

Beyond economics, some chief executive officers believe they have a responsibility to partner with social organizations. "Corporations can and *should* change the world for the better," says John Paul DeJoria, who heads hair care company John Paul Mitchell Systems.[6] When Salesforce.com CEO Marc Benioff started his company, he put 1 percent of the equity into a public charity and said that 1 percent of future profits would go to nonprofits. He also designated 1 percent of each employee's working time for paid volunteer efforts. When the company went public, the foundation was vested with more than $15 million and 12,000 hours of employee volunteerism.[7]

Profit–nonprofit relationships are almost always positive and productive, but there are exceptions. Officials with One Laptop Per Child publicly expressed its disappointment when Intel severed ties with the group. Noted outside observer Kathy Rogers of the American Heart Association, "Everyone needs to realize that you go into [these relationships] with a commitment, but that goals and objectives might change."[8]

Perhaps one of the easiest ways to differentiate between a **for-profit organization** and a **nonprofit organization** is by determining what happens to any monies that are not spent on overhead and operating expenses. In a for-profit organization, this money is called "profit" and distributed on a prorated basis to those who own the company. Thus, someone who owns 20 percent of the company will get more of the profit than someone who owns 1 percent. Examples of for-profit companies include large ones such as Microsoft, Starbucks, and McDonald's as well as many locally owned restaurants, tire centers, or appliance stores. In a nonprofit, the excess monies are called "surplus." Surplus funds are reinvested in the organization, to strengthen and expand the scope of the work.

Beyond dollars, the goals of for-profits and nonprofits are different. A for-profit develops products and services that will make money for its owners, as a way of financially rewarding them for their investment in the company. A nonprofit organization focuses on fulfilling an educational or charitable mission, recognizing that all organizations must maintain positive bottom lines to exist. The terms *nonprofit* and *not-for-profit* can be used synonymously and interchangeably, the former a result of the American urge to truncate.

Some nonprofits would like to think that their mission-oriented agenda provides some flexibility in evaluating programs and overall effectiveness, allowing nonprofits to measure success in subjective and intangible ways. Yet some for-profits, such as The Body Shop and Patagonia, have successfully merged mission and profit. The reality is that today's nonprofits must go beyond warm, fuzzy stories to achieve their mission. Nonprofits that expect to thrive must run well-managed, fiscally sound operations, deliver quality services, and be accountable to the publics they serve. Michael Ertel, manager of public relations for Quest, a nonprofit servicing the disabled in Florida, suggests that the implications for communicators is that "nonprofit is a tax code, not a way of doing public relations."[9]

THE NONPROFIT ENVIRONMENT

Because not all nonprofits are required to file with the U.S. Internal Revenue Service, it's difficult to grasp the true size and scope of the sector. By any measurement, however, it's huge. In 2006 there were approximately 1.48 million nonprofits in the United States.[10] The largest—YMCA of the USA—is a $5.1 billion network. This would place it in the Fortune 500 list, ranking with network and communications equipment company Avaya and commercial bank Marshall & Illsley Corp., were it a for-profit company.[11] See figure 15.1 for a list of the top 10 revenue-generating nonprofits.

Nonprofits include hospitals, museums, research centers, homeless shelters, rehabilitation centers, symphony orchestras, and many other organizations in every community across the nation. Human service organizations comprise 35 percent of the category, followed by education (18 percent), health care (13 percent), public and societal benefit (12 percent), and arts, culture, and humanities (11 percent).[12]

Top 10 Revenue-Generating Nonprofits

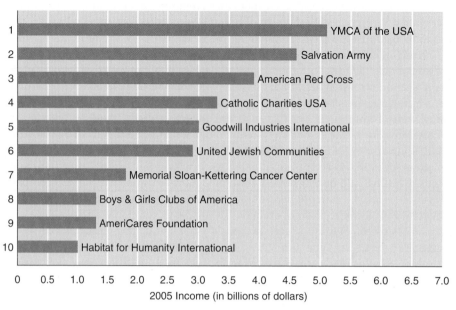

1	YMCA of the USA
2	Salvation Army
3	American Red Cross
4	Catholic Charities USA
5	Goodwill Industries International
6	United Jewish Communities
7	Memorial Sloan-Kettering Cancer Center
8	Boys & Girls Clubs of America
9	AmeriCares Foundation
10	Habitat for Humanity International

2005 Income (in billions of dollars)

FIGURE 15.1 **Revenue-Generating Nonprofits** *Source:* Paul Clolery and Mark Hrywna, "Special Report: The NPT Top 100. An In-Depth Study of America's Nonprofits," *Nonprofit Times,* www.nptimes.com, November 1, 2006.

Multi-ethnic group of Paramount Pictures volunteers reads to Hispanic school children during Viacommunity Day at the Santa Monica Boulevard Community Charter School, Santa Monica, CA.

Nonprofits have been on a public relations fast-learning curve in recent years, hiring practitioners and integrating the communication function into their strategic plans. The importance of job factor priorities across the nonprofit and for-profit sectors is strikingly similar, with practitioners citing access to technology, creative opportunity, and professional development opportunities as most essential. Many factors affect salaries, including the size and culture of the organization, its geographical location, the area of the nonprofit's endeavor, and the qualifications and experience level of the candidate. The pay range on Salary.com for entry-level practitioners was $32,000 to $52,000.[13] The 2008 *PRWeek* salary survey reported that those working in the nonprofit sector had a median annual salary of $71,200. While this figure is lower than some practice areas, the pay is in the same bracket as those working in entertainment, education, travel and tourism, trade associations, government/public services, and retail.[14] As a general rule, smaller, local nonprofit organizations tend to have fewer resources so they pay less, provide little access to professional development opportunities, and are less likely to contribute to retirement plans. Those who choose to work in nonprofits, though, are willing to sacrifice some benefits to work for a cause they believe in. "There is a huge desire for people to do [jobs] that make them feel good," said Shonali Burke of the American Society for the Prevention of Cruelty to Animals.[15]

This section provides an overview of public relations in the more predominant nonprofit sectors, including those relating to health and human services, membership associations, educational facilities, religious organizations, and miscellaneous others.

THE PRACTICE OF NONPROFIT PUBLIC RELATIONS

Health and Human Services

Health and human services organizations are the most common kind of nonprofit. Nationally, more than one in three public charities is a human services organization. Health constitutes 18 percent of all public charities, and nonprofits spend approximately 63 percent of their revenues on health activities.[16] Understandably, areas with dense populations have more nonprofits than do less populated areas. For example, New York will have two to three times as many charities as Idaho. The health and human services sector is very broad, encompassing hundreds of areas, such as help for those with disabilities, food services, temporary shelters and permanent housing, disaster response services, pregnancy care, health care, adoption services, employment assistance, and child and adult day care.

A variety of challenges face the health and human services sector, including high demand, high cost, access, and ethics of criteria used to select those who receive services. Public relations is often called upon to provide positioning statements and to respond to critics. Many look to nonprofits to fill gaps and supplement services provided by government agencies and others. For example, a *Wall Street Journal* headline noted that "Rising Welfare Rolls Prompt States to Make Cuts to Job-Aid Programs." The article notes that "services that help people make the transition from welfare to work—ranging from helping provide cars to substance-abuse treatment—are losing funding."[17] It's at times like this that nonprofits often see an increase in the number of persons seeking their services, creating many public relations opportunities. Notes Steven Rabin, a former public relations practitioner and now assistant to the president of Kaiser Family Foundation, "Health and family get good coverage." He goes on to say, "Issues like poverty, race relations and some of the more thorny issues have a tougher uphill climb."[18]

In general, health and human services topics of interest to the media tend to be episodic and seasonal, a reflection of what is happening at a particular point in time. When Hurricane Katrina forced hundreds of thousands of New Orleans–area residents from their homes in 2005, the American Red Cross along with hundreds of its long-established partners provided help. Public relations played a major role in helping communicate how to receive help as well as how to donate money, time, and other resources.

The Colorado Department of Public Health and Environment wanted to promote influenza prevention and emergency preparedness. Tapping into the reality-show craze, they hosted an online video contest through YouTube.com, allowing real people to share their actions through the new social media. The integrated campaign also included a Web-based tool to help citizens calculate the essentials they would need in case of a disaster, online social marketing techniques, outreach to Hispanics and consumer-generated blogs.[19]

Public relations audiences for health and human services nonprofits are often those who can do something to solve or alleviate the problem. This would put legislators and other government officials high on the list, as they can allocate monies or sponsor laws and public policies. And this group is particularly sensitive to constituents' suffering as might be shared through human interest stories. Poor families who can't afford to pay their electric bills in the winter, sick people who don't have money to buy their lifesaving prescriptions, foster children who have been placed in abusive households—all can make for compelling media drama.

Membership Associations

Membership associations are organizations that allow those with similar interests and goals to join together to address common needs, often in the areas of legislation, law, education, and training. There are thousands of different kinds of membership associations for lawyers, teachers, health care professionals, food producers, consumer safety personnel, and the like. Some well-known ones are the American Medical Association, Chambers of Commerce, and the AARP, formerly known as the American Association for Retired Persons. There are also associations for associations. The American Society of Association Executives represents the more than 25,000 members who lead trade, professional, and philanthropic associations. The National Council of Nonprofit Associations is a network of 37 established state and regional associations of nonprofits serving more than 22,000 nonprofits in the United States.[20]

At the heart of any successful membership association are relationships, and this is where public relations efforts are often focused. Practitioners are always looking for new and effective ways to build and maintain a sense of community, a task made increasingly difficult by the broad range of membership demographics and the pressures of time, schedules, technology, and proximity. To accomplish this, groups often use a combination of "old" technology such as newsletters, magazines, and brochures; "new" technology such as e-mail, Web sites, and chat rooms; and face-to-face communication at statewide and regional meetings. Beyond communications vehicles, operational decisions can affect relationships. The Missouri State Teachers Association, for example, has made a conscious decision not to have an automated voice attendant. The receptionist, who is considered the "manager of first impressions," greets and personally connects callers with the best person or department to meet their needs.

Associations might be called upon to comment on current events within the sector. For example, the Magazine Publishers of America was surprised to learn the U.S. Postal Service planned to raise the postal rate for periodicals an average of 15 percent, after being told to expect a single-digit hike. On behalf of its members, MPA worked to convince the USPS to stick to its original promise. A public relations campaign was created that included contact with reporters who cover politics and government, advertising, a luncheon with key influentials, and lobbying. The rate was reduced to 9.9 percent.[21]

Associations may respond publicly on behalf of all of their members to personal news involving one of their high-profile members. When Dave Thomas, the founder of Wendy's restaurants, died, the National Restaurant Association expressed sympathy and noted that Thomas's death was a loss that would be felt by the whole food-service industry.

Associations receive an annual report card of sorts at membership renewal time as members decide if the organization is worth joining for another year. Public relations must communicate how the organization has met and will continue to meet the needs of its members.

Educational Institutions

Public schools, as well as higher education institutions, have found that public relations is increasingly important to them as they seek funds, deal with crises, or face many of the special situations revolving around education.

Elementary and Secondary Public Schools   A quick glance at the headlines highlights the need for public relations in public elementary and secondary schools. School bond issues are being voted down, teachers and bus drivers are striking, students and teachers are being shot and killed, there's concern about curriculum and standardized test scores, teachers are in short supply, and teacher competency is questioned. School districts realize that part of their responsibility as publicly funded agencies is to keep taxpayers and other publics informed about their operations.

Any issue that affects public schools is likely to affect large segments of the community; even people without school-age children will have an interest in the school system because their taxes support it, and schools are a focus of civic pride and concern. Most people in our society believe it is their right to know and have a voice in what happens in the public schools.

Elementary and secondary schools have numerous, overlapping audiences. For example, a teacher might be a graduate of the school, be a taxpayer, and have children in the school. This means, from a public relations perspective, that publics form opinions based on information from a number of different perspectives. The most important internal audiences for elementary and secondary schools are teachers, students, parents, and district residents. Other key internal and external audiences for public schools include local school administrators and staff; alumni and school board members; local business and industry leaders; service and civic clubs; churches and religious organizations; athletic boosters; legislators; local, state, and federal government agencies; and teachers' organizations and unions.

Beyond education, schools are taking positive steps to address issues that today's young people face. For example, the Drug Abuse Resistance Education (D.A.R.E.) program reaches more than 36 million children in 80 percent of all U.S. school districts and works with educators to present D.A.R.E. in 54 countries. Schools partner with local law enforcement agencies to offer the program. Research supports the effectiveness of the program. In fact, D.A.R.E. graduates are five times less likely than others to start smoking.[22] When officials at Timken High School in Canton, Ohio, learned that 64 of its 490 female students, or 13 percent, were pregnant, the school rolled out a three-prong program to address pregnancy, prevention, and parenting.[23]

When policies of elementary and secondary schools are questioned, public relations must respond. Almost all Arizona school districts follow the Arizona School Boards Association's zero-tolerance rule for any type of druglike substance, including vitamins and nutritional supplements, except when special provisions have been made.[24] When parents of students with drug-related offenses publicly challenge the policy, public relations must communicate the rationale and sustain continued support.

Higher Education   From a public relations perspective, the culture of an institution of higher education is both a blessing and a curse. On the plus side, it's a great environment for creatives because scholars are developing new knowledge and processes, students are creating trends, and there's an openness to exploring new concepts and ideas. On the down side, there is no clear-cut hierarchy of power, but, rather, one that is diffused among a variety of internal groups, such as administration, faculty, and students. Communicators often walk a tightrope in trying to balance the wishes, desires, and needs of internal audiences and external constituents of the campus departments.

Successful public relations practitioners in colleges and universities involve representatives from areas that will be affected by the issue or activity. The following list gives examples of which college or university departments might be involved in planning a campus event and what each might contribute.

- *Public relations:* Identify goals and purpose for the event; ensure appropriate university administration is present at the event; secure a master of ceremonies and suggest program content (including overseeing protocol); develop a schedule of related activities; draft speeches/write scripts.
- *News bureau:* Promote the event; respond to media inquiries.
- *Government affairs:* Identify legislators or other government officials who might need to be present; determine what information needs to be sent to them prior to the event; spot them at the event because they will probably need to be introduced.
- *Events staff:* Reserve rooms, plan menus, manage any catering and decorations, and handle RSVPs; accommodate the needs of visitors, from directions and parking to handling VIP guests and distributing materials.
- *Web editor:* Post the event on the institution's main site or create a special site for a major event.
- *Development and alumni relations:* Identify which segments of the alumni/friends audience should be included, how they should be contacted, and the role of alumni at the event; answer questions.
- *Special interests:* Depending on the scope of the event, various representatives from special interest or other campus groups might need to be involved to ensure the event is handled properly and if any representatives from those areas need to be involved in the program. Especially for major outdoor events, campus facilities staff will need to be involved to handle setup.
- *Campus police:* Ensure safety for all participants and to accommodate any special law enforcement needs.

Colleges and universities face increased security risks that have public relations challenges. The April 2007 killing of 32 students at Virginia Tech by a fellow student redefined emergency response and communications systems for colleges and universities and initiated debate about numerous issues, including gun violence, gun and privacy laws, responsibility of college administrations, journalism ethics, and treatment of the mentally ill. Northern Illinois University had a multifaceted system in place that included the Web site, e-mail, voice-mail, crisis hotline, media, and alarm systems to notify students about potential threats, but after a gunman killed five students there in February 2008, its president noted, "I don't know if any plan can prevent this kind of tragedy."[25]

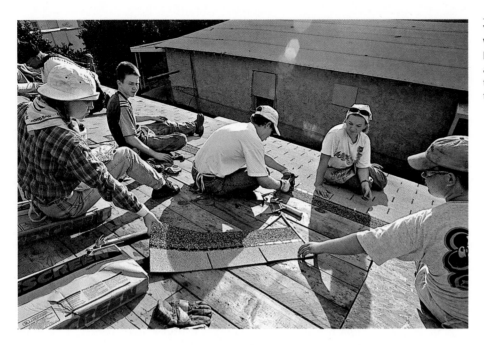

Young people working with World Changers assist in building churches as a mission activity to learn to give their talents and time as well as their money to the church.

The public can misunderstand the research done in universities. When *The Times* of London printed a story that said a researcher at the Oregon Health & Science University sought to "cure" some sheep of their attraction to other sheep of the same gender, inaccuracies and misunderstandings about the data quickly spiraled out of control on the blogosphere. The unit's communications coordinator took immediate action by sharing the scientific facts with two of the primary bloggers, both of whom quickly corrected their information. He corrected the errors in a letter to the editor of *The Times* and followed up with a personal phone call. The scientist also participated in media interviews in order to shed some light on his research. The controversy made such public noise that a *New York Times* article documented the publicity storm, and the university had the opportunity to explain how scientific research works and how grants applications are written to contain language mentioning human implications.[26]

Beyond events, colleges and universities are concerned about their image. While at a football game against Yale in the early 2000s, Cornell students were somewhat envious of the cool hats and other gear worn by their rival fans. The branded items were symbolic of a general sense of Cornell being underappreciated as an Ivy League school. Students formed an image committee to address ways the 13th-ranked school could rise in national rankings and have worked with administrators on Cornell's visual identity, class size, student recruitment, diversity, and other areas related to the *U.S. News & World Report* standing.[27]

Religious Public Relations

Religious organizations must generally rely on public relations to promote their work because funds are usually not available for large-scale advertising efforts. On the local level, public relations helps congregations promote their worship services, Sunday and vacation Bible schools, music programs, and other activities. State, national, and international efforts often focus on denominational, evangelical, and larger social issues. Jews, Presbyterians, Unitarians, and people from other denominations and belief systems are involved in literacy programs, hunger programs, after-school programs, and shelters for battered women, among others. The best intentions, though, may not be enough to overcome legal and political issues and other policies. When the tsunami hit Thailand in December 2004, thousands of aid workers and foreign governments responded with pledges to help and provide billions of dollars for recovery. Nine months later, nearly 150,000 survivors were still living in tents and emergency shelters. Squabbles over land rights, poor coordination, and unclear policies were cited as reasons for the inefficiencies.[28] It is hoped that a solid public relations plan can be developed in this and similar situations, to help communicate long after the tragedy has been replaced by more recent disasters.

Given their nature, religious organizations are often held to standards higher than those for other organizations. Internal quarreling, wrongdoings of leaders and members, and other such scandals can threaten beliefs and destroy the foundations of the denomination's principles and values—the very opposite of what they want to accomplish. For example, some Catholic priests have been accused of and have admitted to being pedophiles. Some married ministers have committed adultery and sought divorces from their spouses. The challenge for religious public relations is to separate the poor judgment and mistakes that its human leaders and members make from the divine meaning and purpose of faith.

At the time of this writing Catholic colleges expect a stern rebuke from Pope Benedict XVI for not teaching and supporting the Church's values. From holding a conference on teen pregnancy and having professors and student organizations that support abortion and embryonic stem cell rights to opening gay resource centers and showing questionable plays, the school presidents have a tough time being authentic and meeting the needs of a diverse student body.[29]

Larger denominations have well-defined and well-organized communication functions. For example, the Church of Jesus Christ of Latter-Day Saints (Mormons) provides story packages, TV/video clips, radio sound bites, broadcast fillers, photos, news releases, facts, and background and contact information to the media.

Other Nonprofit Sectors

The multitude of other nonprofit sectors that actively engage in public relations are too numerous to provide detail on each one in this chapter. For example, some nonprofits promote economic development and tourism. The Irish Tourist Board developed an "Ireland Is Open for Business" public relations campaign to reassure tourists that the country was free of foot-and-mouth disease.[30] Historically, nonprofits like the Colonial Williamsburg Foundation attract the attention of tourists by generating a national dialogue about history education.[31] Others like the Montgomery [Alabama] Improvement Association focus on racial equality.

Nonprofit activist and environmental groups also use public relations. "Boardroom activism" is a guerrilla public relations technique in which activists become shareholders, infiltrate annual meetings, and present their demands in shareholder proposals.[32] As an activist organization, Mothers Against Drunk Driving (MADD) used grassroots support to push for tougher alcohol laws and enforcement and related legislative issues. As a result, alcohol-related traffic deaths have dropped by 40 percent since the early 1980s, and MADD has broadened its public relations efforts to include a proposed constitutional amendment on crime victims' rights and a federally funded anti–youth-drinking advertising campaign.[33] Volvo partnered with the Caribbean Conservation Corporation to initiate a major educational and environmental campaign to conserve sea turtles.[34]

Like their for-profit counterparts, nonprofit organizations face a multitude of public relations challenges, all of which can affect their ability to survive and thrive. They include the following.

PUBLIC RELATIONS CHALLENGES FACED BY NONPROFITS

Gaining Recognition in a Crowded Environment

The sheer number of nonprofits makes for an extremely competitive environment. A 2001 Independent Sector report, the most recent one as of this writing, noted that the number of charities grew 74 percent between 1987 and 1998 to a total of 1.6 million organizations.[35] A Johns Hopkins University study estimates that nonprofits (e.g., teaching hospitals, home health care, universities, cultural institutions) have created one of every four new jobs in Pennsylvania. Nonprofits of all sizes are challenged to gain a significant share of voice and receive support and recognition for their work in such a crowded marketplace.

One valuable tool that nonprofits use to communicate is information technology. Web sites, e-mail, and Internet access allow organizations to conduct research, to share information with key constituents, to raise funds, to network with affiliates, to attract employees and volunteers, to provide training, to sponsor 24/7 information services, and to enhance their overall ability to carry out their programs and mission.

Effective Web sites focus on audience needs. The search engine for the Habitat for Humanity International Web site allows visitors to access information in 11 languages. The site includes a special events calendar, the opportunity to sign up for house-building trips worldwide, stories about work completed and in progress, and much more.[36] The Cystic Fibrosis Foundation recognizes that many of its visitors will use their site for background information. Their Web site provides facts about the genetic disease that affects 1 out of every 31 Americans, information about research and clinical trials, and human interest stories about persons affected by cystic fibrosis. Those wishing to make a donation to this cause can do so online, and details about other fund-raising events and activities are included.[37]

Competing for Resources

Nonprofits compete with other nonprofits and for-profits for a variety of needs and resources, including good employees, conscientious volunteers, steady contributions, and proper recognition. Catherine Palmquist, executive director of the YWCA of Chester County, Pennsylvania, notes that one of her biggest challenges is finding people to hire. "Corporations are trying to hire people and they're paying these bizarre salaries, which we can't compete with," she explains.[38] Competition in all of these areas can be intensified in other ways, such as through job terminations, layoffs, a drop in the value of stocks, and plant closures. For example, when one of the largest employers in Rochester, New York, shut down and layoffs were occurring at other local businesses, the area's United Way fell $1.8 million short of its $38 million goal.[39] The volunteer base was also affected, because some people needed to leave the community to find jobs.

National emergencies can affect local resources, too. In 2005 the federal government diverted 80 percent of the Second Harvest food products to assist those in hurricane-damaged areas. This move affected the ability of local food banks such as the one in Central Missouri to serve its citizens. A $10,000 emergency grant from the United Way allowed the food bank to continue its pantry services to 68,000 people.[40]

Nonprofits always need volunteers to serve in numerous capacities, from serving on boards and fund-raising to working in an office and providing direct services to others.[41]

Although Stan Hutton of nonprofit.com notes that "you haven't really been initiated into nonprofit work until you've done at least two bulk mailings,"[42] most of the more than 110 million people who volunteer[43] aren't content to stuff envelopes. They want to assist senior citizens, cheer up frightened children, work at homeless shelters, help put out fires, clean up roadways, read stories at the library, give tours at museums, serve in the Peace Corps, and help others in myriad ways.

Communicating the need, benefits, and value of volunteerism is one of many tasks for public relations practitioners in nonprofit organizations. Although appeals can be made directly to individuals, many nonprofits are working with community-minded corporations who sponsor volunteer days.

One such company, Atlanta-based Turner Broadcasting System, Inc., hosted a Turner Volunteer Day in 2000, selecting volunteer projects most attractive to employees. Sixteen hundred Turner volunteers, from top-level executives to administrative staff, donned special T-shirts as they volunteered at more than 30 sites in five cities. Public relations efforts, with assistance from Ketchum Public Relations, included an internal campaign to build momentum; media relations before and after the day to tell the story and make employees proud; sponsorships and partnerships with other community members to provide transportation, food, and beverages; and free live remotes and public services announcements. The event was a win-win for everyone. More than 50,000 people of the benefiting nonprofits were affected, employee participation exceeded expectations, and community and organizational leaders praised TBS's efforts. In addition, the company found a new way to retain a loyal employee base by linking itself with something it found within its employee community—a passion for volunteering.[44]

The overriding implication for public relations is clear: Ongoing communication is essential if a nonprofit is to attract its share of scarce resources.

Weathering Crises and Scandals

Nonprofits are treated like any other organization that experiences a crisis or scandal: They get media attention. But when a nonprofit finds itself in such a situation, the whole mission and future existence of the organization can be jeopardized.

The Smithsonian Institution, the world's largest museum and research complex, was criticized about its executive compensation packages and questionable business practices such as travel policies. The board sought new leadership to refocus the organization and strengthen relationships with its employees.[45]

The American Red Cross kept collecting blood it knew it didn't need after the 2001 attacks on the World Trade Center and ended up destroying 50,000 pints. A Red Cross spokesperson tried to defend the action by muttering, "We did our best guess and came within 5 percent of using it all."[46] Such actions can damage the reputation of an organization that depends on the goodwill and support of the nation's citizens.

The bankruptcy of energy giant Enron in early 2002 had serious ramifications for the accounting industry. In response, the 330,000-member-strong American Institute of Certified Public Accountants initiated a public relations campaign to help restore the public's faith in the auditing and accounting system.[47]

Nonprofits of all sizes need to think about how they would handle a potential emergency, an embarrassment, and some other urgent situations *before* they occur. A multitude of training organizations exist that can help nonprofits develop a strategic plan, which would include an assessment of their risks and vulnerabilities, when and how to call the media, how to develop message points, how to prepare for funding alternatives, and how to be specific about what to ask for.

Managing Multiple Publics

Nonprofits are accountable to numerous publics, including corporate and individual donors, board members, employees, volunteers, opinion makers, lawmakers, clients and customers, members, government funders and regulators, neighbors and citizens, foundations and grantees. These complex audiences have different public relations needs, and satisfying all of them isn't easy.

For example, board members of large nonprofits are often wealthy and influential corporate executives. As a group, they use their high-level management expertise to help address the nonprofit's bottom-line issues, and they help support the mission of the organization through substantial gifts. Getting the right composition of board members and satisfying information needs about operations and finances can be difficult.

Bill Lowman, the executive director of the Idyllwild School of Music and the Arts in Idyllwild, California, had such a problem. The school, one of only three residential schools in the country for performing arts, had serious financial problems in 1983, almost to the point of closing. Lowman sought counsel from the affluent weekend residents who had been coming to this mountain retreat for many years. And he did it in an untraditional way: Lowman appointed both spouses to the board instead of the common practice of just one. The result was fresh and frank input and board meetings that resembled social activities, with dinners and concerts by the school's musicians. Today Idyllwild is a 70-building complex with 250 students from 33 states and 23 countries.[48]

Other audiences present equal challenges. Disagreements can erupt over priorities, where and how resources are allocated, ownership issues, different interpretations of the mission, and how results are to be interpreted and evaluated, to name just a few. Practitioners must try to balance these numerous perspectives.

Balancing Multiple Bottom Lines

Nonprofits often use an axiom to describe their bottom line: No margin, no mission. Without sufficient funds to operate the business, the organization is short-lived. Nonprofit public relations efforts go far beyond financial concerns. For example, their publics expect them to meet needs appropriate to the organization; to be a persuasive, unifying voice on key issues; to maintain an ever-readiness in their ability to offer support and services; and to comfort in times of crisis. The National Association of Broadcasters, for example, wanted to help the general public, policymakers, and television executives better understand the implications of switching from the current analog transmission system to a digital format. Their public relations campaign created awareness through special events, media relations, advertising, and other appropriate tactics.[49] For organizations like the Christopher Reeve Paralysis Foundation (CRPF), the only true measure of the organization's success will be effective treatments and a cure for paralysis caused by spinal cord injury.[50] Public relations for CRPF can raise public awareness, keep the issue current, and help increase funding for research.

Building a Brand and an Identity

When you consider the passion that most nonprofit workers have for their particular cause, it's obvious why most resources are allocated to mission-related projects and not public relations. Yet many nonprofits have realized that low name recognition, an obscure image, limited knowledge about their work, and a competitive nonprofit marketplace can significantly affect the amount of support and funding they receive. Strategic public relations is a necessity, not a luxury.

Lutheran Services in America (LSA) is a well-kept secret. What started out, in some cases 150 years ago, as local churches meeting the needs of their communities has grown to more than 300 individual organizations related to the two major Lutheran denominations in the United States. These organizations, together with the two denominations, comprise the network that is Lutheran Services in America. LSA provides a full range of health and human services, serving in thousands of communities with collective operating budgets of over $9 billion, making it one of the nation's largest nonprofits in terms of revenue. LSA member organizations touch the lives of more than 6 million people every year—1 in every 50 Americans.

LSA's challenge is that few recognize who it is and what it does. Its member organizations and board members believe the network must focus on developing a national branding identity as a

way of strengthening its ability to meet community-based needs. In 2003, LSA created a visual identity system and new logo and tagline—*Together we can.* In 2005 LSA began work on a signature fund-raising/awareness-raising event called *Trading Graces.* This annual Lutheran auction on eBay has helped to heighten public awareness of LSA organizations and raise contributions for local member organizations. It received high-profile media attention in its inaugural year, but has struggled to receive attention in subsequent years. In 2008, LSA began a media strategy to create relationships with national reporters covering issues on which LSA is an expert resource, particularly public policy issues such as low-income housing, health care, and aging services. In 2008, LSA also redesigned its Web site to develop more interactive relationships. LSA will also offer resources to members in a restricted Web site.

Lutheran Services in America
Together we can

Here are some of the challenges LSA faces as it works to create a recognized national identity:

- **Tremendous diversity.** Individual LSA organizations are separately incorporated, have very different local identities, use many different names, offer a wide variety of services, and vary greatly in size. Also, trying to describe an entity that involves multiple Lutheran denominations can be confusing to those unfamiliar with the LSA network.

United Way organizations realized this firsthand when contributors were allowed to identify where they wanted their dollars to go. Those groups with little brand awareness began to lose funds, while those who had invested in their brands maintained donor support.[51]

Although nonprofits who undertake branding and identity efforts are often criticized for spending money on such activities, impressive results quell the dissenters. A national branding effort by Volunteers of America allowed the organization to double the number of people served and increased the number of youth and senior volunteers.[52]

Branding issues take on a new perspective as nonprofits join networks while maintaining their own identities. Lutheran Services in America is one of the largest nonprofits in terms of revenue. Mini-case 15.1 outlines the pros and cons of LSA developing a brand identity.

SUCCESS FACTORS FOR NONPROFIT PUBLIC RELATIONS

It's no mystery why some nonprofits are more successful at public relations than others. Those who see measurable results usually incorporate the following into their communication strategies and plans.

Focus on Mission

Like any organization, nonprofits need to revisit their mission statement from time to time to ensure they are fulfilling their purpose. It's easy to take advantage of new opportunities to grow and to dilute the focus on the original purpose and role. Nonprofits

- **Cost.** Developing a national identity is expensive. Some members may be critical of spending money on communications strategies and activities. LSA has hired a seasoned communications director, but she is in great demand for internal communications as well as external.

- **Elective participation in branding efforts.** LSA has no formal authority over member organizations, so it cannot require participation in a brand identity project. Member organizations will have to be persuaded that they can add value to their work by hooking onto this identity and being known as a part of the LSA system. One positive move has been the development of an LSA Communicators Network, made up of PR, marketing, and communication personnel from across member organizations. This network is likely to be supportive of national branding that can have a halo effect on their local efforts.

- **Misunderstandings about messages.** LSA needs to consider how its clients might receive the national brand identity. The religious affiliation, for example, confuses some, leading them to believe they are not eligible for services.

- **Potential negative impact on charitable giving.** When a system such as LSA is seen as large, those who don't understand its federated nature may believe that support isn't needed, resulting in a negative effect on philanthropy.

- **No corporate control.** LSA can provide guidelines, but it has no control over how the identity might be expressed on the local, community level. Yet, some level of branding consistency needs to be present in order to be of any value to member organizations.

As daunting as these challenges may be, LSA feels that it is time for member organizations to highlight their strong witness of faith in action and increasingly to claim their Lutheran identity as that becomes more valuable. A recognized national identity can allow LSA to expand its services and missions. It can enhance the sense of pride among staff, volunteers, Lutherans in the pew, and the clients in the thousands of neighborhoods where LSA member organizations are present.

Questions

1. What are the pros and cons of LSA's approach to introduce new strategies for its identity program over a period of years?
2. Who are the key audiences for this branding effort?
3. Identify other organizations, both for-profit and nonprofit, that face or have faced similar identity problems. What lessons could LSA learn from them?

Source: Jeanean Merkel, Lutheran Services in America, February 2008.

of all sizes are vulnerable to mission erosion, and it can happen even under the watchful eyes of board members and the public.

Scholars and activists demanded the resignation of the Smithsonian Institution's top administrator for commercializing what has been called "the nation's attic," a collection of more than 140 million artifacts. Critics said that corporate and private sponsorship of exhibits and zoo animals allowed outside interests to dictate the Smithsonian's mission, sacrificing integrity and independence. The Smithsonian comprises 16 museums and galleries, the National Zoo in Washington, and research facilities in the United States and abroad.[53]

Strong Internal Public Relations

Fleishman-Hillard executive Dan Barber champions a philosophy that says that all great external public relations begins with great internal public relations.[54] Accomplishing this task with a small staff is an entirely different task than for a national organization with thousands of employees and volunteers in chapters and affiliates around the country. Still, it's important to gain support from those associated with the organization, to add strength to external efforts.

Beyond newsletters, intranets, and other similar tactics, internal public relations can mean involving employees in communication planning efforts. Some test their emergency preparedness, allowing the public relations department to test and evaluate the accuracy and effectiveness of media contact lists, special crisis communications Web sites, and other backup systems, and even to ensure that the batteries in flashlights work. By participating in these scenarios, employees at all levels have a better understanding of what communication systems are in place.

External Public Relations That Unify

Public relations response to issues is usually conducted on an individual nonprofit-by-nonprofit basis; that is, each nonprofit generates communication from its perspective. Often more than one nonprofit is addressing the same issue, increasing the possibility of conflicting messages received by various publics.

During the national anthrax crisis in late 2001, Americans expressed disappointment over how the anthrax scare was handled. There was confusion as to how serious the threat actually was, how contamination could occur, how to safeguard businesses and households, and the like. Given the organization of the U.S. Department of Health and Human Services, it's easy to understand how conflicting messages were created. There are a dozen agencies under the HHS umbrella, most of which have their own, independent communications functions. More than 200 persons are employed in these departments, and HHS has hundreds of millions of dollars' worth of contracts with private public relations firms. It's a system in which few checks and balances exist to ensure that a consistent, single message is delivered.[55]

When the public hears conflicting messages, organizations can lose credibility and trust. Practitioners are urged to look beyond their own agendas when developing message strategies, to better meet the information needs of the public.

Active Participation of Board Members

Board membership usually carries a price tag in that its members are expected to make a substantial financial gift. But their contributions can extend beyond money, as the following example illustrates. Camp Fire USA and Fleishman-Hillard created a special annual one-day awareness campaign called the "Absolutely Incredible Kid Day." Adults are urged to write at least one letter filled with appreciation and love to a child, creating treasured memories that can last a lifetime. National board members helped secure celebrity participation, and they themselves were actively involved in the national call to action. Many celebrities, including Oprah Winfrey, Bill Cosby, and Donald Trump, wrote letters as a result.

Fortune 500 companies generally encourage their employees to serve on boards of nonprofits, and some help train them for board leadership. American Express provides its managers with a toolkit created by the National Center for Nonprofit Boards. The materials include information about the role of the board, an overview of fund-raising activities, its role in strategic planning, and a question-answer book.

Board members of many nonprofits feel pressured to strengthen governance practices and codes of ethics in the shadow of the corporate reform law known as Sarbanes-Oxley. Although this act doesn't apply to nonprofits, many organizations are wanting the same financial controls as are in place for for-profits. Board members see this as a way to protect their reputations should problems occur.[56]

Simple Messages

Nonprofits that break through the clutter are those that focus on one idea. The best messages are those that support the program goals. When a constant barrage of highly publicized high-protein diets cast foods like bread, cereal, and pasta as "high-carbohydrate demons," sales and consumption for wheat and grain products dropped. The Wheat Foods Council, a nonprofit devoted to increasing awareness of dietary grains as an essential component to a healthy diet, developed a simple seal, "Grains: Harvest the Energy." The seal was placed on the packages of grain-food products in grocery stores and resulted in strong sales, with higher margins for the retailers.[57]

Message Points for FAMILY MATTERS 1999

FAMILY MATTERS, an initiative of the Points of Light Foundation in 1999, was ready to spread the word about the benefits of family volunteering and position itself as *the* family volunteering resource. An annual nationwide call to action encouraging families to volunteer together was created. The following message points for national spokespersons provide the rationale for the topic of family volunteering, explain why FAMILY MATTERS is qualified to serve as a liaison between families and their communities, and include a call to action.

Message Points

- *Family volunteering works.*
  - It strengthens the family.
  - It strengthens the community.
- It strengthens local business.
- It strengthens not-for-profits.

- *FAMILY MATTERS connects families and communities.*
  - FAMILY MATTERS, an initiative of the Points of Light Foundation, partnered with the Kellogg Foundation to research how nonprofit agencies nationwide were using family volunteering. We identified an opportunity to fill a need—connecting families to their communities.
  - After implementing and evaluating family volunteering programs in test markets, FAMILY MATTERS established successful models in 20 cities.
  - FAMILY MATTERS sites facilitate family volunteers through link-

ages between neighborhoods, businesses, not-for-profit organizations, and state and local agencies. FAMILY MATTERS can also help individuals start FAMILY MATTERS clubs.
  - FAMILY MATTERS's goal is to make family volunteering the norm in America.

- *Try it, you'll like it.*
  - There's a role for everyone during National Family Volunteer Day.

Source: The Points of Light Foundation and Fleishman-Hillard.

Spotlight 15.1 on FAMILY MATTERS is an example of what message points look like. They organize the key points for the spokespersons and provide a rationale for making the case.

Nonprofits have the same bottom-line accountability as for-profits. As discussed earlier in this chapter, nonprofits manage budgets in the millions and even billions of dollars. Their corporate underwriters, government granters, and donors expect measurable results, those that go far beyond the "do good/feel good" variety. Both qualitative and quantitative research should be used to evaluate public relations results.

EVALUATING NONPROFIT PUBLIC RELATIONS

The nonprofit Habitat for Humanity International worked with Delahaye Medialink to develop a comprehensive measurement process. A team of participants, including communication department heads, senior representatives from fund-raising and development, as well as individuals from other critical areas, was formed to determine how to develop a plan. One of the first issues to be addressed with the team was the fear of measurement and how poor results might reflect on individuals or units. Related to this was an assumption that much work can't be measured. It was important for the team to understand how they valued their work and how their work was valued as well as to consider how and if intangible factors such as feelings and emotions might be indicative of communication effectiveness.

The next step identified eight top effectiveness indicators, including a high percentage of renewals and a high degree of satisfaction with communications and with the program overall and the number of message impressions per month, message tone, and message content. Finally, it was determined how evaluation information could be collected in a timely, efficient manner. This would include assigning an advocate to each of the eight priorities, establishing benchmarks, identifying what's being measured, and determining the presentation format, audience, and frequency.

The end product of this planning is a media measurement device called Media-Scope. Early results are encouraging. This device allows Habitat employees to review all print coverage on a monthly basis and television on a daily basis, making available a valuable source of homeowner stories and testimonials for the work of Habitat departments.[58]

For all nonprofits, the importance of measuring how communication contributes to the bottom line will increase. The competitiveness of the marketplace demands a careful management of resources and results that indicate real effectiveness.

Case Study

NRANews.com: A Case Study in "Branded News"

By Angus McQueen
Chief Executive Officer
Ackerman McQueen, Oklahoma City

What do you do when federal law muzzles your organization's access to political free speech, restricting political advocacy to only politicians and news media?

The National Rifle Association (NRA) faced such a conundrum upon passage of the Bipartisan Campaign Reform Act (BCRA) of 2002. Many questioned its constitutionality, because it banned political broadcast advertising by groups like the NRA 30 days before a primary election and 60 days before a general election.

The law was passed with the NRA specifically in mind, largely in response to its influence upon the presidential race of 2000. The NRA is, by almost any measure, one of the most politically influential grassroots organizations in the country. Its potency is derived from a very broad base of shared opinion among Americans from all demographics.

So communicating with that base—especially during elections—is a critical service to its membership. Silencing the organization precisely when its members needed to speak posed a real threat to the NRA's continued role in national political discourse.

If political free speech is restricted to news media, why not go deeper into the news business yourself?

Imagine a live news network where the lead story, the feature story, almost *every* story is about the Second Amendment right to keep and bear arms.

This real-time network exists at www.NRANews.com, a live daily program featuring news (fact-based, checked, and edited) and opinion about firearm freedoms specifically, and individual freedoms in general.

This is the principle behind "branded news," a bold concept pioneered by Oklahoma City–based agency Ackerman McQueen.

What Is Branded News?

Branded news holds that an established brand is better equipped than traditional media to gather and deliver news about that brand's product category. Who knows more about it than the people who live and breathe it every day?

What's more, branded news provides yet another touch point with customers, regulators, newsmakers, and other influentials important to the brand's value.

In this case, the customers are Second Amendment advocates, the brand is the NRA, and the product is a particular point of view.

Branded news also holds that all news outlets deliver some information with an inevitable bias. Yes, the journalists on NRANews.com are Second Amendment advocates. Like the media exempted by the BCRA, they have a bias. But unlike those media, NRANews.com clearly discloses that bias up front and welcomes opposing points of view, with free access granted to its audience.

Why Now?

With the emerging ubiquity of broadband Internet access, traditional news brands such as CNN, MSNBC, Fox, and other news channels no longer have a monopoly on news delivery. Nor does federal law prohibit it—at least not yet.

Besides, the trust once enjoyed by major news brands is suffering from a blurred distinction between news and commentary. There's a growing perception of media bias, and a widening values gap between the media and the general public.

What's more, most news outlets don't have editors and reporters who specialize in narrow product categories or specific issues. So why shouldn't brand leaders fill this void? Especially when no existing news outlet has the resources or financial incentive to do it.

Finally, traditional news media are constrained by a profit motive, with success measured by revenue enrichment. Branded news doesn't rely on such a return, because its success is measured in brand enrichment.

A New Brand of Free Speech

Publishing and journalism have been core NRA business functions for almost all of its 135-year history. Since 1871, NRA has published magazines that have grown to six titles serving four million members. But passage of the BCRA invited an expanded and equally powerful channel of communication.

Launched live from the organization's annual convention in Pittsburgh in April 2004, NRANews.com became the world's first and only real-time Second Amendment news network. Two months later, the show was picked up for nationwide broadcast on the SIRIUS Satellite Radio network.

NRANews.com delivers all the day's news on firearm freedoms, with in-depth, up-to-the-minute live coverage that's unavailable anywhere else:

- Live, three-hour streaming video newscasts every weekday of "Cam & Company" with host Cam Edwards
- Simulcast nationwide on SIRIUS Satellite Radio, Patriot Channel 144

- In-studio guests range from lawmakers and NRA leaders to authors, legal experts, celebrities, and political adversaries
- Real-time calls, e-mails, and Instant Messaging let viewers interact with host and guests
- Remote live coverage of trade shows, political conventions, shooting competitions, and news events
- Point-and-click access by state for news of local interest, plus show and video archives available 24/7

Skeptics critical at the outset have now quieted, since many traditional news outlets now monitor and cite NRANews as a source for stories.

More validation that branded news is legitimate journalism is that, beginning in 2008, SIRIUS asked NRANews to provide election night coverage for the nation's primary and general elections.

A Higher Standard

How can a brand objectively report on its own industry?

Simply put, a brand can't be enhanced by dishonest news. Audiences know what's legitimate news and what's not. Advertising or hyperbole masquerading as news would damage the brand.

That's why branded news, by definition, must not only meet but also exceed traditional standards of objective journalism.

With a fraction of traditional brand-building investment cost, the NRA now enjoys a daily presence with audiences it could never acquire through traditional public relations and advertising channels.

As American businesses harness the news delivery potential of the Internet, they, too, can cover their industry news for their audiences with more authority, expertise and accuracy than anyone ever before.

In doing so, they add depth, dimension and humanity to their brands, because people who are important to them can reach out and touch them every day. That's the golden ring for good PR practitioners *and* good journalists.

Questions

1. What are the distinguishing characteristics of traditional news and branded news? What are the advantages and disadvantages of each?

2. Select a company or issue you're interested in. If you were to create a branded news site for them, what features would you include?

3. Assume you're the director of an automotive branded news site sponsored by Mercedes. The Mercedes CEO asks you not to run a story about a Mercedes recall. What would you do?

4. How do you rate the bias of today's national broadcast news media? Would you expect branded news to be generally more, or less, biased? Why or why not?

Public relations plays an essential role in helping a nonprofit organization gather support for its mission and in communicating with its key publics. Nonprofits face challenges unique to this sector. Public relations helps nonprofits balance multiple fickle publics and quantitative and qualitative bottom lines.

Public relations tactics in nonprofits include media relations activities, employee and volunteer communication, special events, and the Internet. Public relations is expected to deliver real bottom-line results to nonprofit ventures.

For self-testing and additional chapter resources, go to the Online Learning Center at **www.mhhe.com/lattimore3e.**

for-profit organization

nonprofit organization

1. Adapted from Christie Casalino, "Children's Museum Puts Its PR Creativity on Display," *PRWeek*, August 8, 2005, p. 8.

2. John N. Frank, "Tide Launches Grassroots Drive for Its New Detergent," *PRWeek*, February 7, 2005, p. 5.

3. Ted McKenna, "NCPC, GlobalFluency Team in Anti-Crime Push," *PRWeek*, July 30, 2007, p. 3.

4. Beth Herskovits, "Post-It Adheres to Its Breast Cancer Awareness Effort," *PRWeek*, June 13, 2005, p. 15.

5. Bob Fernandez and Patricia Horn, "Nonprofits' Job Engine Transforms Pa.

Economy," *The Philadelphia Inquirer*, www.philly.com, August 28, 2005.

6. Mary Rose Almasi, "A Champion for the Planet," *Shape* magazine, August 15, 2005.

7. Steven Levy, "Die, Software!" *Newsweek*, April 18, 2005, p. E6.

8. Tonya Garcia, "Intel-OLPL Split, A Cause for Concern?" *PRWeek*, January 14, 2008, p. 8.

9. As quoted in article by Ana Vargas, "Doing PR for Fun and Nonprofit," *PRWeek*, August 21, 2000, p. 17.

10. The Urban Institute, National Center for Charitable Statistics, Business Master File, January 2006.

11. Fortune 500 annual ranking of America's largest companies, *Fortune* magazine, http://money.cnn.com/magazines/fortune/April 30, 2007.

12. The Urban Institute.

13. Salary.com, "Salary Wizard: Know Your Worth," http://swz.salary.com, March 2008.

14. Aarti Shah, Salary Survey 2008, *PRWeek*, February 28, 2008, p. 24.

15. Shah, Salary Survey 2008, p. 24.

16. Carol J. DeVita, "Viewing Nonprofits Across the States," Charting Civil Society: A Series by the Center on Nonprofits and Philanthropy, Urban Institute (August 1997), no. 1.

17. Russell Gold, "Rising Welfare Rolls Prompt States to Make Cuts to Job-Aid Programs," *The Wall Street Journal*, www.interactive.wsj.com, January 16, 2002.

18. As quoted in article by David Ward, "When It Comes to Social Injustice, Drama Sells," *PRWeek*, June 11, 2001, p. 12.

19. Craig McGuire, "Reality Edges Ads for CDPHE," *PRWeek*, January 28, 2008, p. 15.

20. Web site for National Council of Nonprofit Associations, www.ncna.org, September 24, 2005.

21. Thom Weidlich, "MPA Gets USPS to Deliver Lower Rate," *PRWeek*, December 4, 2000, p. 38.

22. Web site for D.A.R.E., www.dare.com, September 24, 2005.

23. Rick Senften, "Mustard Seeds: The 'Irresponsible' Should Get the Blame," *The Repository*, www.cantonrep.com, August 21, 2005.

24. Kristen Go, "No Drugs, Vitamins," *The Arizona Republic*, December 12, 2001.

25. Elia Powers and Elizabeth Redden, "6 Killed in Northern Illinois Shooting," www.insidehighered.com, February 15, 2008.

26. Marc Longpre, "OHSU's Newman Clears Up Coverage of Sheep Study," *PRWeek*, May 14, 2007, p. 10.

27. Alan Finder, "Cornell's Worried Image Makers Wrap Themselves in Ivy," www.nytimes.com, *The New York Times*, April 2, 2006.

28. "Conditions for Homeless Tsunami Survivors Unacceptable: UN," *The China Post*, www.chinapost.com, September 23, 2005.

29. Jacqueline L. Salmon and Michelle Boorstein, "Catholic College Leaders Expect Pope to Deliver Stern Message," washpost.com, March 14, 2008, p. A01.

30. David Rovella, "Irish Tourist Board Springs into Action," *PRWeek*, July 23, 2001, p. 19.

31. Larry Dobrow, "History Revisited for Future's Sake," *PRWeek*, October 15, 2001, p. 19.

32. Douglas Quenqua, "When Activists Attack," *PRWeek*, June 11, 2001, p. 15.

33. Sherri Deatherage Green, "MADD's Efforts Continue to Drive into New Territory," *PRWeek*, January 21, 2002, p. 8.

34. Eric Arnold, "Volvo Races to Aid the Environment," *PRWeek*, January 21, 2002, p. 19.

35. "Number of Charities Grows 74% in Just Over Decade," Independent Sector, www.independentsector.org, July 18, 2001.

36. Web site for Habitat for Humanity International, www.habitat.org, accessed January 5, 2002.

37. Web site for the Cystic Fibrosis Foundation, www.cff.org, accessed January 5, 2002.

38. As quoted by Gina Bernacci, "Nonprofits Weathering Economic Storm, Recession," *NonProfit Times*, www.nptimes.com, December 15, 2001.

39. David Cay Johnston, "United Way Is Reporting a 3.8% Increase in Donations," *The New York Times*, August 8, 2001, p. C2.

40. Michelle Brooks, "United Way's $10,000 Grant Puts Food Back on Bare Shelves at Food Bank," *Jefferson City News Tribune*, www.newstribune.com, September 23, 2005.

41. Stan Hutton, "Volunteers: The Heart of Nonprofit Work, Typical Board Positions," www.nonprofit.about.com, April 19, 2001.

42. Stan Hutton, "Volunteers: The Heart of Nonprofit Work, Part 1: How Many Americans Volunteer Each Year?" *NonProfit Times*, www.nonprofit.about.com, April 19, 2001.

43. "The Nonprofit Almanac IN BRIEF."

44. Ketchum Public Relations; and Yusuf Davis, "1,100 TBS Volunteers Tackle Tasks; Employees, Families, Pals Devote Saturday to Projects Citywide; Turner: Volunteers Span the City," *Atlanta Journal and Constitution,* September 14, 2000, p. 1JD.

45. Associated Press, "Troubled Smithsonian Institution Picks Ga. Tech President Clough as Its New Leader," *Jefferson City News Tribune,* March 16, 2008, p. A9.

46. Gilbert M. Gaul and Mary Pat Flaherty, "Red Cross Kept Asking for More; 5% of Blood Given After Attacks Was Discarded; Donor Backlash Feared," *Washington Post,* December 16, 2001, p. A34.

47. Julia Hood, "Accountancy Body Hopes to Rebuild Post-Enron Confidence with PR," *PRWeek,* January 21, 2002, p. 1.

48. Jaye Scholl, "In the Boardroom: No Fistfights, So Far: An Unconventional Board of Trustees Produces Surprising Results at Idyllwild Arts Academy," *The Wall Street Journal,* www.interactive.wsj.com, December 14, 2001.

49. Dougles Quenqua, "NAB Seeks PR Firm to Educate Everyone about Switch to DTV," *PRWeek,* July 23, 2001, p. 2.

50. CRPF news release, "Quality of Life Programs Expands to Offer International Assistance," www.apacure.org, January 16, 2002.

51. Ana Vargas, "Doing PR for Fun and Nonprofit," *PRWeek,* August 21, 2000, p. 17.

52. Ibid.

53. Associated Press, "Scholars, Activists Want Top Administrator Fired for Commercialism of Smithsonian Institution," *Jefferson City News Tribune,* January 17, 2002, p. 10.

54. Telephone conversation with Dan Barber, partner and senior vice president, Fleishman-Hillard, Kansas City, January 11, 2002.

55. Douglas Quenqua, "HHS Makes Strides Toward Consolidated Messaging," *PRWeek,* January 21, 2002, p. 1.

56. Carol Hymowitz, "In Sarbanes-Oxley Era, Running a Nonprofit Is Only Getting Harder," *The Wall Street Journal,* June 21, 2005, p. B1.

57. Fleishman-Hillard public relations agency.

58. Institute for Public Relations.

Corporate Public Relations

OUTLINE

PREVIEW

Today's corporate environment is complex. Companies that succeed are proactive, have well-defined communication strategies linked to business objectives, and practice open, honest communication. One college intern's experience provides a snapshot of corporate public relations.

Warren distributed the handouts to the corporation's top public relations, marketing, and advertising directors who had assembled for their weekly Tuesday afternoon meeting. As a summer intern in the corporate communications office at this Fortune 500 company, he often assisted his boss during these sessions. The meetings were turning out to be tremendous learning opportunities, as Warren could eavesdrop on the strategic thinking and planning that went behind major branding efforts. He saw firsthand how research drove message development. Warren heard spirited discussions about the pros and cons of developing a tag line that could work for all of the disciplines. His public relations campaign team had had similar discussions while working on their project last semester. He found the comparison unsettling, though, as students often went with the first idea that everyone liked. That approach would never have worked here.

Warren's thoughts were interrupted when the account representatives from the public relations agency entered the room. It was almost as if the agency folks worked for the corporation, as they knew the brands, the people, the numbers—well, really knew about everything. The group worked together effectively. His boss valued the agency's strategic insights and how their talents complemented those of the corporate staff. Warren was not sure which direction—corporate or agency—he would like to go when he graduated next year, as he had had good experiences with both.

The meeting lasted for three hours. When Warren got back to his cubicle, he wrote a detailed summary of the meeting, from the research briefing, items discussed, and new assignments to assigning responsibilities, timetables, and budget issues. At first he was amazed at how much was accomplished at these meetings, but he soon grew to appreciate the thorough preparation on the part of the team. Still, overall progress often seemed to inch along as additional research and information needs, time needed to make changes, the approval process, and other such factors slowed things down.

Warren did a final spelling and grammar check on the 10-page summary, attached it in an e-mail, and sent it to the corporate and agency team members. The document would be waiting for them when they got to their offices in the morning, although he knew that most would review it tonight. Warren would have e-mails waiting in his in-box noting the changes that the various team members would like to have incorporated. He followed up on a few messages from earlier in the day before putting his computer to sleep and leaving for the day. Tomorrow Warren would update the summary and finish his work on the stories he was writing for the employee newsletter. There was always plenty to do.

OVERVIEW OF CORPORATE PUBLIC RELATIONS

Business has had to adapt to increasingly complex and dynamic environments such as new product introductions, mergers and acquisitions, layoffs, lawsuits, and new technology. Business leaders must manage relations with a variety of publics and balance their responses to many conflicting demands of these diverse publics.

Public relations helps corporations deal with this complex environment, and it's important that these efforts support the organization's overall business mission and objectives. This is done in a number of ways, including helping corporations anticipate and adapt to societal demands and trends; positively impacting a company's image and reputation, resulting in a better operating environment; and smoothing and enhancing a company's operations, which can lead to an increase in sales.

A Corporation's Audiences

The groups and individuals that corporations communicate with vary from industry to industry. High-technology companies, for example, focus on different media, anticipate different crises, and deal with issues different from those of an organization whose business is health care. While the terms *audiences, publics,* and *markets* are sometimes used interchangeably to identify those to be reached in a campaign, distinctions should be made among these words. **Target audiences** is a term used when the goal is to reach people with media. When the goal is to talk about communal issues, the term **target publics** is used. When communication is supporting the marketing function and is geared toward those who make buying and selling decisions, the term **target markets** is used.

For example, the following organizations debated the safety of mercury levels in seafood, trying to determine what fish was safe to eat and in what quantity.[1]

- Major media, one of which was *The New York Times,* which commissioned two sushi tests[2]
- Governmental agencies such as the Environmental Protection Agency, National Marine Fisheries Service, and the Food and Drug Administration
- The National Fisheries Institute, a trade association for the seafood industry
- Environmental advocacy groups such as Oceana
- Health-related associations such as the American Heart Association
- Those who make their living by fishing
- Scientists
- Health care workers
- Restaurants
- Supermarkets
- Consumers
- Agencies with seafood clients

The Role of the CEO in Corporate Public Relations

The value of a good chief executive officer (CEO) is not to be underestimated, and consumers have high expectations. A study by Ketchum found that consumer trust in corporations and CEOs is at an all-time low. In three areas—environment, ethics, and employees—the public noted a gap between actual and perceived corporate behavior. CEOs can enhance credibility by being transparent, engaging in proactive communications, and supporting corporate social responsibility initiatives.[3]

Respondents to a Burson-Marsteller national study said that the CEO's reputation influences decisions to invest in a company (95 percent), believe a company is under pressure from the media (94 percent), recommend a company as a good alliance/merger partner (93 percent), and maintain confidence in a company when its share price is lagging (92 percent). Moreover, business influentials are more likely to recommend a company as a good place to work (88 percent) if the CEO is favorably regarded.[4]

Scandals have eroded the confidence that the public once had in business and its leaders. In these cases, actions spoke louder than words. Mattel Inc., famous for producing Barbie and Hot Wheels toys, recalled more than 21 million Chinese-made products because of potential dangers to young children. In explaining the company's new three-point check plan to test paint and other manufacturing elements, CEO Bob Eckert said, "Trust is a powerful part of our world; I believe trust is a highly relevant factor to business today."[5]

Thousands of Enron employees lost their life savings in 401(k) plans because the top executives engaged in fraud, conspiracy, and other accounting irregularities, causing the largest bankruptcy in U.S. history. Other companies once held in high esteem—WorldCom, Xerox, KPMG, Arthur Andersen, Halliburton—are among those accused and convicted in shocking front-page headlines of deceit and abuse of office on the part of their executives. To help prevent fraudulent accounting scandals in the future, Congress passed the Sarbanes-Oxley Act in 2002. The act requires corporations to hire separate auditors for parts of businesses that may be in competition with each other.

With time, most people will not be able to associate the name of the wayward executive with the company. But when the company and the CEO are the same, a scandal can make the company more vulnerable to collapse. Volumes could be written about Martha

Stewart, her trial, and subsequent prison sentence for lying during an insider trading investigation and the future of her company. Public opinions are divided as to whether she was a hero, a victim, or a scapegoat. The key, though, is to find a way in which the company benefits from an appealing public personality while building a strong identity that doesn't rely on the individual. Donald Trump, Michael Dell, Mary Kay Ash, Michael Bloomberg, and Calvin Klein are others who have had to determine the best strategies for associating themselves with their companies.[6]

One result of illegal corporate disclosures is that ethical and law-abiding CEOs may have increased visibility. Unfortunately, they may not be prepared to deal with the increased public relations responsibilities because their education did not prepare them for this role. About 60 percent of Fortune 700 CEOs have worked in one of four functions at some point in their career: finance, 22 percent; operations, 14 percent; marketing, 12 percent; and sales, 11 percent.[7] Thus, they may not have much familiarity with communications as a strategic tool and may not understand how it adds value to everyday operations. The organization's top leader must believe in the value of communication and make this function a priority by spending substantial portions of his or her energies and efforts on public relations–related matters.

In a *Wall Street Journal* article, Michael Sands, president of orbitz.com, says he wishes there had been a course on corporate reputation and communication strategy. "I would argue that public relations and word-of-mouth messages are more important than ever," he states. The same article goes on to note that "it is indeed the rare business school that provides master of business administration graduates with a thorough grounding in corporate communications."[8]

Nor is communication training emphasized in some executive leadership development programs. Curriculum topics in these courses often focus on finance, operations, marketing, and negotiations, to the exclusion of public relations. This means that the corporate communication department is often the primary driver of reputation management.

Strong communication leadership is especially important when the company needs to take a position. Media writer Jon Friedman, a columnist for MarketWatch, advises public relations managers to "make your CEO available for as much as possible, on the record, for as long as you need to make people understand your position."[9]

The benefit of having a CEO who values communication and relationships has a trickle-down effect throughout the organization. Employees have the information they need to make better decisions. Better decisions lead to a higher performing organization, which in turn helps attract the best and brightest employees who have the skills and motivation to be successful in a competitive marketplace. Informed people outperform uninformed people, when all else is equal.

Finally, those interviewing for corporate public relations positions are advised to check out how the organization values this function before taking the position. If the senior communicator reports to the highest level in the organization, it is a strong indicator that public relations is considered a vital, strategic function. The public relations aspect of everything that the company does, from its reputation, image, and management of issues to selling products and communicating with its employees, will benefit from this viewpoint.

Public Relations Specialties

The demands placed on large corporations are great and diverse. Business organizations must fulfill a long list of responsibilities and still compete effectively in domestic and international markets.

Mark Davis hoists his first-place trophy after winning the professional division at a Bassmaster tournament in Missouri. Corporations such as Citgo often sponsor sporting events to promote their image or products.

The job of public relations in large corporations is ultimately to ensure that corporate power is maintained by responsible use and to help develop cooperative relationships between corporations and other societal institutions. To promote these goals successfully, public relations practitioners rely on a variety of specialties. We discuss these specialties as they relate to specific publics in part III, "The Publics."

- *Media relations* is used to gain support and sympathy from print and broadcast outlets, to generate positive publicity, and to tell its side of the story.
- *Employee relations* contributes to harmonious labor relations and helps attract and retain good employees. Effective employee communication can also stimulate worker creativity and input, boost attitudes and morale, improve product quality and customer service, and enhance productivity.
- *Community relations* supports sales, attracts employees, improves the quality of public services, provides support for business initiatives, and improves the quality of life for employees and executives.
- *Consumer relations* builds positive relations with customers, responds effectively to consumer complaints and problems, and supports sales and marketing efforts.
- *Financial relations* provides sound financial communication, allowing business to attract capital at the lowest possible cost. Other financial relations goals include ensuring that public firms' stock is appropriately valued, building knowledge and confidence in fund sources, and responding to investor questions or needs.
- *Marketing communications* focuses on activities that support the selling of products and services. Typically a variety of tactics is used, including advertising, public relations, sponsorships, the Internet, and special events.
- *Public affairs* deals with a business's interaction with government on various levels. Government relations have a direct impact on a business's flexibility and

manageability. Regulation, taxation, labor law, and international trade policies are only a few ways in which governmental actions constrain business decision making and success.

In short, **corporate public relations** is a means by which businesses seek to improve their ability to do business. Effective corporate public relations smooths and enhances a company's operations as well as increases its sales. It enables a business to better anticipate and adapt to societal demands and trends. It is the means by which businesses improve their operating environments.

Public Relations Activities

Corporate public relations deals with a variety of activities, issues, and events. The Generally Accepted Practices Study[10] identifies the following as the key responsibilities of the practitioners surveyed:

- Corporate communications (not advertising)—85 percent
- Crisis management—73 percent
- Internal communications—73 percent
- Marketing public relations—73 percent
- Executive communications—69 percent
- Product public relations—62 percent
- Online communications—61 percent
- Community relations—61 percent

Activities that tend to be addressed by fewer than half of those surveyed include issues management, advertising for the corporation and its products and issues, public and consumer affairs, philanthropy, government and investor relations, and ombudsman.

Here is a brief glance at the activities and issues a corporate public relations department might be asked to deal with at any time:

- To establish the hotel chain as a major player in the wedding-planning market, Marriott International created a wedding certification program for its staff.[11]
- With a goal of being the national leader in retail mortgage originations, Bank of America launched its No Fee Mortgage Plus program with traveling block party events, home shows, family-oriented events, and NASCAR race sponsorships.[12]
- Because the western division of Comerica Bank is establishing a stronger West Coast presence, new relationships are being forged with the media while simultaneously introducing the brand to the region.[13]
- Atkins Nutritionals selected a new **agency of record.** The firm will utilize nontraditional approaches, including viral marketing, product placement, and interactive gaming.[14]
- *Newsweek* wants to be known as the magazine that drives the nation's conversation. Its editorial content is promoted to reporters in an attempt to keep the title top-of-mind with the media.[15] Similarly, HBO uses **blogs,** in-theater advertising, mobile devices, billboards, and print promotion to keep the cable network top-of-mind in the pop-culture buzz.[16]

Corporations whose reputations have been damaged due to corporate crises have changed their names. ValuJet became AirTran, Philip Morris Cos. adopted the Altria Group Inc. name. Andersen Consulting transformed itself into Accenture. Communicators oversee the name transition of every aspect of the corporation's being from advertising and signage to letterhead, Web site, and promotional materials.[17]

This is but a mere snapshot of the world of corporate public relations. Businesses deal with and adapt to increasingly complex and dynamic situations, issues, and environments. They manage relations with a variety of publics and balance numerous complicated and pressing issues, including business ethics, equal opportunity, the quality of work life, consumerism, environmentalism, global commerce, and others.

The Role of the Corporate Communicator

While the scope of responsibilities will be tailored to fit the structure of each organization, senior communicators generally oversee, manage, and direct programs and activities that address the organization's reputation and image. A well-rounded team of knowledgeable and skilled communicators is critical for success.

Most corporations (85 percent) will utilize outside counsel for strategic purposes.[18] Says Marci Maule, public relations director for Coinstar, on why they selected their agency, "Certainly strategic business thinkers—an agency that really could get in and understand our business."[19] Beyond strategy, external agencies can balance staff strengths and weaknesses, provide an objective point of view, control costs, and assist with evaluation.

The responsibility of managing the expertise and talent of others on the corporate staff and the agency falls on the top communicator. The first step is to find an agency that meets the corporation's needs. An international company might need a worldwide agency with an extensive network to meet its needs. A regional organization might best utilize the talents of a boutique firm. There is also that intangible quality called *chemistry*. An executive at Kraft calls this "provocateurship," the ability of each side to bring out the best in the relationship.[20] A group that clicks will be more efficient and productive.

The senior communicator will also be working in concert with other organizational functions, such as marketing, human resources, and legal affairs. For example, marketing communications will help support the sales of the company's products and services. Ruder Finn Marketing Practice in New York helped Keurig launch its new single-cup coffee-brewing product by partnering with a bridal magazine, media relations, and taste-testing research.[21] The public relations team might manage the corporation's intranet, an internal electronic network that provides a way for employees to communicate with each other, as well as produce a newsletter and plan employee events.

The Role of Public Relations in Multinational Corporations

In the last decade, U.S. companies have expanded rapidly into global markets. International trade, though, is much more complicated than trade within the United States because different laws and cultural norms often cause considerable confusion. Conditions of competition are often quite different as well. Many barriers not found in American markets are found in international business.

Fortune magazine categorizes corporations into almost 50 industries, from the cutting-edge businesses of telecommunications, computer technology, and pharmaceuticals to the mature sectors of steel, chemicals, and autos. In figure 16.1, you will note that half of the corporations in the top 10 of the 2007 Fortune Global 500 are American. The others are from Britain, the Netherlands, Germany, Japan, and France. Three industry groups are represented: general merchandising, petroleum refining, and motor vehicles and parts. The 2007 Fortune 500 top 10 U.S. corporations, also shown in figure 16.1, make up a slightly more diversified group, representing five different

2007 Largest Global Corporations	2007 America's Largest Corporations
1. Wal-Mart Stores (U.S.) *General merchandising*	1. Wal-Mart Stores *General merchandising*
2. Exxon Mobil (U.S.) *Petroleum refining*	2. Exxon Mobil *Petroleum refining*
3. Royal Dutch Shell (the Netherlands) *Petroleum refining*	3. General Motors *Motor vehicles and parts*
4. BP (Britain) *Petroleum refining*	4. Chevron *Petroleum refining*
5. General Motors (U.S.) *Motor vehicles and parts*	5. ConocoPhillips (U.S.) *Petroleum refining*
6. Toyota Motor (Japan) *Motor vehicles and parts*	6. General Electric *Diversified financials*
7. Chevron (U.S.) *Petroleum refining*	7. Ford Motor *Motor vehicles and parts*
8. DaimlerChrysler (Germany) *Motor vehicles and parts*	8. Citigroup *Diversified financials*
9. ConocoPhillips (U.S.) *Petroleum refining*	9. Bank of America *Diversified financials*
10. Total (France) *Petroleum refining*	10. American International *Insurance: P & C*

FIGURE 16.1   Top 10 Global and U.S. Corporations *Source: Fortune* magazine, April 30 and July 23, 2007.

industries: general merchandising, petroleum refining, motor vehicles and parts, diversified financials, and insurance.[22]

The challenge of global public relations is to eliminate as many of the barriers to effective communication as possible. Thus, that communication must be able to transcend cultural as well as geographic barriers. Three major barriers that often confront business and public relations are differences in language, law, and culture. Other barriers in many countries include extremely bureaucratic governments, multiplicity of languages, and an underdeveloped mass media.

Public relations for multinational corporations is a complex area of practice requiring all the skills discussed elsewhere in this book plus extraordinary cross-cultural sensitivities.

The public relations function in multinational corporations has three distinct aspects. In one role, public relations practitioners represent multinational corporations at home, dealing with public opinion and governmental activities that relate both to specific corporations and to multinational enterprise as a whole. The second role of multinational public relations is to help bridge the communication gap that inevitably exists between foreign operations and top management in the world headquarters. Finally, public relations must be conducted in the various host countries of the corporation. See spotlight 16.1 for 10 best practices for global communication.

John M. Reed concludes that public relations in the host country "has to have three legs upon which it is built: cultural savvy; language savvy; a savvy use of the tools of the craft. Forget one leg and the edifice topples. Use them in balance and success is assured."[23]

Corporations often use public relations agencies to handle the long list of communication responsibilities necessary to compete effectively in domestic and international markets. Strategically placed global agency offices ensure that the corporation has access to experts knowledgeable with the culture, language, government, media, and other important aspects of the country they're trying to operate in. Two major advantages that outside firms bring to a corporation are their unbiased perspective and their depth of experience in dealing with organizational issues.

Dynamic forces reshaping business are redefining corporate communications on a global scale. Driven by innovations in technology and telecommunications, these forces are expanding the quantity, quality, and speed of communication worldwide. As communicators face a world that is greatly influenced by technology, we begin to look at developing new strategies, skills, and tools. Ten of the best practices for global communication are identified below.

1. Communications efforts match the overall business plan.
2. Strategy is integrated with the approach most appropriate for each particular country.
3. The communications plans of best practices companies integrate marketing, media, advertising, government relations, community relations, events, trade relations, customer relations, and overall measurement programs.
4. Best practices companies recognize the sensitive nature of communications with a fine balance between an overall global strategy communicated from corporate headquarters and a local adaptation that is sensitive to the local culture.
5. Public relations practitioners are business savvy and understand that their work must contribute to the firm's bottom line.
6. There is a sharp focus on the customer—business, consumer, partners, and other alliances are linked with communications counsel.
7. Measurement is a strong component of brand communications.
8. A team-based staff is critical to a global mix. Staffing balances an in-country team with the host of those corporate staff elsewhere.
9. Internal communications efforts are innovative because they must bridge a variety of languages, culture, and business practices.
10. Investor relations are recognized as a global communications priority.

The corporate public relations staff manages agencies and other outside consultants. Many times this is by function, such as media relations, employee relations, or government relations.

The Role of Public Relations in Smaller Corporations

The challenge to most small business owners and managers is finding time to devote to public relations. They not only must satisfy their customers, hire dependable employees, and pay their bills, but they must also be a good community citizen, work with suppliers, and find ways to grow the company. Because they are responsible for all aspects of the business, small business owners and managers must focus first on the core business, the part that brings in the profits. Customers and sales come before public relations. This less-than-systematic approach means small businesses may not realize the consistent benefits that a planned public relations program could deliver.

Most small businesses have lean public relations staffs. This demands that its practitioners be generalists. For example, the corporate communicator might perform senior-level tasks like developing a strategic plan for a new plant opening and supervising employees and outside consultants, as well as overseeing junior-level tasks such as the employee newsletter and pitching story ideas to reporters. A practice analysis conducted by the Public Relations Society of America (PRSA) Universal Accreditation Board and Gary Siegel Organization found that corporate communicators spent most of their time on strategic planning, supervision, and doing the work.[24]

Skills Necessary for Success in Corporate Public Relations

To be successful in corporate public relations, a practitioner must have a broad range of skills and abilities and be able to apply them as the situation demands. Those new to public relations, such as recent college graduates, often start as **technicians.** Technicians develop and polish their writing, research, and other foundational public relations skills by finding information about the company's industry, writing press releases, coordinating production schedules, developing marketing communications materials, and assisting with special events. Technicians also begin to understand how senior practitioners diagnose communication problems and develop strategic plans.

As technicians assume greater managerial responsibilities, other qualities assume higher importance. Gerald C. Meyers, former American Motors chairman and chief executive officer, identifies five key attributes for senior corporate public relations professionals. First, this person must keep the boss informed and offer advice on appropriate actions. Being at the top of the organizational pyramid often isolates CEOs from others, notes one in that position. "It is very lonely being CEO because everyone you come in daily contact with is working for you," said Frank Newman, former chairman, president, and CEO of Eckerd, JCPenney's drugstore chain.[25]

Other critical qualities Meyers identifies for public relations professionals include being a sounding board to the CEO, providing early warning about potential problems, rethinking the value of conventional wisdom, and being objective and dependable.[26] These points are reinforced by John C. Knapp, president of Knapp Inc.: "PR serves clients best when it raises uncomfortable questions, introduces competing points of view and offers an unbiased interpretation of actions and implications."[27]

Corporate Public Relations Budgets

The corporate communication budget is usually a mere fraction of what the company may spend on advertising. Still, a number of factors affect the cost of communication, causing corporate communication budgets to increase an average of 3 percent in 2004 versus 2003.[28] These include staffing new offices, penetrating new markets, increased competition, investing in technology, and dealing with inefficiencies in reporting structures.

Unlike consumer companies, business-to-business companies often combine their marketing efforts with public relations. A placement in the industry's premier trade publication, for example, can raise the image of the company as well as generate sales.

Tactics Used by Corporate Public Relations

Corporate public relations departments work with public relations agencies to develop comprehensive communication plans. Freelancers often supplement the corporate staff to execute the tactical aspects of the plan. Dallas-based Spaeth Communications recommends that communicators evaluate both the controlled and uncontrolled routes of communication when determining appropriate tactics. Notes Merrie Spaeth, president, "The first step in leveraging communication is to understand how a target constituency can receive conflicting messages."[29] Controlled routes are those that the corporation has editorial discretion over, such as its annual report, newsletters, advertising, Internet site, and marketing communication materials. The uncontrolled route, that which the practitioner is not able to control, represents the most powerful and credible vehicles for communicating—that is, the media and groups that influence the intended audiences.

Thus, communicators should consider **cross-disciplinary integration** and **tool integration** when determining the appropriate mix of controlled and uncontrolled tactics for the company's key audiences. Cross-disciplinary integration allows all messages communicated through advertising, media channels, or any other method to be consistent and constant. A communicator might use, for example, the disciplines of advertising and marketing communications in addition to public relations. Tool integration means that the communicator will use whatever means is available and appropriate to send a message to external and internal audiences. News releases, advertisements, e-mail, posters on bulletin boards, in-person meetings, newsletters, brochures, the Internet, and the

Former WorldCom Chief Financial Officer Scott Sullivan (center) is escorted to a court appearance. He was sentenced to five years in prison for his role in the WorldCom accounting scandal.

company's intranet are all possibilities. See figure 12.1 in chapter 12, "Consumer Relations and Marketing," for a larger list of tactics.

A first-ever study about corporate funding of publications found that the average amount that companies of all sizes spend annually on corporate publications is close to $800,000. Approximately 81 percent of this figure, or $631,865, is tagged for print publications, with 19 percent, or $168,135, earmarked for electronic publications. The study also found that the average salary of a professional working on corporate publications is $51,500.[30]

CORPORATE CREDIBILITY AND REPUTATION

If business and private enterprise are to exert positive influence on public attitudes toward business, they must be perceived as honest and responsible.

Today's marketplace is one of intense pressure—to grow, to reward stockholders, to create new jobs, to be exciting—quarter after quarter, year after year. These expectations demand that established companies constantly develop new business models in order to survive. The result is that old notions of the value of a reputation, of a brand, and of dependability are challenged and often sacrificed for short-term gain. "The most important thing is to educate them (the public) not only on where the industry is going, but what your company's role will be," says Lynn Kettleson of Clarke & Company, a public relations agency.[31]

One timeless truth is reinforced in this unsettling business environment: A corporation's best tool in achieving its business objectives and in establishing and reinforcing credibility is an excellent reputation. See mini-case 16.1. Fleishman-Hillard, one of

Mini·Case 16.1 New Brand Vision for Greyhound Aims High with "Elevated" Campaign

By Erin Braxton
The Richards Group

Greyhound is a venerable American brand with a strong history and a rich, iconic identity like no other. For generations, passengers trusted the bus company to provide safe, affordable, and enjoyable transportation to more than 3,100 locations in the continental United States. Sales reached an all-time high in 2000, following seven years of consecutive growth.

In 2004, after three years of declining sales and customer base, Greyhound knew a change was in order. The company sought the help of The Richards Group, a 30-year-old Dallas-based agency dedicated to creating and building strong brands. Together, this partnership would work to improve Greyhound's standing with its current and potential passengers by improving brand perceptions and, ultimately, Greyhound's overall business.

Research

Greyhound conducted research to focus its brand revitalization efforts on specific problems. In broad terms, the study identified that overall passenger satisfaction and brand perceptions suffered because of the company's failure to refresh products, services, and image.

Specifically, Greyhound conducted a quantitative survey in six key markets: Chicago, Dallas, New York, Orlando, Phoenix, and Portland. The purpose of the survey was threefold:

- To learn about existing brand perceptions among riders and nonriders in the United States.
- To obtain a level of understanding surrounding the key drivers of these brand perceptions.
- To identify rider and potential rider segments for future targeted marketing and communication efforts.

The survey revealed several key findings about Greyhound:

- Among current riders and nonriders, an improvement of their overall Greyhound experience by providing a more enjoyable one would result in more positive brand perceptions.
- Among nonriders, improvements in "coolness" and a faster, more enjoyable experience would improve their overall brand perception.
- Greyhound identified six segments that defined its ridership base: pragmatic riders, student travelers, ethnic enthusiasts (Hispanic and African American riders), no-choice travelers, senior travelers, and rejecters. Their primary focus would be on pragmatics, students, and ethnic enthusiasts.

Planning

Once Greyhound pinpointed its key audience and recognized some of its consumers' key concerns, it developed a new brand vision: "Making enjoyable travel possible for everyone." The new focus would serve as a catalyst to upgrade the overall customer experience.

Implementation

Beginning as a test in three key markets for bus travel (Minneapolis, Milwaukee, and Chicago), the execution of Greyhound's new brand vision included

- Making changes that improved and enhanced existing terminals to create a more pleasant experience for its customers.
- Refurbishing buses both internally and externally.
- Training personnel to create a more positive customer service experience.
- Developing marketing and advertising to support all of the improvements and new customer experiences.

Greyhound made a departure from its previous advertising creative by taking a more lighthearted approach with the launch of its new "Elevated" campaign. The campaign touted the tag line, "We've elevated everything." Greyhound utilized well-known celebrity comedienne Wanda Sykes in radio and television media to excite consumers about the new changes happening at Greyhound. Sykes used her sarcastic comedic style to poke fun at everyday-life situations, like high gas prices and current fashion trends. The cleverly written spots put a spin on these everyday observations and related them to the new, improved, hassle-free Greyhound. Newspaper print and outdoor advertising were also significant parts of the media plan.

During the launch of the new rollout campaign, Greyhound elevated one of its refurbished buses at its Chicago terminal to communicate its strong commitment to "making over" the business. The press coverage, from this public relations event, produced numerous broadcast and print stories and reached more than 40 million people.

Evaluation

While it is too soon to measure the effectiveness of Greyhound's "Elevated" campaign, the marketing team is optimistic that this effort will be an overall success by not only increasing customer ridership and brand perceptions but by also increasing those customers' likelihood to continue riding Greyhound after such a positive and enjoyable customer experience.

Questions

1. What questions do you think The Richards Group might have asked Greyhound when first approached about the campaign?
2. What were the advantages and disadvantages of using quantitative methodology for the survey?
3. The research identified six categories of bus riders. Develop a demographic and lifestyle profile for each.
4. Why would Greyhound focus its communication efforts on only three of its identified customer segments?
5. Identify other tactics the company might use to convey its new brand vision.
6. What are the pros and cons of using a celebrity comedienne as the spokesperson?

the world's top public relations agencies, notes that "all the goals a corporation can set—higher stock multiple, stronger ability to attract and retain good employees, better margins, more attractive partners for mergers or acquisitions, more customers—benefit from a strong, well-managed reputation."[32]

Public relations helps a corporation build a world-class reputation. The positive relationships with key publics and the resultant mutual understanding on policies and issues can enhance a corporation's stature within its community and industry. There is a correlation between a good reputation and a healthy bottom line. However, as Ivy Lee, the "father of public relations," pointed out in the early years of the development of the discipline, it is actions, not words, that count. Reputations are earned by following through, by being trustworthy, and by taking the right actions. Public relations helps counsel management to consider its publics in determining the correct course to take.

One study that illustrates this point is the *Fortune* magazine annual report, "The 2007 Global Most Admired Companies" (see figure 16.2). Business executives and analysts who study corporations rank companies according to nine multifaceted attributes:

- Innovation
- People management
- Use of corporate assets
- Community/environment
- Quality of management
- Financial soundness
- Long-term investment
- Quality of products and services
- Globalness

2007 Global Most Admired Companies

1. General Electric (U.S.) *Electronics*
2. Toyota Motor (Japan) *Motor vehicles*
3. Procter & Gamble (U.S.) *Household and personal products*
4. Johnson & Johnson (U.S.) *Pharmaceuticals*
5. Apple (U.S.) *Computers*
6. Berkshire Hathaway (U.S.) *Insurance: P & C*
7. FedEx (U.S.) *Delivery*
8. Microsoft (U.S.) *Computers*
9. BMW (Germany) *Motor vehicles*
10. PepsiCo (U.S.) *Consumer food products*

FIGURE 16.2 **World's Most Admired Companies**
Source: Fortune magazine, March 19, 2007.

The Challenge of Earning a Good Reputation

Confidence levels have been falling for most major American institutions since the early 1970s, as tracked by the Gallup Organization.[33] There are a variety of reasons for this. Big business can be seen as evading issues, disclaiming responsibility, exaggerating facts, or overpromising results. It's easy for the general public to think that corporations are only looking out for themselves, supporting persuasion research that says disinterested parties are perceived as more credible than interested ones.

It could be argued that big business's problems began in the early 1930s, when President Hoover and American business promised "prosperity is right around the corner." When the promises proved false, the American public invited Franklin Roosevelt and the New Deal to change the face of American business, government, and society. In the ensuing years, American business made promises it could not keep, accepted credit for accomplishments that were not really its own, pushed costs and problems into a future that has now arrived, oversold and underdelivered, and kept score with a crooked measuring stick. Whether such mistakes and misdemeanors are intentional, and whether business is the perpetrator or the victim of these circumstances, is not the point. What matters is that public and consumer expectations have been pumped up in thousands of small ways—through corporate statements, advertising, marketing techniques, and public relations—and that those expectations have not been fulfilled. Such is the power of promises perceived to be broken.

As Hill & Knowlton executive William A. Durbin has commented, "The single most critical problem facing us today is . . . lost credibility."[34]

Restoring Credibility

Credibility once lost is difficult to regain. Nevertheless, a number of policies, if implemented and practiced by businesses individually and collectively, can substantially contribute to the reestablishment of public trust.

Dr. Leslie Gaines-Ross, the chief reputation strategist for Weber-Shandwick, a global public relations firm, outlines 12 steps a company can take to recover its reputation and restore credibility:

1. **Take the heat-leader first.** A single corporate leader, almost always the CEO, must serve as the official spokesperson during troubled times. By acting promptly with one voice, transparently, and decisively, CEOs can stabilize an unstable situation and set the right tone that, in many cases, ultimately defines the crisis.

2. **Communicate tirelessly.** Communicating effectively and often during a crisis is essential. Rescuing reputation and taking the first steps on the path to long-term recovery require a greater level of communications than is typical in less stressful times.

3. **Don't underestimate your critics and competitors**. A company should not ignore or diminish what its critics and enemies have to say. Critics do not come and go but have a staying power that can last for years.

4. **Reset the company clock.** Instilling a sense of urgency often requires getting the senior team to focus more on what has to happen next and less on what went wrong in the first place.

5. **Analyze what went wrong *and* right.** By studying one's own mistakes and those of others, companies can avoid repeating and encountering even larger problems that may lie ahead.

6. **Measure, measure, and measure again.** To track progress once reputation loss has occurred, benchmarks are necessary. Companies and their leaders need real-time, hard evidence that the company is moving in the right direction.

7. **Right the culture.** Most chroniclers of corporate failure will readily admit that the company's culture is what failed the organization in the first place and that the only way to ensure recovery is by altering the corporate culture.

8. **Seize the shift.** Business models and practices often need changing. A surprising number of crises can be traced to shifts in the business climate that leaders did not see, ignored, or did not take seriously enough.

9. **Brave the media.** Companies now have numerous channels to get their messages heard without exclusively relying on the major media as they did in the past.

10. **Build a drumbeat of good news.** Recovering reputation typically does not come from one major event or announcment, but rather from a series of small incremental steps that slowly generate positive momentum.

11. **Commit to a marathon, not a sprint.** Reputation recovery is a long-term process that does not end after a quick burst of success.
12. **Minimize reputation risk.** As the recovery process turns the final corner and the company feels healthier, reputation risk should be faithfully monitored. Minimizing reputation risk now becomes everyone's responsibility.[35]

Consumer Relations

Consumer relations is an essential component of corporate communication. The quality of the average individual's daily experiences with a company's products, services, employees, and other aspects should be outstanding, but that isn't always the case. The role of public relations in this effort is to advise top management of appropriate responses to alienated consumers and to work with management to ensure the problems aren't repeated. Consumer relations is discussed in detail in chapter 12.

Promoting Public Understanding

If we want the public to understand profits or private enterprise, we must see to it that communicators present information in terms the public can understand. Statistics must illuminate, not exaggerate. Here again, public relations practitioners should heed the basic tenets of their creed: Consider the audience, carefully word the communication, and be consistent. We cannot achieve public economic understanding by blocking it with statistics, generalities, technical language, and the like. Frequently, such communication does more harm than good.

One example is a newspaper headline that reported a major company's "Profits Up 273 Percent." During the next few days, other corporations' second-quarter earnings were reported in similar terms: an automaker's profits were up 313 percent; three chemical companies' profits were up 109 percent, 430 percent, and 947 percent, respectively. Various sources reported that all industries enjoyed average profit increases ranging from 31 percent to 36 percent. People who have business experience understand these figures and can immediately put them in perspective. Indeed, such statistics are designed to impress knowledgeable stockholders and investors. But these astronomically high figures also reach the general public who interpret them as big, even "obscene," profits.

An insurance company offered another example of inflammatory rhetoric, reporting "operating earnings . . . almost four times greater than . . . a year earlier." Consumers who do not understand the statistics that follow this claim consider their higher insurance premiums and conclude that they are being ripped off. With the help of a calculator, however, one can see that the company's margins rose from 0.92 percent to 2.57 percent. An informed emotional response changes from hostility to sympathy. But the company cannot assume that the ordinary consumer will understand such figures. As Disraeli said, there are lies, damn lies, and statistics.

Other major issues facing corporate public relations in the early part of the 21st century include globalization of business operations, with resulting globalization of public relations; unprecedented technological change; increased emphasis on diversity issues; and intensified crises and disasters.

Technology and Corporate Public Relations

Emerging technologies are revolutionizing the way public relations people do business and communicate with their key publics. The Internet, chat rooms, intranet, Web sites, e-mails, blogs, and other computer-based tools as well as wireless technology provide numerous opportunities for disseminating information, giving and receiving feedback, purchasing goods and services, tapping into what consumers are thinking, providing access to corporate materials, updating consumers and employees, and more. Two of these channels are discussed in detail here.

Corporate Blogs   Corporate blogs are "the new Op-Ed page."[36] Short for Web logs, blogs are journals that allow authors to post thoughts, philosophies, and opinions to a Web site for public consumption. Companies such as GM, Boeing, and Microsoft have developed them as a means to nurture relationships with their stakeholders and as an inexpensive way to get customer feedback about the company. But disgruntled employees, activists, customers, and others also create blogs to voice their sentiments on topics that involve corporate activities. Two companies that measure and index blogs, Technocrati[37] and Blogpulse, each counted more than 15 million blogs as this text was written.

Yet, the number of corporate blogs is low. An eMarketer survey puts the estimate at 4 percent.[38] The 2005 *PRWeek*/Weber Shandwick Corporate Survey indicates that only 7.9 percent of the companies surveyed have a blog and that nearly half of these companies are in the tech sector. Of those who do sponsor a blog, two-thirds consider the most important audiences to be existing and potential customers. Approximately 75 percent of corporate communicators do not monitor the blogosphere at all (45.6 percent) or very little (32 percent). Roughly the same percentage do not have a strategy for responding to blog entries.[39]

Organic yogurt company Stonyfield Farm Inc. hired a chief blogger to produce two blogs: one about the company, called the Daily Scoop, and the other about healthy foods in schools, called Creating Healthy Kids. Job responsibilities include researching, linking to news, and providing personal insight. One of Microsoft's 1,500-plus bloggers helps recruit employees by sharing what it's like to work at the company, jobs she is trying to fill, and hiring trends. Salary estimates for corporate bloggers range from low to mid $40s to as high as $70,000. The higher salaries usually carry other communication responsibilities.[40]

Here are some guidelines to consider for corporate blogs:

- *Commit adequate resources to its development and maintenance.* A blog is a long-term investment. Once in place, "it's a big responsibility," says Richard Cline, chief executive officer of Voce Communications. "It's not like putting up a website. You are creating a transparent medium to customers."[41]

- *Monitor blogs to uncover new trends in your industry.* Tracking services such as Bacon's, PR Newswire, and others have software that can track search terms and keywords on blogs, discussion boards, and other **consumer-generated media.** "Such information allows companies to pick up on the important issues before competitors do," says Andrew Bernstein, CEO of Cymphony.[42]

- *Be open and honest.* "You can hear what the unofficial word is," says one tech-savvy blogger. "You can watch the buzz happen."[43] In this environment, there is no place to hide. Cover-ups, insincerity, a self-serving attitude, factual errors, and other discrepancies can be recognized quickly by users. A blog can be a powerful tool to develop a meaningful dialogue with stakeholders.[44]

- *Stay focused on your key publics.* "You need to know what is influencing your constituencies to behave in the manner you desire," says K. D. Paine.[45] Your key publics, not the blog, should drive your communications agenda.

- *Don't be afraid to respond to bloggers who post incorrect information.* Some travel companies have their employees monitor FlyerTalk.com, a travel Web site where travelers discuss their experiences. The corporate bloggers respond as authorized representatives to the commentary, clarifying incorrect information and reporting hot topics back to management.[46]
- *Don't treat blogs like a separate entity.* They are another media source.
- *Correlate blog coverage of your company to mainstream coverage.*

Corporate RSS Feeds   **Real Simple Syndication (RSS)** feeds can be a useful tool for the corporate public relations department. It allows editors and reporters, employees, consumers, and others to use the Web to access, display, and distribute news headlines, articles, listings, and information that a corporation provides. While the adoption rate is fairly low as of this writing, the use of RSS promises to grow in the years to come.

The problems that RSS feeds currently experience are typical of those encountered by newcomers to the technology environment. These include not being mainstream enough, users not having the right software to use and view, difficult to use by non-techies, and poor ability to find the feeds in the first place.

As these challenges are overcome, more corporations will use RSS to communicate with their external and internal publics. The benefits will include the following:

- Organized information (incoming information can be categorized).
- Online press room. Journalists can access your information 24/7.
- Customer information, especially product support information such as specifications, troubleshooting, and security updates.
- Specialized information for those who are interested in only certain brands or topics.
- Time-sensitive material such as early-bird specials, limited-time-only product discounts, and the like.
- Real-time buzz. An RSS feed can capture what is being said about a corporation as it happens.[47]

Corporate Social Responsibility

Corporate social responsibility (CSR) is not a random act of kindness. "In order to be truly meaningful, CSR has to be layered into everything, from labor relations to plant operations. It's not about doing good; it's about business."[48]

CSR is emerging as an important business tenet. Eight in 10 Americans say that corporate support of causes wins their trust in that company, a 21 percent increase since 1997.[49]

CSR has its roots in corporate philanthropy. Companies would sponsor a program or donate funds to a worthwhile effort. Today, the number of multinational corporations who define their CSR efforts in that manner is diminishing. From the global perspective, there are too many challenges and issues, including a borderless media network, how to structure communications teams around the world, political implications, integration of marketing disciplines, and corporate reputation concerns.[50] "The speed with which issues travel these days [requires] global coordination," says Rob Flaherty.[51]

Says Edelman's CSR director Chris Deri, "The fact is that we're having to do that not just to have a social license to operate, but also a legal license to operate."[52]

Smart corporations should heed the advice of a Cone executive: "It's clear from our research that the public wants to know through a variety of channels what a company is doing in the community—good and bad. Making a strong, focused commitment to one relevant social issue is a smart business strategy that will have resonance with a variety of stakeholders as it infuses emotion and trust into the brand."[53]

Diversity

Diversity, or inclusion as it is sometimes referred to, encompasses the mix of race, age, gender, sexual orientation, religious beliefs, national origin, and disability. J. Donald Turk, APR, a public relations manager for ExxonMobil Corporation, expresses his belief in the future: "There will be greater diversity of employees, customers, and constituencies." Turk has served as the chair of the Corporate Section of the PRSA and anticipates that the global economy will be a place where "diversity will be characteristic of the workforce and customer mix, as well as one in which diversity will be valued and even required to be a successful business."[54]

Diversity means different things in different countries. For example, almost one-fourth of Lucent Technologies's workforce is employed outside of the United States. Whereas Hispanic, African, and Native American issues receive much attention in the United States, most non-Dutch employees in the Lucent Netherlands office are from North Africa, the Middle East, or Europe. Local employment laws and practices create difficulties in transferring training programs from one country to another.[55] Because of Lucent's commitment to global diversity, the company developed a New Realities Diversity Campaign.

Global companies like Hilton Hotels Corporation (HHC) operate hotels around the world. The HHC diversity mission statement emphasizes the importance of "developing and maintaining a workplace culture which reflects awareness and sensitivity to individual abilities and appreciation of ethnic, gender, racial, religious, and cultural differences."[56]

Commitment to diversity affects how corporations do business. Bank of America, for example, commits 15 percent of its total procurement budget with businesses owned by minorities, women, and disabled individuals. The program, initiated in 1999, has already led to increases in revenue and cash flow and stronger market positions.

Business can perhaps borrow from former commerce secretary Ron Brown's seven tenets for planning to achieve diversity. At the U.S. Census Bureau the following guidelines are used to achieve a diverse workforce:

1. *Inclusion.* Valuing all employees regardless of race, gender, color, religious belief, national origin, age, disability, or sexual orientation.

2. *Opportunity.* Recruiting aggressively and developing career programs to ensure a diverse pool of qualified candidates for the job.

3. *Comprehensiveness.* Considering diversity in business affairs such as training, seminar procurement, grant processes, trade missions, regulatory matters, business liaisons, and every other program of the department.

4. *Accessibility.* Strengthening equal employment opportunity complaint procedures to ensure fair and timely processing of complaints.

5. *Training.* Encouraging participation of senior managers in training on diversity policies and conflict resolution techniques.

6. *Management.* Adding diversity efforts as a factor to job performance evaluations of management personnel.

7. *Evaluation and Communication.* Establishing a diversity council to monitor, evaluate, and facilitate programs to implement diversity.[57]

MasterCard Project Math

Summary

The current state of U.S. math achievement has serious implications for to-morrow's workforce, especially for technology-based companies such as MasterCard Worldwide. In St. Louis, home to the MasterCard global technology and operations headquarters, the company's communications team with its agency colleagues at Weber Shandwick examined local math achievement and decided to focus its local support of education on one cause—improving the teaching of math—that not only helps the community but is also good for business. The result was Project Math, a community program to maximize the visibility and impact of the company's local grants while helping advance regional math achievement and build workforce employability.

Case Study

Research

Research was critical to the success of the program, as MasterCard did not consider itself in a position to dictate a solution for advancing the teaching of math, but rather, to serve as the means to activate a solution defined by math education experts. The team conducted both primary and secondary research in order to ensure that the program was relevant, meaningful, and successful.

Secondary Research

The team researched the state of math achievement in Missouri and St. Louis and reached out to Missouri Governor Matt Blunt's Math, Engineering, Technology and Science (METS) initiative for data to illustrate the need for improvement.

The team also conducted an informal audit of other technology companies that support math and science education and discovered that its focus on the teaching of math was not shared by other local companies.

Primary Research

In undertaking Project Math, the planning team interviewed education leadership including university professors, K-12 administrators and teachers, not-for-profit organizations, and the Math Educators of Greater St. Louis, which confirmed the need for professional development and corporate support for local math teachers. The team conducted additional primary research in order to fulfill an important program strategy—sharing national and international expertise. In order to plan a relevant, actionable Math Education Summit, obtaining feedback from teachers, school administrators, and subject-matter experts was critical. As such, the team assembled a Project Math advisory group, consisting of community leaders, teachers, education organizations, district administrators, and thought leaders. The advisory group provided guidance that helped concentrate the event focus and contributed insights on invitees, speakers, topics, and event format.

Planning

Strategy

By streamlining its support of education in St. Louis into a strategic program that is aligned with its business, MasterCard helped maximize the impact of its grant money while positioning the company as a leader in actively addressing a pressing education issue and raising visibility for its community efforts.

Objectives

The goal of Project Math is straightforward: expand resources and development opportunities for math educators to advance the teaching of math in order to bolster student achievement. Excellence in teaching encourages student interest in math, improves math comprehension, and better prepares students to manage their finances, navigate everyday life, and qualify for career opportunities in today's environment of globalization. The communications objectives were as follows:

- Build community and employee support for Project Math
- Encourage local companies to focus on the teaching of math
- Raise local awareness of the MasterCard commitment to the issue of math achievement

Audience

- Math teachers, math coaches, curriculum coordinators, school administrators, and board members
- MasterCard employees
- Legislators, community and business leaders, including MasterCard customers and vendors

- Local media
- Students were not a focus of the campaign, as MasterCard takes care to refrain from promoting its brand to minors.

Execution

In late 2006, MasterCard announced Project Math, pledging $1 million over three years towards empowering St. Louis-area teachers to more effectively teach math. The team defined five strategies for the program as follows:

Share national and international expertise. The global presence of MasterCard uniquely positions the company to connect international expertise with local educators with the goal of sharing best practices. In 2007, MasterCard convened a Math Education Summit, assembling presenters from around the world to share expertise and help St. Louis mine local possibilities for advancing math achievement. (See implementation section below for a brief event description.)

Facilitate regional partnerships. Through partnerships with universities and math and science organizations, MasterCard supports coaching and professional development opportunities for local math teachers. In 2007, MasterCard awarded such grants to Washington University in St. Louis, University of Missouri-St. Louis and Saint Louis Science Center.

Assist local districts. MasterCard underwrites solutions to address pressing math needs of local school districts. In 2007, MasterCard awarded grants to add math teachers to the Teach For America St. Louis corps in urban schools and to provide teacher training and implementation of an innovative after-school math program at the school district in which the MasterCard facility is situated.

Share intellectual resources through employee volunteer opportunities. Whether volunteering to provide financial literacy lessons or guide students in a robotics competition, MasterCard employees have engaged in supporting the goals of Project Math by helping students connect academics to careers. In 2007, more than 265 MasterCard employees taught Junior Achievement classes and helped plan, staff, and judge FIRST (For Inspiration and Recognition of Science and Technology) Robotics competitions.

Donate technology. MasterCard distributes computers to local schools as equipment upgrades are completed at its technology headquarters in St. Louis. MasterCard has donated more than 1,100 computers since 2001, including 260 in 2007.

Summary of Tactics

Employee Announcement (December 15, 2006): MasterCard announced Project Math at an all-employee meeting, leveraging the company's 40th anniversary as an opportunity to celebrate its commitment to the community and make a deeper impact through focused dedication to a cause that not only is good for the community but also represents enlightened self-interest. Support included working closely with technology and communications leadership to plan and produce a global employee Webcast to introduce the program, identifying opportunities for volunteers to participate in the initiative, publishing an intranet feature article, including information for employees to help their own children, and managing post-event feedback in order to further develop the program.

Project Math Kick-Off Luncheon (December 15, 2006): MasterCard launched Project Math with a luncheon at its St. Louis technology headquarters. More than 80 local education, community, business, and legislative leaders attended the event, at which MasterCard executives announced the company's million-dollar commitment to the cause and hosted a panel discussion on the need for expanded support of local math achievement. The panel included the governor's education policy analyst, a professor of mathematics education and the superintendent of a local school district. The team engaged executive representation, built strategic relationships with diverse community stakeholders, selected grant recipients, prepared event speakers, planned event logistics, invited attendees, and conducted media outreach, as well as created a Project Math brochure, a short presentation, and a video as collateral to be used when sharing information about the program with external audiences.

Math Education Summit (October 24, 2007): To fulfill the first program strategy, the team planned a Math Education Summit to gather education, business and community leaders from the St. Louis region to network and learn from presentations by internationally recognized teachers and curriculum experts. The crux of the event involved sharing expertise from an expert from Singapore, the country that leads the world in math achievement. The event consisted of a keynote address from Dr. Lianghuo Fan, Singapore National Institute of Education, on the approach to math education in Singapore, as well as presentations from nationally recognized math teachers Jason Kamras, special assistant to the chancellor for teacher performance in the District of Columbia Public Schools and 2005 National Teacher of the Year, and Frank Corcoran, founding teacher of KIPP Academy in New York. Additional speakers and breakout sessions focused on successful math curriculum, math resources for students and teachers, business-education collaboration, and real-world applications of math. Support included engaging an advisory group to set the scope and agenda, researching subject matter experts, working with speakers, producing a video featuring several local experts, coordinating all logistics, managing post-event feedback, and assessing resulting opportunities.

Project Math Employee Family Event (October 27, 2007): MasterCard sponsored a day-long event for its employees and their children to engage in math-oriented activities at the Saint Louis Science Center. Included were math-focused workshops, puzzles, and games. More than 700 employees and family members participated. Approximately 20 employees volunteered their time to help plan the event agenda, coordinate logistics, manage registration, produce a highlights video, and administer surveys for participant feedback.

Evaluation

MasterCard continues to advance its commitment to investing in education globally. As a result of the first year of Project Math, the company is evaluating it as a model to consider for expanding citizenship efforts in additional locations.

The team measured the success of year one of Project Math by analyzing employee reactions, community developments, event attendance, and media coverage of the program. Evaluation of the success of individual grant recipients included short-term criteria defined by each beneficiary, and, in the long term, improvement in regional math scores. The team achieved each of its short-term communication objectives:

1. **Engage community and employee support for Project Math.** Careful strategy helped employees feel involved in the program from day one. As the company was stepping out of supporting several causes unrelated to math, the team prepared to address employee concerns, and yet, employees were extremely supportive. In fact, more than 265 employees participated in Project Math volunteer opportunities in 2007, and more than 700 employees and family members participated in the Project Math Family Day. Community response included endorsement from education and business leaders, development of business-education partnerships, and enthusiastic participation by teachers and students in selected projects. In addition, MasterCard Project Math received the Education Progress award from Partners for Progress, a regional organization of business associations and civic leaders.

2. **Encourage other companies to focus on the teaching of math.** Project Math events have served as an effective forum for dialogue to increase business–education collaboration, with strong representation from a range of industries as attendees and panelists. Business and civic leaders, as well as consortiums representing regional business leadership, have spoken highly of the leadership role that MasterCard has taken in highlighting the importance that math achievement has for business and community success. While Project Math received strong attendance by business and civic leaders at the kick-off event and at the Math Education Summit, MasterCard was also pleased with the readiness of business leaders from the Regional Business Council, Citi, Boeing, and AT&T/METS to serve as speakers at the Math Education Summit and on the Project Math advisory group. Additionally, since MasterCard has successfully created an effective forum for dialogue to increase business–education collaboration and brought awareness of this issue to other companies, MasterCard representatives were asked to join the planning committee of Missouri Governor Matt Blunt's Regional Business–Education Summit launching the METS St. Louis Network.

3. **Raise local awareness of the MasterCard commitment to the issue of math achievement.** Driving media coverage communicating the MasterCard commitment to the issue of math achievement was imperative. Coverage of the kick-off included articles in the *St. Louis Post-Dispatch, St. Louis Business Journal,* and *St. Charles Journal.* The team also secured coverage of the Math Education Summit in the Missouri Chamber of Commerce newsletter, *MissouriBusiness,* as well as on major regional talk radio stations, KTRS-AM and KMOX-AM, and two local television stations, KSDK-NBC and KTVI-FOX.

   Another important way to raise local awareness included driving attendance for the kick-off luncheon, employee family event, and math education summit. The team executed three well-attended Project Math events. More than 80 education, community, business, and legislative leaders attended the kick-off luncheon; the family event attracted more than 700 employees and family members; and the Math Education Summit brought together 84 teachers, school administrators, and community leaders.

Source: Weber Shandwick

Questions

1. How does Project Math support MasterCard's strategic goals?
2. Identify possible obstacles MasterCard might have faced in launching Project Math.
3. If you were to implement Project Math in your local community, what challenges would you face in selecting those to participate in the advisory groups?
4. Identify the Corporate Social Responsibility aspects of the Project Math project.

Summary

For self-testing and additional chapter resources, go to the Online Learning Center at **www.mhhe.com/lattimore3e.**

This chapter explores the aspects of public relations practice that apply to corporations. Effective public relations must begin with the CEO. The CEO who values communication has a trickle-down effect, enabling employees to make better decisions, which in turns helps to attract the best employees who apply their skills and talents in a competitive environment.

Effective corporate public relations has a positive impact on the bottom line. Customers want to do business with companies that have good reputations.

Global public relations, diversity, technological change, and crisis management are major issues facing corporate public relations practitioners. How they prepare to deal with these issues may well be the margin of success or failure in the next decade.

Key Terms

agency of record
blog
consumer-generated media (CGM)
corporate public relations
cross-disciplinary integration

Really Simple Syndication (RSS)
target audiences
target markets
target publics
technicians
tool integration

Notes

1. Ted McKenna, "Mercury Level Discussion Fires Up Seafood Sector Marketers," *PRWeek,* February 11, 2008, p. 9.

2. Marian Burros, "More Testing of Seafood to Address Mercury Concerns," *The New York Times,* www.nytimes.com, January 30, 2008.

3. John Weckenmann, "Op-ed: CEO Efforts Key to Consumer Trust," *PRWeek,* January 14, 2008, p. 10.

4. Peter Himler and Melanie Driscoll, "CEOs Have Only Five Quarters to Prove Themselves According to National Study of Business Influentials," Burson-Marsteller proprietary research, Building CEO Capital, www.CEOgo.com, 2001.

5. Jacquelyn Ryberg, "Mattel CEO Talks Trust, Meets Business Leaders," *The Badger* (Wisc.) *Herald,* http://badgerherald.com/, October 26, 2007.

6. "When the CEO Is the Brand, But Falls from Grace, What's Next?" Knowledge @ Wharton, http://knowledge.wharton.upenn.edu, April 7, 2004.

7. Tom Neff and Dayton Ogden, "Sixth Annual Route to the Top: Anatomy of a CEO," Chief Executive/Spencer Stuart, February 2001.

8. Ronald J. Alsop, "Communication Skills Are Critical to M.B.A.s," *The Wall Street Journal Online,* February 8, 2005.

9. "Journalist Q & A," *PRWeek,* June 6, 2005, p. 14.

10. Third Annual Public Relations Generally Accepted Practices Study, conducted by the USC Annenberg Strategic Public Relations Center and sponsored by the Council of Public Relations Firms, 2003, p. 7.

11. Alex Garinger, "Marriott Certifies Its Staff's Savvy at Wedding Planning," *PRWeek,* June 6, 2005.

12. Craig McGuire, "BoA Drives Big Rigs to Gain Hype," *PRWeek,* February 25, 2008, p. 27.

13. Anita Chabria, "Comerica's Padilla Takes Pride in His Passion for PR," *PRWeek,* August 1, 2005, p. 13.

14. John N. Frank, "Atkins Nutritionals Taps Magnet AOR as Comms Chief Ponders Exit," *PRWeek,* August 29, 2005, p. 1.

15. Erica Iacono, "Weine Positions *Newsweek* as Driver of US Discussion," *PRWeek,* January 10, 2005, p. 11.

16. Brian Steinberg, "Questions for . . . Courteney Monroe," *The Wall Street Journal Online,* www.wsj.com, September 7, 2005, p. B15B.

17. Ronald J. Alsop, "Reputation Renewal," *The Wall Street Journal Online,* www.wsj.com, March 30, 2004.

18. Third Annual Public Relations Generally Accepted Practices Study, p. 11.

19. Hamilton Nolan, "The Top of the List," *PRWeek,* August 1, 2005, p. 15.

20. Stuart Elliott, "Consumer Advice for Advertisers," *The New York Times Online,* www.nytimes.com, October 11, 2004.

21. Jen Adams, "Keurig Gives Media Taste of Its Coffee-Brewer Superiority," *PRWeek,* August 1, 2005, p. 19.

22. The 2007 Fortune 500, *Fortune Online,* www.fortune.com, April 30, 2007; and The 2007 Global 500, *Fortune Online,* www.fortune.com, July 23, 2007.

23. John M. Reed, "International Media Relations: Avoid Self-Binding," *Public Relations Quarterly* (Summer 1989), pp. 12–15.

24. Universal Accreditation Report, www.prsa.org, October 2000.

25. Joann S. Lublin, "Pros Give Advice to Managers Making the Leap to Top Spot," *The Wall Street Journal Online,* www.wsj.com, February 6, 2001.

26. Mike Davis, "Most Desirable PR Traits Told at PRSA," *PRWeek,* November 13, 2000, p. 7.

27. John C. Knapp, "Thinkpiece: Public Relations Will Never Be Considered a True Profession Unless Pros Give Objective Advice," *PRWeek,* June 26, 2000, p. 15.

28. Council of Public Relations Firms, PR on the Upswing After a "Bounce-Back" 2004, Says USC G.A.P. III Study, Los Angeles, May 23, 2005.

29. Merrie Spaeth, Spaeth Communications, Inc. www.spaethcommunications.com, March 6, 2001.

30. McMurry Publications Management survey report, www.pubmgmt.com, March 6, 2001.

31. Lynn Kettleson, as quoted by Craig McGuire, "Switching on to PR," *PRWeek,* October 16, 2000, p. 21.

32. Fleishman-Hillard Web site: www.fleishmanhillard.com, November 25, 2000.

33. The Gallup Organization, www.gallup.com.

34. Hill & Knowlton Executives, *Critical Issues,* p. 223.

35. Leslie Gaines-Ross, *Corporate Reputation: 12 Steps to Safeguarding and Recovering Reputation,* New Jersey: John Wiley & Sons, Inc., 2008. Used with permission.

36. Erica Iacono, "Keeping Both Eyes on the Blogosphere," *PRWeek,* June 20, 2005, p. 16.

37. Technocrati Web site, www.technocrati.com, September 5, 2005.

38. Sarah E. Needleman, "Blogging Becomes a Corporate Job; Digital 'Handshake'?" *The Wall Street Journal,* May 31, 2005, p. B1.

39. Hamilton Nolan, "Broadening Communications," *PRWeek,* June 27, 2005, pp. 16–22.

40. Needleman.

41. As quoted in Julia Hood's editorial, "If Your Only Goal Is Instant Gratification for the Company, Stay off the Blog Bandwagon," *PRWeek,* June 13, 2005, p. 6.

42. Iacono.

43. Vauhini Vara, "New Search Engines Help Users Find Blogs," *The Wall Street Journal,* September 7, 2005, p. D1

44. Julia Hood, "Citizens of the World," *PRWeek,* July 18, 2005, p. 14.

45. K. D. Paine, "It Just Doesn't Matter. Don't Bother Measuring Blogs." The Measurement Standard, www .themeasurementstandard.com, August 29, 2005.

46. Susan Stellin, "On Board the Message Board," *The New York Times Online,* www .nytimes.com, June 14, 2005.

47. Elizabeth Albrycht, "Ten Ideas for Corporate RSS Feeds," *Public Relations TACTICS,* June 2005, p. 15.

48. Hood.

49. Alison DaSilva, "The 2004 Cone Corporate Citizenship Study," Cone, www.coneinc.com, December 8, 2004.

50. Hood.

51. As quoted by Hood, "Citizens of the World," p. 16.

52. Ibid., p. 14.

53. DaSilva.

54. J. Donald Turk, quoted in Susan Bovet, "Forecast 2001," *Public Relations Journal,* October 1995, p. 13.

55. Jan Neuteboom, "Reliving Diversity in a Multi-Local Company," *Profiles in Diversity Journal,* February 2001.

56. Dorothy Hayden-Watkins, "Diversity— The Right Thing," *Profiles in Diversity Journal,* February 2001.

57. Carol Shaw, "Achieving Diversity After Work Force Downsizing," *Government Communications,* November 1995, p. 18.

Issues in Public Relations: Crisis Communication, Social Media, and Global Advances

OUTLINE

What do you want to know? Whether it's election results, the Super Bowl score, the latest negotiations in the Middle East, or a simple weather forecast, everyone wants to find out something every day. Where do you get your news? Do you listen to the radio, watch television, or buy a newspaper or news magazine?

A growing number of people in the United States are getting their news and opinions every day from the Internet. As Internet access becomes more widespread and more portable, thanks to handheld devices and even cell phones, we draw closer and closer to an unrecognizable future.

Some writers believe we are only a few years away from a new definition of public relations work, as not only Internet technology but also **globalization** and organizational restructuring continue at rapid rates. Any one of these factors has the power to change the relationship-building business that we know as public relations today.

New communication technologies, of which the Internet is only one, offer speed, pinpoint targeting, and nearly costless repetition of messages. Globalization includes not just the lowering of trade barriers but also a reminder of the powerful social, economic, political, and cultural changes now taking place in market economies around the world. And wide-scale restructuring within organizations responding to the recent wave of mergers and acquisitions, as well as to the dot.com boom and bust, have only increased our reliance on communications technology.

Grupp/PR Strategist predicts that in a couple of years 95 percent of all information will be generated by machines and only 5 percent in face-to-face communication. If true, that won't change the fact that effective public relations is grounded in two-way communication. But it might just change everything else.

PUBLIC RELATIONS CHALLENGES

Public Relations in the 21st century faces continual challenges, including

1. The increased need for effective strategies for crisis communication.
2. Keeping up with the increasing avenues of interaction with stakeholders through the new social media.
3. The evolving global public relations community and practice.
4. The changing organizational structure needed to meet these challenges.

CRISIS COMMUNICATION

Crisis communication involves using all the public relations tools available to preserve and strengthen an organization's long-term reputation whenever it's threatened. Organizations deal with problems every day. Late shipments, unhappy customers, unfilled job vacancies, rising prices, and disrupted services are some of the challenges of being in business—but they don't necessarily constitute a crisis. **Crises** are different than everyday problems in that they attract public scrutiny through news coverage. This can disrupt the organization's normal operations and have political, legal, financial, and governmental impacts on its business.[1]

The Nashville, Tennessee–based Institute for Crisis Management identifies four basic causes of a business crisis:

1. **Acts of God.** Storms, earthquakes, volcanic action, floods, and the like fall into this category.
2. **Mechanical problems.** Examples include a ruptured pipe or a falling skywalk.
3. **Human errors.** An employee opens the wrong valve and causes an oil spill, or miscommunication about how to perform a task results in serious injuries.
4. **Management decisions/indecisions.** Senior-level executives sometimes don't take the problem seriously enough, or they think that no one will find out.[2]

Table 17.1 shows the business crises covered by the media in 2006 compared with the same categories in 1990. White-collar crime remains the top category of crises in business with mismanagement second. Workplace violence has almost tripled in this period, and catastrophes and casualty accidents have also gone up considerably.

There is often considerable overlap of categories. For example, ICM notes that the class action lawsuits they studied are often the result of management decisions/indecisions in that management didn't take action when informed of a problem.

Crises can be anticipated or even prevented when organizations build and maintain ongoing relationships with key stakeholders, including employees, customers, government, and general and trade media. Regular, two-way communication with these groups is the glue that translates into credibility and positive expectations should an unpredictable crisis hit. Thus, the more consistently an organization does what it tells its stakeholders it will do, the better its reputation.

For example, the Coca-Cola company had to weigh the value of relationship building with the educational community against the cost of pursuing a marketing strategy involving exclusive arrangements in schools to ensure only its products would be sold on campus. Coca-Cola came down on the side of preserving its long-term reputation and franchise by concluding that it needed to support nonexclusive agreements in schools, allowing a range of beverages and brands to be available to students. As a result, there was no crisis with national education associations or parent-teacher groups, because the soft drink company listened, assessed the facts, and made a decision.

TABLE 17.1   Crisis Categories Compared 1990–2006 (% of total crises each year)

	1990	2006
Catastrophes	5.5	9.0
Casualty accidents	4.8	7.0
Environmental	7.8	2.0
Class action lawsuits	2.2	7.0
Consumer activism	2.8	4.0
Defects & recalls	5.4	4.0
Discrimination	3.3	4.0
Executive dismissal	1.3	2.0
Financial damages	4.2	4.0
Hostile takeover	2.6	1.0
Labor disputes	10.3	10.0
Mismanagement	24.1	14.0
Sexual harassment	0.4	2.0
Whistle-blowers	1.1	1.0
White-collar crime	20.4	21.0
Workplace violence	3.8	9.0

Source: Institute for Crisis Management, "Annual ICM Crisis Report," June 2007. Retrieved from www.crisisexperts.com on March 10, 2008.

After a tanker collision in the San Francisco Bay in the late 1960s, Standard Oil immediately spent whatever resources were necessary to clean up the mess. The rapid positive action led to newspaper editorials saying things like "Beaches never were cleaner before." At the other extreme, Exxon paid a heavy public relations price for not immediately facing up to the crisis prompted by the oil its tanker *Valdez* spilled off the Alaskan coast. Organizational credibility crises are often long-term issues more than they are responses to emergencies.

Two keys to crises or disaster public relations are having an up-to-date, workable crisis plan, and taking positive action that will move your corporation off the defensive and onto the offensive.

Public relations practitioners deal with crisis communication by starting with a **crisis plan** that spells out how the entire organization will respond. When a crisis occurs, a written and rehearsed communication plan will speed up response time by having all the background information available and by having all crisis response duties pre-assigned. For example, chances are that almost all of the public relations staff will be working with the media, and much of this work will be to provide up-to-the-minute online responses to the general media, the trade press, and financial writers. At least one public relations or human resource specialist will be providing employees with up-to-the-minute reports via e-mail over the intranet. With sufficient staffing, others will be assigned to provide Web site updates for customers and investors, but this will likely involve staff support from other departments.

TABLE 17.2	Key Audiences Who Might Be Affected by a Crisis	
Employees	Licensees	Community leaders
Investors	Vendors	Law enforcement officials
Bankers	Union officials	Dealers and distributors
Suppliers	Neighbors	Competitors
Adversarial groups	Retirees/pension recipients	Plaintiff attorneys
Franchisees	Stockholders	Regulatory officials
Customers/clients	Security analysts	Educators
Business groups	Politicians	Industry-at-large

Source: www.crisisexperts.com, Institute for Crisis Management.

Cohn & Wolfe, an international public relations firm, recommends to its clients that they begin their crisis planning with an audit of potential internal and external problems. This would include identifying key publics who might be affected by the crisis. See table 17.2 for a sample listing.

The agency then develops a tailor-made plan that addresses

- How to increase support from allies.
- Creation of a response manual to use if and when a crisis occurs.
- Formation of a crisis committee.
- Development of simulation and training exercises.
- Formation of a contingency plan.
- Determination of how the corporation's position can be strengthened during the crisis.[3]

Other more specific plan elements and guidelines include the following:

1. Putting the public interest first and especially the needs of all people directly concerned, including accident victims and their families and employees and their families. This means resolving the emergency and protecting the people affected until it is completely resolved.

2. Taking responsibility for correcting the situation. Seldom, if ever, should the organizational response to the media or affected stakeholders be "no comment."

3. Being as open as possible with all stakeholder groups, including governmental agencies, investors, employees and their families, victims and their families, customers, neighboring businesses, residences, and communities affected by the crisis.

4. Having a designated spokesperson whose job is to manage the accuracy and consistency of the messages coming from the organization.

5. Establishing a central media or information center, although circumstances may require multiple centers that would include the corporate office, the crisis location, and the metropolitan area nearest the crisis location.

6. Responding to all media inquiries according to predetermined guidelines. Do respond to all media inquiries, but if you don't know the answer, say so. Then promise to get back as soon as possible with the answer. Do not release the names of the dead or injured until relatives have been notified by appropriate police or public safety officials.

7. Do not speculate.

Crisis Management: Chinese Toys Found to Be Fatal for Kids

By Laurie Lattimore-Volkmann, Ph.D.
Dominican University

China manufactured each of the 24 kinds of toys recalled for safety reasons in the United States in 2007, a record that is causing alarm among consumer advocates, parents, and regulators.

One recall involved 1.5 million Thomas & Friends trains and rail components because the toys were coated at a factory in China with lead paint, which can damage brain cells, especially in children.

Over all, the number of products made in China that are being recalled in the United States by the federal Consumer Product Safety Commission has doubled in the last five years, driving the total number of recalls in the country to a record 467 last year.

It also means that China today is responsible for about 60 percent of all product recalls, compared with 36 percent in 2000.

Toys made in China make up 70 to 80 percent of all the toys sold in the United States, according to the Toy Industry Association. This string of toy recalls is inspiring new demands for better safety enforcement by U.S. regulators and importers, as well as by the government and industry in China.

As the vice president of public relations for a major American toy company that sends more than half its toy manufacturing to China (and who has had to do a recall in the last year), how do you handle this crisis with the following publics:

- *Shareholders:* What changes do you make to ensure safe products going forward? How do you avoid another multimillion-dollar loss from a product recall?
- *Consumers:* What do you do to (1) reassure them about current products and (2) approach marketing of future products?
- *Government:* How will you approach regulators to convince them you are taking care of the problem and assure them this will not be a continuing problem with your Chinese plant?
- *Employees:* What kinds of changes in process need to be made to be absolutely sure your toys are safe? Are these realistic from a business standpoint? What challenges will you face in implementing these?
- Knowing that future recalls will paralyze the company, but that changes are likely to cost millions of dollars and higher costs could decrease sales and profit, what would your argument be to your CEO that it is important to incur such costs versus the potential public relations cost of doing nothing?

Source: Eric S. Lipton and David Barboza, "As More Toys Are Recalled, Trail Ends in China," www.nytimes.com, June 19, 2007.

As with real crises, **rumors** can have severe impacts on organizations. When faced with a rumor, a corporate communicator rarely has any statistical data available to guide decision making. There's little hard evidence to guide the practitioner in trying to figure out who is saying what, who is listening, the harshness of the comments, how long the rumors are likely to persist, and, ultimately, if something should be done to counteract what is being spread. Although corporate public relations practitioners should expect rumors to circulate, it is important to address them. Corporations can face Securities and Exchange Commission actions if rumors are allowed to persist. This is because rumors can affect the company's stock price and, in some cases, the market in general.

The best defense is a good offense. Here are some practical ways to manage rumors:

1. Strive to increase and maintain trust and credibility.
2. Keep audiences regularly informed through a variety of communication channels.
3. Tailor each message to the audience receiving it so there's less likelihood of it being misunderstood.
4. Establish an ongoing rumor hotline and other two-way communication channels to seek questions and concerns from key publics. Use written communication to answer the questions posed.
5. Monitor possible effects of rumors so early intervention can be enacted if necessary.

See mini-case 17.1 for an application of the crises principles.

SOCIAL MEDIA

New communication technologies have always influenced public relations practice, but perhaps none so profoundly as the **Internet,** e-mail, and the new social media. Budgets have been reallocated to make optimal use of digital technology. An array of new practices capitalizes on Internet speed and currency to keep key constituencies aware of current developments. These include crisis management programs, multimedia campaigns, round-the-clock media relations programs, and partnerships and alliances with new and existing groups. The results show up in sales to new customers, in repeated sales to existing ones, and in lower operating costs because technology helped create a dialogue between organizations and activist groups.

First, let's consider the Internet—its rate of adoption, the way it has intensified the nature of relationship building with key constituencies, and how it has changed specific practice areas in public relations, including media relations and crisis communication, employee and internal communication, investor relations, marketing communication, and communication with activist groups in the community and throughout the world. Conservative forecasts suggest that more than one billion users are now surfing the Net.[4] That's close to 15 percent of the world's population. Carried further, seven people log onto the Internet for the first time every second. A profile of Internet users suggests that the average user is a white male who speaks English. Approximately two-thirds of all Internet users are male. They tend to be in the middle- to upper-income classes, with the largest percentage of users in the 35–44 age bracket. Users spend approximately 5.5 hours a week online.[5] The fastest growth in Internet use is now outside the United States. One billion users are expected before 2010. However, the United States still leads in Internet use, with 68.5 percent of the total population online. China is second to the United States in total Internet users. Australia and the Netherlands are close behind the United States in total Internet penetration of their countries' populations.

In the United States the number of hours Internet users are online continues to increase. In 2007, the number of hours increased 1 hour per week to an average of 15.3 hours according to the University of Southern California's Digital Media Project.[6] Of the total U.S. Internet users, this includes 96 percent using e-mail weekly, 71 percent surfing the Web without a specific destination, 60 percent looking for news online, and 43 percent finding product information.[7]

What these statistics don't show are the ways the Internet has fundamentally changed how journalists and businesses operate. Grasping this involves knowing a few basics. First, the Internet alters the way people get information from organizations. Communicating through the Internet means that the general public or members of an organization's constituencies are pulling information off the Net about the organization rather than the organization pushing information onto them as is the case with regular news release dissemination.

Second, communication is not just top-down and one-to-many. Making all appropriate information available on the Web site, along with accompanying links, means that customers, media reporters, investors, industry analysts, employees, government regulators, activists, and others can get whatever information they want and put it together in any order they want without going through a public relations practitioner. In this sense, the Internet has noticeably displaced the "gatekeeping" functions previously provided both by editors and by public relations practitioners.

In short, the Internet offers channel capabilities unequaled by other media. Some believe that being able to pull information from the Internet gives busy people better control of their time—they get their news when they want it and where they want it; thus, individuals are relying more heavily on the Internet as the news source versus traditional print or broadcast media outlets.

The Internet is considered a rich medium in that its interactive qualities give it many of the characteristics of interpersonal communication or the sense of actually being there in face-to-face conversation. Thus, **rich media** "touch" more of the senses, and their messages can be personalized enough to convey a sense of conversing with someone as if you were building a long-term relationship.

Because of fast, direct, and consistent contact with key constituencies, Internet technology advances almost every facet of public relations practice. Seen this way, the practice areas discussed in this section, although not representing the full scope of public relations work, nevertheless highlight common new uses of Internet technology for public relations. A discussion of Internet uses in public relations would be incomplete, however, without mention of common misuses. Unfortunately, the Internet generally and e-mail in particular are too often used for spamming or blitzing the immediate world with overly one-sided or near-useless information.

Besides Internet use, e-mail has become a mainstay for public relations practice, especially in media relations. A majority of reporters and editors prefer to get news releases by e-mail and even to contact their own story sources at least initially through e-mail. In fact, e-mail has replaced the fax as the principal source of company news releases. Digitally edited video is transmitted over satellite or through fiber-optic cables laid by the telephone, telecom, and cable companies. Like other professionals, public relations practitioners make significant use of blogs, although it's too early to forecast all the uses blogging can have in public relations.

Implications for Media Relations

Media relations work, more than other practice areas, has benefited from Internet technology and the **World Wide Web.** That's because journalists and other insiders have come to expect news and information to be announced seven days a week on a round-the-clock basis. What a switch from the days when news releases were fully developed and then sent by mail, fax, or courier. Thus, the Internet provides stiff competition for all traditional media because of its ability to transmit news virtually instantaneously. The old "news cycle" is obsolete. The media day has turned into the media hour and now into the media minute or second, says Carole Howard.[8] Internet technology has created access to and demand for immediate information and frequent updates. The upshot is that as many people now get their breaking news online as those who read it in the newspapers. Today, half of all print and broadcast media allow their Web sites to scoop their parent publications, networks, or stations.

At least three new media relations benchmarks took hold in the early 21st century.[9] For the first time, journalists covering breaking stories said in 2000 that they are more likely to turn first to an organization's Web site than to a live source at the company or in the community. Also, for the first time, e-mail became journalists' preferred medium when working with new or unknown sources. Unfortunately, journalists have often resorted to taking information from chat rooms and blogs as secondary sources.

Perhaps the most common uses of the Internet by public relations practitioners involve story pitching and story development. The typical process would involve a public relations practitioner pitching a story idea via e-mail to a New York trade magazine editor. If they knew each other, they might phone. The trade magazine reporter assigned to this segment or beat would then scope out the information and story possibilities by viewing the organization's Web site. This is followed by another e-mail exchange or phone call to the practitioner, asking for the names of other sources, including industry analysts and perhaps financial analysts. From this point on, the public relations practitioner is likely to be responding to specific information requests from the reporter.

Musician Slash, left, and musician Steven Tyler, with microphone, perform during the 4th Annual MusiCares benefit concert in Hollywood to help provide access to addiction recovery treatment for members of the music community.

Another common practice is for the public relations consultant to pitch particular stories to particular media based on knowing their editorial calendars or schedules of stories or themes for upcoming issues. Second only to story pitching and development is for media relations experts to use the Internet to track their media coverage and that of the competitors. As well, tracking services peruse chat rooms and discussion groups so they can report what the media and other influential citizens or groups are saying about an organization and its competitor organizations.

Implications for Investor Relations

Raising the necessary capital to develop markets worldwide, as well as 24-hour financial markets, has transformed investor relations into a markedly more integral public relations function over the course of the last decade. Online media are proving to be especially useful in investor relations because they connect the organization to the business and financial press, shareholders, and institutional investors.

Public relations practitioners, especially those in investor relations departments, focus on Internet audiences that matter most in building credibility and awareness—media, industry analysts, venture capitalists, individual investors, and the financial community, writes Internet public relations expert Don Middleberg.[10] He believes that the Internet helps explain why organizations put more money into public relations and communication programs prior to the dot-com bust and subsequent recession.

Implications for Marketing Communication

The Internet has undoubtedly done more than any other communication technology to strengthen relationships with customers through relationship marketing. In fact, Middleberg maintains that public relations consistently plays a bigger role in branding products and companies than do any other communication tools, including advertising.[11] That is, public relations is utilized to demonstrate market demand primarily through third-party endorsements from industry analysts and other experts. Moreover, public relations practitioners have become astute at building brand acceptance by attracting customers to the company Web site through contests and continuous information updates. Creating this online "buzz" may also involve working through message boards and postings to newsgroups.

Unlike other elements in the marketing communications process (advertising, sales promotions, corporate sponsorships, direct selling), Web site updating does not take months of planning and production and, therefore, becomes a principal tool for increasing market share. All of this promotes customer loyalty that translates into repeat purchases by existing customers, thereby cutting the number of advertising dollars that must be spent to attract new, replacement customers. It's little wonder then that companies build market share by being online first with a Web site geared to attracting new customers and keeping old ones.

Internet and e-mail technologies are used increasingly to maintain contact with existing customers through a process called **relationship marketing.** Relationship marketing is based on the premise that keeping an existing customer is less costly and more profitable than finding a new one. Unfortunately, the process routinely breaks down when companies fail to respond to their customers' e-mails in a timely way.

Implications for Internal Communication

Though less apparent, using the Internet to improve employee productivity and loyalty is making a major bottom-line contribution to organizational success. In fact, providing useful on-the-job information has become the source of about three-fourths of the value added in manufacturing, according to James Brian Quinn of Dartmouth's Amos Tuck School of Business Administration.[12]

Writing in *Communication World,* Richard Nemec describes this work as *knowledge management,* a set of processes that organizes knowledge and makes it easy to use, distribute, and share either from an individual workstation, by a "virtual team" of employees linked by a listserv, or with far-flung agency subsidiaries and branch operations.[13] We'll return to knowledge management practices later in this chapter.

Implications for Activists and New Stakeholders

Because of its ability to personalize messages, the Internet offers opportunities for relationship building or connecting people and organizations in ways not feasible with traditional media. Listservs, electronic bulletin boards, or blogs are helping community groups, community leaders, and organizations understand one another's concerns and the common ground among them.

Public relations scholar Timothy Coombs has identified the Internet as a potential equalizer for activist organizations because now they can communicate directly with the organizations whose practices they oppose.[14] That's because the Internet is an affordable communication channel open to everyone, including groups and social movements that can't afford expensive public relations services. When organizations respond to queries and comments from activist groups, they begin to establish dialogue, to better understand each other's viewpoint, and to interact more in areas of common concern—all of which may lead to greater long-term interdependence, writes scholar Maureen Taylor.[15]

A Paradigm Shift Among Practitioners

All of these new Internet-based communication opportunities have led Dr. Donald Wright to argue that the Internet represents a paradigmatic shift in corporate communications, opening the door to full two-way communication between a corporation and its publics. Therefore, it is incumbent upon corporate officers, he says, to develop policies supporting and effecting more interactive communication. To support this claim, Wright reports the following results from a study of senior-level public relations practitioners conducted for the Institute of Public Relations:

- Seventy-nine percent of respondents said the Internet has already improved two-way communication between their company and its publics.
- Eighty-nine percent believe that the Internet (including intranets and extranets) will change how communications/public relations resources are deployed at their companies from now until the foreseeable future.
- Seventy-two percent of the surveyed communication policymakers believe that the Internet has forced their companies to consider broader social policy issues, including electronic privacy, security, commerce, and civil rights in cyberspace.
- Ninety-two percent said that their companies had developed guidelines for managing their organization's Web site development.[16]

We should not close this discussion regarding the Internet's implications without first underscoring the need for some organizational unit not only to manage the Web site but also to enhance the organization's long-term reputation among its constituencies by ensuring that its key messages stand out among all the other Web site information. Because of their primary interest in reputation management, public relations practitioners may be best positioned to assume these responsibilities.

And finally, future public relations practitioners should be alerted to the fact that a joint IABC-PRSA study on the status and future of the profession conducted in 2000 reported that knowing technology uses offers the greatest opportunity for career advancement in public relations in coming years.[17] See mini-case 17.2 for an example of a company that used the Internet strategically to accomplish its objectives.

PUBLIC RELATIONS AND GLOBAL MARKETS

The opening of worldwide markets throughout the latter part of the 20th century was a financial boon that redirected public relations practice and the structure of the industry. Consider, for instance, that most of the world's largest public relations agencies are now owned by advertising agencies. In turn, some of these already-big advertising/public relations firms are owned by or linked to other multinational conglomerates. The result is that these firms have sufficient resources to mount extensive public relations initiatives almost anywhere at any time. And that's exactly what's happening with 40 to 50 percent of annual revenue from leading U.S. advertising/public relations firms now coming from outside the United States.

Writing in *Communication World,* Brian Heiss and Edie Fraser reported that in world-class companies, the communication function leads in supporting the corporation in its globalization effort: "In the current era of globalization, corporations are faced with pressure to gain international market share and stockholders have made it increasingly important to keep global sales and stock prices high. The claims seem reflected in practice."[18]

Ray Kotcher, Ketchum's CEO, noted that in the mid-1990s the share of business at Ketchum on a worldwide basis was less than 25 percent. In 2001 the business that was shared across two or more geographies and/or practices was almost 50 percent.[19]

To meet these challenges and to elevate a corporation's global reputation, corporate communication teams need to be part of designing and implementing global strategy as described in the Starbucks case study at the end of the chapter. Doing public relations

MusicCity: From Zero to Napster in 30 Days

After Internet file-sharing company Napster announced its transition to a paid-subscription service, frustrated users tested other free networks such as Lime Wire, Gnutella, AIMster, and MusicCity. The crunch of new users forced MusicCity to develop a new software application called Morpheus that allowed users to trade digital files freely.

MusicCity asked KVO Public Relations (now Fleischman-Hillard) to help move at least 1,000 current users to Morpheus in 30 days before these users could switch to competing services. The agency's idea was to work directly with file sharers to request that they sign up their friends; more than 1 million people were encouraged to download and use Morpheus in less than a month.

But the bigger story was the type of Internet-based media relations approach that made this possible. MusicCity could not afford a large-scale media outreach plan, and its own team of 10 employees would be busy with development and operating issues. How to develop a media-based campaign "on the cheap" was a huge challenge.

Research and Planning

Initial research indicated that aggressive media relations such as extensive story pitching, press release distribution, and executive/founder exposure often resulted in coverage focusing on the company rather than the products' features. By studying Internet chat rooms, bulletin boards, relevant articles, and the reactions of file-sharing experts, KVO professionals discovered that Morpheus wasn't much different and certainly no better than competing services. KVO decided that the most feasible approach wouldn't be extensive media relations, but would instead be to approach users on a grassroots level, similar to Napster's beginnings. This approach would also help preserve MusicCity's independent or "indie" reputation, differentiating it from its overexposed competitors.

Objectives

With a total budget of only $20,000 and two months to execute the program, KVO set three campaign objectives for Morpheus:

1. Encourage at least 1,000 MusicCity users to download the Morpheus application. (Evaluation measure: download figures)
2. Preserve MusicCity's "indie" credibility and user-friendly brand. (Evaluation measure: user approval ratings)
3. Communicate with media economically. (Evaluation measure: substantial coverage of the product using a streamlined proactive effort)

Strategy

Considering the objectives and limited budget, the agency advised MusicCity to reach out to users through the Internet: Web site, e-mail, instant messaging, and bulletin boards. The plan was to secure coverage in consumer technology and file-sharing publications while keeping a low profile in mainstream media to draw attention and intrigue from mainstream media who'd heard about Morpheus's high user interest. Media inquiries were responded to with a combination of e-mail, phone, and Internet bulletin boards.

Once Morpheus launched, KVO was flooded with phone calls and e-mails from users. Users appreciated the quick, meaningful customer support replies delivered through e-mail and acknowledged that Morpheus was a great alternative to Napster. These "converts" were then persuaded to spread the word to friends and asked that they rate Morpheus highly on Downloads.com where the application was available. Soon afterward the old users replied with tallies of new Morpheus converts, which in turn led to favorable ratings appearing on Downloads.com.

Agency staff studiously contacted consumer-technology and file-sharing publications regarding the launch and rapid growth of Morpheus. At this point, mainstream journalists noticed the Morpheus underground buzz on the Internet and then contacted KVO for information. What followed were myriad articles announcing the launch. Thus, by highlighting the product's features and popularity first to niche publications, the mainstream media became enticed. And the product-centered articles preserved MusicCity's "indie" credibility. As a result, MusicCity appeared not only exotic but also an attractive subject among otherwise overly promotional start-ups clamoring for mainstream attention.

Consider the following results in light of the campaign objectives:

1. Approximately 1 month into the grassroots campaign, CNET's Downloads.com reported nearly 1 million downloads to Morpheus.
2. Morpheus's approval rating jumped 50 percent at launch to 74 percent in 30 days. On January 25, 2002, the approval rating was at 92 percent.
3. Morpheus appeared in hundreds of articles, including coverage in mainstream and consumer-technology publications.

Lessons

Public relations can help organizations make big changes even with small budgets. The key was the strategy by which KVO received such substantial media coverage by directing the story first to the niche consumer technology and file-sharing publications. In turn, mainline media reporters picked up the story once their sources indicated the existence of a significant audience for file-sharing music services. The Web site, e-mail, chat rooms, and bulletin board channels were very useful as well. In addition, mainline journalists scored with their stories by illustrating the magnitude of the underground buzz among file sharers and the extent to which these users rely on Internet media largely unknown to the general public. And finally, the KVO professionals incorporated a consumer response plan that followed up with e-mail contact to users who switched to Morpheus. E-mails acknowledged the importance of these users who doubtlessly contributed to their willingness to pass the word on to friends.

Questions

1. Suggest an environmental group that might want to use similar tactics in reaching its target audiences.
2. Are there other tactics that use technology to directly reach the target audiences that you would suggest to use?

Source: Interview with Jeffrey Hardison, Fleischman-Hillard (formerly KVO Public Relations), Portland, Oregon.

internationally involves infinitely more coordination and synchronization with foreign business partners, overseas local public relations firms, and a host of cultural norms and regulations not adhered to in the United States.

Heiss and Fraser have noted some of the ways in which public relations efforts are coordinated between headquarters and local subsidiaries on a global scale: "Globalization has increased the need for clear, consistent, and central corporate messages with adaptation at the local level. Companies must reach customers, potential customers, alliances, partners, employees, stakeholders, the investment community, distributors, media, government, trade, and professional constituencies.[20] The trick seems to be for the multinational corporations to enhance their overall reputations and brand identities in ways that take advantage of local cultures, media availability, and political climates.

At the corporate level, the public relations function has three distinct aspects. In one role public relations practitioners represent multinational corporations at home, dealing with public opinion and governmental activities that relate both to specific corporations and to multinational enterprises as a whole. The second role of multinational public relations is to help bridge the communication gap that inevitably exists between foreign operations and top management in the world headquarters. Finally, public relations must be conducted in the corporation's various host countries. All this points to better internal communication.

Though public relations has been a critical component in the unfolding of the global economy, many practitioners are skeptical about the future. For example, will the big marketing/advertising/public relations conglomerates give disproportionate emphasis to customers at the expense of such other key constituencies as employees, local and national governments, and community and activist groups in the overseas communities where these firms are doing business for their corporate clients? Concerns of at least equal import arise at the societal level, where thoughtful observers in other countries fear that economic globalization will lower their nations' and their citizens' economic viability by promoting consumer expectations that can't be met given substandard wages, cultural differences, and infrastructures that don't readily accommodate the global economy.

THE CHANGING INSTITUTION OF PUBLIC RELATIONS

At the outset of this chapter, we asserted that public relations practice by 2010 would be very unlike what it has been. Already we have seen that new communication technologies speed up every dimension of the practice as well as encourage new and uncharted relationship building with established and emergent constituencies.

The capital that's been required to finance and shape the global economy into a more or less single market system places enormous pressures on short-term profits, on cutting planning cycles from years to months to weeks, not to mention the rush to adapt public relations procedures and practices to fit the cultural prerequisites of countries and regions of the world that businesses enter.

Taken together, these societal-level changes signal whole new formulations for public relations work. Today, public relations and corporate communications work is being integrated into broader communication processes to integrate organizations' operations as never before. By redefining themselves as communication experts and consultants—rather than more narrowly defined technical specialists in public relations—today's university communication and public relations majors will find themselves working within a more comprehensive public relations and communication management practice.

Try to imagine the extent of the long-range reputation management tasks facing organizations in light of the dot-com bulge and bust as well as the recent unscrupulous accounting practices to inflate stock prices. While all this was going on, most public relations practitioners—technically competent and highly motivated as they were—failed to understand and communicate the adverse effects of short-term profit taking on the protection and enhancement of the long-term reputation, the brands, and the franchise.

At least some of the blame might go to the mixed messages that people receive from organizations because content is added to their organizational intranets and extranets in such a haphazard manner. Rarely has a single unit been given responsibility for coordinating corporate Internet content so that the core themes and messages would dominate or at least be present most of the time. Instead, intranet and extranet sites became filled with submissions coming directly from the CEO's office, from the finance and legal offices, from marketing, from human resources, from various operating and production units, from public relations—not to mention the thousands of many and varied individual submissions.

Under these conditions, is it any wonder that users found it difficult to see the organization's big picture? To overcome the clutter and to highlight key messages, Jack Bergen, first president of the Council of Public Relations Firms, believes that intranet and extranet content control should reside in public relations and corporate communication, rather than either the information technology (IT) or human resources (HR) departments:

> The website is your company in cyberspace. You should control it. It helps you manage coalitions and it's the cheapest way of getting to a lot of people at one time. Use internal and external websites to develop communities of interest, building coalitions and establishing relationships with employees, customers, and other stakeholders.[21]

Rethinking Internal Communication

Loss of shareholder value and declining consumer confidence and organizational support have prompted many corporations, nonprofit organizations, and government agencies to reexamine their core communication processes and ways of doing things. In doing so, they can't help but note that increased employee productivity gains have boosted the bottom line. Using communication to increase productivity introduces whole new directions for the internal communication work taken on by public relations practitioners.

One such new direction, as noted earlier, is called knowledge management. **Knowledge management** is a collection of practices for getting products out the door faster by better ensuring that all employees have the right information they need at the right time. Knowledge management accounts for the ways an organization captures, stores, shares, and delivers information using appropriate software. Thus, as Kate Vitale has noted, knowledge management boosts the bottom line by creating smarter employees.[22] Knowledge management practices provide access to all who need it while simultaneously cutting information overload for those who don't. Behind these processes, then, are beliefs that employees come to feel more empowered and satisfied the more quickly they get the information they need.

To date, however, corporate communicators have not embraced knowledge management work, even though a recent IABC report[23] called it one of the three principal areas for organizational communication research. Ironically, corporate communicators are perhaps best trained and qualified to match the capabilities of different communication technologies with message types and desired outcomes.

Becoming a knowledge management consultant is only one such new internal communication role for public relations practitioners and communication managers. Another is to become a **change management expert,** someone who uses a wide range of communication skills to help change organizational cultures, to increase employee loyalty, and to assist the organization in adapting to intercultural conditions. For instance, the recent-year economic downturns have prompted companies to merge. When two or more previously separate organizations must now work together to accomplish the same goals, the skills of communication consultants become in real demand to build the new shared culture or dominant values and themes that must be communicated up, down, and across the organization.

Public relations professionals with some training in organizational communication are pivotal corporate change agents. They often begin with communication audits or diagnostic tools designed to assess the effectiveness of various internal communication processes. Audits uncover mismatches between information sought and information received, between channels used and channels preferred, satisfaction with the communication climate, and the most appropriate communication networks for different types of information.

Results from communication audits help public relations practitioners and communication managers to improve organizational effectiveness by incorporating new ideas more quickly and by being more responsive to changes in the overall environment(s) in which the organization operates. The need for this type of public relations expertise appears to be supported in findings from the 2002 Middleberg/Ross survey showing that 81 percent of respondents agreed that the ability to manage change would be the most fundamental component of business success in coming years.[24]

Changing Organizational Structures and Settings

The work and structure of public relations firms or agencies and corporate or organizational departments are changing relatively quickly as well and largely in response to technology, globalization, and the new publics whose interests have been previously shortsighted or overlooked.

One reason for the changes is that it is not altogether clear that existing public relations work captures a significant amount of the communication activity in organizations. In recent years, for example, corporations have willingly parceled out traditional public relations functions such that (1) the investor or financial relations component reports through either the financial or the legal department, (2) the employee and newsletter work reports through the HR department, which also takes on all sorts of communication training, (3) the product publicity and consumer relations work gets assigned to the marketing division, and (4) the public affairs and government relations work is directed to the legal department. Some believe that these varied reporting relationships represent encroachment on the public relations function, whereas others argue that such placement reflects the decentralized nature of communication work in organizations.

Another persistent and growing trend is for alternative work arrangements outside traditional firms and departments. This might include public relations specialists working as part of virtual teams on some sort of global project where the only contact with team members is through the Internet. Such work often requires dual reporting relationships, with the project supervisor being in charge until the work is completed, when the public relations practitioner again becomes more the direct responsibility of managers in her or his home department.

The 1980s and 1990s saw the rise of thousands of independent public relations and communication consultants who either work totally on their own or distribute some of their extra work to other independent consultants on a contract basis. Within the public relations field, independent consultants are now thought to represent the largest single job category or classification.

Within firms and agencies one clear trend is the move toward specialization by industry or by general practice areas such as health care or technology. Today, account coordinators and account managers are assigned to fewer clients and oftentimes within the same industry such as health care, technology, consumer goods, or financial services.

As well, the opening of global markets has brought about intensive consolidation of public relations agencies by advertising agencies. When public relations agencies are merged into advertising ones, the tendency is for relatively more of the work to be focused on product publicity or developing the public relations practices within an overall marketing framework.

Despite mergers and globalization impacts, very few of even the biggest public relations firms have or want the capacity to service their clients' needs in each of the world's cities and regions where the client does business. That's because many clients prefer the combination of having the overall public relations planning done by a single, multinational firm, but then parceling out much of the implementation work to local agencies who no doubt better understand the cultural traditions in their cities, the customary ways of working with local news media, and the community leaders whose support is often useful in mounting community and governmental relations efforts as well as in staging special events. The larger independent public relations firms or agencies respond to the need for localization by becoming partners or affiliates in networks of independent professionals located around the world. The largest of these are PRIO (Public Relations Organization International), Pinnacle Worldwide, IPREX (International Public Relations Exchange), and World Communication Group. Affiliating with networks of other independently owned firms provides opportunities to compete more effectively with multinational public relations and advertising conglomerates.

On the organizational or client side there's an ongoing examination of the mix of communication programs and activities undertaken in-house versus those assigned to firms or independent consultants and vendors. Typically, the communications or public relations department handles the core strategic planning functions in-house while subcontracting specific program planning, execution, and communication support services to firms and independents. In fact, during periods of economic recession corporate communicators are likely to bring more of the planning work back in-house, thereby casting the firm in more supportive and implementing roles.

In more healthy economic periods, though, what's left for the corporate communication department are media relations, managing issues and crises, and consulting with top management on long-term reputation management issues. Work that is typically outsourced includes routine media relations, some product publicity, events management, and selected community relations functions. A few corporations have adopted an in-house creative services model under which corporate communication specialists are assigned to various divisions or brands, where they act like account executives for a firm or agency.

EVOLVING PRACTITIONER ROLES

Against this backdrop of new technology, global markets, and business responsibility issues, it's little wonder that practitioner roles are changing. We end this chapter by considering 10 evolving changes.

From External Counsel to Internal Communication Consultant

The field of public relations was established as a legitimate occupation and worthwhile field of study by a handful of ex-newspapermen and press agents in the early decades of the 20th century. These pioneers, for the most part, set up their own firms and frequently succeeded in building larger-than-life reputations for themselves as well as their clients. This external, independent counselor model of public relations practice quickly became the ideal.

The actual practice of public relations has evolved far beyond this original model. Although counseling firms have flourished, a new breed of practitioner has emerged, primarily within the structures of large, complex organizations. These practitioners are concerned with internal communication as well as external publicity.

Public relations specialists in organizations must understand the concerns and attitudes of customers, employees, investors, managers, special interest groups, and a vast array of publics. The job cannot stop with an understanding of these complex issues; public relations practitioners must be able to integrate their strategic planning skills into the organization's managerial decision-making process. Public relations practitioners of today and tomorrow must continue to exhibit high-quality communication skills to do the jobs for which they are hired. They must also understand both their role as managers affecting the actions of an organization and the importance of public relations input into the process.

Public relations is increasingly the responsibility of CEOs and top executives. Thus, part of the practitioner's job is to train and advise the organization's leaders on the appropriate uses of communication and in talking to the media (see spotlight 17.1).

From One-Way Communication to Two-Way Communication and Interaction

With its roots in rhetoric and persuasion, it's not surprising that campaign theory and concepts were initially designed as one-way publicity blitzes to create awareness and attitude change that might, in turn, influence behavior. Public relations theory development and conceptualization over the last quarter century, though, has focused on two-way communication that is more or less balanced between the organization and its key publics or constituencies.

The two-way symmetric, or balanced, communication formulation has been developed and tested over the past quarter century by James Grunig and colleagues at the University of Maryland.[25] Two-way communication processes involve infinitely broader and more comprehensive roles for public relations practice than one-way persuasion models ever did. Using two-way communication, practitioners now hope that their communication efforts will result in knowledge gain, understanding, and other high-order cognitive effects that are more likely to underpin longer-lasting relationships. Because two-way communication principles involve each group or side understanding the other's point of view, the process is more likely to lead to negotiation, compromise, and a host of win-win outcomes for all.

Two-way communication principles, unlike one-way principles, are best for maximizing the capabilities of e-mail and the Internet, including listservs, chat rooms, electronic bulletin boards, and discussion groups. By promoting dialogue and conversation—rather than one-directional information flows—these new technologies help organizations create and continuously maintain ties to key publics.

New Dimensions in Corporate Social Responsibility

By Robert L. Dilenschneider

You don't have to be a futurist to know that vast societal and worldwide changes, including the September 11, 2001, bombings of the World Trade Center and Pentagon, have tremendous impacts on public relations practice. Over the next 20 years we will have to continue to keep pace with the seemingly endless advances in communication technology that have already speeded up the delivery of messages. But the bigger challenge will be mustering the courage to insist that all organizations adopt a broader, more socially conscious view of their company's responsibilities to their employees, their customers, and the communities in which they operate.

Little attention was focused on corporate responsibility during the past 20 years as the revolution in information and communication technology, and the creation of huge worldwide conglomerates in the banking, investment, insurance, manufacturing, energy, entertainment, media, and information industries, literally transformed the world into a global marketplace. Fortunately, these technological, economic, and political developments have revitalized democracy, reinvigorated capitalism, and generated immense global economic growth; particularly in the United States. And yet, these advances also suggest that large corporations have become so powerful that they no longer feel compelled to consider the public interests as they pursue their goals of maximizing profits.

Some of the elements of public discontent can be easily seen.

1. General prosperity is not being equally shared. It is widely perceived that, while the rich are getting richer, the middle class is working harder than ever to maintain its position, and the poor are getting poorer.

2. The pain of the economic recovery has not been evenly shared. Most of the ruthless downsizing has fallen on the heads of the line workers, the clerks, or the middle managers, not the upper level of management.

3. CEOs are getting paid extraordinary salaries (as evidenced by the Enron downfall), while workers are asked to tighten their belts and suffer cuts in benefits. CEOs are generally raking in extraordinary amounts of money in salaries, bonuses, stock options, and perks.

4. Free trade is already under fire from workers and unions in the industrial nations. Multinational corporations are once again viewed with increasing suspicion in developing countries for fostering sweatshop wages and working conditions, for degrading the environment, and for shipping their profits back to corporate headquarters instead of investing them in host nations.

Unless public relations professionals and leaders address these problems in the next several years, we can expect huge societal problems. This effort will require a great deal of courage because the message concerns the growing discontent with business—and in most cases top management doesn't want to hear about it, and won't readily agree with it, or wants to avoid it. CEOs are pressured by Wall Street, and those waiting to be CEOs cannot afford to break ranks.

I am convinced that our biggest challenge in the next 20 years will be to convince corporate leaders that in order to preserve these economic gains, they need to restrain their pursuit of even larger profits by assuming greater responsibility for the lives their businesses affect.

So the job is on our shoulders to help those in charge of our organizations become leaders. Doing this requires more than rhetoric. It calls for original thinking and original ideas that respond to the following questions:

What can be done, for example, to show how corporations are loyal to the nations they operate in?

How can CEOs step out of isolation in the ivory tower and show compassion for average workers?

How do you muster the best minds in our country and elsewhere to develop ideas for peace and for addressing the burdened of the underclass in this country and around the world?

How do you get those who have made excess wealth in the past 20 years to recognize that they cannot take for their entire life and must start giving back and helping to solve some of society's ills?

How do you take some of the profit motive out of science and encourage those who have the capacity to develop products that can address serious illness?

How do you help CEOs address diversity in the workplace?

How do you help those CEOs who are fearful of stepping forward to overcome their anxieties?

How do you help the big egos—the big "I ams"—to put their personal power to work for good and not for intimidation or self-aggrandizement?

The list can go on, and these are no easy tasks—for you or for those who expect to be leaders. But they must be addressed—and the time is now.

Source: Robert L. Dilenschneider is chief executive of The Dilenschneider Group, the firm he founded in 1991. He was president and CEO of Hill & Knowlton, Inc., from 1986 to 1991.

From Marketing Support to Integrated Communication

Not very long ago, the primary justification for public relations was its effort to sell products. Public relations was seen as an adjunct to the sales effort, concerned primarily with product publicity, special events coordination, and getting free advertising.

For some time, though, the trend has been to move public relations work from a marketing adjunct role to the marketing communication mainstream. Public relations plays different marketing communication roles over the course of a product's life cycle. Prior to product launch, practitioners work with the trade press and through Internet sites to generate news stories and favorable product reviews that will be seen by major customers, distributors, wholesalers, and retailers. Closer to product launch they write product publicity features for publications and programs reaching target audiences. All of this product anticipation buildup happens before consumer advertising is launched.

From Program to Process

Traditionally, public relations has placed tremendous emphasis on programs and campaigns and other tangible outputs of public relations efforts, including news clips. In this sense, the job of the public relations practitioner has consisted of a progression of discrete tasks—media releases, publications, public service announcements, publicity campaigns, and the like. Such products and programs are still a time-consuming responsibility for public relations departments. They are the bulk of the expanding work of public relations agencies. One of the clearest, observable trends in public relations, however, is the growing view that organizational communication is a continuous process, not just a succession of programs.

Although public relations practitioners will still develop and deliver specific products and programs, they will increasingly be involved in broader, less discrete responsibilities and more focused on multiple programs aimed at enhancing and preserving the long-term reputation. They will spend more time and effort developing communication objectives that are consistent with an organization's overall objectives. They will act as counselors to management and serve on teams with managers and other organizational specialists, working closely and cogently on a broad array of organizational programs. They will adopt a long-term, general perspective instead of specific short-term ones.

From Media Craftsperson to Communication Planner

Owing to the traditional emphasis on producing specific products and programs, public relations practitioners have been viewed as possessing a specific set of skills. Writing ability has always led the list, followed by speaking, interpersonal skills, and a potpourri of other abilities, including photography, graphic design, and the like. Over time, the skill base only gets broader and the work more varied. Consider how much there is to know today about Web page design; expanded e-mail uses, including the intranet; and visual communication. And yet the greater the number of media and communication outlets, the greater the need for future practitioners to know how to use each medium most effectively and creatively. Knowing how to best use each of these skill sets or tactics is what makes public relations as much a thinking and planning process as it is a "doing" process.

From Short-Term Items to Long-Term Relationship Development

In times past, public relations practitioners sought to place items in the media and measured their effectiveness by their success. The current trend carries public relations away from that stage, through defending against negative publicity, and toward issues management.

Issues management is the identification of key issues confronting organizations and the management of organizational responses to them. This process involves early identification of potential controversies, development of organizational policy related to these issues, creation of programs to carry out policies, implementation of these programs, and communication with appropriate publics about these policies and programs and evaluation of the results.

The issues management process is an area in which public relations has its greatest potential in terms of contributions to managerial decision making. Organizations can avoid negative publicity and gain positive public notice by adapting in advance to environmental demands. In this way, they are able to reap benefits by being perceived as responsible leaders. Public relations practitioners must be prepared to identify and deal with issues that confront their organizations.

From Firefighters to Crisis Managers

Among the most fully established trends affecting public relations practitioners is the evolution of their role from being "firefighters" to "fire preventers." Effective public relations does not exist merely to clean up messes once they are made but seeks to avoid such situations. Preventive public relations is a widely held ideal among practitioners. Public relations practitioners are moving into positions that allow them to more fully recognize areas of potential danger, to be equipped to deal with those dangers, and to possess sufficient power and influence to effect needed changes before potentials become realities. It is now standard practice for public relations practitioners to prepare and rehearse written crisis communication contingencies. In fact, the crisis planning process gained steam in the months following the September 11, 2001, terrorist attacks on New York's World Trade Center and the U.S. Pentagon in Washington, D.C., and was emphasized again in the crisis debacle of Hurricane Katrina in September 2005.

From Manipulation to Understanding, Negotiation, and Compromise

Public relations was born as a manipulative art. Its intent was to achieve specific results in terms of customer response, election outcomes, media coverage, or public attitudes. Public relations' purpose was to communicate in such ways as to ensure the compliance of relevant publics' behavior and attitudes with an individual or organization's plans. The means, methods, and media of communication were determined by what it took to get the job done and little else. Stunts, sensationalism, and embellished, highly selective truth were the hallmarks of the trade.

Such crass manipulation made for short-term rather than long-term impact, thereby limiting the effectiveness of public relations. The fact is that public relations is still about persuasion and social influence. What's changed are the myriad sophisticated ways in which persuasive techniques are utilized today.

From a Male- to a Female-Dominated Profession

There were still more male than female public relations practitioners in 1983 when this book was first published. Today, however, female practitioners outnumber their male counterparts 71 percent to 29 percent. In recent years, female public relations graduates outnumber males almost 10 to 1. Even so, older males continue to hold a disproportionate number of senior and managerial level positions that carry higher salaries. Ongoing research attempts to understand gender-based differences in salary, rates of promotion, and leadership in the top public relations or communication corporate role.

From U.S. Profession to Global Profession

The last decade has seen worldwide expansion of public relations as a global function. Cultural, language, and legal differences make global public relations more difficult, but rapidly evolving communication technologies have made these barriers less of a factor. Marshall McLuhan's "global village" predicted almost 40 years ago has finally arrived. The future of public relations must take the global community into account in all its efforts.

Case Study

Starbucks Enters Global Markets

Specialty coffee company Starbucks is fast becoming as well known outside the United States as it is within. With more than 3,000 stores outside the United States, Starbucks's international business constitutes about 40 percent of total store units. The company opened its first international stores in 1996 in Japan. Today, Japan has the largest number of Starbucks outlets outside the United States, followed by the United Kingdom. All told, Starbucks operates in 36 countries in Asia, Europe, the Middle East, and Latin America.

Although Starbucks has plenty of room to grow in the United States judging from its 7 percent coffee market share, the company is clearly laying the groundwork for future growth once the U.S. business slows.

Rather than opening company-owned stores or subsidiary operations outside the United States, Starbucks locates business partners around the globe whose management philosophies and cultural sensitivities support Starbucks. And international public relations director Soon Beng Yeap gets in on the ground floor in selecting their overseas business partners:

> We want to know early on if partners help raise our reputation or will have problems. By sitting in on all discussions, I am able to ask questions and pose alternatives to our top executives. In terms of public relations, I am especially concerned with the prospective partner's issues, credibility, strength of his/her current brands, and financials. We need to know if their image is consistent with ours and what we want it to become. At the same time we're sizing up the prospective partner, we're learning more about all the cultural influences impinging on business.

Once the partner is selected, public relations planning moves to overall launch plans, including media relations, internal or employee relations, community relations, corporate philanthropy, and dealing with activist organizations. Together with the business partner and perhaps a local agency, Starbucks's management considers all the cultural ramifications of the launch and seeks input on building community and media support and in attracting the most desirable local employees.

Starbucks does not advertise. Instead, it builds its brand image through effective media relations to gain the credibility that comes with third-party endorsement. Starbucks's credibility shoots up in the marketplace when reporter-written media coverage presents Starbucks favorably. This all comes about because Starbucks hosts elaborate media briefings months prior to a grand opening. A couple of months ahead of the scheduled opening, Starbucks invites top magazine and business editors from that region of the world to gather at

Starbucks's expense for a preview of the new store plans. When the reporters return home and write their stories, the published clips go into the press books that Starbucks distributes to local media just before the scheduled store opening. This process also works as a form of third-party endorsement in that the local media are induced to publicize the topics that have been covered by larger metropolitan, national, and global media.

Local public relations firms or agencies are selected to support on-site media relations and especially follow-up requests from reporters, to implement grand opening event plans, and to help initiate some of the community involvement activities. What's important, though, is that overall strategic planning remains either at corporate headquarters in Seattle or international division offices located in Amsterdam, Hong Kong, and Miami, Florida. By keeping public relations planning centralized, Starbucks hopes to build the brand image with message consistency and to be positioned to handle overall corporate reputation issues.

As corporate public relations director, Soon Beng Yeap also has input into employment issues because work norms vary from culture to culture. In Asia, for example, Starbucks employees wear name tags because uniforms and name tags are highly regarded both by employees and by their families. Elsewhere, employee name tags might be seen as an invasion of privacy and tempting to potential stalkers. Public relations strategies are also employed to position Starbucks as the employer of choice by (1) producing a great working environment, (2) child care, (3) stock options, (4) dress down opportunities, (5) open access to executives, and (6) involvement in corporate-sponsored community service projects.

Starbucks's community relations programs are intended to reflect a corporate sense of social responsibility adjusted to varying laws and cultural and ethnicity issues. For instance, the community relations program begins with a community preopening to show the community that Starbucks wants its blessing and permission to operate there. Preopenings are set up as friends and family events with a guest list made up of community leaders, neighbors, and parents of employees.

In Asia, all first-day sales go to charity as selected by the employees. This simple gesture underscores giving back to the community. Because Starbucks's principal community relations program is the books for children's literacy campaign, the company asks its international business partners if such a program would support community relations efforts there. The fact is that several U.S.-based community relations programs do not work abroad, including recycling, which is not seen as a respected or revered practice in many parts of the world.

This case study underscores several principles for conducting public relations work internationally. First, there's no single pattern governing how businesses expand globally; consequently, there's no single recipe for preparing international public relations programs. Second, the Starbucks case underscores the importance of understanding cultural differences and intercultural communication patterns and then refitting the public relations plan accordingly. And finally, the skillful use of media relations and third-party endorsement principles gives Starbucks sufficient high-level, free media coverage so that it has not yet had to use consumer advertising to implement its business model or to achieve desired profit levels.

Source: Interviews with Soon Beng Yeap, Starbucks's corporate public relations director, by Jim Van Leuwan, 2003.

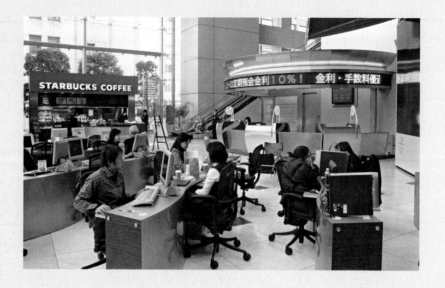

Customers surf the Internet in Shinsei Bank in Tokyo where a Starbucks serves its vast array of coffees. Starbucks has built its brand image without costly advertising.

Questions

1. Following Starbucks's typical plan for public relations when opening a new store in a country outside the United States, what would you as public relations director do if you were to open a new store in Panama City, Panama, in six months?

2. What lessons could you apply from Starbucks if you were opening a retail sub sandwich shop in Frankfurt?

3. Which does Harold Burson in video clip #5 say would be the countries where public relations would have a difficult time accomplishing what Starbucks has done by using public relations efforts to launch a new store?

Summary

For self-testing and additional chapter resources, go to the Online Learning Center at **www.mhhe.com/lattimore3e.**

Public relations today faces continual challenges, including the increased need for effective strategies for crisis communication, keeping up with the increasing avenues of interaction with stakeholders through the new social media, the evolving global public relations community and practice, and the changing organizational structure needed to meet these challenges.

Crises are different than everyday problems in that they attract public scrutiny through news coverage. Learning how to plan and deal with crises is becoming essential for the 21st-century organization.

The public relations profession must also deal with the rising new social media. While still seen as a publicity and media relations function, public relations is becoming both more strategic in nature and more broad based in its communication services. Beyond that, the future of public relations work seems to hinge on planning communication programs that serve an organization's business goals or overall strategic plan.

change management expert
crisis
crisis plan
globalization
Internet
issues management

knowledge management
relationship marketing
rich media
rumor
World Wide Web

Key Terms

Notes

1. Institute for Crisis Management Web site, www.crisisexperts.com, February 25, 2001.

2. Ibid.

3. Cohn & Wolfe Web site, www.cohnwolfe.com, February 25, 2001.

4. Carole Howard, "Technology and Tabloids: How the New Media World Is Changing Our Jobs," *Public Relations Quarterly* 45, no. 1 (Spring 2000), p. 9.

5. O'Reilly & Associates and Nielson NetRatings data from www.Internetworldstats.com, July 23, 2005.

6. University of Southern California's Digital Media Project, "Digital Futures Project: 7th Annual Internet Survey," retrieved from www.digitalmediaproject.com, March 8, 2008.

7. Ibid.

8. Howard, p. 9.

9. Don Middleberg and Steven Ross, "The Middleberg/Ross Media Survey: Change and Its Impact on Communications," Eighth Annual National Survey, 2002.

10. Don Middleberg, *Winning PR in the Wired World: Powerful Communications Strategies for the Noisy Digital Space* (New York: McGraw-Hill, 2001).

11. Ibid.

12. James B. Quinn, "Strategic Outsourcing: Leveraging Knowledge Capabilities," *Sloan Management Review* 40, no. 4 (Summer 1999), p. 9.

13. Richard Nemec, "What's New? Everything," *Communication World* 16, no. 7 (August/September 1999), pp. 21–24.

14. Timothy Coombs, *Ongoing Crisis Communication: Planning, Managing, and Responding* (Thousand Oaks, CA: Sage, 1999).

15. Maureen Taylor, Michael L. Kent, and William J. White, "How Activist Organizations Are Using the Internet to Build Relationships," *Public Relations Review* 27 (2001), p. 264.

16. Donald Wright, "Corporate Communications Policy Concerning the Internet: A Survey of the Nation's Senior-Level Corporate Public Relations Officers," Institute for Public Relations, 1998.

17. An IABC/PRSA Joint Survey of the Profession, "Profile 2000," *Communication World* (June/July, 2000).

18. Brian Heiss and Edie Fraser, "Is Your Company Ready to Go Global?" *Communication World* 17, no. 6 (August/September 2000), p. 29.

19. Ray Kotcher, "Roundtable: Future Perfect? Agency Leaders Reflect on the 1990s and Beyond," *Public Relations Strategist* 8, no. 3 (Summer 2001), p. 11.

20. Heiss and Fraser, pp. 29–30.

21. An interview with Jack Bergen.

22. Kate Vitale, "Knowledge Management: An Executive Summary for Busy Practitioners," *Journal of Communication Management* 3, no. 2 (November/December 1998), pp. 44–51.

23. IABC, "Think Tank Report," www.iabc.com, retrieved November 2002.

24. Middleberg/Ross survey.

25. James Grunig and Todd Hunt, *Managing Public Relations* (New York: Holt, Rinehart & Winston, 1984).

Good writing begins with clear thinking. First, you must logically think through the message you want to tell your target audience. Public relations writing is purposeful; know who your target audiences are and how to relate to them. Then decide what channel is best to use; different writing styles are suited for different media. Finally, use the proper vocabulary and grammar to reflect your purpose in communicating.

Writing forms the basis for most of the work of public relations. In this appendix, we look at the Ten Commandments of Public Relations Writing and some simple rules associated with each. At the conclusion, we list rules for formatting and writing a news release.

The Ten Commandments of Public Relations Writing are as follows:

1. You shall honor truth and accuracy above all else.
2. You shall not commit literature.
3. You shall not demean the English language.
4. You shall always write for audience comprehension.
5. You shall engage audience interest.
6. You shall express thoughts concisely.
7. You shall observe the rules of grammar.
8. You shall spell accurately.
9. You shall observe the rules of punctuation.
10. You shall adhere to the standards of the medium.[1]

1. Truth and Accuracy

Nothing is more important in public relations writing than truth and accuracy; individual and organizational reputations are put on the line with everything that is written. The concepts of truth and accuracy are separate. You can be truthful but inaccurate, or inaccurate yet truthful. But both qualities must be present to give you the credibility the public requires of you and your organization.

If an error is made, apologizing may help, especially for organizations, but as an individual practitioner you will find it hard to regain credibility if a reporter is caught in an error that originated with you.

2. Literature

Poetic prose has no place in public relations practice. Neither does intellectual elitism. The language of the public relations practitioner must be the language of the journalist, which is the language of the masses.

Public relations demands the ability to work in multiple writing styles—those of newspapers, trade magazines, electronic media, the Internet, and many others. But the primary purpose is still to have your audience act on your message. So that message must always be easy to understand, retain, and act upon.

3. Language Usage

Public relations writing must use language properly. "Public relations writing deals in short, declarative sentences. It applies words selected for understanding . . . it conveys information without distraction."[2]

Here are some basic language usage rules and examples[3]:

a. Write with brevity.
    1. Eliminate clichés, stock phrases, and glittering generalities.
        Example: He traveled a distance of 12 miles.
        Better: He traveled 12 miles.
    2. Shorten verbal phrases to simple verbs.
        Example: He made mention of the new contract in today's speech.
        Better: He mentioned the new contract in today's speech.
    3. Delete unnecessary words or phrases.
        Example: Roger W. Murray paid in the neighborhood of $80,000 for his home.
        Better: Roger W. Murray paid about $80,000 for his home.
    4. Eliminate repetition and redundancy.
        Example: The club will meet for its regular monthly meeting tomorrow at 3 P.M. in the auditorium.
        Better: The club will meet tomorrow at 3 P.M. in the auditorium.
    5. Use simple words for clarity.
        Example: He substantiated the facts.
        Better: He checked the facts.
b. Use proper verb tense.
    Present tense makes the writing seem more positive, alive, and up-to-date. It also helps keep sentences shorter, less awkward, and less artificial. But there are times for using past tense or past perfect. You must decide what is appropriate for the material.
c. Choose active over passive voice.
    Passive voice is often a sign of lazy writing. Active voice, by contrast, results in more understandable copy, shorter sentences, and dynamic expression. The differences are easy to see.
    If the subject of the verb receives the action, the verb is in the passive voice.
        Example: The burglar was shot three times by police.
    If the subject of the verb is the doer of the action, the verb is in the active voice.
        Example: Police shot the burglar three times.

d. Use the appropriate vocabulary.

The public relations writer draws from a full, varied vocabulary, rich in specific words that convey exact meaning and connotation. For example, "government" may be more neutral to a reader than "regime." Choose the simple word over the complex and the concrete over the abstract. Avoid slang, foreign words, highly technical words, and clichés.

4. Reader Understanding

To write clearly, write for a specific audience. Then write so your reader will understand. Rudolph Flesch suggests that the average number of words in a sentence should be 20.[4] In *Say What You Mean,* Flesch cites research showing that, above that average, your ability to reach a mass audience declines significantly. He also suggests using fewer prefixes and suffixes to increase audience comprehension.

5. Audience Interest

Thanks to the television remote, we can zap advertising messages we don't want to hear. But it is almost as easy to tune out other kinds of messages as well. The public relations writer's fundamental challenge, then, is to engage the audience with the message. A highly effective way is to invoke the self-interest principle. "What's in it for me?" is the question the audience will ask and the writer must answer.

6. Concise Expression

Conciseness is the ability to communicate clearly in as few words as possible. Whittle your drafts and prune unnecessary words and phrases.

7. Grammar

While a detailed knowledge of grammar is helpful for any writer, it's essential to have at least a working knowledge of the fundamentals. The following 10 basic rules of grammar offer a good review for the public relations writer.[5]

Rule 1: Verbs must agree with their subjects in number (singular or plural) and person (I, you, they).

Example: We **are**; you **are**; she **is**.

Rule 2: Words intervening between the subject and verb do not affect the number of the verb.

Example: Improvements in the mall **have** not increased the cost.

Rule 3: When the subject is one of the following words, the verb must be singular: *anybody, each, every, everybody, nobody, either. Neither* and *none* usually require the singular verb but not always.

Examples: Each of the members **has** filed a report.
Neither of the editors **is** going.

However, if *neither* is used to link plural nouns, then a plural verb is used.

Example: Neither members nor officers **have** come to the national meeting in two years.

Rule 4: When the subject is a collective noun, consider the subject singular or plural depending on the meaning you wish to convey.

> *Examples:* The office staff **is** planning a year-end party. [staff as group]
>
> The office staff **are** listed individually in the directory. [staff as individuals]

Rule 5: Verb tenses should indicate the correct sequence of action; therefore, a verb in a subordinate clause should be consistent with the verb tense in the main clause.

> *Example:* When Governor Ramos **finished** the speech, he realized he had **forgotten** to mention the tax reduction bill.

Rule 6: Active voice is preferred for most verbs.

> *Example:* My team made the decision. [Rather than, The decision was made by my team.]

Rule 7: Modifiers must be located close enough to the word or phrase they modify for the reader to be able to distinguish clearly what they modify.

> *Incorrect:* The president said that he was tired and would return to Washington after the news conference.
>
> *Correct:* After the news conference, the president said he was tired and would return to Washington.

Rule 8: Pronouns must refer to their antecedents.

> *Incorrect:* The alderman told the sheriff that his statement was incorrect. [Whose statement?]
>
> *Correct:* The sheriff's statement was incorrect, the alderman told him.

Rule 9: The case of a pronoun must suit its function.

a. A pronoun used as an object of the preposition must take the objective case.

> *Example:* He came with **me.** [not I]

b. A pronoun must agree with the word it explains.

> *Example:* Only two officers, John and **I,** could go to the meeting. (I refers to the subject; therefore, like the subject, the pronoun must be in the subjective case.)

c. A pronoun modifying a gerund must take the possessive case.

> *Example:* The college administration appreciates **your** [not you] exercising restraint in dealing with the students.

Rule 10: The elements in a series must be grammatically parallel.

Adjectives should be linked with other adjectives, adverbs with adverbs, infinitives with infinitives, and so forth.

> *Incorrect:* The North Sea oil companies plan to install new drilling equipment, to hire additional employees, and computerize lab operations.
>
> *Correct:* The North Sea oil companies plan to install new drilling equipment, to hire additional employees, and to computerize lab operations. (All the verbs are infinitives.)

8. Spelling

You may think you don't need to be able to spell because your computer's spell-checker will protect you. It will most of the time but not when there are multiple spellings of similar words. The spell-checker, for instance, won't catch the difference between its and it's, there and their, and deer and dear. Misspelled words make you look incompetent; proofread carefully.

9. Punctuation

Most word processing programs now have a grammar-checker that will flag major punctuation errors. These applications are far from perfect, however. Here are some key punctuation guidelines to remember:

a. Connect with a comma two independent clauses that are joined by a conjunction.

    Example: The ship's captain went with me to the boat, and he helped me load my gear on board.

b. Connect with a semicolon two independent clauses that are not joined by a conjunction.

    Example: The ship's captain went with me to the boat; he helped me load my gear on board.

c. For public relations writing, separate a series of objects or phrases with a comma before each except the last if the list is short; otherwise put a comma before the last in the list just before the conjunction joining the end item.

    Example: My father, my sister and my mother came to my performance.

d. Use hyphens to make a compound adjective when two or more modifiers precede the noun.

    Example: The three-year-old boy was rushed to the hospital this morning. (But: The boy was three years old.)

e. Use quotation marks around exact quotations. Include closing punctuation within the quotation marks.

    Example: Paul Evans said, "We should fire the financial vice president before another day goes by."

f. Use commas to set off an appositive.

    Example: Tom Wilson, the filmmaker, will receive the highest award given by the Tennessee Film Commission.

g. Use a comma to set off a dependent clause from the independent clause.

    Example: If the state passes the expected budget, the public school teachers will receive a 3 percent salary increase beginning January 1.

h. Use an apostrophe and *s* for a singular possessive. Put an apostrophe after the *s* for a plural possessive. For nouns that are plural in form but singular in meaning, add only an apostrophe. Treat nouns that are the same in singular and plural form as plural in form.

    Examples: The girl's car was stolen by three boys.

    The three boys' shoes were left in the car when they abandoned it trying to escape.

    The blues' influence on American music was profound.

    The deer's tracks were quite obvious. [Whether one or more deer]

10. Media Standards

Writers have personal styles, but organizations often compile style guides to make sure all their written materials conform to the same standards. The media typically use the *Associated Press Stylebook* as their guide, although some individual media organizations may add their own rules to the AP standards. Broadcast media have some style rules that are different from those of newspapers or magazines. Internet writing is still evolving, and while organizations may impose their style on text for their Web site and Web materials, there is no standard Web style. Spotlight 7.2 gives Internet Writing Guidelines as developed from research by a graduate student studying what worked best on the Internet. Your own writing must conform in style to that of the organization for which you are writing.

Preparing News Releases

The simplest and least expensive way to reach the media is the publicity, news, or press release, the heart of any publicity effort. Public relations practitioners can duplicate or e-mail such releases to dozens, even thousands, of news outlets. Releases can convey routine news, provide potential feature or background material, or offer follow-up information.

Publicity releases take many forms depending on the audience and the medium for which they are intended. Still, some general rules apply. A publicity release should focus on one topic only, conform to accepted journalistic style, and begin with an opening paragraph (lead) that can stand by itself.

Here are some tips for writing a news release (also see chapter 8):

1. Use the inverted pyramid style of writing, emphasizing the important or interesting facts first in the story.
2. Answer as many as possible of the basic questions of a news story—the five "W's" and "H"—who, what, where, when, why, and how—early in the news release. (Note that "when" makes for a weaker lead than the others if used alone.)
3. Keep the lead to 25 words or less.
4. Treat information that is not a timely news item as a feature story instead.
5. Be concise; releases should only rarely exceed two pages. Provide supplemental information (if any) on a separate fact sheet.
6. Include only information appropriate to the specific medium.
7. Be strictly accurate. Spell all names correctly; get the facts straight and the quotes correct.
8. Be specific, not general. Use examples; show your point.
9. Do not editorialize or advocate a viewpoint.
10. Vary the length of your paragraphs. A paragraph may be as short as one sentence but should not be more than six typed lines. Sentences should also vary in length but should average no more than 20 words each.

Some stories can lose their impact if too many facts are forced into the lead. In such cases, select one or two major facts that will attract the reader's (and editor's) interest. If the person being written about is not prominent, you may choose not to mention his or her name in the opening; this technique is known as a blind lead. Once you have organized the essential facts into an opening paragraph, follow with details and elaboration in descending order of importance, to allow editors to cut the story to fit the space or time available.

Attention to a few other guidelines will make your publicity more effective.

1. Use standard format with $8\frac{1}{2}$-by-11-inch plain white paper typed double-spaced on only one side.

2. Give your organization's name, address, Web site, and telephone number. The public relations contact person's name, telephone number, and e-mail address should also appear in the top portion of the release.

3. Give a release time. Most releases should be marked, "For Immediate Release." If there is a compelling reason to have a future release time and date, write, "For Release at noon, September 21." Be sure to include the date the release is prepared, in either the top portion of the release or in the dateline (see #6 below).

4. So that the editor can see at a glance what the story is about (and not to suggest a headline), put a summary title or headline above the story.

5. Start your story approximately one-third of the way down the first page.

6. Begin with the dateline. Today wire services use only the name of the city and sometimes the state where the story originated; however, you may also include the date if you prefer. The state is needed if the city of origin has fewer than one million in population. A larger city, such as Chicago, does not need the state name included.

7. Complete a sentence before going to the next page. Put "more" at the bottom of each continued page. Place page numbers on succeeding pages along with a two-to-three-word "slug" identifying the story. This usually goes in the upper left corner of the page. At the end of the story type "-30-." Or you may use ### or END to indicate the conclusion of a story.

8. When appropriate, include high-quality photographs with your release. Attach a caption to the bottom border of the photo, and mark the back with soft felt pen giving the name, address, and phone number of the contact person. If you send the photos electronically, be sure the dots per inch, dpi, is at least 300. Internet dpi is typically 75 dpi, which is not good enough for print reproduction.

NOTES

1. E. W. Brody and Dan Lattimore, *Public Relations Writing* (New York: Praeger, 1990), p. 69.

2. Ibid., p. 72.

3. Dan Lattimore and John Windhauser, *The Editorial Process*, 2nd ed. (Englewood, CO: Morton Publishing Co., 1984), pp. 33–39.

4. Rudolph Flesch, *Say What You Mean* (New York: Harper and Row, 1972), pp. 59–96.

5. James Redmond, Frederick Shook, Dan Lattimore, and Laurie Lattimore-Volkmann, *The Broadcast News Process*, 7th ed. (Englewood, CO: Morton Publishing Co., 2005), pp. 35–36.

Speechmaking

By Dan Reines

Speaking in public isn't easy. For most people, just standing in front of dozens of people can be nerve-wracking. Standing and talking is even worse. And standing, talking, and being interesting, insightful, and memorable . . . all at the same time? Only pros need apply—or so it may seem.

If you're at all comfortable speaking in public, you have a huge edge right out of the blocks. But even if you suffer at the very thought of giving a public presentation, don't worry—because you are far from alone; it won't take much for you to stand out in the crowd. As communications expert Tony Carlson says in *The How of Wow,* "on a beige canvas, even a dash of color makes an impact and becomes memorable."

Of course, you want to give speeches that provide more than just a dash of color. You want to paint masterpieces. That doesn't happen overnight, but it can happen. To get started, you'll want to follow some basic, time-tested techniques, both in preparing your speech and in delivering it.

PREPARING YOUR SPEECH

Pick a Subject

Before you write a word, you'll need to figure out what you're going to talk about. That seems obvious, but this is no small consideration. Whenever possible, pick a subject that fascinates you. As presentation coach Ron Hoff, author of *Do Not Go Naked into Your Next Presentation,* puts it, you've got the right subject if "you'd be reading about it on a beach somewhere if you weren't scheduled to be giving a speech." The more interested in a topic you are, the more you'll know about it, and the more engaging you'll be as a speaker. Nothing bores an audience more quickly than a bored speaker.

Here are some other considerations in choosing a topic for your speech. Does it fit the occasion? Is it an appropriate subject for you? Think about the audience. How many people will be there? Who are they? You'll probably want an entirely different topic if you're speaking to an audience of marketing professionals than you would if you were speaking to a group of elementary school teachers—and even if the topic is the same for both, your angle may differ. Ask yourself, what do your listeners know about your topic? What do you want them to know? And what do *they* want from *you*? Remember, the audience is giving you an investment of its time and attention. Listeners are going to be thinking about what's in it for *them.* You should be too.

Even your physical surroundings are important in choosing a subject. Pick a topic that fits the room. "If you're going to give an instructional talk on how to conduct a safety seminar," Hoff explains, "you should be in a smallish room. You'll look like an idiot talking about safety seminars in a chandeliered ballroom just before a six-course dinner. By the same token, you don't want to deliver a landmark speech on global warming in a committee room that holds twelve people."

Write the Speech

Nearly every how-to manual ever written about speechmaking says the same thing about structuring a presentation: "Tell 'em what you're gonna say . . . say it . . . then tell 'em what you just told 'em." It's a tried-and-true method, but it's not terribly interesting. Tony Carlson offers a different tack. He asks, "Do we really think audience members are so stupid that they need to hear stuff three times? This conventional speech structure is tired." Carlson suggests that you'd be better off starting at the end and working backward: "Begin with what you want the audience to believe or do at the end of the speech, then figure out how to get there," he writes. "Only when you know what you want the audience to do after the speech can you build a speech that the audience will remember, that will build your brand."

The following guidelines will help you to write a more engaging speech:

- *Make sure you have a clear central message.* You know what you want to talk *about,* but what do you want to *say*? Iowa State University's College of Agriculture runs a useful communications Web site at www.ag.iastate.edu /aginfo/speechindex.html. Their advice? "Keep it simple! If you can't state your central message in one or two sentences, you probably haven't narrowed your topic enough." When you've got that message, begin developing a few key points—any more than five will muddy the water. These key points will act as the pegs on which you'll hang your whole presentation.

- *Find a hook with which to begin your presentation.* You're going to be nervous, and your audience is going to be full of anticipation. Don't tell a joke unless you're sure it's relevant and you happen to be a dynamite joke-teller. And resist the temptation to open with a quote from a famous person. As Tony Carlson says, "quoting someone famous doesn't show that that person would agree with you: it shows that you agree with that person."

- *Tell a story.* Make it simple or poignant or funny if you're any good at telling funny stories. The key is, it should be something personal that will allow you to connect with your audience right away. As Caryl Rae Krannich writes in *101 Secrets of Highly Effective Speakers,* "Stories tell of events that have happened to people. Stories personalize a message as listeners can identify with the people and situations you relate."

As you write the body of your speech, keep in mind the basic rules of writing mentioned in appendix 1. Your words should be simple and direct, without unnecessary ornamentation. Stay away from clichés, avoid the passive voice, and use proper grammar. Minimize jargon, and if you do use it, make sure it's appropriate and that your audience will understand what you're talking about. Use conversational language, including contractions and even sentence fragments. In other words, write like you speak—because you *will* be speaking.

Finally, don't just say things, *show* them—tell stories, use examples, or use numbers to illustrate and support your points. Make sure what you're telling your listeners is interesting and useful to *them* and make sure they know it. Develop a strong closing, perhaps one that recalls your introduction in some way.

And most important, keep it short. In most cases, if you talk longer than a half hour, you're begging your audience to tune you out.

Get Ready

The first rule of preparing to deliver a speech is as follows: Know your stuff and know it cold. The better you know your material, the better off you'll be. In *Do Not Go Naked into Your Next Presentation,* Hoff recommends that you have at least seven times as much information as you'll actually use. "When you say to yourself, 'I know more about this subject than anyone else in the room,' it should be true—not just *hopefully* true," he writes. "When you're convinced it's true, you won't be nervous."

Of course, that doesn't mean you should memorize your speech word for word. It's a speech, not a recital. It does, however, mean that you should know your speech well enough to find your way back into it if your laptop fails, or the lights go out for a second, or the guy in the third row has a hacking cough that won't quit. If someone blindfolded you and walked you to a random spot in your home, you'd know where you were when the blindfold was removed, and you'd know how to get to the front door. Know your speech as well as you know your home.

So how do you get to that point of familiarity? Practice, practice, practice. And practice smart. Here are a few tips that nearly every speechmaking expert agrees on:

- *Practice aloud.* Do it at full voice, in the volume you'll be using to give the speech itself. Look out for tongue-twisters and hard-to-pronounce words that you may not notice in your written text. If you're going to be speaking at a podium, practice at a podium.

- *Watch yourself.* Practice in front of a full-length mirror so that you can see your body language. Are you fiddling with your wristwatch? Jangling the coins in your pocket? Tapping your foot to the beat of some unheard drummer? Better yet, videotape yourself. That way you can focus on the presentation now and the fidgeting later.

- *Get feedback.* If watching yourself is good, then having someone else watch you is even better. Find a trusted friend or adviser, preferably someone who's about as familiar with your subject matter as your audience will be. Get feedback on your words and your delivery. And if possible, make sure that person is in the audience when you speak so that you can find her or him when you need a familiar face to connect with.

Even after you've got your speech down, there's room for more preparation. Where are you giving your speech? If possible, run through your talk at the actual site to make sure you know the geography of the room, including any surprises. Is there a podium? If so, how tall is it? Will there be a giant screen behind the stage, or two smaller screens off to the side? How long will it take you to get from your seat to the stage when you're introduced? Even if you're speaking out of town, get a full description of the room. "Find out if it's cheery or dark, open or cavernous," says Ron Hoff. "See if you can determine its personality, sight unseen, then check it out carefully when you arrive."

On the day of your presentation, find a moment to plant yourself by the door as people are arriving to greet some of your audience members. This recommendation comes from the Toastmasters, an international organization that has been helping people overcome their fear of public speaking since the 1920s. After all, the reasoning goes, it's always easier to speak to a group of friends than to a group of strangers.

DELIVERING YOUR SPEECH

Be Presentable

On the day of your speech, you'll want to make sure your presentation is as strong as your words. Dress appropriately. Stand up straight. And read your text confidently and clearly. Better yet, don't read it at all.

Once you've written and practiced your presentation, it's not a bad idea to jettison the script. Pare it down to an extended outline with key phrases and talking points, rather than a word-for-word litany. This will force you to focus on your ideas, not on the specific words. It will also keep you from burying your head in the lectern and droning through 30 minutes of text, and it keeps things fresh if you happen to give the same speech more than once.

Make the Most of Visual Aids

According to Iowa State's communications Web site, research shows that people will remember 65 percent of information they're presented with after five days—if that information is presented with visual support. Without visual support? They retain only 5 percent of the information. Clearly, PowerPoint slides and other visuals can serve a purpose.

In fact, if used correctly, visuals can boost your presentation tremendously. Just make sure you keep them simple and clean, with a minimum of numbers and information. According to Tony Carlson, a single slide can't usefully contain more than about 40 words.

Better yet, though, a single slide can contain one very good image. "If there's a *noun* in your presentation, consider showing us what the noun represents," writes Ron Hoff. "If you're talking about a book, *show us* the book. If you're talking about a typical consumer, *show us* a one-minute videotape of that consumer. If you're talking about a product, *show us* that product."

But Don't Make Too Much of Them

Too many people use PowerPoint because everybody else is doing it, not because it actually adds anything to their presentation. If that's you, then save yourself the trouble. And definitely don't bother with slides that are simply visual bookmarks to let us know where you are in your speech. As Tony Carlson puts it, "All you're doing is helping the audience members gauge how much longer they have to count their teeth with their tongues until you're finished."

Whatever you do, make sure you know your equipment and how to fix it if something goes wrong. If you can't fix it, make sure you can get by without it. Because eventually, something *will* go wrong, and if you can't fix it or do without, you'll be standing on stage alone, exposed and vulnerable.

Finally, wait to pass out handouts until you're done speaking. If you don't, says Ron Hoff, "you are inviting [your audience] to pay *zero* attention to your speech."

Finally: Just Relax

This is the most important advice about public speaking that anyone will ever give you—and the most difficult to follow. For most people, the toughest thing by far about speaking in public is overcoming nerves, and you should expect to be dealing with butterflies no matter how long you've been speaking. Still, there are some things you can do to minimize your jitters and their impact on your speech:

- *Move around.* Before you go on, pace, swing your arms back and forth, do some jumping jacks. Just give your nervous energy an outlet.
- *Take a deep breath.* "When we get nervous, we breathe shallowly," says Ethel M. Cook, a management consultant and a past president of the New England Speakers Association. "If you concentrate on breathing deeply, you'll get enough air to speak and ease your panic."
- *Realize that people want you to succeed.* You're not alone up there. People want you to do well because they want to be entertained and enlightened. Everybody's rooting for you.
- *Don't apologize.* You may feel like there's a softball lodged in your throat, but the audience may not have noticed. Don't call attention to your nerves.
- *Focus on your message.* Think about what you're trying to say, not how you're saying it.
- *Make eye contact.* "You'll be amazed at the calming effect of *one* friendly face when you're trying to connect with a sea of strangers," says Hoff.
- *Get some experience.* The more you speak, the better you'll be. Get as much practice as you can.
- *Just don't worry about it.* You won't be perfect up there—nobody ever is. Don't put undue burdens on yourself.

REFERENCES

Carlson, Tony. (2005). *The How of Wow.* New York: AMACOM.

Cook, Ethel M. *Making Business Presentations Work.* Retrieved September 19, 2005, from www.businessknowhow.com /manage /presentation101.htm.

Hoff, Ron. (1997). *Do Not Go Naked into Your Next Presentation.* Kansas City, MO: Andrews and McMeel.

Krannich, Caryl Rae. (1998). *101 Secrets of Highly Effective Speakers.* Manassas Park, VA: Impact Publications.

Mayer, Lyle U. (2004). *Fundamentals of Voice and Articulation.* New York: McGraw-Hill.

Osborn, Michael, and Suzanne Osborn. (2005). *Public Speaking,* 7th ed. Boston: Houghton Mifflin Co.

Steps to Giving an Effective Speech. Retrieved September 19, 2005, from www.ag.iastate.edu /aginfo/ speechindex.html.

10 Tips for Successful Public Speaking. Retrieved September 19, 2005, from www.toastmasters.org/ pdfs /top10.pdf.

Glossary

A

action implementation   Any attempt to spread information within a target audience as part of a public relations plan.

active public   People who are aware of a problem and will organize to do something about it.

advergaming   Branded, interactive online entertainment used in conjunction with a marketing campaign. This is often delivered via pop-up ads on third-party sites.

advertainment   A branded entertainment experience on the Web.

advocacy communication   Communication techniques used by advocates of a political cause or public policy change.

agency of record   Being designated an "agency of record" usually means that the corporation has an exclusive agreement with an agency to work on a particular product or service.

agenda   Items or ideas the public relations practitioner wants to get across in a media interview.

annual meetings   Yearly meetings at which a corporation's stockholders have the opportunity to meet and vote on various issues related to company management.

annual report   A yearly report to stockholders prepared by publicly held corporations, containing required financial performance information and other material designed to promote the organization.

API (Application Programming Interface)   Ease of creating content and moving it into a variety of Web sites is often the result of using an open API provided by these sites.

B

blog   Short for Web log, blogs are journals that allow authors to post thoughts, philosophies, and opinions to a Web site for public consumption.

blogosphere   The collective universe of bloggers.

boundary spanning   Looking in and outside the organization to anticipate issues, problems and opportunities.

B-roll   Extra video footage often sent along with a video news release (VNR) for use by TV stations to prepare their own video stories about the topic on the video.

brainstorming   A technique of group discussion used to generate large numbers of creative alternatives or new ideas.

branded news   An independent electronic news outlet that uses a corporate-sponsored Web site as its vehicle for

(continued)

appropriation   Commercial use of an entity's picture, likeness, or name without permission.

attitude-action consistency   A set of theories and models accounting for the discrepancies between expressed attitudes and actual behavior.

audience coverage   Whether and how well intended publics were reached, which messages reached them, and who else heard the messages.

audit   An evaluation and inventory of an organizational system.

authoritarian cultures   Centralized decisions made in organizations by top management.

aware public   People who know about a problem but don't act on it.

reporting in-depth news about one particular industry.

brandstanding   Corporate sponsorship of special events as a way of getting publicity and gaining goodwill.

burnout   The idea that a message loses its punch if consumers hear it too often or too far in advance of an event.

C

campaign (project) budget   Zero-based budget where every tactic is given a cost to produce a budget for the public relations campaign.

change management expert   Someone who assists an organization in adapting to various changes, especially in relation to changes in culture.

civil libel   Cases involving published, defamatory information showing negligence and identifying the injured party. Injured party seeks monetary damage under civil statutes.

closed system   Organizations that do not seek new information from their environments.

closed-system evaluation   A pre-/post-event assessment that considers only the controlled message elements.

code of ethics   A formal set of rules governing proper behavior for a particular profession or group.

collective bargaining   A continuing institutional relationship between an employer and a labor organization concerned with the negotiation, administration, interpretation, and enforcement of contracts covering wages, working conditions, and other issues related to employment.

commercial speech Public communication by business organizations through advertising or public relations to achieve sales or other organizational goals.

communication audit Research to determine the flow of communication within an organization.

communication climate The degree of trust and openness that exists in the communication processes of an organization.

communication climate survey A scientific study usually administered through a questionnaire to measure the degree of trust and openness that exists internally in an organization.

communication flow The direction (upward, downward, or horizontal) messages travel through the networks in an organization.

communication load The total amount of communication received and initiated in a given channel.

communication networks The patterns of communication flow between individuals in organizations.

communication policies Final statements of organizational positions related to communication activities and behaviors and information sharing.

communication rules Mutually accepted standards of communication behavior that provide the basis for coordinated interpersonal interaction.

community relations A public relations function consisting of an institution's planned, active, and continuing participation with and within a community to maintain and enhance its environment to the benefit of both the institution and the community.

conference call (financial) Video or phone conference with the chief executive officer (CEO) and the chief financial officer (CFO) of a company and analysts, financial reporters, and other investment stakeholders. The call is usually scheduled the day following the release of a quarterly report. It is for the CEO and CFO to explain the meaning behind the numbers to the financial stakeholders.

conflict resolution Efforts to reduce friction between individuals or organizations and publics.

consumer-generated media (CGM) Online information that is created, developed, initiated, distributed, and used by consumers. Such information is often thought to be unbiased, credible, and objective because it is perceived that its providers only want to be helpful and share personal experiences with products, brands, and issues.

consumer relations The aspect of public relations that improves the organization's relationships and communication with consumers. This includes resolving customer complaints, disseminating consumer information, dealing with outside consumer advocacy groups, and advising management on consumer opinion.

content analysis Systematic coding of questionnaire responses or other written messages into categories that can be statistically analyzed.

contract A legal instrument that protects the rights of two or more parties.

controlled media Those media that the public relations practitioner has actual control over, such as a company newsletter.

copyright Legal protection from unauthorized use of intellectual property fixed in any tangible medium of expression.

corporate philanthropy Recognition of corporate obligations and responsibilities to communities represented by monetary and other contributions to charitable organizations.

corporate public relations Public relations activities that are intended to build a sound relationship between the organization and its employees.

corporate social responsibility A demonstration of a company's commitment to its neighbors, consumers, and others to be a good citizen.

counseling firm A public relations or marketing company hired by another organization to help with campaigns or run an entire public relations function.

criminal libel Public defamatory communication causing breach of the peace or incitement to riot; the state, or the injured party through the government, seeks punishment under criminal statutes, which may result in fine, imprisonment, or both.

crisis A situation, issue, or event that attracts public scruntiny through mass media and disrupts an organization's working environment.

crisis plan A standing public relations action plan to deal with how to react to crisis situations that is instituted the moment a crisis occurs.

critical theory Theories that relate underlying faults of public relations practice to larger social issues and value frameworks.

cross-disciplinary integration Messages from all media are consistent.

cultural interpreter model Model of public relations focused on explaining the culture of an organization's publics or stakeholders.

cybernetics The study of how systems use communication for direction and control.

cyberspace A term used to refer to the place where online conversations and information exchange take place.

D

defamation Any communication that holds a person up to contempt, hatred, ridicule, or scorn.

Delphi Model A technique for reaching consensus through multiple sets of questionnaires or interviews.

descriptive data Data used to describe something, such as a particular group of people (a public).

desk-side briefings A visit made by a public relations practitioner to a member of the media to pitch a story idea, provide background information, and update the reporter on current activities.

diffusion of information The way in which information spreads through a public.

diffusion of innovations Processes by which social changes (technologies, new social behaviors) are introduced into social systems.

diffusion theory Theory that states people adapt an idea only after going through five stages: awareness, interest, evaluation, trial, and adoption.

dominant coalition People who have the power to direct their organizations.

DVD A digital video disc that has a large storage capacity, enough for a full-length, high-resolution movie.

E

economic education Widespread efforts to overcome economic illiteracy.

economic illiteracy A lack of understanding on the part of individuals or the general public concerning economic concepts, relationships, and issues.

ecosystem A system serving as an environment for several smaller systems.

elaborated likelihood model A cognitive processing model that explains whether people skim messages for relevant cues (peripheral processing) or read and think through the material (central processing).

employee benefits Aspects of employee compensation, often including health and life insurance, vacation and sick leave, pension programs, and other valuable considerations.

employee communication A special audience within an organization that management must communicate with in order to have good internal public relations.

employee relations Public relations activities that are intended to build a sound relationship between the organization and its employees.

environment The surrounding social, political, and economic activity in which organizations exist.

environmental mediation Influences that effect a campaign that are outside the control of the public relations practitioner.

environmental monitoring Formal systems for observing trends and changes in public opinion that are used either once, periodically, or continuously.

environmental scanning The monitoring, evaluating, and disseminating of information to key decision makers within an organization.

expectancy value theory A behavioral theory regarding the rewards that people come to expect from messages based on past behavior.

ethics The criteria for determining what is right and wrong based on standards of conduct and morality.

evaluation An examination of the effectiveness of a public relations effort.

experimental research Scientific testing that usually includes an untested control group. Test results from the group or groups tested can be measured against the untested control group to determine the extent of difference.

extranet An Internet-based external communication system that organizations use as a link to the media and other outside stakeholder groups.

F

fair comment A defense against libel, the expression of opinion on matters of public interest.

fair use Permission to use creative expression of others without compensation; it is based on four criteria specified in the 1976 Copyright Law.

false light Part of privacy law that indicates privacy has been invaded if truthful information has been used either in an exaggerated form or out of context.

Federal Communications Commission (FCC) Established in 1934 to regulate television and radio broadcasting.

Federal Trade Commission (FTC) The regulatory body charged with assuring fair dealing in relation to goods and services in terms of such things as truth in advertising; it governs all commercial advertising.

feedback Information received in response to actions or messages about those actions or messages.

financial analysts Investment counselors, fund managers, and others whose function is to gather information about various companies, develop expectations of the companies' performances, and make judgments about how securities markets will evaluate these factors.

financial budget A detailed estimate of how much an organization expects to spend in a given period and where the money will come from.

financial press Media outlets devoted to coverage of business and financial information.

financial public relations The process of creating and maintaining investor confidence and building positive relationships with the financial community through the dissemination of corporate information.

First Amendment The initial section of the U.S. Bill of Rights that guarantees the freedoms of press, speech, assembly, and religion.

flack (or flak) A derogatory term sometimes applied to public relations practitioners, primarily by reporters and editors.

focus group A group of people representative of an organization's various publics who are called together, usually only once, to give advance reaction to a plan.

Food and Drug Administration (FDA) The agency that regulates labeling, packaging, and sale of food, drugs, and cosmetics.

formal research Scientific research or information gathering.

formative evaluation Monitoring of a program or campaign at various intervals as it progresses to determine what is working and what isn't and where changes need to be made.

Forms 10-K, 10-Q, and 8-K Reports required by the Securities and Exchange Commission from publicly traded companies.

for-profit organization An organization in which any extra monies not spent on overhead and operating expense are distributed on a prorated basis to company owners.

forum A gathering place on an online service such as America Online where people "meet" about a topic or theme. Messages are left, other people add to the discussion, and at times people "chat" online.

Freedom of Information Act (FOIA) A law passed in 1966, and amended in 1974, requiring disclosure of certain categories of government information.

FTP File transfer protocol, the principal means by which one retrieves files from the Internet.

G

game theory A framework for understanding outcomes of organizational behavior based on organizations and their publics taking each other's interests into account.

Gantt chart A graphic illustration of the time required to accomplish various jobs in a project.

gatekeeper   An individual positioned within a communication network to control the messages flowing through communication channels.

globalization   The process of developing worldwide markets and overall economic interdependence among the nations of the world.

goals   Basic direction of an organization or other entity. Goals are generally considered to be the top priority within an organization because they provide a sense of direction.

grassroots lobbying   Organizing local constituencies to influence government decision makers.

guerilla tactics   The concept of using nontraditional communication vehicles to gain visibility for a product or service. Sidewalk art, Internet chat rooms, and radio talk shows are some examples of guerilla tactics.

H

hierarchy   A proposition underlying systems theory that maintains that systems are organized in a successively more inclusive and complex pattern and that to understand systems of behavior several appropriate levels should be examined.

home page   A site on the Internet or World Wide Web where one can place data, including words, sound, and graphics, to be retrieved by Internet users.

hostile takeover   Company acquisition through an unfriendly takeover either through a tender offer or management change by a proxy fight.

I

impact analysis   Measuring the results of a public relations effort to determine its effect on an organization's program.

inferential data   Information that not only characterizes a particular group or situation but also allows researchers to draw conclusions about other groups or situations.

informal research   Nonscientific research or information gathering.

information subsidy   The savings in reporter time that media organizations are said to gain when they accept news releases and video materials from organizations.

integrated communications   Coordinating public relations, marketing, and advertising to create and strengthen the relationship the organization has with a consumer while selling the product or service.

integrated marketing communication   The process of using a variety of tactical applications to reach consumers. Choices may include advertising, public relations, endorsements, sponsorships, Web sites, video games, podcasts, and more.

interdependence   A proposition underlying systems theory that maintains that elements of systems cannot act unilaterally and that all elements of a system influence one another. Behavior is the product of systems, not individual system elements.

internal communication   Communication that takes place within an organization.

internal media   Channels of communication controlled by the organization and directed to audiences within the organization.

Internet   A vast, interconnected computer network that allows computers anywhere in the world to communicate instantly with computers in another part of the country or the world.

interorganizational communication   Structured communication among organizations linking them with their environments.

interpersonal communication   The exchange of messages between individuals through which needs, perceptions, and values are shared and by which mutual meanings and expectations are developed.

interpersonal and relational communication   The processes of relationship development between individuals as applied to the study of relationships between organizations and their publics.

intervening publics   People who may make it more difficult for an organization to reach those it aims to influence or gain approval from.

interviews   Gathering of information from a respondent. They may be obtained in person, on the phone, by mail, or on the Internet.

intranet   An Internet-based internal communication system that organizations use as a link to employees and board members.

intrusion   Surreptitious recording or observing of other people's private documents, possessions, activities, or communications.

invasion of privacy   Four areas in which one entity may violate the privacy of another: appropriation, publication of private information, intrusion, or publication of false information.

investment conferences   Meetings attended by investment professionals especially for the purpose of hearing company presentations.

investor relations   Public relations efforts with a company's stockholders.

issue advertising (advocacy advertising)   Advertising designed to communicate an organization's stand on a particular issue and seeking to generate support for that position.

issues management   The process of identifying issues that potentially impact organizations and managing organizational activities related to those issues.

K

key contacts   People who can influence the publics an organization is trying to reach or who have direct power to help the organization.

knowledge management   The computer-based system designed to increase productivity by getting the right information to the right people at the right time.

L

latent public   People who are not aware of an existing problem.

law   The rules of conduct established and enforced by authority in society.

level of analysis   In the systems approach, the magnitude of the system chosen for examination.

liaisons   Individuals who serve as linking pins connecting two or more groups within organizational communication networks. Sometimes referred to as internal boundary spanners.

libel Published defamation by written or printed words or in some other physical form that is communicated to a third party.

licensure A formal certification process that indicates a person measures up to a set of professional standards and qualifications.

line organization A method of structuring organizations as a sequence of ascending levels of responsibility for the production of goods or services.

lobbying The practice of trying to influence governmental decisions, usually done by agents who serve interest groups.

M

malice A requirement of civil libel in cases involving public figures that the plaintiff must show the defendant's knowledge of the falsity of published material or a reckless disregard for the truth.

management by objectives (MBO) A process specifying that supervisors and employees will jointly set goals for employees; usually followed by a joint evaluation of the employee's progress after a set period of time.

manager role Refers to the public relations roles undertaken by public relations managers to identify and solve problems.

marketing Business discipline concerned with building and maintaining a market for an organization's product or services. It focuses externally on selling and how quality and availability of a product or service affect its ability to be sold in the marketplace.

marketing communications Refers to all activities, be they research, strategies, tactics, that support the selling of products and services.

mass opinion The consensus of the public at large.

media agenda The topics chosen by media to report.

media kit See *press kit.*

media relations Activities intended to build open channels of communication between an organization and the media,

as a way of sharing news and features of potential interest to media audiences.

message Words, pictures, and actions to which meaning is attached.

mission Overall direction for an organization.

mission statement An oral or written statement that defines the overall direction for an organization.

model A way of looking at something.

moderating publics Those people who could make it easier for an organization to get its message through to the public it really wants to reach.

mutual expectations Shared similar responses to messages and events.

N

National Labor Relations Board (NLRB) The federal government regulatory body charged with overseeing union activities and union–management relations. It governs communication between unions and employers.

network Two or more computers linked together.

network analysis Research comparing organizational charts and communication policies to reality within the organization.

news conferences Structured opportunities to release news simultaneously to multiple media with an opportunity for the media personnel to ask questions.

news release A news story prepared for the media by the organization.

newsroom An area set aside to provide information, services, and amenities to journalists covering a story.

nonprofit organization A group or company whose primary purpose is not to make a profit, regardless of whether it actually does so in a given year.

O

observations Data or information secured by observing; qualitative evidence as contrasted with experimental or scientific evidence.

off-the-record An agreement with an interviewer not to print information provided.

online A situation where two or more computers are "talking" to each other.

open source The term most commonly applied to the source code of software that is made available to the general public with relaxed or nonexistent intellectual property restrictions. This allows users to create user-generated software content through incremental individual effort or through collaboration. Open source is part of the whole Web 2.0 movement and now means more than just software. It's evolved to mean partly a group of people coming together regardless of traditional organizational structures, to create something all benefit from but none can do alone.

open system Organizations that seek new information and feedback from their environments.

open-system evaluation An ongoing assessment of the effectiveness of public relations actions considering the impact of uncontrolled elements.

operating budget An estimate of the amount and costs of goods and services an organization expects to consume.

opinion leaders People who are instrumental in influencing other people's attitudes or actions.

organizational climate The collective subjective perceptions held by an organization's employees concerning organizational policies, structure, leadership, standards, values, and rules.

organizational communication The exchange and interaction of informal and formal messages within networks of interdependent relationships.

organizational culture The values, symbols, meanings, beliefs, and ways of doing things that integrate a group of people who work together.

P

participative cultures Organizational environment in which employees are empowered to make decisions in the organization.

perception The process of making sense of incoming stimuli.

perceptual screens Filters composed of needs, values, attitudes, expectations, and experiences through which individuals process messages to derive meaning.

personal influence model A model of public relations based on friendships.

persuasion   The communication process intended to change awareness, attitudes, or behavior.

planned publicity   Publicity that is the planned result of a conscious effort to attract attention to an issue, event, or organization.

podcast   Digital media files, audio and/or video, that are distributed over the Internet for playback on portable media players or computers. The term originated with delivery to the Apple iPod combined with the term *broadcast,* but it has much wider appreciation now. Podcasts may be downloaded, streamed, or fed through formats such as RSS. The **podcaster** is the producer or author of the podcast.

policies   Types of standing plans that serve as a guide for decision making and which are usually set by top management.

political action committee (PAC)   A group of people who raise or spend at least $1,000 in connection with a federal election.

portal   A gateway. **Web portal** is a site that functions as a point of access for more information on other pages at that Web site. **Enterprise portal** is a gateway on enterprise Web software to provide a single point of access to a variety of information or tools that the organization wants you to have in one place.

press agent   One who uses information as a manipulative tool, employing whatever means are available to achieve desired public opinion and action.

press clubs   Organizations established by corporations in Japan and elsewhere where media reporters meet corporate public relations practitioners.

press conference   A structured opportunity for an organization to release news to interested news media organizations simultaneously. Only the most newsworthy information or events should be presented in a news or press conference.

press kit   A collection of publicity releases packaged to gain media attention; often called *media kit.*

primary public   The group of people an organization ultimately hopes to influence or gain approval from.

primary research   The gathering of information that is not already available.

prioritize   Put in order of most important to least important.

privacy rights   Protection from unauthorized intrusion into a person's private life.

privilege   A defense against libel; the allowance of what might otherwise be libelous because of the circumstances under which a statement was produced. A person has "qualified privilege" to report fairly and accurately a public meeting or record, even if it turns out to be untrue.

proactive   Taking an action to be on the offensive.

pro bono   Professional services provided without compensation.

procedures   Types of standing plans that consist of standard instructions for performing common tasks; procedures carry out an organization's policies.

product liability   The principle that companies are responsible for any damage or disease that might be caused by the use of their products.

product placement   The process by which marketers pay to have their branded products placed in advertisements, movies, and other such venues as a way to reach and influence consumer buying decisions.

program evaluation and review technique (PERT)   A network representing a plan to accomplish a project showing the sequence, timing, and costs of the various tasks.

project budget   Component of a public relations campaign plan that outlines the cost of each activity or tactic in the campaign.

propaganda of the deed   Provocative actions designed solely to gain attention for ideas or grievances.

proxy   Absentee voting rights. In publicly held companies stockholders may give their "proxy" to someone else to vote based on their shares of stock.

public   A group of individuals tied together by a sense of common characteristics or responses.

public affairs   The aspect of public relations dealing with the political or governmental environment of organizations.

public communication   A multistep, multidirectional process in which messages are disseminated to a broad, and sometimes undifferentiated, audience through complex networks of active transmitters.

public information/public affairs officers (PIOs/PAOs)   Public relations practitioners working for the U.S. government or other institutions using those titles.

public opinion   An attitudinal measure of the image a public holds concerning some person, object, or concept that is a collection of opinions within society.

public opinion surveys   Surveys to measure the attitudes and opinions of specific audiences.

public participation programs or citizen involvement programs   Government-mandated programs to assess the social impacts of proposed changes on affected individuals, groups, and organizations.

public relations   A management function that helps define an organizational philosophy and direction by maintaining communication within a firm and with outside forces and by monitoring and helping a firm adapt to significant public opinion.

public relations audit   A research process to determine what the image of an organization is both internally and externally.

public relations counselor   One who informs both publics and organizations in the effort to create relationships of mutual benefit and support.

publication of private information   Part of privacy law that says even though it is true, some information, such as health records, can't be published without prior consent.

publicity   Publication of news about an organization or person for which time or space was not purchased.

publicity agent   One who serves as a conduit of information from organizations to publics, using the information to promote understanding, sympathy, or patronage for the organization.

Q

qualitative research   A method of delving into audience opinion without relying on formal, rigorous, number-based research methods.

questionnaire   List of questions used to gather information or to obtain a sample of opinion.

R

readability study An assessment of the difficulty an audience should have reading and comprehending a passage.

readership survey A study to determine the characteristics, preferences, and reading habits of an audience.

receiver The recipient of the message.

regulation A proposition underlying systems theory that maintains that the behavior of systems is constrained and shaped by interaction with other systems.

relationship marketing Another term related to integrated marketing. It focuses on building relationships with consumers through marketing, advertising, and public relations.

remix/mashups An open approach to content. the "remix" society takes content, personalizes it by changing it or "mashing" it with other content to make something entirely new.

rhetorician A master of clear, persuasive writing and speaking techniques.

rich media Media channels that more closely resemble face-to-face communication because they allow for continual feedback and touch more of the senses by incorporating words, visuals, and sound.

roles The collection of a person's daily activities.

RSS Real Simple Syndication is a way of distributing information to the Web. Data is pushed to the user when it is new and comes without the receiver having to do anything to get it. The XML file format can be used for Web feeds, Web sites, and blogs.

rules Statements that specify the action to be taken in a particular situation.

rumor An unconfirmed report, story, or statement that gets into general circulation.

S

sample A subset of a population or public.

sanctions Restrictions imposed on a member of a profession by an official body.

Sarbanes-Oxley Act A 2002 federal law that requires that corporations be open with information about their financial institutions.

satellite radio Subscriber-based, commercial-free radio service.

scenario construction A forecasting tool that explores likely consequences of alternative courses of action in a hypothetical, logical future situation.

secondary research The gathering of available information from published sources.

Securities and Exchange Act of 1934 Federal law that requires adequate publicity for sale of stocks and full disclosure of any pertinent information when it becomes available; it set up the Securities and Exchange Commission to regulate financial markets.

Securities and Exchange Commission (SEC) Federal regulatory body established by Congress in 1934 to oversee the trade of stocks and bonds and the operations of financial markets.

selective attention Attending to only a few messages.

selective perception Filters composed of needs, values, attitudes, expectations, and experiences through which individuals selectively process messages to derive meaning.

single-use plans Plans developed for use in one specific situation.

simple random sampling A technique that allows each member of a public an equal chance of being selected.

situational theory A principal technique for segmenting audiences in public relations based on their likelihood of communicating.

slander Oral defamation.

social audit Research to determine the social programs of an organization to determine its ability to be a socially responsible organization.

social bookmarking A method for Web users to store, organize, search, and manage bookmarks of Web pages with the help of metadata.

social exchange theory A theory that assumes individuals and groups choose strategies based on perceived rewards and costs.

social learning theory A theory that attempts to explain and predict behavior by looking at ways individuals process information.

social marketing A special form of public relations that tries to change public attitudes and behaviors on behalf of a social cause whose work benefits society as a whole rather than the sponsoring organization.

social media An umbrella term that refers to new media that use technology to create social interaction through words and/or visual material. The term is sometimes identified with Web 2.0.

source The initiator of the message.

spontaneous publicity Publicity accompanying unplanned events.

staff Organizational personnel employed to provide support and advice to line management.

stakeholder analysis Method for characterizing publics according to their interest in an issue.

stakeholders Individuals or groups who perceive themselves as having an interest in the actions of an organization.

standing plans Plans for dealing with certain types of situations, particularly common situations and emergencies.

strategic plans Long-range plans concerning a group's major goals and ways of carrying them out. These plans are usually made by top management.

subsystem A component of a system.

summative evaluation Measurement to determine the success or failure in reaching a program's or campaign's objectives that is done at the completion of the program.

Sunshine Act A federal law requiring meetings of governmental boards, commissions, and agencies to be open to the public.

supplier relations An aspect of public relations of special importance to the small business owner. Supplier relations helps small businesses maintain inventory, secure financing, and engage in other activities that allow the business to survive.

survey research A formal or scientific study usually accomplished through use of a questionnaire administered to a sample of the audience being studied.

synergy A proposition underlying systems theory that maintains that the whole is greater than the sum of its parts.

system   A set of objects or events grouped together by sets of relationships.

systematic sampling   A technique that uses a list to select a sample at random.

systems theory   A theory that suggests how organizations are made up of interrelated parts and how they use these parts to adapt to the environment.

T

tactical plans   Short-range plans for accomplishing the steps that lead up to achievement of an organization's goals. These plans are carried out at every level of an organization and on an everyday basis.

tagging   A user-generated way of describing content by adding "tags" to writing, images,videos, posts, or other social media content.

target audience   The primary group an organization is trying to influence.

target market   Communication with key publics to support the marketing function.

target publics   Key publics concerned with common issues.

technicians   Public relations practitioners who perform the skills of writing, editing, or producing the public relations materials.

tender offer   An offer above the market price of the company's stock that is high enough to entice shareholders to sell despite their loyalty to the company.

theory   An explanation or belief about how something works.

third-party endorsements   Testimonials or other support for an organization, person, or product by someone outside the organization to give validity to the message.

TiVo   A term that is now being used as a verb to describe users who record television shows and view them at their discretion. TiVo also refers to a popular digital video or televsion screen.

tool integration   Communicator chooses from a mix of media to use the medium or media needed to reach internal and external audiences necessary for a particular campaign.

trademark   A legally protected name, logo, or design registered to restrict its use to the owner.

U

uncontrolled media   Those media whose actions are not under the public relations practitioner's control, such as community newspapers and radio stations.

universe   A system providing the environment for ecosystems.

USA Patriot Act   A 2001 federal law that permits the U.S. government wider powers to access individual records.

uses and gratifications theory   A theory that asserts people are active and selective users of media.

V

variable   An object or event that can be measured or manipulated.

video news release (VNR)   A video package sent as a news story for use on television news broadcasts.

video on demand (VOD)   Allows users the ability to view video at any time on a computer or television screen. Sometimes spelled VoD.

viral marketing   A phenomenon in which consumers share experiences, knowledge, and feelings about a brand through social media such as blogs, discussion boards, personal Web sites, MySpace, and YouTube.

W

Web 2.0   Internet use that facilitates creativity and collaboration among users. It usually involves the new social media such as wikis, blogs, and social-networking sites. Rather than referring to any technical changes, it refers to changes in the ways software developers and other people make use of Web technology.

wiki   Short for wikipedia. A wiki is a technology for creating collaborative Web sites. **Wikipedia** is a term that combines "wiki" with "encyclopedia" to prove an Internet reference site begun in 2001 by Jimmy Wales and Larry Sanger.

whistle-blowing   Insiders telling the media what they know about improper practices by others, usually in the same company, with the hope of improving the situation.

World Wide Web   Another term for the Internet, or interconnected computer system.

written consent   Defense against invasion of privacy and copyright violation when permission is given in writing.

Credits

PHOTO CREDITS

Chapter 1
p. 1: © image100/PunchStock; **p. 6:** © Kayte M. Deioma/PhotoEdit, Inc.; **p. 12:** © Fisher-Thatcher/Getty Images

Chapter 2
p. 21: © Bettmann/Corbis; **p. 33:** © Rachel Epstein/PhotoEdit, Inc.

Chapter 3
p. 45: Photo courtesy of Stacey Smith

Chapter 4
p. 67: Photo by Win McNamee/Getty Images; **p. 73:** © Don Emmert/AFP/Getty Images

Chapter 5
p. 85: © Jeff Greenberg/PhotoEdit, Inc.; **p. 93:** © Spencer Grant/Stock Boston; **p. 99:** © Michael Newman/PhotoEdit, Inc.

Chapter 6
p. 114: © Alex Wong/Getty Images; **p. 117:** © Rachel Epstein/PhotoEdit, Inc.

Chapter 7
p. 131: © Jonathan Nourok/Getty Images; **p. 137:** © Bill Aron/PhotoEdit, Inc.

Chapter 8
p. 163: AP Photo/Ed Andrieski

Chapter 9
p. 169: © Royalty-Free/Corbis; **p. 172:** © Spencer Grant/Stock Boston; **p. 174:** Courtesy of the author; **p. 191:** AP Photo/Steve Helber

Chapter 10
p. 200: © moodboard/Corbis; **p. 205:** © Mary Katz/The Image Works; **p. 214:** © Photo by CNN/Getty Images

Chapter 11
p. 223: AP Photo/Expedia, Ron Wurzer; **p. 235:** © Photodisc/Getty Images

Chapter 12
p. 254: Courtesy of the author

Chapter 13
p. 285: © David Young-Wolff/PhotoEdit, Inc.; **pp. 288, 289:** Courtesy of the author

Chapter 14
p. 295: © John A. Rizzo/Getty Images; **p. 302:** © AFP/Corbis; **p. 309:** Andy Wong-Pool/Getty Images

Chapter 15
p. 322: © Michael Newman/PhotoEdit, Inc.; **p. 327:** Courtesy of North American Mission Board, SBC

Chapter 16
p. 347: AP Photo/Springfield News-Leader, Steve J.P. Liang; **p. 353:** © Reuters NewMedia, Inc./Corbis; **p. 361:** Courtesy of MasterCard and Weber Shandwick Public Relations

Chapter 17
p. 378: AP Photo/Chris Carlson; **p. 392:** AP Photo/Koji Sasahara

Index